CW00970560

TEMPUS
SPEEDWAY
YEARBOOK 2007

TEMPUS
SPEEDWAY
YEARBOOK2007

EDITED BY ROBERT BAMFORD

First published 2007

Stadia is an imprint of
Tempus Publishing Limited
The Mill, Brimscombe Port,
Stroud, Gloucestershire, GL5 2QG
www.tempus-publishing.com

© Robert Bamford 2007

The right of Robert Bamford to be identified as the Author
of this work has been asserted in accordance with the
Copyrights, Designs and Patents Act 1988.

All rights reserved. No part of this book may be reprinted
or reproduced or utilised in any form or by any electronic,
mechanical or other means, now known or hereafter invented,
including photocopying and recording, or in any information
storage or retrieval system, without the permission in writing
from the Publishers.

British Library Cataloguing in Publication Data.
A catalogue record for this book is available from the British Library.

ISBN 978 07524 4250 1

Typesetting and origination by Tempus Publishing Limited
Printed in Great Britain

CONTENTS

ACKNOWLEDGEMENTS   6
INTRODUCTION   7
ABBREVIATIONS   19

ELITE LEAGUE 2006

ARENA-ESSEX DUGGO 7 HAMMERS   25
BELLE VUE FONESTYLE UK ACES   30
COVENTRY BUILDBASE BEES   35
EASTBOURNE EAGLES SPONSORED BY
   MERIDIAN MARQUEES   40
IPSWICH EVENING STAR WITCHES   45
OXFORD CHEETAHS   49
PETERBOROUGH PANTHERS   53
POOLE RIAS PIRATES   58
READING BULLDOGS   63
SWINDON ROBINS IN ASSOCIATION WITH
   TEAM PARTNERS, PEBLEY BEACH SUZUKI &
   EDGE LOGISTICS LTD   67
WOLVERHAMPTON PARRYS
   INTERNATIONAL WOLVES   72

PREMIER LEAGUE 2006

ANDERSON'S QUALITY BUTCHERS
   BERWICK BANDITS   82
EDINBURGH SCOTWASTE MONARCHS   87
GLASGOW PREMIER TRAVEL INN TIGERS   92
ISLE OF WIGHT WIGHTLINK ISLANDERS   97
KING'S LYNN MONEY CENTRE STARS   101
MILDENHALL ASL FREIGHT FEN TIGERS   106
NEWCASTLE WARBURTONS DIAMONDS   110

EVEREST GROUP NEWPORT WASPS   114
REDCAR BEARS   119
RYE HOUSE SILVER SKI ROCKETS   123
SHEFFIELD PIRTEK TIGERS   128
SOMERSET MIKE MANNING AUDIO REBELS   133
STOKE EASY-RIDER POTTERS   138
WORKINGTON COMETINSURANCE.COM
   COMETS   143

CONFERENCE LEAGUE 2006

BOSTON N.C. WILLIAMS & SON
   INSURANCE BARRACUDA-BRAVES   151
BUXTON HITMEN   155
CLEVELAND SCOTT BROS BAYS   159
MILDENHALL JOLLY CHEF ACADEMY   162
NEWPORT MAVERICKS   165
PLYMOUTH GT MOTORCYCLES DEVILS   168
RYE HOUSE ELMSIDE RAIDERS   173
SCUNTHORPE LINCS FM SCORPIONS   176
SITTINGBOURNE CRUSADERS   180
STOKE SAS SPITFIRES   183
WEYMOUTH DOONANS WILDCATS   187

SOUTHERN AREA LEAGUE 2006   191
MAJOR BRITISH MEETINGS 2006   195
SPEEDWAY GRAND PRIX 2006   218
MAJOR INTERNATIONAL
   MEETINGS 2006   239
RIDER INDEX 2006   255

ACKNOWLEDGEMENTS

Here we go once more with the fourth edition of the *Tempus Speedway Yearbook*, and indeed my fifth successive term in producing such a publication. There are an ever-increasing number of people to thank for their help, with much appreciation to one and all: Ian Adam, Lucy Aubrey, Nick Barber, Ian Belcher, Karen Chappell, Ray Collins, Richard Crowley, Gordon Day, Frank Ebdon, Matt Ford, Colin Goddard, Mike Golding, Roger Hulbert, Mike Hunter, Nathan Irwin, Tracy Irwin, Jeremy Jackson, Tony Jackson, Dick Jarvis, Pam Johnson, Roger Last, Jo Lawson, Charles McKay, Peter Oakes, Gary Patchett, Robert Peasley, Robbie Perks, Lee Poole, Andy Povey, Laurence Rogers, Alun Rossiter, Terry and Wayne Russell, John Sampford, Jeff Scott, Glynn Shailes, George Sheridan, Mike Smillie, Rod Smith, Dave Stallworthy, Barry Stephenson, Norrie Tait, Steve Thorn, Dominic Threlfall, Peter Toogood, Malcolm Vasey, Bob Wayte and Bryn Williams. I am particularly grateful to Matt Jackson for help with numerous dates of birth and, indeed, to all the riders who were more than helpful with similar information when asked. I am very much indebted to Chris Seaward for his assistance throughout the season and also for the superb Grand Prix and World Cup reviews, as well as the magnificent introduction to this work. Once again, statistical genius Mike Moseley has kept me on the straight and narrow as far as the accuracy of averages is concerned and I am deeply indebted for his time and trouble in cross-checking all my figures. I am grateful for the assistance of various photographers, so many thanks indeed to the following for expertly producing all the images contained herein: main photographic content by Mike Patrick (www.mike-patrick.com); other contributions by Les Aubrey, Ian Charles, Phil Hilton, Mick Hinvis, John Hipkiss, Hywel Lloyd, Graham Platten, Matt Sprake and Alan Whale. The internet has proved invaluable in helping to keep right up to the minute with everything in the speedway world, so grateful thanks to all the web-masters for collectively doing such a marvellous job. I also wish to again pay tribute to *Speedway Star* magazine, which has been an excellent and invaluable reference point. For guidance purposes, please note that in the calculation of rider averages, any tactical ride and any tactical substitute points are recorded as those normally given for the relevant finishing position, e.g. 1st = 3 points, 2nd = 2 points and 3rd = 1 point. Appearances are only included in a rider's statistics when he was a member of the side as per the BSPA team declarations. All other appearances are included in the total for guests.

Robert Bamford
31 October 2006

INTRODUCTION

It was more than appropriate in the year Sky Sports announced they would be extending their live coverage of Elite League action for a further five years that British speedway's top flight produced a wonderfully compelling contest and concluded with an incredible Play-Off final. After months of speculation, Reading joined the Elite League under the management of John Postlethwaite and his accomplished Benfield Sports team, who manage the highly successful Grand Prix series. The London-based company, who had been linked to Reading in the past, announced they had purchased the club from long-serving promoter Pat Bliss in November 2005. The Berkshire outfit was immediately rebranded as the Bulldogs and the new promotion implemented several pioneering initiatives that aimed to raise professionalism not just within the club, but in Britain as a whole. On track, the Bulldogs certainly had a year to remember as they were narrowly beaten to the Elite League title in the two-legged Play-Off final by a power-packed Peterborough septet, culminating in a night of unprecedented drama at the Panthers' East of England Showground. The silverware looked to be heading Reading's way, before the Panthers staged a miraculous comeback in the final three heats to clinch what seemed, at one point, an impossible victory and spark sensational scenes of celebration on the packed terraces. Indeed, the second leg of the Play-Off final was one of the most dramatic encounters in the sport's illustrious history and a night that will be talked about for many years to come. Peterborough promoter Colin Horton's investment into the club had certainly paid dividends; the ambitious chief had spent heavily in the winter months and, along with team manager Trevor Swales, constructed a potent outfit that was admirably led by Danish star Hans N. Andersen. The Cambridgeshire side rarely found themselves outside the top four in the league table and much of their success must be attributed to their wonderful team spirit and a well-structured off-track promotion that ensured the crowds returned to the Showground week after week.

Peterborough were many peoples' favourites to scoop the Elite League crown before a wheel had been turned as, on paper, their power-packed line-up was admired throughout the speedway world. Hans N. Andersen and Ryan Sullivan were purchased from Poole for an undisclosed fee, with Niels-Kristian Iversen also joining the Panthers on a full contract. Ulrich Ostergaard made the full-time step up to top-level racing and initially coped extremely well, before suffering from a lull in form as the season came to a conclusion. In contrast, Richard Hall initially found the step from Premier League racing understandably difficult, but as the year progressed the British youngster proved to be a real trump card and his gritty performance in the second leg of the Play-Off final arguably secured the title for his club. The team was completed by Jesper B. Jensen, who suffered a nasty shoulder injury in the middle of the campaign and then made a tentative return in the closing stages of the season, and also former GP rider Tomasz Bajerski. However, the Pole struggled to contribute the scores everyone knew he was capable of and was replaced by Danish youngster Jonas Raun. Polish sensation Karol Zabik was later introduced and made a huge impression during his short stint in the side, before an unpleasant split paved the way for Piotr Swiderski to make a successful return to the side. It was fitting that Sullivan's race victory in heat fifteen of the second leg of the Play-Off final wrapped up the league title for the Panthers, as the Aussie, who successfully recovered from illness the previous season, was a member of the 1999 Championship-winning side and couldn't conceal his understandable elation as he held the league trophy.

Reading, in their first year back in top-league racing since 1996, certainly made a big impression and the Bulldogs came agonisingly close to securing the Championship. Captained by the ever-cheerful Greg Hancock, the Berkshire side purchased the contract of Australian Travis McGowan from former Oxford promoter Nigel Wagstaff and managed to secure the services of the highly-rated Polish Champion Janusz Kolodziej, whose only previous experience of British racing had been with Reading during their Premier League days in 2003. Crucially, the Bulldogs were able to fight off strong interest from other clubs and retain the services of sensational Slovenian Matej Zagar, along with young Czech rider Zdenek Simota. They also drafted in Charlie Gjedde, on loan from Swindon, and completed their septet with Andy Smith, who was signed after a complication with Danny Bird's average meant that the Brit was ineligible to ride for the club. Sam Ermolenko was assigned the innovative role of sporting director and worked closely with experienced team manager Jim Lynch, whilst John Postlethwaite and his BSI team ensured there was a real feel-good factor at Smallmead Stadium. Whilst Reading's attendance figures may have fallen short of the promotions expectations, nobody could deny the effectiveness of their pioneering initiatives. The Bulldogs' fleet of identical vehicles, glossy full-colour programme, team mascot, new website, post-meeting press conference, smart team suits and matching bike covers all epitomise the direction in which British speedway should be heading. No doubt, the Reading promotion will be working on extending the fan-base during the winter and building on what was a phenomenal return to top-flight speedway for the Berkshire team.

Swindon enjoyed arguably their most successful season for several years as the Wiltshire side booked their spot in the Elite League Play-Offs for the first time in their history. However, off-track the Robins were dealt a bitter blow when the owners of the Abbey Stadium announced plans to redevelop the site without the inclusion of speedway. Fans, media and the people of Swindon protested passionately about the potential loss of the sport and, whilst the future of the Robins still remains uncertain, the prestigious club has confirmed they will be competing in the Elite League next season. For a third successive term, the team was captained by nine times Australian Champion Leigh Adams, who yet again was the team's lynchpin and registered a typically hefty league average of 10.58, not to mention plundering an amazing 18 maximums (6 full and 12 paid). Lee Richardson, who had enjoyed such a fruitful 2005 campaign, suffered from a lack of form in 2006 and, whilst there were rare moments of brilliance, it was generally a disappointing campaign for the British rider. Stylish Polish international Seba Ulamek performed extremely well throughout the season and proved to be a very worthwhile signing along with Mads Korneliussen, who coped well with the full-time transition to Elite League racing. The regular absences of Adrian Miedzinski and Renat Gafurov were undoubtedly the most frustrating aspect of Swindon's campaign, as both riders struggled to effectively mix their other racing commitments with the hectic British calendar. When available, the duo proved to be ultimate crowd-pleasers, in particular Gafurov, whose sheer bravery and spectacular racing style brought the Abbey Stadium to life, making him a real favourite on the terraces. The departure of the out-of-form Swedish youngster Seb Alden sparked a revival in the Robins' camp and, bolstered by the signing of former GP rider Tomasz Chrzanowski, the side made a miraculous surge towards the top of the table. Their quest for glory finally came to a halt in the Play-Off semi-final at the hands of local rivals Reading, but it was, nevertheless, a fantastic season for the club, with an upsurge in attendances, a successful junior league programme and the introduction of the Legends' Lounge, which welcomed the stars of yesteryear back to Blunsdon.

Coventry enjoyed a successful 2006 campaign in which they earned themselves a Play-Off spot and lifted the Knock-Out Cup for the first time since 1967. The Midlands side was once again led by skipper Scott Nicholls and fielded an almost identical septet to the one that collected the league title the previous season. The only addition was British youngster Olly Allen, who joined on loan from Swindon and replaced Seba Ulamek in order to ensure the Bees team nestled beneath the points limit. Any doubts that the Bees lacked potency in the heat-leader department quickly vanished as Chris Harris and Rory Schlein matured wonderfully to provide Nicholls with first-rate support throughout the season. Young Australian Schlein did remarkably well to recover from the serious back injury he suffered in 2005 and teammate Harris continued to establish himself as a major force in the Elite League with an array of classy performances. Elsewhere in the side, Billy Janniro once again fulfilled his role as a solid club rider, whilst Allen enjoyed a wonderful season that saw the Brit add a significant amount to his average. The youngster started the campaign phenomenally and, whilst his scores did tail off towards the end of the season, the faith shown in him from the Coventry promotion certainly proved worthwhile as he forged his way into the top five of the team. The remainder of the side was occupied by up-and-coming German Martin Smolinski and Denmark's Morten Risager, who missed much of the concluding third of the season because of a badly broken leg. It was undoubtedly another year of success for the Bees, who also scooped the Elite Shield and reached the latter stages of all the major competitions, before rounding the year off perfectly with a victory over local rivals Wolverhampton in the Midland Trophy.

Belle Vue narrowly missed out on making the Play-Offs, but the Manchester side still enjoyed a relatively successful season. In a replica of the 2005 Play-Off final, the Aces were beaten by Coventry to Knock-Out Cup glory, although the pairing of Simon Stead and Jason Crump did collect the prestigious Elite League Pairs Championship, held at Swindon in June. For a fifth successive year, the Aces were led admirably by Crump, who registered a whopping 11.23 average from 39 league appearances, having plundered an astonishing 522 points. Meanwhile, the fast-rising Stead filled the number one race-jacket and coped with the pressure of a heat-leader berth well. Danish youngster Kenneth Bjerre made a good recovery from the badly broken leg that had curtailed his 2005 campaign and fans' favourite Joe Screen enjoyed a steady season that was eventually ended prematurely by a collarbone injury. James Wright 'doubled-up' with the Manchester club when his commitments with Workington in the Premier League allowed, and at the Kirkmanshulme Lane circuit weighed in with impressive scores, although he understandably found points harder to come by on his travels. Nevertheless, it was good experience for the talented youngster, whose notable progression through British speedway must be accredited to the fabulous work of Buxton in the Conference League, where Wright began his competitive career. Phil Morris and Tom P. Madsen completed the Aces' line-up and spent most of the season in the reserve positions, along with club number eight riders Tommy Allen and, towards the latter stages, Joel Parsons.

Ipswich made possibly the highest profile signing of the winter when they acquired the services of 2000 World Champion Mark Loram to spearhead their campaign. After the departure of Scott Nicholls the previous season and the announcement that Hans N. Andersen would transfer to Peterborough in 2006, the Witches responded in the perfect possible manner by securing the signature of the British star. Indeed, Ipswich started the season well and looked to be heading for a spot in the Play-Offs, before a dismal period in the closing stages eradicated their hopes of qualification. The Suffolk side boasted a powerful-looking top three as Loram was joined by Grand Prix rider Piotr Protasiewicz and Ipswich legend Chris Louis, along with two very able second-string riders, namely Kim Jansson and 2004 World Under-21 Champion

Robert Miskowiak. Added to that, Daniel King returned to a reserve spot and once again made steady progress, whilst his partner Jan Jaros, after making an electric start to the season, was released by the Witches in June following a string of much-reduced returns. Tobias Kroner, who spent a period at Oxford in 2005, was brought into the Ipswich line-up and justified his inclusion within the side with several eye-catching scores. It is hard to pinpoint just why Ipswich didn't mount a more serious challenge for honours in 2006, because, on paper, they undoubtedly boasted one of the most attractive septets in the league and oozed potential.

Poole looked as if they would bag a position in the Play-Off berths until a dismal end-of-season run ruined their hopes of qualification and relegated the Dorset club to seventh spot in the Elite League table. In an uncanny resemblance to 2005, the Pirates faltered in the final third of their league campaign and were hindered by injuries to top riders, along with problems generating a potent reserve pairing. However, the Pirates did finish the term on a high as they took victory in the Craven Shield competition after easing through the group stage and then defeating Eastbourne and Coventry in a three-legged final. The Dorset side were once again led by Bjarne Pedersen, who was the model of consistency throughout the season and the unassuming Danish rider struck a wonderful riding relationship with experienced Australian Craig Boyce, who lined up at number two for the Pirates. Boyce rolled back the years and quickly refamiliarised himself with top-division racing, proving to be a competent second-string rider, contributing a handful of paid double-figure scores. The Pirates' unluckiest rider was undoubtedly Polish youngster Krzysztof Kasprzak, who missed a significant chunk of the season courtesy of a reoccurring collarbone injury, however, when fit, the stylish twenty-two-year-old continued to showcase his phenomenal talent. The availability of Kasprzak's compatriot Grzegorz Walasek and Brazilian-born Swede Antonio Lindback was a very prominent concern for the Dorset outfit, who often struggled to adequately cover the absences of such a potent pairing. A further problem was the hit-and-miss form of reserve rider Jonas Davidsson, whose expected progression into the top five of the team didn't materialise and the Swedish youngster, who has so much obvious talent, yet again endured a frustrating season. Finding a rider to occupy the number seven race-jacket also proved tricky, and after the Pirates parted company with the out-of-form Daniel Davidson, the elder of the two racing brothers, a number of riders were used to fill the position, although, in truth, the Pirates struggled to construct any sort of continuity.

By their high standards, Wolverhampton endured a disappointing 2006 campaign and didn't enforce their authority on any of the league's competitions. The side's major winter acquisition was the experienced American Billy Hamill, who linked with the Swedish duo of Peter Karlsson and Fredrik Lindgren in what looked a strong top three. They were joined by Magnus Karlsson, who was looking to build upon his fruitful 2005 campaign, and also Krzysztof Pecyna, who had quietly elevated himself into the top five of the team during the previous season. However, Pecyna left the club in the early part of the season due to personal reasons, which paved the way for popular Californian Ronnie Correy to make a welcome return to the Wolverhampton septet, following a short loan spell at Swindon whilst Renat Gafurov's visa was sorted out. The number six spot was allocated to young German talent Christian Hefenbrock and the position of his partner at number seven was usually alternated between two of Britain's rising stars, William Lawson and Ben Wilson. Despite occasional flashes of brilliance, Peter Adams' men generally underperformed and whilst the Monmore Green faithful enjoyed witnessing the vintage form of Peter Karlsson, they will have been ultimately disappointed not to have collected any silverware. On the plus side, there were positives to come from Wolverhampton's campaign, including the remarkable progress of young Scotsman William Lawson, the continued progress of Lindgren and the high levels of entertainment on offer each week at Britain's most intriguing race circuit.

It is hard to pin point why Eastbourne ended up a lowly ninth in the Elite League since, on paper, their cosmopolitan team certainly looked attractive. Led by 2003 World Champion Nicki Pedersen, the Eagles welcomed back Arlington favourite David Norris and the popular Adam Shields. However, the Australian endured rotten luck with injury and twice suffered a broken pelvis whilst riding in Poland, although he thankfully made a full recovery and was back in the saddle before the end of the season. Possibly the most exciting signing for the East Sussex side was young teenage sensation Lewis Bridger, who handled the huge step up from Conference League racing remarkably well and sensationally earned a spot in the top five of the side for part of the season. Bridger's leap of faith into the Elite League certainly created a buzz around Arlington Stadium and the young man further underlined his talent as he eased to victory in the British Under-18 Championship at Wolverhampton. Another British rider who didn't have such a successful season was Andrew Moore, who quit the club partway through the season due to financial difficulties. It was certainly a great loss for British speedway to see one of its young talents walk away from the sport, especially after Moore had done so well to establish himself as an Elite League rider. Moore's departure made way for Edward Kennett to make a return to his spiritual home and the British rider generally performed well in his 'doubling-up' capacity with Rye House. Australian Cameron Woodward was drafted into the side after a nasty injury had ruled out Brent Werner in the early part of the 2006 campaign. It was a baptism of fire for young Woodward, who hadn't previously experienced the ferocity of Elite League racing, but his gritty performances will have done his quest for a team spot in 2007 no harm at all.

Oxford, under the ownership of new promoter Aaron Lanney, reverted back to their traditional Cheetahs nickname and came to the tapes with a brand new septet in 2007. With the installation of a new colour-coded air safety barrier, a professional-looking website and a wonderful-looking set of team kevlars, the feel-good factor was most definitely reinstated at Cowley Stadium. The Cheetahs resurgence continued vibrantly as it was announced six-times World Champion Tony Rickardsson had agreed a six-week contract with the club and, after his departure, would be replaced by former club favourite Todd Wiltshire. The Australian returned to England after changes in his personal life provoked a rethink on his retirement and was nothing short of remarkable upon his comeback to domestic racing. Despite the initial off-track buzz, it soon became clear that the Cheetahs would need significant strengthening as victories proved very hard to come by and home form was poor. As things turned out, Rickardsson was to depart before his proposed six-week stint had concluded, which paved the return for Wiltshire and another former Cowley favourite, Freddie Eriksson, who was drafted in to replace the struggling Adam Pietraszko. Unfortunately, the team continued to find the going tough and the promotion had no other option but to dispense with the out-of-form Eriksson and draft in much-loved Czech international Ales Dryml, whose arrival certainly saw a drastic improvement in terms of performance. However, the speedway world was horrified when Dryml was seriously hurt in a track accident on Wednesday 12 July during Oxford's home encounter against Wolverhampton and was subsequently placed in an intensive care unit at the John Radcliffe Hospital. Remarkably, and against all the odds, the Czech recovered from his severe head injuries and was thankfully able to return to his homeland where he began his recuperation. The only bright spot in the Cheetahs' season was the progression of young Swedish rider Eric Andersson, who caught the attention of many, with bundles of enthusiasm and a flamboyant style in what was his inaugural season of British racing.

Ronnie Russell's Arena-Essex side collected their second successive wooden spoon and endured a season plagued with dismal fortune. The Thurrock-based side signed Swedish Grand Prix star Andreas Jonsson for the opening six weeks of the season, who was then replaced by compatriot Mikael Max on loan from Wolverhampton, after recovering from a badly-broken leg suffered at the end of the previous season. The Hammers welcomed a new sponsor in the form of award-winning movie company Duggo 7, but, in truth, struggled all season to establish a solid run of form and endured a depressing spell on their home patch at the Purfleet raceway. Tragedy engulfed the club when news filtered through from Poland that talented young reserve Lukasz Romanek had committed suicide in his homeland. His shocking death continued the disturbing record of Polish speedway riders taking their own lives and raised question marks about just how much pressure these individuals face from the media, fans and clubs within their homeland. Even the close-season acquisition of newly appointed captain Steve Johnston couldn't raise the spirits of the club, who lost Paul Hurry to injury and were blighted by the lengthy absence of exciting Finnish rider Joonas Kylmakorpi due to a collarbone problem. The reliable Leigh Lanham enjoyed a steady campaign, as did Henning Bager who, despite suffering from a shoulder injury, made a good return to the club at which he enjoyed so much success in 2003 at Premier League level. Another rider to be struck by the injury jinx was Mariusz Puszakowski, who had enjoyed a stint at Ipswich in 2005. The enthusiastic Pole was drafted in by the Hammers' management but suffered a badly-broken leg whilst riding at Poole on 19 June. Even Rhys Naylor, the young club mascot, couldn't avoid getting hurt in a season that saw every member of the Arena-Essex side miss at least one match because of injury – and some of them, unfortunately, many more. Since their inclusion amongst the top flight in 2004, the team hasn't enjoyed a whole lot of luck and it would surely be beneficial for the league to witness a successful and injury-free campaign for the Hammers next season.

The Premier League welcomed two more clubs to its number in 2006, namely the Redcar Bears and Mildenhall Fen Tigers, which set the number of teams competing in the division at a healthy fourteen, one lower than 2005. After the unfortunate closures of Exeter and Hull, along with the departure of Reading to the Elite League, there were serious concerns about the long-term future of the division, but, thankfully, the arrivals of Mildenhall and Redcar steadied the ship. In fact, it proved to be a good year for the sport's second tier, which saw numerous homegrown youngsters make encouraging progress due to the resounding success of the graded British reserve initiative. Under Peter Oakes' system, every Premier League club had to track British riders at their number six and seven team slots, with each rider receiving a grading in accordance to their ability. Additionally, the league introduced a similar Play-Off system to the one that has proved so successful in the sport's higher tier, with the top eight teams progressing through to the knock-out system after their 26 league matches.

Kings Lynn enjoyed a wonderful 2006 campaign in which they were victorious in all three of the division's major competitions. Firstly, the Stars gained success in the Premier Trophy, which was quickly followed by a dominant performance in the Knock-Out Cup and an emphatic victory over Sheffield in the league decider. Promoter Buster Chapman didn't only get things right on track, but also ensured the fans flocked to the Norfolk Arena each week as he invested heavily in spectator facilities and worked closely with the local media. His achievements were recognised when the club collected the Promotion of the Year award at the Speedway Riders' Association ceremony, held in Coventry. The Stars' septet were, in many peoples' eyes, one of the greatest teams to ever grace the Premier League, and with riders like Troy Batchelor and Tomas Topinka, they demonstrated a wonderful balance between raw talent and invaluable experience. King's Lynn made just the one team change as the season progressed, replacing Simon Lambert with young Australian John Oliver, who proved to be an absolute revelation as the season reached its vital stages. Kevin Doolan performed phenomenally for the Norfolk side throughout the year and his compatriot Trevor Harding also made notable progress in the number two position.

The experience of Topinka and Daniel Nermark was priceless, along with the great talent of Batchelor, who seems destined for a wonderful future in the sport.

Despite not collecting any silverware, Sheffield enjoyed a generally successful 2006 campaign and reached the final in two of the division's major competitions. One of the most surprising aspects of the winter was the exclusion of long-serving Tiger Sean Wilson from the northern club's 1-7, who, instead, opted for a top two of Andre Compton and Ricky Ashworth. Argentine-born Emiliano Sanchez joined the Sheffield ranks after the unfortunate demise of Hull and Canadian Kyle Legault was invited back to Yorkshire after enjoying a successful inaugural season in 2005. The talented Ben Wilson continued his impressive progress up the speedway ladder as he enjoyed a fantastic domestic season and underlined his undisputed potential with victory in the British Under-21 Championship. The Tigers lost just once at their plush Owlerton Stadium all season and their tradition of nurturing young British riders continued to reap significant rewards. Furthermore, the club built strong links with Scunthorpe in the Conference League and provided opportunities for some of the Scorpions' youngsters to experience the intensity of Premier League racing.

Glasgow enjoyed an excellent season and, thankfully, in the club's sixtieth year of operation, the promotions attendance concerns of 2005 were eradicated. The Tigers were able to capture the signature of highly-rated British rider Danny Bird, who found himself unattached after a miscalculation of averages at Reading. Dependable Aussie Shane Parker returned to the side for a third successive year, which gave the Scottish outfit a mighty powerful top two, who, predictably, reigned victorious in the Premier League Pairs Championship, held on their home Ashfield circuit. Kauko Nieminen joined from Workington and proved to be an acute signing along with Robert Ksiezak, who was taken on loan from local rivals Edinburgh. The superb season-long progression of young Aussie Ksiezak, together with some flashes of brilliance from the talented James Cockle, were undoubtedly highlights for Glasgow, who were surprisingly knocked-out of the Play-Offs by the Isle of Wight at the quarter-final stage.

Rye House were dealt a bitter blow when they lost dependable captain Stuart Robson in the early part of the season with a nasty arm injury. The experienced British rider did make a return to the saddle towards the end of the campaign but, whilst absent, was initially replaced by the experienced Ross Brady, before Lee Smethills had a stint in the side. Yet again, Len Silver's faith in British riders was wonderfully rewarded as many of the Rockets' septet made significant progress in 2006, most of all Steve Boxall, who elevated himself from a reserve berth to a heat-leader spot. The youngster, who also gained some Elite League experience with Ipswich, was the talk of the Hertfordshire side's terraces and is sure to be a target for many clubs in the higher echelon. Edward Kennett continued his steady progress and certainly benefited from his 'doubling-up' experience with Eastbourne, whilst Chris Neath's successful campaign served to emphasise his potential to succeed in the Elite League, should he decide to further his career. The most unfortunate rider of the Rye House campaign was young Luke Bowen, who was making encouraging progress when he was struck down by a nasty injury in early June and was consequently sidelined for the remainder of the speedway year.

Somerset were led for a second successive year by Magnus Zetterstrom and enjoyed a fruitful term that saw them reach the final of the Knock-Out Cup and gain a spot in the Play-Offs. The Rebels did suffer some injuries during the early part of the season and in the first month of the campaign lost both Pavel Ondrasik and Jamie Smith. Stephan Katt was drafted in to replace Ondrasik and the German, who had previously represented the club in 2003, proved to be a real fans' favourite with his bundles of courage and never-say-die attitude. Elsewhere in the side, Paul Fry was the victim of a badly-broken leg sustained on 2 June during a home encounter against Berwick and his replacement was the experienced Swede Emil Kramer, who generally performed well at the Oak Tree Arena. Reserve riders Simon Walker and Ben Barker made encouraging progress, as did Glen Phillips in a second-string role after coming into the side as the replacement for Smith. A highlight of the Rebels' campaign was their inter-league challenge with Swindon on Friday 1 September, which was watched by a bumper crowd and, despite being well beaten, Somerset gave a good account of themselves, underlining what a fantastic team spirit they enjoy. The loveable Zetterstrom concluded his second season with the club in memorable fashion by romping to victory in the Premier League Riders' Championship at Sheffield on 24 September.

Speedway made a welcome and successful return to Teesside after planning permission was granted to construct a track at the South Tees Motorsports Park in Redcar. Wolverhampton chief Chris Van Straaten was primary promoter of the club and his wealth of ideas and close working relationship with the local council was undoubtedly a deciding factor in the smooth approval of authorisation for the site. Gary Havelock, who had begun his career in Middlesbrough over two decades earlier, aptly led the Bears and an attractive-looking side was constructed around the former World Champion's hefty average. Frenchman Mathieu Tresarrieu joined Havelock in a heat-leader berth and proved to be immensely popular at Redcar, so much so that by the end of the season his contract had been purchased by the Bears promotion. American rookie Chris Kerr was handed a team spot after impressing immensely on the USA Dream Team tour in 2005 and, considering it was his first season in British racing, the Californian posted a respectable average. Elsewhere in the team, southern-based youngster Daniel Giffard made wonderful progress and the experienced Kevin Little enjoyed his last year in the sport as he registered an array of impressive scores. After successfully making the Play-Offs, Redcar eventually crashed out in the quarter-final stages at the hands of a dominant King's Lynn side, however, the season was about much more than on-track success. Healthy crowds attended the South Tees Motorsports Park each week and the promotion progressively improved stadium facilities at the arena, which has the potential to be one of the plushest speedway venues in the country.

Tipped by many to be languishing near the bottom of the table, the Isle of Wight silenced their doubters as they reached the semi-final of the Play-Offs and enjoyed a thoroughly compelling campaign. The Islanders continued their tradition of unearthing raw speedway talent as they handed a team spot to Australian youngster Chris Holder, who hadn't previously been part of a British team. The exciting rookie exceeded all expectations in his debut season and posted a wonderful league average of 9.19, along with reaching the final of the World Under-21 Championship. Compatriot Jason Doyle also enjoyed a steady, if unspectacular, second term with the club and undoubtedly benefitted from his occasional outings with Poole in the Elite League. Jason Bunyan joined the Islanders after Robert Kasprzak, the younger brother of Krzysztof, hadn't produced the form that had been hoped for and was quickly released. After making a favourable impression towards the conclusion of the 2005 campaign, Krzysztof Stojanowski was welcomed back to the club and the Pole revelled in the wide-open spaces of the pacy Smallbrook arena. Overshadowed by the scintillating progress of Holder was the improvement made by young reserve Chris Johnson, who developed in terms of consistency and maturity as the season went along.

For a second successive season, Newport lost the services of their influential Australian Craig Watson in the early part of their campaign, this time due to a badly broken arm received at Stoke's Loomer Road raceway on 6 May. The Welsh side never realistically recovered from such a bitter blow and it was cruel misfortune for Watson, whose 2005 season had been prematurely curtailed because of a broken ankle, ironically when he was riding against Stoke at Newport's Queensway Meadows arena. The Wasps welcomed back the experienced Neil Collins who, as always, proved to be the ultimate entertainer and Tony Atkin, who continued his reputation as a solid second-string rider. Carl Wilkinson, after enjoying a sensational spell with Berwick in 2005, was recalled to Newport and, whilst he didn't enjoy such a rapid improvement, the British rider, nevertheless, performed solidly for the Wasps throughout. The brightest aspect of the Welsh side's otherwise miserable campaign was the progress of both Chris Schramm and Joel Parsons. In particular, the latter, who recovered well from multiple leg fractures sustained in the previous year and adapted to life at the Queensway Meadows circuit smoothly, which helped establish him as one of the most formidable reserves in the Premier League.

Mildenhall joined the Premier League under the promotion of former Peterborough chief Mick Horton and quickly announced the signing of one of the division's top men, experienced Australian Jason Lyons. Joining him in the Fen Tigers' line-up was the highly-rated Daniel King, together with his elder brother, Jason. The side's potential potency was added to with the inclusion of West Row favourite Jon Armstrong and Shaun Tacey, yet it was surprising that Mildenhall struggled to stamp their authority on the league. An out-of-form Tacey was released in mid-May, which allowed Andrew Moore to join the club in a 'doubling-up' capacity with Elite League club Eastbourne. However, Moore abruptly quit the sport and the Fen Tigers instead introduced American international Brent Werner. Unfortunately, James Brundle didn't make the progress many had hoped for, while the struggling Barry Burchatt was eventually replaced by Dorset-based youngster Jordan Frampton. Despite the changes, Mildenhall still found it hard going and were worryingly vulnerable on their home patch, which led to a concern over attendance levels. Thankfully, promoter Mick Horton has confirmed the club will again be lining up in the Premier League in 2007 and has stated that he will be constructing a more cost-efficient team.

Stoke captured the experienced Australian Mark Lemon to spearhead their 2006 charge for honours and the former Exeter man rode wonderfully in the Potters race-jacket. However, Lemon's success wasn't replicated throughout the rest of the side, as the Staffordshire outfit missed out on a spot in the Play-Offs and ended up finishing in tenth position in a season that was marred by the horrific injuries suffered by reserve rider Luke Priest. The youngster was badly hurt while riding for Stoke's Conference League side and confined to hospital for several months with pelvic, elbow and ankle injuries in addition to internal damage, although, thankfully, he was released as the season drew to a close. The Potters' promotion was ruthless in the quest for success and even released long-serving club favourite Alan Mogridge, drafting in Paul Thorp as a replacement. Earlier in the season, the underperforming Michael Coles was replaced by Trent Leverington and the Australian was a dependable second-string throughout the campaign. Robbie Kessler and Paul Clews enjoyed steady campaigns and British reserve rider Barrie Evans produced the occasional flash of brilliance in what was a generally disappointing year for Stoke.

By their high standards, Workington didn't enjoy an overly successful 2006 league campaign and the Comets' season was blighted by injuries. Mancunian Carl Stonehewer was still sidelined with the serious arm injury he suffered in 2005 and his professional presence was certainly missed at the top-end of the northern side. On the plus side, British youngster James Wright continued his wonderful progress to head the side's Premier League averages with an impressive 8.61 figure. Tenacious Pole Tomasz Piszcz returned for his second spell at the Derwent Park arena, while Garry Stead joined from the defunct Hull Vikings and generally rode very well, along with Aidan Collins who posted a respectable average. Former club favourite Rusty

Harrison made a late-season switch back to the Comets after he and Edinburgh had come to a parting of the waves, with Paul Thorp making way for the Australian's return. Richard Juul also had a short stint with the side, while Alan Mogridge concluded his career with the Comets after he had been released from Stoke. A highlight of Workington's campaign was victory in the Premier League Four-Team Championship, staged at their home track in front of a bumper crowd. The team's unluckiest rider of the season was Ritchie Hawkins, who joined the side after enjoying a fruitful 2005 campaign with Somerset. The British rider was proving to be a real favourite until a tangle with Glasgow's Danny Bird at Derwent Park on 15 July unfortunately left him with a badly bruised brain and he spent the remainder of the season on the sidelines. Breaking both legs in a serious smash at Sheffield regrettably caused Lee Derbyshire's extended absence at reserve, which ensured the Comets' supporters saw quite a number of guests from early May until the season's conclusion.

Berwick promoter Peter Waite left it to the last possible minute before confirming that his Bandits team would be competing in the 2006 Premier League, after a desperate hunt to gain the necessary sponsorship proved successful. The northern team chopped and changed their line-up throughout the campaign, following the early-season departure of fans' favourite Adrian Rymel. Fellow Czech Michal Makovsky proved to be the model of consistency and newly recruited Swede Andreas Bergstrom enjoyed a relatively successful inaugural term in British speedway. Poland's Stainslaw Burza, who is a top-flight rider in his homeland, joined the Bandits late in April and certainly enjoyed the large Shielfield Park bowl, along with a few opportunities to prove his talent with Oxford in the Elite League. Jacek Rempala, another Pole, arrived in August and was hugely impressive, not least when called upon by Coventry for some top-flight outings. It wasn't the most successful of campaigns for Waite's men, who struggled with consistency and injuries to the desperately unlucky James Birkinshaw. Young reserve Danny Warwick deservedly scooped the club's Rider of the Year award, the Dorset-based youngster making notable progress and proving to be a very dependable rider.

Edinburgh missed out on a Play-Off spot but still enjoyed a campaign that saw impressive progression from a number of their riders. Young Scotsman William Lawson established himself as a second-string cum heat-leader and his compatriot Derek Sneddon was an absolute revelation in the reserve department. Dutchman Theo Pijper returned for a fifth successive season with the club and topped the team averages, whilst Australian Matthew Wethers' form continued to head in the right direction. Rusty Harrison left the club in July, allowing talented young Italian Daniele Tessari to enjoy his first taste of league racing in Britain. Henrik Moller made the final of the World Under-21 Championship and demonstrated his potential for the future with some useful scores over the course of the Monarchs' campaign.

On paper, Newcastle looked to have a team that was capable of challenging for major honours, but the Diamonds failed to make the Play-Offs and endured a campaign full of frustration. A series of rain-offs meant a fixture backlog and a hectic end-of-season spell for the Tyneside team, who ended up just three points outside the eighth and final Play-Off qualification spot. The Diamonds septet was led by the experienced Czech pairing of Josef Franc and George Stancl, together with Australian Christian Henry who had successfully recovered from the nasty injury that prematurely curtailed his 2005 season. James Grieves neatly slotted into the cosmopolitan side, along with talented Austrian youngster Manuel Hauzinger, who, after a steady campaign, quit the club towards the end of the season as the fixture backlog began to takes its toll. In the reserve department, Jamie Robertson didn't make the progress many had hoped for, while in his first season in the Premier League, Adam McKinna endured an uphill struggle, although doubtless the youngster will have learnt an awful lot from such a tough year. On the plus side,

Newcastle enjoyed the local derby clashes with newly formed Redcar and the significantly larger crowds that accompanied them.

The Premier League received a phenomenal boost towards the end of the season, when it was announced that planning permission had been granted by Birmingham City Council to construct a new speedway track at the Perry Barr Greyhound Stadium, which, of course, had previously hosted the sport in three spells (1928, 1946-1957 and 1960), when known as the Alexander Sports Stadium. It was a case of second time lucky for promoter Tony Mole, whose original proposal had been rejected. A revamped plan was met with approval from the councillors and a three-year lease was granted for the Brummies. Mole quickly appointed Graham and Denise Drury to run the sport in the Second City and the venture is an extra special boost for not only the Premier League, but for British speedway in general. The news wasn't quite as positive for Exeter, who have ruled out a return to competitive action in 2007. The Falcons were hoping to receive planning permission to build a track at Haldon Racecourse, but were held up because of complications with approval. However, they have a solid and passionate backer in Allen Trump, who has pledged his future to the Falcons' plight and there is a real hope the prestigious side will take to the track again in 2008.

The Play-Off system was also introduced into the Conference League and, in an eight-team set-up, it was Scunthorpe who eased past newly reformed Plymouth in the two-legged grand final. The Scorpions have been a huge success story since their rebirth in 2005, and in 2006 were victorious in all four of the division's major competitions. Their septet included highly-rated British youngster Josh Auty and hot prospect Tai Woffinden, son of former Scunthorpe rider Rob. The promotion at the Lincolnshire track must take great credit for ensuring large crowds flocked to the Normanby Road arena each week, investing money to improve facilities and building close links with local media outlets. Joining Auty and Woffinden were South African Bryon Bekker, the continually improving Richie Dennis, Isle of Man-born Andrew Tully, experienced captain Wayne Carter and Benji Compton, the younger brother of Sheffield lynchpin Andre. The Scorpions were by far the best team in the league and it was refreshing to see so many young British riders contributing to the club's success and making such rapid progress. Praise must be particularly heaped on Woffinden, who only turned sixteen years of age in August and had no previous experience of riding a 500cc machine before he came to Britain, yet forged his way into the Scunthorpe team and, by the end of the season, had signed a professional contract with Elite League giants Wolverhampton, as well as one with the Premier League's major hotbed for youth development, Rye House.

The Plymouth Devils made a highly successful return to British speedway and the new St Boniface Arena provided much in the way of cracking entertainment. Mike Bowden's side actually topped the standings after their fourteen league matches but, as previously mentioned, were well-beaten by Scunthorpe in the Play-Off final. The Devils were captained and led admirably by former Exeter favourite Seemond Stephens, who suffered a wrist injury towards the end of the season which, unfortunately, prevented his participation in the Play-Off showdown. Joining the skipper were Lee Smart, Tom Brown and Rob Smith, together with the rapidly improving Shane Waldron.

Another couple of youngsters that caught the eye in 2006 were Chris Johnson and Ben Barker, who both reaped the benefits of the 'doubling-up' system that allowed them to gain experience with the Isle of Wight and Somerset respectively. Johnson began the Conference League campaign with Plymouth, but later transferred to Weymouth whilst Barker was the master of Stoke's Loomer Road circuit as he registered an array of impressive scores for the SAS Spitfires. Yet again, Len Silver's Rye House Raiders did a wonderful job in nurturing young talent and, whilst the team didn't collect any silverware in 2006, the emergence of Robert Mear was an overriding positive.

Midway through the year, Weymouth gained the necessary planning permission to once again begin racing at their Radipole Lane circuit after complications with ownership and noise had prevented them from competing at the start of the season. All being well, the Wildcats should come to tapes in 2007, along with Oxford who announced, as the season came to a conclusion, that they would be reintroducing Conference League speedway at Cowley next year. As always, rumour suggests that more clubs could be joining the Conference League in 2007 and they would certainly be welcomed with open arms. Whilst the division continues to offer wonderful assistance for younger riders, it would undoubtedly benefit from the inclusion of additional teams to provide a smoother learning curve for the stars of tomorrow.

Certainly, speedway in Britain did take encouraging steps forward in 2006 and the sport is slowly but surely beginning to enjoy increased recognition amongst the media. BBC local radio must be praised for their increased involvement during the season; not only did they establish the nation's first weekly speedway show, but noticeably became significantly more associated with the sport. The traditionalists may gripe, but the benefits of the Play-Off system significantly outweigh the drawbacks, and promoters of the sport must build upon the interest generated by the coverage of Sky Sports by implementing initiatives to ensure the public is tempted to the terraces. After its recent overhaul, British speedway's youth structure continues to make good progress and the extraordinary development of Lewis Bridger emphasises just how much can be achieved with the correct schemes in place. Promotions like Redcar must be praised for their innovative 'community days' that allow anyone of any age to come and try the sport free of charge; it is this sort of spirit that will increase participation at grass-roots level. However, to further safeguard the future of the sport it is paramount to continue offering youngsters an attractive and harmonious route into speedway, which means investing additional resources into this already improving dimension.

Chris Seaward
31 October 2006

ABBREVIATIONS

GENERAL

AL	Amateur League
BSPA	British Speedway Promoters' Association
CL	Conference League
CLKOC	Conference League Knock-Out Cup
CS	Craven Shield/Conference Shield
CT	Conference Trophy
DNA	Did Not Arrive
DNR	Did Not Ride
EL	Elite League
ELKOC	Elite League Knock-Out Cup
FIM	Federation Internationale de Motorcyclisme
KOC	Knock-Out Cup
PL	Premier League
PLKOC	Premier League Knock-Out Cup
PO	Play-Offs
R/R	Rider Replacement
YS	Young Shield

AVERAGE TABLES

Mts	Matches
Rds	Rides
Pts	Points
Bon	Bonus Points
Tot	Total Points
Avge	Average
Max	Maximums

SCORE TABLES

DNA	Did Not Arrive
DNR	Did Not Ride
R	Reply
R/R	Rider Replacement
15(5)	Maximum (Applies to any underlined total)

LEAGUE TABLES

Mts	Matches
Won	Won
Drn	Drawn
Lst	Lost
For	For
Agn	Against
Pts	Points
Bon	Bonus Points
Tot	Total Points

RACE POSITIONS

Ex	Excluded
F	Fell
Ns	Non-starter
Rem	Remounted
Ret	Retired

RACE SCORES TABLES

F	Fell
M	Excluded, 2 minutes
N	Non-starter
R	Retired
X	Excluded
T	Excluded, tapes

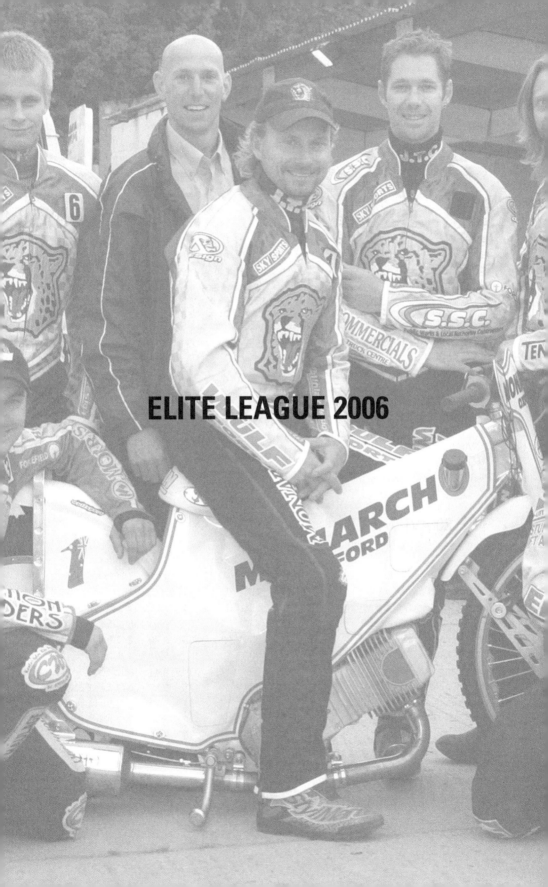

ELITE LEAGUE 2006

SKY SPORTS ELITE LEAGUE TABLE

Team	Mts	Won	Drn	Lst	For	Agn	Pts	Bon	Tot
Peterborough	40	24	0	16	1,942	1,731	48	16	64
Reading	40	25	1	14	1,934	1,756	51	13	64
Swindon	40	23	1	16	1,893	1,786	47	14	61
Coventry	40	23	1	16	1,861	1,835	47	11	58
Belle Vue	40	21	0	19	1,880	1,761	42	15	57
Wolverhampton	40	20	2	18	1,827	1,840	42	10	52
Poole	40	19	0	21	1,880	1,811	38	13	51
Ipswich	40	19	0	21	1,847	1,837	38	8	46
Eastbourne	40	20	1	19	1,791	1,860	41	5	46
Oxford	40	12	0	28	1,696	1,989	24	2	26
Arena-Essex	40	11	0	29	1,658	2,003	22	3	25

PLAY-OFFS

SEMI-FINALS

Peterborough	52	Coventry	40
Reading	51	Swindon	43

FINAL

Reading	49	Peterborough	47	
Peterborough	48	Reading	45	(Peterborough won 95-94 on aggregate)

TOP 20 AVERAGES

(Elite League only. Minimum qualification: 6 matches.)

Rider	Mts	Rds	Pts	Bon	Tot	Avge	Max
Jason Crump (Belle Vue)	39	188	522	6	528	11.23	16 (15 full; 1 paid)
Leigh Adams (Swindon)	40	197	498	23	521	10.58	18 (6 full; 12 paid)
Hans N. Andersen (Peterborough)	38	198	508	13	521	10.53	9 (3 full; 6 paid)
Peter Karlsson (Wolverhampton)	38	184	442	15	457	9.93	8 (3 full; 5 paid)
Nicki Pedersen (Eastbourne)	28	136	329	4	333	9.79	2 (2 full)
Tony Rickardsson (Oxford)	6	29	70	0	70	9.66	1 (1 full)
Greg Hancock (Reading)	36	179	396	25	421	9.41	Nil
Bjarne Pedersen (Poole)	38	202	454	19	473	9.37	4 (2 full; 2 paid)
Jesper B. Jensen (Peterborough)	23	106	224	20	244	9.21	2 (1 full; 1 paid)
Scott Nicholls (Coventry)	36	181	396	16	412	9.10	3 (2 full; 1 paid)
Mark Loram (Ipswich)	40	200	439	7	446	8.92	Nil
Antonio Lindback (Poole)	29	146	289	26	315	8.63	2 (2 paid)
Billy Hamill (Wolverhampton)	38	179	358	20	378	8.45	3 (2 full; 1 paid)
Fredrik Lindgren (Wolverhampton)	38	178	346	22	368	8.27	Nil
Piotr Protasiewicz (Ipswich)	34	155	299	19	318	8.21	1 (1 paid)
Matej Zagar (Reading)	38	187	347	32	379	8.11	1 (1 full)

Ryan Sullivan (Peterborough)	38	185	340	35	375	8.11	4 (1 full; 3 paid)
Simon Stead (Belle Vue)	39	181	344	22	366	8.09	2 (1 full; 1 paid)
Joonas Kylmakorpi (Arena-Essex)	30	149	281	19	300	8.05	1 (1 paid)
Tomasz Chrzanowski (Swindon)	9	52	92	12	104	8.00	Nil

CRAVEN SHIELD

SEMI-FINALS
FIRST LEG (at Swindon) Reading 37, Swindon 36, Poole 35
SECOND LEG (at Poole) Poole 41, Swindon 37, Reading 29
THIRD LEG (at Reading) Poole 40, Reading 37, Swindon 31
AGGREGATE: Poole 116, Swindon 104, Reading 103

FIRST LEG (at Wolverhampton) Eastbourne 38, Ipswich 37, Wolverhampton 33
SECOND LEG (at Ipswich) Ipswich 46, Eastbourne 38, Wolverhampton 23
THIRD LEG (at Eastbourne) Eastbourne 42, Ipswich 33, Wolverhampton 33
AGGREGATE: Eastbourne 118, Ipswich 116, Wolverhampton 89

FIRST LEG (at Coventry) Coventry 42, Belle Vue 40, Peterborough 26
SECOND LEG (at Peterborough) Peterborough 45, Coventry 37, Belle Vue 26
THIRD LEG (at Belle Vue) Belle Vue 41, Coventry 34, Peterborough 33
AGGREGATE: Coventry 113, Belle Vue 107, Peterborough 104

FINAL
FIRST LEG (at Coventry) Poole 41, Coventry 38, Eastbourne 29
SECOND LEG (at Eastbourne) Coventry 38, Eastbourne 35, Poole 35
THIRD LEG (at Poole) Eastbourne 41, Poole 38, Coventry 29
AGGREGATE: Poole 114, Coventry 105, Eastbourne 105

KNOCK-OUT CUP

ROUND ONE

Oxford	43	Wolverhampton	47	
Wolverhampton	54	Oxford	40	(Wolverhampton won 101-83 on aggregate)
Arena-Essex	59	Peterborough	35	
Peterborough	57	Arena-Essex	37	(Arena-Essex won 96-92 on aggregate)
Reading	47	Swindon	43	
Swindon	40	Reading	50	(Reading won 97-83 on aggregate)

QUARTER-FINALS

Ipswich	48	Coventry	42	
Coventry	56	Ipswich	40	(Coventry won 98-88 on aggregate)

| Eastbourne | 55 | Wolverhampton | 38 | |
| Wolverhampton | 41 | Eastbourne | 51 | (Eastbourne won 106-79 on aggregate) |

| Poole | 58 | Reading | 34 | |
| Reading | 51 | Poole | 42 | (Poole won 100-85 on aggregate) |

| Arena-Essex | 44 | Belle Vue | 46 | |
| Belle Vue | 56 | Arena-Essex | 38 | (Belle Vue won 102-82 on aggregate) |

SEMI-FINALS

| Belle Vue | 53 | Poole | 41 | |
| Poole | 43 | Belle Vue | 34 | (Belle Vue won 87-84 on aggregate) |

| Eastbourne | 46 | Coventry | 44 | |
| Coventry | 61 | Eastbourne | 31 | (Coventry won 105-77 on aggregate) |

FINAL

| Belle Vue | 45 | Coventry | 45 | |
| Coventry | 56 | Belle Vue | 40 | (Coventry won 101-85 on aggregate) |

ELITE SHIELD

| Coventry | 51 | Belle Vue | 39 | |
| Belle Vue | 51 | Coventry | 41 | (Coventry won 92-90 on aggregate) |

ARENA-ESSEX DUGGO 7 HAMMERS

ADDRESS: Arena-Essex Raceway, A1306 Arterial Road, Thurrock, Essex, RM19 1AE.
PROMOTER: Ronnie Russell.
YEARS OF OPERATION: 1984-1990 National League; 1991 British League Division Two; 1992-1994 British League Division One; 1995 Premier League; 1996 Conference League; 1997-2003 Premier League; 2004-2006 Elite League.
FIRST MEETING: 5 April 1984.
TRACK LENGTH: 252 metres.
TRACK RECORD: 57.2 seconds – Andreas Jonsson (27/04/05).

CLUB HONOURS

LEAGUE CHAMPIONS: 1991.
KNOCK-OUT CUP WINNERS: 1991.
FOUR-TEAM CHAMPIONS: 1991.

RIDER ROSTER 2006

Henning BAGER; Paul HURRY; Steve JOHNSTON; Joonas KYLMAKORPI; Leigh LANHAM; Mikael MAX; Andreas MESSING; Mariusz PUSZAKOWSKI; Brent WERNER.

OTHER APPEARANCES/GUESTS (official matches only)

James BRUNDLE; Daniel GIFFARD; Gary HAVELOCK; Christian HENRY; David HOWE; Andreas JONSSON; Edward KENNETT; Jason KING; Mark LEMON; Chris MILLS; Scott NICHOLLS; David NORRIS; Shane PARKER; James PURCHASE; the late Lukasz ROMANEK; Rory SCHLEIN; Andy SMITH; Shaun TACEY.

ARENA-ESSEX

* Denotes aggregate/bonus-point victory.

NO.	DATE	OPPONENTS	VENUE	COMPETITION	RESULT	JONSSON	BAGER	JOHNSTON	LANHAM	KYLMAKORPI	ROMANEK	HURRY	TACEY	PUSZAKOWSKI	MAX	MESSING	OTHERS
1	17/3	Eastbourne	H	SC	W57-37	12 (5)	8+3 (4)	5+1 (4)	8 (4)	11+2 (5)	1 (3)	12+1 (5)	-	-	-	-	-
2	18/3	Eastbourne	A	SC	L39-51*	11 (5)	3+2 (4)	7+2 (4)	6 (4)	5+1 (5)	0 (4)	7 (4)	-	-	-	-	-
3	22/3	Poole	A	ELA	L33-59	7 (5)	3+3 (5)	R/R	5 (5)	10 (6)	0 (3)	8+1 (6)	-	-	-	-	-
4	24/3	Poole	H	ELA	W55-40	8+1 (4)	11+4 (6)	R/R	10+1 (5)	12+1 (6)	2+1 (4)	12+1 (5)	-	-	-	-	-
5	31/3	Peterborough	H	KOC	W59-35	9 (4)	6+2 (4)	8+1 (4)	13+2 (5)	13+1 (5)	4 (3)	6+2 (5)	-	-	-	-	-
6	4/4	Swindon	H	ELA	W50-40	-	6+2 (4)	7 (4)	12+2 (5)	13+1 (5)	0 (3)	8+3 (5)	-	-	-	-	4 (4)
7	6/4	Peterborough	A	KOC	L37-57*	-	5+2 (4)	8 (5)	4+1 (4)	7 (4)	0 (7)	0 (0)	-	-	-	-	13 (5)
8	14/4	Ipswich	A	ELA	L42-50	-	3 (4)	7+1 (4)	2 (4)	14 (5)	-	-	7 (5)	-	-	-	0 (3)

NO.	DATE	OPPONENTS	VENUE	COMPETITION	RESULT	JONSSON	BAGER	JOHNSTON	LANHAM	KYLMAKORPI	ROMANEK	HURRY	TACEY	PUSZAKOWSKI	MAX	MESSING	OTHERS
9	14/4	Ipswich	H	ELA	W49-41	R/R	7+1 (5)	7+2 (5)	13+1 (6)	13 (6)		9+1 (5)	0 (3)	-			
10	24/4	Belle Vue	A	ELA	L44-46	R/R	5+2 (5)	8+2 (5)	11 (6)	13 (6)		3+2 (4)	4 (4)				
11	28/4	Reading	H	ELA	W58-33	-	11+2 (5)	8+2 (4)	10+1 (4)	14 (5)		6+2 (4)	-	0 (4)	-		9+1 (4)
12	8/5	Reading	A	ELA	L46-50*	15 (5)	2 (4)	6+2 (4)	6 (4)	14+2 (5)		1 (4)	-	2+1 (4)	-		
13	10/5	Wolverhampton	H	ELA	W46-44		11 (5)	6+2 (4)	7 (4)	11+1 (5)		6+2 (4)	-	3 (4)	2 (4)		
14	26/5	Coventry	A	ELA	L43-47		R/R	4 (4)	6+1 (5)	9+2 (5)		7 (5)	-	7+2 (6)	10 (5)		
15	31/5	Coventry	H	ELA	W46-43		R/R	5+1 (4)	8+1 (5)	10 (5)		5+1 (4)	-	8 (7)	10+3 (5)	-	
16	5/6	Wolverhampton	A	ELA	L36-56		-	4+1 (4)	5+1 (4)	10 (5)		8 (5)	1+1 (4)	-	7 (5)	-	1 (3)
17	7/6	Wolverhampton	H	ELB	L44-46		-	4+1 (4)	11+1 (6)	7+1 (4)		10+2 (7)	1+1 (4)		11+1 (5)	-	R/R
18	8/6	Swindon	A	ELA	L38-53		-	13 (6)	4+1 (5)	R/R		1+1 (3)	11 (7)		3+2 (4)	-	6 (5)
19	17/6	Eastbourne	A	ELA	L32-62		-	7+1 (5)	8 (6)	R/R		-		-	10 (6)		7+1 (10)
20	19/6	Poole	A	ELB	L24-66		-	7 (6)	5+1 (5)	R/R		-		0 (2)	9 (6)		2 (11)
21	21/6	Ipswich	H	ELB	L42-48		R/R	4+2 (4)	11 (5)	8 (5)		-		-	-		19+4 (16)
22	22/6	Ipswich	A	ELB	L25-57		R/R	9+2 (5)	3+1 (5)	9+1 (5)		-		-	4 (2)		12+1 (13)
23	28/6	Eastbourne	H	ELA	L40-52		5+2 (5)	5+1 (5)	13 (6)	R/R		8+1 (6)		-	3+1 (4)	-	6+2 (4)
24	3/7	Peterborough	H	ELA	L42-48		6+3 (5)	7+1 (5)	10+1 (6)	R/R		6+2 (5)		-	11+1 (6)	-	2 (3)
25	7/7	Belle Vue	H	KOC	L44-46		6 (5)	13+1 (6)	8+2 (5)	R/R		8+1 (5)		-	9+1 (6)	-	0 (3)
26	10/7	Belle Vue	A	KOC	L38-56		0 (3)	4+1 (5)	8+1 (6)	R/R		6+1 (5)		-	14 (6)	-	6 (5)
27	12/7	Swindon	H	ELB	L43-46		7+1 (4)	9+1 (6)	9+2 (6)	R/R		5+3 (5)		-	6+1 (5)	-	7+1 (4)
28	14/7	Coventry	A	ELB	L29-65		1 (4)	6+1 (6)	5 (5)	R/R		-		-	12 (6)	-	5+1 (9)
29	26/7	Coventry	H	ELB	L44-46		5+1 (4)	7+2 (5)	11 (6)	R/R		-		-	10+1 (6)	-	11+4 (9)
30	27/7	Swindon	A	ELB	L36-57		3+1 (4)	8 (6)	4+2 (5)	R/R		-		-	13 (6)	-	8+1 (9)
31	2/8	Oxford	H	ELA	L39-53		9+3 (7)	7 (5)	6+1 (5)	-		R/R		-	13+1 (5)	-	4 (8)
32	7/8	Reading	A	ELB	L33-60		4+2 (6)	9 (5)	5 (5)	9+1 (5)		R/R		-	4 (4)	-	2 (5)
33	9/8	Reading	H	ELB	L41-51		13+3 (7)	6 (5)	6+2 (5)	3+1 (5)		R/R		-	9+1 (4)	-	4 (4)
34	11/8	Eastbourne	A	ELB	L41-53		9+3 (7)	12+3 (6)	4 (4)	6 (4)		R/R		-	10 (5)	-	
35	18/8	Poole	H	ELB	W50-40		8+2 (5)	8+2 (5)	13+1 (6)	9+2 (5)		-		-	R/R	1+1 (4)	11 (5)
36	21/8	Wolverhampton	A	ELB	L40-54		3+3 (6)	8+2 (5)	5 (5)	6 (4)		R/R		-	14 (5)	4 (5)	-
37	25/8	Belle Vue	H	ELA	W48-41*		12+1 (7)	14 (6)	5+2 (4)	11+1 (5)		R/R		-	1+1 (2)	5+2 (6)	-
38	28/8	Peterborough	A	ELA	L39-56		10+2 (7)	10+1 (6)	3 (3)	7 (5)		R/R		-	9 (4)	0 (2)	-
39	30/8	Oxford	A	ELA	L26-64		7 (6)	4+1 (6)	R/R	2 (3)		-		-	8 (6)	2+2 (5)	3 (4)
40	1/9	Peterborough	H	ELB	W58-38		14+2 (7)	12+1 (5)	8+3 (4)	10+2 (5)		R/R		-	12+1 (5)	2 (4)	-
41	4/9	Belle Vue	A	ELB	L42-51		5+2 (6)	7+1 (5)	8+1 (4)	9 (5)		R/R		-	6+2 (5)	7+1 (5)	-
42	6/9	Belle Vue	H	ELB	L39-56		4+1 (6)	8 (5)	9+1 (4)	6 (5)		R/R		-	9 (5)	3+1 (5)	-
43	7/9	Peterborough	A	ELB	L28-62		8+1 (7)	3+1 (5)	4 (4)	8 (5)		R/R		-	5+1 (5)	0 (4)	-
44	27/9	Oxford	A	ELB	L37-55		7+1 (6)	6+2 (5)	5 (4)	8+1 (5)		R/R		-	9+1 (5)	2+1 (5)	-
45	29/9	Oxford	H	ELB	W62-32*		16+5 (7)	12+1 (5)	8+2 (4)	11+1 (5)		R/R		-	14+1 (5)	1 (1)	-
46	4/10	Eastbourne	H	ELB	W48-42		10+4 (7)	7+1 (5)	10+1 (5)	14+1 (5)		R/R		-	6 (4)	1 (4)	-

NOTE: SC = Spring Challenge. Following the home match against Ipswich on 14 April, Joonas Kylmakorpi lost a bonus point run-off to Piotr Protasiewicz. The away match at Ipswich on 22 June originally ended in a 57-37 defeat, but was amended as Troy Batchelor was not permitted to appear as a guest for the Hammers due to being in Coventry's declared line-up as their number eight rider. His tally on the night was therefore deleted to leave the result as a 57-25 defeat instead.

DETAILS OF OTHER RIDERS

(all guests unless underlined)

Match No. 6: David Norris 4 (4); Match No. 7: Scott Nicholls 13 (5); Match No. 8: Scott Nicholls 9 (5); Jason King 0(3); Match No. 11: David Norris 9+1 (4); Match No. 16: James Brundle 1 (3); Match No. 17: Roman Povazhny R/R; Match No. 18: Andy Smith 6 (5); Match No. 19: Brent Werner 5+1 (6); Jason King 2 (4); Match No. 20: David Howe 2 (5); Brent Werner 1 (6); Match No. 21: Scott Nicholls 11+1 (5); Brent Werner 7+2 (7); Jason King 1+1 (4); Match No. 22: Troy Batchelor 12+1 (7); James Purchase 0 (6); Match No. 23: Brent Werner 6+2 (4); Match No. 24: Brent Werner 2 (3); Match No. 25: Chris Mills 0 (3); Match No. 26: Brent Werner 6 (5); Match No. 27: Brent Werner 7+1 (4); Match No. 28: Shane Parker 5+1 (5); Brent Werner 0 (4); Match No. 29: Gary Havelock 7+1 (5); Brent Werner 4+3 (4); Match No. 30: Mark Lemon 6+1 (5); Christian Henry 2 (4); Match No. 31: Rory Schlein 4 (4); Brent Werner 0 (4); Match No. 32: Brent Werner 2 (5); Match No. 33: Daniel Giffard 4 (4); Match No. 35: Gary Havelock 11 (5); Match No. 39: Edward Kennett 3 (4).

DETAILS OF TACTICAL RIDES AND TACTICAL SUBSTITUTE RIDES

Match No. 3: Jonsson 4 points (TR); Hurry 0 points (TR); Match No. 7: Nicholls 6 points (TR); Kylmakorpi 4 points (TR); Match No. 8: Kylmakorpi 4 points (TR); Nicholls 0 points (TR); Match No. 12: Kylmakorpi 6 points (TR); Jonsson 6 points (TR); Match No. 16: Max 4 points (TR); Hurry 0 points (TR); Match No. 18: Puszakowski 2 points (TR); Johnston 1 point (TR; not doubled); Match No. 19: Max 4 points (TR); Johnston 4 points (TR); Match No. 20: Max 1 point (TR; not doubled); Johnston 1 point (TR; not doubled); Match No. 22: Batchelor 4 points (TR); Johnston 4 points (TR); Match No. 23: Lanham 4 points (TR); Max 0 points (TR); Match No. 26: Max 6 points (TR); Lanham 2 points (TR); Match No. 28: Max 4 points (TR); Parker 4 points (TR); Match No. 30: Max 6 points (TR); Johnston 0 points (TR); Match No. 31: Max 4 points (TR); Lanham 1 point (TR; not doubled); Match No. 32: Johnston 6 points (TR); Max 1 point (TR; not doubled); Match No. 33: Max 4 points (TR); Kylmakorpi 0 points (TR); Match No. 34: Johnston 6 points (TR); Max 4 points (TR); Match No. 36: Max 4 points (TR); Johnston 4 points (TR); Match No. 38: Max 6 points (TR); Johnston 4 points (TR); Match No. 39: Kylmakorpi 0 points (TR); Match No. 41: Lanham 6 points (TR); Match No. 42: Johnston 6 points (TR); Lanham 4 points (TR); Match No. 43: Johnston 0 points (TR); Bager 0 points (TR); Match No. 44: Max 4 points (TR); Kylmakorpi 1 point (TR; not doubled).

AVERAGES
(40 Elite League, 4 Knock-Out Cup = 44 fixtures)

Rider	Mts	Rds	Pts	Bon	Tot	Avge	Max
Joonas Kylmakorpi	32	158	299	20	319	8.08	1 paid
Mikael Max	32	156	248	20	268	6.87	1 paid
Leigh Lanham	43	209	313	37	350	6.70	1 paid
Steve Johnston	42	209	297	44	341	6.53	-
Paul Hurry	20	92	123	26	149	6.48	-
Henning Bager	35	189	242	61	303	6.41	1 paid
Brent Werner	11	52	40	9	49	3.77	-
Mariusz Puszakowski	8	38	31	4	35	3.68	-
Andreas Messing	12	50	28	8	36	2.88	-

Also rode (in alphabetical order):

Rider	Mts	Rds	Pts	Bon	Tot	Avge	Max
Andreas Jonsson	4	18	34	1	35	7.78	-
Lukasz Romanek	5	20	6	1	7	1.40	-
Shaun Tacey	4	16	12	1	13	3.25	-

ARENA-ESSEX: From left to right, back row: Paul Hurry, Leigh Lanham, Ronnie Russell (promoter/team manager), Lukasz Romanek, Henning Bager, Shaun Tacey, Andreas Jonsson. Front row, kneeling: Rhys Naylor (mascot), Joonas Kylmakorpi. On bike: Steve Johnston.

Guests   21   92   95   6   101   4.39   -

(James Brundle [1]; Daniel Giffard [1]; Gary Havelock [2]; Christian Henry [1]; David Howe [1]; Edward Kennett [1]; Jason King [3]; Mark Lemon [1]; Chris Mills [1]; Scott Nicholls [3]; David Norris [2]; Shane Parker [1]; James Purchase [1]; Rory Schlein [1]; Andy Smith [1])

NOTE: Troy Batchelor made a guest appearance for Arena-Essex in the ELB match at Ipswich, scoring 12+1 points from seven rides, including 4 points from a tactical ride, however, his appearance was deemed ineligible and was deleted from the records.

BELLE VUE FONESTYLE UK ACES

ADDRESS: Belle Vue Greyhound Stadium, Kirkmanshulme Lane, Gorton, Manchester, M18 7BA.
PROMOTERS: Ian Thomas, Anthony E. Mole and Redvers T. Mole.
YEARS OF OPERATION: 1928 Open; 1988-1990 British League; 1991-1994 British League Division One; 1995-1996 Premier League; 1997 Elite League and Amateur League; 1998-2006 Elite League.
FIRST MEETING: 28 July 1928.
TRACK LENGTH: 285 metres.
TRACK RECORD: 57.8 seconds – Jason Crump (07/08/06).

PREVIOUS VENUE: Zoological Gardens, Hyde Road, Manchester.
YEARS OF OPERATION: 1929 English Dirt-Track League; 1930 Northern League; 1931 Northern League and Southern League; 1932-1933 National League; 1934 National League and Reserve League; 1935-1936 National League; 1937 National League and Provincial League; 1938 National League Division One; 1939 National League Division One and National League Division Two; 1940-1945 Open; 1946 National League; 1947-1956 National League Division One; 1957-1964 National League; 1965-1967 British League; 1968-1969 British League Division One and British League Division Two; 1970-1974 British League Division One; 1975-1987 British League.

CLUB HONOURS

LEAGUE CHAMPIONS: 1930, 1931, 1933, 1934, 1935, 1936, 1963, 1970, 1971, 1972, 1982, 1993.
NOTE: The Division Two side were also crowned League Champions in 1968 and 1969.
KNOCK-OUT CUP WINNERS: 1931, 1972, 1973, 1975, 2005.
NOTE: The Division Two side also won their Knock-Out Cup competition in 1969.
NATIONAL TROPHY WINNERS: 1933, 1934, 1935, 1936, 1937, 1946, 1947, 1949, 1958.
ACU CUP WINNERS: 1934, 1935, 1936, 1937, 1946.
BRITISH SPEEDWAY CUP WINNERS: 1939.
BRITANNIA SHIELD WINNERS: 1957, 1958, 1960.
INTER-LEAGUE KNOCK-OUT CUP WINNERS: 1975.
PREMIERSHIP WINNERS: 1983.
LEAGUE CUP WINNERS: 1983.
PAIRS CHAMPIONS: 1984, 2006.
FOUR-TEAM CHAMPIONS: 1992.

RIDER ROSTER 2006

Kenneth BJERRE; Jason CRUMP; Tom P. MADSEN; Phil MORRIS; Joe SCREEN; Simon STEAD; James WRIGHT.

OTHER APPEARANCES/GUESTS (official matches only)

Tommy ALLEN; Craig BRANNEY; James BRUNDLE; Josef FRANC; Gary HAVELOCK; Chris LOUIS; Jason LYONS; Henrik MOLLER; Joel PARSONS; Ryan SULLIVAN; Davey WATT.

BELLE VUE

* Denotes aggregate/bonus-point victory.

NO.	DATE	OPPONENTS	VENUE	COMPETITION	RESULT	BJERRE	SCREEN	STEAD	WRIGHT	CRUMP	MORRIS	MADSEN	ALLEN	PARSONS	OTHERS
1	17/3	Coventry	A	ES	L39-51	13 (5)	0 (1)	7 (4)	3 (4)	8+1 (5)	4+2 (5)	4 (6)	-	-	
2	20/3	Eastbourne	H	ELA	W48-42	8 (6)	R/R	9+1 (5)	3 (4)	15 (5)	11+1 (6)	2 (4)			
3	23/3	Peterborough	A	ELA	L44-46	10+1 (6)	R/R	9 (5)	0 (3)	15 (5)	7 (6)	3+2 (5)			
4	3/4	Peterborough	H	ELA	W50-40*	5+2 (4)	7 (4)	9+1 (5)	6 (4)	15 (5)	3+1 (5)	5 (3)			
5	10/4	Coventry	H	ELA	W58-37	9+3 (5)	10+1 (4)	11+1 (4)	6+1 (4)	15 (5)	4+1 (5)	3 (3)			
6	14/4	Wolverhampton	H	ELA	W54-39	3 (4)	12 (4)	15 (5)	5+1 (4)	13 (5)	3 (1)	3 (7)			
7	19/4	Swindon	H	ELA	W55-41	5+1 (4)	8+1 (4)	11+2 (5)	-	14 (5)	10+2 (5)	7+2 (4)	0 (3)		
8	24/4	Arena-Essex	H	ELA	W46-44	9 (5)	8+1 (4)	8 (4)	5+1 (4)	13+1 (5)	2+1 (4)	1 (4)			
9	26/4	Poole	A	ELA	L38-55	4+2 (4)	6+1 (4)	7 (5)	2 (4)	17 (5)	1 (4)	1 (4)			
10	27/4	Swindon	A	ELA	L43-50*	10+1 (5)	5+2 (4)	6 (4)	3+1 (4)	17 (5)	1 (4)	1 (4)			
11	1/5	Ipswich	A	ELA	L42-53	1+1 (4)	13 (6)	R/R	-	16 (5)	8+2 (7)	0 (3)			4 (5)
12	3/5	Coventry	H	ES	W51-41	8+2 (4)	7+1 (4)	12 (5)	-	13+1 (5)	2 (4)	4+1 (4)	5+1 (4)		
13	8/5	Oxford	H	ELA	W56-38	8 (4)	7 (4)	12 (5)	6+1 (4)	15 (5)	5+2 (4)	3+1 (4)			
14	10/5	Oxford	A	ELA	W50-43*	7 (4)	9+2 (5)	10 (4)	4+1 (4)	15 (5)	3 (4)	2+2 (4)			
15	24/5	Ipswich	H	ELA	W48-42	R/R	8 (5)	13 (6)	1 (4)	16+1 (6)	3 (4)	7+2 (5)			
16	29/5	Reading	A	ELA	L43-52	6+1 (4)	7+2 (5)	6 (4)	-	17 (5)	4 (5)	1+1 (4)			2+1 (3)
17	31/5	Reading	H	ELA	W51-39*	7+1 (4)	8+1 (4)	12+1 (5)	3+1 (4)	14 (5)	1 (3)	6+1 (5)			
18	1/6	Swindon	A	ELB	L42-51	7+1 (5)	5 (4)	7 (4)	3 (4)	16 (5)	2+1 (4)	2 (4)			
19	5/6	Peterborough	H	ELB	W52-43	6 (5)	4+2 (4)	11 (4)	-	13 (5)	11+2 (6)	6+2 (4)	1 (3)		
20	9/6	Coventry	A	ELA	L42-49*	6 (4)	10+1 (5)	9 (4)	1+1 (4)	13+1 (5)	2 (5)	1 (3)			
21	10/6	Eastbourne	A	ELA	L42-48*	1+1 (4)	11 (5)	7+1 (4)	-	15 (5)	3 (7)	5+1 (4)	0 (1)		
22	19/6	Eastbourne	H	ELB	W44-30	4+2 (3)	11 (4)	10 (4)	4 (3)	9 (3)	3 (3)	3+1 (4)			
23	22/6	Peterborough	A	ELB	L39-55	9+1 (4)	2+2 (4)	8 (5)	3+2 (4)	14 (5)	3+1 (7)	0 (1)			
24	26/6	Swindon	H	ELB	W43-30*	7 (3)	7+2 (4)	8 (4)	4+1 (3)	9 (3)	3 (3)	5 (4)			
25	28/6	Wolverhampton	H	ELB	W61-35	9+3 (5)	12+2 (5)	9+1 (4)	6+1 (4)	12 (4)	6+2 (4)	7+2 (4)			
26	3/7	Poole	H	ELA	W53-37	8 (4)	9+1 (4)	8+3 (5)	8+3 (5)	14 (5)	2+2 (4)	4+1 (4)			
27	6/7	Ipswich	A	ELB	L43-52	7 (4)	9+1 (5)	2+1 (4)	6+1 (6)	18 (5)	1+1 (3)	0 (3)			
28	7/7	Arena-Essex	A	KOC	W46-44	-	11 (6)	R/R	2+1 (4)	18 (6)	3 (4)	4+1 (5)			8+1 (5)
29	10/7	Arena-Essex	A	KOC	W56-38*	12+2 (5)	8+1 (4)	9+1 (4)	5+1 (4)	14 (5)	4+1 (4)	4+1 (4)			
30	12/7	Poole	A	ELB	L44-50	6 (4)	4 (4)	10+1 (5)	6 (6)	18 (5)	0 (3)	0 (3)			
31	24/7	Poole	H	ELB	L42-48	10+1 (5)	3 (4)	8 (5)	7+1 (7)	11+1 (5)	R/R	3 (4)			
32	27/7	Coventry	A	ELB	L44-49	9 (5)	R/R	15 (6)	4+1 (6)	11+1 (5)	-	0 (3)			5 (5)
33	31/7	Coventry	H	ELB	W49-41*	8 (5)	9 (5)	6+1 (4)	10+1 (7)	15 (5)	R/R	1 (4)			
34	7/8	Ipswich	H	ELB	W51-39*	7+3 (4)	9 (4)	10+2 (5)	4+1 (4)	15 (5)	-	5+2 (5)			1 (3)
35	9/8	Oxford	A	ELB	L44-46	6 (4)	4 (4)	7+1 (5)	4+2 (4)	15 (5)	-	5+1 (5)			3 (3)

NO.	DATE	OPPONENTS	VENUE	COMPETITION	RESULT	BJERRE	SCREEN	STEAD	WRIGHT	CRUMP	MORRIS	MADSEN	ALLEN	PARSONS	OTHERS
36	14/8	Wolverhampton	A	ELA	L44-46*	8 (4)	7+1 (4)	8 (5)	3+2 (4)	13 (5)	-	3 (5)	-	-	2 (3)
37	21/8	Oxford	H	ELB	W53-39*	7+1 (4)	12+1 (5)	9+2 (5)	6+2 (4)	11 (4)	6+1 (4)	2 (4)	-	-	-
38	25/8	Arena-Essex	A	ELA	L41-48	10 (5)	5 (4)	5 (5)		-	3+3 (4)	8+3 (6)		1 (3)	9 (3)
39	28/8	Reading	A	ELB	L40-55	9+1 (6)	7 (4)	8 (4)	-	15 (5)	R/R	1 (6)	-	-	0 (5)
40	2/9	Eastbourne	A	ELB	L36-42*	4+2 (4)	9 (3)	6 (3)	-	11 (3)	2+2 (4)	2 (3)	-	2 (4)	-
41	4/9	Arena-Essex	H	ELB	W51-42	9+2 (4)	9+1 (4)	10+2 (5)	6 (4)	15 (5)	1+1 (4)	1 (4)	-	-	-
42	6/9	Arena-Essex	A	ELB	W56-39*	13+1 (5)	7+2 (4)	7+1 (4)	5 (4)	15 (5)	4+2 (4)	5+1 (4)	-	-	-
43	11/9	Poole	H	KOC s/f	W53-41	15+1 (6)	R/R	9+2 (5)	8+2 (5)	14 (5)	3+1 (3)	4+1 (6)	-	-	-
44	18/9	Wolverhampton	A	ELB	L39-52*	13+1 (6)	R/R	10 (6)	2 (5)	11 (5)	3+1 (6)	0 (2)	-	-	-
45	20/9	Reading	H	ELB	W59-34*	10 (5)	R/R	15 (6)	9+3 (5)	14+1 (5)	4+2 (5)	7+1 (4)	-	-	-
46	28/9	Poole	A	KOC s/f	L34-43*	12+1 (5)	R/R	14 (4)	1+1 (4)	-	2 (2)	1 (6)	-	-	4 (3)
47	6/10	Coventry/ Peterborough	Cov	CS s/f	2nd – 40	7+1 (4)	-	8 (4)	4 (4)	12 (4)	2 (4)	-	-	-	7+1 (4)
48	9/10	Coventry	H	KOC f	D45-45	9+1 (5)	R/R	9 (6)	3+1 (5)	14 (5)	7+2 (6)	3 (3)	-	-	-
49	12/10	Coventry/ Peterborough	Peter	CS s/f	3rd – 26	-	-	8 (4)	1+1 (4)	12 (4)	1 (4)	-	-	-	4 (8)
50	13/10	Coventry	A	KOC f	L40-56	-	R/R	12 (6)	4+1 (5)	15 (5)	1 (3)	-	-	1 (5)	7 (6)
51	16/10	Coventry/ Peterborough	H	CS s/f	1st – 41	5+2 (4)	-	9 (4)	5+1 (4)	12 (4)	-	-	-	5+2 (4)	5+1 (4)

NOTE: ES = Elite Shield. Following the away match at Eastbourne on 10 June, Jason Crump defeated Nicki Pedersen in a run-off for the bonus point. The home league match versus Eastbourne on 19 June was abandoned after heat twelve, with the result permitted to stand. The home league match versus Swindon on 26 June was abandoned after heat twelve, with the result permitted to stand. The away league match at Eastbourne on 2 September was abandoned after heat twelve, with the result permitted to stand. The away Knock-Out Cup semi-final tie at Poole on 28 September was abandoned after heat twelve, with the result permitted to stand.

DETAILS OF OTHER RIDERS

(all guests)

Match No. 11: James Brundle 4 (5); Match No. 16: James Brundle 2+1 (3); Match No. 28: Gary Havelock 8+1 (5); Match No. 32: Josef Franc 5 (5); Match No. 34: Joel Parsons 1 (3); Match No. 35: Joel Parsons 3 (3); Match No. 36: Joel Parsons 2 (3); Match No. 38: Chris Louis 9 (3); Match No. 39: Henrik Moller 0 (5); Match No. 46: Ryan Sullivan 4 (3); Match No. 47: Jason Lyons 7+1 (4); Match No. 49: Jason Lyons 3 (4); Craig Branney 1 (4); Match No. 50: Davey Watt 7 (6); Match No. 51: Jason Lyons 5+1 (4).

DETAILS OF TACTICAL RIDES AND TACTICAL SUBSTITUTE RIDES

Match No. 9: Crump 6 points (TR); Screen 1 point (TR; not doubled); Match No. 10: Crump 6 points (TR); Match No. 11: Screen 6 points (TR); Crump 4 points (TR); Match No. 16: Crump 6 points (TR); Screen 4 points (TR); Match No. 18: Crump 6 points (TR); Match No. 20: Bjerre 2 points (TR); Match No. 23: Crump 4 points (TR); Bjerre 4 points (TR); Match No. 27: Crump 6 points (TR); Screen 4 points (TR); Match No. 30: Crump 6 points (TR); Stead 2 points (TR); Match No. 32: Stead 6 points (TR); Match No. 39: Stead 6 points (TR); Crump 4 points (TR); Match No. 40: Crump 6 points (TR); Screen 6 points (TR); Match No. 44: Crump 2 points (TS); Match No. 46: Stead 6 points (TR); Bjerre 4 points (TR); Match No. 50: Crump 6 points (TR); Stead 6 points (TR); Watt 1 point (TS; not doubled).

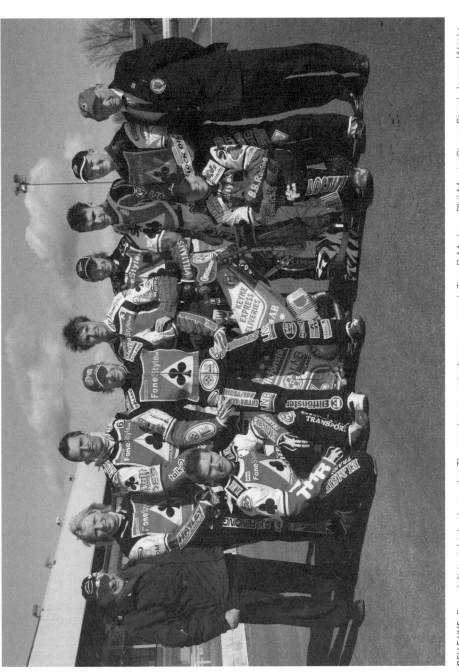

BELLE VUE: From left to right, back row: Ian Thomas (co-promoter/team manager), Tom P. Madsen, Phil Morris, Simon Stead, James Wright, Aidan Collins, Joe Screen, Tony Mole (club owner/promoter). Front row, kneeling: Tommy Allen, Kenneth Bjerre. On bike: Jason Crump.

AVERAGES
(40 Elite League, 6 Knock-Out Cup, 3 Craven Shield, 2 Elite Shield = 51 fixtures)

Rider	Mts	Rds	Pts	Bon	Tot	Avge	Max
Jason Crump	49	236	651	8	659	11.17	19 full; 1 paid
Simon Stead	49	227	435	25	460	8.11	1 full; 1 paid
Joe Screen	39	165	289	29	318	7.71	1 full
Kenneth Bjerre	47	212	361	43	404	7.62	-
James Wright	42	183	181	38	219	4.79	-
Phil Morris	43	186	154	37	191	4.11	-
Tom P. Madsen	47	194	145	30	175	3.61	-

Also rode (in alphabetical order):							
Tommy Allen	4	11	6	1	7	2.55	-
Joel Parsons	4	16	9	2	11	2.75	-

Guests	15	60	61	4	65	4.33	-

(Craig Branney [1]; James Brundle [2]; Josef Franc [1]; Gary Havelock [1]; Chris Louis [1]; Jason Lyons [3]; Henrik Moller [1]; Joel Parsons [3]; Ryan Sullivan [1]; Davey Watt [1]).

NOTE: Tom P. Madsen was ever-present throughout the 40-match Elite League programme.

INDIVIDUAL MEETINGS

6 March: Peter Craven Memorial Trophy

    1st Jason Crump (after run-off) 14; 2nd Bjarne Pedersen 14; 3rd Joe Screen 13; Simon Stead 10; Mark Loram 9; Niels-Kristian Iversen 9; Andy Smith 9; David Howe 7; Kenneth Bjerre 7; Rusty Harrison 6; Andre Compton 5; James Wright 5; Tom P. Madsen 4; Tobias Kroner 4; Phil Morris 3; Tommy Allen 1; Aidan Collins (reserve) 0.

17 July: Greggs Junior Championship

    1st Adam Roynon 14; 2nd Tai Woffinden 13; 3rd Josh Auty (on race wins) 12; John Oliver 12; Adam McKinna 11; Barry Burchatt 9; Paul Burnett 7; John Branney 7; Karl Mason 7; Byron Bekker 6; Jack Roberts 5; David Haigh 5; Ben Taylor 5; Ben Hopwood 3; Grant Hayes 1; Karl Langley 1.

17 September: Foxy's Fun-Day – Andy Smith Testimonial

    QUALIFYING SCORES: Simon Stead <u>15</u>; Mark Loram 12; Jason Crump 12; James Wright 11; Travis McGowan 10; Olly Allen 9; Stuart Robson 8; Steve Johnston 8; Billy Janniro 8; Richard Hall 7; Ricky Ashworth 6; Lubos Tomicek 6; Tai Woffinden 3; Trevor Harding 3; Rusty Harrison 1; John Oliver 1. SEMI-FINAL: 1st Crump; 2nd McGowan; 3rd Allen; 4th Wright. FINAL: 1st Stead; 2nd Crump; 3rd McGowan; 4th Loram.

COVENTRY BUILDBASE BEES

ADDRESS: Coventry International Motor Speedway, Rugby Road, Brandon, Nr Coventry, Warwickshire, CV8 3GJ.
PROMOTERS: Colin Pratt and Jeremy Heaver.
YEARS OF OPERATION: 1928 Open; 1929-1931 Southern League; 1932-1933 National League; 1934 Open; 1936 Open; 1948 National League Division Three; 1949-1956 National League Division Two; 1957-1964 National League; 1965-1967 British League; 1968-1974 British League Division One; 1975-1990 British League; 1991-1994 British League Division One; 1995-1996 Premier League; 1997-2003 Elite League; 2004 Elite League and Conference Trophy; 2005-2006 Elite League.
FIRST MEETING: 29 September 1928.
TRACK LENGTH: 301 metres.
TRACK RECORD: 58.0 seconds – Leigh Adams (30/06/06) and Chris Harris (15/09/06).

CLUB HONOURS

LEAGUE CHAMPIONS: 1953, 1968, 1978, 1979, 1987, 1988, 2005.
KNOCK-OUT CUP WINNERS: 1967, 2006.
PAIRS CHAMPIONS: 1978 (Shared with Cradley Heath).
LEAGUE CUP WINNERS: 1981, 1985, 1987.
PREMIERSHIP WINNERS: 1986.
CRAVEN SHIELD WINNERS: 1997, 2000.
ELITE SHIELD WINNERS: 2006.

RIDER ROSTER 2006

Olly ALLEN; Troy BATCHELOR; Chris HARRIS; Billy JANNIRO; Scott NICHOLLS; Rory SCHLEIN; Martin SMOLINSKI;

OTHER APPEARANCES/GUESTS (official matches only)

James BRUNDLE; Paul CLEWS; Daniel GIFFARD; Christian HENRY; Pawel HLIB; Jason KING; Emil KRAMER; Mark LORAM; Bjarne PEDERSEN; Tomasz PISZCZ; Jacek REMPALA; Chris SCHRAMM; Mathieu TRESARRIEU; Danny WARWICK; Davey WATT; Todd WILTSHIRE.

COVENTRY

* Denotes aggregate/bonus-point victory

NO.	DATE	OPPONENTS	VENUE	COMPETITION	RESULT	HARRIS	JANNIRO	SCHLEIN	RISAGER	NICHOLLS	SMOLINSKI	ALLEN	BATCHELOR	HLIB	REMPALA	OTHERS
1	17/3	Belle Vue	H	ES	W51-39	4 (4)	7+2 (4)	11 (5)	7+2 (4)	13 (5)	8+2 (6)	1 (4)	-	-	-	-
2	20/3	Reading	A	ELA	W49-41	9+2 (5)	8+1 (4)	9+2 (4)	6 (4)	11 (5)	5 (5)	1+1 (4)	-	-	-	-

NO.	DATE	OPPONENTS	VENUE	COMPETITION	RESULT	HARRIS	JANNIRO	SCHLEIN	RISAGER	NICHOLLS	SMOLINSKI	ALLEN	BATCHELOR	HLIB	REMPALA	OTHERS
3	24/3	Reading	H	ELA	L42-48*	8 (5)	5+1 (4)	7 (4)	1 (4)	11+1 (5)	7+1 (5)	3 (3)	-	-	-	-
4	7/4	Ipswich	H	ELA	W48-45	3+2 (4)	10 (5)	6 (4)	4+1 (4)	10+1 (5)	7 (4)	8 (4)	-	-	-	-
5	10/4	Belle Vue	A	ELA	L37-58	4+1 (4)	4 (4)	9 (5)	4+1 (4)	10 (5)	1 (4)	5+1 (4)	-	-	-	-
6	14/4	Wolverhampton	H	ELA	W53-40	9+2 (5)	6+2 (4)	5 (4)	4+1 (4)	14 (5)	3+2 (3)	12+1 (5)	-	-	-	-
7	17/4	Wolverhampton	A	ELA	L40-53*	6 (4)	7+1 (4)	12+1 (5)	1+1 (3)	11 (6)	-	3 (5)	0 (3)	-	-	-
8	26/4	Oxford	A	ELA	L43-47	10+2 (5)	7+1 (4)	7 (4)	2+1 (4)	13+1 (5)	4 (4)	0 (4)	-	-	-	-
9	28/4	Oxford	H	ELA	W50-42*	6+1 (4)	5+2 (4)	10+1 (5)	0 (1)	15 (5)	4+2 (5)	10 (6)	-	-	-	-
10	1/5	Poole	A	ELA	L38-55	4+1 (4)	4+1 (4)	11+1 (5)	5+2 (4)	8 (5)	-	6+2 (5)	-	-	-	0 (3)
11	3/5	Belle Vue	A	ES	L41-51*	5+1 (4)	4 (2)	6 (5)	3+1 (4)	13 (6)	6+2 (7)	4+1 (4)	-	-	-	-
12	8/5	Eastbourne	A	ELA	L41-47	9 (5)	4+2 (4)	5 (4)	4 (4)	6+1 (5)	4+1 (4)	9 (4)	-	-	-	-
13	11/5	Swindon	A	ELA	L39-56	8+1 (5)	1+1 (3)	9 (4)	1 (3)	13 (5)	3+1 (5)	4+2 (5)	-	-	-	-
14	15/5	Peterborough	H	ELA	W48-44	9+2 (5)	3+1 (4)	8+1 (4)	3+2 (4)	9 (5)	6 (3)	10+2 (5)	-	-	-	-
15	18/5	Ipswich	A	ELA	L42-51	2 (4)	4+2 (4)	7+1 (5)	1 (3)	16 (5)	3+1 (3)	9 (6)	-	-	-	-
16	25/5	Peterborough	A	ELA	L32-62	1 (4)	3 (4)	11 (5)	5+1 (4)	9 (5)	-	2 (5)	-	-	-	1 (3)
17	26/5	Arena-Essex	H	ELA	W47-43	7 (4)	7+2 (4)	12+2 (5)	6+1 (4)	10+1 (5)	-	1 (1)	-	-	-	4 (7)
18	29/5	Eastbourne	H	ELA	W56-40*	6 (4)	2+1 (4)	12+1 (5)	7+1 (4)	15 (5)	8+2 (4)	6+1 (4)	-	-	-	-
19	31/5	Arena-Essex	A	ELA	L43-46*	1 (4)	6 (4)	9+2 (5)	2 (3)	12 (5)	11+1 (6)	2+1 (3)	-	-	-	-
20	1/6	Ipswich	A	KOC	L42-48	7+1 (4)	2+1 (4)	10 (5)	5+2 (4)	10 (5)	5+2 (5)	3 (3)	-	-	-	-
21	9/6	Belle Vue	H	ELA	W49-42	9 (5)	7+1 (4)	7 (4)	5+1 (4)	11 (5)	6+2 (5)	4+2 (4)	-	-	-	-
22	14/6	Oxford	A	ELB	W51-44	10+2 (5)	4+1 (5)	9+1 (4)	R/R	10 (5)	4+2 (5)	14+1 (6)	-	-	-	-
23	16/6	Reading	H	ELB	W47-46	10+1 (5)	4+2 (5)	10 (5)	R/R	8+1 (4)	5+1 (5)	10+1 (6)	-	-	-	-
24	26/6	Wolverhampton	A	ELB	L43-53	6 (5)	6+1 (4)	11 (5)	-	13 (5)	-	4 (4)	-	3+1 (4)	-	-
25	28/6	Poole	A	ELB	L46-47	9 (4)	2 (4)	15+1 (5)	-	8+2 (5)	2 (3)	9+1 (6)	-	1 (3)	-	-
26	30/6	Swindon	H	ELA	W51-43	7 (4)	5+2 (4)	13 (5)	-	11+1 (5)	4+2 (4)	8 (5)	-	3+2 (3)	-	-
27	6/7	Peterborough	A	ELB	L41-49	4+1 (4)	4+2 (4)	7+2 (5)	-	12 (5)	8 (5)	4+1 (4)	2+1 (3)	-	-	-
28	7/7	Ipswich	H	KOC	W56-40*	12+1 (6)	-	R/R	-	13+1 (6)	12+1 (5)	3+2 (4)	5+2 (4)	-	-	11+1 (5)
29	10/7	Poole	H	ELA	W47-42	9+1 (5)	7+3 (4)	4 (3)	-	14 (5)	3+1 (5)	5+2 (4)	-	5+1 (4)	-	-
30	14/7	Arena-Essex	H	ELB	W65-29	8+1 (4)	12+2 (5)	8+1 (4)	-	11+3 (5)	11+1 (4)	9+1 (4)	-	-	-	6 (4)
31	24/7	Swindon	H	ELB	D45-45	12+1 (5)	4+1 (4)	8 (4)	-	11 (5)	-	5+1 (4)	2+1 (5)	-	-	3 (3)
32	26/7	Arena-Essex	A	ELB	W46-44*	12 (5)	7+3 (4)	9 (4)	-	14 (5)	-	2 (4)	-	-	-	2+1 (8)
33	27/7	Belle Vue	H	ELB	W49-44	10 (4)	5+1 (4)	9+1 (5)	-	11 (5)	-	5+2 (4)	7+1 (4)	2 (4)	-	-
34	31/7	Belle Vue	A	ELB	L41-49	8+1 (4)	6+2 (4)	7+1 (5)	-	11 (5)	-	3+1 (4)	0 (3)	-	-	6 (5)
35	4/8	Ipswich	H	ELB	W46-44	7+2 (4)	7+3 (4)	12+1 (5)	-	10+1 (5)	-	7+1 (4)	-	-	-	3+1 (8)
36	5/8	Eastbourne	A	ELB	L46-47	8+1 (5)	5 (4)	7 (4)	-	12+1 (5)	-	9+1 (4)	2 (4)	-	-	3+2 (5)
37	10/8	Swindon	A	ELB	L40-53	14 (5)	3 (4)	5 (4)	-	9 (5)	-	1 (4)	-	-	5+3 (4)	3+1 (4)
38	21/8	Peterborough	H	ELB	W49-47	12+1 (6)	8+2 (5)	R/R	-	13 (5)	7+2 (5)	3+2 (4)	-	-	6+2 (5)	-
39	28/8	Eastbourne	H	ELB	W56-39*	15+1 (6)	9 (5)	R/R	-	-	4+2 (4)	9+2 (5)	-	-	-	19+3 (10)
40	31/8	Ipswich	A	ELB	W50-44*	15+2 (6)	8+3 (5)	R/R	-	-	1 (3)	3 (5)	-	-	8+1 (5)	15+1 (6)
41	1/9	Poole	H	ELB	W54-42*	14+1 (6)	7+3 (5)	R/R	-	-	-	9+2 (5)	-	-	9 (4)	15+4 (10)
42	4/9	Reading	A	ELB	W46-44*	17 (6)	4+3 (5)	R/R	-	-	4+1 (4)	4 (4)	-	-	6+1 (5)	11+1 (6)
43	15/9	Oxford	H	ELB	W54-38*	12+3 (6)	10+2 (5)	R/R	1 (3)	17+1 (6)	4+1 (5)	10 (5)	-	-	-	-
44	16/9	Eastbourne	A	KOC s/f	L44-46	10+1 (6)	8+2 (5)	R/R	1+1 (3)	12 (6)	10+2 (6)	3+1 (4)	-	-	-	-
45	19/9	Wolverhampton	H	ELB	W51-42	10+1 (5)	6+2 (4)	5+1 (4)	-	11+1 (5)	12 (5)	4 (4)	3+1 (3)	-	-	-

NO.	DATE	OPPONENTS	VENUE	COMPETITION	RESULT	HARRIS	JANNIRO	SCHLEIN	RISAGER	NICHOLLS	SMOLINSKI	ALLEN	BATCHELOR	HLIB	REMPALA	OTHERS
46	25/9	Peterborough	A	PO s/f	L40-52	3 (4)	7+1 (6)	5+1 (4)	-	15 (5)	5 (4)	2 (4)	3+2 (3)	-	-	-
47	29/9	Eastbourne	H	KOC s/f	W61-31*	8+3 (4)	5+3 (4)	12+2 (5)	-	8 (4)	9+2 (5)	11 (4)	8+1 (4)	-	-	-
48	6/10	Belle Vue/ Peterborough	H	CS s/f	1st – 42	10 (4)	4+2 (4)	9 (4)	-	10 (4)	4+2 (4)	5 (4)	-	-	-	-
49	9/10	Belle Vue	A	KOC f	D45-45	7 (5)	4+1 (4)	8 (4)	-	13 (5)	8+1 (5)	2+1 (4)	-	-	-	3+2 (3)
50	12/10	Belle Vue/ Peterborough	Peter	CS s/f	2nd – 37	8+2 (4)	3+2 (4)	8 (4)	-	11 (4)	1+1 (4)	6+1 (4)	-	-	-	-
51	13/10	Belle Vue	H	KOC f	W56-40*	12+1 (5)	5+1 (4)	8+1 (4)	-	9 (5)	9+1 (5)	5+2 (4)	8+3 (4)	-	-	-
52	16/10	Belle Vue/ Peterborough	BV	CS s/f	2nd – 34*	7 (4)	4+1 (4)	11 (4)	-	9+1 (4)	-	2+1 (4)	1 (4)	-	-	-
53	20/10	Poole/ Eastbourne	H	CS f	2nd – 38	8 (4)	5+1 (4)	9 (4)	-	10+1 (4)	-	6+1 (4)	-	-	-	0 (4)
54	23/10	Wolverhampton	A	MT	W45-43	13 (5)	8+2 (4)	6 (4)	-	11+2 (5)	-	4+1 (4)	3+1 (5)	-	-	0 (3)
55	24/10	Poole/ Eastbourne	East	CS f	1st – 38	10+1 (4)	5+1 (4)	9 (4)	-	8 (4)	-	4 (4)	2+1 (4)	-	-	-
56	26/10	Poole/ Eastbourne	Poole	CS f	3rd – 29	9 (4)	-	6 (4)	-	10 (4)	-	1 (4)	-	-	-	3+2 (8)
57	27/10	Wolverhampton	H	MT	D45-45*	6+1 (4)	6+2 (4)	11+1 (5)	-	14+1 (5)	-	7+1 (4)	-	-	-	1 (8)

NOTE: ES = Elite Shield; MT = Midland Trophy. Following the away match at Wolverhampton on 17 April, Scott Nicholls defeated Peter Karlsson in a bonus point run-off. In the away match at Wolverhampton on 26 June, Martin Smolinski arrived just before heat eleven, but not in time to take his final programmed ride. Prior to that, he had been excluded three times for exceeding the two-minute time allowance, with Coventry tracking one rider only on each occasion. This is not counted as a match appearance in Smolinski's total for the season.

DETAILS OF OTHER RIDERS

(all guests)

Match No. 10: Jason King 0 (3); Match No. 16: Jason King 1 (3); Match No. 17: Tomasz Piszcz 4 (7); Match No. 28: Davey Watt 11+1 (5); Match No. 30: Christian Henry 6 (4); Match No. 31: Christian Henry 3 (3); Match No. 32: Christian Henry 1+1 (5); James Brundle 1 (3); Match No. 34: Mathieu Tresarrieu 6 (5); Match No. 35: Paul Clews 2 (4); Chris Schramm 1+1 (4); Match No. 36: Chris Schramm 3+2 (5); Match No. 37: Troy Batchelor 3+1 (4); Match No. 39: Todd Wiltshire 12+1 (6); Troy Batchelor 7+2 (4); Match No. 40: Bjarne Pedersen 15+1 (6); Match No. 41: Todd Wiltshire 10+2 (6); Troy Batchelor 5+2 (4); Match No. 42: Mark Loram 11+1 (6); Match No. 49: Emil Kramer 3+2 (3); Match No. 53: Paul Clews 0 (4); Match No. 54: Emil Kramer 0 (3); Match No. 56: Danny Warwick 2+1 (4); Daniel Giffard 1+1 (4); Match No. 57: Ben Barker 1 (4); Christian Henry 0 (4).

DETAILS OF TACTICAL RIDES AND TACTICAL SUBSTITUTE RIDES

Match No. 5: Nicholls 6 points (TR); Schlein 4 points (TR); Match No. 7: Schlein 6 points (TR); Nicholls 1 point (TS; not doubled); Harris 1 point (TR; not doubled); Match No. 10: Schlein 6 points (TR); Nicholls 1 point (TR; not doubled); Match No. 11: Nicholls 4 points (TS); Match No. 13: Nicholls 6 points (TR); Schlein 4 points (TR); Match No. 15: Nicholls 6 points (TR); Match No. 16: Schlein 4 points (TR); Nicholls 4 points (TR); Match No. 24: Nicholls 6 points (TR); Schlein 6 points (TR); Harris 0 points (TS); Match No. 25: Schlein 6 points (TR); Match No. 36: Allen 6 points (TR); Match No. 37: Harris 6 points (TR); Nicholls 1 point (TR; not doubled); Match No. 46: Nicholls 4 points (TR); Janniro 1 point (TS; not doubled); Allen 0 points (TR).

COVENTRY: From left to right, back row: Colin Pratt (co-promoter/team manager), Olly Allen, Rory Schlein, Morten Risager, Billy Janniro, Peter Oakes (team manager). Front row, kneeling: Chris Harris, Martin Smolinski. On bike: Scott Nicholls.

AVERAGES

(40 Elite League, 1 Play-Offs, 6 Knock-Out Cup, 6 Craven Shield, 2 Elite Shield = 55 fixtures) ◆ Denotes ever-present.

Rider	Mts	Rds	Pts	Bon	Tot	Avge	Max
Scott Nicholls	51	252	556	19	575	9.13	2 full; 1 paid
Rory Schlein	47	208	389	25	414	7.96	-
Chris Harris ◆	55	255	457	45	502	7.87	-
Billy Janniro	53	222	289	75	364	6.56	-
Martin Smolinski	38	173	218	42	260	6.01	1 paid
Olly Allen ◆	55	234	287	42	329	5.62	-
Troy Batchelor	13	48	43	13	56	4.67	-
Morten Risager	23	83	78	19	97	4.67	-

Also rode (in alphabetical order):

	Mts	Rds	Pts	Bon	Tot	Avge	Max
Pawel Hlib	5	18	14	4	18	4.00	-
Jacek Rempala	5	23	34	7	41	7.13	-

	Mts	Rds	Pts	Bon	Tot	Avge	Max
Guests	23	102	108	19	127	4.98	-

(Troy Batchelor [3]; James Brundle [1]; Paul Clews [2]; Daniel Giffard [1]; Christian Henry [3]; Jason King [2]; Emil Kramer [1]; Mark Loram [1]; Bjarne Pedersen [1]; Tomasz Piszcz [1]; Chris Schramm [2]; Mathieu Tresarrieu [1]; Danny Warwick [1]; Davey Watt [1]; Todd Wiltshire [2]).

NOTE: Billy Janniro was ever-present throughout the 40-match Elite League programme.

OTHER MEETING

29 October: Celebrate with the Cup Kings

Scott Nicholls' Select 38: Scott Nicholls 11+2 (5); David Howe 8+1 (4); Billy Janniro 7+1 (4); Troy Batchelor 6 (4); Stuart Robson 5+1 (5); Ben Barker 1+1 (2); Davey Watt 0 (2). Chris Harris' Select 40: Chris Harris 12 (5); Olly Allen 11+1 (5); Rory Schlein 10 (5); Edward Kennett 5 (5); Lewis Bridger 2+1 (3); Trevor Harding 0 (3); Tomas Topinka R/R.

EASTBOURNE EAGLES SPONSORED BY MERIDIAN MARQUEES

ADDRESS: Arlington Stadium, Arlington Road West, Hailsham, East Sussex, BH27 3RE.
PROMOTERS: Terry Russell and Jon Cook.
YEARS OF OPERATION: 1929-1930 Open; 1932-1937 Open; 1938 Sunday Dirt-Track League; 1939 Open; 1946 Open; 1947 National League Division Three; 1948-1953 Open; 1954-1957 Southern Area League; 1958 Open; 1959 Southern Area League; 1960-1963 Open; 1964 Metropolitan League; 1965 Training; 1969-1974 British League Division Two; 1975-1978 National League; 1979-1984 British League; 1985-1990 National League; 1991-1994 British League Division One; 1995 Premier League; 1996 Premier League and Conference League; 1997-2006 Elite League.
FIRST MEETING: 5 August 1929.
TRACK LENGTH: 275 metres.
TRACK RECORD: 55.1 seconds – Tony Rickardsson (10/05/03).

CLUB HONOURS

LEAGUE CHAMPIONS: 1938, 1947, 1959, 1971, 1977, 1986, 1987, 1995, 2000.
KNOCK-OUT CUP WINNERS: 1975, 1977, 1978, 1985, 1986, 1987, 1994, 1997, 2002.
PREMIERSHIP WINNERS: 1995, 1996.

RIDER ROSTER 2006

Dean BARKER; Lewis BRIDGER; Edward KENNETT; Andrew MOORE; David NORRIS; Nicki PEDERSEN; Adam SHIELDS; Cameron WOODWARD.

OTHER APPEARANCES/GUESTS (official matches only)

Leigh ADAMS; Andrew APPLETON; Jason CRUMP; Kevin DOOLAN; Daniel GIFFARD; Trevor HARDING; David HOWE; Peter KARLSSON; Joonas KYLMAKORPI; Mark LORAM; Joel PARSONS; Bjarne PEDERSEN; Glen PHILLIPS; Chris SCHRAMM; Joe SCREEN; Brent WERNER.

EASTBOURNE

* Denotes aggregate/bonus-point victory.

NO.	DATE	OPPONENTS	VENUE	COMPETITION	RESULT	NORRIS	MOORE	BARKER	SHIELDS	N. PEDERSEN	WERNER	BRIDGER	APPLETON	WOODWARD	KENNETT	DOOLAN	OTHERS
1	17/3	Arena-Essex	A	SC	L37-57	9 (4)	1+1 (4)	2+1 (4)	9 (5)	6 (4)	9 (5)	1 (4)	-	-	-	-	-
2	18/3	Arena-Essex	H	SC	W51-39	6+1 (4)	8+2 (5)	8+1 (4)	7 +1 (4)	15 (5)	4 (4)	3+1 (4)	-	-	-	-	-
3	20/3	Belle Vue	A	ELA	L42-48	6 (4)	5+2 (4)	6+1 (4)	11+1 (5)	9+1 (5)	2+1 (5)	3 (3)	-	-	-	-	-
4	1/4	Peterborough	H	ELA	W47-46	7 (4)	2 (4)	7+1 (4)	9+2 (5)	17 (5)	5+1 (5)	0 (3)	-	-	-	-	-

NO.	DATE	OPPONENTS	VENUE	COMPETITION	RESULT	NORRIS	MOORE	BARKER	SHIELDS	N. PEDERSEN	WERNER	BRIDGER	APPLETON	WOODWARD	KENNETT	DOOLAN	OTHERS
5	8/4	Wolverhampton	H	ELA	W46-44	5+1 (4)	3+1 (4)	8+2 (4)	9+1 (5)	13 (5)	3 (2)	5 (6)	-	-	-	-	-
6	12/4	Oxford	A	ELA	W48-42	6+1 (4)	5+1 (4)	6+2 (4)	12+1 (5)	-		3+1 (5)	2 (3)	-			14 (5)
7	14/4	Poole	A	ELA	L36-54	5 (4)	4+2 (4)	2 (4)	9 (5)	11 (5)		4+1 (5)	1+1 (3)	-			
8	14/4	Poole	H	ELA	W49-41	8+1 (5)	4 (4)	9 (4)	8+1 (4)	14 (5)		4 (5)	2+1 (3)	-			
9	21/4	Oxford	H	ELA	W60-32*	14+3 (6)	6 (5)	12+2 (5)	R/R	-		8+2 (4)	5+1 (5)	-			15 (5)
10	24/4	Wolverhampton	A	ELA	L45-48	11 (6)	4+1 (5)	9+3 (5)	R/R			14 (7)	2+2 (3)	-			5 (4)
11	27/4	Peterborough	A	ELA	L33-59	11 (6)	3+1 (5)	6 (5)	R/R			3+3 (5)					10+1 (9)
12	29/4	Swindon	H	ELA	L41-55	9+1 (7)	4+1 (4)	10+2 (5)	R/R			5+1 (5)					13 (9)
13	8/5	Coventry	H	ELA	W47-41	11+2 (6)	4+1 (5)	8 (5)	R/R	15 (5)		9+2 (6)		0 (3)			-
14	13/5	Ipswich	H	ELA	W51-39	13+1 (6)	4+1 (5)	9 (5)	R/R	14 (5)		9+2 (6)		2+1 (3)			-
15	15/5	Reading	A	ELA	L34-61	12 (6)	2+1 (5)	-	R/R	12 (5)		3 (5)		0 (4)			5+1 (5)
16	25/5	Ipswich	A	ELA	L38-57	11 (6)	-	2 (3)	R/R			3 (5)		3+1 (6)	3 (5)		16 (5)
17	27/5	Reading	H	ELA	L42-48	11 (6)	-	8+2 (5)	R/R	11 (5)		8+1 (6)		2+1 (3)	2+1 (5)		-
18	29/5	Coventry	A	ELA	L40-56	14 (6)	1 (4)	8 (5)	R/R	12 (5)		4 (5)		1 (5)			-
19	5/6	Swindon	H	ELB	W53-43	7+3 (5)	-	13+2 (6)	R/R	13 (5)		7 (5)		5+1 (4)	8+2 (5)		-
20	10/6	Belle Vue	H	ELA	W48-42	8+1 (5)	-	6+2 (4)	8 (4)	12 (5)		7+2 (4)		6+1 (4)	1+1 (4)		-
21	12/6	Wolverhampton	A	ELB	L43-47	R/R	-	7+4 (6)	5+1 (5)	15 (6)		8+1 (5)		3+1 (3)	5+1 (5)		-
22	17/6	Arena-Essex	H	ELA	W62-32	13+2 (5)	-	8+2 (4)	15 (5)	12 (4)		6 (4)		2+1 (3)	-		6+1 (5)
23	19/6	Belle Vue	A	ELB	L30-44	7 (3)	-	5 (3)	2+2 (3)	7 (3)		0 (4)		-			9+1 (8)
24	23/6	Peterborough	H	ELB	W55-35	8+1 (4)	-	6+4 (4)	13 (5)	-		6+1 (5)		3+1 (3)	7 (4)		12+1 (5)
25	28/6	Arena-Essex	A	ELA	W52-40*	9+1 (4)	-	9+1 (4)	9+1 (5)	-		5 (4)		0 (4)	5 (4)		15 (5)
26	29/6	Swindon	A	ELA	L39-51	R/R	-	8+1 (6)	10 (6)	-		1 (3)		7+1 (5)	4 (5)		9+1 (5)
27	1/7	Wolverhampton	H	KOC	W55-38	9 (4)	-	4+1 (4)	15 (5)	13+1 (5)		4 (4)		4 (4)	6 (4)		-
28	3/7	Wolverhampton	A	KOC	W51-41*	9 (4)	-	6+2 (4)	10 (5)	14 (5)		8+2 (5)		0 (3)	4+1 (4)		-
29	8/7	Reading	H	ELB	W46-44	11 (5)	-	8+1 (5)	R/R	11+1 (5)		7 (5)		3+2 (4)		6+2 (6)	-
30	10/7	Reading	A	ELB	L41-54	4 (4)	-	8+2 (5)	R/R	11 (5)		1 (3)		4+1 (7)	13 (6)		-
31	23/7	Oxford	H	ELB	W50-45	10+2 (5)	-	10 (4)	2+1 (2)	14 (5)		6+1 (7)		1 (3)	7+2 (4)		-
32	26/7	Oxford	A	ELB	L42-50	9+1 (5)	-	8 (5)	R/R	13+1 (5)		4+1 (7)		1 (3)	7+1 (5)		-
33	2/8	Poole	A	ELB	L44-49	11+1 (5)	-	5+1 (4)	5 (4)	12 (5)		5+1 (4)		1+1 (4)	5+1 (4)		-
34	5/8	Coventry	H	ELB	W47-46	10 (5)	-	4+2 (4)	8 (4)	14 (5)		2 (4)		5+1 (4)	-	4+1 (4)	-
35	11/8	Arena-Essex	H	ELB	W53-41	11+2 (5)	-	9 (4)	12+1 (5)	-		6+1 (5)		1+1 (3)	3 (4)		11+1 (4)
36	14/8	Peterborough	A	ELB	L32-61	0 (3)	-	5 (4)	4 (5)	15 (5)		1+1 (4)		3 (4)	4 (4)		-
37	19/8	Poole	H	ELB	W53-41*	12+1 (5)	-	3+2 (4)	10 (4)	13+1 (5)		6 (4)		3+1 (4)	6+2 (4)		-
38	25/8	Wolverhampton	H	ELB	D45-45	6+3 (4)	-	10+1 (5)	5+2 (4)	-		8+2 (5)		3 (3)	4 (4)		9 (5)
39	28/8	Coventry	A	ELB	L39-56	9 (4)	-	2+1 (4)	8 (5)	16 (5)		3+1 (4)		0 (4)			1 (4)
40	31/8	Swindon	A	ELB	L32-58	7 (4)	-	3+1 (4)	3 (3)	11 (5)		1+1 (4)		6+1 (6)	1 (4)		-
41	2/9	Belle Vue	H	ELB	W42-36	6+1 (3)	-	10 (4)	5 (3)	8 (3)		6+1 (4)		5+1 (4)	-		2+1 (3)
42	9/9	Ipswich	H	ELB	W54-39	17 (6)	-	7+3 (5)	11+1 (6)	R/R		8+1 (4)		3+1 (4)	8+2 (5)		-
43	14/9	Ipswich	A	ELB	W48-42*	6+1 (4)	-	5+2 (4)	11 (5)	10 (5)		7+2 (4)		4+3 (4)	5+1 (4)		-
44	16/9	Coventry	H	KOC s/f	W46-44	9+1 (5)	-	4 (4)	8 (4)	15 (5)		0 (3)		5 (4)	5+2 (5)		-
45	25/9	Wolverhampton/ Ipswich	Wolv	CS s/f	1st – 38	7+1 (4)	-	3+1 (4)	5 (4)	12 (4)		4+1 (4)		-	7+1 (4)		-
46	28/9	Wolverhampton/ Ipswich	Ips	CS s/f	2nd – 38	8+1 (4)	-	4+2 (4)	10 (4)	10 (4)		2+1 (4)		-	4+1 (4)		-

NO. DATE	OPPONENTS	VENUE	COMPETITION	RESULT	NORRIS	MOORE	BARKER	SHIELDS	N. PEDERSEN	WERNER	BRIDGER	APPLETON	WOODWARD	KENNETT	DOOLAN	OTHERS
47 29/9	Coventry	A	KOC s/f	L31-61	3 (4)	-	2 (4)	5 (5)	14 (5)		3+1 (4)	-	2+1 (5)	-	2 (4)	-
48 4/10	Arena-Essex	A	ELB	L42-48*	7+2 (4)	-	8 (5)	6 (4)	11 (5)		4+1 (5)	-	0 (3)	6+2 (4)	-	
49 7/10	Wolverhampton/ Ipswich	H	CS s/f	1st – 42*	9 (4)	-	6+1 (4)	10+1 (4)	11 (4)		3+2 (4)	-	3 (4)	-	-	
50 20/10	Coventry/Poole	Cov	CS f	3rd – 29	6+1 (4)	-	3+1 (3)	5 (4)	11 (4)		2 (5)	-	-	2 (4)	-	
51 24/10	Coventry/Poole	H	CS f	= 2nd – 35	9 (4)	-	4+1 (4)	5 (4)	12 (4)		3+1 (4)	-	-	2+1 (4)	-	
52 26/10	Coventry/Poole	Poole	CS f	1st – 41	6+2 (4)	-	4 (4)	4 (4)	12 (4)		6+3 (4)	-	-	9+1 (4)	-	

NOTE: SC = Spring Challenge. Following the home match against Belle Vue on 10 June, Nicki Pedersen was beaten by Jason Crump in a run-off for the bonus point. The away league match at Belle Vue on 19 June was abandoned after heat twelve, with the result permitted to stand. The home league match versus Belle Vue on 2 September was abandoned after heat twelve, with the result permitted to stand.

DETAILS OF OTHER RIDERS

(all guests)

Match No. 6: Jason Crump 14 (5); Match No. 9: Peter Karlsson 15 (5); Match No. 10: David Howe 5 (4); Match No. 11: Joonas Kylmakorpi 8 (5); Trevor Harding 2+1 (4); Match No. 12: Peter Karlsson 13 (5); Trevor Harding 0 (4); Match No. 15: Edward Kennett 5+1 (5); Match No. 16: Bjarne Pedersen 16 (5); Match No. 22: Glen Phillips 6+1 (5); Match No. 23: Kevin Doolan 7 (4); Joel Parsons 2+1 (4); Match No. 24: Mark Loram 12+1 (5); Match No. 25: Leigh Adams 15 (5); Match No. 26: Joe Screen 9+1 (5); Match No. 35: Mark Loram 11+1 (4); Match No. 38: Mark Loram 9 (5); Match No. 39: Daniel Giffard 1 (4); Match No. 41: Chris Schramm 2+1 (3).

DETAILS OF TACTICAL RIDES AND TACTICAL SUBSTITUTE RIDES

Match No. 1: Shields 4 points (TR); Norris 4 points (TR); Match No. 4: N. Pedersen 6 points (TR); Match No. 7: N. Pedersen 1 point (TR; not doubled); Shields 1 point (TR; not doubled); Match No. 11: Norris 4 points (TR); Barker 0 points (TR); Match No. 12: Norris 4 points (TS); Barker 4 points (TR); Karlsson 4 points (TR); Match No. 15: Norris 6 points (TR); N. Pedersen 4 points (TR); Match No. 16: Norris 6 points (TR); B. Pedersen 6 points (TR); Match No. 18: N. Pedersen 6 points (TR); Norris 6 points (TR); Match No. 23: Norris 4 points (TR); Match No. 30: N. Pedersen 6 points (TR); Kennett 4 points (TR); Match No. 32: Norris 4 points (TR); Match No. 33: Norris 6 points (TR); Match No. 36: N. Pedersen 6 points (TR); Barker 1 point (TS; not doubled); Shields 0 points (TR); Match No. 39: N. Pedersen 6 points (TR); Norris 4 points (TR); Match No. 40: Shields 1 point (TR; not doubled); Norris 0 points (TR); Match No. 47: N. Pedersen 6 points (TR); Shields 0 points (TR).

EASTBOURNE: From left to right, back row: Adam Shields, Dean Barker, Edward Kennett, Lewis Bridger, Trevor Geer (team manager). Front row: Nicki Pedersen, David Norris, Cameron Woodward.

AVERAGES

(40 Elite League, 4 Knock-Out Cup, 6 Craven Shield = 50 fixtures) ◆ Denotes ever-present.

Rider	Mts	Rds	Pts	Bon	Tot	Avge	Max
Nicki Pedersen	38	180	450	5	455	10.11	6 full
David Norris	48	224	395	38	433	7.73	1 paid
Adam Shields	36	159	287	16	303	7.62	2 full
Dean Barker	49	214	315	56	371	6.93	-
Edward Kennett	27	117	136	21	157	5.37	-
Lewis Bridger ◆	50	229	235	42	277	4.84	-
Andrew Moore	14	62	51	12	63	4.06	-
Cameron Woodward	34	134	91	23	114	3.40	-
Also rode (in alphabetical order):							
Andrew Appleton	5	17	12	5	17	4.00	-
Kevin Doolan	4	19	17	5	22	4.63	-
Brent Werner	3	12	10	2	12	4.00	-
Guests	19	86	147	8	155	7.21	2 full; 1 paid

(Leigh Adams [1]; Jason Crump [1]; Kevin Doolan [1]; Daniel Giffard [1]; Trevor Harding [2]; David Howe [1]; Peter Karlsson [2]; Edward Kennett [1]; Joonas Kylmakorpi [1]; Mark Loram [3]; Joel Parsons [1]; Bjarne Pedersen [1]; Glen Phillips [1]; Chris Schramm [1]; Joe Screen [1]).

IPSWICH EVENING STAR WITCHES

ADDRESS: Foxhall Heath Stadium, Foxhall Road, Ipswich, Suffolk, IP4 5TL.
PROMOTER: John Louis.
YEARS OF OPERATION: 1950-1951 Open; 1952-1953 Southern League; 1954-1956 National League Division Two; 1957-1958 National League; 1959 Southern Area League; 1960-1962 National League; 1964 Metropolitan League; 1965 Open; 1969-1971 British League Division Two; 1972-1974 British League Division One; 1975-1988 British League; 1989-1990 National League; 1991-1994 British League Division One; 1995-1996 Premier League; 1997 Elite League and Amateur League; 1998-2006 Elite League.
FIRST MEETING: 25 October 1950.
TRACK LENGTH: 305 metres.
TRACK RECORD: 57.5 seconds – Jaroslaw Hampel (12/09/02).

CLUB HONOURS

KNOCK-OUT CUP WINNERS: 1970, 1971, 1976, 1978, 1981, 1984, 1998.
LEAGUE CHAMPIONS: 1975, 1976, 1984, 1998.
PAIRS CHAMPIONS: 1976, 1977.
INTER-LEAGUE KNOCK-OUT CUP WINNERS: 1977.
FOUR-TEAM CHAMPIONS: 1991.
CRAVEN SHIELD WINNERS: 1998.

RIDER ROSTER 2006

Kim JANSSON; Jan JAROS; Daniel KING; Tobias KRONER; Mark LORAM; Chris LOUIS; Robert MISKOWIAK; Piotr PROTASIEWICZ; Carl WILKINSON.

OTHER APPEARANCES/GUESTS (official matches only)

Steve BOXALL; Ales DRYML; Daniel GIFFARD; Chris HARRIS; David HOWE; Joonas KYLMAKORPI; Scott NICHOLLS; Glen PHILLIPS; Adam SKORNICKI; Todd WILTSHIRE.

IPSWICH

* Denotes aggregate/bonus-point victory.

NO.	DATE	OPPONENTS	VENUE	COMPETITION	RESULT	LOUIS	JANSSON	PROTASIEWICZ	MISKOWIAK	LORAM	JAROS	WILKINSON	BOXALL	KING	KRONER	OTHERS
1	16/3	Mildenhall	H	SC	W54-40	10+1 (5)	7+2 (5)	12 (4)	1 (4)	10 (4)	7+1 (4)	7+1 (4)	-	-	-	-
2	19/3	Mildenhall	A	SC	W47-43*	8+2 (4)	2 (4)	8+1 (5)	7 (4)	12 (5)	5+1 (4)	-	5+2 (4)	-	-	-
3	22/3	Oxford	A	ELA	W51-42	12+1 (5)	6+2 (4)	11+1 (5)	5+2 (4)	4 (4)	5 (4)	-	-	8+2 (4)	-	-
4	23/3	Oxford	H	ELA	W60-30*	8 (4)	5+1 (4)	14+1 (5)	10+2 (4)	13+1 (5)	6+1 (4)	-	-	4+2 (4)	-	-
5	28/3	Swindon	A	ELA	L40-53	4 (4)	5+1 (4)	13+2 (5)	5 (4)	9 (5)	0 (3)	-	-	4+2 (5)	-	-

NO.	DATE	OPPONENTS	VENUE	COMPETITION	RESULT	LOUIS	JANSSON	PROTASIEWICZ	MISKOWIAK	LORAM	JAROS	WILKINSON	BOXALL	KING	KRONER	OTHERS
6	30/3	Swindon	H	ELA	W48-45	10 (5)	6+2 (4)	8+2 (5)	6 (4)	8+1 (4)	4+1 (3)	-	-	6+4 (5)	-	-
7	3/4	Reading	A	ELA	L40-50	R/R	3 (5)	12 (6)	5 (5)	13 (6)	1+1 (4)	-	-	6 (4)	-	-
8	6/4	Reading	H	ELA	L43-47	5+1 (4)	4+2 (3)	11 (5)	3+2 (4)	12 (5)	2+1 (4)	-	-	6+2 (5)	-	-
9	7/4	Coventry	A	ELA	L45-48	3 (4)	8 (4)	16+1 (5)	6 (4)	7+1 (5)	2 (3)	-	-	3+2 (5)	-	-
10	14/4	Arena-Essex	H	ELA	W50-42	4+1 (4)	9+1 (4)	9 (5)	6+1 (4)	12 (5)	4+1 (4)	-	-	6+3 (4)	-	-
11	14/4	Arena-Essex	A	ELA	L41-49*	5+1 (4)	1 (3)	10 (5)	6+1 (4)	10 (5)	3+1 (4)	-	-	6+1 (5)	-	-
12	24/4	Poole	H	ELA	W50-40	11+1 (6)	5+2 (5)	R/R	9+1 (5)	13 (5)	-	8+1 (5)	-	4+1 (4)	-	-
13	1/5	Belle Vue	H	ELA	W53-42	8+1 (4)	8+4 (5)	9 (4)	7 (4)	13 (5)	5 (4)	-	-	3+1 (4)	-	-
14	4/5	Peterborough	A	ELA	L38-55	0 (3)	9 (5)	13 (5)	0 (3)	7 (4)	4+1 (5)	5+2 (5)	-	-	-	-
15	11/5	Wolverhampton	H	ELA	W50-42	10+2 (5)	7+1 (4)	10 (4)	5+1 (4)	11+1 (5)	3+1 (4)	4 (4)	-	-	-	-
16	13/5	Eastbourne	A	ELA	L39-51	7 (5)	6+2 (4)	9 (4)	-	11 (5)	1 (5)	-	-	-	-	5+2 (7)
17	18/5	Coventry	H	ELA	W51-42*	7+3 (5)	10+1 (4)	11 (4)	5+2 (4)	13 (5)	0 (3)	-	-	5+1 (5)	-	-
18	24/5	Belle Vue	A	ELA	L42-48*	8 (5)	6+1 (4)	10 (5)	8+2 (4)	6 (4)	0 (3)	-	-	4 (5)	-	-
19	25/5	Eastbourne	H	ELA	W57-38*	10+2 (5)	9+3 (5)	13+1 (5)	R/R	11 (5)	2+1 (4)	-	-	12+4 (6)	-	-
20	1/6	Coventry	H	KOC	W48-42	15 (5)	6 (4)	4 (4)	5+1 (4)	13+1 (5)	2 (6)	-	-	3 (2)	-	-
21	5/6	Reading	A	ELB	L38-57	14 (5)	3 (4)	5 (4)	3 (4)	12 (5)	0 (4)	1 (4)	-	-	-	-
22	8/6	Peterborough	H	ELA	W48-42	12+1 (6)	4+1 (5)	R/R	10+2 (5)	13 (6)	-	5+2 (4)	-	4+1 (5)	-	-
23	12/6	Swindon	H	ELB	W56-37	10+3 (5)	6+3 (4)	14 (5)	10+1 (4)	9 (4)	-	5 (4)	-	2+2 (4)	-	-
24	21/6	Arena-Essex	A	ELB	W48-42	17 (6)	R/R	7 (3)	6+2 (5)	10 (5)	-	-	-	6+1 (7)	2+1 (4)	-
25	22/6	Arena-Essex	H	ELB	W57-25*	14+1 (5)	7 (4)	9+2 (5)	8 (4)	11 (4)	-	-	-	6+1 (4)	2 (4)	-
26	29/6	Peterborough	A	ELB	L40-50	6 (4)	2 (4)	-	7+1 (5)	7 (4)	-	-	-	9 (5)	2+1 (3)	7 (5)
27	6/7	Belle Vue	H	ELB	W52-43	10+2 (5)	8+1 (4)	8+2 (4)	5 (4)	11+1 (5)	-	-	8+1 (5)	-	2+1 (4)	-
28	7/7	Coventry	A	KOC	L40-56	12+1 (5)	5 (4)	12+1 (5)	4 (4)	6 (4)	-	0 (4)	-	-	1 (4)	-
29	13/7	Wolverhampton	H	ELB	W53-43	5+2 (4)	7+1 (4)	11+1 (5)	11 (5)	9 (4)	-	-	-	6+2 (4)	4+2 (4)	-
30	27/7	Oxford	H	ELB	W52-43	14+2 (6)	7+2 (5)	R/R	9+2 (5)	13 (6)	-	0 (3)	-	-	9+2 (5)	-
31	31/7	Wolverhampton	A	ELA	L35-56	14+1 (5)	4 (4)	2+1 (3)	2 (4)	11 (5)	-	-	-	1+1 (5)	1 (4)	-
32	4/8	Coventry	A	ELB	L44-46	9 (5)	3+1 (4)	5+1 (4)	3+2 (4)	14 (5)	-	-	-	9 (5)	1+1 (3)	-
33	5/8	Peterborough	H	ELB	W51-43	9+2 (5)	6+2 (4)	8 (4)	7 (4)	13 (5)	-	4+2 (4)	-	-	4+1 (4)	-
34	7/8	Belle Vue	A	ELB	L39-51	11 (5)	5+1 (4)	4 (4)	3+1 (4)	10 (5)	-	-	-	5+2 (5)	1+1 (3)	-
35	9/8	Poole	A	ELA	L39-57	3+1 (5)	2 (4)	10 (5)	1 (3)	16 (5)	-	-	-	6 (6)	1+1 (3)	-
36	10/8	Reading	H	ELB	W56-38	13+2 (5)	6+1 (4)	8 (4)	9 (4)	13 (5)	-	-	-	2+1 (4)	5+1 (4)	-
37	17/8	Poole	H	ELB	W52-44	10+1 (6)	9+3 (5)	R/R	10 (5)	16 (6)	-	-	-	1 (3)	6+1 (5)	-
38	28/8	Swindon	A	ELB	L38-57	R/R	4+1 (4)	7 (5)	8+1 (5)	16 (6)	-	-	-	3+1 (6)	0 (4)	-
39	30/8	Poole	A	ELB	L36-54	R/R	5+1 (4)	9+2 (5)	6 (5)	12 (6)	-	3+1 (5)	-	-	1 (4)	-
40	31/8	Coventry	H	ELB	L44-50	R/R	6+1 (5)	4+1 (4)	10+1 (6)	17 (6)	-	3+1 (4)	-	-	4 (5)	-
41	9/9	Eastbourne	A	ELB	L39-54	-	7 (5)	R/R	3+1 (5)	12+1 (6)	-	-	-	-	1 (4)	16 (10)
42	11/9	Wolverhampton	A	ELB	L46-47*	R/R	9+3 (6)	6+1 (5)	10+1 (5)	9 (5)	-	-	-	6+2 (4)	6+1 (5)	-
43	14/9	Eastbourne	H	ELB	L42-48	0 (2)	7+1 (4)	6 (4)	11 (5)	14 (5)	-	0 (3)	-	-	4 (6)	-
44	20/9	Oxford	A	ELB	L44-46*	R/R	4+1 (5)	9 (5)	11 (6)	8+1 (5)	-	-	-	8+1 (5)	4+2 (4)	-
45	25/9	Wolverhampton/Eastbourne	Wolv	CS s/f	2nd – 37	-	5 (4)	-	7+1 (4)	10+1 (4)	-	-	-	5+1 (4)	-	10 (8)
46	28/9	Wolverhampton/Eastbourne	H	CS s/f	1st – 46	-	0 (3)	-	8+1 (4)	11+1 (4)	-	-	-	7+2 (5)	-	20+1 (8)
47	7/10	Wolverhampton/Eastbourne	East	CS s/f	= 2nd – 33	-	2 (4)	-	4 (4)	8 (4)	-	2+2 (4)	-	-	-	17+1 (8)

IPSWICH: From left to right, back row: Daniel King, Tobias Kroner, Piotr Protasiewicz, Mark Loram, Kim Jansson, Robert Miskowiak, Mike Smillie (team manager). On bike: Chris Louis.

NOTE: SC = Suffolk Cup. Following the away match at Arena-Essex on 14 April, Piotr Protasiewicz defeated Joonas Kylmakorpi in a bonus point run-off. The home match against Arena-Essex on 22 June originally ended in a 57-37 victory, but was amended as Troy Batchelor was not permitted to appear as a guest for the visiting side due to being in Coventry's declared line-up as their number eight rider. His tally on the night was therefore deleted to leave the result as a 57-25 success instead. Following the away match at Swindon on 28 August, Mark Loram was defeated by Leigh Adams in a run-off for the bonus point.

DETAILS OF OTHER RIDERS

(all guests)

Match No. 16: Glen Phillips 4+2 (4); Daniel Giffard 1 (3); Match No. 26: Ales Dryml 7 (5); Match No. 41: Todd Wiltshire 16 (6); Daniel Giffard 0 (4); Match No. 45: Adam Skornicki 8 (4); David Howe 2 (4); Match No. 46: Scott Nicholls 11 (4); Adam Skornicki 9+1 (4); Match No. 47: Chris Harris 10+1 (4); Joonas Kylmakorpi 7 (4).

DETAILS OF TACTICAL RIDES AND TACTICAL SUBSTITUTES

Match No. 5: Protasiewicz 6 points (TR); Louis 0 points (TR); Match No. 9: Protasiewicz 6 points (TR); Match No. 14: Protasiewicz 6 points (TR); Loram 1 point (TR; not doubled); Match No. 21: Louis 6 points (TR); Loram 4 points (TR); Match No. 28: Protasiewicz 6 points (TR); Louis 6 points (TR); Match No. 31: Louis 6 points (TR); Loram 1 point (TR; not doubled); Match No. 35: Louis 6 points (TR); Protasiewicz 6 points (TR); Match No. 38: Loram 6 points (TR); Miskowiak 4 points (TR); Match No. 39: Loram 1 point (TR; not doubled); Miskowiak 1 point (TR; not doubled); Match No. 40: Miskowiak 6 points (TR); Loram 4 points (TR); Match No. 41: Wiltshire 6 points (TR).

AVERAGES

(40 Elite League, 2 Knock-Out Cup, 3 Craven Shield = 45 fixtures) ♦ Denotes ever-present.

Rider	Mts	Rds	Pts	Bon	Tot	Avge	Max
Mark Loram ♦	45	221	487	10	497	9.00	1 paid
Piotr Protasiewicz	36	164	312	20	332	8.10	1 paid
Chris Louis	35	166	301	32	333	8.02	1 full; 2 paid
Robert Miskowiak	43	187	272	32	304	6.50	1 paid
Kim Jansson	44	187	246	47	293	6.27	-
Daniel King	32	148	166	43	209	5.65	-
Carl Wilkinson	12	49	39	11	50	4.08	-
Tobias Kroner	21	85	61	16	77	3.62	-
Jan Jaros	18	71	44	9	53	2.99	-
Also rode:							
Steve Boxall	2	9	9	1	10	4.44	-
Guests	11	46	72	4	76	6.61	-

(Ales Dryml [1]; Daniel Giffard [2]; Chris Harris [1]; David Howe [1]; Joonas Kylmakorpi [1]; Scott Nicholls [1]; Glen Phillips [1]; Adam Skornicki [2]; Todd Wiltshire [1]).

INDIVIDUAL MEETING

12 October: 16-Lap Classic

QUALIFYING SCORES: Robert Miskowiak 11; Adam Shields 9; David Howe 9; Tobias Kroner 8; Leigh Lanham 8; Kim Jansson 7; Lewis Bridger 7; Shaun Tacey 5; Davey Watt 4; Carl Wilkinson 2; Claus Vissing 2; Matthew Wright 0. FINAL: 1st Jansson (14); 2nd Lanham (12); 3rd Shields (10+2); 4th Howe (8+2); 5th Tacey (6); 6th Kroner (4+2); 7th Miskowiak (2+2); 8th Bridger (0). OVERALL RESULT: 1st Shields 21 (due to starting from the back grid in the final); 2nd Jansson 21; 3rd Lanham 20; Howe 19; Miskowiak 15; Kroner 14; Tacey 11; Bridger 7. CONSOLATION FINAL: 1st Watt; 2nd Wilkinson; 3rd Vissing; 4th Wright.

OXFORD CHEETAHS

ADDRESS: Oxford Stadium, Sandy Lane, Cowley, Oxford, Oxfordshire, OX4 6LJ.
PROMOTER: Aaron Lanney.
YEARS OF OPERATION: 1939-1941 Open; 1949-1950 National League Division Three; 1951-1952 National League Division Two; 1953 Southern League; 1954-1956 National League Division Two; 1957-1964 National League; 1965-1967 British League; 1968-1974 British League Division One; 1975 British League; 1976-1983 National League; 1984-1990 British League; 1991-1992 British League Division One; 1993-1994 British League Division Two; 1995-1996 Premier League; 1997 Premier League and Amateur League; 1998-2002 Elite League; 2003-2005 Elite League and Conference League; 2006 Elite League.
FIRST MEETING: 8 April 1939.
TRACK LENGTH: 297 metres.
TRACK RECORD: 56.2 seconds – Hans Nielsen (13/10/88).

CLUB HONOURS

LEAGUE CHAMPIONS: 1950, 1964, 1985, 1986, 1989, 2001.
NOTE: The Conference League side were also crowned League Champions in 2005.
NATIONAL TROPHY (DIVISION THREE) WINNERS: 1950.
NATIONAL TROPHY WINNERS: 1964.
BRITANNIA SHIELD WINNERS: 1964.
PAIRS CHAMPIONS: 1985, 1986, 1987.
KNOCK-OUT CUP WINNERS: 1985, 1986 (Shared with Cradley Heath).
LEAGUE CUP WINNERS: 1986 (Shared with Cradley Heath).
PREMIERSHIP WINNERS: 1987.
GOLD CUP WINNERS: 1989.
FOUR-TEAM CHAMPIONS: 1994, 1996.
CRAVEN SHIELD WINNERS: 2005.

RIDER ROSTER 2006

Eric ANDERSSON; Stanislaw BURZA; Freddie ERIKSSON; David HOWE; Adam PIETRASZKO; Tony RICKARDSSON; Adam SKORNICKI; Lubos TOMICEK; Davey WATT; Todd WILTSHIRE.

OTHER APPEARANCES/GUESTS (official matches only)

Leigh ADAMS; Olly ALLEN; Paul CLEWS; Jamie COURTNEY; Ales DRYML; Niels-Kristian IVERSEN; Krzysztof KASPRZAK; Stephan KATT; Chris LOUIS; Krister MARSH; Sam MARTIN; David NORRIS; Tomasz PISZCZ; Adam SHIELDS; Lee SMART; Mathieu TRESARRIEU.

OXFORD

* Denotes aggregate/bonus-point victory

NO.	DATE	OPPONENTS	VENUE	COMPETITION	RESULT	HOWE	ANDERSSON	WATT	SKORNICKI	RICKARDSSON	PIETRASZKO	TOMICEK	WILTSHIRE	ERIKSSON	DRYML	BURZA	OTHERS
1	15/3	Swindon	H	Chal	L39-51	7+1 (5)	3+1 (4)	7+2 (4)	7+1 (4)	9 (5)	4 (4)	2 (4)	-	-	-	-	-
2	16/3	Swindon	A	Chal	L28-61	2 (5)	5 (4)	7 (5)	2+1 (4)	7 (4)	3 (4)	2 (4)	-	-	-	-	-
3	22/3	Ipswich	H	ELA	L42-51	4 (4)	1 (4)	9+1 (4)	6+2 (4)	16 (5)	0 (3)	6 (5)	-	-	-	-	-
4	23/3	Ipswich	A	ELA	L30-60	5+1 (5)	2 (4)	3 (4)	4+1 (4)	8 (5)	4 (3)	4 (5)			-		-
5	29/3	Wolverhampton	H	KOC	L43-47	9+1 (5)	6 (4)	5+2 (4)	7+1 (4)	-	4+1 (4)	2+1 (4)			-		10+1 (5)
6	3/4	Wolverhampton	A	KOC	L40-54	8 (5)	4+2 (4)	7+1 (4)	7+1 (4)	13 (5)	0 (3)	1 (5)	-		-		-
7	5/4	Peterborough	H	ELA	L42-47	7+2 (5)	7+1 (4)	6+1 (4)	5 (4)	13 (5)	0 (3)	4+1 (5)	-		-		-
8	12/4	Eastbourne	H	ELA	L42-48	4+1 (4)	7 (5)	5+1 (4)	6 (4)	13 (5)	3 (3)	-			-		4 (5)
9	14/4	Reading	H	ELA	W50-44	7 (4)	7+1 (4)	7 (4)	11+1 (5)	15 (5)	0 (2)	3+2 (6)	-		-		-
10	14/4	Reading	A	ELA	L28-67	7 (5)	2+1 (4)	3 (5)	3 (4)	11 (4)	-	2 (4)	-		-		0 (4)
11	21/4	Eastbourne	A	ELA	L32-60	5 (4)	1 (4)	10+1 (5)	11 (5)	-	-	0 (3)	3+1 (5)	2 (4)	-		-
12	25/4	Peterborough	A	ELA	L31-63	0 (3)	2 (4)	6+2 (4)	4+2 (4)	-	-	5+1 (6)	7 (4)	7 (5)	-		-
13	26/4	Coventry	H	ELA	W47-43	8 (4)	4+1 (4)	6+2 (5)	7 (4)	-	-	-	11+1 (5)	5+1 (4)	-		6+1 (4)
14	28/4	Coventry	A	ELA	L42-50	9+1 (5)	4+1 (4)	6+2 (4)	6 (4)	-	-	-	11 (5)	4+2 (4)	-		2 (4)
15	4/5	Swindon	A	ELA	L38-56	8+1 (5)	8 (4)	5+3 (4)	6 (4)	-	-	3 (4)	6 (5)	2+1 (4)	-		-
16	8/5	Belle Vue	A	ELA	L38-56	2 (4)	4 (4)	10 (5)	2+1 (4)	-	-	13+1 (5)	6+2 (5)	1 (3)	-		-
17	10/5	Belle Vue	H	ELA	L43-50	5+1 (5)	6+1 (6)	5+2 (5)	8 (4)	-	-	-	12 (5)	7+1 (4)	-		0 (3)
18	29/5	Wolverhampton	A	ELA	L37-53	4 (4)	4+1 (4)	6+3 (4)	9 (5)	-	-	-	8 (5)	4+1 (4)	-		2 (2)
19	31/5	Swindon	H	ELA	W47-43	3+1 (4)	9+3 (5)	2+1 (2)	12 (5)	-	-	7+1 (5)	11 (5)	3+1 (4)	-		-
20	7/6	Poole	A	ELA	L40-55	5 (4)	5+2 (5)	6+1 (5)	5 (4)	-	-	-	15 (5)	2 (4)	-		2+1 (3)
21	8/6	Poole	H	ELA	W50-43	12+1 (5)	5+1 (4)	9+1 (4)	5 (4)	-	-	5+2 (4)	12+1 (5)	2+1 (4)	-		-
22	12/6	Reading	A	ELB	L42-50	4+3 (4)	0 (3)	13 (5)	2+1 (4)	-	-	9 (6)	12 (5)	2 (3)	-		-
23	14/6	Coventry	H	ELB	L44-51	6+1 (4)	3+1 (4)	7+1 (4)	5+1 (5)	-	-	3 (5)	17 (5)	3+2 (4)	-		-
24	21/6	Reading	H	ELB	L39-54	5+1 (5)	-	R/R	14 (6)	-	-	-	7 (4)	-	12 (6)		1 (9)
25	28/6	Peterborough	H	ELB	L41-49	6+1 (4)	6+3 (7)	5+3 (4)	6+1 (4)	-	-	1 (1)	9 (5)	-	8 (5)		-
26	12/7	Wolverhampton	H	ELB	L41-51	4 (4)	1 (6)	7+1 (4)	12 (5)	-	-	4+1 (4)	10 (5)	-	3 (2)		-
27	23/7	Eastbourne	A	ELB	L45-50	4 (5)	7+4 (5)	-	9+1 (5)	-	-	4+1 (4)	12 (6)	-	R/R		9+1 (5)
28	26/7	Eastbourne	H	ELB	W50-42*	7+2 (5)	6 (4)	-	13+1 (6)	-	-	5+2 (5)	13+1 (6)	-	R/R	6+2 (4)	-
29	27/7	Ipswich	A	ELB	L43-52	11 (6)	4+1 (5)	-	5+1 (5)	-	-	1 (4)	17 (6)	-	R/R	5 (4)	-
30	31/7	Poole	H	ELB	W49-47	8+2 (5)	4+2 (4)	12+1 (6)	9 (5)	-	-	5+2 (4)	11+1 (6)	-	R/R		-
31	2/8	Arena-Essex	A	ELA	W53-39	8 (4)	5+2 (4)	9+1 (4)	6+1 (4)	-	-	4+1 (4)	6+1 (5)	-	-		15 (5)
32	3/8	Swindon	A	ELB	L38-52	0 (1)	1 (5)	6 (4)	7 (4)	-	-	8+2 (6)	8+1 (5)	-	-		8 (5)
33	7/8	Wolverhampton	A	ELB	L44-46	9 (4)	9+1 (5)	5+2 (4)	1+1 (4)	-	-	0 (3)	9+1 (5)	-	-		11 (5)
34	9/8	Belle Vue	H	ELB	W46-44	4+2 (4)	9 (5)	7+1 (4)	9 (5)	-	-	1 (3)	11+1 (5)	-	-		5 (4)
35	16/8	Swindon	H	ELB	W48-47	6+1 (4)	8+2 (5)	11+1 (5)	9+1 (5)	-	-	-	6+2 (4)	-	-	3 (3)	5 (4)
36	21/8	Belle Vue	A	ELB	L39-53	9 (4)	-	10 (5)	2+2 (4)	-	-	3+1 (4)	5 (4)	-	-	4+1 (4)	6 (5)
37	30/8	Arena-Essex	H	ELA	W64-26*	10+2 (4)	5+1 (4)	9 (4)	14+1 (5)	-	-	6+1 (4)	11+4 (5)	-	-		9 (4)
38	31/8	Peterborough	A	ELB	L34-55	7 (4)	9+1 (7)	7+1 (4)	4+1 (4)	-	-	4 (5)	3 (3)	-	-	0 (4)	-
39	6/9	Poole	A	ELB	L42-49	3 (4)	4+2 (5)	5+1 (4)	5+1 (4)	-	-	-	12+2 (5)	-	-		13 (8)
40	7/9	Wolverhampton	H	ELB	L44-46	9+2 (5)	12+1 (5)	3 (4)	7+1 (4)	-	-	2+1 (3)	7 (5)	-	-		4 (4)
41	15/9	Coventry	A	ELB	L38-54	4+1 (4)	10+2 (7)	4+1 (4)	6+1 (4)	-	-	1 (3)	8 (4)	-	-		5 (4)
42	20/9	Ipswich	H	ELB	W46-44	8 (4)	1+1 (5)	10+1 (5)	6+1 (4)	-	-	-	14+1 (5)	-	-	1 (3)	6+1 (4)
43	27/9	Arena-Essex	H	ELB	W55-37	13+1 (6)	4+1 (4)	9+1 (5)	11+2 (5)	-	-	-	R/R	-	-	3+2 (4)	15 (6)
44	29/9	Arena-Essex	A	ELB	L32-62	5+1 (4)	1+1 (4)	13 (7)	6+1 (6)	-	-	2 (4)	5+1 (5)	-	R/R		-

OXFORD: From left to right, back row: Ales Dryml, Lubos Tomicek, Graeme Gordon (team manager), Davey Watt, Adam Skornicki. Front row, kneeling: David Howe, Eric Andersson. On bike: Todd Wiltshire.

DETAILS OF OTHER RIDERS

(all guests unless underlined)

Match No. 5: Leigh Adams 10+1 (5); Match No. 8: Tomasz Piszcz 4 (5); Match No. 10: Jamie Courtney 0 (4); Match No. 13: Tomasz Piszcz 6+1 (4); Match No. 14: Paul Clews 2 (4); Match No. 17: Krister Marsh 0 (3); Match No. 18: Sam Martin 2 (2); Match No. 20: Mathieu Tresarrieu 2+1 (3); Match No. 24: Mathieu Tresarrieu 1 (5), Stephan Katt 0 (4); Match No. 27: Olly Allen 9+1 (5); Match No. 31: Chris Louis 15 (5); Match No. 32: Krzysztof Kasprzak 8 (5); Match No. 33: David Norris 11 (5); Match No. 34: David Norris 5 (4); Match No. 35: Niels-Kristian Iversen 5 (4); Match No. 36: Adam Shields 6 (5); Match No. 37: Adam Shields 9 (4); Match No. 39: Adam Shields 13 (5); Lee Smart 0 (3); Match No. 40: Adam Shields 4 (4); Match No. 41: Adam Shields 5 (4); Match No. 42: Adam Shields 6+1 (4); Match No. 43: Adam Shields 15 (5); Sam Martin 0 (1).

DETAILS OF TACTICAL RIDES AND TACTICAL SUBSTITUTE RIDES

Match No. 2: Rickardsson 1 point (TR; not doubled); Howe 0 points (TR); Match No. 3: Rickardsson 6 points (TR); Match No. 4: Rickardsson 0 points (TR); Howe 0 points (TR); Match No. 6: Howe 4 points (TR); Watt 4 points (TR); Match No. 10: Rickardsson 6 points (TR); Howe 4 points (TR); Match No. 11: Watt 4 points (TR); Howe 1 point (TR; not doubled); Wiltshire 0 points (TS); Match No. 12: Watt 4 points (TR); Eriksson 4 points (TR); Match No. 14: Wiltshire 4 points (TR); Match No. 15: Andersson 4 points (TR); Howe 4 points (TR); Match No. 16: Watt 4 points (TR); Tomicek 4 points (TR); Match No. 17: Eriksson 6 points (TR); Match No. 20: Wiltshire 6 points (TR); Watt 4 points (TR); Match No. 22: Watt 6 points (TR); Match No. 23: Wiltshire 6 points (TR); Watt 4 points (TR); Match No. 24: Skornicki 6 points (TR); Wiltshire 0 points (TR); Dryml 0 points (TS); Match No. 26: Skornicki 4 points (TR); Wiltshire 1 point (TR; not doubled); Match No. 27: Allen 6 points (TR); Skornicki 6 points (TR); Match No. 29: Wiltshire 6 points (TR); Skornicki 4 points (TR); Match No. 36: Howe 4 points (TR); Skornicki 0 points (TR); Match No. 38: Howe 1 point (TR; not doubled); Skornicki 0 points (TR); Match No. 39: Wiltshire 4 points (TR); Howe 1 point (TR; not doubled); Match No. 41: Skornicki 4 points (TR); Match No. 44: Howe 4 points (TR); Watt 4 points (TS); Wiltshire 0 points (TR).

AVERAGES
(40 Elite League, 2 Knock-Out Cup = 42 fixtures) ◆ Denotes ever-present.

Rider	Mts	Rds	Pts	Bon	Tot	Avge	Max
Tony Rickardsson	7	34	83	0	83	9.76	1 full
Todd Wiltshire	33	162	302	21	323	7.98	2 paid
Davey Watt	38	167	251	40	291	6.97	-
Adam Skornicki ◆	42	187	280	29	309	6.61	1 paid
David Howe ◆	42	180	252	30	282	6.27	1 paid
Eric Andersson	40	185	195	41	236	5.10	-
Stanislaw Burza	7	26	22	5	27	4.15	-
Lubos Tomicek	31	133	116	21	137	4.12	-
Freddie Eriksson	13	51	39	10	49	3.84	-
Adam Pietraszko	7	21	11	1	12	2.29	-

Also rode (in alphabetical order):

Rider	Mts	Rds	Pts	Bon	Tot	Avge	Max
Ales Dryml	3	13	23	0	23	7.08	-
Mathieu Tresarrieu	2	8	3	1	4	2.00	-

	Mts	Rds	Pts	Bon	Tot	Avge	Max
Guests	23	94	132	4	136	5.79	2 full

(Leigh Adams [1]; Olly Allen [1]; Paul Clews [1]; Jamie Courtney [1]; Niels-Kristian Iversen [1]; Krzysztof Kasprzak [1]; Stephan Katt [1]; Chris Louis [1]; Krister Marsh [1]; Sam Martin [2]; David Norris [2]; Tomasz Piszcz [2]; Adam Shields [7]; Lee Smart [1]).

PETERBOROUGH PANTHERS

ADDRESS: East of England Showground, Alwalton, Peterborough, Cambridgeshire, PE2 0XE.
PROMOTERS: Colin Horton and Neil Watson, with the latter standing down at the end of April due to business commitments.
YEARS OF OPERATION: 1970-1974 British League Division Two; 1975-1990 National League; 1991-1994 British League Division Two; 1995 Premier League; 1996 Premier League and Conference League; 1997 Elite League and Amateur League; 1998 Premier League; 1999 Elite League; 2000-2003 Elite League and Conference League; 2004-2006 Elite League.
FIRST MEETING: 12 June 1970.
TRACK LENGTH: 336 metres.
TRACK RECORD: 59.2 seconds – Hans N. Andersen (14/04/06).

CLUB HONOURS

FOUR-TEAM CHAMPIONS: 1977, 1978, 1988, 1989, 1992, 1997, 1998.
LEAGUE CHAMPIONS: 1992, 1998, 1999, 2006.
NOTE: The Amateur League team won their League Championship in 1997; the Conference League side won their League Championship in 2002.
KNOCK-OUT CUP WINNERS: 1992, 1999, 2001.
PREMIERSHIP WINNERS: 1993.
PAIRS CHAMPIONS: 1998.
CRAVEN SHIELD WINNERS: 1999.

RIDER ROSTER 2006

Hans N. ANDERSEN; Richard HALL; Niels-Kristian IVERSEN; Jesper B. JENSEN; Ulrich OSTERGAARD; Ryan SULLIVAN; Piotr SWIDERSKI; Karol ZABIK.

OTHER APPEARANCES/GUESTS (official matches only)

Jon ARMSTRONG; Tomasz BAJERSKI; James COCKLE; Billy HAMILL; Rusty HARRISON; Gary HAVELOCK; Alan MOGRIDGE; Henrik MOLLER; Joel PARSONS; Tomasz PISZCZ; Jonas RAUN; Lee RICHARDSON; Adam SKORNICKI; Mark THOMPSON; Todd WILTSHIRE.

PETERBOROUGH

* Denotes aggregate/bonus-point victory

NO.	DATE	OPPONENTS	VENUE	COMPETITION	RESULT	ANDERSEN	BAJERSKI	JENSEN	IVERSEN	SULLIVAN	HALL	OSTERGAARD	ARMSTRONG	RAUN	SWIDERSKI	ZABIK	OTHERS
1	16/3	Wolverhampton	H	Chal	W51-42	10 (5)	6+2 (4)	8+1 (5)	7 (4)	7 (4)	4+3 (4)	9+1 (4)	-		-		-
2	23/3	Belle Vue	H	ELA	W46-44	11+1 (5)	3+1 (4)	7 (4)	6 (4)	8+1 (5)	2+1 (3)	9+1 (5)	-		-	-	

NO.	DATE	OPPONENTS	VENUE	COMPETITION	RESULT	ANDERSEN	BAJERSKI	JENSEN	IVERSEN	SULLIVAN	HALL	OSTERGAARD	ARMSTRONG	RAUN	SWIDERSKI	ZABIK	OTHERS
3	30/3	Reading	H	ELA	L41-52	10 (4)	1 (4)	6+2 (4)	13 (5)	8+1 (4)	3 (6)	0 (3)	-	-	-	-	-
4	31/3	Arena-Essex	A	KOC	L35-59	11 (5)	0 (1)	11 (5)	4 (4)	4 (4)	2+1 (7)	3 (4)	-	-	-	-	-
5	1/4	Eastbourne	A	ELA	L46-47	10 (5)	R/R	14+1 (6)	8+2 (4)	6 (4)	3+1 (5)	5+2 (6)	-	-	-	-	-
6	3/4	Belle Vue	A	ELA	L40-50	10+1 (6)	0 (3)	5+1 (4)	9+1 (4)	6 (4)	4+1 (4)	6 (5)	-	-	-	-	-
7	5/4	Oxford	A	ELA	W47-42	14 (5)	1 (3)	10+3 (5)	8 (4)	6 (4)	1 (3)	7+2 (6)	-	-	-	-	-
8	6/4	Arena-Essex	H	KOC	W57-37	11+1 (5)	R/R	11+1 (5)	8 (4)	15 (5)	3+1 (3)	9+3 (7)	0 (1)	-	-	-	-
9	10/4	Wolverhampton	A	ELA	L42-48	12 (5)	R/R	11+1 (6)	6+2 (4)	6 (4)	2 (4)	5+2 (7)	-	-	-	-	-
10	14/4	Swindon	H	ELA	W55-40	11 (4)	-	14+1 (5)	11+2 (5)	10 (4)	3 (4)	6+1 (4)	-	0 (4)	-	-	-
11	19/4	Reading	A	ELA	W51-39*	15 (5)	-	12+2 (5)	9+2 (4)	4 (4)	1 (3)	10+2 (6)	-	0 (3)	-	-	-
12	25/4	Oxford	H	ELA	W63-31*	14+1 (5)	-	10 (4)	10+2 (4)	14+1 (5)	5+1 (4)	9+3 (4)	-	1 (4)	-	-	-
13	27/4	Eastbourne	H	ELA	W59-33*	15 (5)	-	10+1 (4)	9+2 (4)	10 (4)	4+1 (4)	11+2 (5)	-	0 (4)	-	-	-
14	4/5	Ipswich	H	ELA	W55-38	14+1 (5)	-	9+1 (4)	9 (4)	13 (5)	3+1 (4)	6+1 (5)	-	1 (3)	-	-	-
15	10/5	Poole	A	ELA	L42-48	12 (5)	-	10+1 (4)	5 (4)	10+2 (5)	3+1 (7)	0 (0)	-	-	2 (4)	-	-
16	11/5	Poole	H	ELA	W48-42	11+1 (5)	-	13+1 (5)	6+1 (4)	10 (4)	2 (5)	-	2+1 (3)	-	4 (4)	-	-
17	15/5	Coventry	A	ELA	L44-48	10 (5)	-	12 (5)	6 (4)	10 (4)	2+1 (5)	-	-	-	4+1 (4)	-	0 (3)
18	25/5	Coventry	H	ELA	W62-32*	9+1 (4)	-	15+2 (6)	9+1 (4)	14+1 (5)	6+2 (5)	9+2 (6)	R/R	-	-	-	-
19	1/6	Wolverhampton	H	ELA	W54-38*	14+1 (5)	-	9 (4)	7+1 (4)	15 (5)	7+1 (5)	2+1 (4)	0 (3)	-	-	-	-
20	5/6	Belle Vue	A	ELB	L43-52	14 (6)	-	R/R	9+1 (5)	11+2 (6)	5 (5)	2+2 (5)	2+1 (4)	-	-	-	-
21	8/6	Ipswich	A	ELA	L42-48*	13+1 (5)	-	11 (5)	5 (4)	7+1 (4)	2+1 (4)	4 (4)	-	-	-	-	0 (4)
22	19/6	Wolverhampton	A	ELB	W46-44	18 (6)	-	R/R	12 (6)	9+1 (5)	3 (4)	0 (3)	-	-	-	4+1 (6)	-
23	22/6	Belle Vue	H	ELB	W55-39*	14 (5)	-	R/R	11+2 (6)	12 (5)	2+1 (3)	3+2 (4)	-	-	-	13 (7)	-
24	23/6	Eastbourne	A	ELB	L35-55	-	-	R/R	-	8 (6)	0 (4)	3+1 (5)	-	-	-	3 (4)	21 (11)
25	28/6	Oxford	A	ELB	W49-41	17 (6)	-	R/R	10+4 (6)	13 (5)	5+1 (5)	2+1 (5)	-	-	-	-	2+1 (3)
26	29/6	Ipswich	H	ELB	W50-40	17 (6)	-	R/R	13+1 (6)	9+2 (5)	5+1 (5)	6+2 (5)	-	-	-	-	0 (3)
27	3/7	Arena-Essex	H	ELA	W48-42	17 (6)	-	R/R	11+1 (5)	13 (6)	5+1 (6)	2 (4)	-	-	-	0 (3)	-
28	6/7	Coventry	H	ELB	W49-41	17 (6)	-	R/R	13 (6)	5+2 (5)	5 (5)	6+1 (4)	-	-	-	-	3+1 (4)
29	13/7	Swindon	A	ELA	L34-58	-	-	R/R	11 (5)	4+3 (5)	4 (6)	2 (4)	-	-	-	-	13 (10)
30	26/7	Poole	A	ELB	W56-36	17 (6)	-	R/R	7+1 (5)	11+2 (5)	3+1 (3)	5+2 (5)	-	-	-	13+2 (6)	-
31	31/7	Reading	A	ELB	L42-51	18 (6)	-	R/R	11 (6)	4+1 (5)	3+1 (4)	1 (4)	-	-	-	5 (5)	-
32	5/8	Ipswich	A	ELB	L43-51*	20 (7)	-	R/R	6 (4)	7+3 (6)	4+1 (6)	3+1 (4)	-	-	-	-	3+1 (3)
33	10/8	Poole	H	ELB	W47-46*	19 (6)	-	R/R	-	9 (6)	8 (5)	5+3 (5)	-	-	-	6+1 (7)	0 (1)
34	14/8	Eastbourne	H	ELB	W61-32*	14 (5)	-	R/R	14 (5)	10+4 (5)	7+3 (5)	4+2 (5)	-	-	-	12+1 (5)	-
35	17/8	Wolverhampton	H	ELB	W47-42*	16+2 (6)	-	R/R	13 (6)	5 (5)	7 (7)	6 (5)	-	-	-	0 (1)	-
36	21/8	Coventry	A	ELB	L47-49*	17 (6)	-	R/R	6 (5)	10+1 (6)	3+1 (4)	7+2 (5)	-	4 (4)	-	-	-
37	24/8	Swindon	A	ELA	L46-47	16+1 (6)	-	R/R	5+2 (5)	14 (6)	9+1 (7)	0 (3)	-	2+1 (3)	-	-	-
38	28/8	Arena-Essex	H	ELA	W56-39*	14+1 (5)	-	12 (4)	7 (4)	6+1 (4)	7+2 (4)	5 (4)	-	-	-	5+1 (5)	-
39	31/8	Oxford	H	ELB	W55-34*	11+1 (4)	-	12+2 (5)	6+1 (4)	R/R	14+1 (7)	5+1 (4)	-	-	-	7+2 (6)	-
40	1/9	Arena-Essex	A	ELB	L38-58	8 (4)	-	5 (5)	14 (6)	R/R	9+2 (7)	1 (5)	1+1 (3)	-	-	-	-
41	7/9	Arena-Essex	H	ELB	W62-28*	9 (4)	-	8 (4)	11+1 (5)	13+2 (5)	11+2 (5)	2 (3)	-	-	-	8+2 (4)	-
42	11/9	Reading	H	ELB	L43-49	16 (5)	-	3 (4)	4 (4)	8+2 (5)	6 (4)	2 (4)	-	-	-	-	4+3 (4)
43	18/9	Swindon	H	ELB	W53-37*	10 (4)	-	6+1 (4)	6+2 (4)	12+2 (5)	9+1 (4)	2+1 (4)	-	-	-	8+1 (5)	-
44	25/9	Coventry	H	PO s/f	W52-40	9+1 (4)	-	9 (4)	8+1 (5)	9+2 (4)	11 (5)	1 (3)	-	-	-	5 (5)	-
45	2/10	Reading	A	PO f	L47-49	14+1 (5)	-	1 (4)	R/R	15 (6)	6+1 (5)	3 (5)	-	-	-	8 (5)	-

NO.	DATE	OPPONENTS	VENUE	COMPETITION	RESULT	ANDERSEN	BAJERSKI	JENSEN	IVERSEN	SULLIVAN	HALL	OSTERGAARD	ARMSTRONG	RAUN	SWIDERSKI	ZABIK	OTHERS
46	6/10	Coventry/ Belle Vue	Cov	CS s/f	3rd – 26	-	-	7+1 (4)		4+1 (4)	0 (4)	2 (4)	-		6+1 (4)	-	7 (4)
47	9/10	Reading	H	PO f	W48-45*	14+2 (5)	-	2+1 (3)	5+1 (4)	12+1 (5)	10+1 (6)	1 (3)			4+1 (4)	-	
48	12/10	Coventry/ Belle Vue	H	CS s/f	1st –45	10+1 (4)	-	7+3 (4)	9+1 (4)	6 (3)	4 (5)				9+2 (4)		
49	16/10	Coventry/ Belle Vue	BV	CS s/f	3rd –33	11 (4)	-		8+2 (4)	-	1 (4)		-	-	4 (4)	-	9+2 (8)
50	20/10	King's Lynn	A	CC	W49-44	15 (5)		5+1 (3)	6 (4)	8+3 (5)	7+1 (4)	4 (5)			4 (4)	-	

NOTE: CC = Champion of Champions Challenge; Following the home match against Poole on 11 May, Jesper B. Jensen lost a bonus point run-off to Antonio Lindback.

DETAILS OF OTHER RIDERS

(all guests)

Match No. 17: Tomasz Piszcz 0 (3); Match No. 21: James Cockle 0 (4); Match No. 24: Todd Wiltshire 11 (6); Billy Hamill 10 (5); Match No. 25: Mark Thompson 2+1 (3); Match No. 26: Mark Thompson 0 (3); Match No. 28: Henrik Moller 3+1 (4); Match No. 29: Adam Skornicki 11 (6); Henrik Moller 2 (4); Match No. 32: Joel Parsons 3+1 (3); Match No. 33: James Cockle 0 (1); Match No. 42: Alan Mogridge 4+3 (4); Match No. 46: Lee Richardson 7 (4); Match No. 49: Gary Havelock 7+1 (4); Rusty Harrison 2+1 (4).

DETAILS OF TACTICAL RIDES AND TACTICAL SUBSTITUTE RIDES

Match No. 3: Iversen 6 points (TR); Match No. 4: Jensen 4 points (TR); Andersen 4 points (TR); Match No. 6: Andersen 0 points (TS); Match No. 17: Sullivan 4 points (TR); Match No. 20: Iversen 6 points (TR); Sullivan 4 points (TR); Match No. 24: Sullivan 1 point (TR; not doubled); Zabik 0 points (TR); Match No. 29: Iversen 6 points (TR); Skornicki 1 point (TR; not doubled); Match No. 31: Andersen 6 points (TR); Sullivan 0 points (TR); Match No. 32: Iversen 4 points (TR); Andersen 4 points (TS); Match No. 33: Andersen 6 points (TR); Match No. 36: Andersen 6 points (TR); Sullivan 6 points (TR); Match No. 37: Sullivan 6 points (TR); Match No. 40: Andersen 6 points (TR); Iversen 6 points (TR); Match No. 42: Andersen 4 points (TR); Iversen 0 points (TR); Match No. 45: Andersen 6 points (TR); Sullivan 6 points (TR); Match No. 47: Andersen 6 points (TR).

AVERAGES

(40 Elite League, 3 Play-Offs, 2 Knock-Out Cup, 3 Craven Shield = 48 fixtures)

♦ Denotes ever-present.

Rider	Mts	Rds	Pts	Bon	Tot	Avge	Max
Hans N. Andersen	45	230	580	19	599	10.42	3 full; 6 paid
Jesper B. Jensen	30	135	270	26	296	8.77	1 full; 1 paid
Ryan Sullivan	45	216	402	39	441	8.17	2 full; 3 paid
Niels-Kristian Iversen	44	203	364	37	401	7.90	1 paid
Piotr Swiderski	15	65	80	12	92	5.66	-
Karol Zabik	9	44	56	5	61	5.55	-
Ulrich Ostergaard	44	195	182	43	225	4.62	1 paid
Richard Hall ♦	48	229	224	36	260	4.54	-

PETERBOROUGH: From left to right, back row: Ryan Sullivan, Ulrich Ostergaard, Richard Hall, Niels-Kristian Iversen. Front row, on bikes: Jesper B. Jensen, Hans N. Andersen, Tomasz Bajerski.

Also rode (in alphabetical order):

Jon Armstrong	5	14	5	3	8	2.29	-
Tomasz Bajerski	5	15	5	1	6	1.60	-
Jonas Raun	5	18	2	0	2	0.44	-
Guests	15	58	62	8	70	4.83	-

(James Cockle [2]; Billy Hamill [1]; Rusty Harrison [1]; Gary Havelock [1]; Alan Mogridge [1]; Henrik Moller [2]; Joel Parsons [1]; Tomasz Piszcz [1]; Lee Richardson [1]; Adam Skornicki [1]; Mark Thompson [2]; Todd Wiltshire [1]).

OTHER MEETING

2 April: The King of the Showground Spectacular - Ryan Sullivan Testimonial
Peterborough 43: Niels-Kristian Iversen 12 (4); Ryan Sullivan 11 (4); Jesper B. Jensen 11 (4); Hans N. Andersen 9 (4); Poole 19. Great Britain 18: Mark Loram 6 (4); Gary Havelock 5 (4); Scott Nicholls 4 (4); David Norris 3 (4). Rest of the World 16: Sean Wilson 7 (4); Peter Karlsson 6 (4); Steve Johnston 3 (4); Tomasz Bajerski 0 (4). Individual tournament: FIRST SEMI-FINAL: 1st Iversen; 2nd Jensen; 3rd Loram; 4th Havelock; SECOND SEMI-FINAL: 1st Grzegorz Walasek; 2nd Karlsson; 3rd Bjarne Pedersen; 4th Bajerski; FINAL: 1st Jensen; 2nd Karlsson; 3rd Iversen; 4th Walasek.

OTHER DETAILS

Denmark Select scorers in Match No. 1: Charlie Gjedde 14 (5); Mads Korneliussen 11 (5); Tom P. Madsen 4+1 (4); Morten Risager 4 (4); Jonas Raun 3+1 (4); Jonathan Bethell 3+1 (5); Henrik Moller 2 (4). Gjedde's total includes 4 points from a TR.

POOLE RIAS PIRATES

ADDRESS: Poole Stadium, Wimborne Road, Poole, Dorset, BH15 2BP.
PROMOTERS: Matt Ford and Mike Golding.
YEARS OF OPERATION: 1948-1951 National League Division Three; 1952-1955 National League Division Two; 1956 National League Division One; 1957 Open; 1958-1959 National League; 1960-1963 Provincial League; 1964 Provincial League and Metropolitan League; 1965-1967 British League; 1968-1974 British League Division One; 1975-1984 British League; 1985-1990 National League; 1991-1994 British League Division One; 1995-1996 Premier League; 1997-2006 Elite League.
FIRST MEETING: 26 April 1948.
TRACK LENGTH: 299.1 metres.
TRACK RECORD: 56.91 seconds – Antonio Lindback (14/06/06).

CLUB HONOURS

LEAGUE CHAMPIONS: 1951, 1952, 1955, 1961, 1962, 1969, 1989, 1990, 1994, 2003, 2004.
NATIONAL TROPHY (DIVISION TWO) WINNERS: 1952, 1955.
KNOCK-OUT CUP WINNERS: 1990, 2003, 2004.
FOUR-TEAM CHAMPIONS: 1994.
CRAVEN SHIELD WINNERS: 2001, 2002, 2006.
BRITISH LEAGUE CUP WINNERS: 2003.

RIDER ROSTER 2006

Tommy ALLEN; Craig BOYCE; Daniel DAVIDSSON; Jonas DAVIDSSON; Krzysztof KASPRZAK; Antonio LINDBACK; Bjarne PEDERSEN; Shaun TACEY; Grzegorz WALASEK; Matthew WETHERS.

OTHER APPEARANCES/GUESTS (official matches only)

Dean BARKER; Jason DOYLE; Gary HAVELOCK; Steve JOHNSTON; Robert KSIEZAK; Fredrik LINDGREN; Jason LYONS; Travis McGOWAN; David NORRIS; Lee RICHARDSON; Adam SHIELDS; Simon STEAD; Ryan SULLIVAN; Davey WATT; Magnus ZETTERSTROM.

POOLE

* Denotes aggregate/bonus-point victory

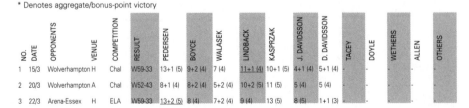

NO.	DATE	OPPONENTS	VENUE	COMPETITION	RESULT	PEDERSEN	BOYCE	WALASEK	LINDBACK	KASPRZAK	J. DAVIDSSON	D. DAVIDSSON	TACEY	DOYLE	WETHERS	ALLEN	OTHERS
1	15/3	Wolverhampton	H	Chal	W59-33	13+1 (5)	9+2 (4)	7 (4)	11+1 (4)	10+1 (5)	4+1 (4)	5+1 (4)	-	-	-	-	-
2	20/3	Wolverhampton	A	Chal	W52-43	8+1 (4)	8+2 (4)	5+2 (4)	10+2 (5)	11 (5)	5 (4)	5 (4)	-	-	-	-	-
3	22/3	Arena-Essex	H	ELA	W59-33	13+2 (5)	8 (4)	7+2 (4)	9 (4)	13 (5)	8 (5)	1+1 (3)	-	-	-	-	-

NO.	DATE	OPPONENTS	VENUE	COMPETITION	RESULT	PEDERSEN	BOYCE	WALASEK	LINDBACK	KASPRZAK	J. DAVIDSSON	D. DAVIDSSON	TACEY	DOYLE	WETHERS	ALLEN	OTHERS
4	24/3	Arena-Essex	A	ELA	L40-55*	12+1 (5)	3+1 (4)	5 (4)	3+1 (4)	15 (5)	2+1 (5)	0 (3)	-	-			
5	5/4	Swindon	H	ELA	W48-42	13 (5)	3+1 (4)	4+2 (4)	8 (4)	9+1 (5)	3+2 (3)	8 (5)	-	-			
6	6/4	Swindon	A	ELA	L43-52	11 (5)	1 (4)	6 (4)	8+1 (4)	10 (4)	7 (6)	0 (3)	-	-			
7	14/4	Eastbourne	H	ELA	W54-36	13+1 (5)	5 (4)	5+3 (4)	9+1 (4)	12+1 (5)	9 (5)	1 (3)	-	-			
8	14/4	Eastbourne	A	ELA	L41-49*	10 (5)	4 (4)	6+1 (4)	7 (5)	6+1 (4)	5+2 (5)	3 (3)	-	-			
9	24/4	Ipswich	A	ELA	L40-50	7 (4)	6 (4)	3+1 (4)	9 (6)	10 (5)	1+1 (3)	4 (4)	-	-			
10	26/4	Belle Vue	H	ELA	W55-38	12 (5)	5+2 (4)	4+1 (4)	12+1 (5)	8+1 (4)	7+2 (4)	7+3 (4)	-	-			
11	1/5	Coventry	H	ELA	W55-38	11+1 (4)	7 (4)	14+1 (5)	12+3 (5)	5 (4)	3+1 (4)	3 (4)	-	-			
12	10/5	Peterborough	H	ELA	W48-42	-	8+1 (4)	8 (4)	10+1 (5)	10 (5)	5+1 (6)	6+2 (4)	-	-			1+1 (2)
13	11/5	Peterborough	A	ELA	L42-48*	-	6 (5)	8+2 (5)	10 (6)	R/R	9 (5)	1+1 (3)	-	-			8+1 (6)
14	15/5	Wolverhampton	A	ELA	L41-52	10 (6)	6+2 (5)	5 (5)	12 (5)	R/R	7+2 (5)	1+1 (3)	-	-			
15	31/5	Wolverhampton	H	ELA	W47-43	11+1 (6)	8 (5)	5+2 (5)	13+2 (6)	R/R	7+2 (5)	3 (3)	-	-			
16	7/6	Oxford	H	ELA	W55-40	13+2 (6)	12+2 (5)	9 (5)	16+2 (6)	R/R	1 (4)	-	4+1 (4)	-			
17	8/6	Oxford	A	ELA	L43-50*	11 (6)	3+2 (5)	-	19 (6)	R/R	0 (3)	-	6+1 (5)	-			4 (5)
18	14/6	Swindon	H	ELB	W58-36	16+1 (6)	11+1 (5)	-	14+2 (6)	R/R	3+1 (4)	-	4 (4)	-			10+3 (5)
19	19/6	Arena-Essex	H	ELB	W66-24	18 (6)	7+1 (5)	-	14+3 (6)	R/R	8+4 (4)	-	6 (4)	-			13+1 (5)
20	26/6	Reading	A	ELA	L40-50	16 (6)	9+1 (5)	4 (5)	-	R/R	3 (5)	-	1 (3)	-			7 (6)
21	28/6	Coventry	H	ELB	W47-46	12+1 (6)	8 (5)	8+1 (5)	14+1 (6)	R/R	5+2 (5)	-	0 (3)	-			
22	3/7	Belle Vue	A	ELA	L37-53*	11 (5)	2+1 (5)	9+1 (5)	12 (6)	R/R	0 (3)	-	3+1 (6)	-			
23	5/7	Reading	H	KOC	W58-34	10+2 (5)	8+2 (5)	16+2 (6)	10+1 (5)	R/R	13+2 (6)	-	1 (3)	-			
24	6/7	Swindon	A	ELB	L44-49*	10 (4)	5+1 (5)	13+1 (6)	11+2 (6)	R/R	5+2 (6)	-	0 (3)	-			
25	7/7	Reading	A	KOC	L42-51*	10 (4)	7+1 (5)	11 (6)	3 (5)	R/R	7+2 (6)	-	4 (4)	-			
26	10/7	Coventry	A	ELA	L42-47*	9 (5)	7+2 (5)	13 (6)	7 (5)	R/R	4 (6)	-	2 (3)	-			
27	12/7	Belle Vue	H	ELB	W50-44	11 (6)	8+3 (5)	10+3 (6)	-	R/R	10+3 (5)	-	1 (3)	-			10+2 (5)
28	23/7	Rest of World	H	TRF	L44-52	14+1 (6)	5 (4)	-	5 (4)	10+1 (6)	5+1 (6)	-	-	-			5 (6)
29	24/7	Belle Vue	A	ELB	W48-42*	13+1 (5)	6+2 (4)	7+2 (4)	9+1 (5)	7+1 (4)	5+2 (5)	-	1 (3)	-			
30	26/7	Peterborough	H	ELB	L36-56	10+1 (4)	2 (4)	7 (4)	10 (5)	6+1 (5)	-	-	0 (4)	1 (4)			
31	31/7	Oxford	A	ELB	L47-49	14+1 (5)	2 (4)	1 (3)	10+2 (5)	9 (4)	8 (5)	-	-	3 (4)			
32	2/8	Eastbourne	H	ELB	W49-44	13 (5)	3+1 (4)	10+1 (5)	9 (4)	9+1 (4)	5+1 (5)	-	-	-			0 (3)
33	9/8	Ipswich	H	ELA	W57-39*	14+1 (6)	11 (5)	9+1 (5)	R/R	12+2 (6)	10+2 (5)	-	-	-	1+1 (3)	-	
34	10/8	Peterborough	A	ELB	L46-47	12+1 (6)	7+1 (5)	11+1 (6)	R/R	8+1 (5)	4 (4)	-	-	-	4+2 (4)	-	
35	14/8	Reading	A	ELA	L41-53	13 (6)	6+1 (5)	-	R/R	11 (6)	2 (4)	-	-	-	2+1 (3)	-	7+1 (5)
36	16/8	Reading	H	ELA	L45-48	13 (6)	7+2 (5)	-	R/R	14 (6)	5 (5)	-	-	-	3+1 (3)	-	3+1 (5)
37	17/8	Ipswich	A	ELB	L44-52	18 (6)	6+1 (5)	-	R/R	11 (6)	4+1 (5)	-	-	-	-	1+1 (3)	4 (5)
38	18/8	Arena-Essex	A	ELB	L40-50*	17 (6)	6+1 (5)	-	R/R	9 (6)	1+1 (4)	-	-	-	-	2 (4)	5 (5)
39	19/8	Eastbourne	A	ELB	L41-53	15 (6)	4+2 (5)	-	R/R	9 (6)	5 (5)	-	-	-	-	0 (3)	8 (5)
40	28/8	Wolverhampton	A	ELB	L40-52	13 (5)	4 (4)	5 (4)	11+1 (5)	3 (4)	3 (4)	-	-	-	1 (4)	-	
41	30/8	Ipswich	H	ELB	W54-36*	10+1 (4)	6 (4)	10+2 (5)	6 (4)	12+1 (5)	9+2 (5)	-	-	-	1 (3)	-	
42	1/9	Coventry	A	ELB	L42-54	21 (6)	3 (5)	4 (5)	R/R	-	0 (4)	-	-	-	-	2 (4)	12 (6)
43	6/9	Oxford	H	ELB	W49-42*	8 (4)	5 (4)	8+1 (4)	9+2 (5)	3+2 (4)	15 (6)	-	-	-	-	1 (3)	
44	11/9	Belle Vue	A	KOC s/f	L41-53	14 (5)	3+2 (4)	9 (5)	4 (3)	4 (4)	4 (5)	-	-	-	3+2 (4)	-	
45	14/9	Reading	H	ELB	W47-43	11+1 (5)	7+1 (4)	6 (4)	5 (3)	8 (5)	7+1 (5)	-	-	-	3+1 (4)	-	
46	20/9	Wolverhampton	H	ELB	W59-34*	14+2 (6)	9+1 (5)	7+1 (5)	R/R	15+2 (6)	11+2 (5)	-	-	-	3 (4)	-	

NO.	DATE	OPPONENTS	VENUE	COMPETITION	RESULT	PEDERSEN	BOYCE	WALASEK	LINDBACK	KASPRZAK	J. DAVIDSSON	D. DAVIDSSON	TACEY	DOYLE	WETHERS	ALLEN	OTHERS
47	21/9	Swindon/ Reading	Swin	CS s/f	3rd – 35	-	11 (4)	7 (4)	-	6 (4)	2 (4)	-	-	6+3 (4)	3+1 (4)	-	-
48	28/9	Belle Vue	H	KOC s/f	W43-34	-	13 (5)	11 (4)	R/R	6+2 (4)	6+1 (4)	-	-	-	-	3+1 (3)	4+3 (4)
49	4/10	Swindon/ Reading	H	CS s/f	1st – 41	11+1 (4)	4 (4)	7+1 (4)	-	9+2 (4)	1 (4)	-	-	-	-	-	9 (4)
50	16/10	Swindon/ Reading	Read	CS s/f	1st – 40*	8+2 (4)	8+2 (4)	-	-	10 (4)	4+2 (5)	-	2+1 (3)	-	-	-	8 (4)
51	20/10	Coventry/ Eastbourne	Cov	CS f	1st – 41	11 (4)	7+2 (4)	2 (4)	-	8+1 (4)	-	-	-	-	-	3 (4)	10+1 (4)
52	24/10	Coventry/ Eastbourne	East	CS f	= 2nd – 35	8 (4)	4+2 (4)	4 (4)	-	9+1 (4)	-	-	-	-	-	0 (4)	10 (4)
53	26/10	Coventry/ Eastbourne	H	CS f	2nd – 38*	12 (4)	5 (4)	4+1 (4)	-	11 (4)	-	-	-	-	-	1 (2)	5+2 (4)

NOTE: TRF = Tony Rickardsson Farewell. Following the away match at Peterborough on 11 May, Antonio Lindback won a bonus point run-off against Jesper B. Jensen. The Knock-Out Cup semi-final tie at home to Belle Vue on 28 September was abandoned after heat twelve, with the result permitted to stand.

DETAILS OF OTHER RIDERS

(all guests)

Match No. 12: Lee Richardson 1+1 (2); Match No. 13: Simon Stead 8+1 (6); Match No. 17: Dean Barker 4 (5); Match No. 18: Adam Shields 10+3 (5); Match No. 19: Gary Havelock 13+1 (5); Match No. 20: Adam Shields 7 (6); Match No. 27: Ryan Sullivan 10+2 (5); Match No. 28: Tony Rickardsson 5 (2); Marc Andrews 0 (4); Match No. 32: Robert Ksiezak 0 (3); Match No. 35: Jason Lyons 7+1 (5); Match No. 36: David Norris 3+1 (5); Match No. 37: Steve Johnston 4 (5); Match No. 38: Travis McGowan 5 (5); Match No. 39: Davey Watt 8 (5); Match No. 42: Simon Stead 12 (6); Match No. 48: Davey Watt 4+3 (4); Match No. 49: Magnus Zetterstrom 9 (4); Match No. 50: Davey Watt 8 (4); Match No. 51: Fredrik Lindgren 10+1 (4); Match No. 52: Fredrik Lindgren 10 (4); Match No. 53: Fredrik Lindgren 5+2 (4).

DETAILS OF TACTICAL RIDES AND TACTICAL SUBSTITUTE RIDES

Match No. 4: Kasprzak 6 points (TR); Pedersen 4 points (TR); Match No. 6: Kasprzak 6 points (TR); Pedersen 4 points (TR); Match No. 9: Lindback 1 point (TS; not doubled); Match No. 14: Lindback 6 points (TR); Match No. 17: Lindback 6 points (TR); Match No. 24: Pedersen 6 points (TR); Match No. 25: Walasek 6 points (TR); Match No. 30: Pedersen 4 points (TR); Lindback 1 point (TR; not doubled); Match No. 31: Lindback 6 points (TR); Pedersen 6 points (TR); Match No. 35: Pedersen 4 points (TR); Kasprzak 4 points (TR); Match No. 37: Pedersen 6 points (TR); Kasprzak 6 points (TR); Match No. 39: Pedersen 4 points (TR); Watt 4 points (TR); Match No. 40: Pedersen 6 points (TR); Match No. 42: Pedersen 6 points (TR); Stead 6 points (TR); Match No. 44: Pedersen 4 points (TR); Walasek 4 points (TR).

OTHER DETAILS

Rest of the World scorers in Match No. 28: Jason Crump 14 (5); Leigh Adams 9+1 (5); Nicolai Klindt 9 (5); Rory Schlein 7+2 (5); Steve Johnston 5+1 (4); Chris Holder 4+1 (4); Jason Doyle 4 (4).

POOLE: From left to right, back row: Grzegorz Walasek, Tommy Allen, Neil Middleditch (team manager), Krzysztof Kasprzak, Antonio Lindback. Front row, kneeling: Jonas Davidsson, Craig Boyce. On bike: Bjarne Pedersen.

AVERAGES

(40 Elite League, 4 Knock-Out Cup, 6 Craven Shield = 50 fixtures) ◆ Denotes ever-present.

Rider	Mts	Rds	Pts	Bon	Tot	Avge	Max
Bjarne Pedersen	46	236	536	24	560	9.49	3 full; 3 paid
Antonio Lindback	32	159	306	27	333	8.38	2 paid
Krzysztof Kasprzak	34	160	296	21	317	7.93	-
Grzegorz Walasek	41	189	297	34	331	7.01	2 paid
Craig Boyce ◆	50	225	306	45	351	6.24	-
Jonas Davidsson	46	217	243	45	288	5.31	1 paid
Daniel Davidsson	13	45	38	8	46	4.09	-
Matthew Wethers	10	36	24	9	33	3.67	-
Shaun Tacey	14	52	33	3	36	2.77	-
Tommy Allen	9	30	13	2	15	2.00	-
Also rode:							
Jason Doyle	4	15	12	4	16	4.27	-
Guests	20	92	133	16	149	6.48	-

(Dean Barker [1]; Gary Havelock [1]; Steve Johnston [1]; Robert Ksiezak [1]; Fredrik Lindgren [3]; Jason Lyons [1]; Travis McGowan [1]; David Norris [1]; Lee Richardson [1]; Adam Shields [2]; Simon Stead [2]; Ryan Sullivan [1]; Davey Watt [3]; Magnus Zetterstrom [1]).

OTHER MEETING

2 April: The King of the Showground Spectacular – Ryan Sullivan Testimonial

Peterborough 43. Poole 19: Bjarne Pedersen 10 (4); Craig Boyce 4 (4); Grzegorz Walasek 3 (4); Edward Kennett 2 (4). Great Britain 18. Rest of the World 16.

INDIVIDUAL MEETING

19 July: Wessex Marine Young Guns Championship

1st Ricky Ashworth 14; 2nd Nicolai Klindt 11; 3rd Tomas Suchanek 10; Ben Wilson 9; Carl Wilkinson 9; Jason Doyle 9; Robert Ksiezak 8; Chris Kerr 7; Chris Holder 7; Chris Schramm 7; Tommy Allen 6; Shaun Tacey 6; Jordan Frampton (reserve) 5; Adam Allott 4; Krzysztof Kasprzak 3; James Cockle 3; Danny Warwick 2.

READING BULLDOGS

ADDRESS: Smallmead Stadium, A33 Relief Road, Smallmead, Reading, Berkshire, RG2 0JL.
PROMOTERS: John Postlethwaite and Jim Lynch.
YEARS OF OPERATION: 1975-1990 British League; 1991-1994 British League Division
One; 1995 Premier League; 1996 Premier League and Conference League; 1997 Premier
League and Amateur League; 1998-2005 Premier League; 2006 Elite League.
FIRST MEETING: 28 April 1975.
TRACK LENGTH: 307 metres.
TRACK RECORD: 58.1 seconds – Per Jonsson (12/10/87).

PREVIOUS VENUE: Reading Greyhound Stadium, Oxford Road, Tilehurst, Reading,
Berkshire.
YEARS OF OPERATION: 1968-1970 British League Division Two; 1971-1973 British
League Division One.

CLUB HONOURS

LEAGUE CHAMPIONS: 1980, 1990, 1992, 1997.
KNOCK-OUT CUP WINNERS: 1990, 1998.
PREMIERSHIP WINNERS: 1991, 1993.
BSPA CUP WINNERS: 1992.
FOUR-TEAM CHAMPIONS: 1993.
PAIRS CHAMPIONS: 2004.

RIDER ROSTER 2006

Charlie GJEDDE; Greg HANCOCK; Janusz KOLODZIEJ; Mark LEMON; Travis McGOWAN;
Zdenek SIMOTA; Andy SMITH; Matej ZAGAR.

OTHER APPEARANCES/GUESTS (official matches only)

Hans N. ANDERSEN; Ben BARKER; Dean BARKER; Glenn CUNNINGHAM; Chris HARRIS;
Gary HAVELOCK; Edward KENNETT; Kyle LEGAULT; Chris LOUIS; Chris MILLS; Kauko
NIEMINEN; Shane PARKER; Chris SCHRAMM; Mathieu TRESARRIEU; Davey WATT; Todd
WILTSHIRE.

READING

* Denotes aggregate/bonus-point victory

NO.	DATE	OPPONENTS	VENUE	COMPETITION	RESULT	HANCOCK	SMITH	McGOWAN	ZAGAR	GJEDDE	SIMOTA	KOLODZIEJ	MILLS	CUNNINGHAM	LEMON	OTHERS
1	13/3	GB Select	H	Chal	W60-32	9+1 (4)	8+2 (4)	7+1 (4)	12 (5)	11+2 (5)	5+1 (4)	8+3 (4)	-	-	-	-
2	20/3	Coventry	H	ELA	L41-49	12+1 (5)	4+1 (4)	4+1 (4)	3 (4)	9 (5)	1+1 (3)	8+3 (5)	-	-	-	-
3	24/3	Coventry	A	ELA	W48-42	13 (5)	2 (3)	6+1 (4)	12+1 (5)	7 (4)	0 (3)	8+1 (6)	-	-	-	-
4	30/3	Peterborough	A	ELA	W52-41	12+1 (5)	6 (4)	5+1 (4)	13 (5)	3+2 (4)	3 (3)	10+3 (5)	-	-	-	-
5	3/4	Ipswich	H	ELA	W50-40	12+2 (5)	5 (4)	5 (4)	7+2 (4)	4 (3)	2 (3)	15+3 (7)	-	-	-	-
6	6/4	Ipswich	A	ELA	W47-43*	12+1 (5)	6+1 (4)	9 (5)	5+1 (4)	3 (4)	4 (3)	8+2 (5)	-	-	-	-
7	10/4	Swindon	H	KOC	W47-43	9 (5)	7+1 (4)	8+3 (5)	9 (4)	7 (4)	2 (3)	5+3 (5)	-	-	-	-
8	13/4	Swindon	A	KOC	W50-40*	9 (4)	4+3 (4)	7+1 (5)	8+1 (4)	9+1 (5)	0 (3)	13+1 (5)	-	-	-	-
9	14/4	Oxford	A	ELA	L44-50	11 (5)	2 (4)	8 (5)	5 (4)	8+2 (4)	2+1 (3)	8 (5)	-	-	-	-
10	14/4	Oxford	H	ELA	W67-28*	10+1 (4)	6+2 (4)	8+3 (4)	15 (5)	12+2 (5)	8+1 (4)	8+3 (4)	-	-	-	-
11	19/4	Peterborough	H	ELA	L39-51	10 (5)	3+2 (4)	7 (5)	6 (4)	4+3 (4)	-	9+2 (5)	0 (3)	-	-	-
12	24/4	Swindon	H	ELA	W46-44	9+1 (5)	3+1 (4)	2+1 (4)	13+1 (5)	7 (4)	-	10+1 (5)	2+1 (4)	-	-	-
13	28/4	Arena-Essex	A	ELA	L33-58	5 (5)	6+1 (4)	10 (5)	-	3+1 (4)	-	8+1 (6)	1+1 (3)	-	-	0 (3)
14	1/5	Wolverhampton	A	ELA	L44-47	14 (5)	3+2 (4)	5+1 (4)	7 (5)	4+1 (4)	3+1 (3)	8+1 (5)	-	-	-	-
15	8/5	Arena-Essex	H	ELA	W50-46	12 (5)	4 (4)	4+1 (5)	8 (4)	7 (4)	7+1 (4)	8+3 (4)	-	-	-	-
16	15/5	Eastbourne	H	ELA	W61-34	10+1 (4)	4+1 (4)	9+2 (4)	13 (5)	8+3 (5)	5 (4)	12+2 (5)	-	-	-	-
17	27/5	Eastbourne	A	ELA	W48-42*	-	5+3 (5)	12+1 (6)	R/R	6 (4)	10+1 (7)	-	0 (3)	-	-	15 (5)
18	29/5	Belle Vue	H	ELA	W52-43	7+1 (5)	4+2 (4)	8+3 (4)	14 (5)	7+1 (4)	11 (5)	-	1 (3)	-	-	-
19	31/5	Belle Vue	A	ELA	L39-51	10 (5)	6+1 (5)	R/R	7+2 (5)	7+1 (6)	7+1 (6)	-	-	-	-	2+1 (3)
20	5/6	Ipswich	H	ELB	W57-38	15+2 (6)	5+2 (4)	11+1 (5)	13 (6)	5+3 (5)	8+1 (4)	R/R	-	-	-	-
21	12/6	Oxford	H	ELB	W50-42	14+1 (6)	4 (5)	5+1 (5)	11+1 (6)	3 (1)	13+2 (7)	R/R	-	-	-	-
22	16/6	Coventry	A	ELB	L46-47	15+1 (6)	1 (3)	2+1 (5)	17+1 (6)	-	4 (5)	R/R	-	-	-	7+2 (5)
23	19/6	Swindon	H	ELB	W57-35	9+3 (5)	4+1 (4)	9+1 (5)	15+2 (6)	13+1 (6)	7 (4)	R/R	-	-	-	-
24	21/6	Oxford	A	ELB	W54-39*	10+1 (5)	7+3 (5)	11+2 (6)	7 (5)	11+1 (5)	8 (4)	R/R	-	-	-	-
25	22/6	Swindon	A	ELA	W49-44*	12+1 (6)	10+1 (5)	7+3 (6)	8+2 (5)	10+2 (5)	2 (3)	R/R	-	-	-	-
26	26/6	Poole	H	ELA	W50-40	13 (6)	6+1 (4)	4+1 (4)	12+1 (6)	7+4 (5)	8+2 (5)	R/R	-	-	-	-
27	5/7	Poole	A	KOC	L34-58	9+1 (5)	-	3 (4)	12 (5)	-	6+1 (5)	2 (4)	-	1+1 (4)	-	1 (3)
28	7/7	Poole	H	KOC	W51-42	14+1 (5)	-	12+2 (6)	6 (5)	8+2 (5)	6+1 (5)	R/R	-	-	-	5 (4)
29	8/7	Eastbourne	A	ELB	L44-46	12 (5)	-	-	6 (5)	-	4 (6)	R/R	-	1 (3)	-	21+2 (11)
30	10/7	Eastbourne	H	ELB	W54-41*	9+1 (4)	-	11+1 (5)	7+1 (4)	10+3 (5)	7 (4)	7 (4)	-	3+1 (4)	-	-
31	24/7	Wolverhampton	A	ELB	D45-45	14 (5)	-	9+1 (5)	9 (6)	8 (5)	5+2 (6)	R/R	-	0 (3)	-	-
32	26/7	Wolverhampton	H	ELA	L43-47	10+1 (5)	-	6 (4)	3 (3)	9+1 (5)	7 (6)	6+1 (4)	-	2 (3)	-	-
33	31/7	Peterborough	H	ELB	W51-42	11 (5)	0 (1)	6+1 (4)	7+1 (4)	9 (5)	12+3 (7)	6+2 (4)	-	-	-	-
34	7/8	Arena-Essex	H	ELB	W60-33	13+1 (5)	-	9+2 (5)	7+4 (5)	12+2 (6)	9+1 (5)	R/R	-	-	10+1 (4)	-
35	9/8	Arena-Essex	A	ELB	W51-41*	-	-	8+1 (5)	13 (6)	15+1 (6)	3+1 (5)	R/R	-	-	4 (4)	8+1 (4)
36	10/8	Ipswich	A	ELB	L38-56*	-	-	8 (5)	4+2 (5)	4+1 (5)	0 (4)	R/R	-	-	10+2 (7)	12 (5)
37	14/8	Poole	H	ELB	W53-41	14 (5)	-	10 (6)	9+2 (5)	-	9+2 (6)	R/R	-	-	2 (3)	9 (5)
38	16/8	Poole	A	ELA	W48-45*	16 (5)	-	15+1 (6)	9+1 (5)	-	7+2 (5)	R/R	-	-	0 (3)	1+1 (5)
39	17/8	Swindon	A	ELB	L40-53*	11 (4)	3 (4)	9+1 (6)	11+2 (6)	-	2+1 (5)	R/R	-	-	-	4+2 (5)
40	28/8	Belle Vue	H	ELB	W55-40	11+2 (5)	-	12+2 (6)	10+1 (5)	9+1 (5)	9+1 (6)	R/R	-	-	-	4+3 (3)
41	4/9	Coventry	H	ELB	L44-46	-	-	1 (4)	10+1 (5)	9 (5)	8+1 (5)	8 (4)	-	-	3+1 (3)	5+1 (4)
42	6/9	Wolverhampton	H	ELB	W58-37*	10 (4)	-	10+2 (5)	14 (5)	8+1 (4)	-	7+2 (4)	-	-	9+2 (5)	0 (3)

NO.	DATE	OPPONENTS	VENUE	COMPETITION	RESULT	HANCOCK	SMITH	McGOWAN	ZAGAR	GJEDDE	SIMOTA	KOLODZIEJ	MILLS	CUNNINGHAM	LEMON	OTHERS
43	11/9	Peterborough	A	ELB	W49-43*	9+2 (4)	-	11+1 (5)	7+1 (5)	5 (4)	0 (3)	8+2 (4)	-	-	9+2 (5)	-
44	14/9	Poole	A	ELB	L43-47*	13 (5)	-	7+2 (5)	9+2 (5)	R/R	0 (3)	2+1 (5)	-	-	12 (7)	-
45	20/9	Belle Vue	A	ELB	L34-59	7 (5)	-	3 (4)	7 (4)	9 (5)	-	0 (4)	-	-	4+1 (5)	4+1 (4)
46	21/9	Swindon/Poole	Swin	CS s/f	1st - 37	-	-	9 (4)	-	11 (4)	1 (4)	-	-	-	4 (4)	12+1 (8)
47	25/9	Swindon	H	PO s/f	W51-43	R/R	-	6+1 (5)	16 (6)	13 (6)	3 (3)	5+2 (5)	-	-	8+2 (5)	-
48	2/10	Peterborough	H	PO f	W49-47	12 (6)	-	6+1 (5)	R/R	13+1 (6)	6+2 (4)	8+2 (5)	-	-	4 (4)	-
49	4/10	Swindon/Poole	Poole	CS s/f	3rd - 29	-	-	6 (4)	-	5 (4)	8 (4)	6+1 (4)	-	-	2+1 (4)	2+2 (4)
50	9/10	Peterborough	A	PO f	L45-48	11 (6)	-	7+1 (5)	R/R	4 (4)	2+1 (3)	9+1 (6)	-	-	12+1 (7)	-
51	16/10	Swindon/Poole	H	CS s/f	2nd - 37	8+2 (4)	-	7+1 (4)	-	7+1 (4)	-	-	-	-	3 (4)	12+2 (8)

DETAILS OF OTHER RIDERS

(all guests)

Match No. 13: Chris Schramm 0 (3); Match No. 17: Hans N. Andersen 15 (5); Match No. 19: Kyle Legault 2+1 (3); Match No. 22: Gary Havelock 7+2 (5); Match No. 27: Chris Schramm 1 (3); Match No. 28: Mathieu Tresarrieu 5 (4); Match No. 29: Chris Louis 16 (6); Davey Watt 5+2 (5); Match No. 35: Dean Barker 8+1 (4); Match No. 36: Todd Wiltshire 12 (5); Match No. 37: Davey Watt 9 (5); Match No. 38: Dean Barker 1+1 (5); Match No. 39: Davey Watt 4+2 (5); Match No. 40: Kyle Legault 4+3 (3); Match No. 41: Todd Wiltshire 5+1 (4); Match No. 42: Ben Barker 0 (3); Match No. 45: Ben Barker 4+1 (4); Match No. 46: Chris Harris 10+1 (4); Kauko Nieminen 2 (4); Match No. 49: Shane Parker 2+2 (4); Match No. 51: Dean Barker 7 (4); Edward Kennett 5+2 (4).

DETAILS OF TACTICAL RIDES AND TACTICAL SUBSTITUTE RIDES

Match No. 2: Zagar 0 points (TR); Match No. 9: Hancock 6 points (TR); Gjedde 4 points (TR); Match No. 13: Kolodziej 2 points (TR); McGowan 1 point (TR; not doubled); Match No. 14: Hancock 4 points (TR); Match No. 22: Zagar 6 points (TR); Match No. 27: Zagar 4 points (TR); Simota 0 points (TR); Match No. 36: Wiltshire 4 points (TR); McGowan 4 points (TR); Match No. 38: Hancock 6 points (TR); Match No. 39: Hancock 6 points (TR); Match No. 45: Zagar 6 points (TR); Kolodziej 0 points (TR).

OTHER DETAILS

GB scorers in Match No. 1: Lee Richardson 12 (5); Mark Loram 7+1 (5); Dean Barker 6 (4); Edward Kennett 5 (4); Chris Louis 1+1 (1); Chris Mills 1 (4); Ricky Ashworth 0 (4). Richardson's total includes 4 points from a TR; Loram's total includes 0 points from a TR.

AVERAGES
(40 Elite League, 3 Play-Offs, 4 Knock-Out Cup, 3 Craven Shield = 50 fixtures)

Rider	Mts	Rds	Pts	Bon	Tot	Avge	Max
Greg Hancock	43	214	468	29	497	9.29	1 paid
Matej Zagar	43	211	396	33	429	8.13	1 full
Janusz Kolodziej	28	134	211	43	254	7.58	-
Charlie Gjedde	43	197	330	42	372	7.55	-
Travis McGowan	48	230	355	50	405	7.04	-
Mark Lemon	16	74	96	13	109	5.89	-
Andy Smith	27	108	120	29	149	5.52	-
Zdenek Simota	44	193	229	31	260	5.39	-

READING: From left to right, back row: Jim Lynch (co-promoter/team manager), Charlie Gjedde, Matej Zagar, Travis McGowan, Zdenek Simota, Sam Ermolenko (sporting director). Front row, kneeling: Andy Smith, Janusz Kolodziej; On bike: Greg Hancock.

Also rode (in alphabetical order):

Glenn Cunningham	5	17	7	2	9	2.12	-
Chris Mills	5	16	4	2	6	1.50	-
Guests	22	92	122	19	141	6.13	1 full

(Hans N. Andersen [1]; Ben Barker [2]; Dean Barker [3]; Chris Harris [1]; Gary Havelock [1]; Edward Kennett [1]; Kyle Legault [2]; Chris Louis [1]; Kauko Nieminen [1]; Shane Parker [1]; Chris Schramm [2]; Mathieu Tresarrieu [1]; Davey Watt [3]; Todd Wiltshire [2]).

SWINDON ROBINS IN ASSOCIATION WITH TEAM PARTNERS, PEBLEY BEACH SUZUKI & EDGE LOGISTICS LTD

ADDRESS: Swindon Stadium, Lady Lane, Blunsdon, Nr Swindon, Wiltshire, SN25 4DN.
PROMOTERS: Terry Russell and Alun Rossiter.
YEARS OF OPERATION: 1949 Open and National League Division Three; 1950-1951 National League Division Three; 1952-1953 Southern League; 1954-1956 National League Division Two; 1957-1964 National League; 1965-1967 British League; 1968-1974 British League Division One; 1975-1990 British League; 1991-1992 British League Division One; 1993-1994 British League Division Two; 1995 Premier League; 1996 Premier League and Conference League; 1997 Elite League and Amateur League; 1998 Elite League; 1999-2001 Premier League; 2002 Premier League and Conference Trophy; 2003 Premier League and Conference League; 2004 Elite League and Conference League; 2005-2006 Elite League.
FIRST MEETING: 23 July 1949.
TRACK LENGTH: 363 metres.
TRACK RECORD: 64.27 seconds – Jason Crump (01/06/06).

CLUB HONOURS

LEAGUE CHAMPIONS: 1956, 1957, 1967.
PAIRS CHAMPIONS: 1994, 2004, 2005.
KNOCK-OUT CUP WINNERS: 2000.
YOUNG SHIELD WINNERS: 2000.
FOUR-TEAM CHAMPIONS: 2003.

RIDER ROSTER 2006

Leigh ADAMS; Sebastian ALDEN; Tomasz CHRZANOWSKI; Renat GAFUROV: Ritchie HAWKINS; Mads KORNELIUSSEN; Adrian MIEDZINSKI; Lee RICHARDSON; Sebastian ULAMEK.

OTHER APPEARANCES/GUESTS (official matches only)

James BRUNDLE; Paul CLEWS; Ronnie CORREY; Christian HENRY; Steve JOHNSTON; Stephan KATT; Edward KENNETT; Travis McGOWAN; Joel PARSONS; Glen PHILLIPS; Jacek REMPALA; Chris SCHRAMM; Krzysztof STOJANOWSKI; Davey WATT.

SWINDON

* Denotes aggregate/bonus-point victory

NO.	DATE	OPPONENTS	VENUE	COMPETITION	RESULT	RICHARDSON	KORNELIUSSEN	CORREY	ULAMEK	ADAMS	MIEDZINSKI	ALDEN	GAFUROV	HAWKINS	CHRZANOWSKI	STOJANOWSKI	OTHERS
1	15/3	Oxford	A	Chal	W51-39	12 (4)	5(4)	8 (4)	8+1 (5)	10+1 (5)	3 (4)	5+1 (4)	-	-	-	-	-
2	16/3	Oxford	H	Chal	W61-28	13+2 (5)	8+2 (4)	4 (4)	13+1 (5)	12 (4)	5+1 (5)	6+1 (4)	-	-	-	-	-
3	23/3	Wolverhampton	H	ELA	W52-42	6+2 (5)	7+1 (4)	3 (4)	11 (4)	12 (5)	5+2 (4)	8+1 (4)	-	-	-	-	-
4	28/3	Ipswich	H	ELA	W53-40	12 (5)	3 (4)	-	5 (4)	14+1 (5)	8 (4)	8+1 (4)	3 (4)	-	-	-	-
5	30/3	Ipswich	A	ELA	L45-48*	7 (4)	1+1 (4)	-	13+1 (5)	18 (5)	0 (3)	5 (5)	1 (4)	-	-	-	-
6	4/4	Arena-Essex	A	ELA	L40-50	6+1 (4)	2+1 (4)	-	11 (5)	10 (5)	9+1 (5)	1 (4)	1+1 (3)	-	-	-	-
7	5/4	Poole	A	ELA	L42-48	7+1 (4)	6+1 (4)	-	5 (5)	14 (5)	4 (4)	2 (4)	4 (4)	-	-	-	-
8	6/4	Poole	H	ELA	W52-43*	11 (5)	6 (4)	-	8 (4)	10+2 (5)	7+1 (4)	4+3 (4)	6+1 (4)	-	-	-	-
9	10/4	Reading	A	KOC	L43-47	13+1 (5)	4+1 (4)	-	2 (4)	12+1 (5)	3+1 (5)	3 (3)	6 (4)	-	-	-	-
10	13/4	Reading	H	KOC	L40-50	6 (4)	1+1 (4)	-	13 (5)	11+1 (5)	-	6 (5)	2+1 (4)	1 (3)	-	-	-
11	14/4	Peterborough	A	ELA	L40-55	5 (4)	R/R	-	10 (5)	10 (5)	3 (5)	6+3 (6)	6+2 (5)	-	-	-	-
12	19/4	Belle Vue	A	ELA	L41-55	1 (4)	3+1 (4)	-	7 (5)	16 (5)	9+1 (6)	-	2 (3)	3+1 (3)	-	-	-
13	24/4	Reading	A	ELA	L44-46	6 (5)	7+3 (4)	-	7+1 (4)	14 (5)	5+1 (4)	2+2 (4)	3+1 (4)	-	-	-	-
14	27/4	Belle Vue	H	ELA	W50-43	R/R	6+1 (5)	-	10+1 (6)	15 (6)	6+1 (4)	9+2 (5)	4+1 (4)	-	-	-	-
15	29/4	Eastbourne	A	ELA	W55-41	10 (5)	1 (4)	-	8 (4)	15 (5)	12+1 (5)	-	7 (4)	-	-	-	2+1 (3)
16	4/5	Oxford	H	ELA	W56-38	9+1 (4)	7+2 (4)	-	15 (5)	13+2 (5)	9 (5)	2 (4)	-	-	-	-	1 (3)
17	11/5	Coventry	H	ELA	W56-39	R/R	7+1 (5)	-	13+1 (6)	17+1 (6)	11+1 (6)	5+2 (4)	-	3+1 (3)	-	-	-
18	18/5	Wolverhampton	H	ELB	W47-43	9 (5)	6+1 (4)	-	6 (4)	14+1 (5)	-	6 (5)	6+1 (4)	-	-	-	0 (3)
19	31/5	Oxford	A	ELA	L43-47*	3 (4)	1 (4)	-	10 (6)	13 (5)	10+1 (6)	6+1 (5)	R/R	-	-	-	-
20	1/6	Belle Vue	H	ELB	W51-42	7 (5)	5+1 (4)	-	6+1 (4)	11 (5)	6+1 (4)	10 (5)	-	6+2 (4)	-	-	-
21	5/6	Eastbourne	A	ELB	L43-53	9 (4)	3+2 (4)	-	9 (5)	14 (5)	3 (4)	5+1 (6)	-	0 (3)	-	-	-
22	8/6	Arena-Essex	H	ELA	W53-38*	13+1 (6)	1+1 (4)	-	R/R	14+1 (5)	-	5 (5)	11+1 (5)	-	-	-	9+1 (5)
23	12/6	Ipswich	A	ELB	L37-56	4 (4)	0 (4)	-	5 (4)	16 (5)	3+2 (4)	3 (3)	6+1 (6)	-	-	-	-
24	14/6	Poole	A	ELB	L36-58	5 (4)	3 (4)	-	6+1 (5)	13 (5)	2 (4)	-	7+1 (5)	0 (3)	-	-	-
25	19/6	Reading	A	ELB	L35-57	9 (5)	1+1 (5)	-	6+1 (5)	12 (5)	R/R	1 (5)	6+1 (5)	-	-	-	-
26	22/6	Reading	H	ELA	L44-49	7 (4)	6+1 (4)	-	8 (5)	18 (5)	-	1 (5)	4+1 (4)	-	-	-	0 (3)
27	26/6	Belle Vue	A	ELB	L30-43	5 (3)	7 (4)	-	2+1 (3)	7+1 (3)	1 (3)	2 (4)	6 (4)	-	-	-	-
28	29/6	Eastbourne	H	ELA	W51-39*	11+1 (6)	12+2 (6)	-	R/R	13+2 (5)	-	6 (4)	-	-	-	-	9+1 (8)
29	30/6	Coventry	A	ELA	L43-51*	7 (4)	-	-	11 (5)	16 (5)	6 (4)	1 (5)	-	-	-	-	2 (7)
30	6/7	Poole	H	ELB	W49-44	8 (5)	8+1 (5)	-	6+1 (5)	15 (5)	R/R	1 (3)	11+5 (7)	-	-	-	-
31	10/7	Wolverhampton	A	ELA	W46-44*	9 (5)	3 (5)	-	8 (4)	13 (5)	10+1 (5)	R/R	3+1 (7)	-	-	-	-
32	12/7	Arena-Essex	A	ELB	W46-43	7+1 (4)	8 (6)	-	11+1 (5)	14+1 (5)	4+1 (5)	R/R	2+1 (5)	-	-	-	-
33	13/7	Peterborough	H	ELA	W58-34*	R/R	2+1 (3)	-	13+1 (6)	13+2 (5)	12+1 (5)	-	10+4 (6)	-	-	-	8+1 (5)
34	24/7	Coventry	A	ELB	D45-45	5 (4)	6+1 (6)	-	11+1 (5)	9+2 (5)	7 (5)	R/R	7+1 (5)	-	-	-	-
35	27/7	Arena-Essex	H	ELB	W57-36*	11+1 (4)	6+1 (6)	-	12+2 (5)	15 (5)	-	R/R	11+2 (6)	-	-	-	2+1 (4)
36	3/8	Oxford	H	ELB	W52-38	6+1 (4)	8 (4)	-	10+1 (5)	9+2 (5)	6+3 (4)	-	-	-	12+2 (5)	-	1 (3)
37	10/8	Coventry	H	ELB	W53-40*	7 (5)	3+2 (5)	-	13+1 (5)	11+1 (4)	R/R	-	-	-	15+1 (6)	-	4 (5)
38	16/8	Oxford	A	ELB	L47-48*	12+1 (5)	1 (5)	-	3+1 (3)	18 (5)	R/R	-	5+1 (5)	-	8 (7)	-	-
39	17/8	Reading	H	ELB	W53-40	11+1 (6)	2+1 (4)	-	9 (4)	14+1 (5)	R/R	-	8+2 (5)	-	9+2 (6)	-	-
40	24/8	Peterborough	H	ELB	W47-46	12+1 (6)	2+1 (4)	-	6 (4)	12+1 (5)	R/R	-	-	-	9+2 (6)	-	6+1 (5)
41	28/8	Ipswich	H	ELB	W57-38*	R/R	7 (4)	-	11+1 (5)	14+1 (5)	-	-	2+1 (4)	-	16+2 (7)	-	7+1 (5)
42	31/8	Eastbourne	H	ELB	W58-32*	R/R	6+1 (5)	-	14+1 (6)	11+1 (4)	-	-	4+3 (5)	-	13+2 (6)	-	10+1 (5)

NO.	DATE	OPPONENTS	VENUE	COMPETITION	RESULT	RICHARDSON	KORNELIUSSEN	CORREY	ULAMEK	ADAMS	MIEDZINSKI	ALDEN	GAFUROV	HAWKINS	CHRZANOWSKI	STOJANOWSKI	OTHERS
43	1/9	Somerset	A	DGC	W54.5-39.5	8.5+2 (5)	3+2 (4)	-	-	12 (4)	-	-	7+2 (4)	-	7+2 (4)	-	17 (9)
44	4/9	Wolverhampton	A	ELB	W49-41*	11+1 (6)	13 (6)	-	3+1 (4)	12 (5)	R/R	-	-	-	5+1 (4)	-	5+1 (5)
45	18/9	Peterborough	A	ELB	L37-53	7 (5)	2+1 (4)	-	10+1 (5)	9 (4)	2+1 (3)	-	2 (4)	-	5 (5)	-	-
46	21/9	Poole/Reading	H	CS s/f	2nd – 36	6+1 (4)	2 (4)	-	12 (4)	-	-	-	6+1 (4)	-	6+1 (4)	4+1 (4)	-
47	25/9	Reading	A	PO s/f	L43-51	13 (5)	9+1 (7)	-	4+1 (4)	11 (5)	0 (3)	-	R/R	-	6+2 (6)	-	-
48	4/10	Poole/Reading	Poole	CS s/f	2nd – 37	6 (4)	4+2 (4)	-	10 (4)	8+1 (4)	-	-	-	-	7 (4)	2 (4)	-
49	16/10	Poole/Reading	Read	CS s/f	3rd – 31	10 (4)	3 (4)	-	-	10+1 (4)	-	-	-	-	3+1 (4)	-	5 (8)
50	19/10	Rest of World	H	Chal	W56-38	13 (5)	6 (4)	-	7+3 (4)	12 (5)	3 (4)	-	-	-	6+1 (4)	-	9+3 (4)

NOTE: DGC = David and Goliath Challenge. The away league match at Belle Vue on 26 June was abandoned after heat twelve, with the result permitted to stand. Following the home match versus Ipswich on 28 August, Leigh Adams defeated Mark Loram in a run-off for the bonus point.

DETAILS OF OTHER RIDERS

(all guests)

Match No. 15: Chris Schramm 2+1 (3); Match No. 16: Stephan Katt 1 (3); Match No. 18: James Brundle 0 (3); Match No. 21: Travis McGowan 9+1 (5); Match No. 26: James Brundle 0 (3); Match No. 28: Travis McGowan 8 (5); Glen Phillips 1+1 (3); Match No. 29: Christian Henry 1 (4); Glen Phillips 1 (3); Match No. 33: Edward Kennett 8+1 (5); Match No. 35: Joel Parsons 2+1 (4); Match No. 36: Joel Parsons 1 (3); Match No. 37: Edward Kennett 4 (5); Match No. 40: Jacek Rempala 6+1 (5); Match No. 41: Davey Watt 7+1 (5); Match No. 42: Travis McGowan 10+1 (5); Match No. 43: Travis McGowan 13 (5); Lewis Bridger 4 (4); Match No. 44: Edward Kennett 5+1 (5); Match No. 49: Steve Johnston 5 (4); Paul Clews 0 (4); Match No. 50: Charlie Gjedde 9+3 (4).

DETAILS OF TACTICAL RIDES AND TACTICAL SUBSTITUTE RIDES

Match No. 5: Adams 6 points (TR); Match No. 11: Adams 6 points (TR); Ulamek 4 points (TR); Match No. 12: Adams 6 points (TR); Ulamek 6 points (TR); Match No. 21: Adams 6 points (TR); Richardson 6 points (TR); Match No. 23: Adams 6 points (TR); Richardson 1 point (TR; not doubled); Match No. 24: Adams 6 points (TR); Gafurov 2 points (TR); Match No. 25: Adams 4 points (TR); Richardson 1 point (TR; not doubled); Match No. 26: Adams 6 points (TR); Match No. 27: Adams 2 points (TR); Match No. 29: Adams 6 points (TR); Ulamek 2 points (TR); Match No. 38: Adams 6 points (TR); Richardson 4 points (TR); Match No. 45: Richardson 0 points (TR); Match No. 47: Adams 4 points (TR); Richardson 4 points (TR).

OTHER DETAILS

Rest of the World scorers in Match No. 50: Jason Crump 14 (5); Travis McGowan 7+2 (4); Chris Holder 6+2 (5); Chris Harris 5+1 (5); Ryan Sullivan 4 (4); Steve Johnston 2 (4); Nicolai Klindt 0 (3). McGowan's total includes 4 points from a TR: Crump's total includes 4 points from a TR.

SWINDON: From left to right, back row: Sebastian Ulamek, Tomasz Chrzanowski, Renat Gafurov, Mads Korneliussen, Alun Rossiter (co-promoter/team manager), Terry Russell (club owner/promoter). Front row, kneeling: Lee Richardson, Adrian Miedzinski. On bike: Leigh Adams.

AVERAGES

(40 Elite League, 1 Play-Offs, 2 Knock-Out Cup, 3 Craven Shield = 46 fixtures)

Rider	Mts	Rds	Pts	Bon	Tot	Avge	Max
Leigh Adams	45	220	548	27	575	10.45	6 full; 12 paid
Sebastian Ulamek	43	200	367	22	389	7.78	2 full
Tomasz Chrzanowski	13	70	114	16	130	7.43	-
Lee Richardson	41	188	322	16	338	7.19	1 paid
Adrian Miedzinski	28	123	163	21	184	5.98	-
Renat Gafurov	31	142	161	35	196	5.52	-
Mads Korneliussen	44	196	201	36	237	4.84	-
Sebastian Alden	25	111	108	16	124	4.47	-
Ritchie Hawkins	7	20	13	4	17	3.40	-
Also rode (in alphabetical order):							
Ronnie Correy	1	4	3	0	3	3.00	-
Krzysztof Stojanowski	2	8	6	1	7	3.50	-
Guests	19	77	71	9	80	4.16	-

(James Brundle [2]; Paul Clews [1]; Christian Henry [1]; Steve Johnston [1]; Stephan Katt [1]; Edward Kennett [3]; Travis McGowan [3]; Joel Parsons [2]; Glen Phillips [2]; Jacek Rempala [1]; Chris Schramm [1]; Davey Watt [1]).

NOTE: Leigh Adams was ever-present throughout the 40-match Elite League programme.

OTHER MEETING

28 September: Mike Broadbank Benefit

Swindon 33: Leigh Adams 9 (3); Mads Korneliussen 7 (3); Olly Allen 6+1 (3); Brian Karger 6 (3); Steve Johnston 4 (3); Shawn McConnell 1+1 (4); Steve Masters 0 (3): Australia Select 33: Chris Holder 8 (4); Jason Doyle 7+2 (4); Travis McGowan 7 (3); Richard Hall 5+1 (3); Cameron Woodward 3+2 (3); Shane Parker 3+2 (3); Tai Woffinden 0 (1) – meeting abandoned after heat eleven.

WOLVERHAMPTON PARRYS INTERNATIONAL WOLVES

ADDRESS: Ladbroke Stadium, Sutherland Avenue, Wolverhampton, West Midlands, WV2 2JJ.
PROMOTERS: Chris Van Straaten, Peter Adams and John Woolridge.
YEARS OF OPERATION: 1928-1930 Open; 1950 Open; 1951 National League Division
Three; 1952 Southern League; 1953-1954 National League Division Two; 1961-1964
Provincial League; 1965-1967 British League; 1968-1974 British League Division One;
1975-1980 British League; 1981 National League; 1984-1990 British League; 1991-
1994 British League Division One; 1995-1996 Premier League; 1997 Elite League and
Amateur League; 1998-2001 Elite League; 2002 Elite League and Conference Trophy;
2003 Elite League and Conference League; 2004-2006 Elite League.
FIRST MEETING: 30 May 1928.
TRACK LENGTH: 264 metres.
TRACK RECORD: 55.05 seconds – Peter Karlsson (26/06/06).

CLUB HONOURS

LEAGUE CHAMPIONS: 1963, 1991, 1996, 2002.
PREMIERSHIP WINNERS: 1992, 1997.
GOLD CUP WINNERS: 1992.
KNOCK-OUT CUP WINNERS: 1996.

RIDER ROSTER 2006

Ronnie CORREY; Billy HAMILL; Christian HEFENBROCK; Magnus KARLSSON; Peter
KARLSSON; William LAWSON; Fredrik LINDGREN; Ben WILSON.

OTHER APPEARANCES/GUESTS (official matches only)

Henning BAGER; Dean BARKER; Troy BATCHELOR; Paul CLEWS; Barrie EVANS; Daniel
GIFFARD; Christian HENRY; Chris KERR; Jason KING; Trent LEVERINGTON; Kevin LITTLE;
Chris LOUIS; David NORRIS; Krzysztof PECYNA; Rory SCHLEIN; Chris SCHRAMM; Lee
SMETHILLS; Simon STEAD; Tomas SUCHANEK; Mathieu TRESARRIEU; Matthew WETHERS.

WOLVERHAMPTON

* Denotes aggregate/bonus-point victory

NO.	DATE	OPPONENTS	VENUE	COMPETITION	RESULT	P. KARLSSON	PECYNA	M. KARLSSON	LINDGREN	HAMILL	LAWSON	HEFENBROCK	WILSON	CORREY	SMETHILLS	TRESARRIEU	OTHERS
1	15/3	Poole	A	Chal	L33-59	4 (4)	6+1 (4)	3 (4)	10 (4)	8 (5)	0 (4)	2+1 (4)	-	-	-	-	-
2	16/3	Peterborough	A	Chal	L42-51	14 (5)	0 (2)	4 (4)	12 (5)	8 (4)	2 (5)	2 (4)	-	-	-	-	-
3	20/3	Poole	H	Chal	L43-52	16 (5)	3+1 (4)	3 (4)	4+1 (4)	12 (5)	4 (4)	1+1 (4)	-	-	-	-	-

NO.	DATE	OPPONENTS	VENUE	COMPETITION	RESULT	P. KARLSSON	PECYNA	M. KARLSSON	LINDGREN	HAMILL	LAWSON	HEFENBROCK	WILSON	CORREY	SMETHILLS	TRESARRIEU	OTHERS
4	23/3	Swindon	A	ELA	L42-52	13 (5)	1+1 (4)	5+1 (4)	13+1 (5)	5 (4)	1 (3)	4+1 (5)	-	-	-	-	-
5	29/3	Oxford	A	KOC	W47-43	14 (5)	4 (4)	4+1 (4)	8 (4)	9+1 (5)	-	4+2 (4)	4 (4)	-	-	-	-
6	3/4	Oxford	H	KOC	W54-40*	11 (4)	-	4 (4)	13 (5)	10+1 (5)	-	8+1 (4)	3+2 (4)	5+2 (4)	-	-	-
7	8/4	Eastbourne	A	ELA	L44-46	9 (4)	-	5+1 (4)	11 (5)	12 (5)	-	4+1 (5)	-	3+1 (4)	-	-	0 (3)
8	10/4	Peterborough	H	ELA	W48-42	14 (5)	-	2 (4)	8 (4)	11+1 (5)	-	10+1 (5)	1 (3)	2+1 (4)	-	-	-
9	14/4	Belle Vue	A	ELA	L39-54	6 (4)	-	1+1 (3)	13+1 (5)	5 (5)	-	8+1 (6)	-	4+2 (4)	2 (3)	-	-
10	14/4	Coventry	A	ELA	L40-53	12 (5)	-	0 (1)	6+1 (5)	10 (4)	-	6 (7)	-	5+2 (4)	1 (4)	-	-
11	17/4	Coventry	H	ELA	W53-40	15 (5)	-	R/R	9 (4)	10+1 (5)	9+3 (7)	3+1 (4)	-	7+1 (5)	-	-	-
12	24/4	Eastbourne	H	ELA	W48-45*	19+2 (6)	-	3 (4)	6 (4)	11 (5)	4 (4)	0 (3)	-	5+1 (4)	-	-	-
13	1/5	Reading	H	ELA	W47-44	12 (5)	-	4 (4)	10 (4)	11 (5)	-	5+1 (5)	-	5+2 (4)	0 (3)	-	-
14	10/5	Arena-Essex	A	ELA	L44-46	15 (6)	-	0 (3)	-	R/R	9+2 (6)	2+1 (4)	-	5 (5)	-	-	13 (6)
15	11/5	Ipswich	A	ELA	L42-50	21 (7)	-	4 (5)	-	R/R	-	2 (4)	-	3+2 (5)	-	-	12 (9)
16	15/5	Poole	H	ELA	W52-41	14+1 (5)	-	3 (4)	8+1 (4)	12 (5)	5+4 (4)	3 (4)	-	7+1 (5)	-	-	-
17	18/5	Swindon	A	ELB	L43-47	10 (5)	-	4 (4)	9+2 (5)	5+1 (4)	2+1 (4)	11+1 (5)	-	2+1 (3)	-	-	-
18	29/5	Oxford	H	ELA	W53-37	13+2 (5)	-	4+1 (4)	6+1 (4)	15 (5)	-	11+1 (5)	1 (3)	3+1 (4)	-	-	-
19	31/5	Poole	A	ELA	L43-47*	12+1 (5)	-	1+1 (4)	10+1 (4)	8 (5)	-	6+2 (5)	1+1 (3)	5 (4)	-	-	-
20	1/6	Peterborough	A	ELA	L38-54	7+1 (5)	-	0 (0)	9 (6)	10 (4)	-	6+2 (7)	-	1+1 (3)	-	-	5+2 (5)
21	5/6	Arena-Essex	H	ELA	W56-36*	12 (4)	-	6+1 (4)	12 (5)	13+1 (5)	-	-	-	8+2 (4)	-	-	5+1 (8)
22	7/6	Arena-Essex	A	ELB	W46-44	-	-	1 (3)	8 (5)	6+1 (4)	-	13+3 (6)	-	5+1 (4)	-	-	13 (7)
23	12/6	Eastbourne	H	ELB	W47-43	13 (5)	-	3 (4)	7+1 (4)	9+2 (5)	-	6+1 (5)	0 (3)	9+1 (4)	-	-	-
24	19/6	Peterborough	H	ELB	L44-46	11 (5)	-	5+2 (4)	5+2 (4)	5 (5)	-	9+3 (5)	1+1 (3)	8 (4)	-	-	-
25	26/6	Coventry	H	ELB	W53-43	10+1 (4)	-	2+1 (3)	10 (5)	14 (5)	4+2 (4)	9+3 (5)	-	4+2 (4)	-	-	-
26	28/6	Belle Vue	A	ELB	L35-61	-	-	0 (3)	13 (5)	6 (6)	0 (4)	4 (5)	-	4 (4)	-	-	8 (4)
27	1/7	Eastbourne	A	KOC	L38-55	9+1 (4)	-	3+2 (5)	9+1 (6)	11 (5)	2 (5)	R/R	-	4+1 (5)	-	-	-
28	3/7	Eastbourne	H	KOC	L41-51	14 (5)	-	7+1 (5)	5 (6)	4 (3)	1 (3)	3+2 (4)	-	7+1 (4)	-	-	-
29	10/7	Swindon	H	ELA	L44-46	10 (5)	-	8+2 (5)	10+2 (5)	7+1 (4)	-	2+1 (4)	-	7 (4)	-	-	0 (3)
30	12/7	Oxford	A	ELA	W51-41*	9 (4)	-	13+2 (7)	12 (6)	10+2 (5)	-	R/R	-	4+1 (3)	-	-	3 (5)
31	13/7	Ipswich	A	ELB	L43-53	17 (5)	-	3+2 (5)	13+1 (6)	5 (4)	-	R/R	-	-	-	-	5 (9)
32	24/7	Reading	H	ELB	D45-45	13 (5)	-	5+2 (4)	10 (5)	6+2 (4)	5 (4)	2 (4)	-	4+2 (4)	-	-	-
33	26/7	Reading	A	ELA	W47-43*	12 (5)	-	6 (5)	9+1 (5)	10+1 (4)	0 (3)	5+1 (4)	-	5+1 (4)	-	-	-
34	31/7	Ipswich	H	ELA	W56-35*	11 (5)	-	6+1 (4)	14 (5)	9+1 (4)	7+2 (4)	4+1 (4)	-	5+2 (4)	-	-	-
35	7/8	Oxford	H	ELB	W46-44	12+1 (5)	-	4 (5)	7+1 (4)	13 (5)	5 (6)	5+1 (5)	-	R/R	-	-	-
36	14/8	Belle Vue	H	ELA	W46-44	12 (5)	-	4+1 (4)	10+2 (5)	6+3 (4)	3 (4)	5+1 (4)	-	6 (4)	-	-	-
37	17/8	Peterborough	A	ELB	L42-47	10 (5)	-	8+1 (5)	4 (4)	9+1 (5)	-	4+2 (4)	-	4+2 (4)	-	-	3 (3)
38	21/8	Arena-Essex	H	ELB	W54-40*	11+1 (4)	-	11+1 (6)	13+1 (5)	14 (6)	-	R/R	0 (4)	5+2 (4)	-	-	-
39	25/8	Eastbourne	A	ELB	D45-45*	14 (5)	-	5+2 (6)	12+2 (5)	12 (5)	-	R/R	0 (4)	2+1 (5)	-	-	-
40	28/8	Poole	H	ELB	W52-40	14 (5)	-	3+1 (3)	5 (4)	12 (5)	7+1 (4)	6+1 (4)	-	5+3 (4)	-	-	-
41	4/9	Swindon	H	ELB	L41-49	10+2 (5)	-	2 (4)	13 (5)	7 (4)	5 (5)	0 (3)	-	4+1 (4)	-	-	-
42	6/9	Reading	A	ELB	L37-58	12 (5)	-	3+1 (5)	3 (4)	12 (5)	6+1 (5)	1+1 (3)	-	0 (3)	-	-	-
43	7/9	Oxford	A	ELB	W46-44*	15 (5)	-	-	8 (4)	14+1 (5)	2 (5)	3 (4)	-	2 (4)	-	-	2 (2)
44	11/9	Ipswich	H	ELB	W47-46	17+1 (5)	-	-	9+1 (4)	15 (5)	-	1 (4)	0 (3)	2 (4)	-	3 (5)	-
45	18/9	Belle Vue	H	ELB	W52-39	7+1 (4)	-	8+2 (4)	13 (5)	11 (5)	6+1 (4)	1+1 (4)	-	6+3 (4)	-	-	-
46	19/9	Coventry	A	ELB	L42-51*	10+1 (5)	-	1+1 (4)	10 (5)	11 (5)	2+1 (3)	4 (4)	-	4 (4)	-	-	-

NO.	DATE	OPPONENTS	VENUE	COMPETITION	RESULT	P. KARLSSON	PECYNA	M. KARLSSON	LINDGREN	HAMILL	LAWSON	HEFENBROCK	WILSON	CORREY	SMETHILLS	TRESARRIEU	OTHERS
47	20/9	Poole	A	ELB	L34-59	3 (2)	-	-	14 (5)	6+1 (5)	4 (6)	3+1 (4)	-	4+1 (4)	-	0 (5)	-
48	25/9	Eastbourne/ Ipswich	H	CS s/f	3rd – 33	-	-	-	7 (4)	5 (4)	1 (3)	5+1 (4)	-	6+2 (4)	-	-	9+1 (4)
49	28/9	Eastbourne/ Ipswich	Ips	CS s/f	3rd – 23	-	-	-	7 (4)	3 (4)	-	3 (4)	-	3 (4)	-	-	7+2 (8)
50	7/10	Eastbourne/ Ipswich	East	CS s/f	3rd – 33	8 (4)	-	-	10 (4)	-	-	-	-	2 (4)	-	-	13+2 (12)
51	23/10	Coventry	H	MT	L43-45	11 (5)	-	10+1 (4)	4 (5)	7 (4)	3 (4)	6+1 (4)	-	2+1 (4)	-	-	-
52	27/10	Coventry	A	MT	D45-45	9 (5)	-	10+1 (5)	7+2 (5)	7 (4)	2+1 (3)	7 (4)	-	3+1 (4)	-	-	-

NOTE: MT = Midland Trophy; Following the home match against Coventry on 17 April, Peter Karlsson lost a bonus point run-off to Scott Nicholls.

DETAILS OF OTHER RIDERS

(all guests)

Match No. 7: Daniel Giffard 0 (3); Match No. 14: Dean Barker 13 (6); Match No. 15: David Norris 10 (6); Jason King 2 (3); Match No. 20: Christian Henry 5+2 (5); Match No. 21: Matthew Wethers 3 (4); Kevin Little 2+1 (4); Match No. 22: Chris Louis 13 (5); Daniel Giffard 0 (2); Match No. 26: Chris Louis 8 (4); Match No. 29: Tomas Suchanek 0 (3); Match No. 30: Tomas Suchanek 3 (5); Match No. 31: Troy Batchelor 4 (5); Barrie Evans 1 (4); Match No. 37: Trent Leverington 3 (3); Match No. 43: Chris Schramm 2 (3); Match No. 48: Simon Stead 9+1 (4); Match No. 49: Henning Bager 4+1 (4); Chris Kerr 3+1 (4); Match No. 50: Rory Schlein 8 (4); Chris Kerr 4+1 (4); Paul Clews 1+1 (4).

DETAILS OF TACTICAL RIDES AND TACTICAL SUBSTITUTE RIDES

Match No. 1: Lindgren 4 points (TR); P. Karlsson 0 points (TR); Match No. 2: P. Karlsson 6 points (TR); Hamill 0 points (TR); Match No. 3: Hamill 6 points (TR); P. Karlsson 4 points (TR); Match No. 4: P. Karlsson 4 points (TR); Lindgren 4 points (TR); Match No. 9: Lindgren 6 points (TR); Hamill 1 point (TR; not doubled); Match No. 10: Hamill 6 points (TR); P. Karlsson 1 point (TR; not doubled); Match No. 12: P. Karlsson 6 points (TR); Match No. 15: P. Karlsson 4 points (TS); Match No. 20: Hamill 4 points (TR); Lindgren 1 point (TS; not doubled); Match No. 26: Louis 6 points (TR); Lindgren 6 points (TR); Match No. 27: P. Karlsson 4 points (TR); Hamill 4 points (TR); Match No. 28: P. Karlsson 4 points (TR); Hefenbrock 0 points (TR); Lindgren 0 points (TS); Match No. 31: P. Karlsson 6 points (TR); Lindgren 6 points (TR); Match No. 42: Hamill 6 points (TR); P. Karlsson 4 points (TR); Match No. 44: P. Karlsson 6 points (TR); Match No. 46: Lindgren 4 points (TR); Hamill 2 points (TS); Match No. 47: Lindgren 6 points (TR); Hamill 1 point (TR; not doubled).

AVERAGES
(40 Elite League, 4 Knock-Out Cup, 3 Craven Shield = 47 fixtures)

Rider	Mts	Rds	Pts	Bon	Tot	Avge	Max
Peter Karlsson	43	206	494	16	510	9.90	3 full; 5 paid
Billy Hamill	44	205	398	22	420	8.20	2 full; 1 paid
Fredrik Lindgren	45	211	405	23	428	8.11	-
Ronnie Correy	43	174	191	47	238	5.47	-
Christian Hefenbrock	40	179	191	40	231	5.16	-
Magnus Karlsson	40	164	161	32	193	4.71	-

WOLVERHAMPTON: From left to right, back row: Billy Hamill, Christian Hefenbrock, Peter Karlsson, Lee Smethills. Front row: Magnus Karlsson, Ben Wilson, Krzysztof Pecyna, William Lawson, Fredrik Lindgren.

William Lawson	23	101	90	18	108	4.28	-
Ben Wilson	10	34	11	4	15	1.76	-

Also rode (in alphabetical order):

Krzysztof Pecyna	2	8	5	1	6	3.00	-
Lee Smethills	3	10	3	0	3	1.20	-
Mathieu Tresarrieu	2	10	3	0	3	1.20	-

Guests	22	89	95	8	103	4.63	-

(Henning Bager [1]; Dean Barker [1]; Troy Batchelor [1]; Paul Clews [1]; Barrie Evans [1]; Daniel Giffard [2]; Christian Henry [1]; Chris Kerr [2]; Jason King [1]; Trent Leverington [1]; Kevin Little [1]; Chris Louis [2]; David Norris [1]; Rory Schlein [1]; Chris Schramm [1]; Simon Stead [1]; Tomas Suchanek [2]; Matthew Wethers [1]).

OTHER MEETING

27 May: Robbie Kessler Testimonial

Stoke 30; Sheffield 25; Hull 24; Wolverhampton 24: David Howe 11 (4); Chris Neath 6 (4); William Lawson 5 (4); Ben Wilson 2 (4). The total for David Howe includes 6 points from a tactical ride.

INDIVIDUAL MEETING

16 October: Banks's Olympique

1st Peter Karlsson 15; 2nd Fredrik Lindgren 12; 3rd Theo Pijper (after run-off) 10; David Howe 10; Christian Hefenbrock 10; Billy Hamill 8; Daniel Nermark 8; Ronnie Correy 8; William Lawson 7; Lewis Bridger 6; Adam Shields 6; Chris Kerr 5; Ricky Kling 4; Kenneth Hansen 3; Claus Vissing 3; Adam Skornicki 2; Jack Hargreaves (reserve) 2; Tai Woffinden (reserve) 1.

PREMIER LEAGUE 2006

PREMIER LEAGUE TABLE

Team	Mts	Won	Drn	Lst	For	Agn	Pts	Bon	Tot
King's Lynn	26	19	2	5	1,409	990	40	13	53
Sheffield	26	16	1	9	1,291	1,101	33	11	44
Glasgow	26	16	1	9	1,241	1,173	33	9	42
Rye House	26	16	0	10	1,250	1,147	32	8	40
Somerset	26	13	1	12	1,243	1,156	27	9	36
Redcar	26	13	1	12	1,220	1,194	27	6	33
Workington	26	13	0	13	1,210	1,199	26	7	33
Isle of Wight	26	13	0	13	1,180	1,211	26	7	33
Newcastle	26	12	1	13	1,129	1,249	25	5	30
Stoke	26	12	0	14	1,127	1,265	24	4	28
Berwick	26	10	1	15	1,140	1,274	21	5	26
Edinburgh	26	8	2	16	1,138	1,270	18	2	20
Mildenhall	26	8	1	17	1,116	1,264	17	2	19
Newport	26	7	1	18	1,087	1,288	15	3	18

PLAY-OFFS

QUARTER-FINALS

Redcar	43	King's Lynn	47	
King's Lynn	63	Redcar	32	(King's Lynn won 110-75 on aggregate)
Sheffield	53	Workington	40	
Workington	46	Sheffield	44	(Sheffield won 97-86 on aggregate)
Isle of Wight	55	Glasgow	39	
Glasgow	52	Isle of Wight	42	(Isle of Wight won 97-91 on aggregate)
Somerset	45	Rye House	45	
Rye House	49	Somerset	43	(Rye House won 94-88 on aggregate)

SEMI-FINALS

Isle of Wight	50	Sheffield	43	
Sheffield	60	Isle of Wight	35	(Sheffield won 103-85 on aggregate)
Rye House	48	King's Lynn	42	
King's Lynn	60	Rye House	35	(King's Lynn won 102-83 on aggregate)

FINAL

Sheffield	52	King's Lynn	37	
King's Lynn	63	Sheffield	30	(King's Lynn won 100-82 on aggregate)

TOP 20 AVERAGES
(Premier League only. Minimum qualification: 6 matches.)

Rider	Mts	Rds	Pts	Bon	Tot	Avge	Max
Magnus Zetterstrom (Somerset)	25	127	331	4	335	10.55	9 (7 full; 2 paid)
Shane Parker (Glasgow)	26	133	318	17	335	10.08	7 (4 full; 3 paid)
Gary Havelock (Redcar)	26	126	310	7	317	10.06	4 (2 full; 2 paid)
Tomas Topinka (King's Lynn)	26	127	305	13	318	10.02	4 (3 full; 1 paid)
Andre Compton (Sheffield)	22	107	257	9	266	9.94	6 (3 full; 3 paid)
Danny Bird (Glasgow)	21	103	233	22	255	9.90	4 (4 paid)
Daniel Nermark (King's Lynn)	24	103	234	9	243	9.44	5 (2 full; 3 paid)
Jason Lyons (Mildenhall)	26	122	275	11	286	9.38	3 (1 full; 2 paid)
Kevin Doolan (King's Lynn)	26	122	252	32	284	9.31	4 (1 full; 3 paid)
Chris Holder (Isle of Wight)	25	134	288	20	308	9.19	2 (2 paid)
Mark Lemon (Stoke)	24	119	264	8	272	9.14	4 (4 full)
Steve Boxall (Rye House)	23	114	231	29	260	9.12	5 (1 full; 4 paid)
Ricky Ashworth (Sheffield)	26	120	233	31	264	8.80	6 (1 full; 5 paid)
Troy Batchelor (King's Lynn)	25	107	210	25	235	8.79	3 (3 paid)
Daniel King (Mildenhall)	22	125	262	10	272	8.70	2 (1 full; 1 paid)
James Wright (Workington)	24	118	244	10	254	8.61	4 (2 full; 2 paid)
Edward Kennett (Rye House)	23	113	232	10	242	8.57	6 (3 full; 3 paid)
Paul Fry (Somerset)	6	26	51	4	55	8.46	Nil
Chris Neath (Rye House)	26	121	238	15	253	8.36	3 (1 full; 2 paid)
Ben Wilson (Sheffield)	26	115	210	29	239	8.31	Nil

KNOCK-OUT CUP

ROUND ONE

Isle of Wight	53	Rye House	41	
Rye House	66	Isle of Wight	26	(Rye House won 107-79 on aggregate)
Edinburgh	56	Newport	40	
Newport	55	Edinburgh	31	(Newport won 95-87 on aggregate)
Somerset	57	Stoke	38	
Stoke	51	Somerset	41	(Somerset won 98-89 on aggregate)
Berwick	47	King's Lynn	43	
King's Lynn	70	Berwick	20	(King's Lynn won 113-67 on aggregate)
Workington	54	Newcastle	40	
Newcastle	55	Workington	40	(Newcastle won 95-94 on aggregate)

QUARTER-FINALS

King's Lynn	54	Rye House	41	
Rye House	49	King's Lynn	44	(King's Lynn won 98-90 on aggregate)
Somerset	52	Mildenhall	43	
Mildenhall	40	Somerset	53	(Somerset won 105-83 on aggregate)
Glasgow	55	Newcastle	41	
Newcastle	48	Glasgow	42	(Glasgow won 97-89 on aggregate)
Sheffield	59	Newport	33	
Newport	39	Sheffield	50	(Sheffield won 109-72 on aggregate)

SEMI-FINALS

Glasgow	45	King's Lynn	45	
King's Lynn	67	Glasgow	27	(King's Lynn won 112-72 on aggregate)
Somerset	55	Sheffield	40	
Sheffield	55	Somerset	41	(Somerset won 96-95 on aggregate)

FINAL

Somerset	45	King's Lynn	45	
King's Lynn	62	Somerset	32	(King's Lynn won 107-77 on aggregate)

PREMIER TROPHY

PREMIER TROPHY (SOUTH) TABLE

Team	Mts	Won	Drn	Lst	For	Agn	Pts	Bon	Tot
Rye House	10	6	0	4	477	428	12	4	16
King's Lynn	10	5	0	5	478	432	10	5	15
Somerset	10	6	0	4	481	437	12	2	14
Mildenhall	10	5	1	4	465	452	11	3	14
Newport	10	4	1	5	434	497	9	0	9
Isle of Wight	10	3	0	7	411	500	6	1	7

PREMIER TROPHY (NORTH) TABLE

Team	Mts	Won	Drn	Lst	For	Agn	Pts	Bon	Tot
Workington	14	10	1	3	675	599	21	6	27
Sheffield	14	8	0	6	696	606	16	6	22
Glasgow	14	8	0	6	682	620	16	5	21
Edinburgh	14	8	0	6	668	610	16	5	21
Newcastle	14	7	0	7	643	657	14	3	17
Stoke	14	5	0	9	610.5	686.5	10	2	12
Redcar	14	5	0	9	613.5	680.5	10	1	11
Berwick	14	4	1	9	585	714	9	0	9

SEMI-FINALS

Sheffield	61	Rye House	31	
Rye House	61	Sheffield	31	(Aggregate 92-92, with Sheffield winning run-off decider)

Workington	51	King's Lynn	39	
King's Lynn	59	Workington	35	(King's Lynn won 98-86 on aggregate)

FINAL

King's Lynn	63	Sheffield	32	
Sheffield	48	King's Lynn	45	(King's Lynn won 108-80 on aggregate)

ANDERSON'S QUALITY BUTCHERS BERWICK BANDITS

ADDRESS: Shielfield Park Stadium, Shielfield Terrace, Tweedmouth, Berwick-upon-Tweed, Northumberland, TD15 2EF.
PROMOTER: Peter Waite.
YEARS OF OPERATION: 1968-1974 British League Division Two; 1975-1980 National League; 1995 Demonstration; 1996 Conference League; 1997 Premier League and Amateur League; 1998-2006 Premier League.
FIRST MEETING: 18 May 1968.
TRACK LENGTH: 368 metres.
TRACK RECORD: 64.2 seconds – Sean Wilson (21/08/99).

PREVIOUS VENUE: Berrington Lough Stadium, Nr Ancroft, Northumberland.
YEARS OF OPERATION: 1982-1990 National League; 1991 British League Division One; 1992 British League Division Two; 1993 Open; 1994 British League Division Three; 1995 Academy League.

CLUB HONOURS

KNOCK-OUT CUP WINNERS: 1980, 1989, 1995.
GOLD CUP WINNERS: 1991.
LEAGUE CHAMPIONS: 1994, 1995.
FOUR-TEAM CHAMPIONS: 2002.

RIDER ROSTER 2006

Andreas BERGSTROM; Craig BRANNEY; Stanislaw BURZA; Michal MAKOVSKY; David MELDRUM; Jacek REMPALA; Adrian RYMEL; Lee SMETHILLS; Danny WARWICK.

OTHER APPEARANCES/GUESTS (official matches only)

Jon ARMSTRONG; James BIRKINSHAW; Luke BOWEN; John BRANNEY; Tom BROWN; Gary FLINT; John MORRISON; John OLIVER; Adam ROYNON; Mark THOMPSON.

BERWICK

* Denotes aggregate/bonus-point victory

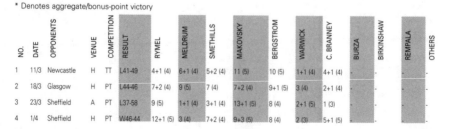

NO.	DATE	OPPONENTS	VENUE	COMPETITION	RESULT	RYMEL	MELDRUM	SMETHILLS	MAKOVSKY	BERGSTROM	WARWICK	C. BRANNEY	BURZA	BIRKINSHAW	REMPALA	OTHERS
1	11/3	Newcastle	H	TT	L41-49	4+1 (4)	6+1 (4)	5+2 (4)	11 (5)	10 (5)	1+1 (4)	4+1 (4)	-			-
2	18/3	Glasgow	H	PT	L44-46	7+2 (4)	9 (5)	7 (4)	7+2 (4)	9+1 (5)	3 (4)	2+1 (4)	-			-
3	23/3	Sheffield	A	PT	L37-58	9 (5)	1+1 (4)	3+1 (4)	13+1 (5)	8 (4)	2+1 (5)	1 (3)	-			-
4	1/4	Sheffield	H	PT	W46-44	12+1 (5)	3 (4)	7+2 (4)	9+3 (5)	8 (4)	2 (3)	5+1 (5)	-			-

NO.	DATE	OPPONENTS	VENUE	COMPETITION	RESULT	RYMEL	MELDRUM	SMETHILLS	MAKOVSKY	BERGSTROM	WARWICK	C. BRANNEY	BURZA	BIRKINSHAW	REMPALA	OTHERS
5	8/4	Newcastle	H	PT	L42-48	8+1 (5)	3+1 (4)	5+3 (4)	9 (5)	7 (4)	1+1 (3)	9+1 (5)	-	-	-	-
6	15/4	Workington	H	PT	D45-45	7 (5)	5 (4)	5+1 (4)	14 (5)	6 (4)	2+1 (3)	6+2 (5)	-	-	-	-
7	17/4	Workington	A	PT	L29-63	3 (4)	3 (4)	9 (5)	4+1 (4)	7 (5)	0 (3)	3+2 (5)	-	-	-	-
8	22/4	Redcar	H	PT	W53-43	-	6+2 (4)	6+2 (4)	14+1 (5)	6+1 (4)	4+1 (4)	10 (4)	7 (5)	-	-	-
9	26/4	Redcar	A	PT	L39-54	-	0 (3)	15 (5)	7+2 (4)	4 (4)	1 (4)	4 (5)	8 (5)	-	-	-
10	29/4	Edinburgh	H	PT	W51-42	-	4 (4)	9+3 (4)	13+1 (5)	10+1 (5)	3 (4)	4+1 (4)	8 (4)	-	-	-
11	6/5	Glasgow	H	PL	W51-44	-	7+3 (4)	7 (4)	10+1 (5)	6 (4)	7+3 (4)	5+3 (4)	9 (5)	-	-	-
12	7/5	Newcastle	A	PT	L44-51	-	3+1 (4)	6+2 (4)	8+1 (4)	7+1 (6)	1 (4)	6+1 (3)	13 (5)	-	-	-
13	13/5	Stoke	H	PT	W46-44	-	7 (4)	8+1 (5)	13+1 (5)	6+1 (4)	1+1 (3)	8+1 (6)	3+1 (4)	-	-	-
14	14/5	Stoke	A	PT	L37-58	-	2 (4)	-	R/R	3 (6)	1 (4)	15 (6)	9 (5)	-	-	7+2 (5)
15	20/5	King's Lynn	H	KOC	W47-43	-	6 (4)	6+2 (4)	10+1 (5)	8+1 (5)	3+2 (3)	9+2 (5)	5+1 (4)	-	-	-
16	21/5	Glasgow	A	PT	L38-57	-	9 (5)	8+1 (4)	13+1 (5)	4 (4)	0 (4)	3 (4)	-	-	-	1 (4)
17	27/5	Isle of Wight	H	PL	L44-46	-	7 (4)	5+2 (4)	10+1 (5)	10+1 (5)	1 (3)	10+2 (6)	-	-	-	1 (3)
18	29/5	Rye House	A	PL	L27-65	-	0 (3)	2 (4)	7 (5)	5 (5)	0 (4)	1 (4)	12 (5)	-	-	-
19	30/5	Isle of Wight	A	PL	L42-53	-	2 (4)	6+1 (4)	12+2 (5)	-	4+1 (4)	4+2 (5)	12 (5)	-	-	2 (3)
20	31/5	King's Lynn	A	KOC	L20-70	-	2 (4)	1 (4)	6 (5)	4+1 (5)	0 (3)	5 (5)	2 (4)	-	-	-
21	2/6	Somerset	A	PL	L39-53	-	2+1 (4)	11 (5)	7+1 (4)	4+2 (4)	0 (3)	6 (5)	9 (5)	-	-	-
22	4/6	Stoke	A	PL	L37-56	-	1+1 (3)	4 (4)	8+1 (5)	6 (4)	0 (4)	11+2 (6)	7 (4)	-	-	-
23	10/6	King's Lynn	H	PL	L46-51	-	1+1 (3)	0 (3)	12+2 (6)	7 (4)	1+1 (3)	10+2 (6)	15 (5)	-	-	-
24	16/6	Edinburgh	A	PT	L34-61	-	-	R/R	9 (6)	7+1 (5)	2+1 (7)	0 (1)	11 (5)	5+2 (5)	-	-
25	17/6	Newcastle	H	PL	W51-45	-	-	R/R	12+1 (6)	5 (4)	5+1 (4)	10+2 (7)	14 (5)	5+2 (4)	-	-
26	22/6	Sheffield	A	PL	L39-56	-	-	R/R	13 (6)	5+1 (4)	1+1 (3)	-	0 (4)	13 (6)	-	7+1 (7)
27	24/6	Sheffield	H	PL	L43-47	-	-	7+1 (4)	12+1 (5)	8 (5)	9+1 (7)	-	5+1 (4)	0 (1)	-	2 (4)
28	6/7	Redcar	A	PL	L26-64	-	-	6 (4)	5+2 (5)	5 (5)	2 (7)	2 (4)	6 (5)	R/R	-	-
29	8/7	Rye House	A	PL	W54-42	-	-	9+2 (4)	9+2 (5)	10+1 (5)	11+1 (6)	-	10 (5)	R/R	-	5+1 (5)
30	15/7	Stoke	H	PL	W49-44	-	-	7 (4)	9+1 (5)	6+2 (4)	8+1 (6)	11+3 (6)	8+1 (5)	0 (1)	-	-
31	21/7	Edinburgh	H	PL	L43-53	-	-	3+1 (4)	5 (4)	13 (6)	1+1 (4)	6+1 (7)	15 (5)	R/R	-	-
32	22/7	Redcar	H	PL	W50-41	-	-	9 (4)	12+1 (5)	8 (5)	5+1 (5)	5+1 (5)	11 (5)	R/R	-	-
33	23/7	Glasgow	A	PL	L37-53	-	-	6+1 (4)	7 (5)	8+1 (5)	5 (5)	5+4 (5)	6 (6)	R/R	-	-
34	29/7	Somerset	H	PL	W55-40*	-	-	9 (4)	7+1 (5)	11+2 (5)	7 (4)	9+4 (7)	12 (5)	R/R	-	-
35	5/8	Edinburgh	H	PL	W58-37*	-	-	-	8+1 (4)	8+2 (5)	11+3 (6)	4 (5)	15 (5)	R/R	12+2 (5)	-
36	6/8	Newcastle	A	PL	L44-49*	-	-	-	8 (4)	7 (5)	1 (4)	9+2 (7)	12+1 (5)	R/R	7+1 (5)	-
37	12/8	Mildenhall	H	PL	W50-40	-	-	-	11 (5)	12+1 (5)	4+1 (4)	11+3 (7)	7 (5)	R/R	5+3 (4)	-
38	26/8	Workington	H	PL	L41-49	-	-	-	11+1 (5)	3+2 (5)	1 (4)	11+2 (7)	6 (4)	R/R	9 (5)	-
39	28/8	Workington	A	PL	L43-50	-	-	-	7+1 (5)	7+2 (5)	0 (4)	17+1 (7)	4 (4)	R/R	8+1 (5)	-
40	3/9	Newport	A	PL	W49-41	-	-	-	9 (4)	13+2 (6)	5+2 (6)	6+1 (5)	10+1 (5)	R/R	6 (4)	-
41	6/9	King's Lynn	A	PL	L27-66	-	-	-	3 (4)	8 (6)	1 (6)	2 (5)	3 (4)	R/R	10 (5)	-
42	9/9	Newport	H	PL	D47-47*	-	-	-	9+2 (5)	12+1 (6)	8+1 (7)	0 (1)	13 (5)	R/R	5+1 (2)	0 (3)
43	17/9	Mildenhall	A	PL	W48-42*	-	-	-	9 (5)	11+2 (6)	1+1 (3)	10+2 (5)	13+1 (6)	-	R/R	4 (5)

NOTE: TT = Tyne-Tweed Trophy.

DETAILS OF OTHER RIDERS

(all guests)

Match No. 14: Luke Bowen 7+2 (5); Match No. 16: John Branney 1 (4); Match No. 17: Gary Flint 1 (3); Match No. 19: Tom Brown 2 (3); Match No. 26: John Oliver 7+1 (7); Match No. 27: Jon Armstrong 2 (4); Match No. 29: Adam Roynon 5+1 (5); Match No. 42: John Morrison 0 (3); Match No. 43: Mark Thompson 4 (5).

DETAILS OF TACTICAL RIDES AND TACTICAL SUBSTITUTE RIDES

Match No. 3: Makovsky 6 points (TR); Bergstrom 4 points (TR); Match No. 7: Smethills 4 points (TR); Match No. 9: Smethills 6 points (TR); Burza 0 points (TR); Match No. 12: Burza 6 points (TR); C. Branney 4 points (TR); Bergstrom 0 points (TS); Match No. 14: C. Branney 6 points (TR); Burza 4 points (TR); Match No. 16: Makovsky 6 points (TR); Meldrum 4 points (TR); Match No. 18: Makovsky 4 points (TR); Bergstrom 1 point (TS; not doubled); Burza 1 point (TR; not doubled); Match No. 19: Burza 6 points (TR); Makovsky 4 points (TR); Match No. 20: Makovsky 1 point (TR; not doubled); Smethills 0 points (TR); Match No. 21: Smethills 6 points (TR); Match No. 22: C. Branney 6 points (TR); Burza 1 point (TR; not doubled); Match No. 23: Burza 6 points (TR); Branney 4 points (TR); Makovsky 4 points (TS); Match No. 24: Burza 4 points (TR); Makovsky 4 points (TR); Bergstrom 2 points (TS); Match No. 26: Makovsky 6 points (TR); Birkinshaw 4 points (TR); Match No. 28: Smethills 1 point (TR; not doubled); Burza 1 point (TR; not doubled); Match No. 31: Burza 6 points (TR); Bergstrom 6 points (TR); Match No. 33: Burza 0 points (TS); Match No. 36: Burza 6 points (TR); Match No. 39: C. Branney 6 points (TR); Match No. 41: Rempala 6 points (TR); Bergstrom 1 point (TR; not doubled).

AVERAGES

(26 Premier League, 2 Knock-Out Cup, 14 Premier Trophy = 42 fixtures)

♦ Denotes ever-present.

Rider	Mts	Rds	Pts	Bon	Tot	Avge	Max
Michal Makovsky	41	199	364	37	401	8.06	1 paid
Jacek Rempala	8	35	59	8	67	7.66	-
Adrian Rymel	6	28	46	4	50	7.14	-
Stanislaw Burza	34	162	281	7	288	7.11	1 full
Lee Smethills	29	119	178	26	204	6.86	1 paid
Andreas Bergstrom	41	196	296	30	326	6.65	-
Craig Branney	39	196	242	49	291	5.94	-
David Meldrum	22	86	81	11	92	4.28	-
Danny Warwick ♦	42	182	125	28	153	3.36	-
Also rode:							
James Birkinshaw	5	17	21	4	25	5.88	-
Guests	9	39	29	4	33	3.38	-

(Jon Armstrong [1]; Luke Bowen [1]; John Branney [1]; Tom Brown [1]; Gary Flint [1]; John Morrison [1]; John Oliver [1]; Adam Roynon [1]; Mark Thompson [1]).

NOTE: Michal Makovsky was ever-present throughout the 26-match Premier League programme.

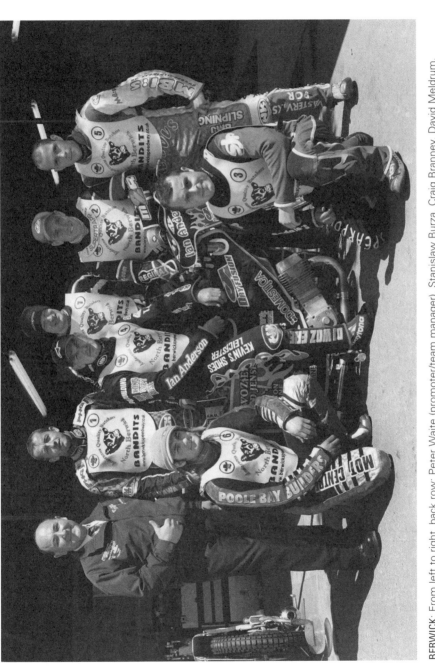

BERWICK: From left to right, back row: Peter Waite (promoter/team manager), Stanislaw Burza, Craig Branney, David Meldrum, Andreas Bergstrom. Front row, kneeling: Danny Warwick, Lee Smethills. On bike: Michal Makovsky.

OTHER MEETINGS

16 September: Tweed-Wear Trophy

Berwick 47: Andrew Tully 18 (6); John Morrison 10+3 (5); John MacPhail 10+2 (6); Alan Ferrow 3 (3); Johnny Grey 3 (2); David Pye 2 (4); Maurice Crang 1 (3). Sunderland 46: Keiran Morris 12+1 (6); Gary Flint 10+1 (5); Peter Johnson 7+2 (4); Cal McDade 6+1 (4); David Haigh 6 (3); Scott Nettleship 3+1 (4); Mark White 2+1 (4). Tully's total includes 6 points from a TS outing.

23 September: Anderson's Quality Butchers Northern Fours

Berwick 37: Michal Makovsky 10 (4); Andreas Bergstrom 10 (4); Stanislaw Burza 9 (4); Danny Warwick 8 (4). Isle of Wight 21. Hull Select 20: Lee Smethills 11 (4); Lee Dicken 5 (4); James Birkinshaw 2 (4); Adam McKinna 2 (4). Edinburgh Select 18.

30 September: Challenge

Scottish Junior Select 42: Adam McKinna 11 (4); Andrew Tully 7 (4); Keiran Morris 7 (4); John MacPhail 5+2 (4); Greg Blair 4+1 (4); Gary Beaton 4+1 (3); Cal McDade 4 (4). English Junior Select 37: Jamie Robertson 11 (4); Johnny Grey 8+1 (7); Steven Jones 6 (4); Rob Grant 6 (4); Gary Flint 3+2 (4); Alan Ferrow 3+1 (4); John Morrison 0 (0) – meeting abandoned after heat fourteen.

INDIVIDUAL MEETING

1 July: Bordernapolis

QUALIFYING SCORES: Todd Wiltshire 12; Shane Parker 11; Simon Stead 8; Kevin Doolan 8; Adrian Rymel 7; Travis McGowan 5; Theo Pijper 5; Josef Franc 4; Chris Holder 4; Carl Wilkinson 4; Krzysztof Stojanowski 3; George Stancl 1. SEMI-FINAL: 1st Stead; 2nd Rymel; 3rd McGowan; 4th Doolan. FINAL: 1st Wiltshire; 2nd Parker; 3rd Stead; 4th Rymel.

EDINBURGH SCOTWASTE MONARCHS

ADDRESS: Armadale Stadium, 2 Bathgate Road, Armadale, West Lothian, EH48 2PD.
PROMOTERS: John Campbell and Alex Harkess.
YEARS OF OPERATION: 1997-2002 Premier League; 2003 Premier League and
Conference Trophy; 2004-2005 Premier League and Conference League; 2006 Premier
League.
FIRST MEETING: 4 April 1997.
TRACK LENGTH: 260 metres.
TRACK RECORD: 54.6 seconds – Theo Pijper (22/09/06).

PREVIOUS VENUES:
(1) ADDRESS: Old Meadowbank Stadium, Clockmill Road, Edinburgh.
YEARS OF OPERATION: 1948-1954 National League Division Two; 1957 Training; 1959
Open; 1960-1964 Provincial League; 1965-1967 British League; 1998 Demonstration.

(2) ADDRESS: Cliftonhill Stadium, Main Street, Coatbridge, ML5 3RB.
YEARS OF OPERATION: 1968-1969 British League Division One
NOTE: The team rode as Coatbridge Monarchs.

(3) ADDRESS: Powderhall Stadium, Beaverhall Road, Edinburgh, EH7 4JE.
YEARS OF OPERATION: 1977-90 National League; 1991-94 British League Division Two;
1995 Premier League.

(4) ADDRESS: Shawfield Stadium, Glasgow Road, Rutherglen, Glasgow, G73 1SZ.
YEARS OF OPERATION: 1996 Premier League.
NOTE: The team rode under the name of Scottish Monarchs.

CLUB HONOURS

QUEEN'S CUP WINNERS: 1953.
FOUR-TEAM CHAMPIONS: 1981, 1993.
KNOCK-OUT CUP WINNERS: 1981, 1997, 1999.
PAIRS CHAMPIONS: 1986.
PREMIERSHIP WINNERS: 1998.
LEAGUE CHAMPIONS: 2003.
CONFERENCE TROPHY: 2005.

RIDER ROSTER 2006

Rusty HARRISON; William LAWSON; Henrik MOLLER; Theo PIJPER; Derek SNEDDON; Sean
STODDART; Daniele TESSARI; Matthew WETHERS.

OTHER APPEARANCES/GUESTS (official matches only)

Richie DENNIS; Kevin LITTLE; Adam ROYNON; Andrew TULLY; Shane WALDRON.

EDINBURGH

* Denotes aggregate/bonus-point victory

NO.	DATE	OPPONENTS	VENUE	COMPETITION	RESULT	MOLLER	PIJPER	WETHERS	LAWSON	HARRISON	STODDART	SNEDDON	TESSARI	OTHERS
1	31/3	Glasgow	H	ST	W42-36	3 (3)	10+1 (4)	6+2 (4)	5 (3)	7+1 (3)	1+1 (3)	10+1 (4)	-	-
2	1/4	Workington	A	PT	L34-41	2 (3)	10 (4)	6+1 (4)	0 (2)	8 (3)	0 (3)	8 (5)		
3	6/4	Sheffield	A	PT	L40-52	1+1 (4)	10 (5)	5+2 (4)	7+1 (4)	9 (5)	1+1 (3)	7+1 (5)		
4	9/4	Newcastle	A	PT	W47-46	4+2 (4)	6 (4)	4+2 (4)	14+1 (5)	11 (5)	0 (3)	8 (5)		
5	14/4	Workington	H	PT	L44-45	5+1 (4)	6 (4)	3+2 (4)	12 (5)	8+1 (5)	2 (3)	8+3 (5)		
6	20/4	Redcar	A	PT	L44-45	7 (4)	8 (4)	9+2 (5)	7+1 (5)	1 (3)	0 (3)	12+1 (6)		
7	21/4	Redcar	H	PT	W52-40*	8+2 (6)	13+1 (6)	9+2 (5)	11+1 (5)	R/R	0 (3)	11 (5)		
8	22/4	Stoke	A	PT	W49-44	8+1 (4)	9+2 (5)	6+1 (4)	6+1 (4)	9 (5)	0 (3)	11+1 (6)		
9	23/4	Newport	A	PL	L31-62	1 (4)	12 (5)	2 (4)	8+1 (5)	7+1 (5)	0 (3)	1 (4)		
10	28/4	Newcastle	H	PT	W51-44*	5+1 (4)	15 (5)	5+1 (4)	11 (5)	3 (4)	5+2 (3)	7+1 (5)		
11	29/4	Berwick	A	PT	L42-51	1 (4)	9 (5)	6 (4)	7 (4)	9+1 (5)	-	8 (5)	-	2 (3)
12	30/4	Glasgow	A	PT	L44-49	4+2 (4)	13+1 (6)	2+1 (4)	7+1 (4)	9 (5)	-	9+2 (6)	-	0 (3)
13	5/5	Glasgow	H	PT	W48-44	3+2 (4)	10 (5)	6+2 (4)	10 (5)	9 (4)	7+2 (4)	3+1 (4)		
14	12/5	Stoke	H	PT	W58-36*	8+2 (5)	9+3 (4)	9 (4)	9+1 (4)	13 (5)	1 (4)	9+2 (4)		
15	19/5	Newport	H	KOC	W56-40	8+3 (4)	12+1 (5)	6+2 (4)	10+1 (4)	12 (5)	1 (3)	7+1 (5)		
16	26/5	Isle of Wight	H	PL	W56-35	5 (4)	5+1 (4)	7+1 (4)	10+1 (5)	14+1 (5)	7+1 (4)	8 (5)		
17	29/5	Glasgow	A	ST	L41-49	5+1 (4)	7+2 (5)	5+1 (4)	4 (4)	8 (5)	1+1 (3)	11+2 (5)		
18	2/6	Sheffield	H	PT	W54-39*	9+1 (5)	14+1 (6)	9+4 (5)	R/R	6+1 (4)	0 (3)	16+1 (7)		
19	8/6	Redcar	A	PL	L38-56	12+1 (5)	8+1 (6)	8 (5)	R/R	5 (4)	2+1 (4)	1+1 (4)	-	2 (2)
20	9/6	King's Lynn	H	PL	D45-45	8+2 (5)	12+1 (6)	8+2 (5)	R/R	5+1 (4)	4 (3)	8+4 (7)		
21	16/6	Berwick	H	PT	W61-34*	13+1 (5)	12+3 (5)	15 (5)	R/R	11+1 (5)	4 (4)	5+2 (4)	-	1 (2)
22	17/6	Workington	A	PL	L39-57	5+1 (4)	7+1 (7)	10 (5)	R/R	13 (5)	0 (3)	4+2 (6)		
23	23/6	Sheffield	H	PL	W52-44	6+2 (4)	9+1 (4)	6+3 (4)	12 (5)	12+1 (5)	4 (3)	3+2 (5)		
24	27/6	Newport	A	KOC	L31-55	0 (1)	5 (4)	9 (4)	5+1 (4)	1 (4)	-	9+1 (7)	-	2+1 (4)
25	30/6	Newport	H	PL	W53-37	R/R	12+1 (5)	11+2 (6)	13 (6)	9 (5)	3+2 (4)	5 (4)		
26	7/7	Rye House	H	PL	L42-47	10+1 (5)	8 (5)	7+3 (4)	6 (4)	2+1 (2)	8+1 (5)	1 (4)		
27	10/7	Newcastle	A	PL	L42-50	8+1 (5)	12+1 (5)	6+2 (5)	9 (6)	R/R	3 (3)	4+2 (6)		
28	14/7	Redcar	H	PL	W53-39	9+4 (5)	12 (5)	9+2 (5)	11+3 (6)	R/R	0 (3)	12+1 (6)		
29	15/7	Rye House	A	PL	L37-55	9 (5)	4 (4)	7+2 (6)	10 (6)	R/R	0 (3)	7+1 (6)		
30	16/7	Mildenhall	A	PL	L41-52	4 (5)	13+1 (5)	6+1 (5)	5+1 (5)	R/R	2+1 (3)	11+1 (7)		
31	21/7	Berwick	H	PL	W53-43	17 (6)	7 (4)	8+2 (5)	12+2 (6)	R/R	2+1 (4)	7+1 (5)		
32	28/7	Somerset	H	PL	W57-36	11+2 (5)	-	16+1 (6)	11+1 (6)	R/R	2 (3)	8+2 (6)	-	9+2 (4)
33	1/8	Isle of Wight	A	PL	L41-55*	0 (0)	14 (5)	12 (5)	5 (4)		1 (5)	3+1 (7)	6+1 (4)	
34	2/8	Somerset	A	PL	L34-59	7 (5)	12+1 (5)	0 (2)	5+1 (4)	-	2 (4)	7+1 (7)	1+1 (4)	
35	5/8	Berwick	A	PL	L37-58	5 (5)	12 (4)	R/R	7+1 (6)	-	0 (4)	12+1 (6)	1 (5)	
36	11/8	Mildenhall	H	PL	L44-46	5+1 (4)	14 (5)	6+1 (4)	6+1 (5)	-	0 (3)	11+1 (5)	2 (4)	
37	17/8	Sheffield	A	PL	L31-61	5 (4)	4 (4)	10+1 (5)	2 (4)	-	0 (4)	8+1 (5)	2 (4)	
38	26/8	King's Lynn	A	PL	L33-61	7 (5)	9+1 (6)	10+1 (6)	R/R	-	1 (4)	6 (5)	0 (4)	

NO.	DATE	OPPONENTS	VENUE	COMPETITION	RESULT	MOLLER	PIJPER	WETHERS	LAWSON	HARRISON	STODDART	SNEDDON	TESSARI	OTHERS
39	1/9	Glasgow	H	PL	D45-45	6 (4)	14 (5)	6+2 (4)	6+1 (5)	-	7 (4)	4+2 (5)	2+1 (4)	-
40	3/9	Glasgow	A	PL	L44-49	3 (3)	8+2 (5)	7+2 (4)	6 (4)	-	2 (4)	11+2 (6)	7+2 (4)	-
41	8/9	Stoke	H	PL	W52-40	6+1 (4)	15 (5)	10+1 (5)	7+1 (4)	-	3+1 (3)	9 (6)	2 (3)	-
42	9/9	Stoke	A	PL	L43-47*	5+2 (4)	2 (4)	9+1 (5)	11 (5)	-	2+1 (3)	9+3 (5)	5 (4)	-
43	15/9	Newcastle	H	PL	W51-45	5+1 (4)	11+1 (5)	10+1 (4)	13 (5)	-	4 (4)	3+1 (4)	5+1 (4)	-
44	22/9	Workington	H	PL	L44-46	6+1 (4)	11+1 (4)	0 (0)	10 (5)	-	5+1 (6)	3+1 (6)	9+1 (5)	-
45	6/10	Glasgow	H	SC	W47-43	5 (4)	9 (5)	-	10+2 (5)	-	2+1 (3)	6+1 (5)	-	15+2 (8)
46	15/10	Glasgow	A	SC	W47-43*	-	8+2 (5)	-	9 (4)	-	1+1 (3)	6+1 (5)	-	23+3 (13)

NOTE: ST = Spring Trophy; SC = Scottish Cup. The home Spring Trophy match versus Glasgow on 31 March was abandoned after heat twelve, with the result permitted to stand. The away Premier Trophy match at Workington on 1 April was abandoned after heat twelve, with the result permitted to stand. The away Knock-Out Cup tie at Newport on 27 June was abandoned after heat fourteen, with the result permitted to stand.

DETAILS OF OTHER RIDERS

(all guests)

Match No. 11: Richie Dennis 2 (3); Match No. 12: Richie Dennis 0 (3); Match No. 19: Adam Roynon 2 (2); Match No. 21: Andrew Tully 1 (2); Match No. 24: Shane Waldron 2+1 (4); Match No. 32: Kevin Little 9+2 (4); Match No. 45: Chris Kerr 9+1 (4); Kevin Little 6+1 (4); Match No. 46: Trent Leverington 13+1 (5); Kevin Little 6+1 (4); Chris Kerr 4+1 (4).

DETAILS OF TACTICAL RIDES AND TACTICAL SUBSTITUTE RIDES

Match No. 2: Pijper 6 points (TR); Match No. 3: Lawson 4 points (TR); Match No. 4: Lawson 6 points (TR); Match No. 9: Pijper 6 points (TR); Harrison 1 point (TR; not doubled); Lawson 1 point (TS; not doubled); Match No. 11: Harrison 6 points (TR); Match No. 12: Pijper 6 points (TR); Match No. 19: Moller 4 points (TR); Pijper 4 points (TR); Match No. 22: Harrison 6 points (TR); Wethers 4 points (TR); Pijper 2 points (TS); Match No. 24: Wethers 4 points (TR); Pijper 0 points (TR); Match No. 27: Pijper 6 points (TR); Lawson 4 points (TR); Match No. 29: Moller 4 points (TR); Wethers 0 points (TR); Match No. 30: Pijper 6 points (TR); Match No. 33: Pijper 6 points (TR); Wethers 6 points (TR); Match No. 34: Pijper 6 points (TR); Moller 1 point (TR; not doubled); Match No. 35: Pijper 6 points (TR); Sneddon 4 points (TR); Match No. 37: Wethers 4 points (TR); Pijper 0 points (TR); Match No. 38: Moller 4 points (TR); Wethers 4 points (TR).

AVERAGES

(26 Premier League, 2 Knock-Out Cup, 14 Premier Trophy = 42 fixtures)

♦ Denotes ever-present.

Rider	Mts	Rds	Pts	Bon	Tot	Avge	Max
Theo Pijper	41	198	381	26	407	8.22	2 full; 3 paid
Matthew Wethers	41	181	289	53	342	7.56	1 full
William Lawson	36	171	294	23	317	7.42	-
Rusty Harrison	23	102	180	9	189	7.41	1 paid
Henrik Moller	41	173	245	39	284	6.57	-
Derek Sneddon ♦	42	226	302	48	350	6.19	-
Daniele Tessari	12	49	42	7	49	4.00	-
Sean Stoddart	39	138	85	15	100	2.90	-

EDINBURGH: From left to right, back row: William Lawson, John Campbell (co-promoter/team manager), Theo Pijper (on bike), Matthew Wethers, Sean Stoddart. Front row, kneeling: Derek Sneddon, Henrik Moller.

Guests   6   18   16   3   19   4.22 -
(Richie Dennis [2]; Kevin Little [1]; Adam Roynon [1]; Andrew Tully [1]; Shane Waldron [1]).

INDIVIDUAL MEETING

4 August: Keyline Scottish Open

QUALIFYING SCORES: Stanislaw Burza 14; Andre Compton 12; Danny Bird 11; Shane Parker 11; Jason Lyons 10; Magnus Karlsson 10; Theo Pijper 10; Chris Kerr 8; William Lawson 7; Tomas Suchanek 7; David Howe 5; Kevin Little 5; George Stancl 3; Trent Leverington 3; Derek Sneddon 2; Daniele Tessari 1; Sean Stoddart (reserve) 1. SEMI-FINAL: 1st Lyons; 2nd Karlsson; 3rd Bird; 4th Parker. FINAL: 1st Burza; 2nd Lyons; 3rd Compton; 4th Karlsson.

OTHER MEETING

23 September: Anderson's Butchers Northern Fours (at Berwick)

Berwick 37; Isle of Wight 21; Hull Select 20; Edinburgh Select 18: Derek Sneddon 9 (4); Kyle Legault 4 (4); David Meldrum 4 (4); Rob Grant 1 (4).

GLASGOW PREMIER TRAVEL INN TIGERS

ADDRESS: Ashfield Stadium, Saracen Park, 404 Hawthorn Street, Possilpark, Glasgow, G22 6RU.
PROMOTERS: Alan C. Dick, Stewart Dickson and Gordon Pairman.
YEARS OF OPERATION: 1949-1952 National League Division Two; 1953 Open; 1999-2006 Premier League.
NOTE: Between 1949 and 1953, the track was home to Ashfield Giants; Ashfield Stadium also played host to a second team in the 2000 Conference League, under the banner of Lightning Ashfield Giants.
FIRST MEETING: 19 April 1949.
TRACK LENGTH: 302 metres.
TRACK RECORD: 57.6 seconds – Shane Parker (18/05/04).

PREVIOUS VENUES:
(1) ADDRESS: White City Stadium, Paisley Road West, Ibrox, Glasgow.
YEARS OF OPERATION: 1928-1929 Open; 1930-1931 Northern League; 1939 Union Cup; 1940 Open; 1945 Open; 1946 Northern League; 1947-1953 National League Division Two; 1954 Northern Shield; 1956 Open; 1964 Provincial League; 1965-1967 British League; 1968 British League Division One.
NOTE: Glasgow first acquired the Tigers moniker in 1946.

(2) ADDRESS: Hampden Park, Mount Florida, Glasgow, G42 9BA.
YEARS OF OPERATION: 1969-1972 British League Division One.

(3) ADDRESS: Cliftonhill Stadium, Main Street, Coatbridge, ML5 3RB.
YEARS OF OPERATION: 1973 British League Division One; 1974 British League Division Two; 1975-1977 National League.
NOTE: The team rode as Coatbridge Tigers throughout their stay at the venue.

(4) ADDRESS: Blantyre Sports Stadium, Glasgow Road, Blantyre, Nr Glasgow.
YEARS OF OPERATION: 1977-1981 National League.
NOTE: Coatbridge moved to Blantyre mid-way through the 1977 season, reverting back to the name of Glasgow Tigers.

(5) ADDRESS: Craighead Park, Forrest Street, Blantyre, Nr Glasgow.
YEARS OF OPERATION: 1982-1986 National League.

(6) ADDRESS: Derwent Park Stadium, Workington, Cumbria, CA14 2HG.
YEAR OF OPERATION: 1987 National League.
NOTE: The side began year as Glasgow Tigers, before becoming Workington Tigers.

(7) ADDRESS: Shawfield Stadium, Glasgow Road, Rutherglen, Glasgow, G73 1SZ.
YEARS OF OPERATION: 1988-1990 National League; 1991-1994 British League Division Two; 1995 Premier League; 1997-1998 Premier League.
NOTE: In 1996, Shawfield Stadium was used by the Scottish Monarchs, who participated in the Premier League.

CLUB HONOURS

NATIONAL SERIES WINNERS: 1990.
LEAGUE CHAMPIONS: 1993, 1994.
KNOCK-OUT CUP WINNERS: 1993, 1994.
PAIRS CHAMPIONS: 2005, 2006.

RIDER ROSTER 2006

Danny BIRD; James COCKLE; Lee DICKEN; Robert KSIEZAK; David McALLAN; Kauko NIEMINEN; Shane PARKER.

OTHER APPEARANCE/GUEST (official matches only)

Danny WARWICK.

GLASGOW

* Denotes aggregate/bonus-point victory

NO.	DATE	OPPONENTS	VENUE	COMPETITION	RESULT	BIRD	McALLAN	DICKEN	NIEMINEN	PARKER	KSIEZAK	COCKLE	OTHERS
1	18/3	Berwick	A	PT	W46-44	10+2 (5)	5+1 (4)	1 (3)	5 (4)	14 (5)	6 (4)	5+1 (6)	-
2	31/3	Edinburgh	A	ST	L36-42	11 (3)	3 (4)	3 (4)	4+1 (3)	9 (3)	6+1 (5)	0 (2)	-
3	2/4	Sheffield	H	PT	W51-44	5+1 (4)	4+1 (3)	1 (4)	11 (5)	14+1 (5)	7+1 (5)	9+2 (5)	-
4	8/4	Workington	A	PT	L45-51	12 (5)	2 (3)	3+1 (4)	10 (4)	13 (6)	3+1 (5)	2+1 (3)	-
5	9/4	Workington	H	PT	L44-46	10 (5)	R/R	2+2 (5)	10 (5)	13+1 (5)	8+2 (6)	1+1 (5)	-
6	16/4	Newcastle	H	PT	W54-36	10+1 (5)	5 (4)	2+1 (3)	11 (4)	12+2 (5)	3+1 (4)	11+1 (6)	-
7	17/4	Newcastle	A	PT	L42-53*	6 (5)	3+1 (5)	R/R	12 (5)	14 (5)	0 (3)	7+1 (7)	-
8	23/4	Stoke	H	PT	W56-36	7+1 (5)	9 (4)	2+2 (3)	10 (4)	12+2 (5)	10+1 (5)	6+2 (4)	-
9	27/4	Sheffield	A	PT	L41-54	10 (5)	1+1 (3)	1+1 (3)	14 (5)	8 (5)	1 (4)	6 (5)	-
10	30/4	Edinburgh	H	PT	W49-44	11 (5)	2 (4)	3+1 (4)	11 (4)	13 (5)	5+1 (4)	4 (4)	-
11	5/5	Edinburgh	A	PT	L44-48*	12 (5)	2 (3)	0 (3)	6 (4)	15+2 (6)	5 (5)	4+1 (4)	-
12	6/5	Berwick	A	PL	L44-51	19+2 (6)	1 (5)	2 (4)	R/R	16 (5)	0 (4)	6+1 (6)	-
13	11/5	Redcar	A	PT	L44-46	9 (6)	7 (5)	2+2 (4)	R/R	12+1 (5)	7 (5)	7+1 (5)	-
14	14/5	Redcar	H	PT	W58-36*	15+3 (6)	7 (5)	6+3 (4)	R/R	15 (5)	8 (5)	7+2 (5)	-
15	21/5	Berwick	H	PT	W57-38*	14+2 (6)	7+2 (5)	4+1 (4)	R/R	13+2 (5)	11+1 (5)	8+1 (5)	-
16	28/5	Stoke	H	PL	W61-32	13+2 (5)	6+1 (4)	5+1 (4)	7+1 (4)	15 (5)	7+1 (4)	8+1 (4)	-
17	29/5	Edinburgh	H	ST	W49-41*	14+1 (5)	1 (4)	3 (4)	8 (4)	13+2 (5)	8 (5)	2+1 (4)	-
18	2/6	Newport	A	PL	W46-44	12 (5)	2+1 (3)	3+1 (4)	7+1 (4)	11+1 (5)	3 (3)	8+1 (6)	-
19	4/6	Mildenhall	A	PL	L44-49	R/R	3 (4)	6 (4)	12+1 (5)	11 (6)	5+2 (6)	7+1 (5)	-
20	10/6	Stoke	A	PT	W51-44*	13+1 (5)	3 (4)	1 (3)	7 (4)	8+1 (4)	14 (6)	5+1 (4)	-
21	11/6	Somerset	H	PL	W50-40	11+1 (5)	4 (4)	3+1 (3)	11 (5)	9+1 (4)	10+2 (5)	2 (4)	-
22	15/6	Redcar	A	PL	L36-59	15+1 (5)	2 (4)	2+1 (4)	8 (5)	6 (4)	3 (4)	0 (4)	-
23	25/6	Newcastle	H	KOC	W55-41	11+2 (5)	4+2 (4)	4+2 (4)	8 (4)	15 (5)	9+3 (5)	4 (3)	-

NO.	DATE	OPPONENTS	VENUE	COMPETITION	RESULT	BIRD	McALLAN	DICKEN	NIEMINEN	PARKER	KSIEZAK	COCKLE	OTHERS
24	26/6	Newcastle	A	KOC	L42-48*	11 (5)	4+1 (4)	3 (4)	7+1 (4)	9 (5)	5 (4)	3+2 (4)	-
25	29/6	Newport	H	PL	W52-38*	10+2 (5)	3 (4)	1+1 (3)	8 (4)	14+1 (5)	9+1 (5)	7 (4)	-
26	2/7	Isle of Wight	H	PL	W52-38	14+1 (5)	6+1 (4)	0 (4)	9 (4)	13+1 (5)	9+1 (5)	1 (3)	-
27	9/7	Rye House	H	PL	W59-35	13+2 (5)	7+1 (4)	2 (4)	12 (4)	15 (5)	5 (4)	5 (4)	-
28	15/7	Workington	A	PL	W46-44	11+1 (6)	4+1 (4)	4 (4)	R/R	15 (5)	9+1 (7)	3+1 (4)	-
29	17/7	Sheffield	H	PL	W49-44	10+1 (5)	3+1 (4)	1 (3)	6 (4)	18+1 (6)	3 (3)	8+2 (5)	-
30	21/7	Somerset	A	PL	L36-58	7 (4)	2+2 (4)	5+2 (5)	13 (5)	5 (4)	4 (5)	0 (3)	-
31	22/7	Rye House	A	PL	L40-54*	13 (5)	2+1 (4)	3+1 (4)	7 (4)	11+1 (5)	0 (3)	4+1 (5)	-
32	23/7	Berwick	H	PL	W53-37*	11+2 (5)	8 (4)	4+1 (4)	6 (4)	14+1 (5)	10+1 (5)	0 (3)	-
33	29/7	Stoke	A	PL	W55-38*	11+1 (5)	8 (4)	6+2 (4)	9+2 (5)	10+1 (4)	6+1 (4)	5 (4)	-
34	30/7	King's Lynn	H	PL	W50-46	12 (5)	5 (4)	4+3 (4)	7 (4)	9+2 (5)	12 (5)	1 (3)	-
35	6/8	Workington	H	PL	W54-41*	12+2 (5)	3+1 (4)	2 (3)	9 (4)	15 (5)	7 (5)	6+1 (4)	-
36	8/8	Isle of Wight	A	PL	L45-49*	14+1 (5)	1 (3)	2 (3)	6+1 (4)	15+1 (6)	1+1 (4)	6+1 (5)	-
37	9/8	King's Lynn	A	PL	L28-62	5 (4)	0 (3)	2 (4)	4 (4)	8 (5)	6 (6)	3 (5)	-
38	13/8	Mildenhall	H	PL	W60-36*	11+3 (5)	8+2 (4)	5+2 (4)	10 (4)	13+1 (5)	9+2 (4)	-	4+2 (4)
39	20/8	Redcar	H	PL	W53-42	13 (5)	5+2 (4)	7+3 (4)	12 (5)	9+1 (4)	3+1 (4)	4 (4)	-
40	24/8	Sheffield	A	PL	L39-57	R/R	2+1 (4)	0 (4)	14 (6)	15+1 (6)	4 (6)	4+2 (4)	-
41	27/8	Newcastle	H	PL	W55-40	9 (3)	5+1 (4)	3+2 (4)	13 (5)	14+1 (5)	5 (6)	6 (4)	-
42	28/8	Newcastle	A	PL	L40-50*	R/R	4+2 (4)	7+1 (5)	5+1 (5)	14+1 (6)	9 (6)	1 (4)	-
43	1/9	Edinburgh	A	PL	D45-45	R/R	4+1 (5)	2+2 (4)	13+1 (6)	16 (6)	7+1 (6)	3 (3)	-
44	3/9	Edinburgh	H	PL	W49-44*	R/R	1 (3)	0 (3)	6+3 (5)	22+1 (7)	13+1 (7)	7+1 (5)	-
45	10/9	King's Lynn	H	KOC s/f	D45-45	11 (5)	1 (3)	2+2 (4)	7+1 (4)	13+1 (5)	10 (6)	1 (3)	-
46	17/9	Rest of World	H	60A	L41-46	15 (5)	0 (2)	3 (4)	9+1 (4)	12 (5)	1 (4)	1 (4)	-
47	20/9	King's Lynn	A	KOC s/f	L27-67	6 (4)	R/R	2 (5)	4 (5)	10 (5)	4 (7)	1 (4)	-
48	26/9	Isle of Wight	A	PO	L39-55	9 (5)	1 (3)	0 (3)	16+1 (5)	6 (5)	7 (5)	0 (4)	-
49	1/10	Isle of Wight	H	PO	W52-42	10+1 (5)	1 (3)	3+1 (3)	7+1 (4)	12+1 (5)	13 (6)	6+3 (4)	-
50	6/10	Edinburgh	A	SC	L43-47	7+1 (4)	7+2 (4)	0 (3)	9 (5)	12 (5)	7+1 (5)	1+1 (4)	-
51	15/10	Edinburgh	H	SC	L43-47	11+1 (5)	6+1 (4)	0 (3)	-	2+1 (4)	12+1 (6)	4 (4)	8 (4)

NOTE: ST = Spring Trophy; SC = Scottish Cup; 60A = 60th Anniversary meeting. The away Spring Trophy match at Edinburgh on 31 March was abandoned after heat twelve, with the result permitted to stand.

DETAILS OF OTHER RIDERS

(all guests)

Match No. 38: Danny Warwick 4+2 (4); Match No. 51: Rusty Harrison 8 (4).

DETAILS OF TACTICAL RIDES AND TACTICAL SUBSTITUTE RIDES

Match No. 2: Bird 6 points (TR); Parker 6 points (TR); Match No. 4: Bird 6 points (TR): Nieminen 4 points (TR); Parker 4 points (TS); Match No. 7: Nieminen 6 points (TR); Parker 6 points (TR); Bird 0 points (TS); Match No. 9: Nieminen 6 points (TR); Bird 4 points (TR); Parker 0 points (TS); Match No. 11: Parker 4 points (TS); Match No. 12: Bird 6 points (TR); Parker 4 points (TR); Match No. 19: Nieminen 6 points (TR); Match No. 22: Bird 6 points (TR); Nieminen 4 points (TR); Match No. 29: Parker 6 points (TS); Match No. 30: Nieminen 4 points (TR); Bird 4 points (TR); Match No. 31: Parker 4 points (TR); Bird 4 points (TR); Match No. 36: Bird 6 points (TR); Parker 4 points (TS); Nieminen 1 point (TR; not doubled); Match No. 37: Bird 1 point (TR; not doubled); Parker 0 points (TR); Match No. 40: Parker 6 points (TR); Nieminen 6 points (TR); Match No. 44: Parker 6 points (TS);

GLASGOW: From left to right, back row: Robert Ksiezak, Shane Parker, Lee Dicken (on bike), Stewart Dickson (co-promoter/team manager), Kauko Nieminen, Danny Bird, James Cockle, David McAllan.

Match No. 46: Nieminen 6 points (TR); Match No. 47: Bird 4 points (TR); Parker 4 points (TR); Match No. 48: Nieminen 6 points (TR); Parker 2 points (TS); Bird 0 points (TR).

OTHER DETAILS

Rest of the World scorers in Match No. 46: Todd Wiltshire 12 (5); Kyle Legault 8 (4); Matthew Wethers 7+4 (5); Cameron Woodward 7+1 (4); Adam Shields 7 (4); William Lawson 4+3 (4); Emiliano Sanchez 1+1 (2).

AVERAGES
(26 Premier League, 2 Play-Offs, 4 Knock-Out Cup, 14 Premier Trophy = 46 fixtures)
♦ Denotes ever-present.

Rider	Mts	Rds	Pts	Bon	Tot	Avge	Max
Shane Parker ♦	46	234	549	31	580	9.91	6 full; 5 paid
Danny Bird	41	204	428	36	464	9.10	5 paid
Kauko Nieminen	41	183	349	15	364	7.96	1 full
Robert Ksiezak ♦	46	225	295	27	322	5.72	-
James Cockle	45	195	202	33	235	4.82	-
David McAllan	44	171	167	28	195	4.56	-
Lee Dicken	45	170	123	43	166	3.91	-
Guest	1	4	4	2	6	6.00	-

(Danny Warwick [1]).

NOTE: David McAllan and Lee Dicken were ever-present throughout the 26-match Premier League programme.

INDIVIDUAL MEETING

29 October: Heathersfield Golden Helmet

QUALIFYING SCORES: Gary Beaton 12; Matej Kus 11; Cal McDade 9; Steven Jones 8; Keiran Morris 7; John MacPhail 7; Wayne Dunworth 5; Simon Lambert 4; Robert McNeil 4; Greg Blair 2; Rickylee Beecroft 2. FIRST SEMI-FINAL: 1st McDade; 2nd Beaton; 3rd Dunworth; 4th Morris. SECOND SEMI-FINAL: 1st Kus; 2nd Jones; 3rd MacPhail; 4th Lambert. FINAL: 1st Kus; 2nd Jones; 3rd McDade; 4th Beaton.

ISLE OF WIGHT WIGHTLINK ISLANDERS

ADDRESS: Smallbrook Stadium, Ashey Road, Ryde, Isle of Wight, PO33 4BH.
PROMOTERS: Dave Pavitt and Martin Newnham.
YEARS OF OPERATION: 1995 Demonstration; 1996 Conference League; 1997 Amateur
League and Premier League; 1998–2006 Premier League.
FIRST MEETING: 13 May 1996.
TRACK LENGTH: 385 metres.
TRACK RECORD: 67.1 seconds – Chris Holder (08/08/06).

CLUB HONOURS

YOUNG SHIELD WINNERS: 1998, 2001.
PAIRS CHAMPIONS: 2002.
KNOCK-OUT CUP WINNERS: 2003.

RIDER ROSTER 2006

Jason BUNYAN; Jason DOYLE; Chris HOLDER; Chris JOHNSON; Krister MARSH; Ray
MORTON; Nick SIMMONS; Krzysztof STOJANOWSKI.

OTHER APPEARANCES/GUESTS (official matches only)

Andrew BARGH; Troy BATCHELOR; Gary BEATON; Karlis EZERGAILIS; Jordan FRAMPTON;
Daniel GIFFARD; Richard HALL; Robert KASPRZAK; Lee SMART; Shane WALDRON; Simon
WALKER; Matthew WRIGHT.

ISLE OF WIGHT

* Denotes aggregate/bonus-point victory

NO.	DATE	OPPONENTS	VENUE	COMPETITION	RESULT	HOLDER	DOYLE	MARSH	STOJANOWSKI	KASPRZAK	JOHNSON	SIMMONS	BUNYAN	MORTON	OTHERS
1	19/3	Newport	A	PT	L42-47	3+1 (4)	9 (5)	6+1 (4)	8+1 (5)	0 (0)	7+1 (5)	9+1 (7)	-	-	-
2	26/3	Mildenhall	A	PT	L34-58	6+1 (5)	11 (5)	6+1 (4)	6 (4)	1 (4)	2 (4)	2 (4)	-	-	-
3	7/4	Somerset	A	PT	L31-62	14 (5)	2+1 (4)	5 (5)	6 (5)	2 (4)	2 (4)	0 (2)	-	-	-
4	8/4	Rye House	A	PT	L20-52	5 (3)	4+1 (4)	5 (4)	1+1 (3)	2 (3)	1 (3)	2 (4)	-	-	-
5	14/4	King's Lynn	A	PT	L26-67	12 (5)	1 (2)	1 (2)	4 (5)	2 (4)	-	3 (6)	-	-	3+1 (6)
6	18/4	Somerset	H	PT	L34-59	7 (5)	R/R	5 (5)	12 (5)	-	-	-	4 (4)	-	6+1 (11)
7	25/4	Rye House	H	PT	L43-50	14+1 (5)	2 (3)	3+1 (4)	10 (4)	-	-	0 (4)	9+3 (5)	-	5 (5)
8	2/5	Mildenhall	H	PT	W56-39	7+1 (4)	9+2 (4)	5+2 (4)	10+1 (5)	-	-	5+1 (4)	13 (5)	-	7+1 (4)
9	9/5	King's Lynn	H	PT	W64-32	10+5 (5)	15 (5)	9 (4)	9+1 (4)	-	7+1 (4)	4+1 (4)	10+1 (4)	-	-
10	16/5	Rye House	H	KOC	W53-41	13+2 (5)	6+1 (4)	5+1 (4)	11 (4)	-	2+2 (4)	4+1 (4)	12+1 (5)	-	-
11	20/5	Rye House	A	KOC	L26-66	5 (5)	3 (4)	2 (4)	6+1 (4)	-	-	1 (4)	1 (4)	8 (5)	-

NO.	DATE	OPPONENTS	VENUE	COMPETITION	RESULT	HOLDER	DOYLE	MARSH	STOJANOWSKI	KASPRZAK	JOHNSON	SIMMONS	BUNYAN	MORTON	OTHERS
12	23/5	Newcastle	H	PL	W57-35	12+2 (5)	5 (4)	4+1 (4)	9+1 (4)	-	7+2 (4)	5+1 (4)	15 (5)	-	-
13	25/5	Redcar	A	PL	L42-51	8+2 (5)	17+2 (6)	R/R	10 (5)	-	2 (5)	0 (5)	5+1 (4)	-	-
14	26/5	Edinburgh	A	PL	L35-56	9 (5)	8 (5)	R/R	3 (5)	-	5+1 (5)	2+1 (5)	8+1 (5)	-	-
15	27/5	Berwick	A	PL	W46-44	13+1 (5)	8+2 (5)	R/R	13+1 (6)	-	6+2 (6)	3 (4)	3 (4)	-	-
16	30/5	Berwick	H	PL	W53-42*	8+3 (4)	13+1 (6)	R/R	8+1 (5)	-	8+2 (5)	2+2 (4)	14 (5)	-	0 (1)
17	6/6	Workington	H	PL	W52-42	14+1 (5)	11+2 (5)	4+2 (4)	8 (4)	-	3 (3)	4 (5)	8 (4)	-	-
18	9/6	Somerset	A	PL	L42-54	16 (5)	8 (5)	3 (4)	6+1 (4)	-	2+1 (5)	1 (4)	6 (4)	-	-
19	11/6	Newport	A	PL	L43-47	R/R	13 (6)	3+2 (5)	13+1 (6)	-	6+2 (6)	6+1 (6)	2 (1)	-	-
20	13/6	Stoke	H	PL	W60-32	12 (5)	14+3 (6)	8 (5)	15+1 (6)	-	8+3 (5)	3+1 (3)	R/R	-	-
21	22/6	Newport	H	PT	W61-34*	15+1 (6)	12+1 (5)	-	16+2 (6)	-	6+1 (5)	6+1 (4)	R/R	6+1 (4)	-
22	28/6	Sheffield	H	PL	L44-46	13 (6)	8 (5)	-	12+2 (6)	-	5 (5)	2+2 (4)	R/R	4 (4)	-
23	29/6	Sheffield	A	PL	L29-62	10 (5)	5 (4)	-	2 (5)	-	5+1 (4)	2+2 (5)	2 (5)	3 (2)	-
24	30/6	Workington	A	PL	L30-63	8+2 (5)	1 (2)	-	7 (5)	-	4 (4)	1+1 (6)	4 (4)	-	5 (4)
25	2/7	Glasgow	A	PL	L38-52	11 (6)	10+1 (6)	-	4 (5)	-	7+2 (5)	-	5+2 (5)	R/R	1+1 (3)
26	6/7	Mildenhall	H	PL	W51-42	15+1 (6)	11+1 (5)	-	9 (5)	-	5+1 (4)	3 (4)	8+2 (6)	R/R	-
27	9/7	Mildenhall	A	PL	L44-49*	15 (6)	6 (5)	-	5+1 (5)	-	5 (4)	2+1 (3)	11+2 (7)	R/R	-
28	11/7	King's Lynn	H	PL	W50-40	13 (6)	7 (5)	-	13+3 (6)	-	9+1 (5)	0 (3)	8+2 (5)	R/R	-
29	18/7	Somerset	H	PL	W43-41	11 (4)	13 (5)	-	6+1 (5)	-	3 (1)	1 (7)	9+2 (5)	R/R	-
30	25/7	Newport	H	PL	W50-40*	15+2 (6)	16+1 (6)	-	7+1 (5)	-	3 (3)	3 (6)	6 (4)	R/R	-
31	1/8	Edinburgh	H	PL	W55-41	13 (6)	0 (0)	-	16+1 (6)	-	10+3 (6)	7+3 (7)	9 (5)	R/R	-
32	8/8	Glasgow	H	PL	W49-45	13 (6)	-	-	8+1 (5)	-	6+1 (4)	6+2 (4)	5+2 (5)	R/R	11+1 (6)
33	12/8	Stoke	A	PL	L39-53*	14 (6)	5+1 (4)	-	5+1 (5)	-	-	3+1 (4)	8+1 (6)	R/R	4 (5)
34	15/8	Rye House	H	PL	W64-29	16+2 (6)	15 (6)	-	11+3 (5)	-	-	9+2 (4)	7 (5)	R/R	6+3 (4)
35	22/8	Redcar	H	PL	W50-40*	13+2 (6)	16 (6)	-	5+2 (5)	-	6+1 (4)	1+1 (4)	9+2 (5)	R/R	-
36	10/9	Newcastle	A	PL	L40-52*	10 (5)	8 (5)	-	R/R	-	5+1 (6)	1 (3)	7+3 (6)	9 (5)	-
37	12/9	Weymouth	H	Chal	W62-32	-	15 (5)	-	-	-	-	9+3 (4)	13+2 (5)	12 (4)	13+2 (12)
38	15/9	King's Lynn	A	PL	L31-63	14 (5)	7+1 (5)	-	2 (4)	-	0 (4)	1 (4)	2 (4)	5 (4)	-
39	16/9	Rye House	A	PL	L43-50*	8+2 (5)	5 (4)	-	10+2 (4)	-	2+2 (4)	3 (4)	6+1 (4)	9+1 (5)	-
40	22/9	Plymouth	A	Chal	L43-51	-	0 (0)	-	5 (4)	-	-	-	17 (5)	5+1 (4)	16+3 (16)
41	26/9	Glasgow	H	PO	W55-39	8 (5)	11+1 (5)	-	7 (4)	-	6+2 (4)	5+1 (4)	10 (4)	8+2 (4)	-
42	1/10	Glasgow	A	PO	L42-52*	15 (5)	6 (5)	-	2+2 (4)	-	1 (4)	3 (3)	7+2 (5)	8 (4)	-
43	3/10	Plymouth	H	Chal	W70-22	11+1 (4)	11+1 (4)	-	12 (4)	-	9+2 (5)	-	9+3 (4)	6+2 (4)	12+1 (5)
44	10/10	Sheffield	H	PO s/f	W50-43	10+1 (5)	14 (5)	-	5+2 (4)	-	0 (3)	7+3 (5)	5+1 (4)	9 (4)	-
45	12/10	Sheffield	A	PO s/f	L35-60	13 (5)	3 (5)	-	4 (4)	-	-	2 (5)	10+1 (5)	1 (4)	2+1 (4)

NOTE: The away Premier Trophy match at Rye House on 8 April was abandoned after heat twelve, with the result permitted to stand. The home Premier League fixture against Somerset on 18 July was abandoned after heat fourteen, with the result permitted to stand.

DETAILS OF OTHER RIDERS

(all guests)

Match No. 5: Matthew Wright 3+1 (6); Match No. 6: Karlis Ezergailis 5 (6); Matthew Wright 1+1 (5); Match No. 7: Daniel Giffard 5 (5); Match No. 8: Simon Walker 7+1 (4); Match No. 16: Shane Waldron 0 (1); Match No. 24: Richard Hall 5 (4); Match No. 25: Gary Beaton 1+1 (3); Match No. 32: Troy Batchelor 11+1 (6); Match No. 33: Lee Smart 4 (5); Match No. 34: Jordan

Frampton 6+3 (4); Match No. 37: Karlis Ezergailis 6+1 (4); Andrew Bargh 5+1 (4); Sam Martin 2 (4); Match No. 40: Andrew Bargh 8+2 (6); Karlis Ezergailis 5 (5); Sam Martin 3+1 (5); Match No. 43: Andrew Bargh 12+1 (5); Match No. 45: Andrew Bargh 2+1 (4).

DETAILS OF TACTICAL RIDES AND TACTICAL SUBSTITUTE RIDES

Match No. 2: Doyle 4 points (TR); Holder 0 points (TR); Match No. 3: Holder 6 points (TR); Stojanowski 1 point (TR; not doubled); Marsh 0 points (TS); Match No. 4: Marsh 1 point (TR; not doubled); Holder 1 point (TR; not doubled); Match No. 5: Holder 6 points (TR); Stojanowski 1 point (TR; not doubled); Match No. 6: Stojanowski 6 points (TR); Holder 0 points (TR); Match No. 7: Holder 6 points (TR); Match No. 11: Bunyan 4 points (TR); Holder 0 points (TR); Match No. 13: Doyle 6 points (TR); Match No. 14: Bunyan 2 points (TR); Doyle 0 points (TR); Match No. 18: Doyle 6 points (TR); Holder 6 points (TR); Match No. 23: Holder 4 points (TR); Doyle 0 points (TR); Stojanowski 0 points (TS); Match No. 24: Holder 6 points (TR); Hall 0 points (TR); Match No. 27: Holder 4 points (TR); Bunyan 2 points (TS); Doyle 0 points (TR); Match No. 33: Holder 4 points (TR); Match No. 36: Holder 4 points (TR); Bunyan 2 points (TS); Doyle 1 point (TR; not doubled); Match No. 38: Holder 4 points (TR); Doyle 4 points (TR); Match No. 39: Stojanowski 6 points (TR); Match No. 40: Bunyan 6 points (TR); Bargh 2 points (TS); Stojanowski 0 points (TR); Match No. 42: Holder 6 points (TR); Bunyan 4 points (TS); Morton 1 point (TR; not doubled); Match No. 45: Bunyan 6 points (TR); Holder 4 points (TR).

AVERAGES
(26 Premier League, 4 Play-Offs, 2 Knock-Out Cup, 10 Premier Trophy = 42 fixtures)

Rider	Mts	Rds	Pts	Bon	Tot	Avge	Max
Chris Holder	41	211	431	33	464	8.80	4 paid
Jason Doyle	40	185	328	22	350	7.57	1 full
Krzysztof Stojanowski	41	196	318	35	353	7.20	1 paid
Jason Bunyan	34	159	245	30	275	6.92	1 full
Ray Morton	10	40	62	4	66	6.60	-
Krister Marsh	16	66	74	11	85	5.15	-
Chris Johnson	35	151	157	33	190	5.03	-
Nick Simmons	40	176	124	30	154	3.50	-
Also rode:							
Robert Kasprzak	5	15	7	0	7	1.87	-
Guests	12	53	50	9	59	4.45	-

(Andrew Bargh [1]; Troy Batchelor [1]; Gary Beaton [1]; Karlis Ezergailis [1]; Jordan Frampton [1]; Daniel Giffard [1]; Richard Hall [1]; Lee Smart [1]; Shane Waldron [1]; Simon Walker [1]; Matthew Wright [2]).

INDIVIDUAL MEETING

17 August: British Under-15 Championship (Round Four)

QUALIFYING SCORES: Ben Hopwood 11; Joe Haines 11; Adam Wrathall 9; George Piper 8; Richard Franklin 8; Kye Norton 6; James Sarjeant 6; Ben Reade (reserve) 5; Daniel Greenwood 4; Scott Meakins 3; Tom Davies (reserve) 3; Jack Butler 0; Sean Paterson 0; Amy Carpenter (reserve) 0; Chris Bint (reserve) 0. FINAL: 1st Haines; 2nd Hopwood; 3rd Wrathall; 4th Norton.

ISLE OF WIGHT: From left to right, back row: Nick Simmons, Jason Doyle, Chris Johnson, Chris Holder, David Croucher (team manager). Front row, kneeling: Robert Kasprzak, Krister Marsh. On bike: Krzysztof Stojanowski.

OTHER MEETING

23 September: Anderson's Butchers Northern Fours (at Berwick)

    Berwick 37; Isle of Wight 21: Ray Morton 8 (4); Jason Doyle 8 (4); Jason Bunyan 5 (4); Andrew Bargh 0 (4); Hull Select 20; Edinburgh Select 18.

KING'S LYNN MONEY CENTRE STARS

ADDRESS: Norfolk Arena, Saddlebow Road, King's Lynn, Norfolk, PE34 3AG.
PROMOTERS: Keith 'Buster' Chapman and Jonathan Chapman.
YEARS OF OPERATION: 1965 Open; 1966-1967 British League; 1968 British League
Division One; 1969-1970 British League Division One and Division Two; 1971-1974
British League Division One; 1975-1990 British League; 1991-1994 British League
Division One; 1995 Premier League; 1996 Training; 1997 Elite League and Amateur
League; 1998-1999 Elite League and Conference League; 2000-2001 Elite League; 2002
Elite League and Conference League; 2003 Premier League; 2004 Premier League and
Conference Trophy; 2005-2006 Premier League.
NOTE: In 1997, King's Lynn shared their Amateur League fixtures with Ipswich, under
the banner of Anglian Angels. The track has also been occupied by Boston for their
Conference League operation from 2000 to 2006.
FIRST MEETING: 23 May 1965.
TRACK LENGTH: 342 metres.
TRACK RECORD: 57.6 seconds – Nicki Pedersen (11/09/02).

CLUB HONOURS

KNOCK-OUT CUP WINNERS: 1977, 2000, 2005, 2006.
INTER-LEAGUE KNOCK-OUT CUP WINNERS: 1978, 1980.
PREMIERSHIP WINNERS: 2001.
YOUNG SHIELD WINNERS: 2005.
PREMIER TROPHY WINNERS: 2006.
LEAGUE CHAMPIONS: 2006.

RIDER ROSTER 2006

Troy BATCHELOR; Kevin DOOLAN; Trevor HARDING; Simon LAMBERT; Chris MILLS; Daniel
NERMARK; John OLIVER; Tomas TOPINKA.

OTHER APPEARANCES/GUESTS (official matches only)

James BRUNDLE; Chris HOLDER; Jason LYONS; Andrew TULLY; Shane WALDRON.

KING'S LYNN

* Denotes aggregate/bonus-point victory

NO.	DATE	OPPONENTS	VENUE	COMPETITION	RESULT	NERMARK	HARDING	BATCHELOR	DOOLAN	TOPINKA	MILLS	LAMBERT	WALDRON	OLIVER	OTHERS
1	15/3	Sheffield	H	PIT	W55-37	7 (4)	6+2 (4)	9+1 (4)	11+1 (5)	14 (5)	7+2 (4)	1 (4)	-	-	-
2	22/3	Newport	H	PT	W52-44	5+2 (4)	6+1 (4)	6+2 (4)	13+1 (5)	13 (5)	4+2 (4)	5 (4)	-	-	-
3	24/3	Somerset	A	PT	L34-38	6 (3)	0 (3)	6+1 (4)	9 (3)	5 (3)	8+2 (5)	-	0 (3)	-	-
4	29/3	Somerset	H	PT	W51-43*	7+1 (5)	8 (4)	7+1 (4)	11+2 (5)	11 (4)	7 (5)	0 (3)	-	-	-
5	1/4	Rye House	A	PT	L40-50	7+1 (4)	1+1 (3)	4+1 (4)	10 (5)	11 (5)	7+2 (6)	0 (3)	-	-	-
6	5/4	Rye House	H	PT	W65-28*	10+1 (4)	6+2 (4)	13+2 (5)	11+1 (4)	11+1 (4)	9+1 (5)	5+3 (4)	-	-	-
7	14/4	Isle of Wight	H	PT	W67-26	9+1 (4)	7+2 (4)	11+1 (4)	12+2 (5)	11 (5)	8+3 (4)	9+3 (4)	-	-	-
8	26/4	Mildenhall	H	PT	W48-42	6 (4)	8+1 (4)	1+1 (2)	12+1 (5)	14 (5)	6+2 (6)	1+1 (4)	-	-	-
9	30/4	Mildenhall	A	PT	L44-49*	9+1 (5)	3+1 (3)	8+1 (4)	4+1 (4)	16 (5)	1+1 (5)	-	-	3 (4)	-
10	9/5	Isle of Wight	A	PT	L32-64*	-	2+1 (4)	10 (5)	9 (5)	9 (5)	1 (5)	-	0 (3)	1 (3)	-
11	10/5	Redcar	H	PL	W70-22	11+1 (4)	8+2 (4)	9+1 (4)	13+2 (5)	14 (5)	8+3 (4)	-	-	7+3 (4)	-
12	11/5	Sheffield	A	PIT	L32-59	10+1 (5)	0 (1)	3+1 (4)	8+1 (5)	3 (4)	6 (6)	-	-	2+1 (6)	-
13	14/5	Newport	A	PT	L45-48*	12+1 (6)	3+2 (5)	R/R	16+1 (6)	7 (5)	4+1 (4)	-	-	3 (4)	-
14	20/5	Berwick	A	KOC	L43-47	8 (4)	2+1 (4)	3 (4)	12+1 (5)	12 (5)	6 (5)	-	-	0 (3)	-
15	26/5	Somerset	A	PL	L39-51	3+1 (4)	2 (3)	7 (4)	10 (5)	10 (5)	5+2 (6)	-	-	2+1 (3)	-
16	28/5	Mildenhall	A	PL	W47-45	4+1 (4)	7+1 (4)	9 (5)	11+1 (5)	8 (4)	5+3 (4)	-	-	3+2 (4)	-
17	31/5	Berwick	H	KOC	W70-20*	8+2 (4)	14+1 (5)	11+1 (4)	10+2 (4)	12 (4)	8+4 (4)	-	-	7+1 (5)	-
18	1/6	Sheffield	A	PL	D45-45	6+1 (4)	4+1 (4)	3+1 (4)	12 (5)	10 (5)	3 (3)	-	-	7+1 (5)	-
19	7/6	Workington	H	PL	W63-30	8 (3)	6+2 (4)	10+2 (4)	13+2 (5)	15 (5)	6+1 (5)	-	-	5+2 (4)	-
20	9/6	Edinburgh	A	PL	D45-45	R/R	4 (4)	3 (4)	14 (6)	16+1 (6)	8 (7)	-	-	0 (3)	-
21	10/6	Berwick	A	PL	W51-46	R/R	3 (5)	10 (5)	13+1 (6)	17 (6)	7 (5)	-	-	1 (3)	-
22	14/6	Sheffield	H	PL	W62-33*	11 (4)	8+3 (4)	7+2 (4)	15 (5)	13+2 (5)	4 (4)	-	-	4+2 (4)	-
23	17/6	Stoke	A	PL	L43-47	6 (4)	5 (4)	7 (5)	11 (5)	8 (4)	4+2 (5)	-	-	2 (3)	-
24	21/6	Rye House	H	KOC	W54-41	R/R	5 (5)	10+1 (5)	14+1 (6)	18 (6)	4+1 (4)	-	-	3+1 (4)	-
25	24/6	Rye House	A	KOC	L44-49*	R/R	6+2 (5)	2+1 (5)	20 (6)	12 (6)	5 (5)	-	-	0 (3)	-
26	28/6	Somerset	H	PL	W56-39*	10 (4)	7 (4)	7+2 (4)	12+1 (5)	10+2 (5)	6+1 (4)	-	-	4+2 (4)	-
27	11/7	Isle of Wight	A	PL	L40-50	9 (5)	4 (4)	5+1 (4)	6 (4)	9 (5)	3 (4)	-	-	4+3 (5)	-
28	12/7	Stoke	H	PL	W66-26*	14+1 (5)	4+2 (4)	9 (4)	9+3 (4)	15 (5)	8+2 (4)	-	-	7+2 (4)	-
29	16/7	Newport	A	PL	W54-39	9 (4)	9+2 (4)	8+1 (4)	11+3 (5)	14 (5)	3+1 (4)	-	-	0 (4)	-
30	19/7	Mildenhall	H	PL	W52-41*	10 (4)	4+2 (3)	11+2 (5)	5+2 (4)	14 (5)	6 (5)	-	-	2 (4)	-
31	29/7	Workington	A	PT s/f	L39-51	8 (4)	3+2 (4)	6+2 (5)	11 (5)	6 (3)	4 (6)	-	-	1+1 (3)	-
32	30/7	Glasgow	A	PL	L46-50	12 (4)	1 (4)	12+2 (5)	5 (4)	9 (5)	6 (6)	-	-	1+1 (3)	-
33	4/8	Workington	H	PT s/f	W59-35*	14 (5)	7+2 (4)	4+1 (4)	10 (5)	12 (4)	6+1 (5)	-	-	6+1 (4)	-
34	9/8	Glasgow	H	PL	W62-28*	11+1 (5)	7+1 (4)	11 (4)	6+3 (4)	14 (5)	6 (4)	-	-	7+1 (4)	-
35	16/8	Rye House	H	PL	W64-28	12 (4)	4+1 (4)	9+1 (4)	10+2 (5)	15 (5)	7+1 (4)	-	-	7+1 (4)	-
36	25/8	Newcastle	H	PL	W62-31	11 (4)	4+1 (4)	13+2 (5)	9+1 (4)	13+1 (5)	6+1 (4)	-	-	6+1 (4)	-
37	26/8	Edinburgh	H	PL	W61-33*	10+1 (4)	8+1 (4)	14+1 (5)	9+3 (5)	11 (4)	-	-	-	5+2 (4)	4+1 (4)
38	30/8	Sheffield	H	PT f	W63-32	9 (4)	6+2 (4)	12+3 (5)	7 (4)	14+1 (5)	8 (4)	-	-	7+3 (4)	-
39	31/8	Sheffield	A	PT f	L45-48*	9+1 (5)	4+1 (4)	8 (4)	9 (5)	5+1 (4)	6+2 (4)	-	-	4+2 (4)	-
40	2/9	Rye House	A	PL	W46-44*	16+1 (6)	8+1 (5)	R/R	8 (4)	8+1 (5)	5+1 (7)	-	-	1+1 (3)	-
41	4/9	Newcastle	A	PL	L44-46*	6 (4)	2+1 (3)	6+2 (4)	11+1 (5)	8+1 (5)	3 (4)	-	-	8+2 (5)	-
42	6/9	Berwick	H	PL	W66-27*	15 (5)	8+4 (5)	9+1 (4)	9+1 (4)	10+1 (4)	8+1 (4)	-	-	7+2 (4)	-

NO.	DATE	OPPONENTS	VENUE	COMPETITION	RESULT	NERMARK	HARDING	BATCHELOR	DOOLAN	TOPINKA	MILLS	LAMBERT	WALDRON	OLIVER	OTHERS
43	7/9	Redcar	A	PL	W49-44*	11 (4)	4 (4)	5+1 (4)	10+1 (5)	13 (5)	4 (4)	-	-	2+1 (4)	-
44	9/9	Workington	A	PL	W49-43*	6 (4)	5+2 (4)	8+2 (4)	10+2 (5)	11+1 (5)	6+2 (4)	-	-	-	3+2 (4)
45	10/9	Glasgow	A	KOC s/f	D45-45	7 (4)	7+2 (4)	6+3 (4)	9 (5)	11+1 (5)	0 (2)	-	-	5+3 (6)	-
46	13/9	Newport	H	PL	W64-26*	14+1 (5)	9+3 (4)	11 (4)	3+1 (4)	7+2 (4)	10+1 (4)	-	-	10+2 (5)	-
47	15/9	Isle of Wight	H	PL	W63-31*	12 (5)	7+1 (4)	10+1 (4)	7+2 (4)	13+1 (5)	5+2 (4)	-	-	9+1 (4)	-
48	20/9	Glasgow	H	KOC s/f	W67-27*	12 (4)	6+1 (4)	13+2 (5)	9+1 (4)	12+1 (5)	10+2 (4)	-	-	5+2 (4)	-
49	21/9	Redcar	A	PO	W47-43	8 (4)	4+1 (4)	3+2 (4)	11+1 (5)	10+1 (5)	9 (4)	-	-	2 (4)	-
50	27/9	Redcar	H	PO	W63-32*	9+2 (4)	9 (4)	13+1 (5)	7+1 (4)	13+1 (5)	6+2 (4)	-	-	6+1 (4)	-
51	6/10	Somerset	A	KOC f	D45-45	5 (4)	1 (3)	11 (4)	9+3 (5)	-	4 (4)	-	-	7 (6)	8+1 (4)
52	11/10	Somerset	H	KOC f	W62-32*	11 (4)	5+3 (4)	8+2 (4)	11+2 (5)	-	8 (4)	-	-	10+2 (5)	9+1 (4)
53	14/10	Rye House	A	PO s/f	L42-48	11+1 (5)	1 (3)	2 (4)	8+1 (5)	-	3+1 (4)	-	-	10+1 (5)	7+1 (4)
54	18/10	Rye House	H	PO s/f	W60-35*	10 (4)	5 (4)	4+1 (3)	13+1 (4)	12 (4)	12+3 (6)	-	-	4+1 (4)	-
55	20/10	Peterborough	H	CC	L44-49	7+1 (4)	2+1 (4)	11 (5)	3 (4)	12 (5)	8+2 (5)	-	-	1 (3)	-
56	26/10	Sheffield	A	PO f	L37-52	9 (5)	3+1 (4)	6 (4)	6+2 (5)	6 (4)	5 (4)	-	-	2+1 (4)	-
57	27/10	Sheffield	H	PO f	W63-30*	11 (4)	7+3 (4)	13 (5)	9+1 (4)	10 (4)	7+3 (5)	-	-	6+1 (4)	-

NOTE: PIT = Pirtek Trophy; CC = Champion of Champions Challenge. The away Premier Trophy match at Somerset on 24 March was abandoned after heat twelve, with the result permitted to stand.

DETAILS OF OTHER RIDERS

(all guests)

Match No. 37: James Brundle 4+1 (4); Match No. 44: Andrew Tully 3+2 (4); Match No. 51: Chris Holder 8+1 (4); Match No. 52: Jason Lyons 9+1 (4); Match No. 53: Jason Lyons 7+1 (4).

DETAILS OF TACTICAL RIDES AND TACTICAL SUBSTITUTE RIDES

Match No. 9: Topinka 6 points (TR); Match No. 10: Batchelor 4 points (TR); Topinka 4 points (TR); Doolan 4 points (TS); Match No. 12: Nermark 4 points (TR); Doolan 1 point (TR; not doubled); Match No. 13: Doolan 4 points (TR); Nermark 2 points (TS); Topinka 0 points (TR); Match No. 25: Doolan 6 points (TR); Match No. 32: Batchelor 6 points (TR); Nermark 6 points (TR); Match No. 39: Batchelor 6 points (TR); Match No. 55: Topinka 6 points (TR).

AVERAGES

(26 Premier League, 6 Play-Offs, 8 Knock-Out Cup, 14 Premier Trophy = 54 fixtures)
◆ Denotes ever-present.

Rider	Mts	Rds	Pts	Bon	Tot	Avge	Max
Tomas Topinka	51	242	573	20	593	9.80	7 full; 3 paid
Kevin Doolan ◆	54	256	537	58	595	9.30	1 full; 5 paid
Daniel Nermark	49	210	453	23	476	9.07	3 full; 3 paid
Troy Batchelor	52	221	406	55	461	8.34	8 paid
Trevor Harding ◆	54	215	280	64	344	6.40	2 paid
Chris Mills	53	240	308	57	365	6.08	2 paid
John Oliver	46	185	203	54	257	5.56	-
Simon Lambert	6	22	20	7	27	4.91	1 paid

KING'S LYNN: From left to right, back row: Chris Mills, Troy Batchelor, Simon Lambert, Shane Waldron, Daniel Nermark. Front row, kneeling: Kevin Doolan, Trevor Harding. On bike: Tomas Topinka.

Also rode:

Shane Waldron	2	6	0	0	0	0.00	-
Guests	5	20	31	6	37	7.40	-

(James Brundle [1]; Chris Holder [1]; Jason Lyons [2]; Andrew Tully [1]).

NOTE: Tomas Topinka was ever-present throughout the 26-match Premier League programme.

INDIVIDUAL MEETINGS

12 April: Ashley Jones Memorial

QUALIFYING SCORES: Olly Allen 13; Jason Doyle 12; Shane Parker 12; Tomas Topinka (after run-off) 11; Rory Schlein 11; Daniel Nermark 11; Adam Allott 8; Troy Batchelor 8; Trevor Harding 6; Kevin Doolan 6; Matthew Wethers 6; Craig Watson 5; Chris Holder 5; Jason Lyons 3; Shaun Tacey 2; Chris Mills 1. FINAL: 1st Parker; 2nd Topinka; 3rd Allen; 4th Doyle.

5 July: International Young Guns

QUALIFYING SCORES: Lewis Bridger 15; Ulrich Ostergaard 13; Adam Allott 12; Richard Hall 12; James Brundle 10; Mark Thompson 10; Mark Jones 8; Nathan Irwin 7; Shane Waldron 6; Matt Browne 6; Chris Mills 4; Andrew Bargh 4; Wayne Dunworth 4; John Oliver 3; James Purchase 2; Darren Mallett 0. FINAL: 1st Bridger; 2nd Ostergaard; 3rd Allott; 4th Hall.

4 October: Pride of the East

QUALIFYING SCORES: Davey Watt 14; Daniel Nermark 12; Troy Batchelor 12; Chris Holder 10; Theo Pijper 9; Chris Mills 9; Paul Lee 8; David Howe 7; Tomas Topinka 6; Kevin Doolan 5; Jason King 5; Trevor Harding 5; James Brundle 5; Shaun Tacey 4; John Oliver 3; Mark Jones 3; Nathan Irwin (reserve) 2. FINAL: 1st Watt; 2nd Nermark; 3rd Batchelor; 4th Holder.

MILDENHALL ASL FREIGHT FEN TIGERS

NOTE: The information below relates only to the main Mildenhall team. For details of the second side, please refer to the Conference League section.

ADDRESS: Mildenhall Stadium, Hayland Drove, West Row Fen, Mildenhall, Suffolk, IP28 8QU.
PROMOTER: Mick Horton.
YEARS OF OPERATION: 1973 Training; 1974 Open and Training; 1975–1989 National League; 1990–1991 Training; 1992 British League Division Two; 1994 British League Division Three; 1995 Academy League; 1996 Conference League; 1997 Amateur League; 1998–2005 Conference League; 2006 Premier League and Conference League.
FIRST MEETING: 18 May 1975.
TRACK LENGTH: 260 metres.
TRACK RECORD: 50.25 seconds – Paul Lee (16/05/04).

CLUB HONOURS

LEAGUE CHAMPIONS: 1979, 2003, 2004.
FOUR-TEAM CHAMPIONS: 1984, 1987, 2004.
PAIRS CHAMPIONS: 1987.
LEAGUE CUP WINNERS: 2000.
CONFERENCE TROPHY WINNERS: 2002, 2004.
KNOCK-OUT CUP WINNERS: 2003, 2004.

RIDER ROSTER 2006

Jon ARMSTRONG; James BRUNDLE; Barry BURCHATT; Jordan FRAMPTON: Daniel KING; Jason KING; Jason LYONS; Andrew MOORE; Ben POWELL; Shaun TACEY; Brent WERNER; Matthew WRIGHT.

OTHER APPEARANCES/GUESTS (official matches only)

Mark BASEBY; Craig BRANNEY; Richard HALL; Shane HENRY; Joel PARSONS; Scott RICHARDSON.

MILDENHALL

* Denotes aggregate/bonus-point victory

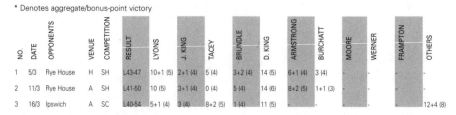

NO.	DATE	OPPONENTS	VENUE	COMPETITION	RESULT	LYONS	J. KING	TACEY	BRUNDLE	D. KING	ARMSTRONG	BURCHATT	MOORE	WERNER	FRAMPTON	OTHERS
1	5/3	Rye House	H	SH	L43-47	10+1 (5)	2+1 (4)	5 (4)	3+2 (4)	14 (5)	6+1 (4)	3 (4)	-	-	-	-
2	11/3	Rye House	A	SH	L41-50	10 (5)	3+1 (4)	0 (4)	5 (4)	14 (6)	8+2 (5)	1+1 (3)	-	-	-	-
3	16/3	Ipswich	A	SC	L40-54	5+1 (4)	3 (4)	8+2 (5)	1 (4)	11 (5)	-	-	-	-	-	12+4 (8)

NO.	DATE	OPPONENTS	VENUE	COMPETITION	RESULT	LYONS	J. KING	TACEY	BRUNDLE	D. KING	ARMSTRONG	BURCHATT	MOORE	WERNER	FRAMPTON	OTHERS
4	19/3	Ipswich	H	SC	L43-47	11 (5)	7+1 (4)	5 (4)	5+2 (4)	7 (5)	7 (4)	1 (4)	-	-	-	-
5	26/3	Isle of Wight	H	PT	W58-34	8+2 (4)	7+1 (4)	11+1 (5)	3+2 (4)	12 (4)	10+2 (5)	7+2 (4)	-	-	-	-
6	31/3	Somerset	A	PT	L43-50	13 (5)	1 (4)	7+2 (4)	2 (3)	7+1 (5)	13 (7)	0 (3)	-	-	-	-
7	2/4	Newport	A	PT	D45-45	12 (5)	5+2 (4)	4 (4)	5+1 (4)	8+1 (5)	8 (5)	3 (3)	-	-	-	-
8	8/4	Newport	H	PT	W49-40*	15 (5)	5+1 (4)	7 (4)	5+1 (4)	12+2 (5)	5+1 (4)	0 (3)	-	-	-	-
9	16/4	Rye House	H	PT	W46-44	10+2 (5)	5+2 (4)	6+1 (4)	6 (4)	9+1 (5)	10+1 (6)	0 (2)	-	-	-	-
10	17/4	Rye House	A	PT	L40-50	9+1 (4)	4 (4)	4 (4)	2 (4)	7 (5)	13 (6)	1 (2)	-	-	-	-
11	23/4	Somerset	H	PT	W54-41*	12+1 (5)	9 (4)	0 (3)	8+2 (4)	11+2 (5)	13+2 (6)	1+1 (3)	-	-	-	-
12	26/4	King's Lynn	A	PT	L42-48	8+2 (5)	6 (4)	7+1 (4)	7 (4)	7 (5)	7+3 (5)	0 (3)	-	-	-	-
13	30/4	King's Lynn	H	PT	W49-44	6 (5)	9+2 (4)	5 (4)	7 (4)	4 (4)	15+2 (7)	3 (3)	-	-	-	-
14	2/5	Isle of Wight	A	PT	L39-56*	16 (5)	2 (4)	8 (5)	2 (4)	10 (4)	1 (4)	0 (4)	-	-	-	-
15	13/5	Rye House	A	PL	L40-53	13 (5)	6 (4)	1 (3)	0 (3)	12 (5)	8+4 (7)	0 (3)	-	-	-	-
16	28/5	King's Lynn	H	PL	L45-47	16 (5)	2 (4)	-	2+1 (4)	11+2 (5)	8+1 (5)	2+1 (3)	4 (4)	-	-	-
17	4/6	Glasgow	H	PL	W49-44	14+1 (5)	5+1 (4)	-	5 (5)	9+1 (6)	13+1 (7)	3+1 (3)	R/R	-	-	-
18	10/6	Newcastle	H	PL	W51-41	13 (5)	-	-	4+2 (5)	R/R	18+1 (7)	3 (3)	-	9+2 (6)	-	4 (4)
19	11/6	Newcastle	A	PL	L32-48	15 (5)	-	-	2+1 (5)	R/R	10+1 (7)	0 (1)	-	5+1 (5)	-	10 (6)
20	23/6	Somerset	A	KOC	L43-52	10+1 (5)	4+1 (4)	-	3+1 (4)	12 (5)	6+2 (5)	2+1 (3)	-	6 (4)	-	-
21	25/6	Somerset	H	KOC	L40-53	11+1 (5)	6+2 (4)	-	5 (4)	10 (5)	3 (4)	2+1 (4)	-	3 (4)	-	-
22	2/7	Redcar	H	PL	D45-45	9 (5)	5+1 (5)	-	7+1 (6)	15 (6)	R/R	0 (4)	-	9+1 (4)	-	-
23	6/7	Isle of Wight	A	PL	L42-51	10+1 (4)	4 (5)	-	2 (5)	13 (6)	R/R	-	-	10+1 (5)	-	3+2 (5)
24	7/7	Somerset	A	PL	W48-42	14 (5)	6+1 (5)	-	8+4 (7)	13 (6)	R/R	-	-	7 (4)	-	0 (3)
25	9/7	Isle of Wight	H	PL	W49-44	11 (5)	11+2 (5)	-	9+3 (7)	7 (6)	R/R	3 (3)	-	8 (4)	-	-
26	16/7	Edinburgh	H	PL	W52-41	14 (5)	6+3 (5)	-	8+1 (7)	17+1 (6)	R/R	0 (3)	-	7 (4)	-	-
27	19/7	King's Lynn	A	PL	L41-52	17 (5)	3+1 (5)	-	11 (7)	9 (6)	-	-	-	R/R	-	1+1 (7)
28	22/7	Newport	H	PL	W55-39	14+1 (5)	7+3 (5)	-	15 (7)	12 (6)	R/R	-	-	5 (4)	-	2+2 (3)
29	23/7	Newport	A	PL	L44-45*	12+2 (5)	5+1 (5)	-	7 (7)	15 (6)	R/R	-	-	5 (4)	0 (3)	-
30	27/7	Redcar	A	PL	L38-57	11 (5)	4 (5)	-	3 (6)	16 (6)	R/R	-	-	3 (4)	1+1 (4)	-
31	5/8	Workington	A	PL	L42-53	6 (4)	9+1 (5)	-	3 (6)	13 (6)	R/R	-	-	8 (5)	-	3+1 (4)
32	6/8	Stoke	H	PL	W51-44	7+2 (4)	6+1 (5)	-	8+1 (6)	13+1 (6)	R/R	-	-	11 (5)	6+1 (4)	-
33	11/8	Edinburgh	A	PL	W46-44*	10+1 (5)	6+2 (5)	-	7+1 (7)	14+1 (6)	R/R	-	-	7+1 (4)	2 (3)	-
34	12/8	Berwick	A	PL	L40-50	12 (5)	5 (5)	-	2+1 (5)	13+1 (6)	R/R	-	-	7 (4)	1 (5)	-
35	13/8	Glasgow	A	PL	L36-60	9 (4)	0 (5)	-	1 (4)	19 (6)	R/R	-	-	2 (4)	5 (7)	-
36	20/8	Rye House	H	PL	L44-48	3 (2)	7+2 (4)	-	3 (1)	10 (5)	6 (5)	-	-	6+1 (4)	9+2 (7)	-
37	27/8	Sheffield	H	PL	L44-46	12+1 (5)	4 (4)	-	2 (5)	15 (5)	6+1 (4)	-	-	3+1 (4)	2+1 (3)	-
38	3/9	Workington	H	PL	L44-46	17 (6)	5+1 (4)	-	0 (4)	R/R	5+1 (5)	-	-	12+1 (6)	5 (5)	-
39	9/9	Somerset	H	PL	L40-50	8+1 (4)	9 (5)	-	6 (5)	10+2 (5)	3 (3)	-	-	3+1 (4)	1 (4)	-
40	14/9	Sheffield	A	PL	L27-63	8 (5)	6 (4)	-	4 (5)	6+1 (5)	2 (4)	-	-	0 (3)	-	1 (5)
41	17/9	Berwick	H	PL	L42-48	7+1 (4)	10 (5)	-	4+1 (4)	14 (5)	2+1 (4)	-	-	-	5+1 (5)	0 (3)
42	30/9	Stoke	A	PL	L29-63	5 (5)	6+1 (6)	-	4+1 (4)	R/R	10 (6)	-	-	-	2+2 (4)	2 (5)
43	21/10	Rye House	A	A11	L32-62	13 (5)	0 (4)	-	2 (4)	-	-	-	-	6+1 (5)	4 (4)	7+1 (8)

NOTE: SH = Suffolk-Herts Trophy; SC = Suffolk Cup; A11 = A11 Trophy. The result of the away league match at Newcastle on 11 June was altered after Craig Branney's appearance as a guest for Mildenhall was deemed ineligible. The original result had been a 48-42 defeat for the Fen Tigers.

DETAILS OF OTHER RIDERS

(all guests unless underlined)

Match No. 3: Stuart Robson 7+3 (4); Chris Neath 5+1 (4); Match No. 18: Joel Parsons 4 (4); Match No. 19: Craig Branney 10 (6); Match No. 23: Ben Powell 3+2 (5); Match No. 24: Matthew Wright 0 (3); Match No. 27: Ben Powell 1+1 (3); Richard Hall 0 (4); Match No. 28: Ben Powell 2+2 (3); Match No. 31: Ben Powell 3+1 (4); Match No. 40: Scott Richardson 1 (5); Match No. 41: Shane Henry 0 (3); Match No. 42: Mark Baseby 2 (5); Match No. 43: Rusty Harrison 6 (4); Paul Lee 1+1 (4).

DETAILS OF TACTICAL RIDES AND TACTICAL SUBSTITUTE RIDES

Match No. 2: D. King 4 points (TS); Match No. 3: D. King 4 points (TR); Robson 4 points (TR); Match No. 6: Lyons 6 points (TR); J. King 0 points (TR); Match No. 14: D. King 6 points (TR); Lyons 4 points (TR); Match No. 15: D. King 6 points (TR); Lyons 1 point (TR; not doubled); Match No. 16: Lyons 4 points (TR); Moore 0 points (TR); Match No. 20: D. King 6 points (TR); Lyons 4 points (TR); Match No. 21: Lyons 6 points (TR); Werner 0 points (TR); Match No. 23: Lyons 4 points (TR); D. King 4 points (TR); Match No. 27: Lyons 6 points (TR); Match No. 30: D. King 6 points (TR); Lyons 4 points (TR); Match No. 31: D. King 6 points (TR); J. King 4 points (TR); Match No. 35: Lyons 6 points (TR); D. King 6 points (TR); Match 40: D. King 1 point (TR; not doubled); Lyons 0 points (TR); Match No. 42: Armstrong 4 points (TR); Lyons 0 points (TR); Match No. 43: Harrison 4 points (TR); Lyons 4 points (TR).

AVERAGES

(26 Premier League, 2 Knock-Out Cup, 10 Premier Trophy = 38 fixtures)

♦ Denotes ever-present.

Rider	Mts	Rds	Pts	Bon	Tot	Avge	Max
Jason Lyons ♦	38	180	395	21	416	9.24	2 full; 2 paid
Daniel King	34	182	365	17	382	8.40	2 full; 1 paid
Jon Armstrong	24	128	193	24	217	6.78	-
Brent Werner	22	95	136	10	146	6.15	-
Shaun Tacey	11	44	60	5	65	5.91	-
Jason King	36	162	198	32	230	5.68	-
James Brundle ♦	38	184	182	25	207	4.50	-
Jordan Frampton	12	54	39	8	47	3.48	-
Barry Burchatt	20	60	30	7	37	2.47	-
Also rode (in alphabetical order):							
Andrew Moore	1	4	4	0	4	4.00	-
Ben Powell	1	4	3	1	4	4.00	-
Matthew Wright	1	3	0	0	0	0.00	-
Guests	8	32	13	5	18	2.25	-

(Mark Baseby [1]; Richard Hall [1]; Shane Henry [1]; Joel Parsons [1]; Ben Powell [3]; Scott Richardson [1]).

NOTE: Craig Branney guested for Mildenhall in the PL match at Newcastle, scoring 10 points from six rides, however, his appearance was deemed ineligible and was deleted from the records.

MILDENHALL: From left to right, back row: Jason Lyons, Jason King, Daniel King, James Brundle. Front row, kneeling: Jon Armstrong, Barry Burchatt. On bike: Shaun Tacey.

INDIVIDUAL MEETING

10 September: Shaun Tacey's 'Back with a Bang!' Testimonial

QUALIFYING SCORES: Leigh Lanham 11; Daniel King 11; Shaun Tacey 9; Jason Lyons 9; Jason King 8; James Brundle 8; Billy Janniro 7; Daniel Giffard 6; Mark Jones 6; Jimmy Jansson 5; Linus Eklof 5; Mark Baseby 4; Nicki Glanz 2; Andrew Bargh 2; Gary Cottham 1; Matt Browne 1. 12-LAP FINAL: 1st Janniro (8 points); 2nd Lanham (7); 3rd Giffard (6); 4th Brundle (5); 5th D. King (4); 6th J. King (3); 7th Tacey (2); 8th Jones (1). OVERALL SCORES: Lanham 18; Janniro 15; D. King 15; Brundle 13; Giffard 12; J. King 11; Tacey 11; Jones 7.

NEWCASTLE WARBURTONS DIAMONDS

ADDRESS: Brough Park Stadium, The Fossway, Byker, Newcastle-upon-Tyne, Tyne and Wear, NE6 2XJ.

PROMOTERS: Darryl Illingworth, George English and Barry Wallace.

YEARS OF OPERATION: 1929 English Dirt-Track League; 1930 Open; 1938-1939 National League Division Two; 1945 Open; 1946 Northern League; 1947-1951 National League Division Two; 1961-1964 Provincial League; 1965-1967 British League; 1968-1970 British League Division One; 1975-1983 National League; 1984 British League; 1986-1987 National League; 1989-1990 National League; 1991-1994 British League Division Two; 1997-2001 Premier League; 2002-2004 Premier League and Conference League; 2005-2006 Premier League.

FIRST MEETING: 17 May 1929.

TRACK LENGTH: 300 metres.

TRACK RECORD: 62.1 seconds – Kenneth Bjerre (20/07/03).

CLUB HONOURS

LEAGUE CHAMPIONS: 1964, 1976, 1982, 1983, 2001.

PAIRS CHAMPIONS: 1975.

FOUR-TEAM CHAMPIONS: 1976, 1982, 1983.

KNOCK-OUT CUP WINNERS: 1976, 1982.

SUPERNATIONAL WINNERS: 1982, 1983.

GOLD CUP WINNERS: 1991, 1992.

RIDER ROSTER 2006

Josef FRANC; James GRIEVES; Manuel HAUZINGER; Christian HENRY; Adam McKINNA; Jamie ROBERTSON; George STANCL.

OTHER APPEARANCES/GUESTS (official matches only)

Craig BRANNEY; Ashley JOHNSON; Emil KRAMER; David McALLAN; Chris MILLS; Glen PHILLIPS; Emiliano SANCHEZ; Derek SNEDDON; Sean STODDART.

NEWCASTLE

* Denotes aggregate/bonus-point victory

NO.	DATE	OPPONENTS	VENUE	COMPETITION	RESULT	STANCL	HENRY	HAUZINGER	FRANC	GRIEVES	McKINNA	ROBERTSON	OTHERS
1	11/3	Berwick	A	TT	W49-41	8+1 (5)	7+1 (4)	4+1 (4)	14 (5)	10 (4)	1 (4)	5 (4)	-
2	19/3	Workington	H	PT	W47-46	11+1 (5)	2 (4)	3 (3)	12+1 (5)	13 (5)	1 (3)	5+1 (5)	-
3	30/3	Sheffield	A	PT	L30-64	11 (5)	2+1 (5)	1 (3)	8+1 (5)	4 (4)	1+1 (4)	3 (4)	-
4	1/4	Stoke	A	PT	L44-45	12+2 (5)	7 (4)	4 (3)	5 (4)	11 (5)	2 (5)	3+2 (4)	-

NO.	DATE	OPPONENTS	VENUE	COMPETITION	RESULT	STANCL	HENRY	HAUZINGER	FRANC	GRIEVES	McKINNA	ROBERTSON	OTHERS
5	8/4	Berwick	A	PT	W48-42	7+1 (4)	9 (5)	R/R	15 (5)	11+1 (5)	2 (5)	4+1 (6)	-
6	9/4	Edinburgh	H	PT	L46-47	10 (5)	5+1 (4)	R/R	12 (5)	5 (4)	5 (6)	9+2 (6)	-
7	16/4	Glasgow	A	PT	L36-54	10 (5)	4+1 (4)	5 (4)	3+1 (4)	8 (5)	2+1 (4)	-	4+1 (4)
8	17/4	Glasgow	H	PT	W53-42	12 (5)	5+1 (4)	4+1 (4)	15 (5)	4 (4)	2 (4)	-	11+1 (5)
9	21/4	Workington	A	PT	L40-50	7+2 (4)	5 (4)	3+1 (4)	10 (5)	10+1 (5)	4 (5)	1+1 (3)	-
10	23/4	Redcar	H	PT	W53-42	7+1 (4)	8+1 (4)	3+1 (4)	8 (5)	13 (5)	3+1 (3)	11+3 (5)	-
11	28/4	Edinburgh	A	PT	L44-51	14+1 (5)	9+1 (5)	R/R	11 (5)	7 (4)	1 (5)	2 (6)	-
12	30/4	Newport	A	PL	L44-46	10 (5)	3 (4)	1+1 (3)	10+2 (5)	9 (4)	2+1 (4)	9 (5)	-
13	1/5	Sheffield	H	PT	W53-38	6+1 (4)	10+1 (4)	4 (4)	12 (5)	12 (4)	1 (4)	8+2 (5)	-
14	4/5	Redcar	A	PT	L44-51*	5+1 (4)	R/R	5 (5)	18 (6)	9 (6)	0 (1)	7+1 (7)	-
15	7/5	Berwick	H	PT	W51-44*	15 (5)	R/R	1 (4)	11+1 (5)	8+1 (4)	-	9+1 (6)	7 (6)
16	23/5	Isle of Wight	A	PL	L35-57	2+1 (4)	4 (4)	9 (4)	8 (5)	10 (5)	0 (3)	2+1 (5)	-
17	27/5	Workington	A	KOC	L40-54	7 (4)	13 (5)	4+1 (4)	10+2 (5)	3 (4)	-	2 (4)	1 (4)
18	28/5	Workington	H	KOC	W55-40*	8+1 (4)	9+1 (4)	7+1 (4)	9+2 (5)	13 (5)	-	9+3 (5)	0 (3)
19	5/6	Newport	H	PL	W53-37*	8 (4)	10+1 (5)	2 (4)	8 (4)	13+1 (5)	-	11+2 (5)	1 (3)
20	10/6	Mildenhall	A	PL	L41-51	10 (5)	7+1 (4)	3+1 (4)	11+1 (5)	7 (4)	1+1 (4)	2 (4)	-
21	11/6	Mildenhall	H	PL	W48-32*	3+1 (4)	9+1 (4)	9+2 (4)	9+2 (5)	10+1 (5)	3+1 (4)	5+1 (4)	-
22	19/6	Rye House	H	PL	W47-42	9 (5)	9+1 (4)	5+1 (4)	5+1 (4)	11 (5)	2+1 (3)	-	6 (5)
23	25/6	Glasgow	A	KOC	L41-55	5 (4)	9+1 (5)	0 (1)	6 (4)	14 (5)	1 (4)	-	6+1 (7)
24	26/6	Glasgow	H	KOC	W48-42	10 (5)	11+1 (5)	R/R	11+2 (5)	11 (4)	0 (5)	-	5+1 (6)
25	29/6	Redcar	A	PL	L43-49	12 (5)	6 (3)	0 (1)	5+1 (5)	10 (4)	1 (5)	-	9+2 (7)
26	2/7	Stoke	H	PT	W54-41*	13+2 (5)	12 (5)	R/R	8+3 (4)	13 (5)	0 (4)	-	8 (7)
27	10/7	Edinburgh	H	PL	W50-42	15 (6)	13+2 (5)	-	15+1 (6)	R/R	0 (3)	-	7+1 (10)
28	13/7	Sheffield	A	PL	L32-60	6 (4)	10+1 (6)	R/R	3 (5)	4+1 (4)	1+1 (4)	-	8+4 (7)
29	16/7	Redcar	H	PL	W49-42*	12+1 (5)	10+1 (5)	R/R	7 (4)	13 (5)	3+1 (7)	4 (4)	-
30	22/7	Stoke	A	PL	L42-47	5+2 (4)	6 (3)	10 (5)	5+2 (4)	7+1 (5)	3 (3)	6+1 (6)	-
31	23/7	Workington	H	PL	W53-39	7+1 (4)	10+2 (4)	7+1 (4)	10+2 (5)	11 (5)	4 (4)	4+3 (4)	-
32	30/7	Somerset	H	PL	D45-45	13 (5)	6 (4)	3 (4)	9+2 (5)	5 (4)	5 (4)	4+1 (4)	-
33	6/8	Berwick	H	PL	W49-44	12 (5)	10 (5)	R/R	11+2 (5)	8 (4)	1+1 (5)	7+2 (6)	-
34	11/8	Somerset	A	PL	L37-57	9+1 (4)	10+1 (5)	4+1 (4)	8+1 (5)	4 (4)	0 (4)	2 (4)	-
35	25/8	King's Lynn	A	PL	L31-62	5 (4)	7 (5)	2 (4)	10 (5)	5 (4)	0 (4)	2+1 (4)	-
36	27/8	Glasgow	A	PL	L40-55	10 (5)	8 (4)	2 (3)	10+1 (5)	4+1 (4)	5 (6)	1+1 (3)	-
37	28/8	Glasgow	H	PL	W50-40	11+1 (4)	9+1 (4)	0 (3)	11+2 (5)	11+1 (5)	0 (3)	8+2 (6)	-
38	3/9	Sheffield	H	PL	W47-46	6+1 (4)	13+2 (6)	R/R	10+1 (5)	7 (4)	3+1 (4)	8+1 (7)	-
39	4/9	King's Lynn	H	PL	W46-44	6 (4)	11+2 (5)	R/R	12+2 (5)	13 (5)	0 (4)	4+1 (7)	-
40	8/9	Rye House	A	PL	L21-69	5 (4)	R/R	-	5 (6)	6 (5)	1 (5)	1 (5)	3+1 (5)
41	10/9	Isle of Wight	H	PL	W52-40	5 (3)	14+1 (5)	R/R	13+2 (5)	13+1 (5)	2 (5)	5+1 (7)	-
42	15/9	Edinburgh	A	PL	L46-51*	2 (2)	9 (5)	R/R	16 (5)	6 (5)	1 (2)	11+2 (7)	0 (1)
43	16/9	Workington	A	PL	L35-60	-	0 (2)	R/R	15 (5)	3 (4)	-	7 (7)	10+2 (12)
44	17/9	Stoke	H	PL	W49-41*	-	R/R	-	17 (6)	11 (5)	-	5+1 (5)	16+2 (14)
45	14/10	Redcar	A	TTT	L42-54	19 (6)	5+1 (5)	-	14 (5)	R/R	3+1 (5)	1 (3)	0 (5)
46	22/10	Redcar	H	TTT	L41-49	12 (5)	11+1 (6)	-	10+2 (6)	R/R	2+1 (5)	6 (5)	0 (3)

NOTE: TT = Tyne-Tweed Trophy; TTT = Tyne-Tees Trophy. The result of the home league match versus Mildenhall on 11 June was altered after Craig Branney's appearance as a guest for the visitor's was deemed ineligible. The original result had been a 48-42 victory for the Diamonds.

NEWCASTLE: From left to right: Josef Franc, George Stancl, Adam McKinna, George English (co-promoter/team manager), James Grieves (on bike), Christian Henry, Jamie Robertson, Manuel Hauzinger.

DETAILS OF OTHER RIDERS

(all guests)

Match No. 7: Derek Sneddon 4+1 (4); Match No. 8: Derek Sneddon 11+1 (5); Match No. 15: Sean Stoddart 7 (6); Match No. 17: Sean Stoddart 1 (4); Match No. 18: Sean Stoddart 0 (3); Match No. 19: Sean Stoddart 1 (3); Match No. 22: Craig Branney 6 (5); Match No. 23: Derek Sneddon 6+1 (7); Match No. 24: Chris Mills 5+1 (6); Match No. 25: Chris Mills 9+2 (7); Match No. 26: Derek Sneddon 8 (7); Match No. 27: Chris Mills 4 (5); David McAllan 3+1 (5); Match No. 28: Chris Mills 8+4 (7); Match No. 40: Glen Phillips 3+1 (5); Match No. 42: Ashley Johnson 0 (1); Match No. 43: Emiliano Sanchez 8 (5); Sean Stoddart 2+2 (7); Match No. 44: Emil Kramer 8+1 (4); Sean Stoddart 6+1 (6); Ashley Johnson 2 (4); Match No. 45: Lee Dicken 0 (5); Match No. 46: Sean Stoddart 0 (3).

DETAILS OF TACTICAL RIDES AND TACTICAL SUBSTITUTE RIDES

Match No. 2: Franc 6 points (TR); Stancl 1 point (TS; not doubled); Match No. 3: Stancl 4 points (TR); Franc 4 points (TR); Henry 0 points (TS); Match No. 11: Franc 6 points (TR); Stancl 4 points (TR); Match No. 14: Franc 6 points (TR); Grieves 4 points (TR); Match No. 16: Grieves 4 points (TR); Stancl 0 points (TR); Match No. 17: Henry 6 points (TR); Franc 2 points (TR); Match No. 20: Franc 6 points (TR); Match No. 23: Henry 6 points (TR); Grieves 6 points (TR); Match No. 25: Grieves 6 points (TR); Match No. 28: Henry 4 points (TR); Franc 0 points (TR); Match No. 34: Stancl 4 points (TR); Henry 4 points (TR); Match No. 35: Franc 4 points (TR); Henry 2 points (TR); Match No. 36: Henry 6 points (TR); Franc 4 points (TR); Match No. 40: Stancl 1 point (TR; not doubled); Franc 1 point (TR; not doubled); Match No. 42: Franc 6 points (TR); Henry 6 points (TR); Match No. 43: Franc 6 points (TR); Sanchez 4 points (TR); Match No. 45: Stancl 6 points (TR); Franc 6 points (TR).

AVERAGES

(26 Premier League, 4 Knock-Out Cup, 14 Premier Trophy = 44 fixtures)

Rider	Mts	Rds	Pts	Bon	Tot	Avge	Max
Josef Franc	43	211	402	38	440	8.34	2 full; 1 paid
George Stancl	42	187	362	22	384	8.21	1 full; 2 paid
James Grieves	43	197	370	12	382	7.76	1 full
Christian Henry	40	177	299	27	326	7.37	3 paid
Jamie Robertson	35	180	184	38	222	4.93	-
Manuel Hauzinger	28	104	110	13	123	4.73	-
Adam McKinna	38	155	63	11	74	1.91	-
Guests	21	106	100	16	116	4.38	-

(Craig Branney [1]; Ashley Johnson [2]; Emil Kramer [1]; David McAllan [1]; Chris Mills [4]; Glen Phillips [1]; Emiliano Sanchez [1]; Derek Sneddon [4]; Sean Stoddart [6]).

EVEREST GROUP NEWPORT WASPS

NOTE: The information below relates only to the main Newport team. For details of the second side, please refer to the Conference League section.

ADDRESS: Hayley Stadium, Plover Close, Nash Mead, Queensway Meadows, Newport, South Wales, NS19 4SU.
PROMOTER: Tim Stone.
YEARS OF OPERATION: 1997–2006 Premier League.
FIRST MEETING: 4 May 1997.
TRACK LENGTH: 285 metres.
TRACK RECORD: 58.38 seconds – Craig Watson (03/08/03).

PREVIOUS VENUE: Somerton Park Stadium, Somerton Park, Newport, Gwent, South Wales.
YEARS OF OPERATION: 1964 Provincial League; 1965-1967 British League; 1968-1974 British League Division One; 1975-1976 British League; 1977 National League.

CLUB HONOURS

PREMIER NATIONAL TROPHY WINNERS: 1999.

RIDER ROSTER 2006

Tony ATKIN; Neil COLLINS; Sam HURST; Billy LEGG; Joel PARSONS; Chris SCHRAMM, Craig WATSON; Carl WILKINSON.

OTHER APPEARANCES/GUESTS (official matches only)

Andre COMPTON; Kevin DOOLAN; Josef FRANC; Chris HOLDER; Stephan KATT; Mads KORNELIUSSEN; Emil KRAMER; Mark LEMON; Phil MORRIS; Chris NEATH; Ulrich OSTERGAARD.

NEWPORT

* Denotes aggregate/bonus-point victory

NO.	DATE	OPPONENTS	VENUE	COMPETITION	RESULT	COLLINS	SCHRAMM	WILKINSON	ATKIN	WATSON	PARSONS	LEGG	HURST	OTHERS
1	10/3	Somerset	A	BCA	L41-52	3+1 (4)	10 (5)	4+1 (4)	5 (4)	11 (5)	8+3 (7)	0 (1)	-	-
2	19/3	Isle of Wight	H	PT	W47-42	11+1 (5)	3+1 (4)	8+1 (4)	8+1 (4)	12 (5)	5+1 (5)		0 (3)	-
3	22/3	King's Lynn	A	PT	L44-52	4+2 (4)	7 (4)	12 (5)	1+1 (4)	15 (5)	5+1 (5)		0 (3)	-
4	2/4	Mildenhall	H	PT	D45-45	9+1 (5)	6+1 (4)	8+2 (4)	5 (4)	12 (5)	4 (6)		1+1 (3)	-
5	8/4	Mildenhall	A	PT	L40-49	2 (4)	5+1 (4)	9+1 (5)	5+2 (4)	7 (5)	12+3 (7)	0 (0)	-	-
6	9/4	Rye House	H	PT	W47-46	7+2 (4)	7+2 (4)	14+1 (5)	4+2 (4)	10 (5)	4+1 (5)		1 (3)	-

NO.	DATE	OPPONENTS	VENUE	COMPETITION	RESULT	COLLINS	SCHRAMM	WILKINSON	ATKIN	WATSON	PARSONS	LEGG	HURST	OTHERS
7	14/4	Somerset	A	PT	L40-55	8 (5)	4+1 (4)	12 (4)	4+2 (4)	10 (5)	2 (5)	0 (3)	-	-
8	16/4	Somerset	H	PT	W51-44	9+2 (5)	9+1 (4)	10+1 (5)	7+1 (4)	8 (4)	7 (5)	1+1 (3)	-	-
9	23/4	Edinburgh	H	PL	W62-31	10+2 (5)	9+2 (4)	10+1 (4)	6+1 (4)	12 (5)	9+1 (5)	6+3 (3)	-	-
10	30/4	Newcastle	H	PL	W46-44	7+2 (5)	7+2 (4)	5 (4)	6+1 (4)	15 (5)	6+1 (6)	0 (2)	-	-
11	1/5	Rye House	A	PT	L38-58	1+1 (1)	6 (4)	10 (5)	4+1 (4)	11 (5)	6 (7)	-	0 (4)	-
12	6/5	Stoke	A	PL	L36-50	R/R	5+1 (5)	12 (5)	3 (5)	12 (5)	4+1 (5)	0 (3)	-	-
13	7/5	Stoke	H	PL	L44-52	R/R	8 (6)	12 (5)	15+1 (6)	-	3 (4)	1 (3)	-	5 (5)
14	13/5	Workington	A	PL	L39-51	R/R	4+1 (5)	9+1 (6)	6+3 (5)	-	3 (4)	1+1 (3)	-	16 (7)
15	14/5	King's Lynn	H	PT	W48-45	R/R	11+1 (5)	14 (6)	4+1 (5)	-	4+1 (5)	-	2+1 (3)	13+1 (6)
16	18/5	Sheffield	A	PL	L30-63	R/R	1+1 (5)	12 (6)	5+1 (5)	-	6 (5)	-	0 (3)	6 (6)
17	19/5	Edinburgh	A	KOC	L40-56	R/R	5 (5)	12 (6)	2+2 (5)	-	6+1 (5)	-	0 (3)	15+1 (6)
18	2/6	Glasgow	H	PL	L44-46	R/R	7+2 (5)	7 (6)	11+1 (5)	-	4+1 (6)	2+1 (3)	-	13 (5)
19	5/6	Newcastle	A	PL	L37-53	R/R	6 (5)	10+1 (6)	6+2 (5)	-	6+1 (5)	0 (4)	-	9+1 (5)
20	11/6	Isle of Wight	H	PL	W47-43	-	10 (6)	R/R	12+1 (5)	-	3+1 (4)	3 (4)	-	19+3 (11)
21	22/6	Isle of Wight	A	PT	L34-61	R/R	7+1 (5)	13+1 (6)	9 (5)	-	3 (6)	-	0 (4)	2 (4)
22	27/6	Edinburgh	H	KOC	W55-31*	6+2 (4)	9+3 (4)	10+1 (4)	9 (4)	-	9+2 (5)	0 (3)	-	12 (4)
23	29/6	Glasgow	A	PL	L38-52	7 (4)	8+2 (4)	8 (5)	7+1 (4)	-	2 (5)	0 (3)	-	6 (5)
24	30/6	Edinburgh	A	PL	L37-53*	2+1 (4)	4 (4)	9 (5)	4+1 (4)	-	10 (5)	0 (3)	-	8 (5)
25	2/7	Workington	H	PL	W58-35*	7+3 (4)	6 (4)	8 (3)	8 (4)	-	14+2 (7)	1 (3)	-	14+1 (5)
26	6/7	Sheffield	A	KOC	L33-59	4 (4)	3+1 (4)	5 (5)	3+2 (4)	-	7+1 (5)	0 (3)	-	11 (5)
27	9/7	Sheffield	H	KOC	L39-50	8+1 (5)	7+1 (5)	8 (4)	2+2 (4)	-	4 (5)	3+1 (2)	-	7 (4)
28	13/7	Redcar	A	PL	W51-39	7+2 (4)	10+1 (5)	6 (4)	5+2 (4)	-	9+1 (5)	1 (3)	-	13 (5)
29	16/7	King's Lynn	H	PL	L39-54	5+1 (4)	10+2 (5)	4 (4)	4+2 (4)	-	9+2 (7)	1 (3)	-	6 (4)
30	22/7	Mildenhall	A	PL	L39-55	1+1 (3)	4 (4)	5+2 (5)	3+2 (4)	-	13 (6)	0 (3)	-	13 (5)
31	23/7	Mildenhall	H	PL	W45-44	6+1 (4)	4+2 (4)	7+1 (5)	6+1 (4)	-	14 (6)	1 (3)	-	7+1 (4)
32	25/7	Isle of Wight	A	PL	L40-50	5 (4)	8+1 (4)	8 (5)	4+3 (4)	-	8+2 (6)	0 (3)	-	7 (4)
33	6/8	Redcar	H	PL	L47-49*	7+2 (4)	8+1 (4)	7 (5)	6+1 (4)	-	7+3 (5)	0 (3)	-	12+1 (5)
34	18/8	Somerset	A	PL	L35-58	7 (5)	1 (4)	5 (4)	1 (4)	-	6 (5)	1+1 (3)	-	14 (5)
35	27/8	Somerset	H	PL	L43-47	9+1 (4)	2+1 (4)	10 (5)	7+1 (4)	-	9+2 (5)	0 (3)	-	6+1 (5)
36	28/8	Rye House	A	PL	L28-64	3 (4)	6 (6)	7 (6)	7 (5)	R/R	5+2 (6)	0 (3)	-	-
37	3/9	Berwick	H	PL	L41-49	4+3 (4)	8 (5)	6 (4)	4+3 (4)	-	9 (5)	0 (3)	-	10+1 (5)
38	9/9	Berwick	A	PL	D47-47	3+1 (3)	5 (4)	11+1 (5)	8+1 (4)	-	9 (5)	4+2 (4)	-	7+1 (5)
39	10/9	Sheffield	H	PL	W45-44	R/R	10+2 (5)	9+3 (6)	5+1 (5)	-	13+1 (6)	0 (3)	-	8 (5)
40	13/9	King's Lynn	A	PL	L26-64	R/R	2+1 (5)	6+1 (6)	3 (5)	-	4 (6)	0 (3)	-	11 (5)
41	17/9	Rye House	H	PL	L43-51	R/R	14 (6)	2 (3)	5+4 (5)	-	11+1 (7)	0 (4)	-	11 (5)

NOTE: BCA = BCA Vehicle Remarketing Trophy. The away league match at Stoke on 6 May was abandoned after heat fourteen, with the result permitted to stand. The home Knock-Out Cup tie versus Edinburgh on 27 June was abandoned after heat fourteen, with the result permitted to stand

DETAILS OF OTHER RIDERS

(all guests)

Match No. 13: Chris Neath 5 (5); Match No. 14: Andre Compton 16 (7); Match No. 15: Chris Neath 13+1 (6); Match No. 16: Chris Holder 6 (6); Match No. 17: Andre Compton 15+1 (6); Match No. 18: Chris Neath 13 (5); Match No. 19: Andre Compton

9+1 (5); Match No. 20: Mark Lemon 12 (6); Phil Morris 7+3 (5); Match No. 21: Stephan Katt 2 (4); Match No. 22: Chris Neath 12 (4); Match No. 23: Chris Neath 6 (5); Match No. 24: Mark Lemon 8 (5); Match No. 25: Chris Neath 14+1 (5); Match No. 26: Kevin Doolan 11 (5); Match No. 27: Kevin Doolan 7 (4); Match No. 28: Chris Neath 13 (5); Match No. 29: Chris Neath 6 (4); Match No. 30: Emil Kramer 13 (5); Match No. 31: Chris Neath 7+1 (4); Match No. 32: Mads Korneliussen 7 (4); Match No. 33: Chris Neath 12+1 (5); Match No. 34: Chris Neath 14 (5); Match No. 35: Chris Neath 6+1 (5); Match No. 37: Chris Neath 10+1 (5); Match No. 38: Josef Franc 7+1 (5); Match No. 39: Chris Neath 8 (5); Match No. 40: Ulrich Ostergaard 11 (5); Match No. 41: Chris Holder 11 (5).

DETAILS OF TACTICAL RIDES AND TACTICAL SUBSTITUTE RIDES

Match No. 1: Schramm 6 points (TR); Match No. 3: Watson 6 points (TR); Wilkinson 6 points (TR); Match No. 6: Wilkinson 6 points (TR); Match No. 7: Wilkinson 6 points (TR); Watson 4 points (TR); Match No. 11: Watson 6 points (TR); Wilkinson 6 points (TR); Match No. 12: Watson 4 points (TR); Atkin 1 point (TR; not doubled); Match No. 13: Wilkinson 6 points (TR); Atkin 6 points (TR); Match No. 14: Compton 1 point (TS; not doubled); Match No. 16: Wilkinson 6 points (TR); Atkin 1 point (TR; not doubled); Match No. 17: Compton 6 points (TR); Wilkinson 6 points (TR); Match No. 19: Schramm 1 point (TR; not doubled); Wilkinson 0 points (TR); Match No. 21: Wilkinson 6 points (TR); Atkin 4 points (TR); Match No. 24: Wilkinson 2 points (TR); Parsons 1 point (TR; not doubled); Match No. 26: Doolan 4 points (TR); Collins 0 points (TR); Match No. 29: Schramm 6 points (TR); Wilkinson 1 point (TR; not doubled); Match No. 30: Kramer 4 points (TR); Parsons 4 points (TR); Match No. 34: Neath 6 points (TR); Collins 1 point (TR; not doubled); Match No. 36: Atkin 4 points (TR); Schramm 0 points (TR); Match No. 38: Atkin 4 points (TR); Wilkinson 4 points (TR); Match No. 40: Ostergaard 1 point (TR; not doubled); Wilkinson 1 point (TR; not doubled); Match No. 41: Schramm 6 points (TR); Parsons 4 points (TR).

AVERAGES

(26 Premier League, 4 Knock-Out Cup, 10 Premier Trophy = 40 fixtures)
♦ Denotes ever-present.

Rider	Mts	Rds	Pts	Bon	Tot	Avge	Max
Craig Watson	11	54	114	0	114	8.44	1 full
Carl Wilkinson	39	190	313	19	332	6.99	-
Neil Collins	27	111	159	32	191	6.88	-
Chris Schramm ♦	40	182	250	36	286	6.29	1 paid
Tony Atkin ♦	40	175	215	51	266	6.08	-
Joel Parsons ♦	40	217	270	33	303	5.59	-
Billy Legg	31	92	26	10	36	1.57	-
Sam Hurst	9	29	4	2	6	0.83	-
Guests	29	145	271	12	283	7.81	1 full; 1 paid

(Andre Compton [3]; Kevin Doolan [2]; Josef Franc [1]; Chris Holder [2]; Stephan Katt [1]; Mads Korneliussen [1]; Emil Kramer [1]; Mark Lemon [2]; Phil Morris [1]; Chris Neath [14]; Ulrich Ostergaard [1])

INDIVIDUAL MEETINGS

9 January: New Year Classic

QUALIFYING SCORES: Brent Werner 12; Chris Neath 12; Leigh Lanham 11; Chris Harris 11; Niels-Kristian Iversen 10; Richard Hall 7; Sean Wilson 7; Robbie Kessler 6; Michael Coles 5; Mads

NEWPORT: From left to right, back row: Chris Schramm, Sam Hurst, Carl Wilkinson, Neil Street (team manager), Craig Watson, Joel Parsons, Neil Collins. Front row, on bike: Tony Atkin.

Korneliussen 4; Paul Clews 4; Neil Collins 1; Karl Mason (Reserve) 0. FINAL: 1st Werner; 2nd Harris; 3rd Lanham; 4th Neath.

4 June: Welsh Open Championship

QUALIFYING SCORES: Zdenek Simota 13; Chris Holder 12; Ricky Ashworth 11; Jason Bunyan 10; Brent Werner 9; Mads Korneliussen 9; Andy Smith 9; Chris Schramm 8; Leigh Lanham 8; Phil Morris 7; Carl Wilkinson 7; Kevin Doolan 5; Krzysztof Stojanowski 4; Adam Shields 3; Tony Atkin 3; Troy Batchelor 2; Tom Hedley (Reserve) 0. FINAL: 1st Holder; 2nd Simota; 3rd Ashworth; 4th Bunyan.

15 October: Inter-League Trophy

QUALIFYING SCORES: Billy Legg 10; Nicki Glanz 10; Karl Mason 8; Carl Wilkinson 8; Joel Parsons 7; Chris Schramm 7; Tony Atkin 6; Sam Hurst 5; Mattie Bates 5; Ben Hopwood 3; Tim Webster 2; Joe Reynolds 1. QUARTER-FINAL: 1st Schramm; 2nd Hurst; 3rd Bates; 4th Atkin. SEMI-FINAL: 1st Schramm; 2nd Mason; 3rd Wilkinson; 4th Parsons. FINAL: 1st Schramm; 2nd Glanz; 3rd Legg; 4th Mason.

REDCAR BEARS

ADDRESS: South Tees Motorsports Park, Dormer Way, South Bank Road, Middlesbrough, Cleveland, TS6 6XH.
PROMOTERS: Chris Van Straaten and Gareth Rogers.
YEARS OF OPERATION: 2006 Premier League.
FIRST MEETING: 13 April 2006.
TRACK LENGTH: 266 metres.
TRACK RECORD: 53.0 seconds – Gary Havelock (31/08/06).

CLUB HONOURS

NONE.

RIDER ROSTER 2006

Daniel GIFFARD; Jack HARGREAVES; Gary HAVELOCK; Richard JUUL; Chris KERR; Kevin LITTLE; Tomas SUCHANEK; Mathieu TRESARRIEU.

OTHER APPEARANCES/GUESTS (official matches only)

Benji COMPTON; Rusty HODGSON; Trent LEVERINGTON: Derek SNEDDON; Matthew WETHERS; Tai WOFFINDEN.

REDCAR

* Denotes aggregate/bonus-point victory

NO.	DATE	OPPONENTS	VENUE	COMPETITION	RESULT	HAVELOCK	JUUL	LITTLE	SUCHANEK	KERR	HARGREAVES	GIFFARD	TRESARRIEU	OTHERS
1	13/4	Sheffield	H	PT	L44-46	15 (5)	2+1 (3)	9 (5)	0 (4)	7 (4)	4 (4)	7+2 (5)	-	-
2	14/4	Sheffield	A	PT	L36-56	15 (5)	3+1 (4)	5 (4)	6+1 (5)	2 (4)	2 (4)	3+1 (4)	-	-
3	15/4	Stoke	A	PT	L43.5-49.5	14 (5)	8.5 (4)	7 (5)	3+1 (4)	4+1 (4)	4 (4)	3+1 (4)	-	-
4	20/4	Edinburgh	H	PT	W45-44	13+1 (5)	2+1 (3)	12+1 (5)	3+2 (4)	7+1 (4)	3 (4)	5+1 (5)	-	-
5	21/4	Edinburgh	A	PT	L40-52	16 (5)	3 (4)	8 (5)	3 (4)	4 (4)	3 (4)	3+2 (4)	-	-
6	22/4	Berwick	A	PT	L43-53	15 (5)	5 (4)	5+1 (4)	10 (5)	4 (4)	1+1 (4)	3 (4)	-	-
7	23/4	Newcastle	A	PT	L42-53	16 (5)	2 (4)	12 (5)	5+1 (5)	2+1 (4)	3 (4)	2 (3)	-	-
8	26/4	Berwick	H	PT	W54-39*	14 (5)	6+2 (4)	9+3 (5)	7 (4)	5+1 (4)	7+1 (4)	6+1 (4)	-	-
9	4/5	Newcastle	H	PT	W51-44	11+1 (5)	5+2 (4)	10 (4)	6+1 (4)	10+2 (5)	3 (4)	6+1 (4)	-	-
10	10/5	King's Lynn	A	PL	L22-70	6 (5)	-	0 (0)	2 (4)	8 (5)	2 (5)	2 (7)	2 (4)	-
11	11/5	Glasgow	H	PT	W46-44	14 (5)	-	R/R	13+1 (6)	5+1 (4)	2+1 (5)	7+1 (5)	5+2 (5)	-
12	12/5	Somerset	A	PL	L41-57	16 (5)	-	R/R	14 (6)	3 (4)	1 (5)	0 (5)	7+1 (5)	-
13	14/5	Glasgow	A	PT	L36-58	8 (4)	-	-	-	4 (6)	3 (5)	1 (4)	R/R	20+2 (11)
14	18/5	Workington	H	PT	L42-49	11 (5)	-	R/R	8 (5)	6+1 (5)	9+1 (6)	5 (6)	3+2 (3)	-

NO.	DATE	OPPONENTS	VENUE	COMPETITION	RESULT	HAVELOCK	JUUL	LITTLE	SUCHANEK	KERR	HARGREAVES	GIFFARD	TRESARRIEU	OTHERS
15	25/5	Isle of Wight	H	PL	W51-42	13 (5)	-	5+1 (4)	10 (5)	5+1 (4)	6+2 (4)	7+3 (4)	5+1 (4)	
16	1/6	Stoke	H	PT	W48-43	14 (5)	-	6+2 (5)	6 (5)	7 (6)	7+1 (5)	8 (4)	R/R	
17	8/6	Edinburgh	H	PL	W56-38	14+1 (5)	-	4+1 (4)	11+1 (5)	6+1 (4)	7 (5)	5+1 (2)	9+1 (4)	
18	15/6	Glasgow	H	PL	W59-36	14 (5)	-	7+3 (4)	12 (5)	6 (4)	5+2 (4)	9+1 (4)	6+3 (4)	
19	17/6	Rye House	A	PL	L40-54	16 (5)	-	5 (4)	9+1 (5)	3 (4)	1 (4)	3 (4)	3+1 (4)	
20	22/6	Rye House	H	PL	W47-43	14+1 (5)	-	6+2 (4)	9+1 (5)	0 (4)	5+1 (4)	6 (4)	7+2 (4)	
21	23/6	Workington	A	PT	L43-50	16 (5)	-	3+2 (5)	7+1 (6)	6 (5)	5+2 (4)	6 (5)	R/R	
22	29/6	Newcastle	H	PL	W49-43	14 (5)	-	4+1 (4)	9+2 (5)	5 (4)	6 (4)	10 (5)	1+1 (3)	
23	2/7	Mildenhall	A	PL	D45-45	5+1 (4)	-	7+1 (4)	11 (5)	3+1 (4)	1 (3)	9+1 (5)	9+2 (5)	
24	6/7	Berwick	H	PL	W64-26	15 (5)	-	7+2 (4)	9 (4)	8+4 (5)	10+1 (4)	9+1 (4)	6+2 (4)	
25	8/7	Stoke	A	PL	W53-42	13 (5)	-	5+1 (5)	7 (4)	7+2 (4)	6+2 (4)	6+2 (4)	9+1 (4)	
26	13/7	Newport	H	PL	L39-51	13 (5)	-	3+1 (4)	5+1 (5)	5+2 (6)	5 (5)	8+1 (5)	R/R	
27	14/7	Edinburgh	A	PL	L39-53*	16 (5)	-	7 (5)	7 (5)	3 (5)	4 (6)	2+1 (4)	R/R	
28	16/7	Newcastle	A	PL	L42-49	13 (5)	-	9 (5)	8+2 (6)	4+2 (5)	0 (3)	8 (6)	R/R	
29	20/7	Stoke	H	PL	W56-40*	12 (4)	-	4 (4)	14 (5)	8+2 (4)	3+1 (4)	9+4 (5)	6+2 (4)	
30	22/7	Berwick	A	PL	L41-50*	10 (4)	-	7+1 (5)	9+1 (6)	5 (4)	0 (3)	4 (4)	6+1 (4)	
31	27/7	Mildenhall	H	PL	W57-38*	10 (4)	-	9+1 (4)	13+2 (5)	1 (4)	4+2 (4)	9+1 (4)	11 (5)	
32	6/8	Newport	A	PL	W49-47	17 (5)	-	11+1 (4)	5 (4)	2+1 (4)	4 (4)	6 (5)	4+1 (4)	
33	10/8	Sheffield	A	PL	L41-49	13 (5)	-	1+1 (4)	5+1 (4)	4+1 (4)	3+1 (3)	7+1 (5)	8+1 (5)	
34	11/8	Sheffield	H	PL	W48-42	14 (5)	-	6 (4)	11+2 (5)	2+1 (4)	2+1 (3)	8 (5)	5+1 (4)	
35	17/8	Somerset	H	PL	W54-39	12 (5)	-	5 (4)	7+1 (4)	6+2 (4)	1 (3)	11+3 (5)	12 (5)	
36	20/8	Glasgow	A	PL	L42-53*	15 (5)	-	7 (5)	2 (4)	7 (4)	1 (4)	8+1 (5)	-	2+1 (3)
37	22/8	Isle of Wight	A	PL	L40-50	9 (5)	-	4 (4)	4 (4)	4+1 (4)	0 (3)	9+2 (5)	10+1 (5)	
38	31/8	Workington	H	PL	W59-36	12+2 (5)	-	7+1 (4)	4 (4)	8+1 (4)	2+1 (1)	11+2 (7)	15 (5)	
39	2/9	Workington	A	PL	L42-52*	12 (5)	-	6 (5)	4 (4)	13+1 (6)	-	7+3 (7)	R/R	0 (3)
40	7/9	King's Lynn	H	PL	L44-49	7+2 (5)	-	5+3 (4)	3 (4)	7 (4)	-	6+1 (5)	15 (5)	1 (3)
41	21/9	King's Lynn	H	PO	L43-47	13 (5)	-	5 (5)	3 (4)	5+1 (4)	4 (4)	6+2 (5)	7+1 (3)	
42	27/9	King's Lynn	A	PO	L32-63	12 (6)	-	4 (5)	R/R	6 (5)	1 (4)	2+1 (4)	-	7 (6)
43	14/10	Newcastle	H	TTT	W54-42	15+1 (6)	-	9+3 (5)	-	10+1 (5)	-	9+3 (6)	R/R	11+2 (8)
44	22/10	Newcastle	A	TTT	W49-41*	15 (5)	-	12 (6)	-	6 (5)	3+2 (4)	8+1 (5)	R/R	5+4 (5)

NOTE: TTT = Tyne-Tees Trophy.

DETAILS OF OTHER RIDERS

(all guests)

Match No. 13: Matthew Wethers 10+2 (6); Derek Sneddon 10 (5); Match No. 36: Rusty Hodgson 2+1 (3); Match No. 39: Benji Compton 0 (3); Match No. 40: Tai Woffinden 1 (3); Match No. 42: Trent Leverington 7 (6); Match No. 43: Lee Smethills 7 (4); Robert Ksiezak 4+2 (4); Match No. 44: Lee Smethills 5+4 (5).

DETAILS OF TACTICAL RIDES AND TACTICAL SUBSTITUTE RIDES

Match No. 2: Havelock 4 points (TR); Little 0 points (TR); Match No. 3: Juul 6 points (TR); Match No. 5: Havelock 4 points (TR); Little 1 point (TR; not doubled); Match No. 6: Suchanek 6 points (TR); Havelock 6 points (TR); Match No. 7: Havelock 6 points (TR); Little 4 points (TR); Suchanek 0 points (TS); Match No. 10: Kerr 4 points (TR); Havelock 1 point (TR; not doubled); Match No. 12: Havelock 6 points (TR); Suchanek 6 points (TR); Tresarrieu 4 points (TS); Match No. 13: Sneddon 6 points (TR);

REDCAR: From left to right, back row: Tomas Suchanek, Chris Kerr, Mathieu Tresarrieu, Kevin Little. Front row, kneeling: Jack Hargreaves, Daniel Giffard. On bike: Gary Havelock.

Wethers 2 points (TR); Match No. 14: Suchanek 2 points (TR); Match No. 19: Havelock 6 points (TR); Suchanek 4 points (TR); Match No. 21: Havelock 6 points (TR); Match No. 27: Havelock 4 points (TR); Little 0 points (TR); Match No. 28: Little 2 points (TS); Match No. 30: Suchanek 2 points (TS); Match No. 32: Little 6 points (TR); Havelock 6 points (TR); Match No. 36: Kerr 6 points (TR); Havelock 4 points (TR); Match No. 37: Little 0 points (TR); Match No. 39: Kerr 6 points (TR); Havelock 4 points (TR); Match No. 40: Tresarrieu 6 points (TR); Match No. 42: Havelock 6 points (TR); Kerr 4 points (TR).

AVERAGES

(26 Premier League, 2 Play-Offs, 14 Premier Trophy = 42 fixtures) ◆ Denotes ever-present.

Rider	Mts	Rds	Pts	Bon	Tot	Avge	Max
Gary Havelock ◆	42	206	511	9	520	10.10	3 full; 2 paid
Mathieu Tresarrieu	24	102	166	27	193	7.57	1 full
Tomas Suchanek	40	187	274	23	297	6.35	1 paid
Kevin Little	38	164	230	30	260	6.34	-
Daniel Giffard ◆	42	195	252	42	294	6.03	-
Chris Kerr ◆	42	184	207	32	239	5.20	-
Richard Juul	9	34	33.5	7	40.5	4.76	-
Jack Hargreaves	40	161	140	21	161	4.00	-
Guests	6	26	26	3	29	4.46	-

(Benji Compton [1]; Rusty Hodgson [1]; Trent Leverington [1]; Derek Sneddon [1]; Matthew Wethers [1]; Tai Woffinden [1]).

NOTE: Tomas Suchanek was ever-present throughout the 26-match Premier League programme.

INDIVIDUAL MEETINGS

7 October: British Under-15 Championship (Round Six)

QUALIFYING SCORES: Joe Haines 11; Ben Hopwood 10; Adam Wrathall 9; George Piper 9; Daniel Greenwood 8; Richard Franklin 8; Shane Hazelden (Reserve) 4; Jack Butler 4; Brendan Johnson 3; James Sarjeant 3; Scott Meakins 2; Sean Paterson 1; Ben Reade 0. FINAL: 1st Haines; 2nd Hopwood; 3rd Wrathall; 4th Piper. FINAL STANDINGS: 1st Haines 68; 2nd Hopwood 64; 3rd Wrathall 56; Piper 51; Franklin 43; Greenwood 43; Meakins 39; Kye Norton 38; Johnson 37; Sarjeant 36; Reade 33; Butler 31; Paterson 28; Tom Davies 16; Amy Carpenter 16; Hazelden 15; Chris Bint 11.

19 October: South Tees Silver Helmet

1st Richard Hall 14; 2nd Fredrik Lindgren 13; 3rd Gary Havelock (after run-off) 12; David Howe 12; James Wright 11; Chris Kerr 9; George Stancl 9; Lee Smethills 7; Adam Skornicki 6; Theo Pijper 6; Daniel Giffard 6; Kenneth Hansen 3; Kevin Little 3; Claus Vissing 3; Jack Hargreaves 3; Ricky Kling 2.

RYE HOUSE SILVER SKI ROCKETS

NOTE: The information below relates only to the main Rye House team. For details of the second side, please refer to the Conference League section.

ADDRESS: Rye House Stadium, Rye Road, Hoddesdon, Hertfordshire, EN11 0EH.
PROMOTERS: Len Silver and Hazal Naylor.
YEARS OF OPERATION: 1958 Open; 1959 Southern Area League; 1960-1966 Open and Training; 1967 Training; 1969-1973 Open and Training; 1974 British League Division Two; 1975-1990 National League; 1991-1993 British League Division Two; 1999-2001; Conference League; 2002-2006 Premier League.
NOTE: In 1999, Rye House staged their home matches at Eastbourne, King's Lynn and Mildenhall.
FIRST MEETING: 3 August 1958.
TRACK LENGTH: 262 metres.
TRACK RECORD: 55.8 seconds – Chris Harris (19/06/04).

PREVIOUS VENUE: Hoddesdon Stadium, Rye Road, Hoddesdon, Hertfordshire.
YEARS OF OPERATION: 1935 Open and Training; 1936-1937 Open; 1938 Sunday Dirt-Track League; 1939-1943 Open; 1945-1953 Open; 1954-1957 Southern Area League.

CLUB HONOURS

KNOCK-OUT CUP WINNERS: 1979.
LEAGUE CHAMPIONS: 1980, 2005.
PREMIER TROPHY WINNERS: 2005.

RIDER ROSTER 2006

Tommy ALLEN; Luke BOWEN: Steve BOXALL; Ross BRADY; Jamie COURTNEY; Edward KENNETT; Chris NEATH; Stuart ROBSON; Lee SMETHILLS.

OTHER APPEARANCES/GUESTS (official matches only)

Jon ARMSTRONG; Josh AUTY; Danny BETSON; Danny BIRD; James BRUNDLE; Barry BURCHATT; James COCKLE; Daniel GIFFARD; Shane HENRY; Ben POWELL; Adam ROYNON; George STANCL; Tai WOFFINDEN.

RYE HOUSE

* Denotes aggregate/bonus-point victory

NO.	DATE	OPPONENTS	VENUE	COMPETITION	RESULT	ROBSON	COURTNEY	KENNETT	ALLEN	NEATH	BOWEN	BOXALL	BRADY	SMETHILLS	ROYNON	OTHERS
1	5/3	Mildenhall	A	SH	W47-43	8+1 (5)	0 (3)	5+3 (4)	9 (4)	10 (5)	6 (4)	9+2 (5)	-	-	-	-
2	11/3	Mildenhall	H	SH	W50-41*	7 (4)	3+1(4)	8+1 (5)	6+1 (4)	12 (5)	1+1 (3)	13+1 (5)	-	-	-	-
3	17/3	Somerset	A	PT	L40-55	11 (5)	0 (3)	6+2 (4)	5 (4)	12 (5)	0 (3)	6 (7)	-	-	-	-
4	18/3	Somerset	H	PT	W59-34*	7+1 (4)	3 (4)	15 (5)	8+4 (5)	10+1 (4)	7+1 (4)	9+1 (4)	-	-	-	-
5	25/3	Sheffield	H	PL	W53-40	9 (4)	3+2 (4)	12+1 (5)	7+2 (4)	4+1 (4)	9 (4)	9+2 (5)	-	-	-	-
6	1/4	King's Lynn	H	PT	W50-40	5 (3)	2 (3)	12+2 (5)	1+1 (3)	14 (5)	8+1 (6)	8+1 (5)	-	-	-	-
7	5/4	King's Lynn	A	PT	L28-65	R/R	1 (5)	1 (1)	2+1 (5)	8 (6)	1+1 (6)	15 (7)	-	-	-	-
8	8/4	Isle of Wight	H	PT	W52-20	R/R	5+3 (4)	15 (5)	3+1 (3)	12 (4)	6+1 (3)	11+3 (5)	-	-	-	-
9	9/4	Newport	A	PT	L46-47	R/R	0 (3)	12 (6)	7+2 (5)	13 (6)	2+1 (4)	12+1 (6)	-	-	-	-
10	16/4	Mildenhall	A	PT	L44-46	-	2 (3)	8 (5)	6+2 (4)	11+1 (5)	1 (3)	13 (6)	3 (4)	-	-	-
11	17/4	Mildenhall	H	PT	W50-40*	-	5+2 (4)	12+1 (5)	6+1 (4)	14 (5)	3+1 (4)	5 (4)	5 (4)	-	-	-
12	21/4	Somerset	A	BCT	L42-53	-	7 (4)	7+1 (4)	9+1 (5)	8+1 (5)	4+1 (4)	6+1 (5)	1 (4)	-	-	-
13	25/4	Isle of Wight	A	PT	W50-43*	-	4+1 (4)	10+1 (5)	7 (4)	7 (5)	2+1 (3)	13+2 (5)	7 (4)	-	-	-
14	29/4	Somerset	H	BCT	W62-30*	-	9+1 (4)	10+1 (5)	9+3 (5)	9+2 (4)	7+2 (4)	7 (4)	11+1 (4)	-	-	-
15	1/5	Newport	H	PT	W58-38*	-	6+1 (4)	11+2 (5)	9+1 (4)	12+1 (5)	6+2 (4)	8+1 (4)	6 (4)	-	-	-
16	6/5	Workington	A	PL	L31-59	-	2+1 (3)	7 (5)	4 (4)	5 (4)	0 (4)	-	2 (3)	-	-	11+1 (7)
17	13/5	Mildenhall	H	PL	W53-40	-	7+1 (4)	9+1 (4)	5+2 (4)	8+2 (5)	11 (5)	8+3 (4)	5 (4)	-	-	-
18	16/5	Isle of Wight	A	KOC	L41-53	-	3+1 (3)	9+1 (6)	2 (4)	7 (6)	0 (4)	20+1 (7)	R/R	-	-	-
19	20/5	Isle of Wight	H	KOC	W66-26*	-	R/R	13+2 (5)	5+2 (5)	15 (5)	11+2 (5)	11+2 (5)	8+1 (4)	-	-	3 (1)
20	29/5	Berwick	H	PL	W65-27	-	R/R	11+2 (5)	10+2 (5)	10+1 (5)	13+2 (5)	13+2 (5)	7+2 (4)	-	-	1 (1)
21	4/6	Workington	H	PL	W49-41	-	R/R	7 (5)	7+3 (5)	13 (5)	1 (1)	20+1 (7)	0 (0)	-	-	1+1 (3)
22	17/6	Redcar	H	PL	W54-40	-	R/R	10+1 (5)	9+1 (5)	11+1 (5)	-	15+2 (7)	6 (4)	-	-	3+2 (4)
23	19/6	Newcastle	A	PL	L42-47	-	R/R	9 (5)	4+1 (5)	12 (5)	-	12+2 (7)	3 (4)	-	-	2 (4)
24	21/6	King's Lynn	A	KOC	L41-54	-	-	11 (5)	4+1 (5)	8+1 (6)	-	15+2 (7)	R/R	-	-	3 (7)
25	22/6	Redcar	A	PL	L43-47*	-	-	8+1 (5)	2 (4)	12+1 (6)	-	16+3 (7)	R/R	-	-	5+1 (8)
26	24/6	King's Lynn	H	KOC	W49-44	-	-	12+1 (5)	8+4 (6)	9 (5)	-	15+2 (7)	R/R	-	-	5+3 (7)
27	7/7	Edinburgh	A	PL	W47-42	-	-	-	3 (3)	13 (5)	-	6+2 (4)	5 (3)	-	-	20+3(15)
28	8/7	Berwick	A	PL	L42-54*	-	-	-	3 (4)	6 (4)	-	9+1 (5)	3 (4)	-	-	21 (13)
29	9/7	Glasgow	A	PL	L35-59	-	-	-	7 (4)	9 (5)	-	4+2 (4)	3 (4)	-	-	12 (13)
30	14/7	Somerset	A	PL	L41-53	-	-	6 (4)	9 (4)	10 (5)	-	5+1 (5)	6 (4)	-	-	5+1 (9)
31	15/7	Edinburgh	H	PL	W55-37*	-	-	15 (5)	9 (4)	12+1 (5)	-	5+1 (4)	8+1 (4)	-	-	6+1 (8)
32	22/7	Glasgow	H	PL	W54-40	-	-	9 (5)	8+1 (4)	11 (5)	-	10 (4)	8+1 (4)	-	-	8+2 (8)
33	27/7	Sheffield	A	PT s/f	L31-61	-	-	3 (4)	3+1 (4)	5 (5)	-	11 (5)	1 (3)	-	-	8+1 (9)
34	29/7	Sheffield	H	PT s/f	W61-31	-	-	13+2 (5)	9+2 (4)	10+1 (5)	-	10+1 (4)	5+1 (3)	-	-	14+2 (9)
35	5/8	Somerset	H	PL	W56-38*	-	-	12+1 (5)	5 (4)	11 (4)	-	14+1 (5)	3 (4)	-	-	11+1 (8)
36	15/8	Isle of Wight	A	PL	L29-64	-	-	9 (6)	8 (6)	3 (4)	-	R/R	0 (2)	-	-	9 (12)
37	16/8	King's Lynn	A	PL	L28-64	-	-	12 (6)	3 (5)	3 (4)	-	R/R	-	-	-	10+2 (15)
38	20/8	Mildenhall	A	PL	W48-44*	-	-	18 (5)	6 (4)	11+1 (5)	-	6 (4)	-	4+2 (4)	-	3 (8)
39	26/8	Stoke	A	PL	W47-43	-	-	9 (5)	4 (4)	7+1 (4)	-	12 (5)	-	4 (4)	-	11+3 (8)
40	28/8	Stoke	H	PL	W65-27*	-	-	14+1 (5)	6+2 (4)	13+2 (5)	-	12 (4)	-	8+1 (4)	-	12+3 (8)
41	28/8	Newport	H	PL	W64-28	-	-	15 (5)	9+1 (4)	8+1 (4)	-	12+3 (5)	-	5+2 (4)	-	15+1 (8)
42	2/9	King's Lynn	H	PL	L44-46	-	-	6 (4)	10+1 (5)	11+1 (5)	-	7+1 (4)	-	2+1 (3)	2 (4)	6+1 (5)

NO.	DATE	OPPONENTS	VENUE	COMPETITION	RESULT	ROBSON	COURTNEY	KENNETT	ALLEN	NEATH	BOWEN	BOXALL	BRADY	SMETHILLS	ROYNON	OTHERS
43	7/9	Sheffield	A	PL	L35-60	-	-	9 (5)	5+1 (4)	3 (4)	-	10 (5)	-	3 (4)	0 (3)	5+2 (5)
44	8/9	Newcastle	H	PL	W69-21*	-	-	14+1 (5)	11+1 (4)	13+2 (5)	-	9+1 (4)	-	6+1 (4)	7+1 (4)	9+3 (4)
45	16/9	Isle of Wight	H	PL	W50-43	-	-	10 (4)	6 (4)	15 (5)	-	11+1 (5)	-	1 (4)	4 (2)	3+1 (6)
46	17/9	Newport	A	PL	W51-43*	-	-	14+1 (5)	0 (1)	6 (4)	-	11 (5)	-	2+1 (3)	-	18+4 (12)
47	29/9	Somerset	A	PO	D45-45	7+1 (4)	-	11+1 (5)	3+1 (4)	8+1 (4)	-	11 (5)	-	-	-	5+1 (8)
48	30/9	Somerset	H	PO	W49-43*	8+2 (5)	-	11 (5)	R/R	8+1 (4)	-	12 (5)	-	-	-	10+3 (11)
49	14/10	King's Lynn	A	PO s/f	W48-42	6+1 (4)	-	10+1 (5)	5 (4)	12 (5)	-	7+1 (4)	-	-	-	8+2 (9)
50	18/10	King's Lynn	A	PO s/f	L35-60	2 (4)	-	4 (4)	7 (4)	12 (5)	-	8+2 (5)	-	-	-	2 (8)
51	21/10	Mildenhall	H	A11	W62-32	8+1 (4)	-	10+1 (4)	7+1 (4)	13+1 (5)	-	13+1 (5)	-	-	-	11+3 (8)

NOTE: SH = Suffolk-Herts Trophy; BCT = Battle of the Champions Trophy; A11 = A11 Trophy. The home Premier Trophy match versus Isle of Wight on 8 April was abandoned after heat twelve, with the result permitted to stand. Following the home PT semi-final tie against Sheffield on 29 July, Edward Kennett was defeated in a run-off decider by Andre Compton.

DETAILS OF OTHER RIDERS

(all guests)

Match No. 16: Jon Armstrong 11+1 (7); Match No. 19: Danny Betson 3 (1); Match No. 20: Danny Betson 1 (1); Match No. 21: Danny Betson 1+1 (3); Match No. 22: Ben Powell 2+1 (1); Danny Betson 1+1 (3); Match No. 23: Danny Betson 2 (4); Match No. 24: Ben Powell 3 (4); Danny Betson 0 (3); Match No. 25: Danny Betson 4+1 (4); Ben Powell 1 (4); Match No. 26: Ben Powell 4+2 (3); Danny Betson 1+1 (4); Match No. 27: Danny Bird 14+1 (5); James Cockle 6+2 (7); Danny Betson 0 (3); Match No. 28: Danny Bird 18 (5); James Cockle 3 (5); Danny Betson 0 (3); Match No. 29: George Stancl 9 (5); Danny Betson 3 (5); Daniel Giffard 0 (3); Match No. 30: Adam Roynon 5+1 (6); Ben Powell 0 (3); Match No. 31: Adam Roynon 4 (5); Danny Betson 2+1 (3); Match No. 32: Danny Betson 5+1 (4); Adam Roynon 3+1 (4); Match No. 33: Adam Roynon 8+1 (6); Danny Betson 0 (3); Match No. 34: Danny Betson 13+2 (6); Adam Roynon 1 (3); Match No. 35: Danny Betson 6+1 (4); Adam Roynon 5 (4); Match No. 36: Adam Roynon 7 (7); Danny Betson 2 (5); Match No. 37: Adam Roynon 7+1 (7); James Brundle 2 (4); Ben Powell 1+1 (4); Match No. 38: Adam Roynon 3 (5); Shane Henry 0 (3); Match No. 39: Adam Roynon 6+2 (4); Ben Powell 5+1 (4); Match No. 40: Adam Roynon 7+1 (4); Ben Powell 5+2 (4); Match No. 41: Adam Roynon 9 (4); Ben Powell 6+1 (4): Match No. 42: Ben Powell 6+1 (5); Match No. 43: Ben Powell 5+2 (5); Match No. 44: Ben Powell 9+3 (4); Match No. 45: Ben Powell 3+1 (6); Match No. 46: Daniel Giffard 11+2 (6); Ben Powell 7+2 (6); Match No. 47: Ben Powell 4+1 (4); Daniel Giffard 1 (4); Match No. 48: Daniel Giffard 6+1 (5); Danny Betson 4+2 (5); Barry Burchatt 0 (1); Match No. 49: Daniel Giffard 4+2 (4); Tai Woffinden 4 (5); Match No. 50: Tai Woffinden 2 (5); Josh Auty 0 (3); Match No. 51: Tai Woffinden 6+1 (4); Barry Burchatt 5+2 (4).

DETAILS OF TACTICAL RIDES AND TACTICAL SUBSTITUTE RIDES

Match No. 3: Robson 6 points (TR); Neath 4 points (TR); Match No. 7: Boxall 6 points (TR); Neath 1 point (TR; not doubled); Match No. 12: Allen 6 points (TR); Kennett 4 points (TR); Match No. 16: Neath 1 point (TR; not doubled); Brady 0 points (TR); Match No. 18: Boxall 6 points (TR); Kennett 2 points (TR); Match No. 24: Boxall 6 points (TR); Kennett 4 points (TR); Match No. 28: Bird 6 points (TR); Boxall 6 points (TR); Match No. 29: Neath 4 points (TR); Stancl 4 points (TR); Match No. 30: Kennett 4 points (TR); Allen 4 points (TR); Match No. 33: Boxall 4 points (TR); Neath 1 point (TR; not doubled); Match No. 36: Kennett 6 points (TR); Allen 1 point (TR; not doubled); Match No. 37: Kennett 4 points (TR); Roynon 1 point (TR; not doubled); Match No. 38: Kennett 6 points (TR); Match No. 43: Kennett 6 points (TR); Boxall 4 points (TR); Match No. 50: Boxall 6 points (TR); Neath 4 points (TR).

AVERAGES

(26 Premier League, 4 Play-Offs, 4 Knock-Out Cup, 12 Premier Trophy = 46 fixtures)

♦ Denotes ever-present.

Rider	Mts	Rds	Pts	Bon	Tot	Avge	Max
Steve Boxall	43	221	437	49	486	8.80	1 full; 5 paid
Edward Kennett	43	208	428	26	454	8.73	5 full; 5 paid
Chris Neath ♦	46	221	441	22	463	8.38	3 full; 2 paid
Stuart Robson	8	33	52	5	57	6.91	-
Tommy Allen	45	189	258	42	300	6.35	1 paid
Luke Bowen	17	68	81	13	94	5.53	1 paid
Ross Brady	21	74	94	6	100	5.41	-
Lee Smethills	9	34	35	8	43	5.06	-
Jamie Courtney	14	51	43	12	55	4.31	-
Also rode:							
Adam Roynon	4	13	13	1	14	4.31	-
Guests	62	261	260	45	305	4.67	1 full; 2 paid

(Jon Armstrong [1]; Josh Auty [1]; Danny Betson [18]; Danny Bird [2]; James Brundle [1]; Barry Burchatt [1]; James Cockle [2]; Daniel Giffard [5]; Shane Henry [1]; Ben Powell [15]; Adam Roynon [12]; George Stancl [1]; Tai Woffinden [2]).

NOTE: Tommy Allen was ever-present throughout the 26-match Premier League programme.

INDIVIDUAL MEETINGS

22 April: Championship of Great Britain qualifying round

QUALIFYING SCORES: Edward Kennett 14; Chris Neath 13; Garry Stead 11; Paul Hurry 10; Olly Allen 9; Ricky Ashworth 9; Carl Wilkinson 8; Andre Compton 8; Daniel King 8; Andrew Moore 7; James Grieves 6; Phil Morris 6; Glenn Cunningham 5; James Wright 3; Shaun Tacey 2; Paul Thorp 1. FINAL: 1st Kennett; 2nd Hurry; 3rd Stead; 4th Neath.

1 July: Vic Harding Memorial

QUALIFYING SCORES: Jason Lyons 15; Chris Neath 12; Tommy Allen 10; Daniel King 9; Leigh Lanham 9; Steve Boxall 9; Ross Brady 8; Richard Hall 5; Brent Werner 4; Danny Betson 3; Harland Cook 2; Jon Armstrong 2; Ben Powell 1; Robert Mear 1. FIRST SEMI-FINAL: 1st Lyons; 2nd Lanham; 3rd Allen; 4th Hall. SECOND SEMI-FINAL: 1st Werner; 2nd Neath; 3rd King; 4th Boxall. FINAL: 1st Lyons; 2nd Neath; 3rd Lanham; 4th Werner.

28 October: Ace of Herts Championship

QUALIFYING SCORES: Edward Kennett 14; Davey Watt 13; Steve Boxall 12; Leigh Lanham 11; Chris Neath 8; Lewis Bridger 7; Stuart Robson 6; Tai Woffinden 6; Barry Burchatt 4; Robert Mear 4; Josh Auty 3; Harland Cook 1. FIRST SEMI-FINAL: 1st Boxall; 2nd Kennett; 3rd Robson; 4th Neath. SECOND SEMI-FINAL: 1st Watt; 2nd Lanham; 3rd Bridger; 4th Woffinden. FINAL: 1st Kennett; 2nd Watt; 3rd Lanham; 4th Boxall.

RYE HOUSE: From left to right, back row: Chris Neath, Luke Bowen, John Sampford (team manager), Edward Kennett, Jamie Courtney. Front row, kneeling: Tommy Allen, Steve Boxall. On bike: Stuart Robson.

SHEFFIELD PIRTEK TIGERS

ADDRESS: Owlerton Sports Stadium, Penistone Road, Owlerton, Sheffield, South Yorkshire, S6 2DE.

PROMOTERS: Neil Machin and Malcolm Wright.

YEARS OF OPERATION: 1929 English Dirt-Track League; 1930-1931 Northern League; 1932 Speedway National Association Trophy; 1933 National League; 1938-1939 National League Division Two; 1945 Open; 1946 Northern League; 1947-1950 National League Division Two; 1951-1952 Open; 1960-1964 Provincial League; 1965-1967 British League; 1968-1974 British League Division One; 1975-1988 British League; 1991-1994 British League Division Two; 1995 Premier League; 1996 Premier League and Conference League; 1997-1999 Premier League; 2000-2003 Premier League and Conference League; 2004 Premier League and Conference Trophy; 2005-2006 Premier League.

FIRST MEETING: 30 March 1929.

TRACK LENGTH: 361 metres.

TRACK RECORD: 59.5 seconds − Simon Stead (08/08/04) and Chris Holder (12/10/06).

CLUB HONOURS

BRITISH SPEEDWAY CUP (DIVISION TWO) WINNERS: 1947.

KNOCK-OUT CUP WINNERS: 1974, 2002.

FOUR-TEAM CHAMPIONS: 1999, 2000.

LEAGUE CHAMPIONS: 1999, 2002.

YOUNG SHIELD WINNERS: 1999, 2002.

PREMIERSHIP WINNERS: 2000.

PREMIER TROPHY WINNERS: 2001.

RIDER ROSTER 2006

Ricky ASHWORTH; Andre COMPTON; Benji COMPTON; Paul COOPER; Kyle LEGAULT; Emiliano SANCHEZ; Mark THOMPSON; Ben WILSON.

OTHER APPEARANCES/GUESTS (official matches only)

Mark LEMON; Jason LYONS; Sam MARTIN; Kauko NIEMINEN; David SPEIGHT; Shane WALDRON; Tai WOFFINDEN.

SHEFFIELD

* Denotes aggregate/bonus-point victory

NO.	DATE	OPPONENTS	VENUE	COMPETITION	RESULT	ASHWORTH	WILSON	SANCHEZ	LEGAULT	A. COMPTON	COOPER	B. COMPTON	THOMPSON	WOFFINDEN	OTHERS
1	15/3	King's Lynn	A	PIT	L37-55	9 (5)	5+1 (4)	7 (4)	2+1 (4)	8 (5)	3+1 (4)	3+2 (4)	-	-	-
2	18/3	Workington	A	PT	L45-50	9+2 (5)	R/R	13 (5)	2 (5)	16 (5)	5+1 (7)	0 (3)	-	-	-
3	23/3	Berwick	H	PT	W58-37	12 (5)	6 (4)	5 (4)	11 (4)	14+1 (5)	4+2 (4)	6+1 (4)	-	-	-
4	25/3	Rye House	A	PL	L40-53	7 (5)	5 (4)	7 (4)	3 (4)	13+1 (5)	3 (4)	2 (4)	-	-	-
5	30/3	Newcastle	H	PT	W64-30	8+2 (4)	11+1 (5)	6+1 (4)	12 (4)	15 (5)	3 (4)	9+3 (4)	-	-	-
6	1/4	Berwick	A	PT	L44-46*	5 (4)	9 (5)	7 (4)	3+1 (4)	13 (5)	4+1 (4)	3+1 (4)	-	-	-
7	2/4	Glasgow	A	PT	L44-51	7+1 (4)	6+1 (4)	14 (5)	5+1 (4)	9+1 (4)	1 (4)	2+1 (4)	-	-	-
8	6/4	Edinburgh	H	PT	W52-40	14+1 (5)	6 (4)	7+3 (4)	10 (4)	12+2 (5)	3 (7)	0 (1)	-	-	-
9	8/4	Stoke	A	PT	L42-48	10 (5)	4+1 (4)	12+1 (5)	2 (4)	7 (4)	1 (3)	6+1 (5)	-	-	-
10	13/4	Redcar	A	PT	W46-44	5+1 (4)	3+1 (4)	8+1 (5)	6+2 (4)	11+1 (5)	13+3 (7)	0 (1)	-	-	-
11	14/4	Redcar	H	PT	W56-36*	10+1 (5)	9+2 (4)	9+2 (4)	7+1 (4)	12 (5)	3 (4)	6+1 (4)	-	-	-
12	27/4	Glasgow	H	PT	W54-41*	9+3 (5)	8+1 (4)	4+1 (4)	10 (4)	14+1 (5)	3+1 (4)	6+1 (4)	-	-	-
13	1/5	Newcastle	A	PT	L38-53*	12 (5)	5+2 (4)	8+2 (5)	4+1 (4)	6 (4)	3+1 (4)	0 (4)	-	-	-
14	4/5	Workington	H	PT	W57-38*	12 (5)	5+2 (4)	7+1 (4)	9+1 (4)	14+1 (5)	5+1 (5)	5+1 (4)	-	-	-
15	5/5	Somerset	A	PL	W49-44	13 (5)	9+3 (5)	6+2 (4)	8+1 (4)	7 (4)	6+3 (5)	0 (3)	-	-	-
16	11/5	King's Lynn	H	PIT	W59-32*	13+2 (5)	10 (4)	5+1 (4)	9 (4)	11+1 (4)	2 (4)	9+2 (5)	-	-	-
17	18/5	Newport	H	PL	W63-30	13+2 (5)	8+2 (4)	9 (4)	8+1 (4)	15 (5)	6+1 (4)	4+1 (4)	-	-	-
18	25/5	Somerset	H	PL	W48-45*	11+2 (5)	9+1 (4)	5+2 (4)	6+1 (4)	12 (5)	4 (4)	1 (4)	-	-	-
19	1/6	King's Lynn	H	PL	D45-45	9+2 (5)	6+1 (4)	5 (4)	3+1 (4)	14 (5)	4+2 (4)	4+1 (4)	-	-	-
20	2/6	Edinburgh	A	PT	L39-54	9+1 (5)	R/R	6+1 (4)	6 (5)	14 (5)	1+1 (5)	3+1 (6)	-	-	-
21	8/6	Stoke	H	PT	W57-38*	5+1 (4)	12+1 (5)	6 (4)	9+1 (4)	14+1 (5)	7+2 (4)	4 (4)	-	-	-
22	14/6	King's Lynn	A	PL	L33-62	2 (4)	7 (4)	4 (4)	7+1 (5)	10 (5)	0 (4)	-	3+2 (4)	-	-
23	22/6	Berwick	H	PL	W56-39	13+2 (5)	8+3 (4)	5 (4)	8+1 (4)	14 (5)	5+3 (4)	3 (4)	-	-	-
24	23/6	Edinburgh	A	PL	L44-52	5 (4)	3 (4)	6+1 (4)	11 (5)	15 (5)	1+1 (4)	3+1 (4)	-	-	-
25	24/6	Berwick	A	PL	W47-43*	11+1 (5)	7+2 (4)	6 (4)	4 (4)	14 (5)	5+2 (5)	0 (3)	-	-	-
26	28/6	Isle of Wight	A	PL	W46-44	9+1 (5)	7+3 (4)	8 (4)	3 (3)	13 (5)	5+3 (6)	1+1 (3)	-	-	-
27	29/6	Isle of Wight	H	PL	W62-29*	10+2 (5)	10 (4)	4+2 (4)	9 (4)	13+2 (5)	16+1 (7)	0 (1)	-	-	-
28	6/7	Newport	H	KOC	W59-33	13+2 (5)	R/R	11+1 (5)	12+2 (5)	15 (5)	7+1 (7)	1+1 (3)	-	-	-
29	9/7	Newport	A	KOC	W50-39*	11+1 (5)	R/R	8+1 (5)	9+1 (5)	15 (5)	7+1 (7)	-	-	-	0 (0)
30	13/7	Newcastle	H	PL	W60-32	13+2 (5)	8+1 (4)	9 (4)	10+2 (4)	14+1 (5)	4 (4)	-	2+1 (4)	-	-
31	17/7	Glasgow	A	PL	L44-49	6+2 (5)	9 (4)	10 (4)	5+3 (4)	11 (5)	3 (5)	-	0 (3)	-	-
32	20/7	Workington	H	PL	W53-42	4+2 (4)	13+1 (5)	9+1 (4)	7+1 (4)	15 (5)	5+1 (5)	0 (3)	-	-	-
33	22/7	Workington	A	PL	W46-44*	7 (4)	9+2 (5)	9 (4)	8 (4)	8+2 (4)	5 (6)	0 (3)	-	-	-
34	27/7	Rye House	H	PT s/f	W61-31	11+1 (5)	8+3 (4)	7+2 (4)	8 (4)	15 (5)	8 (6)	4+1 (4)	-	-	-
35	29/7	Rye House	A	PT s/f	L31-61*	1+1 (4)	13+1 (6)	2 (4)	R/R	8 (5)	3 (6)	4+2 (5)	-	-	-
36	3/8	Stoke	H	PL	L44-45	6+1 (4)	5 (4)	8 (4)	8+1 (4)	13+1 (5)	1 (4)	3+1 (4)	-	-	-
37	5/8	Stoke	A	PL	L43-46	7 (4)	4+1 (4)	12+2 (6)	R/R	10+1 (5)	2+1 (5)	8+1 (6)	-	-	-
38	10/8	Redcar	H	PL	W49-41	5+4 (4)	10 (5)	10+1 (5)	R/R	14 (5)	10+2 (7)	-	-	0 (3)	0 (1)
39	11/8	Redcar	A	PL	L42-48*	7 (4)	9+2 (4)	11+1 (6)	R/R	7 (5)	6+1 (7)	2+1 (4)	-	-	-
40	17/8	Edinburgh	H	PL	W61-31*	8+2 (4)	13 (5)	10 (4)	9+2 (4)	14+1 (5)	4+1 (4)	3+1 (4)	-	-	-
41	24/8	Glasgow	H	PL	W57-39*	10+1 (5)	6+1 (4)	8+1 (4)	8+2 (4)	15 (5)	10+2 (5)	0 (3)	-	-	-
42	27/8	Mildenhall	A	PL	W46-44	9+1 (5)	8+1 (5)	8+1 (4)	8 (4)	5 (4)	4+1 (4)	4 (4)	-	-	-

NO.	DATE	OPPONENTS	VENUE	COMPETITION	RESULT	ASHWORTH	WILSON	SANCHEZ	LEGAULT	A. COMPTON	COOPER	B. COMPTON	THOMPSON	WOFFINDEN	OTHERS
43	30/8	King's Lynn	A	PT f	L32-63	2+1 (4)	4 (4)	7+1 (5)	10 (5)	-	2 (5)	0 (3)	-	-	7 (4)
44	31/8	King's Lynn	H	PT f	W48-45	13+1 (5)	7+1 (4)	8+1 (4)	10+1 (5)	-	1 (3)	1+1 (5)	-	-	8 (4)
45	3/9	Newcastle	A	PL	L46-47*	18 (5)	6+1 (5)	9 (4)	R/R	-	5+2 (7)	-	-	-	8+2 (9)
46	7/9	Rye House	H	PL	W60-35*	17+1 (6)	13+3 (6)	10+2 (5)	11+2 (5)	R/R	5+2 (4)	4+1 (4)	-	-	-
47	10/9	Newport	A	PL	L44-45*	2+2 (3)	9 (4)	8 (4)	10+3 (5)	-	-	1 (4)	-	-	14 (10)
48	14/9	Mildenhall	H	PL	W63-27*	14+1 (5)	11+1 (6)	16+1 (6)	10+3 (5)	R/R	5 (4)	7+2 (4)	-	-	-
49	15/9	Somerset	A	KOC s/f	L40-55	16 (5)	8+2 (5)	6 (4)	2 (4)	-	2 (4)	-	-	0 (3)	6+2 (5)
50	21/9	Workington	H	PO	W53-40	7+2 (4)	12+1 (5)	8+2 (4)	9+1 (4)	15 (5)	1 (4)	1 (4)	-	-	-
51	28/9	Somerset	H	KOC s/f	W55-41	14 (5)	8+2 (4)	6+2 (4)	7 (4)	-	7 (4)	-	2+1 (4)	-	11+1 (5)
52	30/9	Workington	A	PO	L44-46*	13 (5)	7+1 (5)	5+1 (4)	6 (4)	-	6 (5)	-	-	-	7+1 (7)
53	10/10	Isle of Wight	A	PO s/f	L43-50	3 (4)	10+2 (5)	8+2 (4)	9 (4)	9 (5)	3 (5)	-	1+1 (4)	-	-
54	12/10	Isle of Wight	H	PO s/f	W60-35*	9+1 (4)	8+2 (4)	7+2 (4)	11+1 (5)	13+1 (5)	3+1 (4)	-	-	9+2 (4)	-
55	19/10	Hull	H	YC	W59-36	12+3 (5)	14+1 (5)	5+1 (4)	9+1 (4)	9+1 (4)	4+1 (4)	-	-	6+1 (4)	-
56	26/10	King's Lynn	H	PO f	W52-37	9+2 (5)	6+1 (4)	4+1 (4)	5+1 (4)	12+1 (5)	2+1 (3)	-	-	14 (5)	-
57	27/10	King's Lynn	A	PO f	L30-63	3+1 (5)	11 (4)	0 (4)	6 (4)	7 (6)	1 (2)	-	2 (5)	-	-

NOTE: PIT = Pirtek Trophy; YC = Yorkshire Cup; Following the away PT semi-final tie at Rye House on 29 July, Andre Compton defeated Edward Kennett in a run-off decider.

DETAILS OF OTHER RIDERS

(all guests)

Match No. 29: Shane Waldron 0 (0); Match No. 38: David Speight 0 (1); Match No. 43: Jason Lyons 7 (4); Match No. 44: Jason Lyons 8 (4); Match No. 45: Mark Lemon 7+1 (5); David Speight 1+1 (4); Match No. 47: Mark Lemon 12 (5); Sam Martin 2 (5); Match No. 49: Mark Lemon 6+2 (5); Match No. 51: Jason Lyons 11+1 (5); Match No. 52: Kauko Nieminen 6+1 (4); David Speight 1 (3).

DETAILS OF TACTICAL RIDES AND TACTICAL SUBSTITUTE RIDES

Match No. 1: Wilson 4 points (TR); A. Compton 1 point (TR; not doubled); Match No. 2: A. Compton 6 points (TR); Sanchez 4 points (TR); Match No. 4: A. Compton 6 points (TR); Legault 1 point (TR; not doubled); Match No. 7: Sanchez 6 points (TR); Legault 4 points (TR); Match No. 13: Ashworth 4 points (TR); A. Compton 0 points (TR); Match No. 20: A. Compton 6 points (TR); Sanchez 1 point (TR; not doubled); Match No. 22: A. Compton 6 points (TR); Wilson 4 points (TR); Match No. 24: A. Compton 6 points (TR); Legault 6 points (TR); Match No. 35: Wilson 4 points (TR); A. Compton 1 point (TR; not doubled); Match No. 43: Legault 6 points (TR); Sanchez 4 points (TR); Match No. 45: Ashworth 6 points (TR); Lemon 1 point (TR; not doubled); Match No. 49: Ashworth 6 points (TR); Wilson 4 points (TS); Lemon 0 points (TR); Match No. 53: Sanchez 6 points (TR); Match No. 57: Wilson 6 points (TR); Legault 1 point (TR; not doubled); A. Compton 1 point (TS; not doubled).

OTHER DETAILS

Hull scorers in Match No. 55: Joel Parsons 14+1 (7); Paul Thorp 13+1 (5); Robbie Kessler 6 (5); Emil Kramer 2 (5); James Birkinshaw 1 (5); David Speight 0 (3); Mark Lemon R/R. Parsons' total includes 6 points from a TR; Thorp's total includes 4 points from a TR.

SHEFFIELD: From left to right: Emiliano Sanchez, Paul Cooper, Andre Compton, Kyle Legault, Ricky Ashworth, Ben Wilson, Benji Compton.

AVERAGES
(26 Premier League, 6 Play-Offs, 4 Knock-Out Cup, 18 Premier Trophy = 54 fixtures)
♦ Denotes ever-present.

Rider	Mts	Rds	Pts	Bon	Tot	Avge	Max
Andre Compton	45	221	531	19	550	9.95	8 full; 7 paid
Ricky Ashworth ♦	54	250	480	57	537	8.59	1 full; 7 paid
Ben Wilson	50	220	389	57	446	8.11	-
Emiliano Sanchez ♦	54	232	401	46	447	7.71	-
Kyle Legault	49	208	356	40	396	7.62	1 full; 1 paid
Paul Cooper	53	254	233	46	279	4.39	-
Benji Compton	41	153	111	27	138	3.61	1 paid
Mark Thompson	6	24	10	5	15	2.50	-

Also rode:

Tai Woffinden	4	15	23	2	25	6.67	-

Guests	12	45	61	6	67	5.96	-

(Mark Lemon [3]; Jason Lyons [3]; Sam Martin [1]; Kauko Nieminen [1]; David Speight [3]; Shane Waldron [1]).

NOTE: Ben Wilson was ever-present throughout the 26-match Premier League programme.

INDIVIDUAL MEETINGS

20 March: The Sean Cracker – Sean Wilson 20-Year Testimonial

QUALIFYING SCORES: Jason Crump 14; Nicki Pedersen 13; Scott Nicholls 12; Simon Stead 11; Leigh Adams 10; Andre Compton 10; Fredrik Lindgren 9; Ryan Sullivan 8; David Norris 6; Sebastian Ulamek 6; Gary Havelock 6; Sean Wilson 6; Chris Harris 4; Kyle Legault 3; Morten Risager 3; Steve Johnston 2; Benji Compton (Res) 0. SEMI-FINAL: 1st Nicholls; 2nd Adams; 3rd Stead; 4th A. Compton. FINAL: 1st Crump; 2nd Pedersen; 3rd Nicholls; 4th Adams.

15 June: Top Gun Championship

QUALIFYING SCORES: Mark Thompson 15; Josh Auty 14; David Speight 11; Mark Jones 11; Tom Hedley 9; Michael Pickering 9; Shane Waldron 9; A Aldridge 8; Jack Roberts 6; Ben Hopwood 6; Grant Hayes 5; Sam Dore 5; Matt Browne 4; R Hodgson 3; Jamie Pickard 2; Tai Woffinden 1; Scott Richardson (Reserve) 0. SEMI-FINAL: 1st Jones; 2nd Hedley; 3rd Speight; 4th Pickering. FINAL: 1st Auty; 2nd Thompson; 3rd Hedley; 4th Jones.

OTHER MEETING

27 May: Robbie Kessler Testimonial

Stoke 30; Sheffield 25: Simon Stead 11 (4); Ricky Ashworth 8 (4); Steve Johnston 4 (4); Adam Allott 2 (4); Hull 24; Wolverhampton 24. The total for Steve Johnston includes 2 points from a tactical ride.

SOMERSET MIKE MANNING AUDIO REBELS

ADDRESS: Oak Tree Arena, Edithmead, Nr Highbridge, Somerset, TA9 4HA.
PROMOTERS: Peter Toogood and Jo Lawson.
YEARS OF OPERATION: 2000–2001 Conference League; 2002–2006 Premier League.
FIRST MEETING: 2 June 2000.
TRACK LENGTH: 300 metres.
TRACK RECORD: 56.40 seconds – Kenneth Bjerre (20/06/03).

CLUB HONOURS

CONFERENCE TROPHY WINNERS: 2001.
KNOCK-OUT CUP WINNERS: 2001.
FOUR-TEAM CHAMPIONS: 2005.

RIDER ROSTER 2006

Ben BARKER; Glenn CUNNINGHAM; Paul FRY; Stephan KATT; Emil KRAMER; Glen PHILLIPS; Simon WALKER; Magnus ZETTERSTROM.

OTHER APPEARANCES/GUESTS (official matches only)

Tony ATKIN; Lee DICKEN; Pavel ONDRASIK; Chris SCHRAMM; Lee SMART; Jamie SMITH; Tomas TOPINKA.

SOMERSET

* Denotes aggregate/bonus-point victory

NO.	DATE	OPPONENTS	VENUE	COMPETITION	RESULT	ZETTERSTROM	ONDRASIK	SMITH	FRY	CUNNINGHAM	WALKER	BARKER	KATT	PHILLIPS	KRAMER	OTHERS
1	10/3	Newport	H	BCA	W52-41	15 (5)	3 (4)	9+1 (5)	9 (4)	8 (4)	7+2 (4)	1 (4)	-	-	-	-
2	17/3	Rye House	H	PT	W55-40	14+1 (5)	8 (5)	7+2 (5)	R/R	12 (6)	9+3 (5)	5+1 (4)	-	-	-	-
3	18/3	Rye House	A	PT	L34-59	7 (5)	1 (1)	15 (6)	R/R	6 (5)	4 (6)	1+1 (7)	-	-	-	-
4	24/3	King's Lynn	H	PT	W38-34	8 (3)	R/R	8+1 (5)	6+2 (4)	8 (3)	4+2 (5)	4 (4)	-	-	-	-
5	29/3	King's Lynn	A	PT	L43-51	15 (5)	-	4+1 (4)	11 (5)	5 (4)	2+2 (4)	5+1 (4)	1+1 (4)	-	-	-
6	31/3	Mildenhall	H	PT	W50-43	14 (5)	-	R/R	8 (4)	9 (5)	9+2 (7)	4+1 (4)	6+2 (5)	-	-	-
7	7/4	Isle of Wight	H	PT	W62-31	14+1 (5)	-	-	4+2 (4)	11+1 (5)	8+3 (4)	9+1 (4)	10 (4)	6+1 (4)	-	-
8	14/4	Newport	H	PT	W55-40	14 (5)	-	-	3 (4)	7+1 (4)	7+1 (4)	7+1 (4)	13+1 (5)	4 (4)	-	-
9	16/4	Newport	A	PT	L44-51*	16 (5)	-	-	7+1 (5)	7 (4)	3 (4)	1 (4)	5 (4)	5+1 (4)	-	-
10	18/4	Isle of Wight	A	PT	W59-34*	15 (5)	-	-	7+1 (4)	10+1 (5)	6+1 (4)	4+1 (4)	9+2 (4)	8+2 (4)	-	-
11	21/4	Rye House	H	BCT	W53-42	14+1 (5)	-	-	5+1 (4)	14+1 (5)	5 (4)	2 (4)	9 (4)	4+1 (4)	-	-
12	23/4	Mildenhall	A	PT	L41-54	16 (5)	-	-	4+1 (4)	4 (5)	2+2 (4)	3+1 (4)	7 (4)	5 (4)	-	-
13	28/4	Workington	H	PL	W50-40	15 (5)	-	-	6 (4)	11+1 (5)	5+1 (5)	1+1 (3)	9+1 (4)	3 (4)	-	-

NO.	DATE	OPPONENTS	VENUE	COMPETITION	RESULT	ZETTERSTROM	ONDRASIK	SMITH	FRY	CUNNINGHAM	WALKER	BARKER	KATT	PHILLIPS	KRAMER	OTHERS
14	29/4	Rye House	A	BCT	L30-62	11+1 (5)	-	-	1 (4)	4 (4)	0 (4)	2+1 (4)	10 (5)	2 (4)	-	-
15	5/5	Sheffield	H	PL	L44-49	15 (5)	-	-	6 (4)	7+1 (5)	3 (4)	5 (4)	6 (4)	2+1 (4)	-	-
16	12/5	Redcar	H	PL	W57-41	13 (5)	-	-	5+1 (4)	9+1 (4)	6+1 (4)	9+3 (4)	10+1 (5)	5+1 (4)	-	-
17	19/5	Stoke	H	KOC	W57-38	13+1 (5)	-	-	9 (5)	7 (4)	4+2 (4)	9+1 (4)	8+2 (4)	7+3 (4)	-	-
18	20/5	Stoke	A	KOC	L41-51*	14 (5)	-	-	7+2 (5)	5 (4)	5 (6)	2+1 (4)	8 (5)	R/R	-	0 (1)
19	25/5	Sheffield	A	PL	L45-48	10 (5)	-	-	15+1 (5)	6 (4)	1 (3)	7 (5)	2+2 (4)	4+3 (4)	-	-
20	26/5	King's Lynn	H	PL	W51-39	15 (5)	-	-	15+1 (6)	8+2 (4)	7 (6)	1+1 (4)	R/R	5+1 (5)	-	-
21	2/6	Berwick	H	PL	W53-39	12 (5)	-	-	7+1 (3)	11+1 (5)	8+1 (4)	3+2 (5)	5 (4)	7+1 (4)	-	-
22	9/6	Isle of Wight	H	PL	W54-42	14 (5)	-	-	R/R	13+1 (6)	10+1 (5)	4+2 (4)	6+2 (5)	7 (5)	-	-
23	10/6	Workington	A	PL	L45-48*	12 (5)	-	-	R/R	15 (6)	6+2 (5)	3+1 (4)	7 (5)	2 (5)	-	-
24	11/6	Glasgow	A	PL	L40-50	13 (6)	-	-	R/R	10 (6)	2+2 (4)	5+1 (5)	5+1 (4)	5+1 (5)	-	-
25	16/6	Exeter Select	H	WCC	W49-42	13 (5)	-	-	R/R	10+1 (5)	5+2 (5)	5 (4)	11 (6)	5+2 (5)	-	-
26	23/6	Mildenhall	H	KOC	W52-43	14+1 (5)	-	-	R/R	14+1 (6)	0 (3)	3+1 (6)	12+1 (5)	9+2 (5)	-	-
27	25/6	Mildenhall	A	KOC	W53-40*	11+1 (5)	-	-	-	9 (4)	-	11+2 (7)	8 (5)	R/R	12+1 (5)	2+1 (4)
28	28/6	King's Lynn	A	PL	L39-56	18 (5)	-	-	-	2 (4)	-	4+1 (4)	5 (4)	1 (4)	7 (5)	2+1 (4)
29	7/7	Mildenhall	H	PL	L42-48	11+1 (5)	-	-	-	6 (4)	1+1 (4)	3 (4)	8+1 (4)	2 (4)	11 (5)	-
30	14/7	Rye House	H	PL	W53-41	14 (5)	-	-	-	8+1 (4)	6 (4)	4+2 (4)	7+1 (4)	5+2 (4)	9+1 (5)	-
31	18/7	Isle of Wight	A	PL	L41-43*	10+1 (4)	-	-	-	9 (4)	4+2 (5)	2+2 (3)	4+2 (4)	4+1 (4)	8 (4)	-
32	21/7	Glasgow	H	PL	W58-36*	14+1 (5)	-	-	-	11+1 (4)	4+1 (4)	3+1 (4)	6+2 (4)	7+2 (4)	13 (5)	-
33	28/7	Edinburgh	A	PL	L36-57	11 (5)	-	-	-	4 (4)	2 (4)	2+1 (4)	4 (4)	2 (4)	11 (5)	-
34	29/7	Berwick	A	PL	L40-55	18 (5)	-	-	-	6 (4)	1 (4)	1+1 (5)	R/R	7+1 (6)	7 (6)	-
35	30/7	Newcastle	A	PL	D45-45	12 (5)	-	-	-	8 (4)	2 (3)	8+1 (5)	4+1 (4)	4+2 (4)	7+2 (5)	-
36	2/8	Edinburgh	H	PL	W59-34*	15 (5)	-	-	-	7 (4)	8+3 (5)	0 (3)	14+1 (5)	7+1 (4)	8+2 (4)	-
37	5/8	Rye House	A	PL	L38-56	-	-	-	-	4 (4)	2+2 (4)	4+1 (4)	6 (4)	3+1 (4)	8+1 (5)	11 (5)
38	11/8	Newcastle	H	PL	W57-37*	15 (5)	-	-	-	10+1 (5)	6 (4)	7+1 (4)	8 (4)	5+2 (4)	6+1 (4)	-
39	17/8	Redcar	A	PL	L39-54*	14 (5)	-	-	-	6 (4)	4 (4)	3 (4)	1 (4)	3 (4)	8 (5)	-
40	18/8	Newport	H	PL	W58-35	15 (5)	-	-	-	8 (4)	6+2 (5)	6+1 (4)	12+2 (5)	4 (3)	7+2 (4)	-
41	25/8	Stoke	H	PL	W58-34	14 (5)	-	-	-	11 (5)	6+1 (4)	8+3 (4)	4+2 (4)	3 (4)	12 (4)	-
42	27/8	Newport	A	PL	W47-43*	14+1 (5)	-	-	-	6 (4)	1+1 (3)	7+1 (5)	5+2 (4)	3 (4)	11 (5)	-
43	1/9	Swindon	H	DGC	L39.5-54.5	13+1 (5)	-	-	-	2.5 (4)	5+1 (4)	2+2 (4)	2 (4)	-	10 (5)	5+1 (4)
44	9/9	Mildenhall	A	PL	W50-40*	12 (6)	-	-	-	R/R	1+1 (3)	10+1 (5)	6 (5)	9+2 (5)	12+2 (6)	-
45	15/9	Sheffield	H	KOC s/f	W55-40	14 (5)	-	-	-	4+1 (4)	7 (5)	10+3 (6)	12+2 (6)	R/R	8+1 (4)	-
46	16/9	Stoke	A	PL	L44-46*	17 (6)	-	-	-	R/R	3+2 (4)	9+1 (6)	-	-	11 (6)	4+1 (8)
47	28/9	Sheffield	A	KOC s/f	L41-55*	18 (6)	-	-	-	R/R	2 (4)	4+3 (6)	2 (5)	4 (4)	11 (6)	-
48	29/9	Rye House	H	PO	D45-45	17 (6)	-	-	-	R/R	3 (4)	9+1 (5)	2+1 (5)	3+1 (4)	11+1 (6)	-
49	30/9	Rye House	A	PO	L43-49*	16+1 (6)	-	-	-	R/R	7 (5)	1+1 (6)	-	0 (1)	14 (6)	5+1 (6)
50	6/10	King's Lynn	H	KOC f	D45-45	15 (5)	-	-	-	3+1 (4)	7 (4)	4+1 (4)	6 (4)	3 (4)	7+1 (5)	-
51	11/10	King's Lynn	A	KOC f	L32-62	7 (4)	-	-	-	8+1 (5)	3+1 (5)	0 (4)	1 (4)	1 (3)	12 (5)	-

NOTE: BCA = BCA Vehicle Remarketing Trophy; BCT = Battle of the Champions Trophy; WCC = West Country Challenge; DGC = David and Goliath Challenge. The home Premier Trophy match against King's Lynn on 24 March was abandoned after heat twelve, with the result permitted to stand. The away Premier League fixture at the Isle of Wight on 18 July was abandoned after heat fourteen, with the result permitted to stand.

DETAILS OF OTHER RIDERS

(all guests)

Match No. 18: Lee Smart 0 (1); Match No. 27: Lee Smart 2+1 (4); Match No. 28: Lee Smart 2+1 (4); Match No. 37: Tomas Topinka 11 (5); Match No. 43: Neil Collins 5+1 (4); Match No. 46: Lee Dicken 4+1 (4); Tony Atkin 0 (4); Match No. 49: Chris Schramm 5+1 (6).

DETAILS OF TACTICAL RIDES AND TACTICAL SUBSTITUTE RIDES

Match No. 3: Smith 6 points (TR); Zetterstrom 1 point (TR; not doubled); Barker 0 points (TS); Match No. 5: Zetterstrom 4 points (TR); Fry 4 points (TR); Match No. 9: Zetterstrom 6 points (TR); Cunningham 4 points (TR); Match No. 12: Zetterstrom 6 points (TR); Katt 4 points (TR); Match No. 14: Zetterstrom 4 points (TR); Cunningham 1 point (TR; not doubled); Match No. 15: Zetterstrom 6 points (TR); Match No. 18: Fry 4 points (TR); Match No. 19: Fry 6 points (TR); Match No. 23: Cunningham 6 points (TR); Match No. 24: Zetterstrom 1 point (TS; not doubled); Match No. 28: Zetterstrom 6 points (TR); Kramer 4 points (TR); Match No. 33: Kramer 6 points (TR); Zetterstrom 1 point (TR; not doubled); Match No. 34: Zetterstrom 6 points (TR); Kramer 4 points (TR); Phillips 1 point (TS; not doubled); Match No. 37: Topinka 4 points (TR); Kramer 4 points (TR); Match No. 39: Zetterstrom 6 points (TR); Kramer 0 points (TR); Match No. 43: Zetterstrom 4 points (TR); Kramer 4 points (TR); Match No. 47: Zetterstrom 6 points (TR); Kramer 6 points (TR); Katt 0 points (TS); Match No. 49: Zetterstrom 6 points (TR); Schramm 0 points (TS); Match No. 51: Kramer 4 points (TR); Zetterstrom 4 points (TR).

OTHER DETAILS

Exeter Select scorers in Match No. 5: Chris Holder 12 (5); Mark Lemon 11+1 (5); Brent Werner 8+1 (4); Jordan Frampton 6 (5); Tommy Allen 4 (4); Luke Priest 1 (5); Michael Coles 0 (2). Holder's total includes 2 points from a TR.

AVERAGES

(26 Premier League, 2 Play-Offs, 8 Knock-Out Cup, 10 Premier Trophy = 46 fixtures)
♦ Denotes ever-present.

Rider	Mts	Rds	Pts	Bon	Tot	Avge	Max
Magnus Zetterstrom	45	227	587	10	597	10.52	9 full; 5 paid
Emil Kramer	24	120	217	15	232	7.73	1 full
Glenn Cunningham	41	184	320	17	337	7.33	1 paid
Paul Fry	16	70	113	13	126	7.20	-
Stephan Katt	39	171	252	33	285	6.67	1 paid
Glen Phillips	37	151	164	32	196	5.19	-
Ben Barker ♦	46	205	215	51	266	5.19	1 paid
Simon Walker	44	191	197	43	240	5.03	-

Also rode (in alphabetical order):

Pavel Ondrasik	2	6	9	0	9	6.00	-
Jamie Smith	4	20	31	4	35	7.00	-

Guests	7	28	22	4	26	3.71	-

(Tony Atkin [1]; Lee Dicken [1]; Chris Schramm [1]; Lee Smart [3]; Tomas Topinka [1]).

SOMERSET: From left to right, back row: Glenn Cunningham, Glen Phillips, Emil Kramer, Stephan Katt. Front row, kneeling: Ben Barker, Simon Walker. On bike: Magnus Zetterstrom.

OTHER MEETINGS

30 June: Conference Challenge

    Somerset 57: Jordan Frampton 14+1 (5); Cory Gathercole 14+1 (5); Jaimie Pickard 8+2 (4); Matt Browne 8+1 (4); Mattie Bates 6+1 (4); Andy Carfield 6 (4); Bob Charles 1 (2) Newport 39.

22 September: Matt Read Farewell

    Matt's Masters 37: Chris Neath 13 (4); Chris Harris 9 (4); Jason King 6 (4); Chris Mills 4+2 (4); Sean Wilson 3 (4); Simon Walker 2 (4); Ben Barker 0 (4); Readie's Racers 55: Simon Stead 10+2 (4); Steve Boxall 10 (4); Magnus Zetterstrom 9+3 (4); Mark Lemon 9 (4); Davey Watt 9 (4); Stephan Katt 7+1 (4); Paul Cooper 1+1 (4). Neath's total includes 8 points from two TR outings (4 + 4); Harris' total includes 4 points from a TR; Mills' total includes 2 points from two TR outings (2 + 0); King's total includes 2 points from a TR; Wilson's total includes 0 points from a TR; Walker's total includes 0 points from a TR.

INDIVIDUAL MEETING

8 September: British Under-15 Championship (Round Five)

    QUALIFYING SCORES: Joe Haines 12; Ben Hopwood 10; Brendan Johnson 10; Scott Meakins 8; Daniel Greenwood 7; Adam Wrathall 6; Richard Franklin 6; James Sarjeant 5; Tom Davies (reserve) 3; Shane Hazelden 2; Chris Bint (reserve) 2; Sean Paterson 1. FINAL: 1st Haines; 2nd Hopwood; 3rd Wrathall; 4th Johnson.

STOKE EASY-RIDER POTTERS

NOTE: The information below relates only to the main Stoke team. For details of the second side, please refer to the Conference League section.

ADDRESS: Chesterton Stadium, Loomer Road, Chesterton, Newcastle-under-Lyme, Staffordshire, ST5 7LB.
PROMOTER: David Tattum
YEARS OF OPERATION: 1972 Training; 1973-1974 British League Division Two; 1975-1990 National League; 1991-1992 British League Division Two; 1994 British League Division Three; 1995 Academy League; 1996-2006 Premier League.
NOTE: The team rode under the name of Chesterton in 1973. The team rode under the name of Cradley Heath & Stoke in 1996.
FIRST MEETING: 12 April 1973.
TRACK LENGTH: 312 metres.
TRACK RECORD: 61.0 seconds – Billy Hamill (11/09/96).

PREVIOUS VENUE: Hanley Stadium, Sun Street, Hanley, Staffordshire.
YEARS OF OPERATION: 1929 English Dirt-Track League and Open; 1939 National League Division Two; 1947-1949 National League Division Three; 1950-1953 National League Division Two; 1960-1963 Provincial League.

CLUB HONOURS

LEAGUE CHAMPIONS: 1949.
PAIRS CHAMPIONS: 1984, 1988, 1989.
FOUR-TEAM CHAMPIONS: 1990.

RIDER ROSTER 2006

Paul CLEWS; Michael COLES; Barrie EVANS; Robbie KESSLER; Mark LEMON; Trent LEVERINGTON; Alan MOGRIDGE; Luke PRIEST; Paul THORP.

OTHER APPEARANCES/GUESTS (official matches only)

Mattie BATES; John BRANNEY; James GRIEVES; Kriss IRVING; Gareth ISHERWOOD; Robert KSIEZAK; Billy LEGG; Adam McKINNA; Robert MEAR; John OLIVER; Andrew TULLY; Shane WALDRON; Brent WERNER; Matthew WRIGHT.

STOKE

* Denotes aggregate/bonus-point victory

NO.	DATE	OPPONENTS	VENUE	COMPETITION	RESULT	LEMON	COLES	CLEWS	KESSLER	MOGRIDGE	EVANS	PRIEST	LEVERINGTON	THORP	OTHERS
1	18/3	Denmark Select	H	Chal	W51-41	14(5)	7+1(4)	6+1(4)	9(5)	7+1(4)	7(4)	1+1(4)	-	-	-
2	1/4	Newcastle	H	PT	W45-44	11(5)	4+2(4)	4+1(4)	8+1(4)	7(5)	6+2(5)	5+1(3)	-	-	-
3	8/4	Sheffield	H	PT	W48-42	13+1(5)	5(4)	6(4)	8+2(4)	9+1(4)	7+1(6)	0(3)	-	-	-
4	15/4	Redcar	H	PT	W49.5-43.5	13(5)	3(4)	4.5+1(4)	10(4)	9+2(5)	5+1(4)	5+2(4)	-	-	-
5	22/4	Edinburgh	H	PT	L44-49	18(7)	2(3)	6(5)	8+2(5)	R/R	8(7)	2+1(3)	-	-	-
6	23/4	Glasgow	A	PT	L36-56	5(3)	3(4)	5(4)	8+1(5)	12+1(5)	3+2(5)	0(4)	-	-	-
7	29/4	Workington	H	PT	W56-37	12(5)	3+1(4)	7+2(4)	9+1(4)	9+1(5)	11+3(5)	5+1(3)	-	-	-
8	1/5	Workington	A	PT	L28-64	12(5)	2+1(4)	4(4)	3(5)	4(4)	1(4)	2(4)	-	-	-
9	6/5	Newport	H	PL	W50-36	15(5)	-	10+1(5)	9+1(5)	R/R	5+2(4)	5(4)	6(5)	-	-
10	7/5	Newport	A	PL	W52-44*	14(5)	-	10+3(5)	12(6)	R/R	7(5)	4+1(4)	5+1(5)	-	-
11	12/5	Edinburgh	A	PT	L36-58	13(5)	-	8+1(5)	7+1(4)	3(4)	2(4)	1+1(4)	2+1(4)	-	-
12	13/5	Berwick	A	PT	L44-46	9+1(5)	-	13(5)	6+2(4)	4(4)	8+1(5)	0(3)	4(4)	-	-
13	14/5	Berwick	H	PT	W58-37*	14(5)	-	10(4)	9+3(5)	7+1(4)	7(4)	5+1(4)	6+1(4)	-	-
14	19/5	Somerset	A	KOC	L38-57	14(5)	-	3+1(4)	11+1(6)	6(4)	1(4)	0(4)	3(4)	-	-
15	20/5	Somerset	H	KOC	W51-41	13(5)	-	5+2(4)	8(4)	10+1(5)	9+2(5)	4(3)	2+1(4)	-	-
16	28/5	Glasgow	A	PL	L32-61	11(5)	-	3(4)	8+1(5)	3(4)	6+1(5)	1(3)	0(4)	-	-
17	29/5	Workington	A	PL	L38-58	13(5)	-	5+2(4)	9+1(5)	3(4)	6(6)	0(3)	2(3)	-	-
18	1/6	Redcar	A	PT	L43-48*	14(5)	3(4)	9+1(5)	4+1(3)	5+1(4)	7(5)	1+1(4)	-	-	-
19	4/6	Berwick	H	PL	W56-37	14(5)	-	11+1(5)	10+2(4)	8+3(4)	7(4)	3+2(4)	3(4)	-	-
20	8/6	Sheffield	A	PT	L38-57	11(5)	-	R/R	10(5)	4+1(4)	2+1(5)	7+2(6)	4+1(5)	-	-
21	10/6	Glasgow	H	PT	L44-51	9(5)	-	R/R	14(5)	3+1(4)	12+2(7)	2+1(4)	4+2(5)	-	-
22	13/6	Isle of Wight	A	PL	L32-60	11+1(5)	-	R/R	5(5)	5(4)	1+1(5)	5(6)	5(5)	-	-
23	17/6	King's Lynn	H	PL	W47-43	9+2(5)	-	R/R	6+1(4)	12+1(5)	6(6)	4+1(5)	10(5)	-	-
24	2/7	Newcastle	A	PT	L41-54	11(5)	-	8(5)	5(4)	8+1(4)	3(4)	3+2(4)	3(4)	-	-
25	8/7	Redcar	H	PL	L42-53	14(5)	-	11(5)	6(4)	5+1(4)	3+1(5)	-	2+1(4)	-	1(3)
26	12/7	King's Lynn	A	PL	L26-66	11(6)	-	7(6)	R/R	1(4)	2(5)	-	5+2(5)	-	0(4)
27	15/7	Berwick	A	PL	L44-49*	14+1(6)	-	1(1)	R/R	7(5)	2(5)	-	16+2(6)	-	4+2(7)
28	20/7	Redcar	A	PL	L40-56	14+1(5)	-	R/R	10+1(6)	5(5)	5(6)	-	6+1(5)	-	0(3)
29	22/7	Newcastle	H	PL	W47-42	15(5)	-	5+1(4)	9(4)	8(5)	6+2(5)	-	4(4)	-	0(3)
30	29/7	Glasgow	H	PL	L38-55	12(5)	-	5(4)	7+1(5)	4+2(4)	6(5)	-	3(4)	-	1+1(3)
31	3/8	Sheffield	A	PL	W45-44	9(5)	-	4+1(4)	12+1(5)	6(4)	4+1(5)	-	8+3(4)	-	2+1(3)
32	5/8	Sheffield	H	PL	W46-43*	13(5)	-	2(4)	11(4)	-	5+2(5)	-	5(4)	10(5)	0(3)
33	6/8	Mildenhall	A	PL	L44-51	6(4)	-	2+1(4)	15(5)	-	-	-	4(4)	14+1(5)	3+1(8)
34	12/8	Isle of Wight	H	PL	W53-39	15(5)	-	5+1(4)	11+1(5)	-	-	-	3(4)	8(4)	11+3(8)
35	20/8	Workington	H	PL	W54-41	12+1(5)	-	4+2(4)	11(4)	-	8+1(5)	-	6+1(4)	12+1(5)	1(3)
36	25/8	Somerset	A	PL	L34-58	4(3)	-	4+3(4)	10(5)	-	1(6)	-	7(4)	8+1(5)	0(3)
37	26/8	Rye House	H	PL	L43-47	-	-	8+1(4)	8+2(5)	-	3+1(5)	-	6+1(4)	6(4)	12(8)
38	28/8	Rye House	A	PL	L27-65	-	-	3+1(4)	9(5)	-	4(4)	-	4(5)	1(4)	6+1(8)
39	8/9	Edinburgh	A	PL	L40-52	9(5)	-	6+3(4)	11(5)	-	0(5)	-	4+1(4)	9(4)	1(3)
40	9/9	Edinburgh	H	PL	W47-43	12+2(5)	-	5(4)	12(5)	-	4(6)	-	5(4)	9(4)	0(2)
41	16/9	Somerset	H	PL	W46-44	12(5)	-	7(4)	6+3(4)	-	6+2(5)	-	4+1(4)	10+2(5)	1(3)

NO.	DATE	OPPONENTS	VENUE	COMPETITION	RESULT	LEMON	COLES	CLEWS	KESSLER	MOGRIDGE	EVANS	PRIEST	LEVERINGTON	THORP	OTHERS
42	17/9	Newcastle	A	PL	L41-49	9 (5)	-	9+1 (5)	R/R	-	4 (6)	-	13 (6)	4+3 (5)	2 (3)
43	30/9	Mildenhall	H	PL	W63-29*	15 (5)		10 (4)	7 (4)	-	7+3 (4)	-	8+2 (4)	13+2 (5)	3 (4)

NOTE: The home league match versus Newport on 6 May was abandoned after heat fourteen, with the result permitted to stand.

DETAILS OF OTHER RIDERS

(all guests)

Match No. 25: Gareth Isherwood 1 (3); Match No. 26: Robert Mear 0 (4); Match No. 27: Adam McKinna 4+2 (7); Match No. 28: Adam McKinna 0 (3); Match No. 29: Andrew Tully 0 (3); Match No. 30: Adam McKinna 1+1 (3); Match No. 31: Shane Waldron 2+1 (3); Match No. 32: Matthew Wright 0 (3); Match No. 33: John Oliver 3+1 (5); Matthew Wright 0 (3); Match No. 34: Robert Ksiezak 10+3 (5); Billy Legg 1 (3); Match No. 35: John Branney 1 (3); Match No. 36: Mattie Bates 0 (3); Match No. 37: James Grieves 12 (5); John Branney 0 (3); Match No. 38: Brent Werner 4 (4); Shane Waldron 2+1 (4); Match No. 39: Kriss Irving 1 (3); Match No. 40: Kriss Irving 0 (2); Match No. 41: Shane Waldron 1 (3); Match No. 42: Shane Waldron 2 (3); Match No. 43: Shane Waldron 3 (4).

DETAILS OF TACTICAL RIDES AND TACTICAL SUBSTITUTE RIDES

Match No. 5: Lemon 6 points (TS); Match No. 6: Mogridge 4 points (TR); Lemon 0 points (TR); Match No. 8: Lemon 4 points (TR); Mogridge 0 points (TR); Match No. 11: Kessler 4 points (TR); Lemon 4 points (TR); Match No. 14: Lemon 6 points (TR); Kessler 4 points (TR); Match No. 16: Lemon 6 points (TR); Mogridge 0 points (TR); Match No. 17: Lemon 6 points (TR); Kessler 6 points (TR); Match No. 18: Lemon 4 points (TR); Match No. 20: Kessler 6 points (TR); Lemon 4 points (TR); Match No. 21: Kessler 6 points (TR); Evans 4 points (TR); Match No. 22: Lemon 4 points (TR); Kessler 1 point (TR; not doubled); Match No. 24: Lemon 6 points (TR); Mogridge 4 points (TR); Match No. 25: Lemon 6 points (TR); Clews 4 points (TR); Match No. 26: Lemon 4 points (TR); Leverington 1 point (TR; not doubled); Match No. 27: Leverington 6 points (TR); Lemon 0 points (TR); Match No. 28: Kessler 6 points (TR); Lemon 6 points (TR); Match No. 30: Lemon 6 points (TR); Clews 1 point (TR; not doubled); Match No. 33: Thorp 6 points (TR); Kessler 4 points (TR); Match No. 36: Kessler 4 points (TR); Thorp 0 points (TR); Match No. 38: Kessler 4 points (TR); Werner 1 point (TR; not doubled); Match No. 39: Kessler 4 points (TR).

OTHER DETAILS

Denmark Select scorers in Match No. 1: Charlie Gjedde 14 (5); Mads Korneliussen 11 (5); Tom P. Madsen 4+1 (4); Morten Risager 4 (4); Jonas Raun 3+1 (4); Jonathan Bethell 3+1 (5); Henrik Moller 2 (4). Gjedde's total includes 4 points from a TR.

AVERAGES

(26 Premier League, 2 Knock-Out Cup, 14 Premier Trophy = 42 fixtures)

Rider	Mts	Rds	Pts	Bon	Tot	Avge	Max
Mark Lemon	40	199	439	10	449	9.03	4 full
Paul Thorp	12	55	101	10	111	8.07	1 paid
Robbie Kessler	39	181	323	30	353	7.80	1 paid
Paul Clews	37	156	221.5	30	251.5	6.45	-
Alan Mogridge	27	116	162	18	180	6.21	-
Trent Leverington	35	152	170	23	193	5.08	-
Barrie Evans	40	200	196	33	229	4.58	-

STOKE: From left to right, back row: Barrie Evans, Mark Lemon, Michael Coles, Paul Clews, Robbie Kessler, Luke Priest. Front row, on bike: Alan Mogridge.

Michael Coles	7	27	22	4	26	3.85	-
Luke Priest	23	90	70	16	86	3.82	-
Guests	23	82	48	9	57	2.78	-

(Mattie Bates [1]; John Branney [2]; James Grieves [1]; Kriss Irving [2]; Gareth Isherwood [1]; Robert Ksiezak [1]; Billy Legg [1]; Adam McKinna [3]; Robert Mear [1]; John Oliver [1]; Andrew Tully [1]; Shane Waldron [5]; Brent Werner [1]; Matthew Wright [2]).

NOTE: Trent Leverington was ever-present throughout the 26-match Premier League programme.

OTHER MEETINGS

27 May: Robbie Kessler Testimonial

Stoke 30: Robbie Kessler 10 (4); Mark Lemon 9 (4); Paul Clews 6 (4); Alan Mogridge 4 (3); Luke Priest 1 (1); Sheffield 25; Hull 24: Rory Schlein 11 (4); Shane Parker 9 (4); Emiliano Sanchez 4 (4); Ross Brady 0 (4); Wolverhampton 24. The total for Shane Parker includes 6 points from a tactical ride. Individual Trophy: FIRST SEMI-FINAL: 1st Schlein; 2nd Lemon; 3rd Kessler; 4th Parker. SECOND SEMI-FINAL: 1st David Howe; 2nd Chris Neath; 3rd Adam Allott; 4th Priest. FINAL: 1st Schlein; 2nd Lemon; 3rd Neath; 4th Howe.

23 September: Clewsy Classic – Paul Clews Testimonial Pairs

1st David Howe (16+1) and Paul Clews (10+3) = 26; 2nd Rory Schlein (18) and Nick Simmons (5+2) = 23; 3rd Trent Leverington (12+1) and Stuart Robson (8+1) = 20; Jack Hargreaves (10+1) and Paul Thorp (8) = 18; Emiliano Sanchez (9) and Joel Parsons (5+2) = 14; Shane Parker (10+1) and Chris Schramm (4+1) = 14; James Grieves (10) and Tom Brown (1) = 11.

WORKINGTON COMETINSURANCE.COM COMETS

ADDRESS: Derwent Park Stadium, Workington, Cumbria, CA14 2HG.

PROMOTERS: Graham Drury and Anthony E. Mole.

YEARS OF OPERATION: 1970-1974 British League Division Two; 1975-1981 National League; 1985 Open; 1987 National League; 1994 Demonstration; 1999-2006 Premier League.

NOTE: In 1987, the track was occupied by Glasgow Tigers, who later that year became known as Workington Tigers.

FIRST MEETING: 3 April 1970.

TRACK LENGTH: 364 metres.

TRACK RECORD: 63.2 seconds – Simon Stead (23/09/06).

CLUB HONOURS

PAIRS CHAMPIONS: 1999, 2000, 2001, 2003.

FOUR-TEAM CHAMPIONS: 2001, 2004, 2006.

RIDER ROSTER 2006

Aidan COLLINS; Lee DERBYSHIRE; Rusty HARRISON; Ritchie HAWKINS; Alan MOGRIDGE; Tomasz PISZCZ; Garry STEAD; Paul THORP; James WRIGHT.

OTHER APPEARANCES/GUESTS (official matches only)

Carl BELFIELD; Steve BOXALL; Craig BRANNEY; John BRANNEY; Richie DENNIS; Josef FRANC; David HAIGH; Richard JUUL; Robert KSIEZAK; Adam McKINNA; Phil MORRIS; John OLIVER: Joel PARSONS; Ben POWELL; Adam ROYNON; Emiliano SANCHEZ; Sean STODDART; Andrew TULLY; Tai WOFFINDEN; Danny WARWICK; Charles WRIGHT; Matthew WRIGHT.

WORKINGTON

* Denotes aggregate/bonus-point victory

NO.	DATE	OPPONENTS	VENUE	COMPETITION	RESULT	THORP	PISZCZ	HAWKINS	J. WRIGHT	STEAD	DERBYSHIRE	COLLINS	HARRISON	JUUL	MOGRIDGE	OTHERS
1	18/3	Sheffield	H	PT	W50-45	6 (4)	7+1 (4)	9+1 (5)	10+1 (5)	9 (4)	3+1 (4)	6+1 (4)	-	-	-	-
2	19/3	Newcastle	A	PT	L46-47	6 (4)	8+1 (5)	2 (4)	11 (5)	7 (4)	1+1 (3)	11+3 (6)	-	-	-	-
3	1/4	Edinburgh	H	PT	W41-34	2 (2)	8+1 (4)	8+2 (4)	9 (3)	6+1 (3)	1+1 (2)	7+1 (6)	-	-	-	-
4	8/4	Glasgow	H	PT	W51-45	10 (4)	6+1 (4)	8+1 (4)	12+1 (5)	9+1 (5)	0 (3)	6 (5)	-	-	-	-
5	9/4	Glasgow	A	PT	W46-44*	5+2 (4)	8+1 (4)	3 (3)	10+1 (5)	12 (5)	0 (3)	8+2 (7)	-	-	-	-
6	14/4	Edinburgh	A	PT	W45-44*	0(0)	9 (4)	4 (4)	11 (5)	14 (5)	2+1 (5)	5+1 (7)	-	-	-	-

NO.	DATE	OPPONENTS	VENUE	COMPETITION	RESULT	THORP	PISZCZ	HAWKINS	J. WRIGHT	STEAD	DERBYSHIRE	COLLINS	HARRISON	JUUL	MOGRIDGE	OTHERS
7	15/4	Berwick	A	PT	D45-45	R/R	9+1 (5)	8 (5)	10+1 (6)	14 (6)	1 (3)	3+1 (5)	-	-	-	-
8	17/4	Berwick	H	PT	W63-29*	8+2 (4)	10 (4)	12+3 (5)	12 (4)	12+1 (5)	3+1 (4)	6+1 (4)	-	-	-	-
9	21/4	Newcastle	H	PT	W50-40*	8+2 (5)	7 (4)	5 (4)	14 (5)	9 (4)	0 (3)	7+1 (5)	-	-	-	-
10	28/4	Somerset	A	PL	L40-50	6 (4)	4 (4)	10+1 (5)	5+1 (4)	8 (5)	1+1 (3)	6+3 (5)	-	-	-	-
11	29/4	Stoke	A	PT	L37-56	3 (4)	4+1 (4)	2+1 (4)	14 (5)	10 (5)	0 (3)	4+1 (6)	-	-	-	-
12	1/5	Stoke	H	PT	W64-28*	12 (4)	8+2 (4)	9+1 (4)	12 (5)	12+2 (5)	3 (4)	8+2 (4)	-	-	-	-
13	4/5	Sheffield	A	PT	L38-57	12 (5)	5+2 (4)	2 (4)	7 (4)	11 (5)	0 (1)	1 (7)	-	-	-	-
14	6/5	Rye House	H	PL	W59-31	13 (5)	6+2 (4)	9+2 (4)	14+1 (5)	9+1 (4)	-	6+2 (5)	-	-	-	2+1 (3)
15	13/5	Newport	H	PL	W51-39	6 (4)	11 (5)	7+1 (4)	11+2 (5)	7 (4)	-	8+3 (5)	-	-	-	1+1 (3)
16	18/5	Redcar	A	PT	W49-42	9 (4)	7+1 (4)	9 (5)	3+1 (4)	14+1 (5)	-	5+1 (5)	-	-	-	2+1 (3)
17	27/5	Newcastle	H	KOC	W54-40	8 (4)	8+1 (4)	6+2 (4)	13 (5)	10+1 (5)	-	6+1 (4)	-	-	-	3+2 (4)
18	28/5	Newcastle	A	KOC	L40-55	6+1 (4)	3 (4)	5+1 (4)	9 (5)	13 (5)	-	3 (5)	-	-	-	1+1 (3)
19	29/5	Stoke	H	PL	W58-38	11+3 (5)	8+1 (4)	13+2 (5)	8 (4)	8+1 (4)	-	8 (5)	-	-	-	2 (3)
20	4/6	Rye House	A	PL	L41-49*	0 (2)	7 (4)	5+3 (4)	-	9+1 (5)	-	6+1 (5)	-	-	-	14+1 (10)
21	6/6	Isle of Wight	A	PL	L42-52	R/R	-	8+1 (6)	5 (4)	15 (6)	-	9+4 (6)	-	-	-	5 (8)
22	7/6	King's Lynn	A	PL	L30-63	R/R	12 (6)	1 (5)	7 (5)	2 (1)	-	6+2 (7)	-	-	-	2 (6)
23	10/6	Somerset	H	PL	W48-45	R/R	12+3 (6)	12 (6)	-	10+1 (5)	-	9+1 (6)	-	-	-	5 (7)
24	17/6	Edinburgh	H	PL	W57-39	R/R	10+2 (5)	14+3 (6)	15 (5)	11 (5)	-	6 (6)	-	-	-	1 (3)
25	23/6	Redcar	H	PT	W50-43*	7 (4)	6+1 (4)	13+1 (5)	12 (5)	8+2 (4)	-	4+1 (4)	-	-	-	0 (4)
26	30/6	Isle of Wight	H	PL	W63-30*	12 (4)	10+1 (4)	8+3 (4)	12+3 (5)	9 (4)	-	9+1 (4)	-	-	-	3 (5)
27	2/7	Newport	A	PL	L35-58	0 (2)	3+1 (4)	5 (4)	8 (5)	11 (4)	-	6+1 (6)	-	-	-	2 (5)
28	15/7	Glasgow	H	PL	L44-46	4+2 (4)	11+1 (5)	2 (1)	8+1 (5)	6 (4)	-	12+4 (7)	-	-	-	1 (4)
29	20/7	Sheffield	A	PL	L42-53	5+2 (4)	13 (6)	R/R	11 (5)	5 (3)	-	5+3 (6)	-	-	-	3+2 (6)
30	22/7	Sheffield	H	PL	L44-46	10+3 (5)	9 (4)	R/R	9 (5)	-	-	9+1 (7)	-	-	-	7+2 (9)
31	23/7	Newcastle	A	PL	L39-53	3+1 (4)	11+1 (6)	R/R	13 (5)	-	-	8+2 (7)	-	-	-	4 (8)
32	29/7	King's Lynn	H	PT s/f	W51-39	-	5 (4)	-	15 (5)	8+1 (4)	-	10+2 (6)	10+3 (5)	3 (3)	-	0 (3)
33	4/8	King's Lynn	A	PT s/f	L35-59	-	4 (4)	-	5 (5)	13 (5)	-	1 (4)	9 (4)	2 (4)	-	1 (4)
34	5/8	Mildenhall	H	PL	W53-42	-	10 (4)	-	14 (5)	10+1 (5)	-	8+2 (6)	8+3 (4)	3+1 (3)	-	0 (3)
35	6/8	Glasgow	A	PL	L41-54	-	11 (5)	-	8 (4)	9 (5)	-	4+2 (6)	5 (4)	4+2 (4)	-	0 (2)
36	20/8	Stoke	A	PL	L41-54*	-	12 (5)	-	12 (5)	5 (4)	-	1 (5)	6+1 (4)	-	3+1 (4)	2 (3)
37	26/8	Berwick	A	PL	W49-41	-	13 (5)	-	6 (4)	7+1 (4)	-	5+1 (5)	10+2 (5)	-	8+2 (4)	0 (3)
38	28/8	Berwick	H	PL	W50-43*	-	6+1 (4)	-	12 (5)	7+3 (4)	-	8+2 (5)	7 (4)	-	9 (5)	1+1 (3)
39	31/8	Redcar	A	PL	L36-59	-	0 (4)	-	11 (5)	6+1 (4)	-	4+1 (5)	5 (4)	-	10 (5)	0 (3)
40	2/9	Redcar	H	PL	W52-42	R/R	-	-	17 (6)	9 (5)	-	0 (0)	11+2 (5)	-	10+2 (5)	5+2 (7)
41	3/9	Mildenhall	A	PL	W46-44*	R/R	-	-	12+1 (6)	7 (5)	-	0 (1)	-	-	6+4 (5)	21+2 (13)
42	9/9	King's Lynn	H	PL	L43-49	-	13 (6)	-	17 (6)	6 (4)	2 (3)	R/R	-	-	5+2 (5)	0 (3)
43	16/9	Newcastle	H	PL	W60-35*	-	10 (4)	-	13+1 (5)	10+1 (5)	-	9+2 (4)	-	-	7+2 (4)	11+2 (8)
44	21/9	Sheffield	A	PO	L40-53	-	6 (5)	-	8 (5)	9+1 (4)	-	1+1 (3)	-	-	1+1 (4)	15+4 (10)
45	22/9	Edinburgh	A	PL	W46-44*	3+2 (4)	-	-	10 (5)	8 (4)	-	11+1 (5)	-	-	4+1 (4)	10+1 (8)
46	30/9	Sheffield	H	PO	W46-44	-	2 (4)	-	8 (5)	13+1 (5)	-	8 (4)	-	-	6 (4)	9+4 (8)

NOTE: The home Premier Trophy match against Edinburgh on 1 April was abandoned after heat twelve, with the result permitted to stand.

DETAILS OF OTHER RIDERS

(all guests)

Match No. 14: Sean Stoddart 2+1 (3); Match No. 15: John Branney 1+1 (3); Match No. 16: John Branney 2+1 (3); Match No. 17: Richie Dennis 3+2 (4); Match No. 18: Richie Dennis 1+1 (3); John Branney 2 (3); Match No. 20: Josef Franc 9+1 (5); Matthew Wright 5 (5); Match No. 21: Steve Boxall 5 (5); Richie Dennis 0 (3); Match No. 22: Richie Dennis 2 (6); Match No. 23: Rusty Harrison 5 (4); John Branney 0 (3); Match No. 24: John Branney 1 (3); Match No. 25: John Branney 0 (4); Match No. 26: John Branney 3 (5); Match No. 27: Richie Dennis 2 (5); Match No. 28: John Branney 1 (4); Match No. 29: John Oliver 3+2 (6); Match No. 30: John Branney 4+2 (6); Phil Morris 3 (3); Match No. 31: Emiliano Sanchez 3 (4); John Branney 1 (4); Match No. 32: John Branney 0 (3); Match No. 33: Richie Dennis 1 (4); Match No. 34: Adam McKinna 0 (3); Match No. 35: Sean Stoddart 0 (2); Match No. 36: Carl Belfield 2 (3); Match No. 37: Carl Belfield 0 (3); Match No. 38: Carl Belfield 1+1 (3); Match No. 39: Ben Powell 0 (3); Match No. 40: Tai Woffinden 5+2 (7); Match No. 41: Adam Roynon 16 (7); Ben Powell 5+2 (6); Match No. 42: Charles Wright 0 (1); David Haigh 0 (2); Match No. 43: Craig Branney 10+2 (4); Tai Woffinden 1 (4); Match No. 44: Joel Parsons 10+2 (5); Ben Powell 5+2 (5); Match No. 45: Robert Ksiezak 9+1 (5); Andrew Tully 1 (3); Match No. 46: Craig Branney 5+2 (5); Danny Warwick 4+2 (3).

DETAILS OF TACTICAL RIDES AND TACTICAL SUBSTITUTE RIDES

Match No. 11: J. Wright 6 points (TR); Stead 1 point (TR; not doubled); Match No. 13: Stead 6 points (TR); Thorp 4 points (TR); Match No. 18: Stead 6 points (TR); J. Wright 4 points (TR); Match No. 20: Hawkins 2 points (TR); Match No. 21: Stead 4 points (TR); J. Wright 4 points (TR); Match No. 22: Piszcz 6 points (TR); Stead 0 points (TR; fell, non-starter); Match No. 27: Stead 6 points (TR); Hawkins 0 points (TR); Match No. 29: Piszcz 6 points (TR); J. Wright 4 points (TR); Match No. 31: J. Wright 4 points (TR); Piszcz 0 points (TR); Match No. 33: Stead 4 points (TR); Harrison 4 points (TR); Match No. 35: Piszcz 6 points (TR); J. Wright 4 points (TR); Match No. 36: Piszcz 6 points (TR); J. Wright 4 points (TR); Match No. 39: Mogridge 6 points (TR); J. Wright 4 points (TR); Match No. 42: J. Wright 4 points (TR); Match No. 44: Stead 4 points (TR).

AVERAGES

(26 Premier League, 2 Play-Offs, 2 Knock-Out Cup, 16 Premier Trophy = 46 fixtures)

Rider	Mts	Rds	Pts	Bon	Tot	Avge	Max
James Wright	44	214	444	15	459	8.58	3 full; 2 paid
Garry Stead	44	196	392	23	415	8.47	1 paid
Rusty Harrison	14	56	98	15	113	8.07	-
Paul Thorp	26	99	170	18	188	7.60	2 full
Ritchie Hawkins	28	122	198	29	227	7.44	2 paid
Tomasz Piszcz	43	191	323	29	352	7.37	-
Alan Mogridge	11	49	66	15	81	6.61	-
Aidan Collins	41	216	246	55	301	5.57	-
Lee Derbyshire	13	41	15	6	21	2.05	-
Also rode:							
Richard Juul	4	14	12	3	15	4.29	-
Guests	44	175	133	27	160	3.66	1 paid

(Carl Belfield [3]; Steve Boxall [1]; Craig Branney [2]; John Branney [11]; Richie Dennis [6]; Josef Franc [1]; David Haigh [1]; Rusty Harrison [1]; Robert Ksiezak [1]; Adam McKinna [1]; Phil Morris [1]; John Oliver [1]; Joel Parsons [1]; Ben Powell [3]; Adam Roynon [1]; Emiliano Sanchez [1]; Sean Stoddart [2]; Andrew Tully [1]; Tai Woffinden [2]; Danny Warwick [1]; Charles Wright [1]; Matthew Wright [1]).

WORKINGTON: From left to right, back row: Paul Thorp, Lee Derbyshire, Graham Drury (co-promoter/team manager), Aidan Collins, James Wright. Front row, kneeling: Tomasz Piszcz, Ritchie Hawkins. On bike: Garry Stead.

INDIVIDUAL MEETING

23 September: Cumberland Classic

1st Simon Stead (after run-off) 13; 2nd Kauko Nieminen 13; 3rd James Wright 13; Josef Franc 11; Chris Holder 10; Richard Hall 10; Kenneth Hansen 9; Robert Ksiezak 8; Chris Kerr 7; Alan Mogridge 5; Craig Branney 5; Garry Stead 4; Daniel King 3; Scott James 3; David Haigh (reserve) 2; Rusty Harrison 2; John MacPhail (reserve) 1; Adam Scott (reserve) 0; Tomasz Piszcz 0.

CONFERENCE LEAGUE 2006

CONFERENCE LEAGUE TABLE

Team	Mts	Won	Drn	Lst	For	Agn	Pts	Bon	Tot
Plymouth	14	11	0	3	719	561	22	7	29
Scunthorpe	14	11	0	3	756	521	22	6	28
Rye House	14	9	0	5	705	581	18	5	23
Stoke	14	7	1	6	599	657	15	3	18
Boston	14	7	0	7	666	616	14	3	17
Buxton	14	5	0	9	639	655	10	3	13
Mildenhall	14	4	1	9	562	722	9	1	10
Newport	14	1	0	13	460	793	2	0	2

PLAY-OFFS

SEMI-FINAL

Rye House	38	Scunthorpe	52	
Scunthorpe	62	Rye House	32	(Scunthorpe won 114-70 on aggregate)

FINAL

Scunthorpe	67	Plymouth	25	
Plymouth	36	Scunthorpe	58	(Scunthorpe won 125-61 on aggregate)

TOP 20 AVERAGES
(Conference League only. Minimum qualification: 6 matches.)

Rider	Mts	Rds	Pts	Bon	Tot	Avge	Max
Chris Johnson (Plymouth)	7	29	75	4	79	10.90	5 (3 full; 2 paid)
Seemond Stephens (Plymouth)	14	67	178	2	180	10.75	7 (6 full; 1 paid)
James Birkinshaw (Boston)	8	43	102	10	112	10.42	1 (1 paid)
Josh Auty (Scunthorpe)	14	76	172	18	190	10.00	5 (1 full; 4 paid)
Wayne Carter (Scunthorpe)	11	51	110	9	119	9.33	2 (2 paid)
Ben Barker (Stoke)	9	49	101	13	114	9.31	1 (1 paid)
Richie Dennis (Scunthorpe)	13	61	132	8	140	9.18	2 (1 full; 1 paid)
Luke Priest (Stoke)	11	52	104	12	116	8.92	1 (1 paid)
Tai Woffinden (Scunthorpe)	12	54	106	14	120	8.89	2 (2 paid)
Lee Smart (Plymouth)	14	64	130	10	140	8.75	5 (5 paid)
Ben Powell (Rye House)	14	71	148	7	155	8.73	Nil
Tom Brown (Plymouth)	14	61	109	21	130	8.52	2 (2 paid)
Barry Burchatt (Rye House)	9	40	76	9	85	8.50	Nil
John Branney (Scunthorpe/Stoke)	7	31	54	11	65	8.39	Nil
Danny Betson (Rye House)	13	59	113	10	123	8.34	1 (1 paid)
Darren Mallett (Boston)	12	61	122	4	126	8.26	1 (1 full)
John Oliver (Boston)	10	53	99	9	108	8.15	1 (1 paid)

Mark Thompson (Mildenhall)	12	56	113	0	113	8.07	1 (1 full)
Harland Cook (Rye House)	14	69	121	18	139	8.06	1 (1 paid)
Adam Roynon (Buxton)	13	65	121	9	130	8.00	1 (1 paid)
Benji Compton (Scunthorpe)	8	39	64	14	78	8.00	1 (1 paid)

KNOCK-OUT CUP

ROUND ONE

| Mildenhall | 32 | Rye House | 58 | |
| Rye House | 50 | Mildenhall | 43 | (Rye House won 108-75 on aggregate) |

| Boston | 54 | Buxton | 39 | |
| Buxton | 56 | Boston | 38 | (Buxton won 95-92 on aggregate) |

| Scunthorpe | 59 | Stoke | 36 | |
| Stoke | 46 | Scunthorpe | 47 | (Scunthorpe won 106-82 on aggregate) |

| Plymouth | 57 | Newport | 37 | |
| Newport | 41 | Plymouth | 48 | (Plymouth won 105-78 on aggregate) |

SEMI-FINALS

| Plymouth | 58 | Buxton | 34 | |
| Buxton | 51 | Plymouth | 42 | (Plymouth won 100-85 on aggregate) |

| Scunthorpe | 52 | Rye House | 36 | |
| Rye House | 45 | Scunthorpe | 45 | (Scunthorpe won 97-81 on aggregate) |

FINAL

| Plymouth | 42 | Scunthorpe | 51 | |
| Scunthorpe | 48 | Plymouth | 24 | (Scunthorpe won 99-66 on aggregate) |

CONFERENCE TROPHY

CONFERENCE TROPHY (EAST) TABLE

Team	Mts	Won	Drn	Lst	For	Agn	Pts	Bon	Tot
Scunthorpe	4	4	0	0	226	144	8	2	10
Mildenhall	4	2	0	2	168	198	4	1	5
Boston	4	0	0	4	156	208	0	0	0

CONFERENCE TROPHY (WEST) TABLE

Team	Mts	Won	Drn	Lst	For	Agn	Pts	Bon	Tot
Plymouth	4	4	0	0	219	129	8	2	10
Buxton	4	1	0	3	151	197	2	1	3
Stoke	4	1	0	3	141	185	2	0	2

FINAL

Plymouth	39	Scunthorpe	51	
Scunthorpe	59	Plymouth	36	(Scunthorpe won 110-75 on aggregate)

CONFERENCE SHIELD

Team	Mts	Won	Drn	Lst	For	Agn	Pts	Bon	Tot
Scunthorpe	10	10	0	0	569	341	20	5	25
Buxton	10	7	0	3	526	398	14	4	18
Stoke	10	6	0	4	489	428	12	3	15
Weymouth	10	3	0	7	429	493	6	2	8
Cleveland	10	2	0	8	398	515	4	1	5
Sittingbourne	10	2	0	8	337	573	4	0	4

BOSTON N.C. WILLIAMS & SON INSURANCE BARRACUDA-BRAVES

ADDRESS: Norfolk Arena, Saddlebow Road, King's Lynn, Norfolk, PE34 3AG.
CLUB CHAIRMEN: Stephen Lambert, Malcolm Vasey and Mick Smith.
TRACK LENGTH: 342 metres.
CL TRACK RECORD: 60.0 seconds – Trevor Harding (15/06/03).
FIRST MEETING: 1 April 2000.
YEARS OF OPERATION: 2000–2006 Conference League.

PREVIOUS VENUE: Boston Sports Stadium, New Hammond Beck Road, Boston, Lincolnshire.
YEARS OF OPERATION: 1970–1974 British League Division Two; 1975–1984 National League; 1986–1987 National League.

CLUB HONOURS

LEAGUE CHAMPIONS: 1973.
KNOCK-OUT CUP WINNERS: 1973, 2000.
PAIRS CHAMPIONS: 1977.
CONFERENCE TROPHY WINNERS: 2003.

RIDER ROSTER 2006

James BIRKINSHAW; Wayne BROADHURST; Scott CAMPOS; Kyle HUGHES; Nathan IRWIN; Cal McDADE; Darren MALLETT; Sam MARTIN; John OLIVER.

OTHER APPEARANCES/GUESTS (official matches only)

Ben JOHNSON; Simon LAMBERT; Sean STODDART.

BOSTON

* Denotes aggregate/bonus-point victory

NO.	DATE	OPPONENTS	VENUE	COMPETITION	RESULT	BIRKINSHAW	IRWIN	LAMBERT	OLIVER	MALLETT	CAMPOS	MARTIN	HUGHES	McDADE	BROADHURST	STODDART	JOHNSON
1	7/4	Scunthorpe	H	EC	L42-47	10 (5)	7+2 (4)	7+1 (4)	5 (4)	9 (5)	3 (4)	1 (4)	-	-	-	-	-
2	17/4	Scunthorpe	A	EC	L40-53	13 (6)	3+1 (4)	3+2 (4)	10 (5)	6+1 (4)	3 (4)	2+2 (3)	-	-	-	-	-
3	28/4	Spalding Select	H	Chal	W55-38	10+4 (5)	10+1 (4)	-	8 (4)	15 (5)	-	9+2 (5)	3 (4)	-	-	-	0 (3)
4	30/4	Buxton	A	CL	L43-47	12+1 (5)	1 (3)	8+1 (5)	-	7 (4)	4 (4)	9+2 (6)	2+1 (3)	-	-	-	-
5	5/5	Newport	H	CL	W65-24	8+1 (4)	6+1 (4)	15 (5)	11+4 (5)	11 (4)	6+2 (4)	8+3 (4)	-	-	-	-	-
6	10/5	Stoke	A	CL	W48-46	11 (5)	-	3 (1)	-	7+1 (4)	5 (5)	9+2 (6)	5+1 (4)	-	-	8 (5)	-
7	12/5	Mildenhall	H	CL	W66-24	14+4 (6)	12+1 (5)	R/R	12+1 (5)	18 (6)	3+1 (4)	7+1 (4)	-	-	-	-	-
8	14/5	Mildenhall	A	CL	W53-37*	16+1 (6)	11 (5)	R/R	-	11 (6)	2+1 (3)	12+3 (6)	1 (4)	-	-	-	-

NO.	DATE	OPPONENTS	VENUE	COMPETITION	RESULT	BIRKINSHAW	IRWIN	LAMBERT	OLIVER	MALLETT	CAMPOS	MARTIN	HUGHES	McDADE	BROADHURST	STODDART	JOHNSON
9	19/5	Rye House	H	CL	L44-49	14+3 (6)	6 (5)	R/R	9+2 (6)	8 (5)	0 (3)	7+3 (6)	-				
10	4/6	Scunthorpe	A	CL	L40-52	17 (5)	3+1 (3)	-	8 (5)	7 (4)	-	3+2 (6)	0 (3)	2 (4)			
11	9/6	Stoke	H	CL	W51-43*	16 (6)	5 (5)	-	-	11+2 (5)	-	7+1 (4)	9 (6)	3+2 (4)	-	R/R	
12	16/6	Plymouth	A	CL	L38-54	-	2 (4)	-	9+1 (5)	6 (6)	-	13+3 (7)	5+1 (5)	3 (4)	-	R/R	
13	23/6	Buxton	H	CL	W47-43	-	-	-	15 (6)	15 (6)	-	5 (5)	6 (5)	1 (3)	5+2 (5)	R/R	
14	30/6	Scunthorpe	H	CL	L40-53	-	-	-	8 (6)	16 (6)	-	4+2 (6)	4 (4)	0 (3)	8+1 (5)	R/R	
15	7/7	Buxton	H	KOC	W54-39	-	14 (6)	-	11+1 (5)	R/R	-	12+2 (6)	10+1 (5)	2+1 (3)	5+3 (5)	-	
16	9/7	Buxton	A	KOC	L38-56	-	-	-	10 (6)	R/R	-	8+1 (6)	0 (4)	3+1 (4)	11 (6)	6+2 (5)	-
17	16/7	Newport	A	CL	W55-37*	-	7+1 (5)	-	7+1 (4)	R/R	-	14+1 (6)	9+2 (5)	6+3 (6)	12+1 (5)	-	
18	30/7	Mildenhall	A	CT	L38-55	-	5 (4)	-	-	4 (4)	-	7+2 (5)	4 (4)	0 (3)	9 (5)	9+1 (5)	-
19	7/8	Scunthorpe	A	CT	L37-57	-	1+1 (4)	-	12 (5)	4 (4)	-	4+1 (4)	2 (4)	2 (4)	12+2 (5)	-	
20	3/9	Plymouth	H	CL	L44-46	-	7+2 (4)	-	11 (5)	8+1 (5)	-	6+2 (4)	7+2 (7)	0 (1)	5+1 (4)	-	
21	8/9	Mildenhall	H	CT	L43-44	-	11+2 (6)	-	R/R	12 (6)	-	9+1 (5)	3+1 (7)	-	8+1 (5)	-	0 (1)
22	23/9	Rye House	A	CL	L32-61	-	1 (4)	-	14 (6)	R/R	-	4+1 (5)	5+3 (6)	3 (4)	5 (5)	-	
23	23/10	Scunthorpe	H	CT	L38-52	-	0 (0)	11 (6)	R/R	12 (7)	2+2 (6)	-	5+3 (5)	8 (6)			

NOTE: EC = Easter Cup. Following the home league match versus Buxton on 23 June, Darren Mallett was beaten by Adam Roynon in a run-off for the bonus point.

DETAILS OF TACTICAL RIDES AND TACTICAL SUBSTITUTE RIDES

Match No. 2: Oliver 6 points (TR); Birkinshaw 1 point (TS; not doubled); Lambert 0 points (TR); Match No. 9: Birkinshaw 6 points (TR); Mallett 1 point (TR; not doubled); Match No. 10: Birkinshaw 6 points (TR); Match No. 12: Oliver 4 points (TR); Mallett 1 point (TR; not doubled); Match No. 14: Mallett 6 points (TR); Match No. 16: Broadhurst 4 points (TR); Oliver 4 points (TR); Match No. 18: Stoddart 6 points (TR); Mallett 0 points (TR); Match No. 19: Oliver 4 points (TR); Broadhurst 4 points (TR); Match No. 22: Oliver 6 points (TR); Broadhurst 0 points (TR); Match No. 23: Mallett 0 points (TS).

OTHER DETAILS

Spalding Select scorers in Match No. 3: Richie Dennis 13 (5); Simon Lambert 8 (6); Robert Hollingworth 5 (4); Scott Campos 4+1 (4); Wayne Dunworth 4+1 (4); Peter Boast 2+1 (4); Daniel Hodgson 2+1 (3). Dennis' total includes 6 points from a TR; Lambert's total includes 0 points from a TS; Hollingworth's total includes 0 points from a TR.

AVERAGES

(14 Conference League, 2 Knock-Out Cup, 4 Conference Trophy = 20 fixtures)

Rider	Mts	Rds	Pts	Bon	Tot	Avge	Max
James Birkinshaw	8	43	102	10	112	10.42	1 paid
John Oliver	13	69	128	10	138	8.00	1 paid
Darren Mallett	16	82	154	4	158	7.71	1 full
Sam Martin	19	101	148	33	181	7.17	-
Wayne Broadhurst	10	50	76	11	87	6.96	-
Nathan Irwin	16	67	92	9	101	6.03	-
Kyle Hughes	17	81	77	15	92	4.54	-
Scott Campos	7	29	22	6	28	3.86	-
Cal McDade	13	49	33	7	40	3.27	-

BOSTON: From left to right, back row: Stephen Lambert (co-promoter), Simon Lambert, Sam Martin, Kyle Hughes, Nathan Irwin, Mick Smith (co-promoter). Front row, kneeling: Scott Campos, Darren Mallett, James Birkinshaw.

Also rode (in alphabetical order):

Ben Johnson	1	1	0	0	0	0.00	-
Simon Lambert	4	17	37	1	38	8.94	1 full
Sean Stoddart	3	15	20	3	23	6.13	-

INDIVIDUAL MEETINGS

29 September: David Nix Memorial

QUALIFYING SCORES: James Birkinshaw 14; Mark Jones 13; Danny Betson 12; Darren Mallett 11; Mark Thompson 10; Nathan Irwin 10; Benji Compton 10; Andrew Bargh 8; Karlis Ezergailis 8; Barry Burchatt 6; Jonathan Bethell 5; Richie Dennis 4; James Purchase 3; Paul Burnett 3; Karl Mason 2; Simon Lambert (reserve) 1; Jessica Lamb 0; Wayne Dunworth (reserve) 0. SEMI-FINAL: 1st Irwin; 2nd Mallett; 3rd Betson; 4th Thompson. FINAL: 1st Irwin; 2nd Jones; 3rd Birkinshaw; 4th Mallett.

14 October: Lincolnshire Trophy

1st Mark Thompson (on fastest time/countback) 14; 2nd Mark Baseby 14; 3rd Nathan Irwin 14; Mark Jones 11; Andrew Bargh 9; Simon Lambert 9; Matthew Wright 9; Darren Mallett 7; Robert Hollingworth 6; Kyle Hughes 6; Joe Haines 5; Dean Felton 5; Andre Cross 5; Wayne Dunworth 2; James Birkinshaw 2; Jaimie Pickard (reserve) 1; Ben Johnson 0.

BUXTON HITMEN

ADDRESS: Buxton Raceway, Dale Head Lane, Axe Edge, Nr Buxton, Derbyshire.
CLUB CHAIRMEN: Richard Moss and Jayne Moss.
TRACK LENGTH: 240 metres.
TRACK RECORD: 52.9 seconds – James Wright (27/06/04).
FIRST MEETING: 19 May 1996.
YEARS OF OPERATION: 1996 Conference League; 1997 Amateur League; 1998-2006
Conference League.

PREVIOUS VENUE: Buxton Stadium, off A53 Leek-to-Buxton Road, Buxton, Derbyshire.
YEARS OF OPERATION: 1994 British League Division Three; 1995 Academy League.

CLUB HONOURS

KNOCK-OUT CUP WINNERS: 2002.

RIDER ROSTER 2006

Carl BELFIELD; Jonathan BETHELL; Lewis DALLAWAY; Danny HODGSON; Scott JAMES; Jack
ROBERTS; Adam ROYNON; Ben TAYLOR; Charles WRIGHT.

OTHER APPEARANCES/GUESTS (official matches only)

Russell BARNETT; Gary BEATON; Andrew BRAITHWAITE; Bob CHARLES; Scott CHESTER;
Luke GOODY; Gareth ISHERWOOD; Jessica LAMB; Adam OUGHTIBRIDGE.

BUXTON

* Denotes aggregate/bonus-point victory

NO.	DATE	OPPONENTS	VENUE	COMPETITION	RESULT	BETHELL	ROBERTS	BELFIELD	BEATON	ROYNON	DALLAWAY	TAYLOR	JAMES	ISHERWOOD	WRIGHT	OTHERS
1	16/4	USA Dream Team	H	Chal	L40-50	6 (5)	6+1 (4)	3+1 (4)	6+1 (4)	11 (5)	4+1 (4)	4+1 (4)	-		-	-
2	23/4	Newport	A	CL	L46-48	10 (5)	2+1 (4)	8+2 (4)	5+2 (4)	7+1 (5)	0 (3)	14+1 (5)	-		-	-
3	30/4	Boston	H	CL	W47-43	14 (5)	5+1 (4)	2 (2)	3 (4)	9+1 (5)	3 (3)	11+2 (7)	-		-	-
4	5/5	Plymouth	A	CL	L36-55	5 (5)	7+3 (6)	R/R	-	5 (6)	2 (3)	16+1 (7)	-		-	1 (3)
5	28/5	Mildenhall	H	CL	W55-38	12+1 (5)	9+1 (4)	-	4+1 (3)	6+2 (4)	2+1 (4)	10+2 (5)	12+1 (5)		-	-
6	10/6	Rye House	A	CL	L38-54	12+2 (5)	2 (5)	-	3+1 (3)	10 (5)	1+1 (3)	4+1 (5)	6 (4)		-	-
7	12/6	Scunthorpe	A	CL	L39-54	13 (5)	1 (3)	5+1 (4)	-	7+1 (5)	1+1 (3)	5 (6)	7 (4)		-	-
8	18/6	Newport	H	CL	W63-31*	3 (3)	10+3 (5)	5+1 (4)	-	11+1 (4)	3 (3)	16+2 (6)	15 (5)		-	-
9	21/6	Stoke	A	CL	L43-50	R/R	2 (4)	1 (5)	-	9 (5)	-	14+1 (7)	16 (6)	1 (3)	-	-
10	23/6	Boston	A	CL	L43-47*	4+1 (5)	5+1 (4)	6+1 (4)	-	11+1 (5)	-	6+1 (4)	5+1 (4)	6+1 (4)	-	-

NO. DATE	OPPONENTS	VENUE	COMPETITION	RESULT	BETHELL	ROBERTS	BELFIELD	BEATON	ROYNON	DALLAWAY	TAYLOR	JAMES	ISHERWOOD	WRIGHT	OTHERS
11 25/6	Rye House	H	CL	W47-43	7+1 (4)	10+3 (6)	2 (2)		13 (5)		10+1 (6)	3+1 (4)	2+1 (3)		
12 2/7	Plymouth	H	CL	W52-43	10 (5)	5+3 (4)	R/R		13+1 (6)		13+3 (7)	9+1 (5)	2+2 (3)		
13 7/7	Boston	A	KOC	L39-54	9 (6)	4+1 (5)	R/R		19 (6)	0 (3)	2 (5)	5+1 (5)			
14 9/7	Boston	H	KOC	W56-38*	12 (5)	2 (3)	R/R		11+3 (6)	1 (3)	13+2 (7)	17+1 (6)			
15 16/7	Stoke	H	CL	L45-46	2 (2)	8+2 (6)		5+2 (4)	8+1 (4)	1 (3)	15 (7)	6+1 (4)			
16 30/7	Plymouth	H	CT	L32-60	7 (5)		R/R		8 (7)	1+1 (1)		15 (6)			1+1 (11)
17 4/8	Plymouth	A	CT	L36-57	3 (5)				14+1 (6)	3+2 (6)	R/R	13 (6)			3 (7)
18 6/8	Scunthorpe	H	CL	L41-52	10+2 (5)	3+2 (6)			15 (6)	3 (4)	R/R	10+1 (6)			0 (3)
19 13/8	Sittingbourne	H	CS	W65-29	10+1 (4)	9+3 (4)			12 (4)	11+2 (5)		11+1 (5)		10+2 (4)	2+1 (4)
20 21/8	Scunthorpe	A	CS	L25-67	2 (1)	2+1 (5)			5 (5)	4 (6)	8+1 (5)	2 (3)			2 (4)
21 27/8	Cleveland	H	CS	W70-20		11+1 (5)			10+2 (4)	11+1 (4)	11+4 (5)	11 (4)		10+2 (4)	6+3 (4)
22 1/9	Plymouth	A	KOC s/f	L34-58		6+1 (4)	1+1 (4)		8 (5)	2 (4)	3+1 (4)	6 (4)		8 (5)	
23 8/9	Weymouth	A	CS	W52-44		9+3 (4)			R/R	9+2 (7)	12+1 (6)	12 (5)		8+2 (5)	2+1 (3)
24 10/9	Plymouth	H	KOC s/f	W51-42		16 (7)			12 (5)	1 (3)	7+1 (4)	7+1 (4)		6+2 (4)	2+1 (3)
25 17/9	Stoke	H	CT	L44-48	8 (4)	10+3 (7)				3+1 (4)	6+1 (4)	10 (5)		7+2 (5)	0 (1)
26 24/9	Scunthorpe	H	CS	L42-48	8 (5)	11+1 (7)			R/R	2+1 (3)	7+1 (5)	11+1 (6)		3+1 (4)	
27 24/9	Weymouth	H	CS	W50-41*	7+1 (3)	7+3 (6)			R/R	7 (5)	13+2 (6)	8+1 (5)		8+2 (5)	
28 1/10	Stoke	H	CS	W55-40	9+1 (5)	7+3 (5)			R/R	4 (4)	13+1 (6)	12+1 (5)		10+1 (5)	
29 7/10	Sittingbourne	A	CS	W63-29*	14 (6)	16+2 (6)			R/R	4+3 (4)	7+1 (5)	13+2 (5)		9+2 (4)	
30 8/10	Stoke	A	CT	W39-32*	5+1 (4)	2 (3)			R/R	7+3 (4)	8+2 (4)	10 (4)		7+1 (5)	
31 15/10	Mildenhall	A	CL	L44-51*	17 (6)	11+3 (7)			R/R	1+1 (4)	8+1 (5)			7 (5)	0 (3)
32 21/10	Stoke	A	CS	L45-48*	15 (6)	9+1 (6)			R/R	8+1 (4)	2+2 (4)			9 (6)	2+2 (4)
33 26/10	Cleveland	A	CS	W59-32*	9 (4)	19+2 (7)			R/R	7+1 (7)	10+1 (6)			14+1 (6)	0 (0)

NOTE: Following the away league match at Boston on 23 June, Adam Roynon defeated Darren Mallett in a run-off for the bonus point. The away Conference Trophy match at Stoke on 8 October was abandoned after heat twelve, with the result permitted to stand.

DETAILS OF OTHER RIDERS

(all guests unless underlined)

Match No. 4: Jessica Lamb 1 (3); Match No. 16: Adam Oughtibridge 1+1 (4); Danny Hodgson 0 (7); Match No. 17: Russell Barnett 2 (3); Scott Chester 1 (4); Match No. 18: Danny Hodgson 0 (3); Match No. 19: Danny Hodgson 2+1 (4); Match No. 20: Danny Hodgson 2 (4); Match No. 21: Danny Hodgson 6+3 (4); Match No. 23: Bob Charles 2+1 (3); Match No. 24: Danny Hodgson 2+1 (3); Match No. 25: Danny Hodgson 0 (1); Match No. 31: Luke Goody 0 (3); Match No. 32: Andrew Braithwaite 2+2 (4); Match No. 33: Andrew Braithwaite 0 (0).

DETAILS OF TACTICAL RIDES AND TACTICAL SUBSTITUTE RIDES

Match No. 2: Belfield 4 points (TR); Taylor 4 points (TS); Match No. 4: Taylor 4 points (TR); Bethell 0 points (TR); Match No. 6: Bethell 4 points (TR); Roynon 1 point (TR; not doubled); Bethell 6 points (TR); Match No. 9: James 6 points (TR); Match No. 13: Roynon 6 points (TR); Bethell 0 points (TR); Match No. 16: James 4 points (TR); Bethell 0 points (TR); Hodgson 0 points (TS); Match No. 17: Roynon 4 points (TR); James 4 points (TR); Match No. 18: Roynon 6 points (TR); James 1 point (TR; not doubled); Match No. 20: Taylor 4 points (TR); Roynon 1 point (TR; not doubled); Match No. 22: Wright 4 points (TR); Roynon 0 points (TR); Match No. 31: Bethell 6 points (TR); Taylor 4 points (TR).

BUXTON: From left to right, back row: Carl Belfield, Ben Taylor, Charles Wright, Adam Roynon, Lewis Dallaway, Jack Lee (team manager). Front row, kneeling: Gary Beaton, Jack Roberts. On bike: Jonathan Bethell.

OTHER DETAILS

USA scorers in Match No. 1: Buck Blair 17 (6); Dale Facchini 14+2 (7); Michael Hull 9 (5); Neil Facchini 7+2 (5); Adam Mittl 2 (4); Matt Browne 1+1 (3); Tim Gomez R/R.

AVERAGES
(14 Conference League, 4 Knock-Out Cup, 4 Conference Trophy, 10 Conference Shield = 32 fixtures)

Rider	Mts	Rds	Pts	Bon	Tot	Avge	Max
Adam Roynon	21	106	207	15	222	8.38	1 full; 2 paid
Scott James	26	125	245	15	260	8.32	1 full; 2 paid
Charles Wright	14	67	114	18	132	7.88	2 paid
Jonathan Bethell	27	123	229	11	240	7.80	-
Ben Taylor	29	154	257	38	295	7.66	2 paid
Jack Roberts	30	152	220	48	268	7.05	4 paid
Carl Belfield	8	29	28	6	34	4.69	-
Lewis Dallaway	28	116	109	21	130	4.48	1 paid
Danny Hodgson	7	26	12	5	17	2.62	-
Also rode (in alphabetical order):							
Gary Beaton	5	18	20	6	26	5.78	-
Andrew Braithwaite	2	4	2	2	4	4.00	-
Bob Charles	1	3	2	1	3	4.00	-
Scott Chester	1	4	1	0	1	1.00	-
Gareth Isherwood	4	13	11	4	15	4.62	-
Adam Oughtibridge	1	4	1	1	2	2.00	-
Guests	3	9	3	0	3	1.33	-

(Russell Barnett [1]; Luke Goody [1]; Jessica Lamb [1]).

NOTE: Jack Roberts was ever-present throughout the 14-match Conference League programme.

INDIVIDUAL MEETING

18 June: British Under-15 Championship (Round One)

QUALIFYING SCORES: Ben Hopwood 11; Joe Haines 11; Adam Wrathall 10; Brendan Johnson 10; Ben Reade 7; Richard Franklin 5; George Piper 4; Scott Meakins 4; Jack Butler 3; Sean Paterson 0; Kye Norton 0; Amy Carpenter 0. FINAL: 1st Haines; 2nd Hopwood; 3rd Wrathall; 4th Johnson.

CLEVELAND SCOTT BROS BAYS

ADDRESS: South Tees Motorsports Park, Dormer Way, South Bank, Road, Middlesbrough, Cleveland, TS6 6XH.
CLUB CHAIRMEN: Chris Van Straaten and Gareth Rogers.
YEARS OF OPERATION: 2006 Conference Shield.
FIRST MEETING: 24 August 2006.
TRACK LENGTH: 266 metres.
TRACK RECORD: 54.9 seconds – Josh Auty (24/08/06).

CLUB HONOURS

NONE.

RIDER ROSTER 2006

Greg BLAIR; Paul BURNETT; Martin EMERSON; Joe HAINES; Jack HARGREAVES; Rusty HODGSON; Steven JONES.

OTHER APPEARANCES/GUESTS (official matches only)

Gary BEATON; Maurice CRANG; Jitendra DUFFILL; Daniel GIFFARD; Gary IRVING; Ashley JOHNSON; Karl LANGLEY; Joe REYNOLDS; Rob SMITH; David SPEIGHT.

CLEVELAND

* Denotes aggregate/bonus-point victory

NO.	DATE	OPPONENTS	VENUE	COMPETITION	RESULT	HARGREAVES	CRANG	BURNETT	GIFFARD	EMERSON	HODGSON	JONES	BLAIR	BEATON	DUFFILL	HAINES	OTHERS
1	24/8	Scunthorpe	H	CS	L45-46	10 (5)	0 (3)	6+1 (4)	21 (6)	1+1 (5)	7 (6)	-	-	-	-	-	0 (1)
2	27/8	Buxton	A	CS	L20-70	-	2 (5)	6 (5)	R/R	2 (4)	4 (6)	2 (3)	4+1 (7)	-	-	-	-
3	3/9	Sittingbourne	A	CS	L43-49	-	3 (3)	12+1 (5)	-	5+1 (5)	14 (6)	7+1 (5)	-	0 (2)	2+1 (4)	-	-
4	13/9	Stoke	A	CS	L42-53	16 (5)	-	5+2 (4)	-	0 (4)	7 (5)	-	1 (3)	-	-	11+1 (5)	2 (4)
5	16/9	Sittingbourne	H	CS	W60-32*	10+2 (4)	-	14 (5)	12 (4)	-	3+1 (4)	-	2+1 (5)	10+2 (4)	-	9+3 (4)	-
6	16/9	Weymouth	H	CS	W50-39	10+2 (4)	-	-	12 (4)	0 (3)	6+2 (5)	10+1 (5)	-	-	1 (3)	11 (6)	-
7	22/9	Weymouth	A	CS	L32-58	-	-	4 (4)	13 (4)	4+2 (6)	-	7 (5)	1 (5)	-	-	-	3+1 (6)
8	25/9	Scunthorpe	A	CS	L31-63	10 (4)	-	-	-	6 (5)	0 (4)	1 (3)	2+1 (6)	-	-	10 (5)	2+1 (4)
9	28/9	Stoke	H	CS	L43-46	15 (5)	-	-	-	1 (4)	5 (4)	6 (4)	1+1 (3)	-	2+2 (4)	13+1 (4)	-
10	26/10	Buxton	H	CS	L32-59	-	-	7 (5)	-	2+1 (4)	0 (1)	6 (4)	2+2 (6)	-	-	15+1 (7)	0 (3)

CLEVELAND: From left to right, back row: Steve Harland (junior development officer), Martin Emerson, Steven Jones, Maurice Crang, Jason Pipe (team manager). Front row, kneeling: Greg Blair, Rusty Hodgson, Paul Burnett.

DETAILS OF OTHER RIDERS

(all guests unless underlined)

Match No. 1: Karl Langley 0 (1); Match No. 4: David Speight 2 (4); Match No. 7:Rob Smith 2 (3); Joe Reynolds 1+1 (3); Match No. 8: Ashley Johnson 2+1 (4); Match No. 10: Gary Irving 0 (3).

DETAILS OF TACTICAL RIDES AND TACTICAL SUBSTITUTE RIDES

Match No. 1: Giffard 6 points (TR); Hargreaves 4 points (TR); Match No. 2: Hodgson 1 point (TR; not doubled); Burnett 0 points (TR); Match No. 3: Burnett 6 points (TR); Match No. 4: Hargreaves 6 points (TR); Haines 4 points (TR); Match No. 7: Giffard 4 points (TR); Burnett 1 point (TR; not doubled); Jones 1 point (TS; not doubled); Match No. 8: Haines 4 points (TR); Hargreaves 4 points (TR); Match No. 10: Haines 4 points (TR); Jones 1 point (TR; not doubled).

AVERAGES
(10 Conference Shield = 10 fixtures)

Rider	Mts	Rds	Pts	Bon	Tot	Avge	Max
Jack Hargreaves	6	27	64	4	68	10.07	1 full; 2 paid
Joe Haines	6	33	63	6	69	8.36	1 paid
Paul Burnett	7	32	51	4	55	6.88	-
Steven Jones	7	29	39	2	41	5.66	-
Rusty Hodgson	9	41	46	3	49	4.78	-
Martin Emerson	9	40	21	5	26	2.60	-
Greg Blair	7	35	13	6	19	2.17	-
Also rode (in alphabetical order):							
Gary Beaton	2	6	10	2	12	8.00	1 paid
Maurice Crang	3	11	5	0	5	1.82	-
Jitendra Duffill	3	11	5	3	8	2.91	-
Daniel Giffard	4	18	53	0	53	11.78	3 full
Gary Irving	1	3	0	0	0	0.00	-
Ashley Johnson	1	4	2	1	3	3.00	-
Karl Langley	1	1	0	0	0	0.00	-
David Speight	1	4	2	0	2	2.00	-
Guests	2	6	3	1	4	2.67	-

(Joe Reynolds [1]; Rob Smith [1]).

MILDENHALL JOLLY CHEF ACADEMY

NOTE: The information below relates only to the second Mildenhall team. For details of the main side, please refer to the Premier League section.

ADDRESS: Mildenhall Stadium, Hayland Drove, West Row Fen, Mildenhall, Suffolk, IP28 8QU.
CLUB CHAIRMAN: Mick Horton.
TRACK LENGTH: 260 metres.
CL TRACK RECORD: 52.00 seconds – Mark Thompson (30/07/06).
FIRST MEETING: 18 May 1975.
YEARS OF OPERATION: 2006 Conference League.

CLUB HONOURS

NONE.

RIDER ROSTER 2006

Andrew BARGH; Mark BASEBY; Trevor HEATH; Ben HOPWOOD; James PURCHASE; Mark THOMPSON; Matthew WRIGHT.

OTHER APPEARANCES/GUESTS (official matches only)

Marc ANDREWS; Jordan FRAMPTON; Luke GOODY; Grant HAYES; Shane HENRY.

MILDENHALL

* Denotes aggregate/bonus-point victory

NO.	DATE	OPPONENTS	VENUE	COMPETITION	RESULT	BARGH	PURCHASE	WRIGHT	BASEBY	THOMPSON	HEATH	HOPWOOD	GOODY	HENRY	OTHERS
1	8/4	USA Dream Team	H	Chal	W55-40	R/R	10+2 (5)	13+1 (6)	6+1 (5)	14+2 (6)	9+1 (4)	3 (4)	-	-	-
2	15/4	Rye House	A	CL	L31-63	2 (4)	2 (4)	13+1 (5)	4 (5)	7 (4)	3 (4)	0 (4)	-	-	-
3	30/4	Stoke	H	CL	L44-46	7+1 (5)	5+2 (4)	11 (5)	0 (2)	4 (4)	10 (5)	7+2 (5)	-	-	-
4	12/5	Boston	A	CL	L24-66	2 (4)	6+1 (5)	3 (4)	4+1 (4)	6 (5)	3 (7)	0 (1)	-	-	-
5	14/5	Boston	H	CL	L37-53	7+3 (5)	6+1 (4)	6+1 (4)	5+1 (4)	10 (5)	3 (4)	0 (4)	-	-	-
6	28/5	Buxton	A	CL	L38-55	2 (4)	5+1 (4)	8 (5)	1+1 (4)	15 (5)	6 (5)	1 (3)	-	-	-
7	25/6	Scunthorpe	H	CL	L41-52	13+2 (6)	3+1 (4)	4 (4)	2 (4)	17 (5)	0 (3)	2+1 (4)	-	-	-
8	26/6	Scunthorpe	A	CL	L34-59	2 (4)	2+1 (4)	6 (4)	-	15 (5)	-	8+1 (5)	1 (4)	-	0 (4)
9	2/7	Rye House	H	KOC	L32-58	4 (5)	4 (4)	3 (4)	5 (4)	0 (1)	9 (6)	7+2 (6)	-	-	-
10	7/7	Plymouth	A	CL	L42-54	4 (5)	9+2 (5)	-	-	R/R	8 (7)	7+2 (4)	-	1 (3)	13+1 (6)
11	12/7	Stoke	A	CL	D45-45	8 (5)	6 (4)	11+1 (5)	2 (4)	9 (4)	1 (3)	8+1 (5)	-	-	-
12	16/7	Plymouth	H	CL	W49-44	6+1 (4)	6+1 (4)	10 (4)	9+2 (5)	12 (5)	3 (4)	3 (4)	-	-	-

NO.	DATE	OPPONENTS	VENUE	COMPETITION	RESULT	BARGH	PURCHASE	WRIGHT	BASEBY	THOMPSON	HEATH	HOPWOOD	GOODY	HENRY	OTHERS
13	23/7	Newport	A	CL	W46-43	12+1 (6)	3+3 (4)	10 (5)	4+1 (5)	R/R	11 (6)	6+1 (4)	-	-	-
14	30/7	Boston	H	CT	W55-38	11 (5)	2 (4)	6+1 (4)	9+1 (4)	15 (5)	6+1 (4)	6+3 (4)	-	-	-
15	30/7	Scunthorpe	H	CT	L36-57	10+1 (5)	0 (4)	1 (4)	6 (5)	14 (4)	0 (3)	5 (5)	-	-	-
16	31/7	Scunthorpe	A	CT	L33-60	2 (4)	1 (4)	6 (5)	4 (4)	16 (5)	1 (4)	3 (4)	-	-	-
17	6/8	Rye House	H	CL	L31-58	7 (5)	-	6 (4)	-	7 (5)	11+1 (7)	0 (1)	-	0 (4)	-
18	26/8	Rye House	A	KOC	L43-50	14 (5)	3+1 (4)	7 (5)	7+1 (4)	9 (5)	3+2 (4)	-	0 (3)	-	-
19	8/9	Boston	A	CT	W44-43*	10+1 (5)	3 (4)	8+1 (4)	6+1 (4)	13 (5)	-	-	0 (0)	4+1 (7)	-
20	8/10	Newport	H	CL	W49-40*	11+1 (5)	3 (4)	7+1 (4)	9+1 (4)	15 (5)	-	-	-	1 (4)	3+1 (4)
21	15/10	Buxton	H	CL	W51-44	13 (5)	5+1 (4)	12 (4)	9+3 (5)	7 (4)	-	-	-	3+1 (4)	2+1 (4)

DETAILS OF OTHER RIDERS

(all guests)

Match No. 8: Grant Hayes 0 (4); Match No. 10: Jordan Frampton 13+1 (6); Match No. 20: Marc Andrews 3+1 (4); Match No. 21: Marc Andrews 2+1 (4).

DETAILS OF TACTICAL RIDES AND TACTICAL SUBSTITUTE RIDES

Match No. 2: Wright 6 points (TR); Thompson 4 points (TR); Match No. 4: Thompson 1 point (TR; not doubled); Purchase 1 point (TR; not doubled); Match No. 5: Baseby 0 points (TR); Match No. 6: Thompson 6 points (TR); Wright 0 points (TR); Match No. 7: Thompson 6 points (TR); Wright 1 point (TR; not doubled); Bargh 1 point (TS; not doubled); Match No. 8:

MILDENHALL: From left to right, back row: Mark Baseby, Matthew Wright, Trevor Heath, James Purchase. Front row, kneeling: Andrew Bargh, Mark Thompson, Ben Hopwood.

Thompson 6 points (TR); Wright 1 point (TR; not doubled); Match No. 10: Purchase 6 points (TR); Frampton 6 points (TR); Match No. 15: Thompson 6 points (TR); Baseby 0 points (TR); Match No. 16: Thompson 6 points (TR); Baseby 1 point (TR; not doubled); Match No. 17: Wright 1 point (TR; not doubled); Bargh 0 points (TR); Match No. 18: Bargh 4 points (TR); Thompson 2 points (TS); Wright 0 points (TR).

OTHER DETAILS

USA scorers in Match No. 1: Tim Gomez 13 (5); Buck Blair 11 (5); Dale Facchini 5+2 (4); Adam Mittl 4+1 (4); Michael Hull 3+1 (4); Matt Browne 3 (4); Neil Facchini 1 (3); Scott Campos 0 (3). Gomez's total includes 6 points from a TR; Blair's total includes 4 points from a TR.

AVERAGES
(14 Conference League, 2 Knock-Out Cup, 4 Conference Trophy = 20 fixtures)
♦ Denotes ever-present.

Rider	Mts	Rds	Pts	Bon	Tot	Avge	Max
Mark Thompson	18	81	173	0	173	8.54	2 full
Matthew Wright	19	83	135	6	141	6.80	1 full
Andrew Bargh ♦	20	96	145	11	156	6.50	-
Mark Baseby	17	71	86	13	99	5.58	-
Ben Hopwood	16	63	63	13	76	4.83	-
James Purchase	19	78	71	15	86	4.41	-
Trevor Heath	16	76	78	4	82	4.32	-

Also rode (in alphabetical order):

	Mts	Rds	Pts	Bon	Tot	Avge	Max
Luke Goody	3	7	1	0	1	0.57	-
Shane Henry	5	22	9	2	11	2.00	-
Guests	4	18	15	3	18	4.00	-

(Marc Andrews [2]; Jordan Frampton [1]; Grant Hayes [1]).

NEWPORT MAVERICKS

NOTE: The information below relates only to the second Newport team. For details of the main side, please refer to the Premier League section.

ADDRESS: Hayley Stadium, Plover Close, Nash Mead, Queensway Meadows, Newport, South Wales, NS19 4SU.
CLUB CHAIRMAN: Tim Stone.
TRACK LENGTH: 285 metres.
CL TRACK RECORD: 60.27 – Scott Pegler (09/09/00).
FIRST MEETING: 30 May 1997.
YEARS OF OPERATION: 1997 Amateur League; 1998–2006 Conference League.
NOTE: In 1997, Newport shared their Amateur League fixtures with Exeter, under the banner of Welsh Western Warriors.

CLUB HONOURS

LEAGUE CHAMPIONS: 1999.

RIDER ROSTER 2006

Karlis EZERGAILIS; Nicki GLANZ; Sam HURST; Billy LEGG; Karl MASON; Joe REYNOLDS; Tim WEBSTER.

OTHER APPEARANCES/GUESTS (official matches only)

Marc ANDREWS; Ben THOMPSON; Matt TUTTON.

NEWPORT

NO.	DATE	OPPONENTS	VENUE	COMPETITION	RESULT	EZERGAILIS	HURST	LEGG	MASON	REYNOLDS	GLANZ	WEBSTER	TUTTON	ANDREWS	OTHERS
1	9/4	Rye House	H	CL	L31-59	17 (6)	3 (6)	0 (0)	6+1 (5)	3 (4)	2+1 (5)	-			R/R
2	23/4	Buxton	H	CL	W48-46	11+1 (5)	9+2 (5)	11 (4)	9 (4)	2+1 (4)	4 (4)	2+1 (4)	-		
3	1/5	Rye House	A	CL	L26-64	6 (5)	4 (3)	-	9+1 (6)	3+2 (4)	4 (5)	0 (4)	-		
4	5/5	Boston	A	CL	L24-65	7 (5)	0 (1)	5 (4)	7 (5)	1 (6)	1 (4)	3+1 (5)	-		
5	7/5	Stoke	H	CL	L31-43	6 (3)	-	7 (3)	9 (3)	1 (3)	5 (4)	1 (4)	2+1 (4)		
6	26/5	Plymouth	A	CL	L29-65	8 (5)	2+1 (4)	4 (4)	9 (5)	3+1 (6)	3+1 (4)	0 (2)	-		
7	29/5	Scunthorpe	A	CL	L15-75	5 (5)	0 (3)	4 (5)	3 (3)	1 (4)	2 (5)	-	-	-	0 (4)
8	11/6	Plymouth	H	CL	L31-49	4 (3)	7 (4)	1+1 (3)	8 (4)	2+1 (4)	8+2 (4)	1+1 (4)	-		
9	18/6	Buxton	A	CL	L31-63	3 (1)	2 (4)	9 (5)	12 (5)	1 (5)	3 (6)	-	1 (4)	-	
10	28/6	Stoke	A	CL	L35-59	8 (5)	4+1 (4)	10 (4)	7 (5)	2+1 (4)	3 (4)	1 (4)	-		
11	30/6	Somerset	A	Chal	L39-57	8 (3)	-	-	11 (4)	7 (7)	1+1 (2)	6+2 (4)	2+1 (5)	4+1 (5)	
12	2/7	Scunthorpe	H	CL	L39-55	R/R	11+1 (6)	13+2 (6)	6 (4)	1+1 (5)	6+2 (6)	2 (4)	-	-	

NO.	DATE	OPPONENTS	VENUE	COMPETITION	RESULT	EZERGAILIS	HURST	LEGG	MASON	REYNOLDS	GLANZ	WEBSTER	TUTTON	ANDREWS	OTHERS
13	16/7	Boston	H	CL	L37-55	0 (4)	11 (5)	9+1 (5)	13 (4)	1 (4)	0 (4)	3 (4)	-	-	
14	23/7	Mildenhall	H	CL	L43-46	5 (4)	10+1 (5)	11 (5)	7+1 (4)	1 (4)	7+2 (5)	2 (5)			
15	28/7	Plymouth	A	KOC	L37-57	2+1 (4)	4+1 (3)	12 (4)	5 (5)	3+2 (4)	9 (6)	2+1 (4)			
16	27/8	Plymouth	H	KOC	L41-48	R/R	-	12 (6)	10+1 (6)	5 (5)	8 (5)	4+3 (4)		2+2 (4)	
17	8/10	Mildenhall	A	CL	L40-49	13 (6)	5+3 (5)	6+1 (5)	R/R	3 (4)	10 (6)	3+2 (4)	-	-	

NOTE: The home league match versus Stoke on 7 May was abandoned after heat twelve, with the result permitted to stand. The home league match versus Plymouth on 11 June was abandoned after heat thirteen, with the result permitted to stand.

DETAILS OF OTHER RIDERS

(all guests unless underlined)

Match No. 1: Jamie Westacott R/R; Match No. 7: Ben Thompson 0 (4).

DETAILS OF TACTICAL RIDES AND TACTICAL SUBSTITUTE RIDES

Match No. 1: Ezergailis 6 points (TR); Match No. 3: Glanz 1 point (TR; not doubled); Mason 1 point (TS; not doubled); Match No. 4: Legg 1 point (TR; not doubled); Mason 0 points (TR); Match No. 5: Mason 4 points (TR); Match No. 6: Mason 4 points (TR); Ezergailis 4 points (TR); Match No. 7: Mason 1 point (TR; not doubled); Ezergailis 1 point (TR; not doubled); Match No. 8: Glanz 4 points (TR); Ezergailis 0 points (TR); Match No. 9: Mason 6 points (TR); Legg 4 points (TR); Match No. 10: Legg 4 points (TR); Ezergailis 4 points (TR); Match No. 11: Ezergailis 6 points (TR); Mason 6 points (TR); Match No. 12: Legg 4 points (TR); Hurst 4 points (TR); Match No. 13: Mason 6 points (TR); Match No. 15: Legg 6 points (TR); Hurst 2 points (TR).

AVERAGES

(14 Conference League, 2 Knock-Out Cup = 16 fixtures) ♦ Denotes ever-present.

Rider	Mts	Rds	Pts	Bon	Tot	Avge	Max
Billy Legg	15	63	105	5	110	6.98	-
Karl Mason	15	68	110	4	114	6.71	-
Karlis Ezergailis	14	61	88	2	90	5.90	-
Sam Hurst	14	58	69	10	79	5.45	-
Nicki Glanz ♦	16	77	73	8	81	4.21	-
Tim Webster	13	52	24	9	33	2.54	-
Joe Reynolds ♦	16	70	33	9	42	2.40	-
Also rode (in alphabetical order):							
Marc Andrews	2	8	3	2	5	2.50	-
Ben Thompson	1	4	0	0	0	0.00	-
Matt Tutton	1	4	2	1	3	3.00	-

PAIRS MEETING

15 October: British Under-15 Pairs Championship

QUALIFYING SCORES: Joe Haines (19) and Shane Hazelden (10) = 29; Daniel Greenwood (17) and

NEWPORT: From left to right, back row: Joe Reynolds, Billy Legg, Sam Hurst, Karlis Ezergailis. Front row, kneeling: Nicki Glanz, Tim Webster. On bike: Karl Mason.

James Sarjeant (10) = 27; Brendan Johnson (19), Scott Meakins (0) and Tom Davies (reserve, 2) = 21; Richard Franklin (14) and Ben Reade (7) = 21; Ben Hopwood (18) and Sean Paterson (2) = 20; Jack Butler (11), Tom Davies (4) and Chris Bint (reserve, 2) = 17. THIRD PLACE RACE-OFF: 1st Johnson; 2nd Reade; 3rd Davies; 4th Franklin. FINAL: 1st Haines; 2nd Sarjeant; 3rd Greenwood; 4th Hazelden. (Scoring system: 4-3-2-0).

PLYMOUTH GT MOTORCYCLES DEVILS

ADDRESS: St Boniface Arena, Coypool Road, Plymouth, Devon, PL7 4NW.
CLUB CHAIRMEN: Mike Bowden and David Short.
TRACK LENGTH: 260 metres.
TRACK RECORD: 51.22 – Jason Bunyan (22/09/06)
FIRST MEETING: 21 April 2006.
YEARS OF OPERATION: 2006 Conference League.

PREVIOUS VENUE: Pennycross Stadium, Pennycross, Plymouth, Devon.
YEARS OF OPERATION: 1931 Open; 1932–1934 National League; 1935 Open; 1936 Provincial League; 1937 Open; 1947–1949 National League Division Three; 1950 National League Division Two; 1951 National League Division Three; 1952–1953 Southern League; 1954 National League Division Two; 1959–1960 Open; 1961–1962 Provincial League; 1968–1969 British League Division Two; 1970 Open.

CLUB HONOURS

NATIONAL TROPHY (SOUTHERN LEAGUE) WINNERS: 1952.

RIDER ROSTER 2006

Russell BARNETT; Tom BROWN; Chris JOHNSON; Jaimie PICKARD; Lee SMART; Rob SMITH; Seemond STEPHENS; Shane WALDRON; Jamie WESTACOTT.

OTHER APPEARANCES/GUESTS (official matches only)

Mattie BATES; Andrew BRAITHWAITE; Bob CHARLES; Michael COLES; Cecil FORBES; Shane HENRY; Jessica LAMB; Ben THOMPSON; Karl WHITE.

PLYMOUTH

* Denotes aggregate/bonus-point victory

NO.	DATE	OPPONENTS	VENUE	COMPETITION	RESULT	STEPHENS	LAMB	WALDRON	SMART	BROWN	BATES	SMITH	JOHNSON	WESTACOTT	BARNETT	PICKARD	OTHERS
1	21/4	USA Dream Team	H	Chal	W47-42	15 (5)	1 (3)	6+1 (4)	11+1 (5)	7 (4)	7+1 (4)	0 (5)	-	-	-	-	-
2	1/5	Scunthorpe	A	CL	W46-44	18 (6)	-	7 (7)	12+1 (6)	6+2 (5)	1+1 (2)	2 (3)	R/R	-	-	-	-
3	5/5	Buxton	H	CL	W55-36	14+1 (5)	-	4 (5)	14+1 (5)	8+2 (4)	2 (4)	1 (2)	12 (4)	-	-	-	-
4	12/5	Club Carmarthen	H	Chal	W61-33	12 (4)	3 (4)	8+1 (4)	13 (5)	9+1 (5)	-	7+2 (4)	9+1 (4)	-	-	-	-
5	26/5	Newport	H	CL	W65-29	15 (5)	3 (4)	7+2 (4)	11+1 (4)	10+2 (4)	-	8+1 (4)	-	11+2 (5)	-	-	-
6	2/6	Exeter Select	H	Chal	W55-40	13+1 (5)	-	3+1 (4)	12+1 (5)	6+3 (4)	-	3 (4)	10 (4)	8+2 (4)	-	-	-

NO.	DATE	OPPONENTS	VENUE	COMPETITION	RESULT	STEPHENS	LAMB	WALDRON	SMART	BROWN	BATES	SMITH	JOHNSON	WESTACOTT	BARNETT	PICKARD	OTHERS
7	9/6	Great Britain U-21	H	Chal	W52-43	14 (6)	-	3+2 (4)	10+2 (5)	15+2 (6)	-	2 (4)	R/R	8+2 (5)	-	-	-
8	11/6	Newport	A	CL	W49-31*	12 (4)	-	7 (4)	10+1 (4)	3+1 (3)	-	4+2 (4)	12 (4)	-	1 (3)	-	-
9	16/6	Boston	H	CL	W54-38	11 (5)	-	6+1 (5)	13+2 (5)	10+2 (4)	-	4 (4)	10 (4)	-	0 (3)	-	-
10	23/6	Stoke	H	CL	W66-26	12 (4)	2 (3)	11+3 (5)	11+1 (4)	8+4 (5)	-	10+1 (6)	12 (4)	-	-	-	-
11	30/6	Rye House	H	CL	W51-43	12 (5)	0 (0)	12+2 (7)	12 (5)	5+1 (4)	-	1+1 (5)	-	9 (4)	-	-	-
12	2/7	Buxton	A	CL	L43-52*	10 (4)	-	4 (6)	8 (5)	6+2 (4)	-	1 (3)	-	14 (5)	0 (3)	-	-
13	2/7	Stoke	A	CL	L44-45*	13 (5)	-	13+1 (7)	2+1(4)	7+1 (5)	-	2+1 (2)	-	7+1 (4)	0 (3)	-	-
14	7/7	Mildenhall	H	CL	W54-42	12+1 (5)	-	7+2 (5)	11+1 (4)	11 (5)	-	3+1 (4)	10+2 (4)	-	0 (3)	-	-
15	8/7	Rye House	A	CL	W46-44*	13 (5)	-	9 (6)	6 (4)	11 (5)	-	2 (3)	-	3+1 (4)	-	-	2+1 (3)
16	14/7	Scunthorpe	H	CL	W56-38*	12 (4)	-	11+1 (6)	11+1 (5)	9+3 (5)	-	2+2 (5)	11+1 (4)	-	0 (1)	-	-
17	16/7	Mildenhall	A	CL	L44-49*	12 (5)	-	10+1 (6)	2 (4)	6 (4)	-	2+1 (3)	11+1 (5)	-	-	-	1 (3)
18	28/7	Newport	H	KOC	W57-37	13+1 (5)	-	-	10+2 (4)	8+3 (4)	-	10 (4)	15 (5)	-	-	1 (4)	0 (4)
19	30/7	Buxton	A	CT	W60-32	11+1 (5)	-	9+2 (4)	15 (5)	5 (4)	-	5+2 (4)	12 (4)	-	-	3+1 (4)	-
20	4/8	Buxton	H	CT	W57-36*	12 (4)	-	6+2 (4)	12 (5)	4+2 (4)	-	9+1 (5)	11 (4)	-	-	3+1 (4)	-
21	9/8	Stoke	A	CT	W38-34	9 (4)	-	9+1 (5)	10 (4)	6+2 (4)	-	4 (4)	R/R	-	-	0 (3)	-
22	18/8	Stoke	H	CT	W64-27*	10 (4)	-	7+2 (4)	12+2 (5)	10+2 (4)	-	11+3 (7)	-	14+1 (5)	-	-	-
23	27/8	Newport	A	KOC	W48-41*	12 (5)	-	-	11+2 (5)	9+2 (4)	3+1 (2)	-	-	10+1 (4)	3 (4)	0 (3)	-
24	1/9	Buxton	H	KOC s/f	W58-34	10+3 (5)	-	10+1 (4)	10+1 (4)	7+2 (4)	-	5+1 (4)	-	14 (5)	-	2+1 (4)	-
25	3/9	Boston	A	CL	W46-44*	15 (5)	-	5+1 (4)	9 (5)	9+1 (4)	1 (1)	7 (7)	-	0 (4)	-	-	-
26	8/9	Scunthorpe	H	CT f	L39-51	13 (5)	-	4+1 (4)	7 (4)	5+2 (4)	-	-	-	9 (5)	0 (4)	1 (4)	-
27	10/9	Buxton	A	KOC s/f	L42-51*	4+3 (4)	-	8 (4)	16 (5)	3+1 (4)	-	-	-	8 (5)	0 (3)	3 (5)	-
28	22/9	Isle of Wight	H	Chal	W51-43	12+1 (5)	-	2 (3)	9+2 (5)	8+1 (5)	-	-	-	8+1 (4)	-	-	12+2 (8)
29	3/10	Isle of Wight	A	Chal	L22-70	7 (4)	-	1 (5)	3 (5)	4 (4)	-	0 (2)	-	0 (3)	-	-	7 (5)
30	13/10	Scunthorpe	H	KOC f	L42-51	12+1 (4)	-	4 (4)	10+1 (5)	9 (4)	0 (3)	7+2 (7)	-	-	-	0 (3)	-
31	15/10	Scunthorpe	A	PO f	L25-67	R/R	-	1 (4)	12 (6)	6 (6)	-	5 (5)	-	-	-	1 (5)	0 (4)
32	22/10	Scunthorpe	A	KOC f	L24-48	-	-	3+1 (5)	9 (4)	5 (4)	-	1+1 (2)	-	R/R	-	1 (4)	5 (4)
33	27/10	Scunthorpe	H	PO f	L36-58	-	-	1 (5)	11 (5)	8+3 (7)	-	-	-	R/R	-	2 (4)	14 (9)
34	29/10	Scunthorpe	A	CT f	L36-59	-	-	1+1 (5)	14+1 (6)	7+1 (6)	-	-	-	R/R	-	1 (4)	13+1 (9)

NOTE: The away league match at Newport on 11 June was abandoned after heat thirteen, with the result permitted to stand. The away Conference Trophy match at Stoke on 9 August was abandoned after heat twelve, with the result permitted to stand. The away leg of the Knock-Out Cup final versus Scunthorpe was abandoned after heat twelve, with the result permitted to stand.

DETAILS OF OTHER RIDERS

(all guests unless underlined)

Match No. 15: Cecil Forbes 2+1 (3); Match No. 17: Shane Henry 1 (3); Match No. 18: Karl White 0 (4); Match No. 28: Lee Smethills 7+1 (4); Nicki Glanz 5+1 (4); Match No. 29: Lewis Bridger 7 (5); Match No. 31: Andrew Braithwaite 0 (4); Match No. 32: Michael Coles 5 (4); Match No. 33: Michael Coles 14 (6); Bob Charles 0 (3); Match No. 34: Michael Coles 12 (6); Ben Thompson 1+1 (3).

DETAILS OF TACTICAL RIDES AND TACTICAL SUBSTITUTE RIDES

Match No. 12: Stephens 6 points (TR); Smart 4 points (TR); Match No. 17: Johnson 6 points (TR); Match No. 27: Smart 6 points (TR); Match No. 29: Stephens 4 points (TR); Bridger 1 point (TR; not doubled); Match No. 30: Stephens 4 points (TR);

Brown 4 points (TR); Match No. 31: Smart 4 points (TR); Brown 1 point (TR; not doubled); Match No. 32: Smart 1 point (TR; not doubled); Coles 1 point (TR; not doubled); Match No. 33: Coles 4 points (TR); Smart 4 points (TR); Brown 0 points (TS); Match No. 34: Smart 6 points (TR); Coles 4 points (TR); Brown 1 point (TS; not doubled).

OTHER DETAILS

USA scorers in Match No. 1: Buck Blair 11 (5); Dale Facchini 10 (6); Adam Mittl 8+1 (4); Michael Hull 4+3 (4); Neil Facchini 4+1 (4); Matt Browne 4 (4); Tom Gomez 1+1 (3); Club Carmarthen scorers in Match No. 4: Michael Coles 8 (4); Dean Felton 7+1 (5); Jamie Westacott 5 (4); Ben Powell 5 (5); Daniel Hodgson 4+1 (6); Gordon Meakins 2 (3); David Gough 2 (3). Powell's total includes 4 points from a TS; Coles' total includes 4 points from a TR; Felton's total includes 1 point from a TR (not doubled); Exeter Select scorers in Match No. 6: Luke Priest 11 (6); Michael Coles 10 (5); Ben Powell 8+1 (5); Karlis Ezergailis 5 (4); Mark Thompson 4+1 (5); Mattie Bates 2+1 (5); Jack Hargreaves R/R. Priest's total includes 6 points from a TR; Coles' total includes 4 points from a TR. Great Britain Under-21 scorers in Match No. 7: Adam Roynon 11+1 (5); Karl Mason 10 (5); Ben Taylor 8 (6); Harland Cook 6+1 (5); Jack Roberts 6 (5); Danny Betson 2+2 (4); Luke Bowen R/R. Roynon's total includes 6 points from a TR; Roberts' total includes 4 points from a TR.

AVERAGES

(14 Conference League, 2 Play-Offs, 6 Knock-Out Cup, 6 Conference Trophy = 28 fixtures)
♦ Denotes ever-present.

Rider	Mts	Rds	Pts	Bon	Tot	Avge	Max
Chris Johnson	10	42	113	4	117	11.14	5 full; 2 paid
Seemond Stephens	24	112	282	11	293	10.46	7 full; 1 paid
Lee Smart ♦	28	131	279	19	298	9.10	1 full; 6 paid
Jamie Westacott	11	50	99	6	105	8.40	1 paid
Tom Brown ♦	28	124	199	41	240	7.74	3 paid
Shane Waldron	26	129	176	25	201	6.23	-
Rob Smith	23	97	106	20	126	5.20	-
Jaimie Pickard	13	51	18	3	21	1.65	-
Russell Barnett	9	27	4	0	4	0.59	-
Also rode (in alphabetical order):							
Mattie Bates	5	12	7	2	9	3.00	-
Andrew Braithwaite	1	4	0	0	0	0.00	-
Bob Charles	1	3	0	0	0	0.00	-
Michael Coles	3	16	27	0	27	6.75	-
Cecil Forbes	1	3	2	1	3	4.00	-
Jessica Lamb	3	7	5	0	5	2.86	-
Ben Thompson	1	3	1	1	2	2.67	-
Guests	2	7	1	0	1	0.57	-

(Shane Henry [1]; Karl White [1]).

NOTE: Shane Waldron was ever-present throughout the 14-match Conference League programme.

PLYMOUTH: From left to right, back row: Shane Waldron, Tom Brown, Jamie Westacott. Front row, kneeling: Rob Smith, Lee Smart, Russell Barnett, Seemond Stephens.

OTHER MEETING

25 August: Four-Team Tournament

Plymouth 36: Seemond Stephens 11 (4); Lee Smart 11 (4); Tom Brown 9 (4); Russell Barnett 5 (4); Premier Select 25: Chris Johnson 9 (4); Nicki Glanz 6 (4); Adam Allott 5 (4); Billy Legg 5 (4); Exeter 20: Adam Roynon 9 (4); Ben Powell 8 (4); Bob Charles 2 (4); Nick Mallett 1 (4); Welsh Dragons 15: Jamie Westacott 9 (4); Jaimie Pickard 3 (4); Karl Mason 2 (4); Andrew Bargh 1 (4).

INDIVIDUAL MEETINGS

28 April: Devils Intermediate Championship

1st Seemond Stephens 15; 2nd Lee Smart (on race wins) 12; 3rd Karlis Ezergailis 12; David Mason 11; Tom Brown 11; Jordan Frampton 9; Shane Waldron 9; Dean Felton 9; Rob Smith 8; Gordon Meakins 7; Russell Barnett 5; James Humby 3; Jessica Lamb 3; Andre Cross 2; Tim Webster 2; Mattie Bates 1; Cecil Forbes (reserve) 1; Marc Andrews (reserve) 0.

21 July: British Under-15 Championship (Round Three)

QUALIFYING SCORES: Ben Hopwood 12; Scott Meakins 9; George Piper 9; Joe Haines 8; Kye Norton 8; Richard Franklin 7; Adam Wrathall 6; Sean Paterson 3; Jack Butler 1; Amy Carpenter 1. FINAL: 1st Hopwood; 2nd Haines; 3rd Piper; 4th Meakins.

RYE HOUSE ELMSIDE RAIDERS

NOTE: The information below relates only to the second Rye House team. For details of the main side, please refer to the Premier League section.

ADDRESS: Rye House Stadium, Rye Road, Hoddesdon, Hertfordshire, EN11 0EH.
CLUB CHAIRMEN: Len Silver and Hazal Naylor.
TRACK LENGTH: 271 metres.
FIRST MEETING: 1 April 2002
CL TRACK RECORD: 57.0 seconds – Edward Kennett (21/04/03).
YEARS OF OPERATION: 2002-2006 Conference League.

CLUB HONOURS

FOUR-TEAM CHAMPIONS: 2003.

RIDER ROSTER 2006

Danny BETSON; Barry BURCHATT; Harland COOK; Daniel HALSEY; Robert MEAR; Ben POWELL; Lee STRUDWICK.

OTHER APPEARANCES/GUESTS (official matches only)

Luke BOWEN; Gary COTTHAM; Karl WHITE.

RYE HOUSE

* Denotes aggregate/bonus-point victory

NO.	DATE	OPPONENTS	VENUE	COMPETITION	RESULT	POWELL	COTTHAM	COOK	BETSON	BURCHATT	STRUDWICK	MEAR	BOWEN	HALSEY	OTHERS
1	9/4	Newport	A	CL	W59-31	10 (4)	4+2 (4)	10+1 (5)	9+2 (4)	8+1 (4)	12+2 (5)	6+1 (4)	-	-	
2	15/4	Mildenhall	H	CL	W63-31	8+2 (4)	-	6+2 (4)	12 (5)	11 (4)	6+3 (4)	10+1 (5)	10+2 (4)	-	
3	17/4	Stoke	H	CL	W53-41	11+1 (5)	-	11+3 (5)	9 (4)	7+1 (4)	3 (4)	8+1 (4)	-	4+1 (4)	
4	1/5	Newport	H	CL	W64-26*	7 (4)	-	14+1 (5)	8+2 (4)	-	8+1 (4)	7+2 (4)	11 (4)	9+3 (5)	
5	19/5	Boston	A	CL	W49-44	6+1 (3)	-	1+1 (3)	11 (5)	12 (5)	-	8+1 (6)	8+1 (4)	3+1 (4)	
6	10/6	Buxton	H	CL	W54-38	9 (5)	-	13+4 (6)	14 (6)	-	0 (2)	13+1 (6)	R/R	5 (5)	
7	14/6	Stoke	A	CL	L43-50*	17 (6)	0 (3)	9 (6)	4+1 (4)	-	-	10+1 (6)	R/R	3+1 (5)	
8	25/6	Buxton	A	CL	L43-47*	14+1 (6)	-	10+1 (6)	6 (5)	-	3 (4)	5 (4)	R/R	5 (5)	
9	30/6	Plymouth	A	CL	L43-51	13 (5)	-	5+1 (4)	8+1 (5)	4+1 (4)	3 (3)	8+3 (6)	-	2+1 (3)	
10	2/7	Mildenhall	A	KOC	W58-32	16+1 (6)	-	10+1 (5)	14+2 (6)	8+1 (5)	3+2 (4)	-	R/R	7+1 (4)	
11	8/7	Plymouth	H	CL	L44-46	12+1 (6)	-	9+1 (6)	-	10+2 (5)	0 (3)	11 (6)	R/R	2 (4)	
12	16/7	Scunthorpe	A	CL	L24-67	9 (6)	-	4 (5)	4 (5)	-	2 (4)	5+1 (7)	R/R	0 (3)	
13	6/8	Mildenhall	A	CL	W58-31*	13 (6)	-	10+2 (5)	12+1 (5)	11+3 (6)	-	0 (0)	R/R	12+4 (7)	
14	11/8	Weymouth	A	Chal	L43-46	-	3+2 (5)	9 (6)	-	-	-	-	R/R	-	31+2 (19)

NO.	DATE	OPPONENTS	VENUE	COMPETITION	RESULT	POWELL	COTTHAM	COOK	BETSON	BURCHATT	STRUDWICK	MEAR	BOWEN	HALSEY	OTHERS
15	19/8	Scunthorpe	H	CL	W47-46	15 (6)	-	10 (4)	2+1 (1)	4+1 (3)	-	6+2 (7)	R/R	10+1 (7)	-
16	26/8	Mildenhall	H	KOC	W50-43*	-	3+1 (4)	15 (6)	-	15 (6)	-	7+4 (5)	R/R	10+1 (6)	0 (2)
17	4/9	Scunthorpe	A	KOC s/f	L36-52	6+1 (4)	-	3+1 (4)	9 (6)	9 (6)	-	8+1 (6)	R/R	1+1 (4)	-
18	23/9	Scunthorpe	H	KOC s/f	D45-45	13+1 (6)	-	3 (4)	8 (5)	7+3 (6)	-	11+4 (7)	R/R	3 (1)	-
19	23/9	Boston	H	CL	W61-32*	12+1 (5)	-	9+1 (5)	16+2 (6)	9 (5)	5+1 (4)	10+2 (4)	R/R	-	-
20	7/10	Scunthorpe	H	PO s/f	L38-52	-	-	1 (3)	5+2 (5)	9 (6)	2 (3)	14+1 (7)	R/R	7+4 (6)	-
21	8/10	Scunthorpe	A	PO s/f	L32-62	-	-	1 (3)	8+1 (6)	6+1 (6)	3+1 (4)	12+1 (7)	R/R	2 (4)	-

DETAILS OF OTHER RIDERS

(all guests)

Match No. 14: Lee Smart 14+1 (6); Sam Martin 10+1 (7); Mark Jones 6 (4); Rob Smith 1 (2); Match No. 16: Karl White 0 (2).

DETAILS OF TACTICAL RIDES AND TACTICAL SUBSTITUTE RIDES

Match No. 7: Powell 6 points (TR); Mear 0 points (TR); Match No. 9: Powell 4 points (TR); Betson 4 points (TR); Match No. 12: Powell 4 points (TR); Mear 1 point (TR; not doubled); Match No. 20: Betson 0 points (TR); Match No. 21: Betson 4 points (TR); Mear 4 points (TR).

AVERAGES

(14 Conference League, 2 Play-Offs, 4 Knock-Out Cup = 20 fixtures)

♦ Denotes ever-present.

Rider	Mts	Rds	Pts	Bon	Tot	Avge	Max
Ben Powell	17	87	184	10	194	8.92	-
Danny Betson	18	87	155	15	170	7.82	1 paid
Barry Burchatt	15	75	130	14	144	7.68	-
Harland Cook ♦	20	94	154	20	174	7.40	1 paid
Robert Mear	19	101	157	27	184	7.29	1 paid
Daniel Halsey	17	77	85	19	104	5.40	-
Lee Strudwick	13	48	50	10	60	5.00	-

Also rode (in alphabetical order):

	Mts	Rds	Pts	Bon	Tot	Avge	Max
Luke Bowen	3	12	29	3	32	10.67	1 paid
Gary Cottham	3	11	7	3	10	3.64	-
Guest	1	2	0	0	0	0.00	-

(Karl White [1]).

INDIVIDUAL MEETING

11 April: British Under-21 Championship qualifying round

1st Ben Barker (after run-off) 14; 2nd Luke Bowen 14; 3rd Steve Boxall 12; Jamie Courtney 12; Robert Mear (reserve) 10; Matthew Wright 9; Karl Mason 8; Lee Smart 8; Sean Stoddart 8; Kyle Hughes 7; Scott Campos 6; James Purchase 5; Marc Andrews 2; Rob Smith 1; Chris Johnson 1; Karl White 0; Gary Cottham 0.

RYE HOUSE: From left to right, back row: Lee Strudwick, Danny Betson, Daniel Halsey, Ben Powell. Front row, kneeling: Robert Mear, Harland Cook.

SCUNTHORPE LINCS FM SCORPIONS

ADDRESS: Normanby Road, Scunthorpe, North Lincolnshire, DN15 8QZ.
CLUB CHAIRMEN: Norman Beeney and Robert Godfrey.
TRACK LENGTH: 285 metres.
TRACK RECORD: 58.24 seconds – Tai Woffinden (16/07/06).
FIRST MEETING: 27 March 2005.
YEARS OF OPERATION: 2004 Training; 2005-2006 Conference League.

PREVIOUS VENUES:
(1) ADDRESS: Quibell Park, Brumby Wood Lane, Scunthorpe, North Lincolnshire.
YEAR OF OPERATION: 1971 Open; 1972-1974 British League Division Two; 1975-1978 National League.

(2) ADDRESS: Ashby Ville Stadium, off Queensway, Ashby, Scunthorpe, North Lincolnshire.
YEARS OF OPERATION: 1979-1985 National League.

CLUB HONOURS

PAIRS CHAMPIONS: 2006. NOTE: The side that took the plaudits of victory were Scunthorpe 'B'.
CONFERENCE SHIELD WINNERS: 2006.
KNOCK-OUT CUP WINNERS: 2006
LEAGUE CHAMPIONS: 2006.
CONFERENCE TROPHY WINNERS: 2006.

RIDER ROSTER 2006

Josh AUTY; Byron BEKKER; Wayne CARTER; Benji COMPTON; Paul COOPER; Richie DENNIS; Scott RICHARDSON; Andrew TULLY; Tai WOFFINDEN.

OTHER APPEARANCES/GUESTS (official matches only)

John BRANNEY; Gary FLINT; Grant HAYES; Ben HOPWOOD; Alex McCLOUD; Michael PICKERING; Simon TILLMAN.

SCUNTHORPE

* Denotes aggregate/bonus-point victory

NO.	DATE	OPPONENTS	VENUE	COMPETITION	RESULT	CARTER	TULLY	COMPTON	BEKKER	DENNIS	RICHARDSON	AUTY	WOFFINDEN	COOPER	OTHERS
1	7/4	Boston	A	EC	W47-42	14 (5)	3+2 (4)	10 (5)	1 (4)	6+2 (4)	2 (3)	11+1 (5)	-	-	-
2	17/4	Boston	H	EC	W53-40*	8 (5)	3+1 (4)	13 (5)	5+3 (4)	8+1 (4)	0 (2)	16+2 (6)	-	-	-
3	23/4	USA Dream Team	H	Chal	W62-33	11+1 (4)	8+2 (4)	-	10+1 (4)	10+1 (4)	5+1 (4)	9+2 (5)	9+1 (5)	-	-
4	1/5	Plymouth	H	CL	L44-46	11 (5)	7+2 (4)	-	6+1 (4)	7+1 (5)	1 (3)	9+1 (5)	-	-	3+1 (4)
5	29/5	Newport	H	CL	W75-15	14+1 (5)	10+2 (4)	8+4 (4)	8+4 (4)	14+1 (5)	-	11+1 (4)	10+2 (4)	-	-
6	4/6	Boston	H	CL	W52-40	9+2 (5)	6+1 (4)	1+1 (4)	5+2 (4)	10+1 (4)	-	11+1 (5)	10 (4)	-	-
7	12/6	Buxton	H	CL	W54-39	13+1 (5)	3 (4)	3+2 (4)	4 (4)	2 (2)	-	18 (6)	11+2 (5)	-	-
8	18/6	Stoke	H	CL	W64-28	11+2 (5)	12+2 (5)	R/R	2+1 (3)	15 (5)	-	12+1 (5)	12+5 (6)	-	0 (1)
9	25/6	Mildenhall	A	CL	W52-41	9+1 (5)	10+2 (6)	6+1 (5)	5+3 (5)	R/R	-	19+1 (7)	3 (2)	-	-
10	26/6	Mildenhall	H	CL	W59-34*	11+1 (4)	6+1 (5)	10+2 (5)	4+1 (4)	11 (4)	1 (1)	16+2 (7)	-	-	-
11	30/6	Boston	A	CL	W53-40*	R/R	7+2 (5)	-	7+2 (5)	13+1 (6)	-	10+1 (5)	16 (6)	-	0 (3)
12	2/7	Newport	A	CL	W55-39*	R/R	9+2 (5)	-	3+1 (4)	11 (5)	-	17+1 (6)	14+1 (7)	-	1 (3)
13	3/7	Cleveland	H	Chal	W53-43	-	2+1 (3)	R/R	7+2 (5)	6+1 (5)	-	17+1 (7)	16+1 (6)	-	5 (4)
14	5/7	Stoke	A	CL	W45-31*	7 (3)	3 (4)	8 (3)	7 (4)	8+1 (3)	-	9+3 (4)	3+2 (4)	-	-
15	14/7	Plymouth	A	CL	L38-56	7+1 (5)	1+1 (4)	R/R	1+1 (3)	11+1 (6)	-	12 (7)	6 (5)	-	-
16	16/7	Rye House	H	CL	W67-24	12 (5)	6+1 (4)	R/R	9+2 (5)	14+2 (6)	-	12+3 (5)	14+1 (5)	-	-
17	23/7	Stoke	H	KOC	W59-36	8+1 (4)	5+3 (4)	5+2 (4)	2 (3)	14+1 (5)	-	15 (5)	10+3 (5)	-	-
18	26/7	Stoke	A	KOC	W47-46*	8 (4)	5+3 (4)	6+1 (4)	3+1 (4)	9+1 (5)	-	10+3 (5)	6+1 (4)	-	-
19	30/7	Mildenhall	A	CT	W57-36	3+1 (3)	8+1 (4)	8+1 (4)	5+2 (4)	12+1 (5)	-	11+2 (5)	10+2 (5)	-	-
20	31/7	Mildenhall	A	CT	W60-33*	5 (2)	6+3 (5)	5+3 (3)	4+1 (4)	12+1 (5)	-	16+1 (6)	12+1 (5)	-	-
21	6/8	Buxton	A	CL	W52-41*	R/R	12 (6)	18+2 (7)	1 (2)	7 (5)	-	7+2 (5)	7+1 (5)	-	-
22	7/8	Boston	H	CT	W57-37	R/R	7+1 (5)	10+1 (5)	5+1 (5)	6+1 (5)	-	15 (5)	14+1 (5)	-	-
23	19/8	Rye House	A	CL	L46-47*	10 (4)	2+1 (4)	10+2 (7)	3 (4)	9 (5)	-	12+1 (5)	0 (1)	-	-
24	21/8	Buxton	H	CS	W67-25	14+1 (5)	10+2 (5)	5+1 (3)	12+1 (6)	R/R	-	13+2 (5)	13+4 (6)	-	-
25	24/8	Cleveland	A	CS	W46-45	8 (4)	9+1 (6)	-	8+3 (7)	R/R	6+1 (7)	15 (6)	-	-	0 (0)
26	1/9	Weymouth	A	CS	W52-41	-	-	11+1 (6)	16+2 (7)	18 (6)	-	-	5+1 (5)	R/R	2 (6)
27	4/9	Rye House	H	KOC s/f	W52-36	-	12+2 (6)	-	0 (1)	8 (5)	9+3 (7)	R/R	18 (6)	5+1 (5)	-
28	8/9	Plymouth	A	CT f	W51-39	-	3+1 (4)	13+2 (6)	2+1 (2)	8+1 (5)	-	11 (5)	9+1 (4)	5 (4)	-
29	10/9	Stoke	H	CS	W48-42	-	6+1 (5)	-	7+3 (5)	11 (6)	7+2 (5)	-	15+1 (6)	R/R	2 (3)
30	17/9	Sittingbourne	H	CS	W64-24	-	16+2 (6)	6+3 (5)	14+4 (7)	11+1 (5)	0 (1)	R/R	-	17+1 (6)	-
31	23/9	Rye House	A	KOC s/f	D45-45	-	9+1 (5)	2 (4)	2 (4)	7+1 (5)	-	R/R	14+1 (6)	11 (6)	-
32	24/9	Buxton	A	CS	W48-42*	-	9 (5)	6 (4)	7+2 (6)	10+1 (6)	0 (3)	R/R	16+2 (6)	-	-
33	25/9	Cleveland	H	CS	W63-31*	-	5+3 (4)	13+2 (5)	6+2 (4)	10+1 (4)	3+1 (4)	R/R	11 (4)	15 (5)	-
34	1/10	Weymouth	H	CS	W70-20*	-	11+2 (5)	12+1 (5)	11+4 (5)	-	10+2 (5)	R/R	11+2 (5)	15 (5)	-
35	7/10	Sittingbourne	A	CS	W63-27*	-	7 (4)	0 (2)	9+3 (5)	14+1 (5)	10+2 (5)	-	13+2 (5)	10+2 (4)	-
36	7/10	Rye House	A	PO s/f	W52-38	-	6 (3)	8 (5)	2+1 (4)	7 (4)	-	12+3 (5)	12+3 (5)	5 (4)	-
37	8/10	Rye House	H	PO s/f	W62-32*	-	12+1 (5)	6+1 (5)	2+1 (3)	8+3 (4)	-	9 (4)	13+2 (5)	12 (4)	-
38	13/10	Plymouth	A	KOC f	W51-42	-	7+2 (5)	7+1 (4)	4 (4)	7 (5)	-	12 (6)	14 (6)	R/R	-
39	14/10	Stoke	A	CS	W48-44*	-	10 (4)	-	8+4 (7)	R/R	8+1 (5)	9 (4)	-	9 (5)	4+2 (5)

NO.	DATE	OPPONENTS	VENUE	COMPETITION	RESULT	CARTER	TULLY	COMPTON	BEKKER	DENNIS	RICHARDSON	AUTY	WOFFINDEN	COOPER	OTHERS
40	15/10	Plymouth	H	PO f	W67-25	-	9+1 (4)	7+2 (4)	7+1 (4)	14+1 (5)	-	10+3 (5)	9+1 (4)	11 (4)	-
41	22/10	Plymouth	H	KOC f	W48-24*	-	11+1 (4)	8+2 (4)	6+2 (3)	6 (3)	-	4+1 (4)	6+1 (3)	7+1 (3)	-
42	23/10	Boston	A	CT	W52-38*	-	-	6+2 (4)	16 (7)	13+1 (5)	1 (5)	-	15 (5)	0 (0)	1 (4)
43	27/10	Plymouth	A	PO f	W58-36*	-	12+1 (5)	7+3 (5)	6 (4)	10+1 (6)	-	11+2 (5)	12 (5)	R/R	-
44	29/10	Plymouth	H	CT f	W59-36*	-	3 (2)	13+2 (5)	5+2 (6)	9+1 (4)	2 (3)	14 (5)	13+2 (5)	R/R	-

NOTE: EC = Easter Cup. The away league match at Stoke on 5 July was abandoned after heat twelve, with the result permitted to stand. The home leg of the Knock-Out Cup final versus Plymouth on 22 October was abandoned after heat twelve, with the result permitted to stand.

DETAILS OF OTHER RIDERS

(all guests unless underlined)

Match No. 4: John Branney 3+1 (4); Match No. 8: Grant Hayes 0 (1); Match No. 11: Michael Pickering 0 (3); Match No. 12: Michael Pickering 1 (3); Match No. 13: Adam McKinna 5 (4); Match No. 25: Michael Pickering 0 (0); Match No. 26: Simon Tillman 2 (3); Alex McCloud 0 (3); Match No. 29: Ben Hopwood 2 (3); Match No. 39: Gary Flint 4+2 (5); Match No. 42: Gary Flint 1 (4).

DETAILS OF TACTICAL RIDES AND TACTICAL SUBSTITUTE RIDES

Match No. 15: Auty 6 points (TR); Carter 2 points (TR); Match No. 23: Carter 6 points (TR).

OTHER DETAILS

USA scorers in Match No. 3: Buck Blair 13+1 (5); Neil Facchini 10 (5); Adam Mittl 5 (4); Matt Browne 2+2 (4); Dale Facchini 2 (4); Tim Gomez 1 (4); Michael Hull 0 (4). Blair's total includes 6 points from a TR; N. Facchini's total includes 4 points from a TR. Cleveland scores in Match No. 13: Jack Hargreaves 14+1 (6); Paul Cooper 14+1 (5); Ben Hopwood 8 (5); Michael Pickering 3+1 (4); Paul Burnett 3 (4); Rusty Hodgson 1 (4); Karl Langley 0 (2). Cooper's total includes 6 points from a TR; Hopwood's total includes 4 points from a TR; Hargreaves' total includes 2 points from a TS.

AVERAGES

(14 Conference League, 4 Play-Offs, 6 Knock-Out Cup, 6 Conference Trophy, 10 Conference Shield = 40 fixtures) ◆ Denotes ever-present.

Rider	Mts	Rds	Pts	Bon	Tot	Avge	Max
Josh Auty	30	156	359	35	394	10.10	3 full; 6 paid
Tai Woffinden	35	169	377	45	422	9.99	2 full; 8 paid
Paul Cooper	13	55	122	5	127	9.24	3 full; 2 paid
Wayne Carter	17	73	156	12	168	9.21	3 paid
Richie Dennis	35	169	356	26	382	9.04	2 full; 4 paid
Benji Compton	30	135	228	45	273	8.09	3 paid
Andrew Tully	38	173	292	49	341	7.88	3 paid
Byron Bekker ◆	40	176	234	59	293	6.66	2 paid
Scott Richardson	13	54	58	12	70	5.19	-

Also rode (in alphabetical order):

John Branney	1	4	3	1	4	4.00	-

SCUNTHORPE: From left to right, back row: Andrew Tully, Josh Auty, Byron Bekker, Wayne Carter, Tai Woffinden. Front row, kneeling: Scott Richardson, Richie Dennis.

Grant Hayes	1	1	0	0	0	0.00	-
Alex McCloud	1	3	0	0	0	0.00	-
Michael Pickering	3	6	1	0	1	0.67	-
Guests	4	15	9	2	11	2.93	-

(Gary Flint [2]; Ben Hopwood [1]; Simon Tillman [1]).

NOTE: Josh Auty and Andrew Tully were ever-present throughout the 14-match Conference League programme.

INDIVIDUAL MEETINGS

2 April: Lincs FM Trophy

QUALIFYING SCORES: John Oliver 13; Simon Lambert 12; Josh Auty 11; Richie Dennis 10; John Branney 10; Byron Bekker 8; Wayne Carter 8; Ricky Scarboro 8; Jonathan Bethell 8; Scott Richardson 8; Michael Pickering 5; Danny Norton 5; Grant Hayes 4; Gary Flint 4; Cal McDade 3; Ashley Johnson (reserve) 1; Andrew Tully 0. SEMI-FINAL: 1st Dennis; 2nd Scarboro; 3rd Branney; 4th Auty. FINAL: 1st Oliver; 2nd Lambert; 3rd Dennis; 4th Scarboro.

11 April: British Under-21 Championship qualifying round

1st Benji Compton 14; 2nd Richie Dennis 13; 3rd Josh Auty (after run-off) 12; Simon Lambert 12; Andrew Tully 9; Shane Waldron 8; Cal McDade 7; Adam Roynon 7; Daniel Halsey 7; John Branney 6; Ben Taylor 6; Jordan Frampton 5; Darren Mallett 5; Trevor Heath 5; Mark Baseby 3; Grant Hayes 1.

9 July: British Under-15 Championship (Round Two)

QUALIFYING SCORES: Ben Hopwood 11; Kye Norton 11; Joe Haines 10; Adam Wrathall 8; George Piper 7; Richard Franklin 7; Daniel Greenwood 5; Ben Reade 4; James Sarjeant 4; Jack Butler 2; Sean Paterson (reserve) 2; Scott Meakins 1. FINAL: 1st Hopwood; 2nd Haines; 3rd Norton; 4th Wrathall.

SITTINGBOURNE CRUSADERS

ADDRESS: The Old Gun Site, Old Ferry Road, Iwade, Sittingbourne, Kent, ME9 8SP.
CLUB CHAIRMAN: Graham Arnold.
TRACK LENGTH: 251 metres.
TRACK RECORD: 58.0 seconds – Paul Hurry (30/10/05).
FIRST MEETING: 5 November 1972.
YEARS OF OPERATION: 1971 Training; 1972-1993 Open and Training; 1994 British League Division Three; 1995 Academy League; 1996 Conference League; 1997-2003 Open and Training; 2004 Conference League Knock-Out Cup, Open and Training; 2005 Conference League; 2006 Conference Shield.

CLUB HONOURS

NONE.

RIDER ROSTER 2006

Aaron BASEBY; Dan BLAKE; Gary COTTHAM; Andre CROSS; Dean FELTON; Dean GARROD; Luke GOODY.

OTHER APPEARANCES/GUESTS (official matches only)

Lewis BLACKBIRD; Martin ELLIOTT; Karl WHITE.

SITTINGBOURNE

NO.	DATE	OPPONENTS	VENUE	COMPETITION	RESULT	FELTON	COTTHAM	BLAKE	GARROD	CROSS	GOODY	BASEBY	WHITE	ELLIOTT	BLACKBIRD
1	6/8	Weymouth	H	CS	W54-41	9+2 (5)	9+1 (5)	8+1 (4)	8+2 (4)	8+2 (4)	6+2 (4)	6+1 (4)	-	-	
2	13/8	Buxton	A	CS	L29-65	10 (5)	1+1 (4)	3 (4)	4+1 (4)	6 (5)	1+1 (4)	4 (4)	-	-	
3	25/8	Weymouth	A	CS	L35-56	10+1 (5)	4+1 (5)	-	5 (4)	5+1 (4)	5+1 (5)	5+1 (4)	1+1 (3)	-	
4	3/9	Cleveland	H	CS	W49-43	10+1 (5)	5+1 (4)	3 (4)	5+2 (4)	10 (5)	8+2 (4)	8 (4)	-	-	
5	3/9	Stoke	H	CS	L29-54	9 (4)	10 (4)	4 (4)	-	2 (4)	1+1 (3)	3+2 (4)	-	0 (3)	
6	16/9	Cleveland	A	CS	L32-60	11 (5)	3+1 (4)	5+1 (4)	3+1 (4)	3 (4)	2 (4)	5+2 (5)	-	-	
7	17/9	Scunthorpe	A	CS	L24-64	5 (4)	5 (5)	1+1 (4)	0 (3)	3 (5)	5 (4)	5+2 (5)	-	-	
8	7/10	Scunthorpe	H	CS	L27-63	5+1 (4)	4+1 (5)	-	2+1 (4)	10 (4)	-	-	1 (4)	3 (5)	2+1 (4)
9	7/10	Buxton	H	CS	L29-63	13 (5)	3 (4)	7 (5)	1 (3)	0 (3)	2 (4)	3 (6)	-	-	
10	28/10	Stoke	A	CS	L29-64	11 (5)	3 (5)	3 (4)		3+2 (4)	3 (4)	5 (4)		1 (4)	

NOTE: The home Conference Shield match against Stoke on 3 September was abandoned after heat thirteen, with the result permitted to stand.

SITTINGBOURNE: From left to right, back row: Aaron Baseby, Chris Hunt (team manager), Dean Garrod, Gary Cottham, Dan Blake. Front row, kneeling: Luke Goody, Andre Cross, Dean Felton.

DETAILS OF TACTICAL RIDES AND TACTICAL SUBSTITUTE RIDES

Match No. 2: Cross 4 points (TR); Felton 4 points (TR); Match No. 3: Felton 4 points (TR); Garrod 0 points (TR); Match No. 5: Cottham 6 points (TR); Felton 4 points (TR); Match No. 6: Felton 4 points (TR); Cross 1 point (TR; not doubled); Match No. 8: Cross 4 points (TR); Felton 1 point (TR; not doubled); Match No. 9: Felton 6 points (TR); Baseby 0 points (TR); Match No. 10: Felton 4 points (TR); Baseby 2 points (TR).

AVERAGES

(10 Conference Shield = 10 fixtures) ◆ Denotes ever-present.

Rider	Mts	Rds	Pts	Bon	Tot	Avge	Max
Dean Felton ◆	10	47	80	5	85	7.23	-
Aaron Baseby	9	40	43	8	51	5.10	-
Andre Cross ◆	10	42	46	5	51	4.86	-
Dean Garrod	8	30	28	7	35	4.67	-
Dan Blake	8	33	34	3	37	4.48	-
Gary Cottham ◆	10	45	44	6	50	4.44	-
Luke Goody	9	36	33	7	40	4.44	-
Also rode (in alphabetical order):							
Lewis Blackbird	1	4	2	1	3	3.00	-
Martin Elliott	3	12	4	0	4	1.33	-
Karl White	2	7	2	1	3	1.71	-

STOKE SAS SPITFIRES

NOTE: The information below relates only to the second Stoke team. For details of the main side, please refer to the Premier League section.

ADDRESS: Chesterton Stadium, Loomer Road, Chesterton, Newcastle-under-Lyme, Staffordshire, ST5 7LB.
CLUB CHAIRMAN: David Tattum.
TRACK LENGTH: 312 metres.
CL TRACK RECORD: 63.0 seconds – Barrie Evans (22/06/05).
FIRST MEETING: 13 April 2003.
YEARS OF OPERATION: 2003 Conference Trophy; 2004–2006 Conference League.

CLUB HONOURS

FOUR-TEAM CHAMPIONS: 2006.

RIDER ROSTER 2006

Adam ALLOTT; Ben BARKER; John BRANNEY; Scott COURTNEY; Sam DORE; David HAIGH; Jack HARGREAVES; Ben HOPWOOD; Kriss IRVING; Gareth ISHERWOOD; Adam LOWE; Luke PRIEST.

OTHER APPEARANCES/GUESTS (official matches only)

Russell BARNETT; Bob CHARLES; Maurice CRANG; Barrie EVANS; Gary FLINT; Rob GRANT; Nick MALLETT; David MELDRUM; John MORRISON; Philip NAYLOR; Jaimie PICKARD; Sam WYATT.

STOKE

* Denotes aggregate/bonus-point victory

NO.	DATE	OPPONENTS	VENUE	COMPETITION	RESULT	PRIEST	BARKER	COURTNEY	IRVING	HARGREAVES	ISHERWOOD	DORE	LOWE	CRANG	BRANNEY	ALLOTT	OTHERS
1	17/4	Rye House	A	CL	L41-53	5+2 (4)	15+1 (6)	10 (5)	4+1 (4)	6 (4)	1 (4)	0 (3)	-	-	-	-	-
2	30/4	Mildenhall	A	CL	W46-44	6+2 (4)	12+2 (5)	4 (4)	6 (4)	11+2 (5)	2 (4)	5+1 (4)	-	-	-	-	-
3	7/5	Newport	A	CL	W43-31	8 (3)	7+2 (4)	8 (3)	7+1 (3)	7 (4)	1 (4)	5+1 (3)	-	-	-	-	-
4	10/5	Boston	H	CL	L46-48	12+1 (6)	12+1 (6)	9 (5)	9+2 (5)	R/R	1 (3)	3 (5)	-	-	-	-	-
5	9/6	Boston	A	CL	L43-51	12 (5)	-	11 (5)	7+2 (4)	9 (4)	1 (4)	2+1 (4)	1 (4)	-	-	-	-
6	14/6	Rye House	H	CL	W50-43	15+2 (6)	9+2 (6)	13 (5)	8+2 (5)	R/R	-	3+1 (5)	2+2 (3)	-	-	-	-
7	18/6	Scunthorpe	A	CL	L28-64	8+1 (6)	-	10 (6)	4 (4)	R/R	1 (4)	3 (4)	1+1 (4)	1+1 (2)	-	-	-
8	21/6	Buxton	H	CL	W50-43	10+2 (5)	12+2 (5)	8 (4)	9 (4)	-	-	6+1 (5)	-	1+1 (3)	4+3 (4)	-	-
9	23/6	Plymouth	A	CL	L26-66	14 (6)	-	4 (5)	2 (4)	R/R	-	3 (6)	-	0 (4)	-	3+1 (6)	-
10	28/6	Newport	H	CL	W59-35*	17+1 (6)	-	17+1 (6)	5+1 (5)	R/R	-	6+1 (4)	3 (4)	-	11+3 (5)	-	-

NO.	DATE	OPPONENTS	VENUE	COMPETITION	RESULT	PRIEST	BARKER	COURTNEY	IRVING	HARGREAVES	ISHERWOOD	DORE	LOWE	CRANG	BRANNEY	ALLOTT	OTHERS
11	2/7	Plymouth	H	CL	W45-44	-	15 (6)	14+2 (6)	3 (5)	R/R	-	5+1 (5)	0 (3)	-	8+3 (5)	-	-
12	5/7	Scunthorpe	H	CL	L31-45	2+1 (1)	-	6 (3)	0 (3)	3 (1)	-	10 (6)	3+2 (4)	-	7 (4)	-	-
13	12/7	Mildenhall	H	CL	D45-45*	-	14+1 (5)	2 (4)	3 (4)	-	-	3+1 (4)	5 (4)	-	8+1 (4)	10 (5)	-
14	16/7	Buxton	A	CL	W46-45*	-	8+2 (6)	R/R	-	-	3 (4)	3+1 (5)	2+1 (4)	-	16 (5)	14 (6)	-
15	23/7	Scunthorpe	A	KOC	L36-59	-	13 (6)	5 (5)	-	R/R	0 (4)	3 (6)	1+1 (3)	-	-	14 (6)	-
16	26/7	Scunthorpe	H	KOC	L46-47	-	21 (6)	7+1 (4)	-	-	-	2 (4)	1 (4)	-	3 (4)	12 (5)	0 (3)
17	9/8	Plymouth	H	CT	L34-38	-	5 (3)	7 (3)	2+1 (4)	-	-	5+1 (4)	1+1 (3)	-	7+2 (4)	7 (3)	-
18	18/8	Plymouth	A	CT	L27-64	-	-	R/R	-	-	-	10 (7)	2 (5)	-	DNA	11+1 (6)	4+1 (11)
19	3/9	Sittingbourne	A	CS	W54-29	-	12 (4)	R/R	11+2 (5)	-	-	5+1 (3)	2+1 (4)	-	11+3 (5)	13 (5)	-
20	6/9	Weymouth	H	CS	W65-29	-	R/R	11+1 (5)	16+2 (6)	-	-	10+1 (6)	11+2 (6)	-	3+1 (2)	14+1 (5)	-
21	10/9	Scunthorpe	A	CS	L42-48	-	16 (6)	9 (4)	R/R	-	1 (4)	5 (7)	0 (4)	-	-	11+1 (5)	-
22	13/9	Cleveland	H	CS	W53-42	-	15 (5)	12 (5)	-	-	3+2 (3)	9 (5)	2+1 (4)	-	-	-	12+3 (8)
23	15/9	Weymouth	A	CS	L33-60*	R/R	-	-	-	-	7 (6)	18+1 (7)	4 (6)	-	-	-	4 (9)
24	17/9	Buxton	A	CT	W48-44	-	19+1 (6)	2+1 (3)	-	-	1 (4)	12+1 (5)	-	-	-	-	14+2 (12)
25	28/9	Cleveland	A	CS	W46-43*	R/R	-	-	3 (2)	-	1+1 (3)	13+2 (7)	-	-	-	-	29+3 (17)
26	1/10	Buxton	A	CS	L40-55	R/R	-	-	-	-	2 (3)	10 (7)	0 (2)	-	-	-	28+2 (18)
27	8/10	Buxton	H	CT	L32-39	9 (3)	-	-	-	-	3 (4)	0 (0)	-	-	-	-	20+1 (16)
28	14/10	Scunthorpe	H	CS	L44-48	13+1 (5)	-	-	-	-	2+1 (3)	-	0 (3)	-	-	-	29 (19)
29	21/10	Buxton	H	CS	W48-45	20 (6)	-	-	-	-	0 (3)	-	1 (4)	-	-	-	27+1 (17)
30	28/10	Sittingbourne	H	CS	W64-29*	11+2 (5)	-	-	-	-	5+1 (4)	-	4+2 (4)	-	-	-	44+3 (17)

NOTE: The away league match at Newport on 7 May was abandoned after heat twelve, with the result permitted to stand. The home league match against Scunthorpe on 5 July was abandoned after heat twelve, with the result permitted to stand. The home match against Plymouth in the Conference Trophy on 9 August was abandoned after heat twelve, with the result permitted to stand. The away Conference Shield match at Sittingbourne on 3 September was abandoned after heat thirteen, with the result permitted to stand. The home match against Buxton in the Conference Trophy on 8 October was abandoned after heat twelve, with the result permitted to stand.

DETAILS OF OTHER RIDERS

(all guests unless underlined)

Match No. 9: Gary Flint 3+1 (6); Match No. 16: John Morrison 0 (3); Match No. 18: Jaimie Pickard 2+1 (6); Russell Barnett 2 (5); David Haigh DNA; Match No. 22: David Meldrum 8+1 (4); David Haigh 4+2 (4); Match No. 23: Bob Charles 2 (3); Nick Mallett 2 (3); Sam Wyatt 0 (3); Match No. 24: David Meldrum 12+1 (5); Philip Naylor 1+1 (3); Gary Flint 1 (4); Match No. 25: David Meldrum 13 (6); Rob Grant 8 (6); Ben Hopwood 8+3 (5); Match No. 26: Barrie Evans 18 (6); Ben Hopwood 8+2 (7); David Haigh 2 (5); Match No. 27: Barrie Evans 9 (3); Ben Hopwood 5+1 (6); Rob Grant 5 (3); David Haigh 1 (4); Match No. 28: Barrie Evans 13 (5); Ben Hopwood 12 (7); Rob Grant 4 (4); David Haigh 0 (3); Match No. 29: Barrie Evans 11+1 (5); Rob Grant 11 (4); Ben Hopwood 3 (5); David Haigh 2 (3); Match No. 30: Rob Grant 14+1 (5); Barrie Evans 11+1 (4); David Haigh 10 (4); Ben Hopwood 9+1 (4).

DETAILS OF TACTICAL RIDES AND TACTICAL SUBSTITUTE RIDES

Match No. 1: Courtney 6 points (TR); Barker 2 points (TS); Match No. 4: Courtney 6 points (TR); Barker 4 points (TR); Match No. 4: Priest 6 points (TR); Irving 4 points (TR); Match No. 7: Courtney 4 points (TR); Priest 1 point (TR; not doubled); Match No. 9: Priest 4 points (TR); Courtney 1 point (TR; not doubled); Match No. 12: Dore 4 points (TR); Courtney 4 points (TR); Match No. 14: Branney 6 points (TR); Match No. 15: Barker 6 points (TR); Allott 4 points (TR); Match No. 16: Barker 6 points

STOKE: From left to right, back row: Kriss Irving, Sam Dore, Ben Barker, Scott Courtney. Front row, kneeling: Gareth Isherwood, Jack Hargreaves. On bike: Luke Priest.

(TR); Match No. 23: Dore 6 points (TR); Lowe 1 point (TR; not doubled); Match No. 24: Barker 4 points (TS); Match No. 26: Evans 6 points (TR); Dore 4 points (TR); Match No. 28: Evans 6 points (TR); Match No. 29: Barker 6 points (TR).

AVERAGES

(14 Conference League, 2 Knock-Out Cup, 4 Conference Trophy, 10 Conference Shield = 30 fixtures)

Rider	Mts	Rds	Pts	Bon	Tot	Avge	Max
Ben Barker	20	104	244	17	261	10.04	3 full; 1 paid
Adam Allott	9	46	104	3	107	9.30	1 paid
Luke Priest	11	52	104	12	116	8.92	1 paid
John Branney	10	42	75	16	91	8.67	-
Scott Courtney	20	90	160	6	166	7.38	1 paid
Kriss Irving	17	71	97	14	111	6.25	1 paid
Ben Hopwood	6	34	45	7	52	6.12	-
Sam Dore	27	131	152	16	168	5.13	-
David Haigh	6	23	19	2	21	3.65	-
Adam Lowe	21	82	46	14	60	2.93	-
Gareth Isherwood	18	68	35	5	40	2.35	-

Also rode (in alphabetical order):

Bob Charles	1	3	2	0	2	2.67	-
Maurice Crang	3	9	2	2	4	1.78	-
Barrie Evans	5	23	56	2	58	10.09	1 paid
Gary Flint	2	10	4	1	5	2.00	-
Rob Grant	5	22	42	1	43	7.82	1 paid
Jack Hargreaves	5	18	36	2	38	8.44	-
Nick Mallett	1	3	2	0	2	2.67	-
David Meldrum	3	15	33	2	35	9.33	-
John Morrison	1	3	0	0	0	0.00	-
Philip Naylor	1	3	1	1	2	2.67	-
Sam Wyatt	1	2	0	0	0	0.00	-
Guests	2	11	4	1	5	1.82	-

(Russell Barnett [1]; Jaimie Pickard [1]).

NOTE: Sam Dore was ever-present throughout the 14-match Conference League programme.

INDIVIDUAL MEETING

5 April: British Under-21 Championship qualifying round

1st Jason King 15; 2nd James Brundle 14; 3rd Joel Parsons (after run-off) 12; Jack Hargreaves 12; Jamie Robertson 12; James Cockle 10; Adam McKinna 9; Luke Priest 8; Barry Burchatt 7; Harland Cook 5; James Clement 5; Gareth Isherwood 4; Kriss Irving 4; Sam Hurst 2; Sam Dore (reserve) 1; Scott Richardson 0.

WEYMOUTH DOONANS WILDCATS

ADDRESS: Wessex Stadium (2), Radipole Lane, Weymouth, Dorset, DT4 9XJ.
CLUB CHAIRMAN: Phil Bartlett.
TRACK LENGTH: 223 metres.
TRACK RECORD: 52.8 seconds – Ben Barker (04/08/06).
FIRST MEETING: 15 August 2003.
YEARS OF OPERATION: 2003 Open; 2004-2005 Conference League; 2006 Conference Shield.

PREVIOUS VENUE: Wessex Stadium (1), Radipole Lane, Weymouth, Dorset.
YEARS OF OPERATION: 1954 Open; 1955 National League Division Two; 1962-1963 Open; 1964 Metropolitan League; 1965 Open; 1966-1967 Training; 1968 British League Division Two; 1969-1970 Training; 1971-1973 Open & Training; 1974 British League Division Two; 1975-1984 National League; 1985 Open & Training.

CLUB HONOURS

PAIRS CHAMPIONS: 1982, 1983.
FOUR-TEAM CHAMPIONS: 2005.
KNOCK-OUT CUP WINNERS: 2005.

RIDER ROSTER 2006

Terry DAY; Adam FILMER; Jordan FRAMPTON; David MASON; Gordon MEAKINS; George PIPER.

OTHER APPEARANCES/GUESTS (official matches only)

Wayne DUNWORTH; Thomas HILL; Chris JOHNSON; Peter JOHNSON; Nick LAURENCE; Scott RICHARDSON; Simon TILLMAN; James WALKER; Danny WARWICK; Martin WILLIAMS.

WEYMOUTH

* Denotes aggregate/bonus-point victory

NO.	DATE	OPPONENTS	VENUE	COMPETITION	RESULT	MASON	PIPER	MEAKINS	FRAMPTON	FILMER	DAY	JOHNSON	WARWICK	OTHERS
1	4/8	Club Carmarthen	H	Chal	L44-45	9+1 (5)	3 (3)	-	14 (5)	5+2 (6)	-		-	13+2 (11)
2	6/8	Sittingbourne	A	CS	L41-54	19 (6)	1 (4)	11 (4)	-	2 (4)	-		-	8+1 (12)
3	11/8	Rye House	H	Chal	W46-43	8 (4)	1+1 (3)	4 (4)	-	4+1 (5)	-		-	29+4 (14)
4	25/8	Sittingbourne	H	CS	W56-35*	15 (5)	4+2 (3)	8 (4)	13+2 (5)	1 (3)	8 (6)	-		7 (4)
5	1/9	Scunthorpe	H	CS	L41-52	12 (5)	2+1 (3)	1 (3)	7+1 (5)	1+1 (4)	5+1 (5)	13 (5)	-	-
6	6/9	Stoke	A	CS	L29-65	R/R	6 (5)	2+1 (5)	11 (6)	5+1 (6)	3+1 (6)	2 (2)	-	-

NO.	DATE	OPPONENTS	VENUE	COMPETITION	RESULT	MASON	PIPER	MEAKINS	FRAMPTON	FILMER	DAY	JOHNSON	WARWICK	OTHERS
7	8/9	Buxton	H	CS	L44-52	17 (5)	2+1 (4)	-	5 (5)	3+1 (4)	3 (4)	14+1 (5)	-	0 (3)
8	12/9	Isle of Wight	A	Chal	L32-62	7 (5)	-		7+1 (5)	-	0 (3)	4 (3)	3+1 (4)	11+3 (10)
9	15/9	Stoke	H	CS	W60-33	18 (6)	4+2 (3)	9+1 (5)	12+3 (6)	8+2 (5)	9 (5)	R/R	-	-
10	16/9	Cleveland	A	CS	L39-50	R/R	8+2 (6)	0 (0)	-	10+2 (7)	4+2 (4)	-	14 (7)	3+2 (5)
11	22/9	Cleveland	H	CS	W58-32*	15+2 (6)	6+1 (4)	-	12+1 (5)	5+3 (5)	3 (4)	17+1 (6)	R/R	-
12	24/9	Buxton	A	CS	L41-50	10+1 (5)	1 (4)	-	6+1 (4)	0 (4)	-	14 (5)	9+1 (4)	1 (4)
13	1/10	Scunthorpe	A	CS	L20-70	4 (5)	-	-	6+1 (6)	-	0 (6)	R/R	8 (6)	2 (7)

DETAILS OF OTHER RIDERS

(all guests unless underlined)

Match No. 1: Daniel Giffard 9 (4); Karlis Ezergailis 3+1 (4); Lee Strudwick 1+1 (3); Match No. 2: James Walker 6 (5); Nick Laurence 2+1 (4); Simon Tillman 0 (3); Match No. 3: Jamie Westacott 12+1 (5); Tom Brown 10+3 (5); Karlis Ezergailis 7 (4); Match No. 4: Martin Williams 7 (4); Match No. 7: Simon Tillman 0 (3); Match No. 8: Lee Smart 10+2 (6); Matt Browne 1+1 (4); Match No. 10: Wayne Dunworth 3+2 (5); Match No. 12: Scott Richardson 1 (4); Match No.13: Peter Johnson 1 (4); Thomas Hill 1 (3).

DETAILS OF TACTICAL RIDES AND TACTICAL SUBSTITUTE RIDES

Match No. 2: Meakins 6 points (TR); Mason 4 points (TS); Walker 0 points (TR); Match No. 5: Johnson 4 points (TS); Mason 4 points (TR); Match No. 6: Frampton 4 points (TR); Piper 4 points (TS); Johnson 0 points (TR); Match No. 7: Johnson 6 points (TR); Mason 6 points (TR); Frampton 1 point (TS; not doubled); Match No. 8: Smart 4 points (TS); Mason 4 points (TR); Johnson 0 points (TR); Match No. 10: Warwick 1 point (TS; not doubled); Match No. 12: Johnson 6 points (TR); Frampton 0 points (TR); Match No. 13: Frampton 1 point (TR; not doubled); Mason 1 point (TR; not doubled).

OTHER DETAILS

Club Carmarthen scorers in Match No. 1: Mark Jones 12 (6); Ben Barker 9 (5); Karl Mason 8 (4); Dean Felton 7+1 (4); Billy Legg 5+2 (5); Gordon Meakins 3+1 (3); Jessica Lamb 1+1 (3).

AVERAGES
(10 Conference Shield = 10 fixtures)

Rider	Mts	Rds	Pts	Bon	Tot	Avge	Max
David Mason	8	43	103	3	106	9.86	2 full
Jordan Frampton	8	42	70	9	79	7.52	1 paid
Gordon Meakins	6	21	28	2	30	5.71	-
George Piper	9	36	32	9	41	4.56	-
Adam Filmer	9	42	35	10	45	4.29	-
Terry Day	8	40	35	4	39	3.90	-

Also rode (in alphabetical order):

	Mts	Rds	Pts	Bon	Tot	Avge	Max
Wayne Dunworth	1	5	3	2	5	4.00	-
Thomas Hill	1	3	1	0	1	1.33	-
Chris Johnson	5	23	52	2	54	9.39	1 paid
Peter Johnson	1	4	1	0	1	1.00	-

WEYMOUTH: From left to right, back row: Phil Bartlett (promoter/team manager), Wayne Dunworth, Gordon Meakins, Adam Filmer. Front row, kneeling: Terry Day, George Piper, David Mason.

Nick Laurence	1	4	2	1	3	3.00	-
Simon Tillman	2	6	0	0	0	0.00	-
James Walker	1	5	6	0	6	4.80	-
Danny Warwick	3	17	31	1	32	7.53	-
Martin Williams	1	4	7	0	7	7.00	-
Guest	1	4	1	0	1	1.00	-

(Scott Richardson [1]).

OTHER MEETING

18 August: Four-Team Tournament

Weymouth 28: David Mason 12 (5); Danny Warwick 8 (4); Gordon Meakins 4 (4); Andrew Bargh 4 (4); Exeter 41: Ben Powell 14 (5); Karlis Ezergailis 10 (4); Lee Smethills 9 (4); Adam Roynon 8 (4); South Wales Select 23: Mark Jones 11 (5); Dean Felton 6 (4); Harland Cook 6 (4); Ben Hopwood 0 (1); Alex McCloud 0 (3); Poole 6: Jordan Frampton 4 (4); Adam Filmer 1 (5); Bob Charles 1 (4); George Piper 0 (4).

INDIVIDUAL MEETING

29 September: Kingswood Hotel Trophy

1st Chris Johnson 11; 2nd Lee Smethills 10; 3rd Michael Coles (on race wins) 9; David Mason 9; Dean Felton 7; Harland Cook 6; Gary Cottham 4; Sam Hurst 3; Adam Filmer 3; Sam Martin 3; Jaimie Pickard (Reserve) 2; George Piper 0 – meeting abandoned prior to the semi-finals, with the rostrum places declared.

SOUTHERN AREA LEAGUE 2006

SOUTHERN AREA LEAGUE TABLE

Team	Mts	Won	Drn	Lst	For	Agn	Pts	Bon	Tot
Oxford	10	8	1	1	200	101	17	4	21
Rye House	10	8	1	1	200	122	17	4	21
Poole	10	6	0	4	202	152	12	4	16
Swindon	10	5	0	5	179	179	10	2	12
Sittingbourne	10	1	0	9	105	233	2	1	3
Eastbourne	10	1	0	9	128	227	2	0	2

RESULTS

4 June: Rye House 26 Eastbourne 10
14 June: Poole 24 Swindon 11
17 June: Eastbourne 16 Swindon 20
28 June: Poole 22 Rye House 13
2 July: Sittingbourne 17 Swindon 19
2 July: Sittingbourne 23 Eastbourne 13
6 July: Swindon 21 Poole 15
8 July: Rye House 20 Swindon 15
8 July: Eastbourne 22 Sittingbourne 14
13 July: Swindon 17 Rye House 19
22 July: Rye House 21 Poole 15
23 July: Eastbourne 6 Rye House 30
26 July: Oxford 26 Eastbourne 10
2 August: Poole 29 Eastbourne 7
3 August: Swindon 13 Oxford 23

6 August: Sittingbourne 8 Poole 28
9 August: Poole 27 Sittingbourne 7
10 August: Swindon 28 Sittingbourne 8
19 August: Eastbourne 16 Poole 18
26 August: Rye House 27 Sittingbourne 9
30 August: Oxford 16 Sittingbourne 0
31 August: Swindon 22 Eastbourne 14
6 September: Poole 12 Oxford 24
7 September: Oxford 24 Poole 12
9 September: Eastbourne 14 Oxford 19
17 September: Sittingbourne 6 Oxford 30
17 September: Sittingbourne 13 Rye House 23
20 September: Oxford 23 Swindon 13
27 September: Oxford 0 Rye House 0
14 October: Rye House 21 Oxford 15

SUMMARY OF SCORERS:

EASTBOURNE: James Walker 46; Nick Laurence 44; Niall Strudwick 29; Sam Heath 9.
OXFORD: Lee Smart 67; Sam Martin 50; James Purchase 46; Andrew Bargh 17; *Awarded points 16*; Olly Gay 3; Daniel Blake 1; Lewis Blackbird 0.
POOLE: Jordan Frampton 46; Rob Smith 41; Shane Waldron 37; Mattie Bates 35; Bob Charles 21; George Piper 10; Tom Hedley 9; Marc Andrews 3.
RYE HOUSE: Daniel Halsey 56; Gary Cottham 33; Danny Betson 29; Lee Strudwick 27; Harland Cook 21; Robert Mear 20; Sam Heath 5; Adam Filmer 4; Alex McLeod 3; Karl White 2.
SITTINGBOURNE: Aaron Baseby 33; Luke Goody 25; Lee Lingham 15; Chris Neame 9; Rikki Mullins 7; Carl Martin 5; Chris Glanville 4; Mark Baseby 3; Martin Elliott 2; Alex McLeod 2.
SWINDON: Nathan Irwin 76; Kyle Hughes 46; Ben Reade 23; Cory Gathercole 15; Marc Andrews 8; Nicki Glanz 4; Olly Gay 3; Cecil Forbes 2; Billy Legg 2.

NOTE: The meeting on 30 August was awarded to Oxford, as Sittingbourne were unable to raise a team. The fixture on 27 September was abandoned after heat two and awarded as a 0-0 draw.

SOUTHERN TRACK RIDERS' MEETINGS 2006

26 March: King's Lynn

Open Pairs: 1st Dean Garrod and Matt Tutton 28; 2nd Michael Holding and Karl Rushen 21; 3rd Rodney Woodhouse and Wayne Dunworth 19; 4th Daniel Blake and Scott Chester 19; 5th Glyn Edwards and Andrew Blackburn 13; 6th Ben Hannon and Dave Lidgett 8.

Novice Pairs: 1st Jason Taylor and Lee Coley 24; 2nd Kevin Garwood and Shawn Taylor 24; 3rd Steve Oakey and Matt Jarman 23; 4th Nigel Knott and Gary Emeny 18; 5th Phil Hindley and Sid Higgins 9; 6th Robin Couzins and Adrian Townsend 9.

Support Class: Gary Fawdrey 12; Steve Lockyer 12; James Humby 9; Ian Hart 8; Ian Stroud 8; Pete Shakespeare 7; James Fear 6; Sam Howett 4; Barry Byles 3; Alec Jones 3; Martin Hartwell 1; Kieren Higgins 0.

16 April: King's Lynn

Open Class: Karl Rushen 12; Michael Holding 11; Matt Tutton 8; Jason Taylor 8; Shawn Taylor 7; Gary Fawdrey 6; Gordon Walker 6; Andrew Blackburn 5; Steve Oakey 3; Dean Wilson 2; David Tutton 2. Final: 1st Rushen; 2nd M. Tutton; 3rd Holding; 4th J. Taylor.

Novice Class: Olly Gay 14; Nigel Knott 13; Greg Walsh 12; Stuart Lauder 11; Stuart Madle 10; Sam Howett 10; Lewis Blackbird 9; Liam Rumsey 8; Barry Byles 8; James Luckman 6; Alec Jones 5; Andrew Lauder 5; Norman Hornblow 4; Kieren Higgins 2; Shane Fawdrey 0.

Support Class: James Humby 12; Paul Chester 11; Sid Higgins 10; Kevin Garwood 8; Gary Emeny 8; Steve Lockyer 6; Matt Jarman 6; Frank Whitby 4; Adrian Townsend 3; Phil Hindley 2; James Fear 2; Pete Shakespeare 0. Final: 1st Humby; 2nd Garwood; 3rd Higgins; 4th Chester.

14 May: King's Lynn

Open Class: Dean Garrod 12; Karl Rushen 11; Wayne Dunworth 9; Michael Holding 9; Rodney Woodhouse 9; Scott Chester 8; Daniel Blake 7; Shawn Taylor 6; Dave Lidgett 6; Paul Chester 5; Gary Fawdrey 4; James Humby 3; Jason Taylor 3; Andrew Blackburn 2; Lee Geary 1; Steve Oakey 0.

Novice Class: Nick Laurence 12; Alec Gooch 11; Liam Rumsey 10; Chris Widman 10; Niall Strudwick 9; Ian Hart 8; Andy Shaw 6; Richard Walsh 6; Frank Whitby 5; Kieren Higgins 5; Barry Byles 3; Shane Fawdrey 3; Andrew Lauder 3; Clive Marshall 2; Rodger Curtis 2; James Fear 1.

Support Class: Olly Gay 11; Stuart Lauder 11; Kevin Garwood 9; Sid Higgins 9; Gary Emeny 8; Greg Walsh 8; Steve Lockyer 8; Matt Jarman 8; Adi Bursill 5; James Luckman 4; Ian Stroud 4; Stuart Madle 4; Phil Hindley 3; Pete Shakespeare 2; Sam Howett 2; Gary Henriksen 0.

29 May: Newport

Open Class: Dean Garrod 12; Daniel Blake 9; Paul Chester 9; Andrew Blackburn 8; Dave Lidgett 7; Lee Gary 7; Stuart Lauder 6; Jason Taylor 5; David Tutton 4; James Humby 2; Shawn Taylor 0. Final: 1st Blake; 2nd Garrod; 3rd Chester; 4th Blackburn.

Support Class: Russell Barnett 11; Nick Laurence 11; Craig Chater 11; Dean Hancox 9; Chris Widman 6; Gary Emeny 6; Greg Walsh 4; Sam Heath 4; Richard Walsh 4; Laurence Fielding 3; Roger Curtis 2; Steve Oakey 1. Final: 1st Barnett; 2nd Hancox; 3rd Laurence; 4th Chater.

Over 40s Class: Sid Higgins 15; Steve Lockyer 14; Pete Shakespeare 13; Sam Howett 11; Barry Byles

11; Gary Henriksen 8; Andy Lauder 8; Dennis Cairns 8; Ted Ede 8; Alec Jones 6; Ian Stroud 5; Norman Hornblow 4; Phil Hindley 2; Frank Whitby 2; Alec Gooch 0.

18 June: King's Lynn

Open Class: Nick Laurence 11; Ben Johnson 10; Karl Rushen 9; Michael Holding 9; Daniel Blake 9; Glyn Edwards 6; Dave Lidgett 6; Wes Sheasby 3; Rodney Woodhouse 3; Paul Chester 3; Andrew Blackburn 2; Lee Geary 1. Final: 1st Rushen; 2nd Holding; 3rd Laurence; 4th Johnson.

Support Class: Shawn Taylor 13; Kevin Garwood 12; Jason Taylor 12; Stuart Lauder 12; Olly Gay 11; Niall Strudwick 9; Sam Heath 8; Chris Widman 8; Matt Jarman 7; Sid Higgins 7; Steve Oakey 7; Gary Emeny 6; Dean Hancox 4; Andy Shaw 2; James Luckman 1; Sam Howett 0.

Novice Class: Gary Henriksen 12; Ian Stroud 11; Derek Jones 9; Pete Shakespeare 9; Kieren Higgins 8; Phil Hindley 6; Pete Rout 5; Frank Whitby 5; James Fear 3; Alec Jones 3; Clive Marshall 1; Mark Consadine 0. Final: 1st Henriksen; 2nd D. Jones; 3rd Stroud; 4th Shakespeare.

9 July: King's Lynn

Open Class: Wayne Dunworth 10; Matt Tutton 9; Adam Filmer 9; Lewis Blackbird 8; Michael Holding 8; Jason Taylor 6; Nick Laurence 5; Paul Chester 4; Glyn Edwards 4; Rodney Woodhouse 4; Scott Chester 3; Ben Johnson 0. Final: 1st Tutton; 2nd Dunworth; 3rd Blackbird; 4th Filmer.

NOTE: Adam Lowe rode two races as a guest, finishing the meeting with 5 points.

Support Class: Niall Strudwick 14; Shawn Taylor 13; Gordon Walker 12; David Tutton 12; Kevin Garwood 11; Alec Gooch 8; Chris Widman 8; Sid Higgins 8; Matt Jarman 7; Sam Heath 6; Gary Emeny 4; Stuart Lauder 4; Greg Walsh 4; Nigel Knott 3; Steve Oakey 2; Sam Howett 2.

Novice Class: Richard Walsh 12; Ian Hart 9; Derek Jones 9; Pete Shakespeare 9; Paul Robinson 7; Pete Rout 7; Andy Lauder 7; Phil Hindley 5; Kieren Higgins 3; Alec Jones 3; Clive Marshall 1; Norman Hornblow 0. Final: 1st Walsh; 2nd Shakespeare; 3rd D. Jones; 4th Hart.

6 August: King's Lynn

Open Class: Karl Rushen 11; Wayne Dunworth 10; Michael Holding 10; Dave Lidgett 8; Matt Tutton 6; Lewis Blackbird 6; Jason Taylor 5; Rodney Woodhouse 4; Andrew Blackburn 3; Paul Chester 3; Lee Geary 2; Adam Lowe 0. Final: 1st Rushen; 2nd Dunworth; 3rd Lidgett.

Intermediate Class: Andy Braithwaite 9; Dean Hancox 9; Chris Widman 8; Craig Chater 7; Sid Higgins 7; Gary Emeny 6; Paul Quarterman 5; Shawn Taylor 5; Stuart Lauder 5; Greg Walsh 4; Pete Shakespeare 3; Matt Jarman 2.

Novice Class: Scott Whittington 15; Richard Walsh 13; Alec Gooch 13; Derek Jones 13; Nigel Knott 11; Paul Robinson 9; Phil Hindley 9; Tony Venables 7; Ian Hart 7; Sam Howett 6; Lawrence Fielding 6; Joe Burdekin 3; Clive Marshall 3; Phil Woodbines 2; Frank Whitby 0; Andy Lauder 0.

20 August: Newport

Open Class: Jamie Westacott 12; Matt Tutton 11; Karl Mason 8; Nick Laurence 8; Glyn Edwards 8; Nick Mallett 5; Karl White 4; Russell Barnett 3; Paul Chester 3; Michael Holding 3; Dave Lidgett 2; Tim Webster 1. Final: 1st Mason; 2nd Westacott; 3rd Tutton.

Intermediate Class: Olly Gay 12; Shawn Taylor 9; Kevin Garwood 9; Craig Chater 8; Sam Heath 7; Dean Hancox 7; Chris Widman 6; Matt Jarman 4; Sid Higgins 4; Lee Geary 3; David Tutton 2. Final: 1st Taylor; 2nd Gay; 3rd Garwood.

Novice Class: Gary Henriksen 15; Pete Shakespeare 13; Sam Howett 12; Tony Venables 12; Ian Stroud 11; Derek Jones 9; Phil Hindley 9; Dennis Cairns 7; Roger Curtis 7; Barry Byles 7; Andy Lauder 5; Phil Woodbines 5; Norman Hornblow 4.

3 September: King's Lynn

Open Class: Lewis Blackbird 12; Karl Rushen 11; Michael Holding 11; Jason Taylor 7; Olly Gay (Guest) 7; Lee Geary 6; Nick Laurence 5; Dave Lidgett 4; Niall Strudwick (Guest) 4; Rodney Woodhouse 4; Kevin Garwood (Guest) 1; Shawn Taylor (Guest) 0. Final: 1st Rushen; 2nd Holding; 3rd Blackbird.

Intermediate Class: Dean Hancox 11; Sam Heath 11; Stuart Lauder 9; Adam Chandler 9; Craig Chater 9; Sid Higgins 8; Ian Hart 5; Matt Jarman 4; Gary Emeny 3; Tony Venables 2; Lee Coley 1. Final: 1st Heath; 2nd Hancox; 3rd Lauder.

Novice Class: Richard Walsh 14; Gary Henriksen 13; Derek Jones 12; Sam Howett 12; Pete Shakespeare 11; Phil Hindley 10; Andy Lauder 9; Nigel Knott 9; Ian Stroud 8; James Fear 6; Andy Shaw (Guest) 4; Alec Jones 4; Frank Whitby 3; Clive Marshall 2; Roger Curtis 2.

24 September: Newport

Open Class: Daniel Blake 11; Tim Webster 9; Nick Laurence 8; Craig Chester 8; Jason Taylor 8; Sam Heath 7; Glyn Edwards 6; Adam Chandler 5; Chris Widman 4; Sid Higgins 2; Olly Gay 2; Stuart Lauder 0. Final: 1st Blake; 2nd Laurence; 3rd Chater.

Novice Class: Derek Jones 15; Paul Robinson 13; Ian Stroud 11; Pete Shakespeare 11; Andy Lauder 11; Sam Howett 10; James Luckman 10; Lawrence Fielding 8; Phil Hindley 7; Alec Jones 6; Kieren Higgins 5; Steve Cook 4; Roger Curtis 4; Steve Oakey 3; Phil Woodbines 1.

1 October: Sittingbourne

Open Class: Nick Laurence 12; Daniel Blake 11; Jason Taylor 2; Lewis Blackbird 2.

Intermediate Class: Shawn Taylor 12; Niall Strudwick 12; Craig Chester 12; Chris Widman 11; Olly Gay 11; Kevin Garwood 10; Sam Heath 9; Dean Hancox 8; Stuart Lauder 7; Sid Higgins 7; Matt Jarman 6; James Luckman 5; Steve Oakey 4; Gary Emeny 1.

NOTE: Lee Coley and Adam Chandler rode as guests, but their points were not recorded.

Novice Class: Daniel Hunt 12; Lawrence Fielding 10; Kieren Higgins 4; Adi Bursill 1.

Over 40s Class: Michael Holding 15; Steve Cook 14; Kevin Garwood 13; Sid Higgins 12; Paul Robinson 11; Tony Venables 10; Andy Lauder 9; Pete Shakespeare 7; Phil Hindley 7; Barry Byles 7; Clive Marshall 5; Alec Jones 4.

NOTE: Phil Olson, Sam Howell and Les Rowland all rode as guests, but their points were not recorded.

15 October: King's Lynn

Intermediate/Open Class: Glyn Edwards 11; Sam Heath 10; Jitendra Duffill 9; Ben Johnson 9; Steve Oakey 8; Andrew Blackburn 6; Sid Higgins 5; Scott Whittington 4; Craig Chater 4; Adam Chandler 3; Derek Jones 2. Final: 1st Duffill; 2nd Heath; 3rd Edwards.

Novice Class: Steve Lockyer 11; Pete Shakespeare 11; Sam Howett 9; Ian Hart 9; Phil Hindley 8; Andy Shaw 8; Ian Stroud 7; Kieren Higgins 5; Joe Burdekin 3; Alec Jones 1; Clive Marshall 0; Lee Coley 0.

Team Event: The All-Stars 48 (Michael Holding 14; Nick Laurence 12; Karl Rushen 10; Olly Gay 8; Gary Henriksen 4); Top Fuel 43 (Adam Filmer 13; Wayne Dunworth 12; Rodney Woodhouse 8; Niall Strudwick 6; Alec Gooch 4); It's Only a Trophy!! 38 (Daniel Blake 13; Jason Taylor 9; Shawn Taylor 6; Kevin Garwood 6; Liam Rumsey 4); Tigers 21 (Lewis Blackbird 12; Adam Lowe 8; Gary Emeny 1; Nigel Knott 0; Dave Lidgett 0).

MAJOR BRITISH MEETINGS 2006

BRITISH UNDER-21 CHAMPIONSHIP FINAL 2006
3 MAY, KING'S LYNN

1st BEN WILSON
2nd DANIEL KING
3rd LEWIS BRIDGER
4th STEVE BOXALL

RIDER	QUALIFYING SCORES					TOTAL
Ben Wilson	2	3	3	3	3	14
Daniel King	3	3	2	3	3	14
Lewis Bridger	3	3	3	2	2	13
Steve Boxall	2	2	3	2	3	12
Jason King	M	3	3	3	1	10
James Wright	2	2	1	3	2	10
Edward Kennett	3	2	1	1	1	8
James Brundle	1	0	2	1	3	7
Richie Dennis	3	1	1	1	0	6
Josh Auty	2	1	0	2	1	6
Ben Barker	1	0	0	2	2	5
Joel Parsons	X	0	2	1	2	5
Jamie Courtney	1	1	2	0	0	4
Benji Compton	0	2	0	X	1	3
Luke Bowen	0	1	1	X	-	2
Simon Lambert	1	0	0	0	0	1
Robert Mear (reserve)	0	-	-	-	-	0
Ben Hopwood (reserve)	0	-	-	-	-	0

RACE DETAILS

HEAT ONE:	(Awarded) Kennett, Wilson, Barker, Parsons (f, ex).
HEAT TWO:	Dennis, Auty, Courtney, Bowen.
HEAT THREE:	Bridger, Wright, Brundle, Compton.
HEAT FOUR:	D. King, Boxall, Lambert, Mear, J. King (ex, 2 mins).
HEAT FIVE:	D. King, Kennett, Dennis, Brundle.
HEAT SIX:	J. King, Wright, Courtney, Parsons.
HEAT SEVEN:	Bridger, Boxall, Auty, Barker.
HEAT EIGHT:	Wilson, Compton, Bowen, Lambert.
HEAT NINE:	Bridger, Courtney, Kennett, Lambert.
HEAT TEN:	Boxall, Parsons, Dennis, Compton.
HEAT ELEVEN:	J. King, Brundle, Bowen, Barker.
HEAT TWELVE:	Wilson, D. King, Wright, Auty.

HEAT THIRTEEN: (Rerun) J. King, Auty, Kennett, Compton (f, ex)
HEAT FOURTEEN: (Rerun) D. King, Bridger, Parsons, Bowen (f, ex).
HEAT FIFTEEN: Wright, Barker, Dennis, Lambert.
HEAT SIXTEEN: Wilson, Boxall, Brundle, Courtney.
HEAT SEVENTEEN: Boxall, Wright, Kennett, Hopwood (f, rem).
HEAT EIGHTEEN: Brundle, Parsons, Auty, Lambert.
HEAT NINETEEN: D. King, Barker, Compton, Courtney.
HEAT TWENTY: Wilson, Bridger, J. King, Dennis.
SEMI-FINAL: Bridger, Boxall, Wright, J. King.
FINAL: Wilson, D. King, Bridger, Boxall.

ROLL OF HONOUR

NOTE: Became known as the British Under-21 Championship in 1987, having previously been called the Junior Championship of Great Britain.

YEAR	FIRST	SECOND	THIRD
1969	Graham Plant	Geoff Ambrose	Mick Bell
1970	Barry Thomas	Dave Jessup	Mick Bell
1971	Ian Turner	Dave Jessup	Peter Ingram
1972	Allen Emmett	Gordon Kennett	Tony Davey
1973	Peter Collins	Barney Kennett	David Gagen
1974	Chris Morton	Steve Bastable	Neil Middleditch
1975	Neil Middleditch	Steve Weatherley	Joe Owen
1976	Michael Lee	Steve Weatherley	Colin Richardson
1977	Les Collins	Phil Collins	Colin Richardson
1978	Phil Collins	Ian Gledhill	Bob Garrad
1979	Kenny Carter	Nigel Flatman	Mel Taylor
1980	Mark Courtney	Kevin Smith	John Barker
1981	Rob Lightfoot	Peter Carr	Neil Evitts
1982	Peter Carr	Martin Hagon	Simon Cross
1983	Keith Millard	Simon Cross	Kenny McKinna
1984	Marvyn Cox	Simon Cross	Andy Smith
1985	Carl Blackbird	David Mullett	Andy Smith
1986	Gary Havelock	Andrew Silver	Daz Sumner
1987	Daz Sumner	David Biles	Mark Loram
1988	Mark Loram	Andy Phillips	Martin Dugard
1989	Martin Dugard	Chris Louis	Dean Barker
1990	Joe Screen	Mark Loram	Chris Louis
1991	Not staged		
1992	Scott Smith	Mark Loram	Joe Screen
1993	Joe Screen	Carl Stonehewer	David Norris
1994	Paul Hurry	Ben Howe	James Grieves
1995	Ben Howe	Paul Hurry	Savalas Clouting
1996	Savalas Clouting	Scott Nicholls	Paul Hurry
1997	Leigh Lanham	Lee Richardson	Scott Nicholls
1998	Scott Nicholls	Lee Richardson	Paul Lee

1999	Scott Nicholls	Lee Richardson	David Howe
2000	David Howe	Lee Richardson	Paul Lee
2001	Simon Stead	David Howe	Paul Lee
2002	Simon Stead	Ross Brady	Olly Allen
2003	Simon Stead	Olly Allen	Edward Kennett
2004	Ritchie Hawkins	Steve Boxall	Edward Kennett
2005	Edward Kennett	Chris Schramm	Richard Hall
2006	Ben Wilson	Daniel King	Lewis Bridger

ELITE LEAGUE PAIRS CHAMPIONSHIP 2006
4 JUNE, SWINDON

1st BELLE VUE
2nd SWINDON

GROUP A	QUALIFYING SCORES					TOTALS
SWINDON 31						
Leigh Adams	4	4	4	4	4	20
Sebastian Ulamek	3*	3*	3*	0	2	11 (3)
PETERBOROUGH 26						
Hans N. Andersen	F	4	4	3	4	15
Niels-Kristian Iversen	4	0	3*	2*	2	11 (2)
EASTBOURNE 25						
Nicki Pedersen	4	4	R	4	3	15
David Norris	3*	3*	2	2	0	10 (2)
COVENTRY 23						
Scott Nicholls	2	3	4	0	2	11
Rory Schlein	0	2*	3*	3	4	12 (2)
IPSWICH 17						
Kim Jansson	3	0	2	2*	X	7 (1)
Piotr Protasiewicz	2*	2	0	3	3	10 (1)
WOLVERHAMPTON 13						
Ronnie Correy	0	0	2	0	R	2
Fredrik Lindgren	2	2	0	4	3	11

GROUP B	QUALIFYING SCORES					TOTALS
BELLE VUE 21						
Jason Crump	4	4	4	4	-	16
Simon Stead	2	X	0	3*	-	5 (1)

POOLE 21

Bjarne Pedersen	2	2*	3	2*	-	9 (2)
Antonio Lindback	4	3	2*	3	-	12 (1)

READING 19

Greg Hancock	0	4	3*	3	-	10 (1)
Matej Zagar	3	0	4	2*	-	9 (1)

OXFORD 15

Todd Wiltshire	3	4	2	4	-	13
Adam Skornicki	0	2	0	0	-	2

ARENA-ESSEX 14

Leigh Lanham	2*	0	0	0	-	2 (1)
Joonas Kylmakorpi	3	3	2	4	-	12

RACE DETAILS

HEAT ONE:	N. Pedersen, Norris, Lindgren, Correy.
HEAT TWO:	Adams, Ulamek, Nicholls, Schlein.
HEAT THREE:	Iversen, Jansson, Protasiewicz (f, rem), Andersen (fell).
HEAT FOUR:	Crump, Zagar, Stead, Hancock.
HEAT FIVE:	Lindback, Wiltshire, B. Pedersen, Skornicki.
HEAT SIX:	Adams, Ulamek, Lindgren, Correy.
HEAT SEVEN:	N. Pedersen, Norris, Protasiewicz, Jansson.
HEAT EIGHT:	Andersen, Nicholls, Schlein, Iversen (f, rem).
HEAT NINE:	Crump, Kylmakorpi, Lanham, Stead (ex, lapped).
HEAT TEN:	Hancock, Lindback, B. Pedersen, Zagar.
HEAT ELEVEN:	Adams, Ulamek, Jansson, Protasiewicz.
HEAT TWELVE:	Nicholls, Schlein, Correy, Lindgren.
HEAT THIRTEEN:	Andersen, Iversen, Norris, N. Pedersen (ret).
HEAT FOURTEEN:	Wiltshire, Kylmakorpi, Skornicki, Lanham.
HEAT FIFTEEN:	Crump, B. Pedersen, Lindback, Stead.
HEAT SIXTEEN:	Lindgren, Protasiewicz, Jansson, Correy.
HEAT SEVENTEEN:	N. Pedersen, Schlein, Norris, Nicholls.
HEAT EIGHTEEN:	Adams, Andersen, Iversen, Ulamek.
HEAT NINETEEN:	Crump, Stead, Wiltshire, Skornicki.
HEAT TWENTY:	Zagar, Hancock, Kylmakorpi, Lanham.
HEAT TWENTY-ONE:	(Rerun) Schlein, Protasiewicz, Nicholls, Jansson (f, ex).
HEAT TWENTY-TWO:	Andersen, Lindgren, Iversen, Correy (ret).
HEAT TWENTY-THREE:	Adams, N. Pedersen, Ulamek, Norris.
HEAT TWENTY-FOUR:	Wiltshire, Hancock, Zagar, Skornicki.
HEAT TWENTY-FIVE:	Kylmakorpi, Lindback, B. Pedersen, Lanham.
GRAND FINAL:	Adams, Crump, Stead, Ulamek.

ROLL OF HONOUR

NOTE: Known as the British League Pairs Championship from 1976-1978 and the British Open Pairs Championship from 1984-1987.

YEAR	FIRST	SECOND
1976	Ipswich (John Louis & Billy Sanders)	Coventry (Ole Olsen & Mitch Shirra)
1977	Ipswich (Billy Sanders & John Louis)	King's Lynn (Michael Lee & David Gagen)
1978	Cradley Heath (Steve Bastable & Bruce Penhall) and Coventry (Ole Olsen & Mitch Shirra) [shared]	
1979-1983	Not staged	
1984	Belle Vue (Peter Collins & Chris Morton)	Reading (Mitch Shirra & Tim Hunt)
1985	Oxford (Hans Nielsen & Simon Wigg)	Reading (John Davis & Mitch Shirra)
1986	Oxford (Simon Wigg & Hans Nielsen)	Coventry (Kelvin Tatum & John Jorgensen)
1987	Oxford (Hans Nielsen & Andy Grahame)	Swindon (Mitch Shirra & Jimmy Nilsen)
1988-2003	Not staged	
2004	Swindon (Leigh Adams & Charlie Gjedde)	Belle Vue (Jason Crump & Joe Screen)
2005	Swindon (Leigh Adams & Lee Richardson)	Belle Vue (Jason Crump & Joe Screen)
2006	Belle Vue (Jason Crump & Simon Stead)	Swindon (Leigh Adams & Sebastian Ulamek)

CHAMPIONSHIP OF GREAT BRITAIN 2006

11 JUNE, BELLE VUE

1st SCOTT NICHOLLS
2nd JOE SCREEN
3rd SIMON STEAD
4th CHRIS HARRIS

RIDER	QUALIFYING SCORES					TOTAL
Chris Harris	3	3	3	1	3	13
Scott Nicholls	2	3	2	3	3	13
Joe Screen	2	2	3	2	3	12
Simon Stead	1	3	2	3	2	11
Andy Smith	1	2	3	3	2	11
Leigh Lanham	3	3	1	2	1	10
Edward Kennett	3	2	0	1	2	8
Lee Richardson	2	0	2	2	2	8
David Howe	0	1	2	1	3	7
Olly Allen	1	1	1	3	0	6
Ricky Ashworth	2	M	3	R	R	5
David Norris	3	2	N	-	-	5
Carl Wilkinson	F	0	0	2	1	3
Garry Stead	0	1	X	1	1	3
Paul Hurry	1	1	N	-	-	2
Chris Neath	0	0	1	X	1	2
Benji Compton (reserve)	F	1	0	-	-	1
Jonathan Bethell (reserve)	0	0	0	-	-	0

RACE DETAILS

HEAT ONE:	Kennett, Richardson, S. Stead, Wilkinson (fell).
HEAT TWO:	Norris, Screen, Allen, Howe.
HEAT THREE:	Harris, Nicholls, Smith, G. Stead.
HEAT FOUR:	Lanham, Ashworth, Hurry, Neath.
HEAT FIVE:	Harris, Kennett, Allen, Compton (fell), Ashworth (ex, 2 mins).
HEAT SIX:	Lanham, Screen, G. Stead, Richardson.
HEAT SEVEN:	Nicholls, Norris, Hurry, Wilkinson (f, rem).
HEAT EIGHT:	S. Stead, Smith, Howe, Neath.
HEAT NINE:	Screen, Nicholls, Neath, Kennett.
HEAT TEN:	(Rerun) Smith, Richardson, Allen, Bethell, Hurry (f, ns).
HEAT ELEVEN:	Harris, Howe, Lanham, Wilkinson.
HEAT TWELVE:	(Rerun) Ashworth, S. Stead, Compton, Norris (f, ns), G. Stead (f, ex).
HEAT THIRTEEN:	Smith, Lanham, Kennett, Bethell.
HEAT FOURTEEN:	Nicholls, Richardson, Howe, Ashworth (ret).
HEAT FIFTEEN:	(Rerun) Allen, Wilkinson, G. Stead (f, rem), Neath (f, ex).
HEAT SIXTEEN:	S. Stead, Screen, Harris, Compton.
HEAT SEVENTEEN:	Howe, Kennett, G. Stead, Bethell.
HEAT EIGHTEEN:	Harris, Richardson, Neath, Compton (fell).
HEAT NINETEEN:	Screen, Smith, Wilkinson, Ashworth (ret).
HEAT TWENTY:	Nicholls, S. Stead, Lanham, Allen.
FINAL:	Nicholls, Screen, S. Stead, Harris.

ROLL OF HONOUR

NOTE: Became known as the Championship of Great Britain in 2002, having previously been called the British Final.

YEAR	FIRST	SECOND	THIRD
1961	Barry Briggs	Peter Craven	Ronnie Moore
1962	Peter Craven	Barry Briggs	Ronnie Moore
1963	Peter Craven	Barry Briggs	Leo McAuliffe
1964	Barry Briggs	Ken McKinlay	Ron How
1965	Barry Briggs	Nigel Boocock	Ken McKinlay
1966	Barry Briggs	Ivan Mauger	Colin Pratt
1967	Barry Briggs	Ivan Mauger	Eric Boocock
1968	Ivan Mauger	Barry Briggs	Eric Boocock
1969	Barry Briggs	Nigel Boocock	Ronnie Moore
1970	Ivan Mauger	Ronnie Moore	Roy Trigg
1971	Ivan Mauger	Barry Briggs	Tony Lomas
1972	Ivan Mauger	Nigel Boocock	Barry Briggs
1973	Ray Wilson	Bob Valentine	Peter Collins
1974	Eric Boocock	Terry Betts	Dave Jessup
1975	John Louis	Peter Collins	Malcolm Simmons
1976	Malcolm Simmons	Chris Morton	Doug Wyer
1977	Michael Lee	Dave Jessup	Doug Wyer
1978	Michael Lee	Dave Jessup	Malcolm Simmons

1979	Peter Collins	Michael Lee	Dave Jessup
1980	Dave Jessup	Michael Lee	Phil Collins
1981	Steve Bastable	Kenny Carter	John Louis
1982	Andy Grahame	Alan Grahame	Kenny Carter
1983	Chris Morton	Michael Lee	Andy Grahame
1984	Kenny Carter	Andy Grahame	Dave Jessup
1985	Kenny Carter	John Davis	Kelvin Tatum
1986	Neil Evitts	Phil Collins	Jeremy Doncaster
1987	Kelvin Tatum	Neil Evitts	Simon Wigg
1988	Simon Wigg	Kelvin Tatum	Chris Morton
1989	Simon Wigg	Kelvin Tatum	Alan Grahame
1990	Kelvin Tatum	Simon Cross	Jeremy Doncaster
1991	Gary Havelock	Kelvin Tatum	Chris Louis
1992	Gary Havelock	Martin Dugard	Andy Smith
1993	Andy Smith	Joe Screen	Gary Havelock
1994	Andy Smith	Joe Screen	Steve Schofield
1995	Andy Smith	Joe Screen	Dean Barker
1996	Joe Screen	Chris Louis	Carl Stonehewer
1997	Mark Loram	Chris Louis	Sean Wilson
1998	Chris Louis	Joe Screen	Paul Hurry
1999	Mark Loram	Joe Screen	Chris Louis
2000	Chris Louis	Paul Hurry	Martin Dugard
2001	Mark Loram	Stuart Robson	Martin Dugard
2002	Scott Nicholls	Lee Richardson	David Howe
2003	Scott Nicholls	Dean Barker	David Norris
2004	Joe Screen	David Norris	Mark Loram
2005	Scott Nicholls	Chris Harris	Joe Screen
2006	Scott Nicholls	Joe Screen	Simon Stead

CORBETT BOOKMAKERS CONFERENCE LEAGUE FOUR-TEAM CHAMPIONSHIP 2006
24 JUNE, STOKE

1st STOKE
2nd PLYMOUTH
3rd MILDENHALL
4th SCUNTHORPE

FIRST SEMI-FINAL	QUALIFYING SCORES				TOTAL
STOKE 18					
Luke Priest	2	3	-	-	5
Ben Barker	2	3	-	-	5
Scott Courtney	2	2	-	-	4
Kriss Irving	2	2	-	-	4

PLYMOUTH 16

Seemond Stephens	3	2	-	-	5
Chris Johnson	3	3	-	-	6
Lee Smart	3	1	-	-	4
Shane Waldron	1	R	-	-	1

BOSTON 10

Wayne Broadhurst	X	1	-	-	1
Sean Stoddart	3	R	-	-	3
Darren Mallett	1	3	-	-	4
Sam Martin	0	2	-	-	2

NEWPORT 4

Karl Mason	1	0	-	-	1
Daniel Blake	1	1	-	-	2
Sam Hurst	0	0	-	-	0
Billy Legg	X	-	-	-	0
Adam Lowe (Reserve)	1	-	-	-	1

RACE DETAILS

HEAT ONE:	(Rerun) Smart, Irving, Blake, Broadhurst (ex, foul riding).
HEAT TWO:	Stoddart, Priest, Waldron, Hurst.
HEAT THREE:	(Rerun) Stephens, Barker, Mallett, Legg (f, ex).
HEAT FOUR:	Johnson, Courtney, Mason, Martin.
HEAT FIVE:	Priest, Stephens, Broadhurst, Mason.
HEAT SIX:	Barker, Martin, Blake, Waldron (ret).
HEAT SEVEN:	Mallett, Courtney, Smart, Hurst.
HEAT EIGHT:	Johnson, Irving, Lowe, Stoddart (ret).

SECOND SEMI-FINAL	QUALIFYING SCORES				TOTAL
SCUNTHORPE 19					
Wayne Carter	3	2	-	-	5
Richie Dennis	2	3	-	-	5
Josh Auty	3	2	-	-	5
Tai Woffinden	1	3	-	-	4

MILDENHALL 12

Andrew Bargh	3	1	-	-	4
Mark Thompson	2	1	-	-	3
Matthew Wright	3	0	-	-	3
James Purchase	2	0	-	-	2

BUXTON 12

Scott James	1	3	-	-	4
Jonathan Bethell	0	0	-	-	0

Ben Taylor	2	3	-	-	5
Adam Roynon	1	2	-	-	3
RYE HOUSE 5					
Daniel Halsey	1	0	-	-	1
Harland Cook	0	1	-	-	1
Barry Burchatt	0	1	-	-	1
Robert Mear	0	2	-	-	2

RACE DETAILS

HEAT ONE: Wright, Dennis, James, Mear.
HEAT TWO: Auty, Purchase, Halsey, Bethell (f, rem).
HEAT THREE: Bargh, Taylor, Woffinden, Cook.
HEAT FOUR: Carter, Thompson, Roynon, Burchatt.
HEAT FIVE: James, Carter, Bargh, Halsey.
HEAT SIX: Dennis, Roynon, Cook, Purchase.
HEAT SEVEN: Taylor, Auty, Burchatt, Wright.
HEAT EIGHT: Woffinden, Mear, Thompson, Bethell.
RUN-OFF: Bargh, Taylor.

FINAL	QUALIFYING SCORES				TOTAL
STOKE 16					
Luke Priest	1	3	-	-	4
Ben Barker	3	3	-	-	6
Scott Courtney	3	2	-	-	5
Kriss Irving	X	1	-	-	1
PLYMOUTH 16					
Seemond Stephens	3	2	-	-	5
Chris Johnson	3	3	-	-	6
Lee Smart	2	F	-	-	2
Shane Waldron	1	2	-	-	3
MILDENHALL 10					
Andrew Bargh	1	0	-	-	1
Mark Thompson	2	2	-	-	4
Matthew Wright	2	3	-	-	5
James Purchase	0	0	-	-	0
SCUNTHORPE 6					
Wayne Carter	R	1	-	-	1
Richie Dennis	N	-	-	-	0
Josh Auty	2	1	-	-	3
Tai Woffinden	0	X	-	-	0
Gareth Isherwood (reserve)	1	1	-	-	2

RACE DETAILS

HEAT ONE: Johnson, Auty, Priest, Purchase.

HEAT TWO: Barker, Smart, Bargh, Woffinden.

HEAT THREE: Courtney, Thompson, Waldron, Carter (ret).

HEAT FOUR: (Rerun) Stephens, Wright, Isherwood, Dennis (f, ns), Irving (ex, foul riding).

HEAT FIVE: Priest, Stephens, Carter, Bargh.

HEAT SIX: (Rerun) Johnson, Thompson, Irving, Woffinden (f, ex).

HEAT SEVEN: Wright, Courtney, Auty, Smart (fell).

HEAT EIGHT: Barker, Waldron, Isherwood, Purchase.

RUN-OFF: (Awarded) Priest, Johnson (f, ex).

ROLL OF HONOUR

YEAR	FIRST	SECOND	THIRD	FOURTH
2003	Rye House	Mildenhall	Peterborough	Boston
2004	Mildenhall	Newcastle & Wimbledon	-	Stoke
2005	Weymouth	Oxford	Armadale	Boston
2006	Stoke	Plymouth	Mildenhall	Scunthorpe

SUPERIOR EXTERIORS/SILVER SKI CONFERENCE LEAGUE RIDERS' CHAMPIONSHIP 2006

9 SEPTEMBER, RYE HOUSE

1st ADAM ROYNON
2nd SEEMOND STEPHENS
3rd LEE SMART
4th SCOTT COURTNEY

RIDER	RACE SCORES					TOTAL
Adam Roynon	3	3	3	3	3	15
Seemond Stephens	3	2	3	3	R	11
Lee Smart	2	3	2	1	2	10
Scott Courtney	2	F	3	1	3	9
John Oliver	3	2	1	2	F	8
Tai Woffinden	1	3	2	2	0	8
Mark Thompson	2	1	1	2	2	8
Ben Powell	X	2	X	3	2	7
Adam Allott	1	2	1	3	0	7
Andrew Bargh	1	0	2	2	1	6
Barry Burchatt	1	T	2	0	1	4
Josh Auty	3	F	X	-	-	3
Scott James	2	1	M	-	-	3
Wayne Broadhurst	0	1	0	0	1	2
Nicki Glanz	0	R	0	0	1	1
Karl Mason	X	-	-	-	-	0
David Mason (reserve)	3	3	1	3	2	12
Gary Cottham (reserve)	1	1	1	0	3	6

RACE DETAILS

HEAT ONE:	Auty, James, Burchatt, Glanz.
HEAT TWO:	(Rerun) Stephens, Thompson, Allott, Powell (f, ex).
HEAT THREE:	(Rerun) Oliver, Courtney, Woffinden, K. Mason (f, ex).
HEAT FOUR:	Roynon, Smart, Bargh, Broadhurst.
HEAT FIVE:	Roynon, Stephens, James, Courtney (fell).
HEAT SIX:	Woffinden, Powell, Broadhurst, Glanz (ret).
HEAT SEVEN:	(Rerun) D. Mason, Allott, Cottham, Bargh, Burchatt (ex, tapes).
HEAT EIGHT:	Smart, Oliver, Thompson, Auty (fell).
HEAT NINE:	(Rerun) D. Mason, Smart, Cottham, Powell (ex, foul riding), James (ex, 2 mins).
HEAT TEN:	Stephens, Bargh, Oliver, Glanz.
HEAT ELEVEN:	Courtney, Burchatt, Thompson, Broadhurst.
HEAT TWELVE:	(Rerun) Roynon, Woffinden, Allott, Auty (f, ex).
HEAT THIRTEEN:	Allott, Oliver, Cottham, Broadhurst.
HEAT FOURTEEN:	Roynon, Thompson, D. Mason, Glanz.
HEAT FIFTEEN:	Stephens, Woffinden, Smart, Burchatt.
HEAT SIXTEEN:	Powell, Bargh, Courtney, Cottham.
HEAT SEVENTEEN:	D. Mason, Thompson, Bargh, Woffinden.
HEAT EIGHTEEN:	Courtney, Smart, Glanz, Allott.
HEAT NINETEEN:	Roynon, Powell, Burchatt, Oliver (fell).
HEAT TWENTY:	Cottham, D. Mason, Broadhurst, Stephens (ret).

ROLL OF HONOUR

NOTE: Previously known as Division Three Riders' Championship (1994), Academy League Riders' Championship (1995) and Amateur League Riders' Championship (1997).

YEAR	FIRST	SECOND	THIRD
1994	Andy Howe	Kevin Little	Colin Earl
1995	Kevin Little	Chris Cobby	Andre Compton
1996	Mike Hampson	Justin Elkins	Graeme Gordon
1997	Jon Armstrong	Bobby Eldridge	David Howe
1998	Steve Bishop	Andrew Appleton	Seemond Stephens
1999	Jonathan Swales	Steve Camden	Scott Courtney
2000	Scott Pegler	Steve Bishop	Adam Allott
2001	David Mason	Scott Pegler	Simon Wolstenholme
2002	James Birkinshaw	Edward Kennett	Jamie Robertson
2003	Barrie Evans	Jamie Robertson	Trevor Harding
2004	James Wright	Mark Burrows	Richard Hall
2005	Steve Boxall	Barrie Evans	Blair Scott
2006	Adam Roynon	Seemond Stephens	Lee Smart

PREMIER LEAGUE RIDERS' CHAMPIONSHIP 2006
24 SEPTEMBER, SHEFFIELD

1st MAGNUS ZETTERSTROM
2nd JASON LYONS
3rd GARY HAVELOCK
4th TOMAS TOPINKA

RIDER	QUALIFYING SCORES					TOTAL
Magnus Zetterstrom	3	3	2	3	3	14
Jason Lyons	3	2	2	3	3	13
Gary Havelock	2	2	3	2	3	12
Tomas Topinka	0	3	3	2	3	11
Chris Holder	2	3	1	3	1	10
Danny Bird	1	2	3	3	0	9
Andre Compton	1	3	3	N	-	7
Josef Franc	3	1	2	0	1	7
James Wright	2	0	1	2	2	7
Shane Parker	3	1	0	1	1	6
Chris Neath	2	2	0	0	2	6
Mark Lemon	0	0	2	2	2	6
Michal Makovsky	1	1	1	1	1	5
Kevin Doolan	1	0	0	1	2	4
William Lawson	0	1	1	0	0	2
Tai Woffinden (Reserve)	1	-	-	-	-	1
Carl Wilkinson	T	0	0	0	0	0
David Speight (Reserve)	0	0	-	-	-	0

RACE DETAILS

HEAT ONE:	(Rerun) Franc, Hlder, Doolan, Speight, Wilkinson (ex, tapes).
HEAT TWO:	(Rerun) Lyons, Neath, Makovsky, Lawson.
HEAT THREE:	Parker, Wright, Compton, Lemon.
HEAT FOUR:	Zetterstrom, Havelock, Bird, Topinka.
HEAT FIVE:	Topinka, Neath, Franc, Lemon.
HEAT SIX:	Holder, Havelock, Makovsky, Wright.
HEAT SEVEN:	Zetterstrom, Lyons, Parker, Doolan.
HEAT EIGHT:	Compton, Bird, Lawson, Wilkinson.
HEAT NINE:	Bird, Franc, Makovsky, Parker.
HEAT TEN:	Compton, Zetterstrom, Holder, Neath.
HEAT ELEVEN:	Havelock, Lemon, Lawson, Doolan.
HEAT TWELVE:	Topinka, Lyons, Wright, Wilkinson.
HEAT THIRTEEN:	(Rerun) Lyons, Havelock, Woffinden, Franc, Compton (f, ns).
HEAT FOURTEEN:	Holder, Topinka, Parker, Lawson.
HEAT FIFTEEN:	Bird, Wright, Doolan, Neath.
HEAT SIXTEEN:	Zetterstrom, Lemon, Makovsky, Wilkinson.

HEAT SEVENTEEN:	Zetterstrom, Wright, Franc, Lawson.
HEAT EIGHTEEN:	Lyons, Lemon, Holder, Bird.
HEAT NINETEEN:	Topinka, Doolan, Makovsky, Speight (f, rem).
HEAT TWENTY:	Havelock, Neath, Parker, Wilkinson.
SEMI-FINAL:	(Rerun) Topinka, Havelock, Holder, Bird (ex, tapes).
FINAL:	Zetterstrom, Lyons, Havelock, Topinka.

ROLL OF HONOUR

NOTE: Became known as the Premier League Riders' Championship in 1997, having previously been known as the Division Two Riders' Championship (1968-74 and 1991-94) and National League Riders' Championship (1975-1990).

YEAR	FIRST	SECOND	THIRD
1968	Graham Plant	Ken Eyre	Graeme Smith
1969	Geoff Ambrose	Mick Bell	Ross Gilbertson
1970	Dave Jessup	Barry Crowson	Gary Peterson
1971	John Louis	Malcolm Shakespeare	Hugh Saunders
1972	Phil Crump	Arthur Price	Bob Coles
1973	Arthur Price	Bobby McNeil	Lou Sansom
1974	Carl Glover	Ted Hubbard	Phil Herne
1975	Laurie Etheridge	Brian Collins	Arthur Browning
1976	Joe Owen	John Jackson	Ted Hubbard
1977	Colin Richardson	Martin Yeates	Tom Owen
1978	Steve Koppe	John Jackson	Ted Hubbard
1979	Ian Gledhill	Steve Wilcock	Andy Grahame
1980	Wayne Brown	Martin Yeates	Steve Finch
1981	Mike Ferreira	Simon Wigg	Bruce Cribb
1982	Joe Owen	Steve Lomas	Bob Garrad
1983	Steve McDermott	Richard Knight	Martin Yeates
1984	Ian Barney	Dave Perks	Martin Yeates
1985	Neil Middleditch	Kevin Hawkins	Trevor Banks
1986	Paul Thorp	Steve Schofield	Les Collins
1987	Andrew Silver	Nigel Crabtree	David Blackburn
1988	Troy Butler	Mark Loram	Kenny McKinna
1989	Mark Loram	Kenny McKinna	David Blackburn
1990	Andy Grahame	Chris Louis	Craig Boyce
1991	Jan Staechmann	David Bargh	Troy Butler
1992	Robert Nagy	Mick Poole	Richard Green
1993	Gary Allan	Mick Poole	Tony Langdon
1994	Paul Bentley	Tony Olsson	Tony Langdon
1995-1996	Not staged		
1997	Peter Carr	Glenn Cunningham	Robert Eriksson
1998	Glenn Cunningham	Carl Stonehewer	Peter Carr
1999	Sean Wilson	Jesper Olsen	Craig Watson
2000	Carl Stonehewer	Peter Carr	Paul Pickering
2001	Carl Stonehewer	Sean Wilson	Bjarne Pedersen
2002	Adam Shields	Craig Watson	Phil Morris

2003	Sean Wilson	Adam Shields	Carl Stonehewer
2004	Andre Compton	Mark Lemon	Simon Stead
2005	Sean Wilson	Alan Mogridge	Tomas Topinka
2006	Magnus Zetterstrom	Jason Lyons	Gary Havelock

ELITE LEAGUE RIDERS' CHAMPIONSHIP 2006
1 OCTOBER, POOLE

1st JASON CRUMP
2nd NICKI PEDERSEN
3rd GREG HANCOCK
4th SCOTT NICHOLLS

RIDER	QUALIFYING SCORES					TOTAL
Jason Crump	3	3	3	3	3	15
Nicki Pedersen	3	2	3	3	2	13
Greg Hancock	2	2	3	2	3	12
Scott Nicholls	2	3	1	2	2	10
Hans N. Andersen	1	1	3	1	3	9
Todd Wiltshire	3	R	2	2	2	9
Leigh Adams	R	3	2	3	0	8
Billy Hamill	1	2	1	1	3	8
Rory Schlein	2	2	1	1	1	7
Adam Shields	1	1	2	2	1	7
Craig Boyce	0	0	0	3	2	5
Krzysztof Kasprzak	0	3	1	-	-	4
Simon Stead	3	R	0	0	1	4
Jesper B. Jensen	R	1	2	1	0	4
Mark Loram	2	1	-	-	-	3
Mikael Max	1	0	0	0	1	2
Mattie Bates (reserve)	0	0	0	0	-	0

RACE DETAILS

HEAT ONE:	Wiltshire, Nicholls, Hamill, Jensen (ret).
HEAT TWO:	Pedersen, Hancock, Shields, Boyce.
HEAT THREE:	Crump, Schlein, Andersen, Kasprzak.
HEAT FOUR:	Stead, Loram, Max, Adams (ret).
HEAT FIVE:	Adams, Hancock, Andersen, Wiltshire (ret).
HEAT SIX:	Crump, Pedersen, Jensen, Stead (ret).
HEAT SEVEN:	Kasprzak, Hamill, Loram, Boyce.
HEAT EIGHT:	Nicholls, Schlein, Shields, Max.
HEAT NINE:	Pedersen, Wiltshire, Kasprzak, Max.
HEAT TEN:	Hancock, Jensen, Schlein, Bates.
HEAT ELEVEN:	(Rerun) Andersen, Shields, Hamill, Stead.
HEAT TWELVE:	(Rerun twice) Crump, Adams, Nicholls, Boyce.

HEAT THIRTEEN:	Boyce, Wiltshire, Schlein, Stead.
HEAT FOURTEEN:	Adams, Shields, Jensen, Bates.
HEAT FIFTEEN:	Crump, Hancock, Hamill, Max.
HEAT SIXTEEN:	Pedersen, Nicholls, Andersen, Bates.
HEAT SEVENTEEN:	Crump, Wiltshire, Shields, Bates.
HEAT EIGHTEEN:	Andersen, Boyce, Max, Jensen.
HEAT NINETEEN:	Hamill, Pedersen, Schlein, Adams.
HEAT TWENTY:	Hancock, Nicholls, Stead, (3 riders only).
SEMI-FINAL:	Hancock, Nicholls, Andersen, Wiltshire.
FINAL:	Crump, Pedersen, Hancock, Nicholls.

ROLL OF HONOUR

NOTE: Became known as the Elite League Riders' Championship in 1997, having previously been known as British League Riders' Championship (1965-1967 and 1975-1990), Division One Riders' Championship (1968-1974 and 1991-1994) and Premier League Riders' Championship (1995-1996).

YEAR	FIRST	SECOND	THIRD
1965	Barry Briggs	Jimmy Gooch	Cyril Maidment
1966	Barry Briggs	Olle Nygren	Norman Hunter
1967	Barry Briggs	Nigel Boocock	Ray Wilson
1968	Barry Briggs	Eric Boocock	Ivan Mauger
1969	Barry Briggs	Ivan Mauger	Jim Airey
1970	Barry Briggs	Anders Michanek	Eric Boocock
1971	Ivan Mauger	Barry Briggs	Jim McMillan
1972	Ole Olsen	Martin Ashby	Ronnie Moore
1973	Ivan Mauger	Ray Wilson	Anders Michanek
1974	Peter Collins	Ivan Mauger	Phil Crump
1975	Peter Collins	Phil Crump	Martin Ashby
1976	Ole Olsen	Peter Collins	John Louis
1977	Ole Olsen	Peter Collins	Michael Lee
1978	Ole Olsen	Peter Collins	Steve Bastable
1979	John Louis	Bruce Penhall	Michael Lee
1980	Les Collins	Bruce Penhall	Larry Ross
1981	Kenny Carter	Chris Morton	Shawn Moran
1982	Kenny Carter	Shawn Moran	Hans Nielsen
1983	Erik Gundersen	Michael Lee	Hans Nielsen
1984	Chris Morton	Hans Nielsen	Erik Gundersen
1985	Erik Gundersen	Peter Collins	Chris Morton
1986	Hans Nielsen	Erik Gundersen	Shawn Moran
1987	Hans Nielsen	Chris Morton	Kelly Moran
1988	Jan O. Pedersen	Erik Gundersen	Hans Nielsen
1989	Shawn Moran	Hans Nielsen	Brian Karger
1990	Hans Nielsen	Kelly Moran	Ronnie Correy
1991	Sam Ermolenko	Hans Nielsen	Joe Screen
1992	Joe Screen	Per Jonsson	Gary Havelock
1993	Per Jonsson	Henrik Gustafsson	Chris Louis

1994	Sam Ermolenko	Hans Nielsen	Martin Dugard
1995	Gary Havelock	Billy Hamill	Jason Crump
1996	Sam Ermolenko	Jason Crump	Leigh Adams
1997	Greg Hancock	Tony Rickardsson	Chris Louis
1998	Tony Rickardsson	Jason Crump	Joe Screen
1999	Jason Crump	Todd Wiltshire	Jason Lyons
2000	Ryan Sullivan	Greg Hancock	Nicki Pedersen
2001	Jason Crump	Scott Nicholls	Nicki Pedersen
2002	Tony Rickardsson	Nicki Pedersen	Jason Crump
2003	Lee Richardson	Andreas Jonsson	Scott Nicholls
2004	Bjarne Pedersen	Ryan Sullivan	Hans N. Andersen
2005	Nicki Pedersen	Scott Nicholls	Peter Karlsson
2006	Jason Crump	Nicki Pedersen	Greg Hancock

BRITISH UNDER-18 CHAMPIONSHIP 2006
2 OCTOBER, WOLVERHAMPTON

1st LEWIS BRIDGER
2nd TAI WOFFINDEN
3rd BEN BARKER
4th JACK HARGREAVES

RIDER	RACE SCORES					TOTAL
Lewis Bridger	3	3	3	3	3	15
Tai Woffinden	3	3	2	3	3	14
Ben Barker	3	2	2	2	3	12
Jack Hargreaves	2	3	3	2	2	12
Danny Betson	3	2	1	2	3	11
Lee Smart	2	3	3	1	1	10
Jamie Westacott	1	2	2	0	2	7
Harland Cook	0	0	3	3	0	6
Ben Taylor	2	0	2	1	1	6
Simon Lambert	2	1	1	1	-	5
Robert Mear	X	1	1	1	2	5
Billy Legg	0	1	X	2	1	4
Jack Roberts (reserve)	3	0	1	-	-	4
Shane Waldron	1	F	0	0	2	3
Joe Haines	1	2	F	0	R	3
Sam Martin	1	0	1	T	0	2
Ben Hopwood	0	1	0	X	-	1
Kyle Hughes (reserve)	T	-	-	-	-	0

RACE DETAILS

HEAT ONE:	(Rerun) Betson, Lambert, Waldron, Mear (f, ex).
HEAT TWO:	Barker, Smart, Martin, Cook.
HEAT THREE:	Woffinden, Taylor, Haines, Hopwood.
HEAT FOUR:	(Rerun) Bridger, Hargreaves, Westacott, Legg.
HEAT FIVE:	Woffinden, Betson, Legg, Cook.
HEAT SIX:	Bridger, Barker, Lambert, Taylor.
HEAT SEVEN:	Smart, Westacott, Hopwood, Waldron (fell).
HEAT EIGHT:	Hargreaves, Haines, Mear, Martin.
HEAT NINE:	Hargreaves, Barker, Betson, Hopwood (f, rem).
HEAT TEN:	Cook, Westacott, Lambert, Haines (fell).
HEAT ELEVEN:	Bridger, Woffinden, Martin, Waldron.
HEAT TWELVE:	(Rerun) Smart, Taylor, Mear, Legg (f, ex).
HEAT THIRTEEN:	Bridger, Betson, Smart, Haines.
HEAT FOURTEEN:	(Rerun twice) Roberts, Legg, Lambert, Hopwood, (f, ex), Martin (ex, tapes).
HEAT FIFTEEN:	Cook, Hargreaves, Taylor, Waldron.
HEAT SIXTEEN:	Woffinden, Barker, Mear, Westacott.
HEAT SEVENTEEN:	Betson, Westacott, Taylor, Martin.
HEAT EIGHTEEN:	(Rerun) Woffinden, Hargreaves, Smart, Roberts, Hughes (ex, tapes).
HEAT NINETEEN:	Barker, Waldron, Legg, Haines (ret).
HEAT TWENTY:	Bridger, Mear, Roberts, Cook.
THIRD PLACE RUN-OFF:	Barker, Hargreaves.

ROLL OF HONOUR

YEAR	FIRST	SECOND	THIRD
2004	Daniel King	James Wright	Edward Kennett
2005	William Lawson	Lewis Bridger	Jack Hargreaves
2006	Lewis Bridger	Tai Woffinden	Ben Barker

J. EDGAR & SON/CFM PREMIER LEAGUE FOUR-TEAM CHAMPIONSHIP 2006

7 OCTOBER, WORKINGTON

1st WORKINGTON
2nd SOMERSET
3rd SHEFFIELD
4th KING'S LYNN

FIRST SEMI-FINAL SHEFFIELD 20	QUALIFYING SCORES				TOTAL
Andre Compton	R	3	-	-	3
Ricky Ashworth	3	3	-	-	6
Ben Wilson	3	2	-	-	5
Kyle Legault	3	3	-	-	6

KING'S LYNN 11

Trevor Harding	2	2	-	-	4
Kevin Doolan	1	2	-	-	3
Daniel Nermark	1	1	-	-	2
Chris Mills	0	2	-	-	2

RYE HOUSE 9

Stuart Robson	2	1	-	-	3
Edward Kennett	2	1	-	-	3
Steve Boxall	1	0	-	-	1
Tommy Allen	1	1	-	-	2

NEWCASTLE 8

George Stancl	2	0	-	-	2
Jamie Robertson	0	R	-	-	0
Josef Franc	0	3	-	-	3
Christian Henry	3	T	-	-	3
Adam McKinna (reserve)	M	-	-	-	0

RACE DETAILS

HEAT ONE: Wilson, Harding, Allen, Robertson.

HEAT TWO: Legault, Robson, Doolan, Franc.

HEAT THREE: Henry, Kennett, Nermark, Compton (ret).

HEAT FOUR: Ashworth, Stancl, Boxall, Mills.

HEAT FIVE: Compton, Harding, Robson, Stancl.

HEAT SIX: Legault, Mills, Kennett, Robertson.

HEAT SEVEN: Franc, Wilson, Nermark, Boxall.

HEAT EIGHT: (Rerun) Ashworth, Doolan, Allen, McKinna (ex, 2 mins), Henry (ex, tapes).

SECOND SEMI-FINAL

WORKINGTON 19	QUALIFYING SCORES				TOTAL
Garry Stead	3	2	-	-	5
James Wright	2	3	-	-	5
Tomasz Piszcz	3	2	-	-	5
Rusty Harrison	1	-	-	-	1
Alan Mogridge (reserve)	3	-	-	-	3

SOMERSET 12

Magnus Zetterstrom	3	3	-	-	6
Glenn Cunningham	X	1	-	-	1
Emil Kramer	1	3	-	-	4
Stephan Katt	1	0	-	-	1

GLASGOW 10

Shane Parker	3	X	-	-	3
Danny Bird	2	2	-	-	4

Lee Dicken	M	1	-	-	1
David McAllan	1	1	-	-	2
Robert Ksiezak (reserve)	0	-	-	-	0

MILDENHALL 7

Jason Lyons	R	1	-	-	1
Brent Werner	2	2	-	-	4
Jason King	2	0	-	-	2
Jon Armstrong	0	-	-	-	0
James Brundle (reserve)	0	-	-	-	0

RACE DETAILS

HEAT ONE: Stead, King, McAllan, Cunningham (ex, no dirt deflector).

HEAT TWO: Parker, Wright, Kramer, Armstrong.

HEAT THREE: Piszcz, Bird, Katt, Lyons (ret).

HEAT FOUR: Zetterstrom, Werner, Harrison, Ksiezak, Dicken (ex, 2 mins).

HEAT FIVE: (Rerun) Zetterstrom, Stead, Lyons, Parker (f, ex).

HEAT SIX: Mogridge, Bird, Cunningham, Brundle.

HEAT SEVEN: Kramer, Piszcz, Dicken, King.

HEAT EIGHT: Wright, Werner, McAllan, Katt.

FINAL	RACE SCORES			TOTAL
WORKINGTON 23				
Garry Stead	1	2	2	5
James Wright	3	3	1	7
Tomasz Piszcz	2	0	2	4
Rusty Harrison	3	1	N	4
Alan Mogridge (reserve)	3	-	-	3
SOMERSET 21				
Magnus Zetterstrom	3	3	3	9
Glenn Cunningham	2	2	0	4
Emil Kramer	3	1	1	5
Stephan Katt	2	0	1	3
SHEFFIELD 16				
Andre Compton	1	1	3	5
Ricky Ashworth	0	3	0	3
Ben Wilson	1	3	0	4
Kyle Legault	0	1	3	4
KING'S LYNN 12				
Trevor Harding	0	0	0	0
Kevin Doolan	2	2	2	6
Daniel Nermark	0	2	2	4
Chris Mills	1	0	1	2

RACE DETAILS

HEAT ONE:	Wright, Katt, Compton, Nermark.
HEAT TWO:	Zetterstrom, Piszcz, Mills, Ashworth.
HEAT THREE:	Harrison, Cunningham, Wilson, Harding.
HEAT FOUR:	Kramer, Doolan, Stead, Legault.
HEAT FIVE:	Zetterstrom, Stead, Compton, Harding.
HEAT SIX:	Wright, Cunningham, Legault, Mills.
HEAT SEVEN:	Wilson, Nermark, Kramer, Piszcz (f, rem).
HEAT EIGHT:	Ashworth, Doolan, Harrison, Katt.
HEAT NINE:	Legault, Piszcz, Katt, Harding.
HEAT TEN:	Compton, Stead, Mills, Cunningham.
HEAT ELEVEN:	(Rerun) Mogridge, Nermark, Kramer, Ashworth, Harrison (f, ns).
HEAT TWELVE:	Zetterstrom, Doolan, Wright, Wilson.

ROLL OF HONOUR

NOTE: Became known as the Premier League Four-Team Championship in 1997, having previously been known as the National League Four-Team Championship (1976-1990) and the Division Two Four-Team Championship (1991-1994).

YEAR	FIRST	SECOND	THIRD	FOURTH
1976	Newcastle	Eastbourne	Ellesmere Port	Workington
1977	Peterborough	Canterbury	Eastbourne	Stoke
1978	Peterborough	Stoke	Canterbury	Ellesmere Port
1979	Ellesmere Port	Mildenhall	Peterborough	Berwick
1980	Crayford	Rye House	Ellesmere Port	Stoke
1981	Edinburgh	Newcastle	Middlesbrough	Wolverhampton
1982	Newcastle	Mildenhall	Middlesbrough	Rye House
1983	Newcastle	Mildenhall	Milton Keynes	Long Eaton
1984	Mildenhall	Stoke	Milton Keynes	Boston
1985	Middlesbrough	Peterborough	Hackney	Stoke
1986	Middlesbrough	Arena-Essex	Hackney	Mildenhall
1987	Mildenhall	Arena-Essex	Eastbourne	Wimbledon
1988	Peterborough	Mildenhall	Eastbourne	Poole
1989	Peterborough	Stoke	Exeter	Eastbourne
1990	Stoke	Poole	Hackney	Ipswich
1991	Arena-Essex	Long Eaton	Edinburgh	Milton Keynes
1992	Peterborough	Edinburgh	Rye House	Glasgow
1993	Edinburgh	Swindon	Long Eaton	Rye House
1994	Oxford	Long Eaton	Peterborough	Edinburgh
1995-1996	Not staged			
1997	Long Eaton	Edinburgh	Oxford	Berwick
1998	Peterborough	Edinburgh	Hull	Reading
1999	Sheffield	Newport	Isle of Wight	Arena-Essex
2000	Sheffield	Isle of Wight	Swindon	Berwick
2001	Workington	Newcastle	Sheffield	Isle of Wight
2002	Berwick	Arena-Essex	Newport	Hull
2003	Swindon	Trelawny	Newport	Glasgow

2004	Workington	Stoke	Glasgow	Rye House
2005	Somerset	Workington	Exeter	Rye House
2006	Workington	Somerset	Sheffield	King's Lynn

PREMIER LEAGUE PAIRS CHAMPIONSHIP 2006

8 OCTOBER, GLASGOW

1st GLASGOW
2nd SHEFFIELD
3rd NEWCASTLE
4th SOMERSET

GROUP A	QUALIFYING SCORES				TOTAL
NEWCASTLE 25					
George Stancl	2	3*	4	2	11 (1)
Josef Franc	4	4	2	4	14
SHEFFIELD 21					
Ricky Ashworth	3*	X	3*	2*	8 (3)
Ben Wilson	4	2	4	3	13
KING'S LYNN 21					
Daniel Nermark	3*	3*	3	4	13 (2)
Kevin Doolan	4	4	F	F	8
EDINBURGH 12					
Derek Sneddon	0	0	0	3	3
William Lawson	2	2	3	2*	9 (1)
GLASGOW 'B' 11					
Robert Ksiezak	3	0	2	X	5
David McAllan	0	2	0	4	6

GROUP B	QUALIFYING SCORES				TOTAL
SOMERSET 26					
Magnus Zetterstrom	2	4	3*	4	13 (1)
Emil Kramer	4	3*	4	2	13 (1)
GLASGOW 20					
Shane Parker	4	2	2*	X	8 (1)
Danny Bird	2	4	3	3	12
WORKINGTON 17					
James Wright	3	4	2	3	12
Tomasz Piszcz	0	3*	R	2*	5 (2)

STOKE 15

| Mark Lemon | 0 | 2 | 2 | 4 | 8 |
| Paul Thorp | 3 | 0 | 4 | 0 | 7 |

MILDENHALL 12

| Jason Lyons | 3 | 2 | 4 | 3 | 12 |
| Jon Armstrong | 0 | X | 0 | 0 | 0 |

RACE DETAILS

HEAT ONE:	Wilson, Ashworth, Lawson, Sneddon.
HEAT TWO:	Parker, Wright, Bird, Piszcz.
HEAT THREE:	Franc, Ksiezak, Stancl, McAllan.
HEAT FOUR:	Kramer, Lyons, Zetterstrom, Armstrong.
HEAT FIVE:	Doolan, Nermark, Lawson, Sneddon.
HEAT SIX:	(Rerun) Bird, Thorp, Parker, Lemon.
HEAT SEVEN:	(Rerun) Franc, Stancl, Wilson, Armstrong (f, ex).
HEAT EIGHT:	Wright, Piszcz, Lyons, Armstrong.
HEAT NINE:	Doolan, Nermark, McAllan, Ksiezak.
HEAT TEN:	Zetterstrom, Kramer, Lemon, Thorp.
HEAT ELEVEN:	Stancl, Lawson, Franc, Sneddon.
HEAT TWELVE:	(Rerun) Lyons, Bird, Parker, Armstrong.
HEAT THIRTEEN:	Wilson, Ashworth, Ksiezak, McAllan.
HEAT FOURTEEN:	Kramer, Zetterstrom, Wright, Piszcz (ret).
HEAT FIFTEEN:	Franc, Nermark, Stancl, Doolan (fell).
HEAT SIXTEEN:	Thorp, Lyons, Lemon, Armstrong.
HEAT SEVENTEEN:	(Rerun) McAllan, Sneddon, Lawson, Ksiezak (f, ex).
HEAT EIGHTEEN:	(Rerun) Zetterstrom, Bird, Kramer, Parker (f, ex).
HEAT NINETEEN:	Nermark, Wilson, Ashworth, Doolan (fell).
HEAT TWENTY:	Lemon, Wright, Piszcz, Thorp.
FIRST SEMI-FINAL:	Stancl, Parker, Bird, Franc.
SECOND SEMI-FINAL:	Ashworth, Kramer, Wilson, Zetterstrom.
CONSOLATION FINAL:	(Rerun) Kramer, Franc, Stancl, Zetterstrom (f, ex).
GRAND FINAL:	Bird, Ashworth, Parker, Wilson.

ROLL OF HONOUR

NOTE: Became known as the Premier League Pairs Championship in 1997, having previously been known as the National League Pairs Championship (1975-1990) and Division Two Pairs Championship (1994).

YEAR	FIRST	SECOND
1975	Newcastle (Tom Owen & Brian Havelock)	Ellesmere Port (John Jackson & Colin Goad)
1976	Ellesmere Port (John Jackson & Chris Turner)	Newcastle (Joe Owen & Tom Owen)
1977	Boston (Robert Hollingworth & Colin Cook)	Newport (Jim Brett & Brian Woodward)
1978	Ellesmere Port (John Jackson & Steve Finch)	Newcastle (Tom Owen & Robbie Blackadder)
1979	Milton Keynes (Andy Grahame & Bob Humphreys)	Ellesmere Port (John Jackson & Steve Finch)

1980	Middlesbrough (Mark Courtney & Steve Wilcock)	Boston (Robert Hollingworth & Gary Guglielmi)
1981	Canterbury (Mike Ferreira & Denzil Kent)	Berwick (Wayne Brown & Steve McDermott)
1982	Weymouth (Martin Yeates & Simon Wigg)	Long Eaton (Alan Molyneux & Dave Perks)
1983	Weymouth (Martin Yeates & Simon Cross)	Glasgow (Jim McMillan & Steve Lawson)
1984	Stoke (Nigel Crabtree & Tom Owen)	Berwick (Bruce Cribb & Steve McDermott)
1985	Ellesmere Port (Joe Owen & Louis Carr)	Poole (Martin Yeates & Stan Bear)
1986	Edinburgh (Les Collins & Doug Wyer)	Hackney (Barry Thomas & Andy Galvin)
1987	Mildenhall (Dave Jessup & Mel Taylor)	Peterborough (Ian Barney & Kevin Hawkins)
1988	Stoke (Graham Jones & Steve Bastable)	Poole (Steve Schofield & David Biles)
1989	Stoke (Nigel Crabtree & Eric Monaghan)	Mildenhall (Preben Eriksen & Peter Glanz)
1990	Hackney (Steve Schofield & Andy Galvin)	Exeter (Steve Regeling & Peter Jeffery)
1991-1993	Not staged	
1994	Swindon (Tony Olsson & Tony Langdon)	Glasgow (Nigel Crabtree & David Walsh)
1995-1996	Not staged	
1997	Long Eaton (Martin Dixon & Carl Stonehewer)	Reading (David Mullett & Lee Richardson)
1998	Peterborough (Glenn Cunningham & Brett Woodifield)	Exeter (Frank Smart & Michael Coles)
1999	Workington (Carl Stonehewer & Brent Werner)	Arena-Essex (Colin White & Leigh Lanham)
2000	Workington (Carl Stonehewer & Mick Powell)	Isle of Wight (Ray Morton & Danny Bird)
2001	Workington (Carl Stonehewer & Peter I. Karlsson)	Newcastle (Bjarne Pedersen & Jesper Olsen)
2002	Isle of Wight (Adam Shields & Danny Bird)	Newport (Frank Smart & Craig Watson)
2003	Workington (Carl Stonehewer & Simon Stead)	Newport (Frank Smart & Niels-Kristian Iversen)
2004	Reading (Danny Bird & Phil Morris)	Stoke (Paul Pickering & Alan Mogridge)
2005	Glasgow (Shane Parker & George Stancl)	Somerset (Magnus Zetterstrom & Glenn Cunningham)
2006	Glasgow (Danny Bird & Shane Parker)	Sheffield (Ben Wilson & Ricky Ashworth)

SPEEDWAY GRAND PRIX 2006

	SLOVENIA	EUROPE	SWEDEN	BRITAIN	DENMARK	ITALY	SCANDINAVIA	CZECH REP.	LATVIA	POLAND	TOTAL
JASON CRUMP (Australia)	20	25	25	25	20	25	16	14	11	7	188
GREG HANCOCK (USA)	5	20	20	16	13	9	12	4	25	20	144
NICKI PEDERSEN (Denmark)	25	14	16	4	6	9	11	6	18	25	134
ANDREAS JONSSON (Sweden)	8	5	10	20	7	9	25	7	16	12	119
LEIGH ADAMS (Australia)	10	7	11	6	12	16	18	12	8	6	106
HANS N. ANDERSEN (Denmark)	-	-	-	-	25	18	20	25	4	9	101
MATEJ ZAGAR (Slovenia)	9	18	4	9	4	10	4	20	11	8	97
TOMASZ GOLLOB (Poland)	18	9	18	7	3	7	4	6	4	18	94
JAROSLAW HAMPEL (Poland)	4	16	8	18	2	4	10	16	7	6	91
ANTONIO LINDBACK (Sweden)	9	2	6	8	16	4	3	18	20	3	89
SCOTT NICHOLLS (Great Britain)	9	9	5	8	8	20	8	-	9	7	83
BJARNE PEDERSEN (Denmark)	5	6	7	12	18	10	8	2	7	7	82
NIELS-KRISTIAN IVERSEN (Denmark)	2	6	4	5	8	5	6	8	4	3	51
TONY RICKARDSSON (Sweden)	16	6	4	10	5	-	-	-	-	-	41
LEE RICHARDSON (Great Britain)	8	4	0	5	9	4	4	3	0	2	39
PIOTR PROTASIEWICZ (Poland)	1	3	3	3	1	3	4	5	4	4	31
WIESLAW JAGUS (Poland)	-	-	-	-	-	-	-	-	-	16	16
RYAN SULLIVAN (Australia)	-	-	-	-	-	1	9	-	-	-	10
FREDRIK LINDGREN (Sweden)	-	-	7	-	-	-	-	-	-	-	7
KRZYSZTOF KASPRZAK (Poland)	-	6	-	-	-	-	-	-	-	-	6
LUBOS TOMICEK (Czech Republic)	-	-	-	-	-	-	-	4	-	-	4
KJASTAS PUODZHUKS (Latvia)	-	-	-	-	-	-	-	-	4	-	4
MATEJ FERJAN (Slovenia)	3	-	-	-	-	-	-	-	-	-	3
SIMON STEAD (Great Britain)	-	-	-	3	-	-	-	-	-	-	3
ADRIAN RYMEL (Czech Republic)	-	-	-	-	-	-	-	2	-	-	2
KENNETH BJERRE (Denmark)	-	-	-	-	1	-	-	-	-	-	1
CHARLIE GJEDDE (Denmark)	-	-	-	-	1	-	-	-	-	-	1
JANUSZ KOLODZIEJ (Poland)	-	0	-	-	-	-	-	-	-	-	0
JONAS DAVIDSSON (Sweden)	-	-	0	-	-	-	-	-	-	-	0
MATTIA CARPANESE (Italy)	-	-	-	-	-	0	-	-	-	-	0
DANIELE TESSARI (Italy)	-	-	-	-	-	0	-	-	-	-	0
ZDENEK SIMOTA (Czech Republic)	-	-	-	-	-	-	-	0	-	-	0
GRIGORIJS LAGUTA (Latvia)	-	-	-	-	-	-	-	-	0	-	0
ANDREJS KOROLOVS (Latvia)	-	-	-	-	-	-	-	-	0	-	0

For the first time in four years the Grand Prix series was staged over ten rounds in 2006, with the competition's penultimate event being held at the impressive Daugavpils arena situated some 250 kilometres from the Latvian capital of Riga. Six times World Champion Tony Rickardsson announced it was to be his final year in the sport and all eyes were firmly focused on the Swede, who was aiming to gain a record seventh title. Rickardsson was combining his speedway commitments with Porsche Cup car racing and many within the sport questioned whether he would be fully devoted to the 2006 Grand Prix series. The competition welcomed the full-time inclusion of Danish youngster Niels-Kristian Iversen, Slovenian sensation Matej Zagar and experienced Pole Piotr Protasiewicz. However, initially, there was controversially no place for highly rated Dane Hans N. Andersen in the line-up, his heavily discussed absence being regarded by some as a 'political exclusion'. The scoring format introduced the previous year was happily retained and, encouragingly, on top of the debut staging at Daugavpils, all the venues that hosted Grand Prix speedway in 2005 again welcomed the series back in 2006.

The series began in explosive fashion at the large Krsko circuit in Slovenia on 22 April and, on a night of awesome racing, 2003 World Champion Nicki Pedersen emerged victorious. The opening GP of the 2006 campaign was simply breathtaking and the perfectly prepared race circuit at the Matije Gubca Stadium provided a classic no-holds-barred meeting that will be remembered for many years to come. Pedersen's emphatic victory was his first GP win since his title-winning season and the Dane's scintillating duel with Jason Crump in the final race of the night was undoubtedly one of the finest examples of speedway racing the GP series has witnessed since its inception in 1995. Tony Rickardsson topped the scorechart in the qualifying heats with an impressive 13-point haul, but the Swede was unable to stamp his authority on the final and was eventually beaten into third spot by a resurgent Tomasz Gollob. The Pole had mustered just two points from his opening two rides, but rode valiantly to record heat wins in his remaining three qualifying outings and then concluded a fantastic night's work with a neat third spot in the final. 2004 World Champion Jason Crump could consider himself slightly fortunate to find himself in the final and, if it hadn't been for fellow Aussie Leigh Adams' ignition failure when the Swindon rider was easing to victory in the second semi-final, then 'Crumpie' would have been eliminated from the contest. Despite Crump's wholehearted efforts, he was unable to forge a route past Pedersen in what was a phenomenal final heat of the night, and instead had to settle for second spot and 20 accompanying World Championship points.

The cream of the world's riders moved on to the Olympic Stadium, Wroclaw, Poland on 6 May, when Jason Crump claimed an impressive European Grand Prix victory. Crump's triumph, combined with the failure of Nicki Pedersen to make the final, provided the tenacious racer with an early six-point series lead. Pedersen showed no ill effects from a recent wrist operation as he topped the qualifying scorechart with an almost perfect 14 points, but, surprisingly, the Dane bowed out of the competition at the first semi-final, where he ran a third in a race won by home favourite Jaroslaw Hampel. For a second Grand Prix in succession, both Leigh Adams and Scott Nicholls were unable to progress past the semi-final stage; however, the flamboyant Matej Zagar booked himself a spot in the final in only his second round as fully-fledged GP rider. Greg Hancock was another rider showing wonderful form and the Californian actually found himself leading the final, before Crump conjured a fantastic pass of the American to earn himself a big 25 points and move his World Championship tally on to 45. Further down the scoring list, wildcard entry Krzysztof Kasprzak notched up a praiseworthy six points and the young Polish rider certainly proved why he is tipped by many in the sport to be a permanent feature of the Grand Prix in the not too distant future.

The rumour mill was in full flow before the third round of the series at the Smed Stadium, Eskilstuna in Sweden on 20 May. Whispers that Tony Rickardsson was to quit the sport with immediate effect were quickly dismissed by his team manager Olli Tyrvainen but, nevertheless, an off-colour six-times Champion could only muster four points in front of his expectant home fans. Jason Crump and Greg Hancock replicated the result of the previous round in Wroclaw as they once again filled the top two places after topping the qualifying scores with 13 and 15 points respectively. Tomasz Gollob continued his bright start to the series with a deserved third place just in front of Nicki Pedersen, who was the victim of a messy first corner in the evening's final. The home fans didn't have much to shout about as none of the Swedish contingent progressed past the semi-finals and were plagued with mechanical gremlins, as well as a controversial exclusion in the case of Andreas Jonsson. At the top of the pile, Crump's second victory in a row provided the Australian with a 15-point lead over nearest rival Nicki Pedersen, whilst leaving Hancock and Gollob locked in third position on 45 points apiece.

The sun always seems to shine brightly on the British Grand Prix and Saturday 3 June was no exception. Just a fortnight earlier, an announcement was made that the event would remain at the Millennium Stadium, Britain's number one arena, for a further five years. Fittingly, a record crowd, officially given as 40,371, converged on the Welsh capital to witness Jason Crump register his third successive series victory and stretch his championship lead. The home round continues to exceed expectations and notably gathers more media attention with each passing year; indeed, the professionalism of the event is undoubtedly helping bolster speedway's profile within Britain. On the night, Crump made the most of a rerun final after the initial staging of the concluding race had been halted when Greg Hancock fell on the third bend of lap two, whilst attempting to pass Jaroslaw Hampel in a bid to gain the lead. It was cruel luck for the young Polish rider, who had to settle for third spot in the restaging of the race; nevertheless, it was a fantastic effort that was warmly received by the huge number of his compatriots within the plush stadium. Crump's victory was in stark contrast to his misfortune of the previous year at the venue and provided the tenacious Australian with a commanding 34-point advantage over his nearest rival, Hancock.

Hans N. Andersen acted out a fairytale in front of his home fans in the Danish Grand Prix at the impressive Parken venue in Copenhagen on 24 June, when he registered an emphatic victory after making the most of his wildcard opportunity. The controversial Peterborough rider who had been left out of the 2006 series sent the ultimate reminder to the series' organisers of his scintillating talent with a classy GP win that sent the reported 25,000 home crowd delirious. Compatriot Bjarne Pedersen made it a memorable night for Danish speedway with a third spot that left series leader Jason Crump sandwiched between in second place as he continued his unbelievable run of form. Andersen's success was the second of his Grand Prix career and followed up his win at Gothenburg some two years earlier. Once again, Crump's strong finish was contrasted by the failure of both Greg Hancock and home favourite Nicki Pedersen to make the final. The Australian moved his overall tally on to 115 points, a mighty 41 ahead of Hancock and 50 ahead of third-placed man Pedersen.

On 29 July, for a second successive year, Lonigo welcomed the Grand Prix series back to Italy and provided a fantastic night's racing on a well-prepared surface. Despite suffering from a painful ankle injury incurred whilst riding for Belle Vue just a few days earlier, Jason Crump romped to his fourth GP win of the campaign after successfully squeezing through the narrowest of gaps to pass Hans N. Andersen in the final. The Dane had been drafted in as a replacement for Tony Rickardsson, who pulled out of the event after still suffering the side effects of a nasty-looking crash in the Danish Grand Prix at Copenhagen some five weeks earlier. Andersen took advantage of his inclusion and, despite not being able to repeat the heroics of his previous success at Parken, he once again looked lightning-quick. Indeed, if it hadn't been for an uncharacteristic mistake in the final, then the Dane would have undoubtedly been celebrating his second successive GP win. Great Britain's Scott Nicholls enjoyed his best result of the 2006 season with a creditable second spot behind Crump, although the Coventry rider could consider himself slightly fortunate to find himself in the final after an audacious move to pass Matej Zagar in the first semi-final had sent the Slovenian sprawling on the back straight. Australian Leigh Adams enjoyed his best result of the season thus far with a thoroughly deserved fourth spot, but will doubtless have been disappointed not to have further enforced his authority on the final after easing through his semi-final encounter. The Italian GP provided possibly the most flamboyant wildcard in local rider Mattia Carpanese, whose pointless contribution was far from indicative of his highly entertaining efforts, under the watchful eye of Armando Castagna, who commands legendary status in his homeland. Crump's victory was made even sweeter by the failure of his nearest rivals, Greg Hancock and Nicki Pedersen, to make the final as they both collected nine-point tallies and allowed the Bristol-born racer to increase his commanding World Championship lead.

In the lead-up to the Scandinavian Grand Prix, it was announced that Tony Rickardsson would be retiring from the series with immediate effect. The legendary Swede, who had missed the previous round because of injury, explained he was acting on medical advice and was unwilling to risk further injury. Hans N. Andersen, who had enjoyed success in the two previous rounds, was announced as the permanent replacement for the Swedish superstar in the remaining four rounds. Similar to the previous year, the 2006 Scandinavian Grand Prix on 12 August was heavily affected by bad weather and, yet again, the event was saved from certain cancellation by the fantastic work of the Malilla track staff. Fittingly, Rickardsson's compatriot, Andreas Jonsson, delighted the home fans by collecting a hard-earned overall victory, his first at GP level. The popular rider, whose Swedish Elite League club Luxo Stars race at the plush Malilla venue, made use of his track knowledge as he carved his way through the field on several occasions, including the final when he capitalised on a small mistake by Andersen to grab the lead. Jonsson was understandably ecstatic with his victory, which elevated him to fourth spot in the overall standings with a healthy 84 points, and celebrated in style amidst the sodden, but elated, 12,000-strong crowd. Series leader Jason Crump battled hard to reach the final, but was a victim of the treacherous conditions and fell in the early stages of the race, whilst compatriot Leigh Adams came home in third position. Andersen celebrated his re-inclusion in the series with another remarkable second-place finish, the hard-charging Dane booking his place in the final after coming off better in a fiesty second semi-final clash with Scott Nicholls. The failure yet again of both Greg Hancock and Nicki Pedersen to make the final extended Crump's lead to a mighty 61 points at the top of the leaderboard and meant the Australian could clinch his second World Championship in Prague two weeks later.

The Marketa Stadium in Prague hosted the eighth round of the series on 26 August and the venue will always be remembered as the one where Jason Crump gained his second World Championship title. The Australian completed the inevitable courtesy of Greg Hancock's unfortunate engine failure at the start of heat fifteen, which concluded a nightmare evening for the American and sparked emotional scenes of celebration amongst the Crump family. In an eventful meeting, Hans N. Andersen continued his sensational run of form to win an emphatic victory ahead of young guns Matej Zagar, Antonio Lindback and Jaroslaw Hampel, all of whom began the night outside the coveted top eight championship positions. Leigh Adams looked destined to make the final, but the unlucky Australian was struck by mechanical gremlins whilst he was easing to victory in the second semi-final and once again bowed out of the competition prematurely. Uncharacteristically, although somewhat understandably, the normally placid Adams subsequently vented his frustration as yet more GP points slipped from his grasp.

Bad weather in the week leading up to the inaugural Latvian Grand Prix hampered track preparation and, consequently, the standard of racing was below par when the big day arrived on 9 September. The hard-packed, slick surface was prone to nasty ruts, which caught many of the riders by surprise as the evening progressed and proved extremely tough on machinery. Despite this, a crowd of around 10,000 witnessed an exciting meeting that justified Latvia's inclusion amongst the series and the ambitious Daugavpils club will certainly have learnt an awful lot from staging such a prestigious event. Lovable American Greg Hancock took victory on the night after conjuring a wonderful passing manoeuvre on the flamboyant Antonio Lindback in a rerun final. It concluded a cruel week for Lindback after he had been the victim of a rerun in the World Under-21 Championship final at Terenzano in Italy – where he was the clear leader – and then at Daugavpils, when the final race was halted whilst the Brazilian-born Swede held a sizeable lead. The youngster had jointly topped the qualifying scores with a fantastic 13-point tally and then progressed through the semi-final stage with ease, but ultimately was denied a first GP victory by the brilliance of Hancock. The initial staging of the final saw a controversial exclusion for Andreas Jonsson, who was adjudged to have clipped Nicki Pedersen's front wheel and sent him tumbling, as he made a pass of the Dane on the notoriously rutted fourth bend. Jason Crump bowed out of the contest in the first semi-final and understandably lacked the killer instinct that had seen him ease to World Championship glory at Prague a fortnight earlier.

The fabulous Bydgoszcz arena hosted the tenth and final round of the Grand Prix series on 23 September, as the all-important race for the top eight seeded positions reached a tense climax. The passionate Polish crowd jammed the terraces and, as always, expected a triumphant performance from their hero, Tomasz Gollob. The enigmatic Pole is the undoubted master of the Bydgoszcz raceway and, whilst he was unable to register his fifth successive GP victory at the circuit, he gave a tremendous full-throttle exhibition to claim third spot behind Nicki Pedersen and Greg Hancock, a performance that was sufficient to earn him eighth spot in the overall standings. The final Grand Prix of 2006 will be remembered as one of the greatest of all time, featuring a stunning array of breathtaking races that made jaws clang and eyes bulge; indeed, it was the perfect way to bring the curtain down on what had been a season full of high drama and wonderful speedway. Fittingly, four of the top five riders from the qualifying races progressed to the evening's grand final and, to the delight of the home fans, Gollob was joined by compatriot Wieslaw Jagus, who had been handed a wildcard entry for the event. Having already booked his spot in next year's competition by progressing through the qualifying rounds, the experienced Jagus underlined what a fantastic addition he will be to the series in 2007 courtesy of a gritty performance that saw him eventually bag fourth spot. Nicki Pedersen's victory on the night was his second of the series, ironically, the first occurring in the opening round in Slovenia, and the 2003 World Champion must have been left wondering what might have been if he had shown more consistency in the middle part of his campaign. Hancock's hard-fought second spot ensured he would be wearing the number two on his back in 2007 and, for the most part, the cheerful Californian enjoyed a phenomenal twelfth successive GP series. In fact, the American's longevity in the tournament is unequalled, as he has remarkably appeared in all 89 rounds since the competition's inception at the Olympic Stadium, Wroclaw in Poland on 20 May 1995.

As always, rumour suggests that new Grand Prix venues are always on the horizon. It is well documented that BSI, the organisers of the series, are keen to take the competition back to Germany, a nation with a strong interest in motorcycling. The talk on the terraces indicates that Russia is showing interest in hosting a round as the popularity of the sport continues to grow in the country thanks to a well-structured league, which is beginning to attract Grand Prix riders. It remains to be seen whether Australia will hold another GP, however, with the confirmation that Jason Crump will participate in the national championship for 2007; it seems that this historic speedway nation is beginning to receive some much-needed nurturing after a glum and detrimental period of neglect. As far as 2006 was concerned, it was a Crump sandwich, laid on two chunks of Pedersen bread with a slice of spicy Andersen, seasoned with a pinch of Jonsson and served with a large glass of vintage Hancock.

Chris Seaward

GRAND PRIX OF SLOVENIA (ROUND ONE)

DATE: 22 April.

VENUE: Matije Gubca Stadium, Krsko.

TRACK LENGTH: 387 metres.

1st NICKI PEDERSEN

2nd JASON CRUMP

3rd TOMASZ GOLLOB

4th TONY RICKARDSSON

RIDER	RACE POINTS					TOTAL
Tony Rickardsson	3	3	2	3	2	13
Jason Crump	3	1	3	3	2	12
Tomasz Gollob	1	1	3	3	3	11
Nicki Pedersen	3	2	2	1	3	11
Leigh Adams	2	3	3	1	1	10
Matej Zagar	1	2	0	3	3	9
Antonio Lindback	1	2	1	2	3	9
Scott Nicholls	2	2	1	2	2	9
Lee Richardson	0	3	3	0	2	8
Andreas Jonsson	2	3	1	2	0	8
Greg Hancock	3	0	0	1	1	5
Bjarne Pedersen	0	1	1	2	1	5
Jaroslaw Hampel	2	0	0	1	1	4
Matej Ferjan	0	1	2	R	0	3
Niels-Kristian Iversen	0	0	2	0	F	2
Piotr Protasiewicz	1	0	0	0	0	1
Izak Santej (reserve)	-	-	-	-	-	-
Jernej Kolenko (reserve)	-	-	-	-	-	-

RACE DETAILS

HEAT ONE: Hancock, Hampel, Gollob, Iversen.

HEAT TWO: Crump, Adams, Protasiewicz, Ferjan.

HEAT THREE: Rickardsson, Jonsson, Lindback, Richardson.

HEAT FOUR: N. Pedersen, Nicholls, Zagar, B. Pedersen.

HEAT FIVE: Adams, Lindback, B. Pedersen, Hampel.

HEAT SIX: Richardson, Zagar, Crump, Hancock.

HEAT SEVEN: Rickardsson, N. Pedersen, Gollob, Protasiewicz.

HEAT EIGHT: Jonsson, Nicholls, Ferjan, Iversen.

HEAT NINE: Crump, Rickardsson, Nicholls, Hampel.

HEAT TEN: Adams, N. Pedersen, Jonsson, Hancock.

HEAT ELEVEN: Gollob, Forjan, Lindback, Zagar.

HEAT TWELVE: Richardson, Iversen, B. Pedersen, Protasiewicz (f, rem).

HEAT THIRTEEN: Zagar, Jonsson, Hampel, Protasiewicz.

HEAT FOURTEEN: Rickardsson, B. Pedersen, Hancock, Ferjan (ret).

HEAT FIFTEEN:	Gollob, Nicholls, Adams, Richardson.
HEAT SIXTEEN:	Crump, Lindback, N. Pedersen, Iversen.
HEAT SEVENTEEN:	N. Pedersen, Richardson, Hampel, Ferjan.
HEAT EIGHTEEN:	Lindback, Nicholls, Hancock, Protasiewicz.
HEAT NINETEEN:	Gollob, Crump, B. Pedersen, Jonsson.
HEAT TWENTY:	Zagar, Rickardsson, Adams, Iversen (fell).
FIRST SEMI-FINAL:	N.Pedersen, Rickardsson, Zagar, Lindback.
SECOND SEMI-FINAL:	Gollob, Crump, Nicholls, Adams.
FINAL:	N. Pedersen, Crump, Gollob, Rickardsson.

GRAND PRIX OF EUROPE (ROUND TWO)

DATE: 6 May.
VENUE: Olympic Stadium, Wroclaw, Poland.
TRACK LENGTH: 387.4 metres.

1st JASON CRUMP
2nd GREG HANCOCK
3rd MATEJ ZAGAR
4th JAROSLAW HAMPEL

RIDER	RACE POINTS					TOTAL
Nicki Pedersen	3	3	3	2	3	14
Jason Crump	3	2	2	3	3	13
Greg Hancock	3	3	3	3	X	12
Jaroslaw Hampel	0	3	3	1	2	9
Scott Nicholls	2	3	2	T	2	9
Tomasz Gollob	1	1	2	2	3	9
Matej Zagar	1	2	1	3	2	9
Leigh Adams	2	1	3	R	1	7
Bjarne Pedersen	1	0	1	3	1	6
Niels-Kristian Iversen	3	1	0	2	0	6
Krzysztof Kasprzak	2	2	0	1	1	6
Tony Rickardsson	2	2	1	0	1	6
Andreas Jonsson	0	0	2	1	2	5
Lee Richardson	1	0	0	R	3	4
Piotr Protasiewicz	0	1	1	1	R	3
Antonio Lindback	0	0	0	2	0	2
Janusz Kolodziej (reserve)	0	-	-	-	-	0
Tomasz Gapinski (reserve)	-	-	-	-	-	-

RACE DETAILS

HEAT ONE:	Crump, Adams, B. Pedersen, Lindback.
HEAT TWO:	Hancock, Nicholls, Gollob, Jonsson.
HEAT THREE:	N. Pedersen, Rickardsson, Zagar, Hampel.
HEAT FOUR:	Iversen, Kasprzak, Richardson, Protasiewicz.

HEAT FIVE: Hampel, Kasprzak, Adams, Jonsson.
HEAT SIX: Nicholls, Zagar, Protasiewicz, B. Pedersen.
HEAT SEVEN: Hancock, Rickardsson, Iversen, Lindback.
HEAT EIGHT: (Rerun) N. Pedersen, Crump, Gollob, Richardson.
HEAT NINE: Adams, Nicholls, Rickardsson, Richardson.
HEAT TEN: N. Pedersen, Jonsson, B. Pedersen, Iversen.
HEAT ELEVEN: Hampel, Gollob, Protasiewicz, Lindback.
HEAT TWELVE: Hancock, Crump, Zagar, Kasprzak.
HEAT THIRTEEN: Hancock, N. Pedersen, Protasiewicz, Adams (ret).
HEAT FOURTEEN: B. Pedersen, Gollob, Kasprzak, Rickardsson.
HEAT FIFTEEN: Zagar, Lindback, Jonsson, Richardson (ret).
HEAT SIXTEEN: (Rerun) Crump, Iversen, Hampel, Kolodziej, Nicholls (ex, tapes).
HEAT SEVENTEEN: Gollob, Zagar, Adams, Iversen.
HEAT EIGHTEEN: (Rerun) Richardson, Hampel, B. Pedersen, Hancock (ex, foul riding).
HEAT NINETEEN: (Rerun) N. Pedersen, Nicholls, Kasprzak, Lindback.
HEAT TWENTY: Crump, Jonsson, Rickardsson, Protasiewicz (ret).
FIRST SEMI-FINAL: Hampel, Zagar, N. Pedersen, Gollob.
SECOND SEMI-FINAL: Hancock, Crump, Adams, Nicholls.
FINAL: Crump, Hancock, Zagar, Hampel.

GRAND PRIX OF SWEDEN (ROUND THREE)

DATE: 20 May.
VENUE: Smed Stadium, Eskilstuna.
TRACK LENGTH: 335 metres.

1st JASON CRUMP
2nd GREG HANCOCK
3rd TOMASZ GOLLOB
4th NICKI PEDERSEN

RIDER	RACE POINTS					TOTAL
Greg Hancock	3	3	3	3	3	15
Jason Crump	3	2	3	3	2	13
Nicki Pedersen	1	3	3	3	2	12
Tomasz Gollob	2	0	3	3	3	11
Leigh Adams	2	2	2	2	3	11
Andreas Jonsson	3	1	2	1	3	10
Jaroslaw Hampel	2	3	2	0	1	8
Bjarne Pedersen	1	2	0	2	2	7
Fredrik Lindgren	1	2	1	2	1	7
Antonio Lindback	3	0	0	1	2	6
Scott Nicholls	T	1	2	1	1	5
Tony Rickardsson	0	3	1	R	0	4
Niels-Kristian Iversen	2	1	1	0	0	4
Matej Zagar	1	1	1	1	0	4
Piotr Protasiewicz	0	0	0	2	1	3

Lee Richardson	0	0	0	0	0	0
Jonas Davidsson (reserve)	0	-	-	-	-	0
Eric Andersson (reserve)	-	-	-	-	-	-

RACE DETAILS

HEAT ONE:	Lindback, Adams, Lindgren, Protasiewicz.
HEAT TWO:	(Rerun) Hancock, Hampel, N. Pedersen, Rickardsson.
HEAT THREE:	(Rerun) Crump, Gollob, B. Pedersen, Davidsson, Nicholls (ex, tapes).
HEAT FOUR:	Jonsson, Iversen, Zagar, Richardson.
HEAT FIVE:	Hampel, Lindgren, Nicholls, Richardson.
HEAT SIX:	N. Pedersen, Crump, Zagar, Lindback.
HEAT SEVEN:	Rickardsson, B. Pedersen, Iversen, Protasiewicz.
HEAT EIGHT:	Hancock, Adams, Jonsson, Gollob.
HEAT NINE:	N. Pedersen, Jonsson, Lindgren, B. Pedersen.
HEAT TEN:	Gollob, Hampel, Iversen, Lindback.
HEAT ELEVEN:	Hancock, Nicholls, Zagar, Protasiewicz.
HEAT TWELVE:	Crump, Adams, Rickardsson, Richardson.
HEAT THIRTEEN:	Gollob, Lindgren, Zagar, Rickardsson (ret).
HEAT FOURTEEN:	Hancock, B. Pedersen, Lindback, Richardson.
HEAT FIFTEEN:	Crump, Protasiewicz, Jonsson, Hampel.
HEAT SIXTEEN:	N. Pedersen, Adams, Nicholls, Iversen.
HEAT SEVENTEEN:	Hancock, Crump, Lindgren, Iversen.
HEAT EIGHTEEN:	Jonsson, Lindback, Nicholls, Rickardsson.
HEAT NINETEEN:	Gollob, N. Pedersen, Protasiewicz, Richardson.
HEAT TWENTY:	Adams, B. Pedersen, Hampel, Zagar.
FIRST SEMI-FINAL:	(Rerun) Hancock, Gollob, Hampel, Jonsson (f, ex).
SECOND SEMI-FINAL:	N. Pedersen, Crump, Adams, B. Pedersen.
FINAL:	Crump, Hancock, Gollob, N. Pedersen.

GRAND PRIX OF GREAT BRITAIN (ROUND FOUR)

DATE: 3 June.
VENUE: Millennium Stadium, Cardiff.
TRACK LENGTH: 275 metres.

1st JASON CRUMP
2nd ANDREAS JONSSON
3rd JAROSLAW HAMPEL
4th GREG HANCOCK

RIDER	RACE POINTS					TOTAL
Greg Hancock	2	3	2	3	2	12
Bjarne Pedersen	3	2	2	2	3	12
Jason Crump	3	1	3	1	3	11
Tony Rickardsson	2	3	3	2	0	10
Andreas Jonsson	0	2	3	3	1	9

Matej Zagar	2	1	1	3	2	9
Jaroslaw Hampel	3	3	X	0	2	8
Scott Nicholls	1	0	3	1	3	8
Antonio Lindback	0	3	1	3	1	8
Tomasz Gollob	1	2	2	2	R	7
Leigh Adams	3	0	2	X	1	6
Niels-Kristian Iversen	1	1	0	F	3	5
Lee Richardson	1	2	1	1	R	5
Nicki Pedersen	0	1	1	R	2	4
Simon Stead	0	0	0	2	1	3
Piotr Protasiewicz	2	0	0	1	R	3
Edward Kennett (reserve)	-	-	-	-	-	-
Ben Wilson (reserve)	-	-	-	-	-	-

RACE DETAILS

HEAT ONE:	B. Pedersen, Rickardsson, Gollob, Stead.
HEAT TWO:	Adams, Hancock, Nicholls, Jonsson.
HEAT THREE:	(Rerun) Hampel, Zagar, Richardson, Lindback.
HEAT FOUR:	(Rerun) Crump, Protasiewicz, Iversen, N. Pedersen.
HEAT FIVE:	Hampel, Gollob, Iversen, Adams.
HEAT SIX:	Lindback, Jonsson, N. Pedersen, Stead.
HEAT SEVEN:	Rickardsson, Richardson, Crump, Nicholls.
HEAT EIGHT:	Hancock, B. Pedersen, Zagar, Protasiewicz.
HEAT NINE:	Jonsson, Gollob, Richardson, Protasiewicz.
HEAT TEN:	Crump, Adams, Zagar, Stead.
HEAT ELEVEN:	(Rerun) Rickardsson, Hancock, N. Pedersen, Hampel (f, ex).
HEAT TWELVE:	Nicholls, B. Pedersen, Lindback, Iversen.
HEAT THIRTEEN:	Zagar, Gollob, Nicholls, N. Pedersen (ret).
HEAT FOURTEEN:	Hancock, Stead, Richardson, Iversen (fell).
HEAT FIFTEEN:	(Rerun) Lindback, Rickardsson, Protasiewicz, Adams (f, ex).
HEAT SIXTEEN:	Jonsson, B. Pedersen, Crump, Hampel.
HEAT SEVENTEEN:	Crump, Hancock, Lindback, Gollob (ret).
HEAT EIGHTEEN:	Nicholls, Hampel, Stead, Protasiewicz (ret).
HEAT NINETEEN:	Iversen, Zagar, Jonsson, Rickardsson.
HEAT TWENTY:	B. Pedersen, N. Pedersen, Adams, Richardson (ret).
FIRST SEMI-FINAL:	Hancock, Hampel, Rickardsson, Zagar (fell).
SECOND SEMI-FINAL:	Crump, Jonsson, B. Pedersen, Nicholls (f, rem).
FINAL:	(Rerun) Crump, Jonsson, Hampel, Hancock (f, ex).

GRAND PRIX OF DENMARK (ROUND FIVE)

DATE: 24 June.

VENUE: Parken, Copenhagen.

TRACK LENGTH: 275 metres.

1st HANS N. ANDERSEN

2nd JASON CRUMP

3rd BJARNE PEDERSEN

4th ANTONIO LINDBACK

RIDER	RACE POINTS					TOTAL
Greg Hancock	2	3	2	3	3	13
Leigh Adams	3	3	3	3	0	12
Hans N. Andersen	1	3	3	3	1	11
Jason Crump	3	1	1	2	3	10
Antonio Lindback	2	2	2	2	2	10
Bjarne Pedersen	0	2	3	1	3	9
Lee Richardson	3	2	0	1	3	9
Scott Nicholls	3	2	1	2	F	8
Niels-Kristian Iversen	2	3	2	F	1	8
Andreas Jonsson	M	0	3	2	2	7
Nicki Pedersen	1	1	0	3	1	6
Tony Rickardsson	2	F	0	1	2	5
Matej Zagar	1	T	1	1	1	4
Tomasz Gollob	0	0	1	0	2	3
Jaroslaw Hampel	0	0	2	0	0	2
Piotr Protasiewicz	0	1	0	0	0	1
Kenneth Bjerre (reserve)	1	-	-	-	-	1
Charlie Gjedde (reserve)	1	-	-	-	-	1

RACE DETAILS

HEAT ONE:	Richardson, Rickardsson, Zagar, Hampel.
HEAT TWO:	Nicholls, Lindback, N. Pedersen, Protasiewicz.
HEAT THREE:	Crump, Iversen, Bjerre, Gollob, Jonsson (ex, 2 mins).
HEAT FOUR:	Adams, Hancock, Andersen, B. Pedersen.
HEAT FIVE:	(Rerun) Adams, Lindback, Gjedde, Jonsson, Zagar (ex, tapes).
HEAT SIX:	Hancock, Richardson, N. Pedersen, Gollob.
HEAT SEVEN:	Iversen, B. Pedersen, Protasiewicz, Rickardsson (fell).
HEAT EIGHT:	Andersen, Nicholls, Crump, Hampel.
HEAT NINE:	Andersen, Iversen, Zagar, N. Pedersen.
HEAT TEN:	B. Pedersen, Lindback, Crump, Richardson.
HEAT ELEVEN:	Jonsson, Hancock, Nicholls, Rickardsson.
HEAT TWELVE:	Adams, Hampel, Gollob, Protasiewicz.
HEAT THIRTEEN:	Hancock, Crump, Zagar, Protasiewicz.
HEAT FOURTEEN:	Adams, Nicholls, Richardson, Iversen (fell).

HEAT FIFTEEN:	Andersen, Lindback, Rickardsson, Gollob.
HEAT SIXTEEN:	N. Pedersen, Jonsson, B. Pedersen, Hampel.
HEAT SEVENTEEN:	B. Pedersen, Gollob, Zagar, Nicholls (fell).
HEAT EIGHTEEN:	Richardson, Jonsson, Andersen, Protasiewicz.
HEAT NINETEEN:	Crump, Rickardsson, N. Pedersen, Adams.
HEAT TWENTY:	Hancock, Lindback, Iversen, Hampel.
FIRST SEMI-FINAL:	Crump, B. Pedersen, Hancock, Richardson.
SECOND SEMI-FINAL:	Andersen, Lindback, Adams, Nicholls.
FINAL:	Andersen, Crump, B. Pedersen, Lindback (fell).

GRAND PRIX OF ITALY (ROUND SIX)
DATE: 29 July.
VENUE: Motorclub Lonigo, Vicenza, Italy.
TRACK LENGTH: 334 metres.

1st JASON CRUMP
2nd SCOTT NICHOLLS
3rd HANS N. ANDERSEN
4th LEIGH ADAMS

RIDER	RACE POINTS					TOTAL
Hans N. Andersen	3	3	3	2	3	14
Jason Crump	3	2	2	3	3	13
Leigh Adams	3	2	3	1	1	10
Matej Zagar	1	3	3	2	1	10
Bjarne Pedersen	2	2	1	2	3	10
Scott Nicholls	2	1	0	3	3	9
Greg Hancock	1	0	3	3	2	9
Nicki Pedersen	2	3	2	1	1	9
Andreas Jonsson	1	1	2	3	2	9
Tomasz Gollob	2	0	1	2	2	7
Niels-Kristian Iversen	1	3	X	0	1	5
Lee Richardson	3	0	1	0	0	4
Antonio Lindback	T	1	1	0	2	4
Jaroslaw Hampel	0	1	2	1	0	4
Piotr Protasiewicz	0	2	0	1	0	3
Mattia Carpanese	0	0	0	X	0	0
Daniele Tessari (reserve)	0	-	-	-	-	0
Simone Terenzani (reserve)	-	-	-	-	-	-

RACE DETAILS
HEAT ONE:	(Rerun) Richardson, Gollob, Hancock, Tessari, Lindback (ex, tapes).
HEAT TWO:	Adams, B. Pedersen, Zagar, Carpanese (f, rem).
HEAT THREE:	Crump, Nicholls, Iversen, Hampel.
HEAT FOUR:	Andersen, N. Pedersen, Jonsson, Protasiewicz.

HEAT FIVE:	Andersen, B. Pedersen, Nicholls, Gollob.
HEAT SIX:	Zagar, Crump, Jonsson, Hancock.
HEAT SEVEN:	Iversen, Protasiewicz, Lindback, Carpanese.
HEAT EIGHT:	N. Pedersen, Adams, Hampel, Richardson.
HEAT NINE:	(Rerun) Zagar, N. Pedersen, Gollob, Iversen (f, ex).
HEAT TEN:	Hancock, Hampel, B. Pedersen, Protasiewicz.
HEAT ELEVEN:	Adams, Jonsson, Lindback, Nicholls.
HEAT TWELVE:	Andersen, Crump, Richardson, Carpanese.
HEAT THIRTEEN:	(Rerun; Awarded) Jonsson, Gollob, Hampel, Carpanese (f, ex).
HEAT FOURTEEN:	Hancock, Andersen, Adams, Iversen.
HEAT FIFTEEN:	Crump, B. Pedersen, N. Pedersen, Lindback.
HEAT SIXTEEN:	Nicholls, Zagar, Protasiewicz, Richardson.
HEAT SEVENTEEN:	Crump, Gollob, Adams, Protasiewicz.
HEAT EIGHTEEN:	Nicholls, Hancock, N. Pedersen, Carpanese.
HEAT NINETEEN:	Andersen, Lindback, Zagar, Hampel.
HEAT TWENTY:	B. Pedersen, Jonsson, Iversen, Richardson.
FIRST SEMI-FINAL:	(Rerun) Andersen, Nicholls, Hancock, Zagar (f, ex).
SECOND SEMI-FINAL:	Adams, Crump, B. Pedersen, N. Pedersen.
FINAL:	Crump, Nicholls, Andersen, Adams.

GRAND PRIX OF SCANDINAVIA (ROUND SEVEN)

DATE: 12 August.
VENUE: G & B Arena, Malilla, Sweden.
TRACK LENGTH: 310 metres.

1st ANDREAS JONSSON
2nd HANS N. ANDERSEN
3rd LEIGH ADAMS
4th JASON CRUMP

RIDER	RACE POINTS					TOTAL
Greg Hancock	3	1	3	3	2	12
Hans N. Andersen	3	3	2	1	3	12
Leigh Adams	2	3	3	0	3	11
Andreas Jonsson	1	3	1	3	3	11
Nicki Pedersen	1	2	2	3	3	11
Jason Crump	3	1	2	3	2	11
Jaroslaw Hampel	0	3	3	2	2	10
Scott Nicholls	1	2	2	2	1	8
Bjarne Pedersen	2	2	1	2	1	8
Niels-Kristian Iversen	2	1	1	2	R	6
Matej Zagar	0	0	3	1	0	4
Lee Richardson	3	0	X	0	1	4
Piotr Protasiewicz	1	2	0	1	0	4
Tomasz Gollob	0	1	R	1	2	4
Antonio Lindback	2	0	1	F	0	3

Ryan Sullivan	0	0	X	0	1	1
Fredrik Lindgren (reserve)	-	-	-	-	-	-
Jonas Davidsson (reserve)	-	-	-	-	-	-

RACE DETAILS

HEAT ONE:	Andersen, B. Pedersen, N. Pedersen, Gollob.
HEAT TWO:	Crump, Adams, Nicholls, Hampel.
HEAT THREE:	Richardson, Iversen, Protasiewicz, Sullivan.
HEAT FOUR:	Hancock, Lindback, Jonsson, Zagar.
HEAT FIVE:	Adams, B. Pedersen, Hancock, Sullivan.
HEAT SIX:	Andersen, Nicholls, Iversen, Lindback.
HEAT SEVEN:	Jonsson, N. Pedersen, Crump, Richardson.
HEAT EIGHT:	Hampel, Protasiewicz, Gollob, Zagar.
HEAT NINE:	(Rerun) Zagar, Nicholls, B. Pedersen, Richardson (f, ex).
HEAT TEN:	Adams, Andersen, Jonsson, Protasiewicz.
HEAT ELEVEN:	(Rerun) Hampel, N. Pedersen, Lindback, Sullivan (f, ex)
HEAT TWELVE:	Hancock, Crump, Iversen, Gollob (ret).
HEAT THIRTEEN:	Crump, B. Pedersen, Protasiewicz, Lindback (fell).
HEAT FOURTEEN:	Hancock, Hampel, Andersen, Richardson.
HEAT FIFTEEN:	N. Pedersen, Iversen, Zagar, Adams.
HEAT SIXTEEN:	Jonsson, Nicholls, Gollob, Sullivan.
HEAT SEVENTEEN:	Jonsson, Hampel, B. Pedersen, Iversen (ret).
HEAT EIGHTEEN:	Andersen, Crump, Sullivan, Zagar.
HEAT NINETEEN:	N. Pedersen, Hancock, Nicholls, Protasiewicz.
HEAT TWENTY:	Adams, Gollob, Richardson, Lindback.
FIRST SEMI-FINAL:	Jonsson, Crump, Hancock, Hampel (ret).
SECOND SEMI-FINAL:	(Rerun; Awarded) Adams, Andersen, Nicholls (ex, foul riding), N. Pedersen (f, ex).
FINAL:	Jonsson, Andersen, Adams, Crump (fell).

GRAND PRIX OF THE CZECH REPUBLIC (ROUND EIGHT)

DATE: 26 August.
VENUE: Marketa Stadium, Prague.
TRACK LENGTH: 353 metres.

1st HANS N. ANDERSEN
2nd MATEJ ZAGAR
3rd ANTONIO LINDBACK
4th JAROSLAW HAMPEL

RIDER	RACE POINTS					TOTAL
Jason Crump	3	3	2	3	3	14
Leigh Adams	2	1	3	3	3	12
Hans N. Andersen	2	2	3	2	3	12
Matej Zagar	3	3	2	1	1	10
Ryan Sullivan	2	3	3	M	1	9

Antonio Lindback	3	1	1	F	3	8
Niels-Kristian Iversen	3	2	F	2	1	8
Jaroslaw Hampel	0	3	2	0	2	7
Andreas Jonsson	0	2	1	2	2	7
Nicki Pedersen	1	T	X	3	2	6
Tomasz Gollob	R	2	2	2	0	6
Piotr Protasiewicz	1	0	1	3	0	5
Greg Hancock	T	0	3	R	1	4
Lubos Tomicek (reserve)	1	1	2	-	-	4
Lee Richardson	2	X	R	1	-	3
Adrian Rymel	1	1	0	0	X	2
Bjarne Pedersen	0	1	X	1	M	2
Zdenek Simota (reserve)	F	0	-	-	-	0

RACE DETAILS

HEAT ONE: Lindback, Adams, N. Pedersen, Gollob (ret).
HEAT TWO: Zagar, Andersen, Rymel, B. Pedersen.
HEAT THREE: Iversen, Sullivan, Protasiewicz, Hampel.
HEAT FOUR: (Rerun) Crump, Richardson, Tomicek, Jonsson, Hancock (ex, tapes)
HEAT FIVE: Zagar, Jonsson, Lindback, Protasiewicz.
HEAT SIX: (Rerun) Crump, Iversen, Rymel, Simota, N. Pedersen (ex, tapes).
HEAT SEVEN: (Rerun) Hampel, Andersen, Adams, Richardson (f, ex).
HEAT EIGHT: Sullivan, Gollob, B. Pedersen, Hancock.
HEAT NINE: Hancock, Hampel, Lindback, Rymel.
HEAT TEN: (Rerun) Sullivan, Zagar, Richardson (ret), N. Pedersen (f, ex).
HEAT ELEVEN: (Rerun) Adams, Crump, Protasiewicz, B. Pedersen (ex, foul riding).
HEAT TWELVE: Andersen, Gollob, Jonsson, Iversen (fell).
HEAT THIRTEEN: Crump, Andersen, Tomicek, Lindback (fell), Sullivan (ex, 2 mins).
HEAT FOURTEEN: N. Pedersen, Jonsson, B. Pedersen, Hampel.
HEAT FIFTEEN: Adams, Iversen, Zagar, Hancock (ret).
HEAT SIXTEEN: Protasiewicz, Gollob, Richardson, Rymel.
HEAT SEVENTEEN: Lindback, Tomicek, Iversen, Simota, B. Pedersen (ex, 2 mins).
HEAT EIGHTEEN: Andersen, N. Pedersen, Hancock, Protasiewicz.
HEAT NINETEEN: (Rerun) Adams, Jonsson, Sullivan, Rymel (f, ex)
HEAT TWENTY: Crump, Hampel, Zagar, Gollob.
FIRST SEMI-FINAL: Lindback, Zagar, Crump, Iversen.
SECOND SEMI-FINAL: Andersen, Hampel, Sullivan, Adams (ret).
FINAL: Andersen, Zagar, Lindback, Hampel.

GRAND PRIX OF LATVIA (ROUND NINE)

DATE: 9 September.
VENUE: Latvian Speedway Centre, Daugavpils.
TRACK LENGTH: 373 metres.

1st GREG HANCOCK
2nd ANTONIO LINDBACK
3rd NICKI PEDERSEN
4th ANDREAS JONSSON

RIDER	RACE POINTS					TOTAL
Antonio Lindback	3	2	3	3	2	13
Nicki Pedersen	3	3	2	2	3	13
Greg Hancock	3	1	2	3	3	12
Jason Crump	2	3	3	2	1	11
Matej Zagar	1	3	3	2	2	11
Andreas Jonsson	0	3	1	2	3	9
Scott Nicholls	2	2	0	3	2	9
Leigh Adams	1	1	0	3	3	8
Jaroslaw Hampel	1	2	3	1	R	7
Bjarne Pedersen	2	2	1	0	2	7
Hans N. Andersen	3	0	R	0	1	4
Tomasz Gollob	2	0	2	0	0	4
Kjastas Puodzhuks	R	1	2	1	0	4
Piotr Protasiewicz	1	0	1	1	1	4
Niels-Kristian Iversen	0	1	1	1	1	4
Lee Richardson	0	R	R	-	-	0
Grigorijs Laguta (reserve)	0	-	-	-	-	0
Andrejs Korolovs (reserve)	0	-	-	-	-	0

RACE DETAILS

HEAT ONE:	Hancock, B. Pedersen, Protasiewicz, Iversen.
HEAT TWO:	N. Pedersen, Crump, Zagar, Jonsson.
HEAT THREE:	Lindback, Nicholls, Adams, Puodzhuks (f, rem, ret).
HEAT FOUR:	Andersen, Gollob, Hampel, Richardson.
HEAT FIVE:	N. Pedersen, B. Pedersen, Adams, Richardson (ret).
HEAT SIX:	Crump, Hampel, Puodzhuks, Protasiewicz.
HEAT SEVEN:	Zagar, Nicholls, Hancock, Andersen.
HEAT EIGHT:	Jonsson, Lindback, Iversen, Gollob.
HEAT NINE:	Crump, Gollob, B. Pedersen, Nicholls.
HEAT TEN:	Lindback, N. Pedersen, Protasiewicz, Andersen (ret).
HEAT ELEVEN:	Hampel, Hancock, Jonsson, Adams.
HEAT TWELVE:	Zagar, Puodzhuks, Iversen, Richardson (ret).
HEAT THIRTEEN:	Lindback, Zagar, Hampel, B. Pedersen.

HEAT FOURTEEN:	Nicholls, Jonsson, Protasiewicz, Laguta.
HEAT FIFTEEN:	Hancock, N. Pedersen, Puodzhuks, Gollob.
HEAT SIXTEEN:	Adams, Crump, Iversen, Andersen.
HEAT SEVENTEEN:	(Rerun) Jonsson, B. Pedersen, Andersen, Puodzhuks.
HEAT EIGHTEEN:	Adams, Zagar, Protasiewicz, Gollob.
HEAT NINETEEN:	Hancock, Lindback, Crump, Korolovs.
HEAT TWENTY:	N. Pedersen, Nicholls, Iversen, Hampel (ret)
FIRST SEMI-FINAL:	Lindback, Jonsson, Nicholls, Crump.
SECOND SEMI-FINAL:	Hancock, N. Pedersen, Zagar, Adams.
FINAL:	(Rerun) Hancock, Lindback, N. Pedersen, Jonsson (ex, foul riding).

GRAND PRIX OF POLAND (ROUND TEN)

DATE: 23 September.
VENUE: Polonia Stadium, Bydgoszcz.
TRACK LENGTH: 348 metres.

1st NICKI PEDERSEN
2nd GREG HANCOCK
3rd TOMASZ GOLLOB
4th WIESLAW JAGUS

RIDER	RACE POINTS					TOTAL
Nicki Pedersen	3	3	3	2	3	14
Greg Hancock	1	3	3	3	2	12
Andreas Jonsson	2	3	2	3	2	12
Tomasz Gollob	2	2	1	3	3	11
Wieslaw Jagus	3	2	3	1	0	9
Hans N. Andersen	1	2	1	3	2	9
Matej Zagar	3	1	1	1	2	8
Jason Crump	3	0	1	0	3	7
Bjarne Pedersen	2	2	R	2	1	7
Scott Nicholls	2	1	2	1	1	7
Jaroslaw Hampel	0	1	3	2	0	6
Leigh Adams	1	0	0	2	3	6
Piotr Protasiewicz	1	0	2	0	1	4
Antonio Lindback	0	3	R	0	0	3
Niels-Kristian Iversen	0	1	0	1	1	3
Lee Richardson	0	0	2	0	0	2
Janusz Kolodziej (reserve)	-	-	-	-	-	-
Karol Zabik (reserve)	-	-	-	-	-	-

RACE DETAILS

HEAT ONE:	Crump, Nicholls, Adams, Iversen.
HEAT TWO:	(Rerun) Zagar, Jonsson, Protasiewicz, Richardson.
HEAT THREE:	Jagus, Gollob, Andersen, Hampel.

HEAT FOUR:	N. Pedersen, B. Pedersen, Hancock, Lindback.
HEAT FIVE:	Hancock, Gollob, Zagar, Crump.
HEAT SIX:	N. Pedersen, Andersen, Nicholls, Protasiewicz.
HEAT SEVEN:	Jonsson, B. Pedersen, Hampel, Adams.
HEAT EIGHT:	Lindback, Jagus, Iversen, Richardson.
HEAT NINE:	Hampel, Protasiewicz, Crump, Lindback (ret).
HEAT TEN:	Jagus, Nicholls, Zagar, B. Pedersen (ret).
HEAT ELEVEN:	N. Pedersen, Richardson, Gollob, Adams.
HEAT TWELVE:	Hancock, Jonsson, Andersen, Iversen.
HEAT THIRTEEN:	Jonsson, N. Pedersen, Jagus, Crump.
HEAT FOURTEEN:	Hancock, Hampel, Nicholls, Richardson.
HEAT FIFTEEN:	Andersen, Adams, Zagar, Lindback.
HEAT SIXTEEN:	Gollob, B. Pedersen, Iversen, Protasiewicz.
HEAT SEVENTEEN:	Crump, Andersen, B. Pedersen, Richardson.
HEAT EIGHTEEN:	Gollob, Jonsson, Nicholls, Lindback.
HEAT NINETEEN:	Adams, Hancock, Protasiewicz, Jagus.
HEAT TWENTY:	N. Pedersen, Zagar, Iversen, Hampel.
FIRST SEMI-FINAL:	N. Pedersen, Gollob, Zagar, Andersen.
SECOND SEMI-FINAL:	Jagus, Hancock, Jonsson, Crump.
FINAL:	N. Pedersen, Hancock, Gollob, Jagus.

GRAND PRIX RECORDS (1995-2006)

TOTAL ROUNDS STAGED: 89

MOST GP APPEARANCES
89 Greg Hancock
85 Tomasz Gollob
84 Tony Rickardsson
82 Leigh Adams
78 Jason Crump

MOST GP WINS
20 Tony Rickardsson
16 Jason Crump
10 Tomasz Gollob
8 Greg Hancock
6 Billy Hamill

MOST GP POINTS
1,401 Tony Rickardsson
1,200 Jason Crump
1,162 Greg Hancock
1,074 Tomasz Gollob
919 Leigh Adams

WORLD CHAMPIONSHIP ROLL OF HONOUR

NOTE: Run as a one-off World Final from 1936-1994 and as the Grand Prix from 1995-2006.

YEAR	FIRST	SECOND	THIRD
1936	Lionel Van Praag	Eric Langton	Bluey Wilkinson
1937	Jack Milne	Wilbur Lamoreaux	Cordy Milne
1938	Bluey Wilkinson	Jack Milne	Wilbur Lamoreaux
1939-1948	Not staged		
1949	Tommy Price	Jack Parker	Louis Lawson
1950	Freddie Williams	Wally Green	Graham Warren
1951	Jack Young	Split Waterman	Jack Biggs
1952	Jack Young	Freddie Williams	Bob Oakley
1953	Freddie Williams	Split Waterman	Geoff Mardon
1954	Ronnie Moore	Brian Crutcher	Olle Nygren
1955	Peter Craven	Ronnie Moore	Barry Briggs
1956	Ove Fundin	Ronnie Moore	Arthur Forrest
1957	Barry Briggs	Ove Fundin	Peter Craven
1958	Barry Briggs	Ove Fundin	Aub Lawson
1959	Ronnie Moore	Ove Fundin	Barry Briggs
1960	Ove Fundin	Ronnie Moore	Peter Craven
1961	Ove Fundin	Bjorn Knutsson	Gote Nordin
1962	Peter Craven	Barry Briggs	Ove Fundin
1963	Ove Fundin	Bjorn Knutsson	Barry Briggs
1964	Barry Briggs	Igor Plechanov	Ove Fundin
1965	Bjorn Knutsson	Igor Plechanov	Ove Fundin
1966	Barry Briggs	Sverre Harrfeldt	Antoni Woryna
1967	Ove Fundin	Bengt Jansson	Ivan Mauger
1968	Ivan Mauger	Barry Briggs	Edward Jancarz
1969	Ivan Mauger	Barry Briggs	Soren Sjosten
1970	Ivan Mauger	Pawel Waloszek	Antoni Woryna
1971	Ole Olsen	Ivan Mauger	Bengt Jansson
1972	Ivan Mauger	Bernt Persson	Ole Olsen
1973	Jerzy Szczakiel	Ivan Mauger	Zenon Plech
1974	Anders Michanek	Ivan Mauger	Soren Sjosten
1975	Ole Olsen	Anders Michanek	John Louis
1976	Peter Collins	Malcolm Simmons	Phil Crump
1977	Ivan Mauger	Peter Collins	Ole Olsen
1978	Ole Olsen	Gordon Kennett	Scott Autrey
1979	Ivan Mauger	Zenon Plech	Michael Lee
1980	Michael Lee	Dave Jessup	Billy Sanders
1981	Bruce Penhall	Ole Olsen	Tommy Knudsen
1982	Bruce Penhall	Les Collins	Dennis Sigalos
1983	Egon Muller	Billy Sanders	Michael Lee
1984	Erik Gundersen	Hans Nielsen	Lance King
1985	Erik Gundersen	Hans Nielsen	Sam Ermolenko
1986	Hans Nielsen	Jan O. Pedersen	Kelvin Tatum
1987	Hans Nielsen	Erik Gundersen	Sam Ermolenko

1988	Erik Gundersen	Hans Nielsen	Jan O. Pedersen
1989	Hans Nielsen	Simon Wigg	Jeremy Doncaster
1990	Per Jonsson	Shawn Moran	Todd Wiltshire
1991	Jan O. Pedersen	Tony Rickardsson	Hans Nielsen
1992	Gary Havelock	Per Jonsson	Gert Handberg
1993	Sam Ermolenko	Hans Nielsen	Chris Louis
1994	Tony Rickardsson	Hans Nielsen	Craig Boyce
1995	Hans Nielsen	Tony Rickardsson	Sam Ermolenko
1996	Billy Hamill	Hans Nielsen	Greg Hancock
1997	Greg Hancock	Billy Hamill	Tomasz Gollob
1998	Tony Rickardsson	Jimmy Nilsen	Tomasz Gollob
1999	Tony Rickardsson	Tomasz Gollob	Hans Nielsen
2000	Mark Loram	Billy Hamill	Tony Rickardsson
2001	Tony Rickardsson	Jason Crump	Tomasz Gollob
2002	Tony Rickardsson	Jason Crump	Ryan Sullivan
2003	Nicki Pedersen	Jason Crump	Tony Rickardsson
2004	Jason Crump	Tony Rickardsson	Greg Hancock
2005	Tony Rickardsson	Jason Crump	Leigh Adams
2006	Jason Crump	Greg Hancock	Nicki Pedersen

NOTE: In 1990, Shawn Moran was subsequently stripped of second place, having tested positive in a drugs test at the Overseas Final.

GRAND PRIX QUALIFICATION
(FOR THE 2007 GRAND PRIX SERIES)

ROUND ONE; 8 JULY, TARNOW, POLAND

QUALIFYING SCORES: Hans N. Andersen 11; Rune Holta 11; Kaj Laukkanen 10; Lukas Dryml 10; Janusz Kolodziej 10; Wieslaw Jagus 10; Renat Gafurov 10; Denis Gizatullin 9; Sebastian Ulamek 8; Rory Schlein 7; Kenneth Bjerre 7; Bohumil Brhel 6; Christian Hefenbrock 6; Stephan Katt 4; Henrik Moller 1; Mikke Bjerk 0. RUN-OFFS: HEAT ONE: 1st Jagus; 2nd Gafurov; 3rd Dryml. HEAT TWO: 1st Kolodziej; 2nd Laukkanen. HEAT THREE: 1st Laukkanen; 2nd Gafurov; 3rd Dryml. HEAT FOUR: 1st Laukkanen; 2nd Jagus; 3rd Kolodziej; 4th Gafurov. FINAL: 1st Holta; 2nd Jagus; 3rd Laukkanen; 4th Andersen.

ROUND TWO: 9 JULY, MISKOLC, HUNGARY

QUALIFYING SCORES: Ales Dryml 15; Simon Stead 11; Peter Karlsson 11; Matej Ferjan 10; Martin Smolinski 10; David Ruud 9; David Howe 8; Mattia Carpanese 7; Peter Ljung 7; Jernej Kolenko 7; Billy Janniro 6; Laszlo Szatmari 6; Thomas Stange 5; Izak Santej 5; Simone Terenzani 3; Sandor Tihanyi 0. FINAL: 1st Ferjan; 2nd Dryml; 3rd Stead; 4th Karlsson.

ROUND THREE: 9 JULY, ZARNOVICA, SLOVAKIA

QUALIFYING SCORES: Charlie Gjedde 12; Ryan Sullivan 12; Piotr Protasiewicz 12; Mikael Max 12; Robert Kosciecha 11; Chris Harris 10; Niels-Kristian Iversen 9; Fredrik Lindgren 9; Jurica Pavlic 8; Tomas Topinka 8; Edward Kennett 5; Travis McGowan 5; Sergey Darkin 4; Heinrich Schatzer 2; Theo Pijper 2; Vladimir Visvader 0. FINAL: 1st Sullivan; 2nd Protasiewicz; 3rd Gjedde; 4th Max.

FINAL; 19 AUGUST, VETLANDA, SWEDEN

RIDER	QUALIFYING SCORES					TOTAL
Hans N. Andersen	3	3	3	3	3	<u>15</u>
Peter Karlsson	3	3	3	2	3	14
Wieslaw Jagus	3	3	1	3	2	12
Rune Holta	3	2	3	1	3	12
Chris Harris	2	1	3	3	2	11
Kaj Laukkanen	1	1	2	2	3	9
Charlie Gjedde	1	2	0	3	2	8
Ryan Sullivan	2	1	1	2	1	7
Piotr Protasiewicz	2	3	2	0	0	7
Matej Ferjan	1	2	0	2	1	6
Simon Stead	2	2	0	1	0	5
Renat Gafurov	1	0	2	0	2	5
Martin Smolinski	R	0	2	1	1	4
Mikael Max	0	0	1	0	1	2
Robert Kosciecha	0	1	1	0	0	2
David Howe	0	0	0	1	0	1
Niels-Kristian Iversen (reserve)	-	-	-	-	-	-
Fredrik Lindgren (reserve)	-	-	-	-	-	-

RACE DETAILS

HEAT ONE:	Karlsson, Harris, Gjedde, Howe.
HEAT TWO:	Jagus, Stead, Gafurov, Max.
HEAT THREE:	Holta, Sullivan, Laukkanen, Kosciecha.
HEAT FOUR:	Andersen, Protasiewicz, Ferjan, Smolinski (ret).
HEAT FIVE:	Jagus, Holta, Harris, Smolinski.
HEAT SIX:	Protasiewicz, Gjedde, Kosciecha, Gafurov.
HEAT SEVEN:	Andersen, Stead, Sullivan, Howe.
HEAT EIGHT:	Karlsson, Ferjan, Laukkanen, Max.
HEAT NINE:	Harris, Gafurov, Sullivan, Ferjan.
HEAT TEN:	Andersen, Laukkanen, Jagus, Gjedde.
HEAT ELEVEN:	Holta, Protasiewicz, Max, Howe.
HEAT TWELVE:	Karlsson, Smolinski, Kosciecha, Stead.
HEAT THIRTEEN:	Harris, Laukkanen, Stead, Protasiewicz.
HEAT FOURTEEN:	Gjedde, Sullivan, Smolinski, Max.
HEAT FIFTEEN:	Jagus, Ferjan, Howe, Kosciecha.
HEAT SIXTEEN:	Andersen, Karlsson, Holta, Gafurov.
HEAT SEVENTEEN:	Andersen, Harris, Max, Kosciecha.
HEAT EIGHTEEN:	Holta, Gjedde, Ferjan, Stead.
HEAT NINETEEN:	Laukkanen, Gafurov, Smolinski, Howe.
HEAT TWENTY:	Karlsson, Jagus, Sullivan, Protasiewicz.
FINAL:	Jagus, Holta, Andersen, Karlsson.

NOTE: Wieslaw Jagus, Rune Holta and Hans N. Andersen qualified for the 2007 GP series.

MAJOR INTERNATIONAL MEETINGS 2006

SPEEDWAY WORLD CUP 2006

QUALIFYING ROUND ONE

27 MAY, DAUGAVPILS, LATVIA

FINLAND 42 (Joonas Kylmakorpi 12; Kaj Laukkanen 11; Kauko Nieminen 8; Tomi Reima 6; Juha Hautamaki 5)

GERMANY 39 (Christian Hefenbrock 12; Thomas Stange 11; Martin Smolinski 9; Tobias Kroner 4; Stephan Katt 3)

RUSSIA 39 (Denis Gizatullin 13; Semen Vlasov 10; Sergey Darkin 9; Ilya Bondarenko 4; Renat Gafurov 3)

LATVIA 30 (Kjastas Puodzhuks 11; Andrey Korolev 10; Maksim Bogdanov 5; Nikolay Kokin 3; Vyacheslav Girutskiy 1)

NOTE: Christian Hefenbrock defeated Denis Gizatullin in a run-off to secure second place for Germany.

QUALIFYING ROUND TWO

28 MAY, MISKOLC, HUNGARY

USA 59 (Greg Hancock 14; Billy Janniro 14; Billy Hamill 13; Sam Ermolenko 11; Ronnie Correy 7)

SLOVENIA 41 (Matej Zagar 17; Jernej Kolenko 10; Izak Santej 8; Denis Stojs 5; Maks Gregoric 1)

HUNGARY 25 (Norbert Magosi 9; Laszlo Szatmari 8; Sandor Tihanyi 8; Zsolt Bencze 0; Jozsef Tabaka 0)

ITALY 25 (Mattia Carpanese 7; Simone Terenzani 7; Daniele Tessari 5; Guglielmo Franchetti 3; Christian Miotello 3)

NOTE: Laszlo Szatmari defeated Mattia Carpanese in a run-off to secure third place for Hungary.

The Speedway World Cup once again provided a fascinating week of entertainment in 2006 and, typical of recent years, served up an array of top quality racing. For a second year in succession, the tournament was staged in three of the sport's major countries, namely Poland, Sweden and Great Britain. However, it was Denmark who were crowned World Champions after emerging victorious from a hotly contested and thoroughly absorbing final at Reading's Smallmead Stadium on Saturday 22 July. In recent seasons, the youthful Danish side have certainly harboured the ability to seize the coveted Ove Fundin Trophy and their deserved success concluded the nation's nine-year absence from glory in the competition. Captained by the stylish and at times controversial Hans N. Andersen, the Danes triumphed on the night by an 8-point margin, securing victory courtesy of a second place from Bjarne Pedersen in the penultimate race of the evening.

The wide, large and fast Rybnik circuit in the south of Poland provided the venue for round one of the competition proper on Saturday 16 July. With a crowd of around 6,000 in attendance, the host nation lined up against Team Great Britain, Australia and a lesser-fancied Finnish outfit. Poland tracked a different team to their 2005 World Cup-winning side and the most notable absence was that of Norwegian-born racer Rune Holta. Meanwhile, Team GB manager Neil Middleditch had the luxury of a fully-fit pool of riders to select from and, similar to 2005, combined a subtle mix of youth and experience. The Aussies welcomed back a resurgent Todd Wiltshire to their squad and team manager Craig Boyce bolstered his line-up with exciting young prospect Rory Schlein. The two new additions joined the potent threesome of Jason Crump, Leigh Adams and Ryan Sullivan to form what many considered a quintet strong enough to ultimately triumph in the competition. Nevertheless, it was still considered a surprise when Australia defeated home nation Poland on their own patch and consequently bagged a direct route into the final. The meeting itself showcased international speedway at its very best with an assortment of wonderful racing, passionate performances and, to top it all off, a last-heat decider that provided Poland, Australia or Great Britain with the opportunity to gain victory. Crump duly won the concluding race, earned his country automatic qualification to the World Cup Final and completed an impeccable 15-point maximum. Team Great Britain and Poland both finished the meeting on 48 points and headed for the Race-Off, whilst Finland's nine-point tally meant they bowed out. Despite their lowly score, the Finnish side were on the pace throughout, but were understandably hindered by the absence of arguably their top rider, Joonas Kylmakorpi, through a nasty shoulder injury.

Event two came from the fabulous G & B Arena at Malilla in Sweden and was fittingly won by the host nation. Andreas Jonsson's team triumphed by three points over a lively Danish side and an American team that was flawlessly led by Greg Hancock. The phenomenal individual efforts of the United States' captain earned the cheery Californian a place in the record books as he blazed to an unprecedented 20-point return. The Czech Republic were dealt a bitter blow in the week prior to the event as Ales Dryml was seriously hurt whilst riding for Oxford in the British Elite League. His brother, Lukas, who was also originally in the Czech quintet, understandably withdrew from the meeting to be at his sibling's bedside. The absence of the Dryml brothers, arguably the lynchpins of Czech speedway, undoubtedly hampered the performance of the side, who struggled to make an impression. Sweden took control of the meeting from the start and, in front of their home supporters, never realistically looked like being challenged. Both Jonsson and the sensational Antonio Lindback dropped just one point all evening and were well supported by talented youngster Fredrik Lindgren. Whilst the meeting didn't compare to the levels of excitement served up in Rybnik, it was an entertaining affair that saw the most exciting and youthful speedway nations finish in the top two positions.

Since the inception of the new World Cup race format in 2001, the tension-packed Race-Off meetings have consistently served up unbelievable speedway. 2006 was to be no exception and, predictably, a large and passionate crowd flocked to Reading to watch two teams earn their spot in the final. As the evening progressed, it soon became evident that Great Britain and Denmark would battle for victory and consign 2005 World Champions Poland to elimination. Tomasz Gollob's men never quite recovered from a dreadful start to the meeting in which they mustered just four points from the opening eight heats. Home track specialist Janusz Kolodziej and talented youngster Krzysztof Kasprzak were drafted in as replacements for Wieslaw Jagus and Piotr Protasiewicz. However, the pairing only collectively mustered two points and offered little support to Gollob and Jaroslaw Hampel's impressive 14 and 11 point contributions respectively. It was a similar story for the USA, whose eventual 28-point total was mainly thanks to a sublime 19-point contribution from their skipper supreme, Greg Hancock. The presence of the Americans certainly added some additional flavour and charisma to the competition, but, in truth, Hancock's men didn't harbour the necessary strength in depth to realistically compete for a spot in the final. The Danes and Brits battled tenaciously against one another throughout the night, with both nations being brilliantly led by their respective captains. Indeed, one of the most memorable races of the night was courtesy of a sublime duel between old rivals Scott Nicholls and Hans N. Andersen in heat thirteen. In the closing stages of the meeting, as the Smallmead circuit began to slicken off, the Danes exerted their authority and took a deserved victory on the night by a seven-point margin.

After a heavy thunderstorm earlier in the afternoon, the sun choose to shine brightly on the Smallmead arena as World Cup Final fever engulfed the estimated 4,000 in attendance on 22 July. With 2005 winners Poland already eliminated, the prospect of crowning new World Champions certainly increased tension and anticipation levels as the riders paraded around the 307-metre circuit. Team Great Britain made just the one change as boss Neil Middleditch opted for experience over youth by replacing Simon Stead with Chris Louis. Australia also made a solitary change, replacing Rory Schlein with Travis McGowan, whose familiarity with the Smallmead raceway made him an attractive option for team manager Craig Boyce. Both Denmark and Sweden stuck with the quintets that had already proved fruitful and it was the two powerhouse sides that made fantastic starts to the evening and found themselves locked together on nine points apiece after the opening five races. However, as the evening progressed, the British lads and Australia both recovered from below-par starts to haul themselves into gold medal contention. After heat twenty-one, just five points separated the four nations as the meeting looked set for a scintillating climax. Beforehand, controversy had engulfed the stadium as Danish captain Hans N. Andersen was excluded from heat eighteen for foul riding. The Dane was adjudged to have caused Britain's Chris Harris to fall as the two racers battled for position in what was a tremendous duel. The decision was met with disbelief by the Danish camp and, at one stage, their elaborate protests threatened to boil over. Thankfully, order was restored and Andersen's team kept their cool and didn't let a resurgent Australian side take advantage of their momentary lull. In fact, Craig Boyce's men suffered a dismal conclusion to the meeting in which they only mustered a solitary point from five races. Indeed, Denmark maintained their momentum and wrapped up the World Cup in the penultimate race, sparking scenes of great jubilation amongst their camp.

If those in attendance hadn't seen enough action already, then additional drama followed in the last heat as Jason Crump, riding on a 'double pointer', fell on the final bend of the fourth lap whilst occupying second spot. The Australian's uncharacteristic fall whilst challenging for the lead handed Sweden the silver medal and Great Britain a bronze. It meant the Aussies left empty-handed after it appeared at one stage they could be cruising towards top spot on the rostrum and their first victory since 2002. For Team Great Britain, the 2006 World Cup was yet again one of frustration that can be summarised by the age-old cliché of so near, yet so far. As always, the exceptional commitment level was apparent from the British quintet and, refreshingly, for a second year in succession, the exciting progress of young Cornishman Chris 'Bomber' Harris was a gleaming positive.

Chris Seaward

EVENT ONE

16 JULY, RYBNIK, POLAND

	RACE SCORES						TOTAL
AUSTRALIA 49							
Ryan Sullivan	3	1	2	2	2	-	10
Rory Schlein	0	2	1	0	0	-	3
Leigh Adams	1	3	3	3	3	-	13
Jason Crump	3	3	3	3	3	-	15
Todd Wiltshire	2	3	R	3	X	-	8
TEAM GREAT BRITAIN 48							
Lee Richardson	1	2	2	3	2	-	10
Simon Stead	3	2	2	1	1	-	9
Chris Harris	3	2	1	1	2	-	9
Scott Nicholls	1	3	3	2	1	-	10
Mark Loram	1	3	1	3	2	-	10
POLAND 48							
Piotr Protasiewicz	2	0	2	2	1	-	7
Sebastian Ulamek	1	2	2	2	3	-	10
Wieslaw Jagus	2	1	1	1	-	-	5
Jaroslaw Hampel	2	1	3	1	3	-	10
Tomasz Gollob	3	1	3	1	6	2	16
FINLAND 9							
Juha Hautamaki	0	0	0	0	0	1	1
Kauko Nieminen	2	1	0	0	0	0	3
Kaj Laukkanen	0	0	1	2	2	0	5
Tomi Reima	X	0	-	-	-	-	0
Juha Makela	0	0	0	0	0	-	0

RACE DETAILS

HEAT ONE:	Sullivan, Protasiewicz, Richardson, Hautamaki.
HEAT TWO:	Stead, Nieminen, Ulamek, Schlein.
HEAT THREE:	Harris, Jagus, Adams, Laukkanen.
HEAT FOUR:	(Rerun) Crump, Hampel, Nicholls, Reima (f, ex).
HEAT FIVE:	Gollob, Wiltshire, Loram, Makela.
HEAT SIX:	Adams, Richardson, Hampel, Makela.
HEAT SEVEN:	(Rerun) Crump, Stead, Gollob, Hautamaki.
HEAT EIGHT:	Wiltshire, Harris, Nieminen, Protasiewicz.
HEAT NINE:	Nicholls, Ulamek, Sullivan, Laukkanen.
HEAT TEN:	Loram, Schlein, Jagus, Reima.
HEAT ELEVEN:	Crump, Richardson, Jagus, Nieminen.
HEAT TWELVE:	Hampel, Stead, Laukkanen, Wiltshire (ret).
HEAT THIRTEEN:	Gollob, Sullivan, Harris, Hautakaki.

HEAT FOURTEEN:	Nicholls, Protasiewicz, Schlein, Makela.
HEAT FIFTEEN:	Adams, Ulamek, Loram, Hautamaki.
HEAT SIXTEEN:	Richardson, Laukkanen, Gollob, Schlein.
HEAT SEVENTEEN:	Adams, Protasiewicz, Stead, Nieminen.
HEAT EIGHTEEN:	Crump, Ulamek, Harris, Makela.
HEAT NINETEEN:	Wiltshire, Nicholls, Jagus, Hautamaki.
HEAT TWENTY:	Loram, Sullivan, Hampel, Nieminen.
HEAT TWENTY-ONE:	(Rerun) Ulamek, Richardson, Laukkanen (tactical joker), Wiltshire (f, ex).
HEAT TWENTY-TWO:	Gollob (tactical joker), Sullivan, Stead, Makela.
HEAT TWENTY-THREE:	Hampel, Harris, Hautamaki, Schlein.
HEAT TWENTY-FOUR:	Adams, Gollob, Nicholls, Nieminen.
HEAT TWENTY-FIVE:	Crump, Loram, Protasiewicz, Laukkanen.

EVENT TWO

18 JULY, MALILLA, SWEDEN

	RACE SCORES						TOTAL
SWEDEN 56							
Antonio Lindback	2	3	3	3	3	-	14
Fredrik Lindgren	3	2	1	1	3	-	10
Andreas Jonsson	3	3	3	3	2	-	14
Mikael Max	3	3	2	2	1	-	11
Peter Karlsson	1	2	1	2	1	-	7
DENMARK 53							
Nicki Pedersen	1	2	6	3	3	-	15
Charlie Gjedde	1	0	2	1	2	-	6
Niels-Kristian Iversen	2	1	1	2	-	-	6
Hans N. Andersen	2	2	2	3	3	-	12
Bjarne Pedersen	2	3	2	3	2	2	14
USA 39							
Greg Hancock	3	3	3	6	2	3	20
Billy Janniro	2	1	1	1	0	-	5
Sam Ermolenko	X	1	1	1	1	-	4
Brent Werner	0	0	0	0	-	-	0
Billy Hamill	3	2	2	2	1	-	10
CZECH REPUBLIC 7							
Tomas Suchanek	0	0	R	0	0	-	0
Bohumil Brhel	T	1	0	0	0	-	1
Adrian Rymel	X	1	0	1	2	-	4
Zdenek Simota	1	0	0	0	0	-	1
Josef Franc	0	0	0	0	1	-	1

RACE DETAILS

HEAT ONE:	Hancock, Lindback, N. Pedersen, Suchanek.
HEAT TWO:	(Rerun twice) Lindgren, Janniro, Gjedde, Brhel (ex, tapes).
HEAT THREE:	(Rerun twice) Jonsson, Iversen, Ermolenko (f, ex), Rymel (f, ex).
HEAT FOUR:	Max, Andersen, Simota, Werner.
HEAT FIVE:	Hamill, B. Pedersen, Karlsson, Franc.
HEAT SIX:	Hancock, Karlsson, Iversen, Simota.
HEAT SEVEN:	Lindback, Andersen, Janniro, Franc.
HEAT EIGHT:	B. Pedersen, Lindgren, Ermolenko, Suchanek.
HEAT NINE:	Jonsson, N. Pedersen, Brhel, Werner.
HEAT TEN:	Max, Hamill, Rymel, Gjedde (f, rem).
HEAT ELEVEN:	Hancock, Andersen, Lindgren, Rymel.
HEAT TWELVE:	Jonsson, B. Pedersen, Janniro, Simota.
HEAT THIRTEEN:	N. Pedersen (tactical joker), Max, Ermolenko, Franc.
HEAT FOURTEEN:	Hancock (tactical joker), Gjedde, Karlsson, Suchanek (ret).
HEAT FIFTEEN:	Lindback, Hamill, Iversen, Brhel.
HEAT SIXTEEN:	Jonsson, Hancock, Gjedde, Franc.
HEAT SEVENTEEN:	B. Pedersen, Max, Janniro, Suchanek.
HEAT EIGHTEEN:	Andersen, Karlsson, Ermolenko, Brhel.
HEAT NINETEEN:	Lindback, B. Pedersen, Rymel, Werner.
HEAT TWENTY:	N. Pedersen, Hamill, Lindgren, Simota.
HEAT TWENTY-ONE:	Hancock, B. Pedersen, Max, Brhel.
HEAT TWENTY-TWO:	N. Pedersen, Rymel, Karlsson, Janniro.
HEAT TWENTY-THREE:	Lindback, Gjedde, Ermolenko, Simota (tactical joker).
HEAT TWENTY-FOUR:	Lindgren, Iversen, Franc, Werner.
HEAT TWENTY-FIVE:	Andersen, Jonsson, Hamill, Suchanek.

RACE-OFF

20 JULY, READING

	RACE SCORES						TOTAL
DENMARK 49							
Bjarne Pedersen	2	3	2	2	2	-	11
Nicki Pedersen	2	3	1	2	F	-	8
Charlie Gjedde	2	1	2	1	3	-	9
Niels-Kristian Iversen	2	2	2	1	0	-	7
Hans N. Andersen	3	3	2	3	3	-	14
TEAM GREAT BRITAIN 42							
Scott Nicholls	1	2	3	2	2	2	12
Chris Harris	3	3	1	0	2	-	9
Lee Richardson	3	3	0	3	0	1	10
Mark Loram	3	1	0	3	0	-	7
Simon Stead	1	2	1	-	-	-	4

POLAND 35

Krzysztof Kasprzak	0	0	-	-	-	-	0
Sebastian Ulamek	1	0	3	1	3	F	8
Janusz Kolodziej	F	0	1	0	1	-	2
Jaroslaw Hampel	1	1	3	1	3	2	11
Tomasz Gollob	2	2	2	2	3	3	14

USA 28

Greg Hancock	3	2	6	3	2	3	19
Ronnie Correy	0	1	0	-	-	-	1
Billy Hamill	1	0	0	2	1	1	5
Brent Werner	0	0	0	0	-	-	0
Billy Janniro	0	1	0	1	1	R	3

RACE DETAILS

HEAT ONE:	Hancock, B. Pedersen, Nicholls, Kasprzak.
HEAT TWO:	Harris, N. Pedersen, Ulamek, Correy.
HEAT THREE:	Richardson, Gjedde, Hamill, Kolodziej (fell).
HEAT FOUR:	Loram, Iversen, Hampel, Werner.
HEAT FIVE:	Andersen, Gollob, Stead, Janniro.
HEAT SIX:	Richardson, Iversen, Janniro, Kasprzak.
HEAT SEVEN:	Andersen, Hancock, Loram, Ulamek.
HEAT EIGHT:	B. Pedersen, Stead, Correy, Kolodziej.
HEAT NINE:	(Rerun) N. Pedersen, Nicholls, Hampel, Hamill.
HEAT TEN:	Harris, Gollob, Gjedde, Werner.
HEAT ELEVEN:	Hancock (tactical joker), Gjedde, Gollob (tactical joker), Loram.
HEAT TWELVE:	Ulamek, Iversen, Stead, Hamill.
HEAT THIRTEEN:	Nicholls, Andersen, Kolodziej, Werner.
HEAT FOURTEEN:	Hampel, B. Pedersen, Harris, Janniro.
HEAT FIFTEEN:	Hancock, Gollob, N. Pedersen, Richardson.
HEAT SIXTEEN:	(Rerun) Andersen, Hamill, Hampel, Harris.
HEAT SEVENTEEN:	Richardson, B. Pedersen, Ulamek, Werner.
HEAT EIGHTEEN:	Loram, N. Pedersen, Janniro, Kolodziej.
HEAT NINETEEN:	Hampel, Hancock, Gjedde, Richardson (tactical joker).
HEAT TWENTY:	Gollob, Nicholls, Iversen, Correy.
HEAT TWENTY-ONE:	Ulamek, Nicholls, Hamill, N. Pedersen (fell).
HEAT TWENTY-TWO:	Gjedde, Nicholls, Janniro, Ulamek (fell).
HEAT TWENTY-THREE:	Hancock, Harris, Kolodziej, Iversen.
HEAT TWENTY-FOUR:	Andersen, Hampel, Richardson, Janniro (ret).
HEAT TWENTY-FIVE:	Gollob, B. Pedersen, Hamill, Loram.

FINAL

22 JULY, READING

	RACE SCORES						TOTAL
DENMARK 45							
Niels-Kristian Iversen	0	1	0	1	3	-	5
Nicki Pedersen	3	2	3	2	3	-	13
Bjarne Pedersen	1	3	1	2	2	-	9
Hans N. Andersen	3	3	3	X	3	-	12
Charlie Gjedde	2	0	2	1	1	-	6
SWEDEN 37							
Andreas Jonsson	3	3	2	2	3	1	14
Antonio Lindback	2	3	0	1	3	2	11
Fredrik Lindgren	2	0	1	0	2	-	5
Mikael Max	1	1	0	0	-	-	2
Peter Karlsson	1	0	1	3	-	-	5
TEAM GREAT BRITAIN 36							
Lee Richardson	2	1	2	2	0	-	7
Mark Loram	1	1	2	2	1	-	7
Scott Nicholls	3	0	3	4	3	2	15
Chris Louis	0	1	0	2	-	-	3
Chris Harris	0	0	0	3	1	-	4
AUSTRALIA 35							
Travis McGowan	1	2	0	0	X	-	3
Ryan Sullivan	0	2	1	1	0	-	4
Todd Wiltshire	0	2	3	2	1	-	8
Leigh Adams	2	2	1	3	0	-	8
Jason Crump	3	3	3	3	F	-	12

RACE DETAILS

HEAT ONE:	Jonsson, Richardson, McGowan, Iversen.
HEAT TWO:	N. Pedersen, Lindback, Loram, Sullivan.
HEAT THREE:	(Rerun) Nicholls, Lindgren, B. Pedersen, Wiltshire.
HEAT FOUR:	Andersen, Adams, Max, Louis.
HEAT FIVE:	Crump, Gjedde, Karlsson, Harris.
HEAT SIX:	B. Pedersen, McGowan, Max, Harris.
HEAT SEVEN:	Andersen, Sullivan, Richardson, Karlsson.
HEAT EIGHT:	Jonsson, Wiltshire, Loram, Gjedde.
HEAT NINE:	Lindback, Adams, Iversen, Nicholls.
HEAT TEN:	Crump, N. Pedersen, Louis, Lindgren.
HEAT ELEVEN:	Andersen, Loram, Lindgren, McGowan.
HEAT TWELVE:	Nicholls, Gjedde, Sullivan, Max.
HEAT THIRTEEN:	Wiltshire, Nicholls (tactical joker), Karlsson, Iversen.

HEAT FOURTEEN:	N. Pedersen, Jonsson, Adams, Harris.
HEAT FIFTEEN:	Crump, Richardson, B. Pedersen, Lindback.
HEAT SIXTEEN:	Nicholls, N. Pedersen, Jonsson (tactical joker), McGowan.
HEAT SEVENTEEN:	Jonsson, B. Pedersen, Sullivan, Louis.
HEAT EIGHTEEN:	(Rerun) Harris, Wiltshire, Lindback, Andersen (ex, foul riding).
HEAT NINETEEN:	Adams, Richardson, Gjedde, Lindgren.
HEAT TWENTY:	Crump, Loram, Iversen, Max.
HEAT TWENTY-ONE:	(Rerun) Lindback, Louis, Gjedde, McGowan (f, ex).
HEAT TWENTY-TWO:	Iversen, Lindgren, Harris, Sullivan.
HEAT TWENTY-THREE:	N. Pedersen, Lindback, Wiltshire, Richardson.
HEAT TWENTY-FOUR:	Karlsson, B. Pedersen, Loram, Adams.
HEAT TWENTY-FIVE:	Andersen, Nicholls, Jonsson, Crump (tactical joker; fell).

ROLL OF HONOUR

NOTE: Formerly known as the World Team Cup (1960-2000).

YEAR	FIRST	SECOND	THIRD	FOURTH
1960	Sweden	Great Britain	Czechoslovakia	Poland
1961	Poland	Sweden	Great Britain	Czechoslovakia
1962	Sweden	Great Britain	Poland	Czechoslovakia
1963	Sweden	Czechoslovakia	Great Britain	Poland
1964	Sweden	Soviet Union	Great Britain	Poland
1965	Poland	Sweden	Great Britain	Soviet Union
1966	Poland	Soviet Union	Sweden	Great Britain
1967	Sweden	Poland	Great Britain & Soviet Union	
1968	Great Britain	Sweden	Poland	Czechoslovakia
1969	Poland	Great Britain	Soviet Union	Sweden
1970	Sweden	Great Britain	Poland	Czechoslovakia
1971	Great Britain	Soviet Union	Poland	Sweden
1972	Great Britain	Soviet Union	Poland	Sweden
1973	Great Britain	Sweden	Soviet Union	Poland
1974	England	Sweden	Poland	Soviet Union
1975	England	Soviet Union	Sweden	Poland
1976	Australia	Poland	Sweden	Soviet Union
1977	England	Poland	Czechoslovakia	Sweden
1978	Denmark	England	Poland	Czechoslovakia
1979	New Zealand	Denmark	Czechoslovakia	Poland
1980	England	USA	Poland	Czechoslovakia
1981	Denmark	England	West Germany	Soviet Union
1982	USA	Denmark	West Germany	Czechoslovakia
1983	Denmark	England	USA	Czechoslovakia
1984	Denmark	England	USA	Poland
1985	Denmark	USA	England	Sweden
1986	Denmark	USA	England	Sweden
1987	Denmark	England	USA	Czechoslovakia

1988	Denmark	USA	Sweden	England
1989	England	Denmark	Sweden	USA
1990	USA	England	Denmark	Czechoslovakia
1991	Denmark	Sweden	USA	England
1992	USA	Sweden	England	Denmark
1993	USA	Denmark	Sweden	England
1994	Sweden	Poland	Denmark	Australia
1995	Denmark	England	USA	Sweden
1996	Poland	Russia	Denmark	Germany
1997	Denmark	Poland	Sweden	Germany
1998	USA	Sweden	Denmark	Poland
1999	Australia	Czech Republic	USA	England
2000	Sweden	England	USA	Australia
2001	Australia	Poland	Sweden	Denmark
2002	Australia	Denmark	Sweden	Poland
2003	Sweden	Australia	Denmark	Poland
2004	Sweden	Great Britain	Denmark	Poland
2005	Poland	Sweden	Denmark	Great Britain
2006	Denmark	Sweden	Great Britain	Australia

WORLD UNDER-21 TEAM CUP 2006

FIRST SEMI-FINAL
5 JUNE, ABENSBERG, GERMANY

DENMARK 46 (Morten Risager 14; Leon Madsen 12; Nicolai Klindt 11; Patrick Hougaard 5; Henrik Moller 4)
GERMANY 40 (Christian Hefenbrock 16; Kevin Wolbert 11; Tobias Kroner 10; Thomas Stange 3; Max Dilger 0)
GREAT BRITAIN 28 (James Wright 9; Daniel King 8; Ben Wilson 5; Ben Barker 4; Jason King 2)
GERMANY II 5 (Frank Facher 3; Stefan Kurz 1; Christoph Demmell 1; Manfred Betz 0)

SECOND SEMI-FINAL
17 JUNE, KUMLA, SWEDEN

SWEDEN 56 (Fredrik Lindgren 15; Antonio Lindback 12; Sebastian Alden 12; Ricky Kling 10; Robert Pettersson 7)
CZECH REPUBLIC 33 (Zdenek Simota 14; Filip Sitera 9; Hynek Stichauer 7; Matej Kus 3)
RUSSIA 27 (Lenar Nigmatzanov 8; Aleksey Kharchenko 7; Danil Ivanov 5; Marat Gatyatov 4; Ruslan Gatyatov 3)
FINLAND 4 (Rene Lehtinen 2; Joni Keskinen 2; Teemu Lahti 0; Jani Eerikainen 0; Aarni Heikkila 0)

FINAL
17 SEPTEMBER, RYBNIK, POLAND

POLAND 41 (Karol Zabik 13; Pawel Hlib 12; Adrian Miedzinski 8; Krzysztof Buczkowski 5; Pawel Miesiac 3)
SWEDEN 27 (Fredrik Lindgren 15; Thomas H. Jonasson 8; Sebastian Alden 4; Robert Pettersson 0; Ricky Kling 0)
DENMARK 26 (Nicolai Klindt 12; Henrik Moller 5; Morten Risager 4; Kenneth Hansen 4; Klaus Jakobsen 1)
GERMANY 25 (Christian Hefenbrock 10; Tobias Kroner 7; Kevin Wolbert 6; Max Dilger 2; Tobias Busch DNR)

ROLL OF HONOUR

YEAR	FIRST	SECOND	THIRD	FOURTH
2005	Poland	Sweden	Denmark	Czech Republic
2006	Poland	Sweden	Denmark	Germany

WORLD UNDER-21 CHAMPIONSHIP 2006

NOTE: Formerly known as the European Junior Championship (1977-1987).

QUALIFYING ROUNDS
ROUND ONE; 13 MAY, GORICAN, CROATIA
QUALIFYING SCORES: Jurica Pavlic 15; Andriy Karpov 14; Tobias Kroner 12; Pawel Hlib 11; Krzysztof Buczkowski 11; Fritz Wallner 10; Guglielmo Franchetti 9; Lubos Tomicek 9; Alexander Lieschke 7; Kjastas Puodzhuks 6; Maks Gregoric 5; Tamas Sike 3; Roland Kovacs 3; Matija Duh 3; Marko Oto 1; Renato Cvetko 0. FINAL: 1st Karpov; 2nd Pavlic; 3rd Hlib; 4th Kroner.

ROUND TWO; 14 MAY, SHEFFIELD
QUALIFYING SCORES: Chris Holder 14; Adrian Miedzinski 13; James Wright 12; Karol Zabik 11; Edward Kennett 10; Troy Batchelor 10; Jason King 9; Rene van Weele 8; Steve Boxall 7; Kyle Legault 6; Filip Sitera 6; Lewis Bridger 3; Mathieu Tresarrieu 3; Skyler Greyson 2; Martin Vaculik 2; Andrew Aldridge 1; Ben Barker (reserve) 1. FINAL: 1st Zabik; 2nd Holder; 3rd Miedzinski; 4th Wright.

ROUND THREE; 14 MAY, HOLSTED, DENMARK
QUALIFYING SCORES: Sebastian Alden 14; Fredrik Lindgren 14; Antonio Lindback 13; Henrik Moller 12; Morten Risager 11; Robert Pettersson 11; Ricky Kling 9; Lars Hansen 8; Patrick Hougaard 7; Kenneth Hansen 6; Sebastian Bengtsson 5; Rene Lehtinen 3; Jan Graversen 3; Joni Keskinen 2; Remi Ueland 1; Klaus Jakobsen 1; Aarne Heikkila (reserve) 0; Jesper Kristiansen (reserve) 0. FINAL: 1st Moller; 2nd Lindgren; 3rd Lindback; 4th Alden.

FIRST SEMI-FINAL; 11 JUNE, LESZNO, POLAND
QUALIFYING SCORES: Sebastian Alden 14; Karol Zabik 13; Fredrik Lindgren 12; Daniel King

11; Pawl Hlib 10; Chris Holder 9; Pawel Miesiac 9; Ricky Kling 7; Lubos Tomicek 7; Andriy Karpov 7; Thomas Stange 6; Krzysztof Buczkowski 4; Lars Hansen 4; James Wright 3; Jason King 3; Dario Galvin 1. FINAL: 1st Zabik; 2nd Lindgren; 3rd Alden; 4th D. King.

SECOND SEMI-FINAL; 2 JULY, POCKING, GERMANY

QUALIFYING SCORES: Zdenek Simota 14; Adrian Miedzinski 14; Antonio Lindback 13; Christian Hefenbrock 11; Jurica Pavlic 11; Robert Pettersson 10; Henrik Moller 9; Troy Batchelor 7; Patrick Hougaard 7; Miroslaw Jablonski 5; Guglielmo Franchetti 5; Rene van Weele 4; Alexander Lieschke 2; Tobias Kroner 2; Fritz Wallner 0. FINAL: 1st Lindback; 2nd Simota; 3rd Miedzinski; 4th Hefenbrock.

NOTE: British riders Edward Kennett and Ben Wilson were due to contest this meeting, however, the former missed the event due to passport problems, while the latter suffered injures in the pre-meeting practice that prevented his participation.

WORLD UNDER-21 CHAMPIONSHIP FINAL 2006
2 SEPTEMBER, TERENZANO, ITALY

1st KAROL ZABIK
2nd ANTONIO LINDBACK
3rd CHRISTIAN HEFENBROCK
4th FREDRIK LINDGREN

RIDER	QUALIFYING SCORES					TOTAL
Fredrik Lindgren	3	3	3	2	3	14
Karol Zabik	3	3	2	2	3	13
Christian Hefenbrock	3	1	3	3	2	12
Antonio Lindback	2	1	3	3	3	12
Pawel Miesiac	3	0	3	1	1	8
Adrian Miedzinski	0	2	1	3	2	8
Pawel Hlib	1	3	1	2	1	8
Zdenek Simota	0	0	2	3	1	6
Ricky Kling	1	0	2	1	2	6
Henrik Moller	0	2	2	1	1	6
Jurica Pavlic	2	0	0	0	3	5
Chris Holder	1	3	1	X	0	5
Mattia Carpanese	2	1	0	2	F	5
Sebastian Alden	2	2	0	0	0	4
Daniel King	1	2	0	1	X	4
Troy Batchelor (reserve)	2	-	-	-	-	2
Robert Pettersson	0	1	1	0	N	2

RACE DETAILS

HEAT ONE: Zabik, Carpanese, King, Miedzinski.
HEAT TWO: Miesiac, Alden, Kling, Moller.
HEAT THREE: Hefenbrock, Lindback, Holder, Pettersson.

HEAT FOUR:	Lindgren, Pavlic, Hlib, Simota.
HEAT FIVE:	Lindgren, King, Lindback, Kling.
HEAT SIX:	Hlib, Miedzinski, Pettersson, Miesiac.
HEAT SEVEN:	Holder, Alden, Carpanese, Pavlic.
HEAT EIGHT:	Zabik, Moller, Hefenbrock, Simota.
HEAT NINE:	Miesiac, Simota, Holder, King.
HEAT TEN:	Hefenbrock, Kling, Miedzinski, Pavlic.
HEAT ELEVEN:	Lindback, Moller, Hlib, Carpanese.
HEAT TWELVE:	Lindgren, Zabik, Pettersson, Alden.
HEAT THIRTEEN:	Hefenbrock, Hlib, King, Alden.
HEAT FOURTEEN:	(Rerun) Miedzinski, Lindgren, Moller, Holder (f, ex).
HEAT FIFTEEN:	Simota, Carpanese, Kling, Pettersson.
HEAT SIXTEEN:	Lindback, Zabik, Miesiac, Pavlic.
HEAT SEVENTEEN:	(Rerun) Pavlic, Batchelor, Moller, Pettersson (f, ns), King (ex, foul riding).
HEAT EIGHTEEN:	Lindback, Miedzinski, Simota, Alden.
HEAT NINETEEN:	Lindgren, Hefenbrock, Miesiac, Carpanese (fell).
HEAT TWENTY:	Zabik, Kling, Hlib, Holder.
GRAND FINAL:	(Rerun) Zabik, Lindback, Hefenbrock, Lindgren (f, ex).

ROLL OF HONOUR

NOTE: Formerly known as the European Junior Championship (1977-1987).

YEAR	FIRST	SECOND	THIRD
1977	Alf Busk	Joe Owen	Les Collins
1978	Finn Jensen	Kevin Jolly	Neil Middleditch
1979	Ron Preston	Airat Faljzulin	Ari Koponen
1980	Tommy Knudsen	Tony Briggs	Dennis Sigalos
1981	Shawn Moran	Toni Kasper	Jiri Hnidak
1982	Toni Kasper	Mark Courtney	Peter Ravn
1983	Steve Baker	David Bargh	Marvyn Cox
1984	Marvyn Cox	Neil Evitts	Steve Lucero
1985	Per Jonsson	Jimmy Nilsen	Ole Hansen
1986	Igor Marko	Tony Olsson	Brian Karger
1987	Gary Havelock	Piotr Swist	Sean Wilson
1988	Peter Nahlin	Henrik Gustafsson	Brian Karger
1989	Gert Handberg	Chris Louis	Niklas Karlsson
1990	Chris Louis	Rene Aas	Tony Rickardsson
1991	Brian Andersen	Morten Andersen	Jason Lyons
1992	Leigh Adams	Mark Loram	Joe Screen
1993	Joe Screen	Mikael Karlsson	Rune Holta
1994	Mikael Karlsson	Rune Holta	Jason Crump
1995	Jason Crump	Dalle Anderson	Ryan Sullivan
1996	Piotr Protasiewicz	Ryan Sullivan	Jesper B. Jensen
1997	Jesper B. Jensen	Rafal Dobrucki	Scott Nicholls
1998	Robert Dados	Krzysztof Jablonski	Matej Ferjan
1999	Lee Richardson	Ales Dryml	Nigel Sadler

2000	Andreas Jonsson	Krzysztof Cegielski	Jaroslaw Hampel
2001	David Kujawa	Lukas Dryml	Rafal Okoniewski
2002	Lukas Dryml	Krzysztof Kasprzak	David Howe
2003	Jaroslaw Hampel	Chris Harris	Rafal Szombierski
2004	Robert Miskowiak	Kenneth Bjerre	Matej Zagar
2005	Krzysztof Kasprzak	Tomas Suchanek	Fredrik Lindgren
2006	Karol Zabik	Antonio Lindback	Christian Hefenbrock

EUROPEAN CHAMPIONSHIP 2006

QUALIFYING ROUND; 10 JUNE, DAUGAVPILS, LATVIA
1st Adrian Miedzinski 14; 2nd Kjastas Puodzhuks (after run-off) 13; 3rd Christian Hefenbrock 13; Grigorijs Laguta 11; Mariusz Puszakowski 10; Jernej Kolenko 9; Mario Jirout 9; Bohumil Brhel 8; Denis Gizatullin 7; Nikolai Kokin 7; Maksim Bogdanovs 6; Denis Stojs 4; Ilya Bondarenko 4; Mathias Schultz 2; Martin Vaculik 2; Wiaczeslaw Gieruckij 0.

FIRST SEMI-FINAL; 18 JUNE, LJUBLJANA, SLOVENIA
1st Ales Dryml (after run-off) 13; 2nd Christian Hefenbrock 13; 3rd Jacek Rempala 12; Matej Zagar (after run-off) 10; Adrian Miedzinski 10; Bohumil Brhel 10; Krzysztof Jablonski 8; Mariusz Puszakowski 8; Andrej Korolev 7; Jernej Kolenko 7; Sergey Darkin 6; Josef Franc 5; Roman Ivanov 5; Mario Jirout 3; Kjastas Puodzhuks 2; Maksim Bogdanovs 1.

SECOND SEMI-FINAL; 29 JULY, OREBRO, SWEDEN
1st Fredrik Lindgren 14; 2nd Nicolai Klindt 13; 3rd Niklas Klingberg 12; Sebastian Alden (after run-off) 11; Mikke Bjerk 11; Mattias Nilsson 11; Rune Sola 9; Juha Hautamaki 8; Claus Vissing 6; Tomi Reima 5; Patrick Hougaard 5; Rickard Sedelius 5; Anders Nielsen 3; Kenneth Hansen 3; Carl-Johan Raugstad 2; Rene Lehtinen 1; Robert Pettersson (reserve) 0; Goran Flood (reserve) 0.

THIRD SEMI-FINAL; 29 JULY, WIENER NEUSTADT, AUSTRIA
1st Grzegorz Walasek 15; 2nd Robert Kosciecha 14; 3rd Damian Balinski 12; Jurica Pavlic 11; Roman Chromik 11; Stephan Katt 8; Matej Ferjan 8; Lubos Tomicek 7; Thomas Stange 6; Norbert Kosciuch 6; Fritz Wallner 6; Guglielmo Franchetti 6; Jannick de Jong 4; Zdenek Simota 4; Sebastien Tresarrieu 1; Manuel Novotny 0.

FINAL; 1 OCTOBER, MISKOLC, HUNGARY
1st Krzysztof Jablonski (after run-off) 13; 2nd Grzegorz Walasek 13; 3rd Christian Hefenbrock 12; Fredrik Lindgren 11; Matej Ferjan (reserve) 9; Adrian Miedzinski 8; Damian Balinski 8; Nicolai Klindt 8; Laszlo Szatmari 7; Niklas Klingberg 7; Mikke Bjerk 6; Jurica Pavlic 6; Robert Kosciecha 4; Mattias Nilsson 3; Roman Chromik 3; Andrej Korolev 2; Matej Zagar 0.

ROLL OF HONOUR

YEAR	FIRST	SECOND	THIRD
2001	Bohumil Brhel	Mariusz Staszewski	Krzysztof Cegielski
2002	Magnus Zetterstrom	Krzysztof Kasprzak	Rafal Szombierski
2003	Krzysztof Kasprzak	Slawomir Drabik	Magnus Zetterstrom

2004	Matej Zagar	Matej Ferjan	Hans N. Andersen
2005	Jesper B. Jensen	Ales Dryml	Kaj Laukkanen
2006	Krzysztof Jablonski	Grzegorz Walasek	Christian Hefenbrock

EUROPEAN UNDER-19 CHAMPIONSHIP FINAL 2006
19 AUGUST, GORICAN, CROATIA

1st Jurica Pavlic 14; 2nd Andrey Karpov 11; 3rd Lars Hansen 10; Adrian Gomolski 9; Jannick de Jong 9; Ricky Kling 9; Klaus Jakobsen 8; Marcin Jedrzejewski 8; Filip Sitera 8; Mateusz Szczepaniak 6; Kevin Wolbert 6; Kenneth Hansen 6; Matej Kus 5; Slawomir Dabrowski 4; Hynek Stichauer 3; Patrick Hougaard 3.

ROLL OF HONOUR

YEAR	FIRST	SECOND	THIRD
1998	Rafal Okoniewski	Ales Dryml	Hans N. Andersen
1999	Rafal Okoniewski	Karol Malecha	Jaroslaw Hampel
2000	Lukas Dryml	Niels-Kristian Iversen	Zbigniew Czerwinski
2001	Lukasz Romanek	Daniel Davidsson	Rafal Kurmanski
2002	Matej Zagar	Kenneth Bjerre	Fredrik Lindgren
2003	Kenneth Bjerre	Janusz Kolodziej	Antonio Lindback
2004	Antonio Lindback	Karol Zabik	Morten Risager
2005	Karol Zabik	Kjastas Puodzhuks	Robert Pettersson
2006	Jurica Pavlic	Andrey Karpov	Lars Hansen

RIDER INDEX 2006

The following is an A-Z list of riders who appeared in 2006, and includes all official meetings at Elite League, Premier League and Conference League level.

ADAMS, Leigh Scott   BORN: 28 April 1971, Mildura, Victoria, Australia.
BRITISH CAREER: (1989) Poole; (1990-1992) Swindon; (1993-1995) Arena-Essex; (1996) London; (1997-1998) Swindon; (1999-2000) King's Lynn; (2001-2002) Oxford; (2003) Poole; (2004-2006) Swindon.
MAJOR HONOURS: Australian Under-16 Champion: 1986; Australian Under-21 Champion: 1988, 1990, 1991, 1992; Victoria State Champion: 1989, 1990, 1991, 1992, 1994, 1995; Australian Champion: 1992, 1993, 1994, 1998, 2000, 2002, 2003, 2005, 2006; World Under-21 Champion: 1992; Commonwealth Champion: 1993; World Team Cup Champion: 1999; Czech Golden Helmet Champion: 1999, 2000, 2001, 2004; World Cup Champion: 2001, 2002.
GRAND PRIX: Challenge Champion: 1995, 1998; Scandinavian GP Champion: 2002; Slovenian GP Champion: 2003; Swedish GP Champion: 2004.

ALDEN, Sebastian (Seb) Carl   BORN: 7 November 1985, Vasteras, Sweden.
BRITISH CAREER: (2005-2006) Swindon.

ALLEN, Oliver (Olly) James   BORN: 27 May 1982, Norwich, Norfolk.
BRITISH CAREER: (1997) Peterborough (Academy League only); (1998) Mildenhall, Norfolk, Peterborough, Arena-Essex; (1999-2001) Swindon; (2002) Swindon, Peterborough; (2003) Swindon, Wolverhampton; (2004) Swindon; (2005) King's Lynn, Swindon, Eastbourne; (2006) Coventry.
MAJOR HONOUR: Queensland State Champion: 2006.
RIDER LINKS: Son of former rider Dave Allen. Brother of fellow rider Tommy Allen.

ALLEN, Thomas (Tommy) David   BORN: 4 September 1984, Norwich, Norfolk.
BRITISH CAREER: (2002) Mildenhall, Swindon (Conference Trophy only); (2003) Swindon (Premier League & Conference League); (2004) Rye House (Premier League & Conference League); (2005) Rye House, Swindon; (2006) Rye House, Belle Vue, Poole.
RIDER LINKS: Son of former rider Dave Allen. Brother of fellow rider Olly Allen.

ALLOTT, Adam Nick   BORN: 19 March 1983, Stockport, Cheshire.
BRITISH CAREER: (1998) Norfolk, Buxton; (1999) Buxton, Sheffield; (2000) Sheffield, Owlerton; (2001) Sheffield; (2002) Sheffield (Conference League only), Swindon, Somerset; (2003) Buxton (Conference Trophy only), King's Lynn; (2004) King's Lynn; (2005) King's Lynn, Eastbourne, Workington, Stoke; (2006) Stoke (Conference League only).
RIDER LINKS: Son of former rider Nicky Allott. Great nephew of former rider Tommy Allott. Grandson of former rider Guy Allott. Nephew of former riders Ian and Trevor Stead. Cousin of fellow rider Simon Stead.

ANDERSEN, Hans Norgaard   BORN: 3 November 1980, Odense, Denmark.
BRITISH CAREER: (2001-2002) Poole; (2003) Peterborough; (2004-2005) Ipswich; (2006) Peterborough.
MAJOR HONOUR: World Cup Champion: 2006.
GRAND PRIX: Scandinavian GP Champion: 2004; Danish GP Champion: 2006; Czech Republic GP Champion: 2006.

ANDERSSON, Eric BORN: 15 June 1984, St Dicka, Fors, Sweden.
BRITISH CAREER: (2006) Oxford.

ANDREWS, Marc James BORN: 23 November 1986, Poole, Dorset.
BRITISH CAREER: (2004) Stoke (Conference League only), Swindon (Conference League only), King's Lynn (Conference Trophy only); (2005) Weymouth, Stoke (Conference League KOC only), Oxford (Conference League only); (2006) Newport (Conference League only).

APPLETON, Andrew BORN: 18 June 1982, Reading, Berkshire.
BRITISH CAREER: (1997) Oxford (Academy League only); (1998) Newport (Conference League & Premier League), Arena-Essex, Edinburgh; (1999) Newport (Premier League & Conference League); (2000) Newport; (2001) Oxford; (2002) Oxford, Reading; (2003) Reading; (2004) Reading, Peterborough; (2005) Reading; (2006) Eastbourne.
MAJOR HONOUR: New Zealand Champion: 2002.
RIDER LINKS: Son of former rider Alan Appleton.

ARMSTRONG, Jon Thomas BORN: 1 August 1974, Manchester, Greater Manchester.
BRITISH CAREER: (1992-1993) Belle Vue; (1994) Coventry; (1996) Buxton, Sheffield; (1997) Buxton, Belle Vue (Academy League only), Swindon, Stoke; (1998) Newport (Conference League & Premier League); (1999) Belle Vue, Stoke; (2000) Newport; (2001) Stoke; (2002) Buxton, Stoke; (2003) Stoke; (2004) Mildenhall, Belle Vue; (2005) Mildenhall, Peterborough; (2006) Mildenhall, Peterborough.
MAJOR HONOUR: Amateur League Riders' Champion: 1997.

ASHWORTH, Richard (Ricky) David BORN: 17 August 1982, Salford, Greater Manchester.
BRITISH CAREER: (2001) Sheffield (Conference League only); (2002) Sheffield (Premier League & Conference League); (2003) Sheffield; (2004) Sheffield, Peterborough; (2005) Sheffield, Poole; (2006) Sheffield.

ATKIN, Anthony (Tony) Neville BORN: 8 April 1966, Wrexham, North Wales.
BRITISH CAREER: (1986) Stoke; (1994) Wolverhampton; (1995) Bradford; (1996) Sheffield, Wolverhampton, Buxton; (1997) Stoke; (1999-2002) Stoke; (2003-2006) Newport.

AUTY, Joshua (Josh) Liam BORN: 8 September 1990, Mirfield, West Yorkshire.
BRITISH CAREER: (2005-2006) Scunthorpe.
MAJOR HONOURS: British Under-15 Champion: 2004, 2005.

BAGER, Henning BORN: 18 February 1981, Esbjerg, Denmark.
BRITISH CAREER: (2001) Glasgow; (2002) Peterborough, Isle of Wight; (2003) Arena-Essex; (2004-2005) Peterborough; (2006) Arena-Essex.

BAJERSKI, Tomasz BORN: 9 September 1975, Torun, Poland.
BRITISH CAREER: (2001) King's Lynn; (2005) Oxford; (2006) Peterborough.
MAJOR HONOURS: Polish Under-21 Champion: 1993, 1996.

BARGH, Andrew Lawrence BORN: 15 April 1986, Napier, New Zealand.
BRITISH CAREER: (2005) Wimbledon, Mildenhall; (2006) Mildenhall (Conference League only).
MAJOR HONOUR: New Zealand Under-21 Champion: 2005.
RIDER LINKS: Nephew of former rider David Bargh.

BARKER, Benjamin (Ben) John BORN: 10 March 1988, Truro, Cornwall.
BRITISH CAREER: (2003) Oxford (Conference League only), Trelawny (Conference Trophy only);

(2004) Oxford (Conference League only), Coventry (Conference Trophy only); (2005) Oxford (Conference League only), Exeter; (2006) Somerset, Stoke (Conference League only).

BARKER, Dean   BORN: 2 August 1970, Isleworth, Middlesex.
BRITISH CAREER: (1986) Eastbourne; (1987-1988) Eastbourne, Cradley Heath; (1989) Eastbourne; (1990-1992) Oxford; (1993-1995) Eastbourne; (1997) Eastbourne; (1999-2003) Eastbourne; (2004) Arena-Essex; (2005-2006) Eastbourne.
RIDER LINKS: Brother of former rider Sean Barker.

BARNETT, Russell Martin   BORN: 26 May 1987, Newport, Gwent, South Wales.
BRITISH CAREER: (2003) Mildenhall (Conference Trophy only), Rye House (Conference League only), Newport (Conference League only), Oxford (Conference League only); (2004-2005) Newport (Conference League only); (2006) Plymouth.

BASEBY, Aaron Henry   BORN: 31 May 1990, Pembury, Kent.
BRITISH CAREER: (2005) Sittingbourne; (2006) Sittingbourne (Conference Shield only).
RIDER LINKS: Brother of fellow rider Mark Baseby.

BASEBY, Mark Charles   BORN: 28 February 1988, Pembury, Kent.
BRITISH CAREER: (2003) Stoke (Conference Trophy only), Swindon (Conference League only); (2004) Rye House (Conference League only), Sittingbourne (Conference League KOC only); (2005) Sittingbourne; (2006) Mildenhall (Conference League only).
RIDER LINKS: Brother of fellow rider Aaron Baseby.

BATCHELOR, Troy Matthew   BORN: 29 August 1987, Brisbane, Queensland, Australia.
BRITISH CAREER: (2005) King's Lynn, Eastbourne; (2006) King's Lynn, Coventry.
MAJOR HONOUR: Australian Under-16 Champion: 2003.

BATES, Matthew (Mattie)   BORN: 26 July 1989, Exeter, Devon.
BRITISH CAREER: (2004) Weymouth, Coventry (Conference Trophy only); (2005) Weymouth, Mildenhall (Conference Trophy only); (2006) Plymouth.

BEATON HAMILTON, Gary   BORN: 20 August 1986, Glasgow, Scotland.
BRITISH CAREER: (2002) Newport (Conference League only), Newcastle (Conference League only); (2003) Newcastle (Conference League only), Wolverhampton (Conference League only), Armadale; (2004-2005) Armadale; (2006) Buxton, Cleveland (Conference Shield only).
RIDER LINKS: Nephew of former riders George, Bobby and Jim Beaton.

BEKKER, Byron Anthony   BORN: 2 July 1987, Johannesburg, South Africa.
BRITISH CAREER: (2004) Newcastle (Conference League only); (2005-2006) Scunthorpe.

BELFIELD, Carl   BORN: 1 September 1977, Stockport, Cheshire.
BRITISH CAREER: (2002) Buxton; (2004-2006) Buxton.

BERGSTROM, Andreas   BORN: 27 August 1978, Avesta, Sweden.
BRITISH CAREER: (2006) Berwick.

BETHELL, Jonathan   BORN: 18 March 1973, Kendal, Cumbria.
BRITISH CAREER: (2003) Oxford (Conference League only), Buxton; (2004) Buxton; (2005) Buxton, Workington; (2006) Buxton.

BETSON, Daniel (Danny) Robert   BORN: 11 January 1988, Eastbourne, East Sussex.
BRITISH CAREER: (2004) Mildenhall, Swindon (Conference League only); (2005) Wimbledon; (2006) Rye House (Conference League only).
RIDER LINKS: Nephew of former rider Scott Swain.

BIRD, Danny Lee   BORN: 16 November 1979, Guildford, Surrey.
BRITISH CAREER: (1998-2001) Isle of Wight; (2002-2003) Isle of Wight, Ipswich; (2004) Reading, Ipswich; (2005) Reading; (2006) Glasgow.

BIRKINSHAW, James Alexander   BORN: 6 March 1980, Sheffield, South Yorkshire.
BRITISH CAREER: (1996) Owlerton, Sheffield, Hull; (1997) Sheffield, Belle Vue (Academy League only), Newcastle; (1998) Newcastle, St Austell; (1999) Workington, Edinburgh, Linlithgow, Stoke, Sheffield; (2000) Glasgow, Sheffield (Premier League & Conference League); (2001) Newcastle, Sheffield (Conference League only); (2002) Sheffield, Boston, Wolverhampton (Conference Trophy only); (2003) Sheffield; (2004) Sheffield, Buxton; (2005) Glasgow, Buxton, Newcastle; (2006) Boston, Berwick.
MAJOR HONOUR: Conference League Riders' Champion: 2002.

BJERRE JENSEN, Kenneth   BORN: 24 May 1984, Esbjerg, Denmark.
BRITISH CAREER: (2002) Newcastle; (2003) Newcastle, Peterborough; (2004-2006) Belle Vue.
MAJOR HONOURS: European Under-19 Champion: 2003; Danish Under-21 Champion: 2000, 2003, 2004, 2005.

BLACKBIRD, Lewis   BORN: 21 February 1987, Peterborough, Cambridgeshire.
BRITISH CAREER: (2006) Sittingbourne (Conference Shield only).
RIDER LINKS: Son of former rider Carl Blackbird. Nephew of former riders Mark and Paul Blackbird.

BLAIR, Greg Sam Andrew   BORN: 14 October 1990, Jedburgh, Scotland.
BRITISH CAREER: (2006) Cleveland (Conference Shield only).

BLAKE, Daniel (Dan) James   BORN: 7 August 1988, Harlow, Essex.
BRITISH CAREER: (2004) Mildenhall; (2005) Sittingbourne; (2006) Sittingbourne (Conference Shield only).

BOWEN, Luke Alex   BORN: 26 January 1986, Harlow, Essex.
BRITISH CAREER: (2002) Rye House (Conference League only), Carmarthen; (2003) Rye House (Conference League only); (2004) Rye House (Conference League only), King's Lynn (Conference League KOC only); (2005) Rye House (Conference League only); (2006) Rye House (Premier League & Conference League).
RIDER LINKS: Son of former rider Kevin Bowen.

BOXALL, Steven (Steve) Shane   BORN: 16 May 1987, Canterbury, Kent.
BRITISH CAREER: (2002-2003) Rye House (Conference League only); (2004-2005) Rye House (Premier League & Conference League); (2006) Rye House.
MAJOR HONOUR: Conference League Riders' Champion: 2005.

BOYCE, Craig   BORN: 2 August 1967, Sydney, New South Wales, Australia.
BRITISH CAREER: (1988-1990) Poole; (1991) Oxford; (1992-1994) Poole; (1995) Swindon; (1996-1998) Poole; (1999) Oxford; (2000) King's Lynn; (2001-2002) Ipswich; (2003) Oxford, Poole (British League Cup only), Ipswich; (2004-2005) Isle of Wight; (2006) Poole.
MAJOR HONOURS: New South Wales State Champion: 1991, 1993, 1994, 1995; Australian Champion: 1991, 1996, 1997; World Cup Champion: 2001.

BRADY, Ross Burns   BORN: 17 February 1981, Winchburgh, Broxburn, Scotland.
BRITISH CAREER: (1997) Lathallan, Peterborough (Amateur League only); (1998) Mildenhall, Peterborough, Berwick; (1999-2000) Edinburgh; (2001-2002) Hull; (2003) Glasgow, Sheffield (Conference League & Premier League); (2004) Hull; (2005) Edinburgh; (2006) Rye House.
RIDER LINKS: Son of former rider Alistair Brady.

BRAITHWAITE, Andrew James   BORN: 26 December 1989, Coventry, Warwickshire.
BRITISH CAREER: (2006) Plymouth (Play-Off only), Buxton (Conference Shield only).

BRANNEY, Craig Harry   BORN: 31 July 1982, Whitehaven, Cumbria.
BRITISH CAREER: (2000) Ashfield; (2001) Workington, Buxton; (2002) Newcastle (Conference League only), Hull; (2003) Newcastle (Premier League & Conference League), Armadale (Conference Trophy only); (2004) Oxford (Conference League only), King's Lynn (Conference Trophy only); (2005) Hull, Oxford (Elite League & Conference League); (2006) Berwick.
RIDER LINKS: Brother of fellow rider, John Branney.

BRANNEY, John James   BORN: 7 November 1985, Whitehaven, Cumbria.
BRITISH CAREER: (2002) Rye House (Conference League only), Newcastle (Conference League only); (2003) Newcastle (Conference League only), Wimbledon (Conference Trophy only), Buxton (Conference Trophy only); (2004) Newcastle (Conference League only), King's Lynn (Conference Trophy only); (2005) Oxford (Conference League only); (2006) Scunthorpe, Stoke (Conference League only).
RIDER LINKS: Brother of fellow rider Craig Branney.

BRIDGER, Lewis Alan   BORN: 4 November 1989, Hastings, Sussex.
BRITISH CAREER: (2005) Weymouth; (2006) Eastbourne.
MAJOR HONOUR: British Under-18 Champion: 2006.

BROADHURST, Wayne Nicholas   BORN: 28 February 1967, Minsterley, Shropshire.
BRITISH CAREER: (1987) Coventry; (1988) Coventry, Stoke; (1989) Coventry; (1999) Stoke, Workington; (2000) Stoke; (2001) Wolverhampton, Stoke; (2002) Mildenhall; (2003) Mildenhall; (2004) Wimbledon; (2005) Stoke (Conference League only); (2006) Boston.

BROWN, Thomas (Tom) David   BORN: 19 June 1984, Pontypool, South Wales.
BRITISH CAREER: (2000) Peterborough (Conference League only), Newport (Conference League only); (2001) Newport (Conference League & Premier League); (2002) Workington, Newport (Conference League only), Swindon (Conference Trophy only), Isle of Wight; (2003) Trelawny (Premier League & Conference Trophy); (2004) Stoke (Conference League only), Berwick; (2005) Weymouth; (2006) Plymouth.

BRUNDLE, James Michael   BORN: 15 December 1986, King's Lynn, Norfolk.
BRITISH CAREER: (2002) King's Lynn (Conference League only), Mildenhall; (2003-2004) King's Lynn, Mildenhall; (2005) King's Lynn; (2006) Mildenhall.

BUNYAN, Jason Michael   BORN: 9 March 1979, Milton Keynes, Buckinghamshire.
BRITISH CAREER: (1995) Poole; (1996) Eastbourne (Conference League only); (1997) Oxford, Isle of Wight, Peterborough (Amateur League only); (1998) Isle of Wight; (1999-2001) Ipswich; (2002) Reading; (2003) Coventry; (2004) Isle of Wight, Coventry; (2005) Isle of Wight (Premier Trophy only); (2006) Isle of Wight.
MAJOR HONOUR: New Zealand Champion: 2004, 2005, 2006.

BURCHATT, Barry Peter   BORN: 25 October 1987, Farnborough, Kent.
BRITISH CAREER: (2003) Newport (Conference League only), Rye House (Conference League only), Wimbledon; (2004-2005) Rye House (Conference League only); (2006) Rye House (Conference League only), Mildenhall.

BURNETT, Paul Antony David   BORN: 24 October 1981, Bradford, West Yorkshire.
BRITISH CAREER: (1997) Buxton, Belle Vue (Academy League only), Western Warriors; (1998-2004) Buxton; (2005) Scunthorpe, Mildenhall; (2006) Cleveland (Conference Shield only)

BURZA, Stanislaw (Stan)   BORN: 26 September 1977, Tarnow, Poland.
BRITISH CAREER: (2006) Berwick, Oxford.

CAMPOS, Scott Dale   BORN: 1 May 1989, Ipswich, Suffolk.
BRITISH CAREER: (2004) Mildenhall, Rye House (Conference League only); (2005) Mildenhall, Boston; (2006) Boston.

CARTER, Wayne Martin   BORN: 19 December 1970, Halifax, West Yorkshire.
BRITISH CAREER: (1989) Mildenhall, Wolverhampton; (1990) Wolverhampton; (1991) Wolverhampton, Middlesbrough; (1992) Wolverhampton; (1993) Middlesbrough; (1994-1995) Wolverhampton; (1996) Middlesbrough, Belle Vue; (1997) Skegness, Isle of Wight, Peterborough, Belle Vue, Wolverhampton, Bradford; (1998-1999) Isle of Wight; (2000) Wolverhampton; (2001) Belle Vue, Berwick; (2002) Coventry, Newcastle; (2003) Wolverhampton (British League Cup only), Edinburgh; (2004) Sheffield (Conference Trophy only), Swindon (Conference League only); (2005-2006) Scunthorpe.
RIDER LINKS: Cousin of former rider Kenny Carter.

CHARLES, Robert (Bob) Lee   BORN: 14 November 1989, St Austell, Cornwall.
BRITISH CAREER: (2006) Buxton (Conference Shield only), Stoke (Conference Shield only), Plymouth (Play-Offs only).

CHESTER, Scott   BORN: 6 January 1982, Leicester, Leicestershire.
BRITISH CAREER: (2004) Buxton, Weymouth (Conference Trophy only), King's Lynn (Conference Trophy only); (2005-2006) Buxton.

CHRZANOWSKI, Tomasz   BORN: 4 February 1980, Torun, Poland.
BRITISH CAREER: (2002) Poole; (2006) Swindon.

CLEWS, Paul Gordon   BORN: 19 July 1979, Coventry, Warwickshire.
BRITISH CAREER: (1995) Coventry; (1996) Peterborough (Conference League & Premier League), Coventry, Oxford, Anglian Angels; (1997) Skegness, Isle of Wight, Peterborough (Amateur League only), Coventry; (1998) Peterborough; (1999-03) Reading; (2004-06) Stoke.
RIDER LINKS: Brother-in-law of former rider Darren Andrews.

COCKLE, James Robert   BORN: 26 May 1986, Enfield, Middlesex.
BRITISH CAREER: (2001-2003) Rye House (Conference League only); (2004) Boston, Sheffield (Conference Trophy only), Reading, Glasgow; (2005) Glasgow, Sittingbourne, Boston; (2006) Glasgow.

COLES, Michael Timothy   BORN: 11 August 1965, Exeter, Devon.
BRITISH CAREER: (1982-1983) Exeter; (1984) Exeter, Weymouth; (1985-1987) Exeter; (1988) Mildenhall; (1989-1993) Edinburgh; (1994) Belle Vue; (1995) Oxford; (1996) Exeter; (1997) Exeter, King's Lynn; (1998-2004) Exeter; (2005) Newport; (2006) Stoke (Premier Trophy only), Plymouth

(Knock-Out Cup only).
RIDER LINKS: Son of former rider Bob Coles.

COLLINS, Aidan   BORN: 21 April 1982, Stockport, Greater Manchester.
BRITISH CAREER: (1998) Newport (Conference League only); (1999) Buxton, Edinburgh; (2000) Glasgow, Ashfield; (2001) Glasgow; (2002) Buxton, Edinburgh; (2003-2004) Workington; (2005) Mildenhall, Workington; (2006) Workington.
RIDER LINKS: Son of former rider Les Collins. Nephew of fellow rider Neil Collins. Nephew of former riders Peter, Phil and Steve Collins. Cousin of former rider Chris Collins.

COLLINS, Neil Jeffrey   BORN: 15 October 1961, Partington, Greater Manchester.
BRITISH CAREER: (1978) Ellesmere Port; (1979) Nottingham, Workington, Sheffield; (1980) Edinburgh, Sheffield; (1981) Edinburgh, Cradley Heath, Belle Vue; (1982-1983) Leicester; (1984-1988) Sheffield; (1989-1990) Wolverhampton; (1991) Belle Vue; (1992) Glasgow; (1993-1994) Long Eaton; (1995) Sheffield; (1996) Belle Vue; (1997) Glasgow; (1998) Stoke; (1999-2000) Swindon; (2001) Belle Vue, Workington; (2002) Somerset; (2003) Hull, Peterborough (British League Cup only), Belle Vue; (2004) Somerset; (2005-2006) Newport.
RIDER LINKS: Brother of former riders Les, Peter Phil and Steve Collins. Uncle of fellow rider Aidan Collins. Uncle of former rider Chris Collins.

COMPTON, Andre Neil   BORN: 15 May 1977, Dewsbury, West Yorkshire.
BRITISH CAREER: (1993) Bradford, Newcastle; (1994) Stoke, Newcastle, Buxton; (1995) Hull, Buxton, Reading, Coventry, Belle Vue; (1996) Buxton, Bradford, Belle Vue; (1997) Newcastle, Berwick; (1998-1999) Sheffield; (2000) Peterborough, Newcastle; (2001) Newcastle; (2002) Newcastle, Poole; (2003) Sheffield, Poole; (2004) Sheffield, Poole, Belle Vue; (2005-2006) Sheffield.
MAJOR HONOUR: Premier League Riders' Champion: 2004.
RIDER LINKS: Brother of fellow rider Benji Compton.

COMPTON, Benjamin (Benji) Mark   BORN: 17 September 1986, Tenerife, Spain.
BRITISH CAREER: (2002) Newcastle (Conference League only); (2003) Sheffield (Conference League only), Mildenhall; (2004) Buxton; (2005) Scunthorpe; (2006) Sheffield.
RIDER LINKS: Brother of fellow rider Andre Compton.

COOK, Harland Ashley   BORN: 6 August 1988, Watford, Hertfordshire.
BRITISH CAREER: (2003) Rye House (Conference League only); (2004) Rye House (Conference League only), Coventry (Conference Trophy only); (2005-2006) Rye House (Conference League only).

COOPER, Paul Robert   BORN: 7 June 1982, York, North Yorkshire.
BRITISH CAREER: (2003) Sheffield (Conference League only); (2004) Oxford (Conference League only), Sheffield (Conference Trophy only); (2005) Sheffield; (2006) Sheffield, Scunthorpe.

CORREY, Ronnie Dean   BORN: 8 November 1966, Bellflower, California, USA.
BRITISH CAREER: (1987-1993) Wolverhampton; (1995) Long Eaton; (1996-1997) Wolverhampton; (1998-1999) Belle Vue; (2000) Wolverhampton; (2004) Belle Vue; (2005) Wolverhampton; (2006) Swindon, Wolverhampton.
MAJOR HONOURS: World Pairs Champion: 1992; World Team Cup Champion: 1992.

COTTHAM, Gary Dominic   BORN: 13 September 1989, Eastbourne, East Sussex.
BRITISH CAREER: (2004-2005) Rye House (Conference League only); (2006) Rye House (Conference League only), Sittingbourne (Conference Shield only).
RIDER LINKS: Son of former rider Gary Cottham (Senior).

COURTNEY, Jamie Mark   BORN: 22 April 1988, Ashington, Northumberland.
BRITISH CAREER: (2003) Rye House (Conference League only), Trelawny (Conference Trophy only); (2004) Swindon (Conference League only), Isle of Wight, Oxford (Conference League only); (2005) Oxford (Conference League only), Workington; (2006) Rye House.
RIDER LINKS: Son of former rider Mark Courtney. Nephew of former rider Sean Courtney. Brother of fellow rider Scott Courtney.

COURTNEY, Scott Lee   BORN: 3 January 1983, Middlesbrough, Cleveland.
BRITISH CAREER: (1999) Glasgow, Linlithgow; (2000) Glasgow, Ashfield; (2001) Glasgow, Buxton, Mildenhall, Trelawny; (2002) Arena-Essex, Rye House (Conference League only); (2003) Poole (British League Cup only), Rye House (Conference League only); (2005) Workington (Premier Trophy only), Oxford (Conference League only); (2006) Stoke (Conference League only).
RIDER LINKS: Son of former rider Mark Courtney. Nephew of former rider Sean Courtney. Brother of fellow rider Jamie Courtney.

CRANG, Maurice Stephen   BORN: 7 October 1987, Darlington, Durham.
BRITISH CAREER: (2006) Stoke (Conference League only), Cleveland (Conference Shield only).
RIDER LINKS: Son of former rider Mark Crang.

CROSS, Andre   BORN: 12 June 1967, Norwich, Norfolk.
BRITISH CAREER: (2002-2004) Wimbledon; (2005) Sittingbourne; (2006) Sittingbourne (Conference Shield only).

CRUMP, Jason Philip   BORN: 6 August 1975, Bristol, Avon.
BRITISH CAREER: (1991) Poole; (1992) Peterborough; (1993) Swindon; (1994-1995) Poole; (1996-1997) Peterborough; (1998) Oxford; (1999) Peterborough; (2000-2001) King's Lynn; (2002-2006) Belle Vue.
MAJOR HONOURS: Australian Under-16 Champion: 1990; Australian Under-21 Champion: 1995; Queensland State Champion: 1995, 1997, 1998, 2001, 2004; Australian Champion: 1995; World Under-21 Champion: 1995; World Team Cup Champion: 1999; Elite League Riders' Champion: 1999, 2001, 2006; World Cup Champion: 2001, 2002; Czech Golden Helmet Champion: 2002, 2006; World Champion: 2004, 2006.
GRAND PRIX: British GP Champion: 1996, 1998, 2006; Swedish GP Champion: 2000, 2001, 2005, 2006; Polish GP Champion: 2001; Czech Republic GP Champion: 2002, 2003, 2004; Danish GP Champion: 2003, 2004; Scandinavian GP Champion: 2005; European GP Champion: 2006; Italian GP Champion: 2006.
RIDER LINKS: Son of former rider Phil Crump. Grandson of former rider Neil Street.

CUNNINGHAM, Glenn Arthur   BORN: 10 June 1975, Bristol, Avon.
BRITISH CAREER: (1991-1992) Oxford; (1993-1996) Swindon; (1997) Reading; (1998) Peterborough; (1999) Swindon; (2000) Peterborough, Belle Vue; (2001) Newport; (2002) Somerset; (2003) Somerset, Eastbourne; (2004) Somerset, Swindon; (2005) Somerset; (2006) Somerset, Reading.
MAJOR HONOUR: Premier League Riders' Champion: 1998.

DALLAWAY, Lewis Steven   BORN: 26 February 1986, Walsall, West Midlands.
BRITISH CAREER: (2004) King's Lynn (Conference Trophy only); (2005) Newport (Conference League only), Weymouth; (2006) Buxton.

DAVIDSSON, Daniel Jan Johan   BORN: 17 March 1983, Mariestad, Sweden.
BRITISH CAREER: (2003) Poole (British League Cup only); (2004) Poole; (2005) Coventry, Peterborough; (2006) Poole.
RIDER LINKS: Son of former rider Jan Davidsson. Brother of fellow rider Jonas Davidsson.

DAVIDSSON, Jonas BORN: 7 August 1984, Motala, Sweden.
BRITISH CAREER: (2003) Reading; (2004) Oxford; (2005) Swindon; (2006) Poole.
MAJOR HONOURS: Finnish Under-21 Champion: 2002; Swedish Under-21 Champion: 2005.
RIDER LINKS: Son of former rider Jan Davidsson. Brother of fellow rider Daniel Davidsson.

DAY, Terry BORN: 26 February 1985, Poole, Dorset
BRITISH CAREER: (2002) Wimbledon; (2003) Newport (Conference League only); (2006) Weymouth (Conference Shield only).

DENNIS, Richie William BORN: 16 April 1988, Boston, Lincolnshire.
BRITISH CAREER: (2003) Peterborough (Conference League only); (2004) Boston, King's Lynn (Conference Trophy only); (2005-2006) Scunthorpe.

DERBYSHIRE, Lee Geoffrey BORN: 3 December 1981, Stockport, Greater Manchester.
BRITISH CAREER: (2002-2004) Buxton; (2005) Buxton, Workington; (2006) Workington.

DICKEN, Lee Charles BORN: 25 August 1978, Hull, East Yorkshire.
BRITISH CAREER: (1994) Buxton; (1995) Hull, Stoke, Peterborough; (1996) Hull, Owlerton, Sheffield; (1997-1998) Hull; (1999) Hull, Exeter; (2000) Hull; (2001) Hull, Arena-Essex; (2002) Newport, Wolverhampton; (2003) Hull, Newcastle; (2004) Newcastle (Conference League & Premier League), Glasgow; (2005) Hull (Premier Trophy only), Sittingbourne, Newport (Premier League & Conference League); (2006) Glasgow.

DOOLAN, Kevin BORN: 30 November 1980, Shepparton, Victoria, Australia.
BRITISH CAREER: (1999-2000) Belle Vue; (2002) Berwick; (2003) Glasgow; (2004) King's Lynn; (2005) King's Lynn, Ipswich; (2006) King's Lynn, Eastbourne.

DORE, Sam Benjamin BORN: 3 January 1987, Warragul, Victoria, Australia.
BRITISH CAREER: (2006) Stoke (Conference League only).

DOYLE, Jason BORN: 6 October 1985, Newcastle, New South Wales, Australia.
BRITISH CAREER: (2005) Isle of Wight; (2006) Isle of Wight, Poole.
RIDER LINKS. Son of former junior rider Kevin Doyle.

DRYML, Ales BORN: 19 October 1979, Pardubice, Czech Republic.
BRITISH CAREER: (2000-02) Oxford; (2003) Belle Vue, Poole; (2004-05) Peterborough; (2006) Oxford.
MAJOR HONOUR: German Under-21 Champion: 1998.
RIDER LINKS: Son of former rider Ales Dryml (senior). Brother of fellow rider Lukas Dryml.

DUFFILL, Jitendra BORN: 19 May 1981, Middlesbrough, Cleveland.
BRITISH CAREER: (1997) Lathallan; (1999) Glasgow, Berwick, Newcastle, Linlithgow, Mildenhall; (2000) Mildenhall; (2006) Cleveland (Conference Shield only).

DUNWORTH, Wayne BORN: 20 January 1967, Nottingham, Nottinghamshire.
BRITISH CAREER: (1984) Boston; (1986) Mildenhall; (2002) Boston, Carmarthen; (2003) Trelawny (Conference Trophy only), Boston, Peterborough (Conference League only), Armadale (Conference Trophy only); (2004) Boston, King's Lynn (Conference Trophy only); (2005) Boston; (2006) Weymouth (Conference Shield only).

ELLIOTT, Martin John   BORN: 30 September 1970, Glasgow, Scotland.
BRITISH CAREER: (2004) Swindon (Conference League only); (2006) Sittingbourne (Conference Shield only)

EMERSON, Martin   BORN: 28 May 1984.
BRITISH CAREER: (2006) Cleveland (Conference Shield only).
RIDER LINKS: Son of former rider Alan Emerson.

ERIKSSON, Freddie Ove   BORN: 23 April 1981, Stockholm, Sweden.
BRITISH CAREER: (2001–2002) King's Lynn; (2003) Ipswich; (2005–2006) Oxford.
MAJOR HONOUR: Swedish Under-21 Champion: 2002.

EVANS, Barrie Charles   BORN: 16 April 1984, King's Lynn, Norfolk.
BRITISH CAREER: (1999) Mildenhall; (2000-2001) Arena-Essex, Mildenhall; (2002) Newport, Rye House (Conference League only); (2003) Hull, Rye House (Conference League only); (2004) Wimbledon, Newport; (2005) Stoke (Premier League & Conference League); (2006) Stoke (Premier League & Conference Shield).
MAJOR HONOUR: Conference League Riders' Champion: 2003.

EZERGAILIS, Karlis Andrejs   BORN: 8 April 1985, Melbourne, Victoria, Australia.
BRITISH CAREER: (2004) Newport (Conference League), Coventry (Conference Trophy only); (2005) Newport (Premier League & Conference League); (2006) Newport (Conference League only).
MAJOR HONOUR: Tasmanian Champion: 2005.

FELTON, Dean Graham   BORN: 18 August 1969, Wolverhampton, West Midlands.
BRITISH CAREER: (1994) Buxton, Oxford, Ipswich; (1995–1996) Buxton; (1997) Buxton, Stoke, Edinburgh, Skegness, Long Eaton, Shuttle Cubs; (1998) Stoke; (1999) Berwick, Glasgow; (2000) Buxton, Berwick; (2001) Stoke, Buxton; (2002–2003) Carmarthen; (2004) Carmarthen, King's Lynn (Conference Trophy only); (2005) Buxton; (2006) Sittingbourne (Conference Shield only).
RIDER LINKS: Nephew of former rider Dave Harvey.

FILMER, Adam   BORN: 26 September 1986, Maidstone, Kent.
BRITISH CAREER: (2005) Weymouth; (2006) Weymouth (Conference Shield only).

FLINT, Gary Georg   BORN: 5 May 1982, Ashington, Durham.
BRITISH CAREER: (1999) Berwick, Linlithgow, St Austell; (2000) Ashfield, Berwick; (2001) Buxton; (2002) Newcastle (Conference League only); (2003) Buxton, Stoke (Conference Trophy only), Sheffield (Conference League only); (2004) Sheffield (Conference Trophy only), Stoke (Conference League only), Oxford (Conference League only); (2005–2006) Stoke (Conference League only).

FORBES, Cecil Roy   BORN: 28 March 1962, Bristol, Avon.
BRITISH CAREER: (2006) Plymouth.

FRAMPTON, Jordan John   BORN: 8 March 1985, Poole, Dorset.
BRITISH CAREER: (2004) Swindon (Conference League only), King's Lynn (Conference Trophy only), Sheffield (Conference Trophy only); (2005) Sittingbourne; (2006) Plymouth, Mildenhall, Weymouth (Conference Shield only).

FRANC, Josef (Pepe)   BORN: 18 January 1979, Kutna Hora, Czech Republic.
BRITISH CAREER: (2001) Berwick; (2003–2004) Berwick; (2005–2006) Newcastle.
MAJOR HONOURS: Czech Republic Under-21 Champion: 1998, 1999, 2000.

FRY, Paul David   BORN: 25 October 1964, Ledbury, Hereford & Worcestershire.
BRITISH CAREER: (1984) Newcastle, Cradley Heath, Arena-Essex; (1986-1987) Cradley Heath; (1988) Stoke; (1989-1990) Long Eaton; (1991) King's Lynn; (1992-1996) Exeter; (1997-1998) Newport; (1999) Stoke; (2000-2002) Swindon; (2003) Swindon, Peterborough; (2004) Somerset, Belle Vue; (2005-2006) Somerset.
RIDER LINKS: Brother of former rider Mark Fry.

GAFUROV, Renat   BORN: 8 October 1982, Oktyabrsky, Russia.
BRITISH CAREER: (2005) Oxford; (2006) Swindon.
MAJOR HONOURS: Russian Under-21 Champion: 2001, 2003; Russian Champion: 2006.

GARROD, Dean John   BORN: 11 October 1975, Norwich, Norfolk.
BRITISH CAREER: (1993) Middlesbrough; (1994) Mildenhall; (1995-1996) Mildenhall, Poole; (1997) Mildenhall, Newport; (1998) Mildenhall, Arena-Essex, Sheffield; (1999) Mildenhall, Buxton; (2000-2003) Boston; (2004) Boston, King's Lynn (Conference Trophy only); Sittingbourne (Conference League KOC only); (2005) Sittingbourne; (2006) Sittingbourne (Conference Shield only).

GIFFARD, Daniel James   BORN: 10 November 1984, Eastbourne, East Sussex.
BRITISH CAREER: (2000) Rye House; (2001) Rye House; (2002) Isle of Wight, Rye House (Conference League & Premier League); (2003) Wimbledon, Eastbourne (British League Cup only), Stoke; (2004) Stoke (Premier League & Conference League), Weymouth; (2005) Weymouth, Hull; (2006) Redcar, Cleveland (Conference Shield only).

GJEDDE, Charlie Rasmussen   BORN: 28 December 1979, Holstebro, Denmark.
BRITISH CAREER: (1998) Swindon; (1999) Coventry, Wolverhampton; (2001) Reading; (2002) Swindon; (2003) Swindon, Oxford; (2004-2005) Swindon; (2006) Reading.
MAJOR HONOURS: Danish Under-21 Champion: 1995; World Cup Champion: 2006.

GLANZ, Nicki Jens   BORN: 6 January 1990, Swindon, Wiltshire.
BRITISH CAREER: (2006) Newport (Conference League only).
RIDER LINKS: Son of former rider Peter Glanz.

GOODY, Luke Steven   BORN: 17 March 1990, Ashford, Kent.
BRITISH CAREER: (2006) Mildenhall (Conference League only), Sittingbourne (Conference Shield only).

GRANT, Alexander Robert (Rob)   BORN: 10 June 1984, Newcastle-upon-Tyne, Tyne and Wear.
BRITISH CAREER: (1999) Linlithgow; (2000) Ashfield, Newcastle; (2001) Newcastle; (2002) Newcastle, Stoke; (2003) Berwick, Sheffield (Conference League only), Stoke; (2004-2005) Stoke (Premier League & Conference League); (2006) Stoke (Conference Shield only).
RIDER LINKS: Son of former rider Rob Grant. Grandson of former rider Alec Grant.

GRIEVES, James Robert   BORN: 28 September 1974, Paisley, Scotland.
BRITISH CAREER: (1991-1995) Glasgow; (1996-1997) Wolverhampton; (1998) Wolverhampton, Berwick; (1999) Edinburgh; (2000-2002) Glasgow; (2003-2004) Glasgow, Wolverhampton; (2005) Newcastle, Wolverhampton; (2006) Newcastle.

HAIGH, David   BORN: 12 December 1984, Whitehaven, Cumbria.
BRITISH CAREER: (2002) Newcastle (Conference League only); (2003) Wimbledon, Newcastle (Conference League only), Peterborough (Conference League only); (2004) Newcastle (Conference League only), Stoke (Conference League only); (2006) Stoke (Conference Shield only).

HAINES, Joseph (Joe) Keir   BORN: 4 September 1991, Bath, Somerset.
  BRITISH CAREER: (2006) Cleveland (Conference Shield only).
  MAJOR HONOUR: British Under-15 Champion: 2006.

HALL, Richard James   BORN: 23 August 1984, Northallerton, North Yorkshire.
  BRITISH CAREER: (2001) Newcastle; (2002) Newcastle (Premier League & Conference League);
  (2003) Sheffield (Conference League only), Coventry (British League Cup only), Boston; (2004) Sheffield
  (Premier League & Conference Trophy), Boston; (2005) Sheffield, Eastbourne; (2006) Peterborough.

HALSEY, Daniel John   BORN: 15 September 1988, Aylesbury, Buckinghamshire.
  BRITISH CAREER: (2005-2006) Rye House (Conference League only).

HAMILL, William (Billy) Gordon   BORN: 23 May 1970, Arcadia, California, USA.
  BRITISH CAREER: (1990-1995) Cradley Heath; (1996) Cradley Heath & Stoke; (1997) Belle Vue;
  (1998-2003) Coventry; (2005) Oxford; (2006) Wolverhampton.
  MAJOR HONOURS: World Team Cup Champion: 1990, 1992, 1993, 1998; World Champion: 1996;
  AMA American Champion: 1999, 2001, 2002; SRA American Champion: 2002.
  GRAND PRIX: Austrian GP Champion: 1995; Swedish GP Champion: 1996; Danish GP Champion:
  1996; Challenge Champion: 1999; Czech Republic GP Champion: 2000, 2001; European GP
  Champion: 2000.

HANCOCK, Gregory (Greg) Alan   BORN: 3 June 1970, Whittier, California, USA.
  BRITISH CAREER: (1989-95) Cradley Heath; (1996) Cradley Heath & Stoke; (1997-01) Coventry;
  (2003-05) Oxford; (2006) Reading.
  MAJOR HONOURS: World Pairs Champion: 1992; World Team Cup Champion: 1992, 1993, 1998;
  AMA American Champion: 1995, 1998, 2000, 2003, 2004, 2005, 2006; World Champion: 1997; Elite
  League Riders' Champion: 1997.
  GRAND PRIX: British GP Champion: 1995, 2004; Czech Republic GP Champion: 1997; Polish GP
  Champion: 1997; Danish GP Champion: 2000; Challenge Champion: 2001; Australian GP Champion:
  2002; Norwegian GP Champion: 2003; Latvian GP Champion: 2006.

HARDING, Trevor Robert   BORN: 1 November 1986, Perth, Western Australia.
  BRITISH CAREER: (2002) Sheffield (Conference League only), Carmarthen; (2003) King's Lynn,
  Boston; (2004) King's Lynn (Premier League & Conference Trophy), Ipswich, Swindon (Conference
  League only); (2005) Rye House (Conference League KOC only), Sheffield, Boston, Somerset,
  Eastbourne; (2006) King's Lynn, Eastbourne.
  MAJOR HONOURS: Australian Under-16 Champion: 2002; Western Australia State Champion: 2005.
  RIDER LINKS: Grandson of former rider Trevor Harding (senior). Brother of fellow rider Daniel Harding.

HARGREAVES, Jack   BORN: 28 May 1988, Shrewsbury, Shropshire.
  BRITISH CAREER: (2003) Wolverhampton (Conference League only); (2004) Stoke (Conference
  League only); (2005) Stoke (Conference League & Premier League); (2006) Redcar, Stoke (Conference
  League only), Cleveland (Conference Shield only).

HARRIS, Christopher (Chris) Calvin   BORN: 28 November 1982, Truro, Cornwall.
  BRITISH CAREER: (1998) St Austell; (1999-2000) Exeter; (2001) Trelawny; (2002-2003) Trelawny,
  Peterborough; (2004-2006) Coventry.

HARRISON, Russell (Rusty) Wade   BORN: 11 October 1981, Adelaide, South Australia, Australia.
  BRITISH CAREER: (2000) Glasgow; (2001-2004) Workington; (2005) Edinburgh, Belle Vue; (2006)
  Edinburgh, Workington.

MAJOR HONOURS: Australian Under-16 Champion: 1995, 1997; Australian Under-21 Champion: 2001; South Australia State Champion: 2003.

HAUZINGER, Manuel   BORN: 3 December 1982, Vienna, Austria.
BRITISH CAREER: (2005) Isle of Wight; (2006) Newcastle.
MAJOR HONOURS: Austrian Champion: 2002, 2005; Austrian/Croatian Champion: 2004.

HAVELOCK, Robert Gary   BORN: 4 November 1968, Eaglescliffe, Yarm, Cleveland.
BRITISH CAREER: (1985) Middlesbrough, King's Lynn, Wolverhampton; (1986) Middlesbrough, Bradford; (1987-1988) Bradford; (1990-1997) Bradford; (1998) Eastbourne, Poole; (1999-2002) Poole; (2003-2004) Peterborough; (2005) Arena-Essex; (2006) Redcar.
MAJOR HONOURS: British Under-21 Champion: 1986; European Junior Champion: 1987; British Champion: 1991, 1992; Overseas Champion: 1992; World Champion: 1992; Premier League Riders' Champion: 1995.
RIDER LINKS: Son of former rider Brian Havelock.

HAWKINS, Ritchie Mark   BORN: 9 November 1983, Peterborough, Cambridgeshire.
BRITISH CAREER: (2000) Sheffield (Conference League only); (2001) Swindon, Sheffield (Conference League only); (2002) Swindon (Premier League & Conference Trophy); (2003) Swindon (Premier League & Conference League), Peterborough (British League Cup only); (2004) Mildenhall, Berwick; (2005) Somerset, Peterborough; (2006) Workington, Swindon.
MAJOR HONOUR: British Under-21 Champion: 2004.
RIDER LINKS: Son of former rider Kevin Hawkins.

HAYES, Grant Lincoln   BORN: 24 January 1989, Halifax, West Yorkshire.
BRITISH CAREER: (2004) Weymouth, Sheffield (Conference Trophy only); (2005-2006) Scunthorpe.
RIDER LINKS: Son of former junior rider Geoff Hayes.

HEATH, Trevor Michael   BORN: 21 March 1989, Cuckfield, West Sussex.
BRITISH CAREER: (2004) Sheffield (Conference Trophy only); (2005-2006) Mildenhall.
RIDER LINKS: Cousin of fellow rider Sam Heath.

HEFENBROCK, Christian   BORN: 15 May 1985, Liebenthal, Germany.
BRITISH CAREER: (2006) Wolverhampton.
MAJOR HONOURS: German Under-21 Champion: 2001, 2005; German Champion: 2006.

HENRY, Christian   BORN: 20 February 1981, Sydney, New South Wales, Australia.
BRITISH CAREER: (2000) Edinburgh, Ashfield; (2001-2002) Edinburgh; (2003) Glasgow; (2005-2006) Newcastle.

HENRY, Shane   BORN: 20 August 1980.
BRITISH CAREER: (2006) Mildenhall (Conference League only).
RIDER LINKS: Son of former rider Robert Henry.

HILL, Thomas Matthew   BORN: 16 September 1986, Sheffield, South Yorkshire.
BRITISH CAREER: (2003) Peterborough (Conference League only), Wolverhampton (Conference League only); (2004) Buxton, Newport (Conference League only), Weymouth; (2006) Weymouth (Conference Shield only).

HLIB, Pawel   BORN: 20 February 1986, Gorzow, Poland.
BRITISH CAREER: (2006) Coventry.
MAJOR HONOUR: World Under-21 Team Cup Champion: 2006.

HODGSON, Daniel (Danny) Lee   BORN: 21 January 1982, Bradford, West Yorkshire.
BRITISH CAREER: (1998) Buxton; (1999) King's Lynn (Conference League only); (2000) Buxton,
Hull; (2001) Sheffield, Newport (Conference League only), Somerset; (2003) Carmarthen; (2004) King's
Lynn (Conference Trophy only); (2006) Buxton.

HODGSON, Russell (Rusty)   BORN: 29 March 1981, Hutton Rudby, Cleveland.
BRITISH CAREER: (2006) Cleveland (Conference Shield only).
RIDER LINKS: Son of former rider Russ Hodgson. Grandson of former rider Frank Hodgson.
Nephew of former rider Jack Hodgson.

HOLDER, Christopher (Chris)   BORN: 24 September 1987, Appin, Sydney, New South Wales,
Australia.
BRITISH CAREER: (2006) Isle of Wight.
MAJOR HONOURS: Australian Under-21 Champion: 2005, 2006; New South Wales State
Champion: 2006.

HOPWOOD, Ben   BORN: 13 March 1991, Salford, Greater Manchester.
BRITISH CAREER: (2006) Mildenhall (Conference League), Stoke (Conference Shield only).

HOWE, David Peter   BORN: 1 March 1982, Leicester, Leicestershire.
BRITISH CAREER: (1997) Peterborough (Academy League only); (1998) Peterborough, Norfolk;
(1999-2001) Peterborough; (2002-2005) Wolverhampton; (2006) Oxford.
MAJOR HONOUR: British Under-21 Champion: 2000.

HUGHES, Kyle Richard   BORN: 15 June 1989, Bath, Somerset.
BRITISH CAREER: (2004) Mildenhall; (2005) Oxford (Conference League only); (2006) Boston.

HURRY, Paul William George   BORN: 9 April 1975, Canterbury, Kent.
BRITISH CAREER: (1991) Arena-Essex; (1992-1993) Peterborough; (1994-1995) Arena-Essex; (1996)
London; (1997) King's Lynn; (1998-1999) Oxford; (2000) Eastbourne; (2001-2002) Wolverhampton;
(2003) Ipswich; (2004-2006) Arena-Essex.
MAJOR HONOUR: British Under-21 Champion: 1994.

HURST, Samuel (Sam) Melvin   BORN: 28 April 1989, Southampton, Hampshire.
BRITISH CAREER: (2004) Newport (Conference League only), King's Lynn (Conference Trophy
only); (2005) Newport (Conference League only); (2006) Newport (Premier League & Conference
League).

IRVING, Gary Michael   BORN: 1 March 1989, Carlisle, Cumbria.
BRITISH CAREER: (2006) Cleveland (Conference Shield only).
RIDER LINKS: Son of former rider Michael Irving.

IRVING, Kriss Jackson   BORN: 3 April 1987, Whitehaven, Cumbria.
BRITISH CAREER: (2003) Newcastle (Conference League only); (2004) Newcastle (Conference
League only), Stoke (Conference League only); (2005-2006) Stoke (Conference League only).
RIDER LINKS: Nephew of former rider Greg Irving.

IRWIN, Nathan Christopher Terence BORN: 28 March 1983, Cuckfield, Sussex.
BRITISH CAREER: (1999) King's Lynn (Conference League only); (2000) Peterborough (Conference League only); (2002) Wimbledon; (2004) Weymouth, Swindon (Conference League only); (2005-2006) Boston.
RIDER LINKS: Nephew of former junior rider Nick Irwin.

ISHERWOOD, Gareth Andrew BORN: 28 November 1988, Manchester, Greater Manchester.
BRITISH CAREER: (2005) Stoke (Conference League only); (2006) Stoke (Conference League only), Buxton.

IVERSEN, Niels-Kristian Trochmann BORN: 20 June 1982, Esbjerg, Denmark.
BRITISH CAREER: (2001) King's Lynn; (2003) Newport, Oxford; (2004-2005) Oxford; (2006) Peterborough.
MAJOR HONOURS: Danish Under-21 Champion: 2002; World Cup Champion: 2006.

JAMES, Scott Terry BORN: 25 May 1984, Adelaide, South Australia.
BRITISH CAREER: (2002) Workington, Mildenhall; (2003) Mildenhall, Coventry (British League Cup only); (2005) Wimbledon, Workington; (2006) Buxton.

JANNIRO, Billy Mitchell BORN: 30 July 1980, Vallejo, California, USA.
BRITISH CAREER: (2001-2004) Coventry; (2005) Peterborough, Coventry; (2006) Coventry.
MAJOR HONOUR: SRA American Champion: 2004.

JANSSON, Kim Patrik BORN: 30 October 1981, Gothenburg, Sweden.
BRITISH CAREER: (2002-2006) Ipswich.

JAROS, Jan BORN: 11 November 1984, Prague, Czech Republic.
BRITISH CAREER: (2003) King's Lynn (British League Cup only); (2004) Belle Vue; (2005) King's Lynn; (2006) Ipswich.

JENSEN, Jesper Bruun BORN: 14 October 1977, Esbjerg, Denmark.
BRITISH CAREER: (1997-2003) Wolverhampton; (2004) Ipswich; (2005) Oxford, Peterborough; (2006) Peterborough.
MAJOR HONOURS: Nordic Under-21 Champion: 1995; World Team Cup Champion: 1997; World Under-21 Champion: 1997; European Champion: 2005.

JOHNSON, Ashley BORN: 29 September 1984, Middlesbrough, Cleveland.
BRITISH CAREER: (2004) Newcastle (Conference League only); (2005) Scunthorpe; (2006) Cleveland (Conference Shield only).

JOHNSON, Benjamin (Ben) BORN: 17 December 1989, Manchester, Greater Manchester.
BRITISH CAREER: (2006) Boston.

JOHNSON, Christopher (Chris) Simon BORN: 13 October 1987, Chichester, Sussex.
BRITISH CAREER: (2002) Wimbledon; (2003) Oxford (Conference League only), Trelawny (Conference Trophy only), Isle of Wight; (2004) Isle of Wight, Swindon (Conference League only), King's Lynn (Conference Trophy only); (2005) Reading, Rye House (Conference League only), Mildenhall; (2006) Isle of Wight, Plymouth, Weymouth (Conference Shield only).

JOHNSON, Peter Collin BORN: 5 December 1976, Middlesbrough, Cleveland.
BRITISH CAREER: (1994) Cleveland; (1995) Berwick, Linlithgow; (1996) Berwick; (1997) Berwick

(Amateur League only); (1998) Berwick; (1999) Newcastle, Mildenhall; (2006) Weymouth (Conference Shield only).
RIDER LINKS: Son of former rider Brian Johnson.

JOHNSTON, Steven (Steve) Paul   BORN: 12 October 1971, Kalgoorlie, Western Australia.
BRITISH CAREER: (1992) Sheffield; (1993) Sheffield, Long Eaton; (1994-1996) Long Eaton; (1997) Ipswich; (1998-2002) Oxford; (2003) Belle Vue; (2004) Swindon; (2005) Wolverhampton; (2006) Arena-Essex.
MAJOR HONOURS: Western Australia State Champion: 1993, 1996, 2004.

JONES, Steven Paul   BORN: 27 September 1979, Gateshead, Tyne and Wear.
BRITISH CAREER: (1997) Lathallan; (1998) Edinburgh, Newcastle; (1999) Newcastle, Linlithgow; (2002-2003) Newcastle (Conference League only); (2004) Carmarthen; (2006) Cleveland (Conference Shield only).

JONSSON, Andreas Karl Rune   BORN: 3 September 1980, Hallstavik, Sweden.
BRITISH CAREER: (1998-1999) Coventry; (2001-2005) Coventry; (2006) Arena-Essex.
MAJOR HONOURS: Swedish Under-21 Champion: 1998, 2000; World Under-21 Champion: 2000; World Cup Champion: 2003, 2004; Swedish Champion: 2006.
GRAND PRIX: Scandinavian GP Champion: 2006.

JUUL SORENSEN, Richard Kristian BORN: 30 October 1970, Copenhagen, Denmark.
BRITISH CAREER: (1991-1994) Newcastle; (1995) Wolverhampton; (1997) Newcastle, Berwick; (1998) Stoke; (1999) Wolverhampton; (2000) Glasgow, Isle of Wight; (2001-2005) Newcastle; (2006) Redcar (Premier Trophy only), Workington.

KARLSSON, Magnus Erik   BORN: 28 December 1981, Gullspang, Sweden.
BRITISH CAREER: (2002) Edinburgh; (2003) Edinburgh, Wolverhampton; (2004) Hull, Wolverhampton; (2005-2006) Wolverhampton.
RIDER LINKS: Son of former rider Gunnar Karlsson. Brother of fellow riders Peter Karlsson and Mikael Max.

KARLSSON, Peter Gunnar   BORN: 17 December 1969, Gullspang, Sweden.
BRITISH CAREER: (1990) Wolverhampton; (1992-1997) Wolverhampton; (1999) Wolverhampton; (2000) Peterborough; (2001) King's Lynn, Belle Vue; (2002-2003) Wolverhampton; (2005) Peterborough; (2006) Wolverhampton.
MAJOR HONOURS: Nordic Under-21 Champion: 1989; Swedish Champion: 1989, 1991; World Team Cup Champion: 2000; World Cup Champion: 2003, 2004.
GRAND PRIX: Challenge Champion: 2000.
RIDER LINKS: Son of former rider Gunnar Karlsson. Brother of fellow riders Magnus Karlsson and Mikael Max.

KASPRZAK, Krzysztof   BORN: 18 July 1984, Leszno, Poland.
BRITISH CAREER: (2003-2006) Poole.
MAJOR HONOURS: European Champion: 2003; World Under-21 Champion: 2005; World Under-21 Team Cup Champion: 2005.
RIDER LINKS: Son of former rider Zenon Kasprzak. Brother of fellow rider Robert Kasprzak.

KASPRZAK, Robert   BORN: 8 April 1987, Leszno, Poland.
BRITISH CAREER: (2006) Isle of Wight (Premier Trophy only).
RIDER LINKS: Son of former rider Zenon Kasprzak. Brother of fellow rider Krzysztof Kasprzak.

KATT, Stephan   BORN: 15 September 1979, Kiel, Germany.
BRITISH CAREER: (2003) Somerset; (2006) Somerset.

KENNETT, Edward David   BORN: 28 August 1986, Hastings, Sussex.
BRITISH CAREER: (2001) Rye House, Mildenhall; (2002-2003) Rye House (Conference League & Premier League), Eastbourne; (2004) Eastbourne; (2005) Rye House, Poole; (2006) Rye House, Eastbourne.
MAJOR HONOUR: British Under-21 Champion: 2005.
RIDER LINKS: Son of former rider Dave Kennett. Nephew of former riders Gordon and Barney Kennett.

KERR, Christopher (Chris) Robert   BORN: 28 June 1984, Grass Valley, California, USA.
BRITISH CAREER: (2006) Redcar.

KESSLER, Robert (Robbie)   BORN: 5 April 1973, Neuwied, Germany.
BRITISH CAREER: (1994) Sheffield; (1996-1997) Sheffield; (1999) King's Lynn; (2000-2001) Sheffield; (2002) Hull; (2003) Stoke; (2004) Stoke, Peterborough; (2005-2006) Stoke.
MAJOR HONOURS: German Under-21 Champion: 1992, 1993.
RIDER LINKS: Son of former rider Johann Kessler.

KING, Daniel Robert   BORN: 14 August 1986, Maidstone, Kent.
BRITISH CAREER: (2001) Peterborough (Conference League only); (2002) Peterborough (Conference League only), Swindon (Conference Trophy only); (2003) Peterborough (Conference League only), Ipswich (British League Cup only), Reading, Mildenhall, Arena-Essex; (2004) Ipswich, Mildenhall; (2005) Rye House, Ipswich; (2006) Mildenhall, Ipswich.
MAJOR HONOUR: British Under-18 Champion: 2004.
RIDER LINKS: Brother of fellow rider Jason King.

KING, Jason Gary   BORN: 13 April 1985, Maidstone, Kent.
BRITISH CAREER: (2000-2001) Peterborough (Conference League only); (2002) Swindon (Premier League & Conference Trophy), Peterborough (Conference League only); (2003) Arena-Essex, Peterborough (Conference League only); (2004) Mildenhall, Rye House; (2005) Somerset, Newport; (2006) Mildenhall.
RIDER LINKS: Brother of fellow rider Daniel King.

KOLODZIEJ, Janusz   BORN: 27 May 1984, Tarnow, Poland.
BRITISH CAREER: (2003) Reading; (2006) Reading.
MAJOR HONOURS: Polish Under-21 Champion: 2004; Polish Champion: 2005; World Under-21 Team Cup Champion: 2005.

KORNELIUSSEN, Mads Klit   BORN: 15 June 1983, Aalborg, Denmark.
BRITISH CAREER: (2003-2004) Newport; (2005) Newport, Swindon; (2006) Swindon.
RIDER LINKS: Brother of former rider Tim Korneliussen.

KRAMER, Emil   BORN: 14 November 1979, Mariestad, Sweden.
BRITISH CAREER: (2002) King's Lynn, Hull; (2003) Hull; (2004-2005) Hull, Oxford; (2006) Somerset.

KRONER, Tobias   BORN: 16 October 1985, Dohren, Nr Bremen, Germany.
BRITISH CAREER: (2005) Oxford; (2006) Ipswich.

KSIEZAK, Robert   BORN: 15 January 1987, Pooraka, Adelaide, South Australia.
  BRITISH CAREER: (2005) Edinburgh; (2006) Glasgow.

KYLMAKORPI, Joonas Nikolai   BORN: 14 February 1980, Stockholm, Sweden.
  BRITISH CAREER: (2001) Eastbourne; (2002) Ipswich; (2003) Arena-Essex, Eastbourne; (2004) Eastbourne; (2005) Peterborough, Coventry; (2006) Arena-Essex.
  MAJOR HONOURS: Swedish Under-21 Champion: 1999; Nordic Under-21 Champion: 2001.

LAMB, Jessica Nancy   BORN: 5 February 1977, Poole, Dorset.
  BRITISH CAREER: (2001) Boston; (2003) Somerset (Conference Trophy only), Trelawny (Conference Trophy only); (2005) Armadale, Scunthorpe; (2006) Plymouth.

LAMBERT, Simon James   BORN: 21 February 1989, Boston, Lincolnshire.
  BRITISH CAREER: (2004) Boston, King's Lynn (Conference Trophy only); (2005) Boston; (2006) King's Lynn (Premier Trophy only), Boston.

LANGLEY, Karl   BORN: 2 June 1981, Whitehaven, Cumbria
  BRITISH CAREER: (2002) Workington; (2003) Newcastle (Conference League only), Armadale, Mildenhall; (2004) Newcastle (Conference League only), Sheffield (Conference Trophy only); (2005) Armadale; (2006) Cleveland (Conference Shield only).

LANHAM, Leigh Stefan   BORN: 15 August 1977, Ipswich, Suffolk.
  BRITISH CAREER: (1993) Ipswich, Arena-Essex; (1994-1996) Ipswich; (1997) Exeter, Bradford, King's Lynn; (1998-1999) Arena-Essex; (2001) Arena-Essex; (2002-2003) Arena-Essex, Ipswich; (2004-2006) Arena-Essex.
  MAJOR HONOUR: British Under-21 Champion: 1997.
  RIDER LINKS: Son of former rider Mike Lanham.

LAURENCE, Nicholas (Nick) Steven   BORN: 14 June 1990, Eastbourne, East Sussex.
  BRITISH CAREER: (2006) Weymouth (Conference Shield only).

LAWSON, William   BORN: 27 February 1987, Perth, Perthshire, Scotland.
  BRITISH CAREER: (2002) Newcastle (Conference League only); (2003) Newcastle (Premier League & Conference League); (2004) Newcastle (Premier League & Conference League); (2005) Edinburgh, Armadale; (2006) Edinburgh, Wolverhampton.
  MAJOR HONOUR: British Under-18 Champion: 2005.

LEGAULT, Kyle Patrick   BORN: 30 May 1985, St Catharines, Ontario, Canada.
  BRITISH CAREER: (2005-2006) Sheffield.
  MAJOR HONOURS: Canadian Champion: 2003, 2004, 2006.
  RIDER LINKS: Son of former rider Fred Legault.

LEGG, Billy Peter   BORN: 6 September 1988, Swindon, Wiltshire.
  BRITISH CAREER: (2003) Swindon (Conference League only); (2004) Newport (Conference League only), Mildenhall, Weymouth; (2005) Newport (Conference League only); (2006) Newport (Premier League & Conference League).

LEMON, Mark Ian John   BORN: 12 February 1973, Bairnsdale, Victoria, Australia.
  BRITISH CAREER: (1990) Poole; (1991) Poole, Middlesbrough; (1992) Middlesbrough, Long Eaton; (1996) Oxford; (1997-1998) Poole; (1999) Eastbourne, Hull; (2000) Oxford; (2002) Oxford; (2003)

Somerset, Belle Vue; (2004) Exeter, Poole; (2005) Exeter; (2006) Stoke, Reading.
MAJOR HONOURS: Victoria State Champion: 1993, 1996.

LEVERINGTON, Trent Ashley   BORN: 13 May 1980, Brisbane, Queensland, Australia.
BRITISH CAREER: (2003) Glasgow, Armadale, Wolverhampton (Conference League only); (2004) Buxton, Stoke; (2005) Glasgow; (2006) Stoke.

LINDBACK, Antonio   BORN: 5 May 1985, Rio De Janeiro, Brazil.
BRITISH CAREER: (2003-2006) Poole.
MAJOR HONOURS: World Cup Champion: 2004; European Under-19 Champion: 2004; Swedish Under-21 Champion: 2006.
GRAND PRIX: Grand Final Champion: 2004.

LINDGREN, Jan Fredrik   BORN: 15 September 1985, Orebro, Sweden.
BRITISH CAREER: (2003-2006) Wolverhampton.
MAJOR HONOURS: Swedish Under-21 Champion: 2003, 2004.
RIDER LINKS: Son of former rider Tommy Lindgren.

LITTLE, Kevin John   BORN: 24 September 1972, Edinburgh, Scotland.
BRITISH CAREER: (1989) Glasgow, Berwick; (1990-1991) Berwick; (1992) Bradford; (1993) Edinburgh; (1994) Edinburgh, Berwick; (1995) Berwick, Belle Vue, Edinburgh, Coventry; (1996) Coventry; (1997) Berwick; (1998-2000) Edinburgh; (2001-2004) Newcastle; (2005) Workington; (2006) Redcar.
MAJOR HONOUR: Academy League Riders' Champion: 1995.

LORAM, Mark Royston Gregory   BORN: 12 January 1971, Mtarfa, Malta.
BRITISH CAREER: (1987) Hackney; (1988) Hackney, King's Lynn, Belle Vue, Reading, Swindon; (1989) Ipswich; (1990-1994) King's Lynn; (1995-1996) Exeter; (1997) Bradford; (1998) Wolverhampton; (1999-2000) Poole; (2001) Peterborough; (2002-2003) Eastbourne; (2004-2005) Arena-Essex; (2006) Ipswich.
MAJOR HONOURS: British Under-21 Champion: 1988; National League Riders' Champion: 1989; Commonwealth Champion: 1994; British Champion: 1997, 1999, 2001; Overseas Champion: 1999; World Champion: 2000.
GRAND PRIX: Danish GP Champion: 1997; Swedish GP Champion: 1999.

LOUIS, Christopher (Chris)   BORN: 9 July 1969, Ipswich, Suffolk.
BRITISH CAREER: (1988) Hackney, Wolverhampton, King's Lynn, Ipswich; (1989-2002) Ipswich; (2004-2006) Ipswich.
MAJOR HONOURS: World Under-21 Champion: 1990; British Champion: 1998, 2000.
RIDER LINKS: Son of former rider John Louis.

LOWE, Adam   BORN: 17 February 1989, Leicester, Leicestershire.
BRITISH CAREER: (2005) Boston; (2006) Stoke (Conference League only).

LYONS, Jason Rodney   BORN: 15 June 1970, Mildura, Victoria, Australia.
BRITISH CAREER: (1990-1991) Glasgow; (1992-2003) Belle Vue; (2004) Poole, Newcastle; (2005) Belle Vue; (2006) Mildenhall.
MAJOR HONOURS: Victoria State Champion: 1997, 1998, 1999; Overseas Champion: 1998, 2001; South Australia State Champion: 1999; World Team Cup Champion: 1999; World Cup Champion: 2002.
RIDER LINKS: Son of former rider Rod Lyons.

McALLAN, David John   BORN: 20 June 1980, Edinburgh, Scotland.
BRITISH CAREER: (1996) Berwick; (1997) Berwick (Premier League & Amateur League), Sheffield; (1998) Berwick, Newcastle; (1999) Edinburgh, Linlithgow; (2000) Ashfield, Stoke; (2001) Berwick, Boston, Workington; (2002) Glasgow, Sheffield (Conference League only); (2003-2004) Glasgow, Boston; (2005) Sittingbourne, Edinburgh, Boston; (2006) Glasgow.

McCLOUD, Alex   BORN: 16 August 1990.
BRITISH CAREER: (2006) Scunthorpe.

McDADE, Cal   BORN: 25 April 1987, Glasgow, Scotland.
BRITISH CAREER: (2004) Swindon (Conference League only); (2005) Armadale; (2006) Boston.

McGOWAN, Travis   BORN: 13 January 1981, Mildura, Victoria, Australia.
BRITISH CAREER: (1999-2000) King's Lynn; (2002) King's Lynn; (2003-2005) Oxford; (2006) Reading.
MAJOR HONOURS: Australian Under-16 Champion: 1993; Australian Under-21 Champion: 1998, 2000, 2002; Victoria State Champion: 2001, 2002, 2003, 2004, 2005.

McKINNA, Adam Kenneth   BORN: 17 August 1986, Crewe, Cheshire.
BRITISH CAREER: (2004-2005) Armadale; (2006) Newcastle, Scunthorpe.
RIDER LINKS: Son of former rider Kenny McKinna. Nephew of former riders Charlie and Martin McKinna.

MADSEN, Tom Paarup   BORN: 24 November 1977, Esbjerg, Denmark.
BRITISH CAREER: (1999) Berwick; (2000-2002) King's Lynn; (2003) Ipswich, King's Lynn; (2004) King's Lynn, Oxford, Berwick; (2005) Oxford, Berwick; (2006) Belle Vue.

MAKOVSKY, Michal   BORN: 6 April 1976, Hradec Kralove, Czech Republic.
BRITISH CAREER: (2001-2004) Berwick; (2005) Berwick, Oxford; (2006) Berwick.
MAJOR HONOUR: Czech Republic Champion: 1999.

MALLETT, Darren Carl   BORN: 25 May 1986, Boston, Lincolnshire.
BRITISH CAREER: (2001) Somerset, Boston; (2002) Boston; (2003) Boston, King's Lynn; (2004) King's Lynn (Premier League & Conference Trophy), Boston; (2005) Boston, King's Lynn (Young Shield only); (2006) Boston.
RIDER LINKS: Son of former rider Dennis Mallett.

MALLETT, Nicholas (Nick) John   BORN: 12 May 1987, Newport, Gwent, South Wales.
BRITISH CAREER: (2002) Swindon (Conference Trophy only); (2003-2004) Newport (Conference League only); (2006) Stoke (Conference Shield only).

MARSH, Krister Lee   BORN: 23 March 1976, Hereford, Hereford & Worcestershire.
BRITISH CAREER: (1995) Devon; (1996) Swindon (Conference League & Premier League), Sheffield, London; (1997) Oxford (AL & Premier League), Reading; (1998) Reading; (1999) Swindon; (2000) Reading, Newcastle; (2001) Newport, Swindon, Exeter; (2002-2003) Exeter; (2004) Isle of Wight; (2005) Isle of Wight, Belle Vue; (2006) Isle of Wight.
RIDER LINKS: Son-in-law of former rider Martin Yeates.

MARTIN, Sam Alan   BORN: 8 February 1989, Bedford Park, Adelaide, South Australia.
BRITISH CAREER: (2004-2005) Oxford (Conference League only); (2006) Boston.
RIDER LINKS: Son of former rider Mark Martin.

MASON, David Lee   BORN: 20 December 1976, Crawley, West Sussex.
BRITISH CAREER: (1995) Sittingbourne, Reading, Arena-Essex, Swindon, Poole, Oxford; (1996) Sittingbourne, London, Reading; (1997) Arena-Essex; (1998) Newport, Stoke, Arena-Essex, Mildenhall; (1999) Swindon, Rye House; (2000) Rye House, Arena-Essex, Poole; (2001-2003) Rye House; (2004–2005) Weymouth; (2006) Weymouth (Conference Shield only).
MAJOR HONOUR: Conference League Riders' Champion: 2001.

MASON, Karl Lewis   BORN: 4 March 1986, Hillingdon, London.
BRITISH CAREER: (2001) Buxton, Mildenhall, Somerset; (2002) Newport (Conference League only); (2003) Newport (Conference League & Premier League); (2004) Newport (Premier League & Conference League), Coventry (Conference Trophy only); (2005) Newport (Conference League & Premier League); (2006) Newport (Conference League only).

MAX, Karl Mikael Karlsson   BORN: 21 August 1973, Amneharad, Gullspang, Sweden.
BRITISH CAREER: (1993-1994) Wolverhampton; (1996-1999) Wolverhampton; (2001-2005) Wolverhampton; (2006) Arena-Essex.
MAJOR HONOURS: Swedish Under-21 Champion: 1992; World Under-21 Champion: 1994; World Team Cup Champion: 1994, 2000; World Cup Champion: 2003, 2004.
RIDER LINKS: Son of former rider Gunnar Karlsson. Brother of fellow riders Peter and Magnus Karlsson.
NOTE: Rode as Mikael Karlsson prior to 2003.

MEAKINS, Gordon   BORN: 18 March 1974, Aylesbury, Buckinghamshire.
BRITISH CAREER: (1999) King's Lynn (Conference League only); (2000) Peterborough (Conference League only); (2001) Buxton; (2002) Carmarthen; (2003) Carmarthen, Somerset (British League Cup only); (2004) Carmarthen; (2006) Weymouth (Conference Shield only).
RIDER LINKS: Father of junior rider Scott Meakins. Son of former junior rider Nigel Meakins.

MEAR, Robert   BORN: 12 January 1989, Welwyn Garden City, Hertfordshire.
BRITISH CAREER: (2004-2006) Rye House (Conference League only).

MELDRUM, David   BORN: 6 October 1977, Berwick-upon-Tweed, Northumberland.
BRITISH CAREER: (1994-1995) Berwick; (1996) Berwick, Eastbourne (Conference League only); (1997) Berwick (Premier League & AL); (1998) Berwick, Buxton; (1999-2001) Berwick; (2002) Somerset, Wimbledon; (2003) Berwick; (2004) Berwick, Newcastle (Premier League & Conference League); (2005) Sittingbourne, Stoke; (2006) Berwick, Stoke (Conference Shield/Trophy only).
RIDER LINKS: Nephew of former rider Andy Meldrum.

MESSING, Andreas   BORN: 28 January 1987, Hallstavik, Sweden.
BRITISH CAREER: (2006) Arena-Essex.

MIEDZINSKI, Adrian   BORN: 20 August 1985, Torun, Poland.
BRITISH CAREER: (2004) Eastbourne; (2006) Swindon.
MAJOR HONOURS: Polish Under-21 Champion: 2005; World Under-21 Team Cup Champion: 2006.
RIDER LINKS: Son of former rider Stanislaw Miedzinski.

MILLS, Christopher (Chris) William   BORN: 29 March 1983, Chelmsford, Essex.
BRITISH CAREER: (2001) Arena-Essex; (2002) King's Lynn (Conference League only), Wimbledon (Conference Trophy only); (2003) Isle of Wight, Oxford (Conference League only); (2004) Reading, Oxford (Conference League only); (2005) Reading (Premier Trophy only), Oxford (EL & Conference League), Somerset; (2006) King's Lynn, Reading.

MISKOWIAK, Robert   BORN: 21 November 1983, Rawicz, Poland.
  BRITISH CAREER: (2005-06) Ipswich.
  MAJOR HONOUR: World Under-21 Champion: 2004.

MOGRIDGE, Alan John   BORN: 6 November 1963, Westminster, London.
  BRITISH CAREER: (1981) Wimbledon; (1982-1983) Crayford, Wimbledon; (1984) Canterbury,
  Wolverhampton; (1985) Hackney; (1986) Canterbury, Rye House, Ipswich, Hackney; (1987)
  Hackney; (1988) Hackney, Sheffield, Bradford; (1989-1990) Ipswich; (1991-1992) Arena-Essex; (1993)
  Peterborough; (1994) Middlesbrough, Sheffield; (1995) Arena-Essex; (1996) London, Eastbourne; (1997)
  Eastbourne; (1999-2000) Berwick; (2001) Swindon; (2002-2005) Stoke; (2006) Stoke, Workington.

MOLLER, Henrik   BORN: 3 September 1985, Fredericia, Denmark.
  BRITISH CAREER: (2004) Peterborough; (2006) Edinburgh.

MOORE, Andrew David   BORN: 6 October 1982, Lincoln, Lincolnshire.
  BRITISH CAREER: (1998) Skegness, Norfolk; (1999) Mildenhall, Sheffield; (2000) Sheffield
  (Conference League & Premier League), Berwick; (2001) Sheffield (Conference League & Premier
  League); (2002-2003) Sheffield; (2004) Sheffield, Swindon, Eastbourne; (2005) Eastbourne; (2006)
  Eastbourne, Mildenhall.
  RIDER LINKS: Son of former junior rider Richard Moore.

MORRIS, Phillip (Phil) William   BORN: 10 September 1975, Newport, Gwent, South Wales.
  BRITISH CAREER: (1991-1996) Reading; (1997) Stoke; (1998-2003) Reading; (2004) Reading, Poole;
  (2005) Newcastle, Arena-Essex; (2006) Belle Vue.

MORRISON, John Robin   BORN: 14 January 1988, Ashington, Northumberland.
  BRITISH CAREER: (2004) Berwick (Premier Trophy only), Isle of Wight, Swindon (Conference
  League only), Newcastle (Conference League only); (2006) Stoke (Conference League KOC only).

MORTON, Raymond (Ray) Paul BORN: 19 June 1968, Peckham, London.
  BRITISH CAREER: (1985-1987) King's Lynn; (1988) Wimbledon, King's Lynn; (1989-1990)
  Wimbledon; (1991-1992) Reading; (1993) Poole; (1994-1995) Reading; (1996) Reading, Hull; (1998)
  Isle of Wight; (1999) Hull; (2000-2003) Isle of Wight; (2004) Isle of Wight, Arena-Essex; (2005) Poole,
  Exeter; (2006) Isle of Wight.

NAYLOR, Philip   BORN: 2 August 1986.
  BRITISH CAREER: (2006) Stoke (Conference Trophy only).

NEATH, Christopher (Chris)   BORN: 29 January 1982, Worcester, Hereford & Worcestershire.
  BRITISH CAREER: (1998-1999) Newport (Conference League & Premier League); (2000-2001)
  Newport; (2002-2003) Swindon, Wolverhampton; (2004) Rye House, Wolverhampton; (2005-2006)
  Rye House.

NERMARK, Daniel Karl   BORN: 30 July 1977, Karlstad, Sweden.
  BRITISH CAREER: (2001-2002) Wolverhampton; (2003) Ipswich; (2004) Wolverhampton; (2005)
  Edinburgh; (2006) King's Lynn.
  RIDER LINKS: Son of former junior rider, Anders Nermark.

NICHOLLS, Scott Karl   BORN: 16 May 1978, Ipswich, Suffolk.
  BRITISH CAREER: (1994) Peterborough; (1995-1998) Ipswich; (1999-2000) Poole; (2001-2004)
  Ipswich; (2005-2006) Coventry.

MAJOR HONOURS: British Under-21 Champion: 1998, 1999; British Champion: 2002, 2003, 2005, 2006; Czech Golden Helmet Champion: 2005.
RIDER LINKS: Brother of former rider Shaun Nicholls.

NIEMINEN, Kauko Tapio   BORN: 29 August 1979, Seinajoki, Finland.
BRITISH CAREER: (2002-2005) Workington; (2006) Glasgow.
MAJOR HONOURS: Finnish Under-21 Champion: 1998, 1999, 2000.

NORRIS, David Michael   BORN: 20 August 1972, Eastbourne, East Sussex.
BRITISH CAREER: (1988-1989) Eastbourne; (1990-1992) Ipswich; (1993) Ipswich, Eastbourne; (1994) Eastbourne; (1995) Reading; (1996-2006) Eastbourne.

OLIVER, John Francis   BORN: 22 July 1987, Melbourne, Victoria, Australia.
BRITISH CAREER: (2003) Carmarthen, Buxton; (2004) King's Lynn (Conference Trophy only), Boston; (2006) King's Lynn, Boston.

ONDRASIK, Pavel   BORN: 10 December 1975, Prague, Czech Republic.
BRITISH CAREER: (2001-2003) Trelawny; (2004) Newport; (2005) Exeter; (2006) Somerset (Premier Trophy only).
MAJOR HONOURS: Czech Republic Under-21 Champion: 1995, 1996.
RIDER LINKS: Son of former rider Petr Ondrasik.

OSTERGAARD, Ulrich   BORN: 19 April 1981, Odense, Denmark.
BRITISH CAREER: (2003) Eastbourne (British League Cup only); (2004) Eastbourne, Isle of Wight; (2005) Isle of Wight, Eastbourne, Swindon; (2006) Peterborough.

OUGHTIBRIDGE, Adam   BORN: 30 November 1980.
BRITISH CAREER: (2006) Buxton.

PARKER, Shane Andrew   BORN: 29 April 1970, Adelaide, South Australia, Australia.
BRITISH CAREER: (1990-1994) Ipswich; (1995-1996) Middlesbrough; (1997-1998) King's Lynn; (1999) Hull; (2000) King's Lynn, Belle Vue; (2001-2002) Peterborough; (2003) King's Lynn, Peterborough; (2004-2006) Glasgow.
MAJOR HONOURS: Australian Under-16 Champion: 1985; South Australia State Champion: 1991, 1994, 2001, 2002.

PARSONS, Joel Lewis   BORN: 24 July 1985, Broken Hill, New South Wales, Australia.
BRITISH CAREER: (2003) Rye House (Conference League only), Wimbledon (Conference Trophy only); (2004) Rye House (Conference League only), Hull, King's Lynn (Conference Trophy only); (2005) Hull, Mildenhall; (2006) Newport, Belle Vue.

PECYNA, Krzysztof   BORN: 14 September 1978, Pila, Poland.
BRITISH CAREER: (2005-2006) Wolverhampton.

PEDERSEN, Bjarne   BORN: 12 July 1978, Ryde, Denmark.
BRITISH CAREER: (2000-2001) Newcastle; (2002) Poole; (2003) Poole, Newcastle; (2004-2006) Poole.
MAJOR HONOURS: Danish Under-21 Champion: 1999; Danish Champion: 2004; Elite League Riders' Champion: 2004; World Cup Champion: 2006.
GRAND PRIX: European GP Champion: 2004.

PEDERSEN, Nicki   BORN: 2 April 1977, Odense, Denmark.
BRITISH CAREER: (1998) Newcastle; (1999-2000) Wolverhampton; (2001-2002) King's Lynn; (2003) Oxford, Eastbourne; (2004-2006) Eastbourne.
MAJOR HONOURS: Danish Under-21 Champion: 1997, 1998; Danish Champion: 2002, 2003, 2005, 2006; World Champion: 2003; Elite League Riders' Champion: 2005; World Cup Champion: 2006.
GRAND PRIX: European GP Champion: 2002; British GP Champion: 2003; Slovenian GP Champion: 2006; Polish GP Champion: 2006.
RIDER LINKS: Brother of former rider Ronni Pedersen.

PHILLIPS, Glen Alan   BORN: 22 November 1982, Farnborough, Kent.
BRITISH CAREER: (1999) Exeter, Isle of Wight, King's Lynn (Conference League only); (2000) Isle of Wight, Somerset; (2001) Isle of Wight; (2002) Wimbledon, Reading; (2003-2005) Isle of Wight; (2006) Somerset.

PICKARD, Jaimie   BORN: 23 February 1990, Stourbridge, Worcestershire.
BRITISH CAREER: (2006) Plymouth.

PICKERING, Michael Philip   BORN: 28 October 1982, Hull, East Yorkshire.
BRITISH CAREER: (1998) Buxton; (2000) Somerset (Conference League Cup only); (2002) Newport (Conference League only); (2003) Hull, Newcastle (Conference League only); (2004) Newcastle (Conference League only), King's Lynn (Conference League KOC only); (2005) Boston, Armadale; (2006) Scunthorpe.
RIDER LINKS: Son of former rider Phil Pickering.

PIETRASZKO, Adam   BORN: 18 August 1982, Czestochowa, Poland.
BRITISH CAREER: (2004) Berwick, Peterborough; (2005) Berwick; (2006) Oxford.

PIJPER, Theo   BORN: 11 February 1980, Dokkum, Holland.
BRITISH CAREER: (2002-2006) Edinburgh.

PIPER, George David   BORN: 3 August 1991, Kettering, Northamptonshire.
BRITISH CAREER: (2006) Weymouth (Conference Shield only).

PISZCZ, Tomasz   BORN: 8 June 1977, Gdansk, Poland.
BRITISH CAREER: (2004) Peterborough, Coventry; (2005-2006) Workington.

POWELL, Benjamin (Ben) Richard   BORN: 29 November 1984, Helensvale, Gold Coast, Queensland, Australia.
BRITISH CAREER: (2002) Sheffield (Conference League only); (2003) Carmarthen; (2004) Carmarthen, Coventry (Conference Trophy only), Boston; (2005) Boston, Rye House (Conference League only); (2006) Rye House (Conference League only), Mildenhall.

PRIEST, Luke Alex James   BORN: 18 June 1985, Birmingham, West Midlands.
BRITISH CAREER: (2000) Ashfield, Owlerton; (2001) Sheffield (Conference League only), Boston; (2002) Sheffield (Conference League only); (2003) Sheffield (Conference League only), Stoke (Conference Trophy only); (2004) Newport, Stoke (Conference League only), Sheffield (Conference Trophy only); (2005) Stoke (Conference League only); (2006) Stoke (Premier League & Conference League).
RIDER LINKS: Son of former rider John Priest.

PROTASIEWICZ, Piotr (Pepe)   BORN: 25 January 1975, Zielona Gora, Poland.
BRITISH CAREER: (1998) King's Lynn; (2002-2003) Peterborough; (2005-2006) Ipswich.

MAJOR HONOURS: World Under-21 Champion: 1996; World Team Cup Champion: 1996; Polish Champion: 1999; World Cup Champion: 2005.
GRAND PRIX: Challenge Champion: 1997; Grand Final Champion: 2003.
RIDER LINKS: Son of former rider Pawel Protasiewicz.

PURCHASE, James   BORN: 21 October 1987, Southampton, Hampshire.
BRITISH CAREER: (2003) Oxford (Conference League only), Peterborough (Conference League only); (2004) Swindon (Conference League only), King's Lynn (Conference Trophy only); (2005) Mildenhall; (2006) Mildenhall (Conference League only).

PUSZAKOWSKI, Mariusz   BORN: 25 May 1978, Torun, Poland.
BRITISH CAREER: (2005) Ipswich; (2006) Arena-Essex.

RAUN, Jonas Lorenzen   BORN: 22 August 1989, Haderslev, Denmark.
BRITISH CAREER: (2006) Peterborough.

REMPALA, Jacek (Jac)   BORN: 16 February 1971, Tarnow, Poland.
BRITISH CAREER: (1992) Ipswich; (2006) Berwick, Coventry.
RIDER LINKS: Brother of fellow riders Grzegorz and Marcin Rempala. Brother of former rider Tomasz Rempala

REYNOLDS, Joseph (Joe) Michael BORN: 20 March 1989, Wordsley, West Midlands.
BRITISH CAREER: (2004) Buxton; (2005) Buxton, Stoke (Conference League only), Weymouth; (2006) Newport (Conference League only).

RICHARDSON, Lee Stewart   BORN: 25 April 1979, Hastings, Sussex.
BRITISH CAREER: (1995) Reading; (1996) Reading (Conference League only), Poole; (1997) Reading, Peterborough, King's Lynn; (1998) Reading; (1999) Poole; (2000-2003) Coventry; (2004) Peterborough; (2005-2006) Swindon.
MAJOR HONOURS: World Under-21 Champion: 1999; Elite League Riders' Champion: 2003.
GRAND PRIX: Grand Final Champion: 2002.
RIDER LINKS: Son of former rider Colin Richardson. Nephew of former rider Steve Weatherley.

RICHARDSON, James Alan Scott   BORN: 16 September 1988, Mirfield, West Yorkshire.
BRITISH CAREER: (2005-2006) Scunthorpe.
RIDER LINKS: Son of former rider Derek Richardson.

RICKARDSSON, Jan Tony Soren   BORN: 17 August 1970, Grytas, Sweden.
BRITISH CAREER: (1991-1994) Ipswich; (1997-1998) Ipswich; (1999) King's Lynn; (2001-2004) Poole; (2005) Arena-Essex; (2006) Oxford.
MAJOR HONOURS: Swedish Champion: 1990, 1994, 1997, 1998, 1999, 2001, 2004, 2005; Nordic Champion: 1992; Czech Golden Helmet Champion: 1992, 1993, 1995; World Pairs Champion: 1993; World Team Cup Champion: 1994, 2000; World Champion: 1994, 1998, 1999, 2001, 2002, 2005; Elite League Riders' Champion: 1998, 2002; World Cup Champion: 2004.
GRAND PRIX: Czech Republic GP Champion: 1998, 2005; German GP Champion: 1998; Swedish GP Champion: 1998, 2002; British GP Champion: 1999, 2001, 2005; Danish GP Champion: 1999, 2001, 2002, 2005; Polish GP Champion: 2000; Norwegian GP Champion: 2002, 2004; European GP Champion: 2003, 2005; Slovenian GP Champion: 2004, 2005; Italian GP Champion: 2005.

RISAGER, Morten   BORN: 30 September 1987, Arhus, Denmark.
BRITISH CAREER: (2004-2006) Coventry.

ROBERTS, Jack Blain   BORN: 27 October 1990, Stockport, Cheshire.
BRITISH CAREER: (2006) Buxton.

ROBERTSON, Jamie   BORN: 8 October 1986, Berwick-upon-Tweed, Northumberland.
BRITISH CAREER: (2002) Newcastle (Conference League only); (2003) Newcastle (Premier League & Conference League); (2004) Newcastle (Premier League & Conference League); (2005) Newcastle, Oxford (Conference League only); (2006) Newcastle.

ROBSON, Stuart Anthony   BORN: 8 November 1976, Sunderland, Tyne and Wear.
BRITISH CAREER: (1993-1994) Newcastle, Edinburgh; (1995) Coventry; (1996) Coventry, Middlesbrough; (1997) Hull; (1998-2002) Coventry; (2003) Coventry, Newcastle; (2004) Coventry; (2005-2006) Rye House.
RIDER LINKS: Son of former rider John Robson. Brother of former rider Scott Robson.

ROMANEK, Lukasz   BORN: 21 August 1983, Rybnik, Poland.
BRITISH CAREER: (2006) Arena-Essex.
MAJOR HONOUR: European Under-19 Champion: 2001; Polish Under-21 Champion: 2003.
NOTE: Committed suicide in his Polish homeland on 3 June 2006.

ROYNON, Adam Wayne   BORN: 30 August 1988, Barrow-in-Furness, Cumbria.
BRITISH CAREER: (2003) Swindon (Conference League only), Armadale (Conference Trophy only); (2004) Newcastle (Conference League only), Mildenhall; (2005) Mildenhall, Boston, Glasgow; (2006) Buxton, Rye House.
MAJOR HONOUR: Conference League Riders' Champion: 2006.
RIDER LINKS: Son of former rider Chris Roynon.

RYMEL, Adrian   BORN: 30 October 1975, Koprivnice, Czech Republic.
BRITISH CAREER: (2001-2003) Berwick; (2004) Berwick, Peterborough; (2005) Berwick, Coventry; (2006) Berwick (Premier Trophy only).
MAJOR HONOUR: Czech Republic Champion: 2006.

SANCHEZ, Emiliano Diebo   BORN: 9 December 1977, Buenos Aires, Argentina.
BRITISH CAREER: (1999-2001) Glasgow; (2002-2003) Trelawny; (2004) Hull, Peterborough; (2005) Hull; (2006) Sheffield.
MAJOR HONOURS: Argentine Champion: 2001, 2002; Italian Champion: 2004, 2005.

SCHLEIN, Rory Robert   BORN: 1 September 1984, Darwin, Northern Territory, Australia.
BRITISH CAREER: (2001-2002) Edinburgh, Sheffield (Conference League only); (2003-2004) Edinburgh, Belle Vue; (2005-2006) Coventry.
MAJOR HONOURS: Australian Under-16 Champion: 2000; Australian Under-21 Champion: 2003, 2004; South Australia State Champion: 2004, 2005, 2006.
RIDER LINKS: Son of former rider Lyndon Schlein.

SCHRAMM, Chris   BORN: 30 May 1984, Maldon, Essex.
BRITISH CAREER: (2000) Peterborough (Conference League only), Berwick, Arena-Essex; (2001-2002) Peterborough (Conference League only), Reading; (2003) Newport, Wimbledon (Conference Trophy only), Peterborough (Conference League only), Oxford (Conference League only); (2004) Reading, Oxford (Conference League only); (2005) Berwick, Peterborough; (2006) Newport.

SCREEN, Joseph (Joe)   BORN: 27 November 1972, Chesterfield, Derbyshire.
BRITISH CAREER: (1989-1993) Belle Vue; (1994-1997) Bradford; (1998) Belle Vue; (1999) Hull; (2000-2002) Eastbourne; (2003) Eastbourne, Belle Vue; (2004-2006) Belle Vue.

MAJOR HONOURS: British Under-21 Champion: 1990, 1993; Division One Riders' Champion: 1992; World Under-21 Champion: 1993; British Champion: 1996, 2004.

SHIELDS, Adam Matthew   BORN: 8 February 1977, Kurri-Kurri, New South Wales, Australia.
BRITISH CAREER: (2000-2002) Isle of Wight; (2003) Isle of Wight, Eastbourne; (2004-2006) Eastbourne.
MAJOR HONOURS: Australian Under-21 Champion: 1997; Premier League Riders' Champion: 2002; New South Wales State Champion: 2005.
RIDER LINKS: Nephew of former rider David Shields. Cousin of former rider Ben Shields.

SIMMONS, Nicholas (Nick) Steven John   BORN: 24 July 1981, Leamington Spa, Warwickshire.
BRITISH CAREER: (1997) Shuttle Cubs, Ryde; (1998) Newport (Conference League & Premier League), Isle of Wight, Exeter; (1999) Isle of Wight, Stoke, Newport (Conference League only); (2000) Arena-Essex; (2001) Newport (Premier League & Conference League), Somerset; (2002) Isle of Wight; (2003) Stoke, Mildenhall; (2004) Exeter, Weymouth; (2005) Exeter, Sittingbourne; (2006) Isle of Wight.
RIDER LINKS: Son of former junior rider Steve Simmons.

SIMOTA, Zdenek (Sam)   BORN: 4 May 1985, Prachatice, Czech Republic.
BRITISH CAREER: (2005-2006) Reading.

SKORNICKI, Adam   BORN: 22 October 1976, Wolsztyn, Poland.
BRITISH CAREER: (2000-2004) Wolverhampton; (2005) Wolverhampton, Arena-Essex; (2006) Oxford.

SMART, Lee Mitchell   BORN: 5 April 1988, Swindon, Wiltshire.
BRITISH CAREER: (2003) Swindon (Conference League only), Stoke (Conference Trophy only); (2004) Mildenhall; (2005) Somerset, Weymouth, Mildenhall; (2006) Plymouth.

SMETHILLS, Lee Kenneth   BORN: 30 March 1982, Bolton, Greater Manchester.
BRITISH CAREER: (1998) Mildenhall; (1999) Workington, Buxton, Rye House, Belle Vue, Newcastle; (2000) Workington, Buxton; (2001) Workington; (2002) Hull, Belle Vue; (2003) Exeter; (2004) Newcastle, Berwick; (2005) Exeter; (2006) Berwick, Wolverhampton, Rye House.

SMITH, Andrew (Andy)   BORN: 25 May 1966, York, North Yorkshire.
BRITISH CAREER: (1982-1988) Belle Vue; (1989-1990) Bradford; (1991) Swindon; (1992-1995) Coventry; (1996) Bradford; (1997) Coventry; (1998) Belle Vue, Swindon; (1999-2001) Belle Vue; (2003) Oxford (Elite League & Conference League); (2004) Swindon; (2005) Belle Vue; (2006) Reading.
MAJOR HONOURS: British Champion: 1993, 1994, 1995.
RIDER LINKS: Brother of former rider Paul Smith.

SMITH, Jamie Paul   BORN: 20 July 1983, Peterborough, Cambridgeshire.
BRITISH CAREER: (1998) Norfolk; (1999) Eastbourne, Glasgow; (2000) Newcastle, Peterborough (Conference League only), Hull, Somerset; (2001) Hull, Somerset; (2002) Hull; (2003) Swindon; (2004) Somerset, Coventry; (2005) Somerset; (2006) Somerset (Premier Trophy only).
RIDER LINKS: Brother of former rider Darren Smith.

SMITH, Robert (Rob) William   BORN: 18 February 1988, Eastbourne, East Sussex.
BRITISH CAREER: (2004) Mildenhall; (2005) Wimbledon; (2006) Plymouth.
RIDER LINKS: Brother of former junior rider Phil Smith.

SMOLINSKI, Martin   BORN: 6 December 1984, Graefelfing, Nr Munich, Germany.
BRITISH CAREER: (2004-2006) Coventry.
MAJOR HONOUR: German Under-21 Champion: 2003.

SNEDDON, Derek   BORN: 27 July 1982, Falkirk, Scotland.
  BRITISH CAREER: (1998) Hull; (1999) Linlithgow, Isle of Wight; (2000) Ashfield, Edinburgh; (2001) Edinburgh, Glasgow; (2002) Newcastle; (2003) Edinburgh; (2004-2005) Armadale; (2006) Edinburgh.

SPEIGHT, David Andrew   BORN: 21 March 1980, Bradford, West Yorkshire.
  BRITISH CAREER: (2000) Owlerton; (2001) Sheffield (Conference League only); (2002) Hull, Sheffield (Conference League only), Wolverhampton (Conference Trophy only); (2003) Sheffield (Conference League only); (2004) Newcastle (Conference League only), Sheffield (Conference Trophy only), Stoke (Conference League only); (2005) Scunthorpe, Stoke (Conference League only); (2006) Cleveland (Conference Shield only).

STANCL, Jiri (George)   BORN: 19 August 1975, Prague, Czech Republic.
  BRITISH CAREER: (1994-1995) Sheffield; (1996-1999) Wolverhampton; (2000) Coventry; (2002-2004) Glasgow; (2005) Glasgow, Ipswich; (2006) Newcastle.
  MAJOR HONOUR: Czech Republic Under-21 Champion: 1993.
  RIDER LINKS: Grandson of former rider Jiri Stancl (1). Son of former rider Jiri Stancl (2).

STEAD, Garry   BORN: 5 January 1972, Holmfirth, West Yorkshire.
  BRITISH CAREER: (1990-1992) Stoke; (1993) Newcastle; (1994) Newcastle, Bradford; (1995) Bradford; (1996) Sheffield; (1997) Bradford; (1998) Wolverhampton; (1999-2002) Hull; (2003) Hull, Eastbourne; (2004-2005) Hull; (2006) Workington.

STEAD, Simon Trevor   BORN: 25 April 1982, Sheffield, South Yorkshire.
  BRITISH CAREER: (1997) Peterborough (Academy League only); (1998) Peterborough (Premier League), Buxton; (1999-2001) Sheffield; (2002) Sheffield, Peterborough; (2003-2004) Workington, Wolverhampton; (2005-2006) Belle Vue.
  MAJOR HONOURS: British Under-21 Champion: 2001, 2002, 2003.
  RIDER LINKS: Son of former rider Trevor Stead. Nephew of former rider Ian Stead. Cousin of fellow rider Adam Allott.

STEPHENS, Seemond Lee   BORN: 9 August 1967, St Austell, Cornwall.
  BRITISH CAREER: (1998) St Austell, Exeter, Sheffield, Swindon; (1999) Eastbourne, Swindon, St Austell; (2000-2001) Exeter; (2002) Trelawny, Exeter; (2003) Exeter, Eastbourne; (2004-2005) Exeter; (2006) Plymouth.

STODDART, Sean   BORN: 20 January 1987, Edinburgh, Scotland.
  BRITISH CAREER: (2003) Armadale, Trelawny (Conference Trophy only), Carmarthen (Conference Trophy only), Newcastle (Conference League only); (2004) Armadale, Edinburgh; (2005) Armadale; (2006) Edinburgh, Boston.

STOJANOWSKI, Krzysztof   BORN: 5 January 1979, Zielona Gora, Poland.
  BRITISH CAREER: (2005) Isle of Wight; (2006) Isle of Wight, Swindon (Craven Shield only).

STRUDWICK, Lee   BORN: 23 July 1988, Pembury, Kent.
  BRITISH CAREER: (2005) Wimbledon; (2006) Rye House (Conference League only).
  RIDER LINKS: Cousin of junior rider Niall Strudwick.

SUCHANEK, Tomas   BORN: 7 April 1984, Pardubice, Czech Republic.
  BRITISH CAREER: (2003) King's Lynn (British League Cup only); (2005) Isle of Wight, Poole; (2006) Redcar, Wolverhampton.
  MAJOR HONOURS: Czech Republic Under-21 Champion: 2002, 2003.

SULLIVAN, Ryan Geoffrey   BORN: 20 January 1975, Melbourne, Victoria, Australia.
BRITISH CAREER: (1994-1997) Peterborough; (1998) Poole; (1999-2003) Peterborough; (2004-2005) Poole; (2006) Peterborough.
MAJOR HONOURS: Australian Under-16 Champion: 1991; Australian Under-21 Champion: 1993, 1996; South Australia State Champion: 1995, 1996, 1997; Overseas Champion: 1995; Inter-Continental Champion: 1997; Czech Golden Helmet Champion: 1997, 2003; World Team Cup Champion: 1999; Elite League Riders' Champion: 2000; World Cup Champion: 2001, 2002; Australian Champion: 2004.
GRAND PRIX: British GP Champion: 2002; Slovenian GP Champion: 2002; Swedish GP Champion: 2003; Scandinavian GP Champion: 2003.

SWIDERSKI, Piotr   BORN: 11 May 1983, Gostyn, Poland.
BRITISH CAREER: (2006) Peterborough.

TACEY, Shaun James   BORN: 27 November 1974, Norwich, Norfolk.
BRITISH CAREER: (1992) Ipswich; (1993) Ipswich, Arena-Essex; (1994-1996) Coventry; (1997) King's Lynn, Isle of Wight, Bradford, Coventry; (1998-2000) Coventry; (2001-2002) Arena-Essex; (2003) Hull; (2004) King's Lynn, Coventry; (2005) Workington; (2006) Mildenhall, Arena-Essex, Poole.

TAYLOR, Benjamin (Ben) Reece   BORN: 7 November 1990, Dewsbury, West Yorkshire.
BRITISH CAREER: (2006) Buxton.
RIDER LINKS: Grandson of former rider Jack Hughes.

TESSARI, Daniele   BORN: 20 August 1984, Albaredo d-Adige, Italy.
BRITISH CAREER: (2006) Edinburgh.
MAJOR HONOUR: Italian Under-21 Champion: 2002.

THOMPSON, Benjamin (Ben) Karl BORN: 10 September 1990, Lincoln, Lincolnshire.
BRITISH CAREER: (2005) Buxton; (2006) Newport (Conference League only); Plymouth (Conference Trophy only).

THOMPSON, Mark   BORN: 8 July 1979, Orsett, Essex.
BRITISH CAREER: (1996) Sittingbourne, Linlithgow, Mildenhall, Eastbourne (Conference League only); (1997) Anglian Angels; (1998) Mildenhall, Newport, Stoke; (1999) King's Lynn (Conference League only), Mildenhall, Newport (Conference League only); (2000) St Austell, Arena-Essex; (2001) Peterborough (Conference League only); (2002) King's Lynn (Conference League only), Mildenhall; (2003) Boston, Peterborough (British League Cup only); (2004) Weymouth, Swindon (Conference League only), King's Lynn (Conference Trophy only); (2005) Mildenhall; (2006) Mildenhall (Conference League only), Sheffield.

THORP, Paul   BORN: 9 September 1964, Macclesfield, Cheshire.
BRITISH CAREER: (1980) Birmingham; (1981) Birmingham, Scunthorpe, Workington; (1982-1983) Berwick, Birmingham; (1984-1985) Stoke, Wolverhampton; (1986) Stoke, Sheffield, Belle Vue; (1987-1988) Belle Vue; (1989-1992) Bradford; (1993) Newcastle; (1994) Bradford; (1995-1996) Hull; (1997) Belle Vue; (1998) Hull; (1999) Hull, Stoke; (2000-2003) Hull; (2004) Hull, Belle Vue; (2005) Hull; (2006) Workington, Stoke.
MAJOR HONOURS: National League Riders' Champion: 1986; World Team Cup Champion: 1989.

TILLMAN, Simon   BORN: 2 October 1988, Redhill, Surrey.
BRITISH CAREER: (2006) Weymouth (Conference Shield only).
RIDER LINKS: Son of former junior rider Ray Tillman.

TOMICEK, Lubos   BORN: 14 March 1986, Prague, Czech Republic.
BRITISH CAREER: (2003) Oxford (British League Cup only); (2004) Newcastle; (2005) Newcastle, Oxford; (2006) Oxford.
RIDER LINKS: Grandson of former rider Lubos Tomicek (1). Son of former rider Lubos Tomicek (2).

TOPINKA, Tomas   BORN: 5 June 1974, Prague, Czech Republic.
BRITISH CAREER: (1993-1995) King's Lynn; (1996) Oxford; (1997-1998) King's Lynn; (1999) King's Lynn, Ipswich; (2001) Belle Vue; (2002) Coventry; (2003-2004) King's Lynn; (2005) King's Lynn, Coventry; (2006) King's Lynn.
MAJOR HONOURS: Czech Republic Under-21 Champion: 1992; Czech Republic Champion: 1996, 2003; Czech Golden Helmet Champion: 1996.

TRESARRIEU, Mathieu   BORN: 2 March 1986, Bordeaux, France.
BRITISH CAREER: (2002) Isle of Wight (Young Shield only); (2003) Isle of Wight; (2005) Reading; (2006) Redcar, Oxford, Wolverhampton.
MAJOR HONOUR: French Champion: 2002.
RIDER LINKS: Brother of fellow riders Sebastien and Stephane Tresarrieu.

TULLY, Andrew Bruce   BORN: 26 May 1987, Douglas, Isle of Man.
BRITISH CAREER: (2003) Armadale (Conference Trophy only); (2004-2005) Armadale; (2006) Scunthorpe.

TUTTON, Matthew (Matt) Anthony   BORN: 19 June 1982, Newport, Gwent, South Wales.
BRITISH CAREER: (2000) Rye House; (2002) Swindon (Conference Trophy only), Wimbledon; (2003) Mildenhall, Buxton, Carmarthen (Conference Trophy only), Newport (Conference League only); (2004-2006) Newport (Conference League only).
RIDER LINKS: Brother of former junior rider David Tutton.

ULAMEK, Sebastian (Seba)   BORN: 20 November 1975, Czestochowa, Poland.
BRITISH CAREER: (2000) Wolverhampton; (2002) King's Lynn; (2003-2004) Oxford; (2005) Coventry; (2006) Swindon.
MAJOR HONOUR: Continental Champion: 2001.

WALASEK, Grzegorz (Greg)   BORN: 29 August 1976, Krosno, Poland.
BRITISH CAREER: (2000-2002) Poole; (2004) Arena-Essex; (2005) Poole (Craven Shield only); (2006) Poole.
MAJOR HONOURS: Polish Under-21 Champion: 1997; Polish Champion: 2004; World Cup Champion: 2005.

WALDRON, Shane Ashley   BORN: 26 October 1989, Swindon, Wiltshire.
BRITISH CAREER: (2005) Rye House (Conference League only), Weymouth; (2006) King's Lynn (Premier Trophy only), Plymouth.

WALKER, James Sam   BORN: 5 April 1990, Eastbourne, East Sussex.
BRITISH CAREER: (2006) Weymouth (Conference Shield only).

WALKER, Simon Mark   BORN: 19 February 1980, Bristol, Avon.
BRITISH CAREER: (2001) Newport (Conference League only); (2002) Newport (Conference League only), Swindon (Conference Trophy only); (2003) Swindon (Conference League only), Trelawny (Conference Trophy only); (2004) Somerset, Swindon (Conference League only), King's Lynn (Conference Trophy only); (2005) Boston, Somerset; (2006) Somerset.

WARWICK, Daniel (Danny) BORN: 21 November 1983, Poole, Dorset.
BRITISH CAREER: (2002) Newport (Conference League only); (2003) Newport (Conference League only), Poole (British League Cup only); (2004) Weymouth, Swindon (Conference League only), King's Lynn (Conference Trophy only); (2005) Newport (Conference League only); (2006) Berwick, Weymouth (Conference Shield only).
RIDER LINKS: Brother of fellow rider Carl Warwick.

WATSON, Craig BORN: 6 August 1976, Sydney, New South Wales, Australia.
BRITISH CAREER: (1997-1999) Newport; (2000-2001) Poole; (2002) Newport; (2003) Newport, Belle Vue; (2004-2006) Newport.
MAJOR HONOUR: New South Wales State Champion: 2004.

WATT, David (Davey) John BORN: 6 January 1978, Townsville, Queensland, Australia.
BRITISH CAREER: (2001) Isle of Wight; (2002) Newcastle; (2003) King's Lynn, Poole; (2004) Rye House, Poole, Eastbourne; (2005) Eastbourne; (2006) Oxford.
MAJOR HONOUR: Queensland State Champion: 2005.

WEBSTER, Timothy (Tim) Mark BORN: 26 May 1989, Walsall, West Midlands.
BRITISH CAREER: (2004) King's Lynn (Conference Trophy only); (2005) Weymouth, Scunthorpe; (2006) Newport (Conference League only).

WERNER, Jeffrey Brent BORN: 15 April 1974, Los Angeles, California, USA.
BRITISH CAREER: (1995-1997) Long Eaton; (1998) Newcastle; (1999-2000) Workington; (2001) Eastbourne; (2002) Rye House; (2003) Rye House, Peterborough; (2004) Rye House, Belle Vue; (2005) Rye House, Oxford; (2006) Eastbourne, Mildenhall, Arena-Essex.
RIDER LINKS: Nephew of former rider Dubb Ferrell.

WESTACOTT, Jamie BORN: 9 April 1988, Newport, Gwent, South Wales.
BRITISH CAREER: (2003) Newport (Conference League only), Stoke (Conference Trophy only); (2004) Newport (Conference League only), Reading; (2005) Newport (Conference League only); (2006) Plymouth.

WETHERS, Matthew James BORN: 30 May 1985, Adelaide, South Australia.
BRITISH CAREER: (2003) Armadale (Conference Trophy only), Wolverhampton (Conference League only), Edinburgh; (2004) Edinburgh, Armadale; (2005) Glasgow, King's Lynn, Edinburgh; (2006) Edinburgh, Poole.

WHITE, Karl David BORN: 1 December 1987, Thurrock, Essex.
BRITISH CAREER: (2004) Rye House (Conference League only); (2005) Rye House (Conference League only), Boston, Wimbledon; (2006) Plymouth, Sittingbourne (Conference Shield only).

WILKINSON, Carl Adam BORN: 16 May 1981, Boston, Lincolnshire.
BRITISH CAREER: (1997) Peterborough (Academy League only); (1998) Norfolk; (1999) King's Lynn (Conference League only); (2000) Boston, Newcastle, Glasgow; (2001) Boston; (2002-2003) Newport (Premier League & Conference League); (2004) Newport; (2005) Boston, Berwick; (2006) Newport, Ipswich.

WILLIAMS, Martin John BORN: 25 October 1979, Gloucester, Gloucestershire
BRITISH CAREER: (1996) Swindon (Conference League only); (1997) M4 Raven Sprockets; (1998) Newport (Conference League only); (1999) St Austell; (2000) Stoke, St Austell, Reading, Swindon, Isle of Wight; (2001) Newport (Premier League & Conference League), Isle of Wight, Stoke; (2002) Wimbledon; (2006) Weymouth (Conference Shield only)

WILSON, Ben Ryan   BORN: 15 March 1986, Sheffield, South Yorkshire.
BRITISH CAREER: (2001-2002) Sheffield (Conference League only); (2003) Sheffield (Premier League & Conference League), Buxton (Conference Trophy only); (2004) Sheffield (Premier League & Conference Trophy), Carmarthen; (2005) Sheffield; (2006) Sheffield, Wolverhampton.
MAJOR HONOUR: British Under-21 Champion: 2006.

WILTSHIRE, Todd William   BORN: 26 September 1968, Bankstown, Sydney, New South Wales, Australia.
BRITISH CAREER: (1988) Wimbledon, Ipswich; (1989) Wimbledon; (1990-1991) Reading; (1998-2001) Oxford; (2003) Oxford; (2006) Oxford.
MAJOR HONOURS: New South Wales State Champion: 1990, 2000, 2001; German Champion: 1997, 1998; Australian Champion: 1999, 2001; World Team Cup Champion: 1999; Inter-Continental Champion: 1999; World Cup Champion: 2001, 2002.

WOFFINDEN, Tai   BORN: 10 August 1990, Scunthorpe, North Lincolnshire.
BRITISH CAREER: (2006) Scunthorpe, Sheffield.
RIDER LINKS: Son of former rider Rob Woffinden.

WOODWARD, Cameron Jackson BORN: 8 January 1985, Mildura, Victoria, Australia.
BRITISH CAREER: (2003) Poole (British League Cup only); (2004-2005) Edinburgh; (2006) Eastbourne.
MAJOR HONOUR: Victoria State Champion: 2006.

WRIGHT, Charles   BORN: 26 October 1988, Stockport, Cheshire.
BRITISH CAREER: (2004-2005) Buxton; (2006) Buxton (Conference Shield only).
RIDER LINKS: Grandson of former rider Jim Yacoby. Brother of fellow rider James Wright.

WRIGHT, James   BORN: 13 June 1986, Stockport, Cheshire.
BRITISH CAREER: (2002) Buxton; (2003) Buxton, Belle Vue (British League Cup only); (2004) Workington, Buxton; (2005-2006) Workington, Belle Vue.
MAJOR HONOUR: Conference League Riders' Champion: 2004.
RIDER LINKS: Grandson of former rider Jim Yacoby. Brother of fellow rider Charles Wright.

WRIGHT, Matthew Paul   BORN: 19 November 1985, Harlow, Essex.
BRITISH CAREER: (2002) Boston, Mildenhall, Carmarthen, Wimbledon (Conference Trophy only); (2003) Mildenhall, Ipswich (British League Cup only); (2004-2005) Wimbledon; (2006) Mildenhall (Conference League & Premier League).

WYATT, Sam   BORN: 11 January 1990.
BRITISH CAREER: (2006) Stoke (Conference Shield only).

ZABIK, Karol   BORN: 25 October 1986, Torun, Poland.
BRITISH CAREER: (2006) Peterborough.
MAJOR HONOURS: European Under-19 Champion: 2005; World Under-21 Team Cup Champion: 2005, 2006; Polish Under-21 Champion: 2006; World Under-21 Champion: 2006.
RIDER LINKS: Son of former rider Jan Zabik.

ZAGAR, Matej   BORN: 3 April 1983, Ljubljana, Slovenia.
BRITISH CAREER: (2003) Trelawny; (2004-2006) Reading.
MAJOR HONOURS: Slovenian Champion: 2002, 2003, 2004, 2005; European Under-19 Champion: 2002; European Champion: 2004.

ZETTERSTROM, Hans Magnus   BORN: 9 December 1971, Eskilstuna, Sweden.
BRITISH CAREER: (1996) Poole; (1998-1999) Poole; (2000) Peterborough; (2001) Poole; (2002) Poole, Peterborough; (2003) Poole (British League Cup only); (2004) Poole; (2005-2006) Somerset.
MAJOR HONOURS: European Champion: 2002; Premier League Riders' Champion: 2006..

PREVIOUS EDITIONS OF THE
TEMPUS SPEEDWAY YEARBOOK
ARE NOW AVAILABLE FOR ONLY £5.99

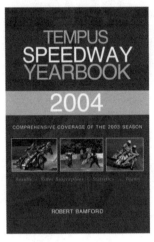

Tempus Speedway
Yearbook 2004
ISBN 07524 29558
RRP £17.99

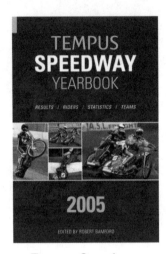

Tempus Speedway
Yearbook 2005
ISBN 07524 33962
RRP £19.99

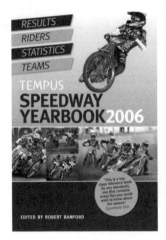

Tempus Speedway
Yearbook 2006
ISBN 07524 36929
RRP £17.99

To order, contact the Tempus Sales Department on
01453 883300

or visit our website at
www.tempus-publishing.com